The Definitive Guide to the .NET Compact Framework

LARRY ROOF AND DAN FERGUS

APress Media, LLC

The Definitive Guide to the .NET Compact Framework
Copyright ©2003 by Larry Roof and Dan Fergus
Originally published by Apress in 2003

ISBN 978-1-59059-095-9   ISBN 978-1-4302-0789-4 (eBook)
DOI 10.1007/978-1-4302-0789-4

Trademarked names may appear in this book. Rather than use a trademark symbol with every occurrence of a trademarked name, we use the names only in an editorial fashion and to the benefit of the trademark owner, with no intention of infringement of the trademark.

Technical Reviewer: Ron Miller

Editorial Board: Dan Appleman, Craig Berry, Gary Cornell, Tony Davis, Steven Rycroft, Julian Skinner, Martin Streicher, Jim Sumser, Karen Watterson, Gavin Wray, John Zukowski

Assistant Publisher: Grace Wong

Project Manager: Tracy Brown Collins

Copy Editor: Ami Knox

Production Manager: Kari Brooks

Compositor, Proofreader, Artist: Kinetic Publishing Services, LLC

Indexer: Ron Strauss

Cover Designer: Kurt Krames

Manufacturing Manager: Tom Debolski

In the United States: phone 1-800-SPRINGER, email orders@springer-ny.com, or visit http://www.springer-ny.com. Outside the United States: fax +49 6221 345229, email orders@springer.de, or visit http://www.springer.de.

For information on translations, please contact Apress directly at 2560 Ninth Street, Suite 219, Berkeley, CA 94710. Phone 510-549-5930, fax 510-549-5939, email info@apress.com, or visit http://www.apress.com.

To Carol, my love, my life. I would not be here without you.

—Larry Roof

To Susie and the boys.
Thanks for putting up with the late nights and the times when I came home
tired after traveling, or staying up too late working on this book. I love you.

—Dan Fergus

Contents at a Glance

Contents

Chapter 10 Data Binding *423*

Chapter 11 Introduction to SQL Server CE *453*

Chapter 12 Working with Server-Based Data *483*

Chapter 13 Working with Device-Based Data *511*

Chapter 14 Working with XML *547*

About the Authors

LARRY ROOF has long been considered an expert in the field of mobile application development. He is a frequent speaker at leading conferences including Microsoft TechEd, the Windows CE Developer's Conference, and the Visual Basic Insider's Technical Conference. He has written for a number of industry-leading magazines and has a monthly MSDN Voices column called "Two for the Road."

Larry heads up one of the premier mobile solution development companies. His company specializes in creating integrated mobile solutions that extend enterprise environments.

In addition to writing and consulting, Larry offers training in both face-to-face and video-based formats. He has been recognized by Microsoft as an eMbedded Most Valuable Professional (eMVP) for his contributions to the mobile development community.

You can contact Larry at larry.roof@larryroof.com and can obtain more information about the consulting and training services offered by his company at http://www.larryroof.com.

It's been a long time since that first computer course in COBOL back in 1973. But instead of getting a degree, **DAN FERGUS** got a little side-tracked and spent the next 12 years as an EMT and paramedic in Hillsborough County, Florida.

After Dan hung up his scissors, he went back to school at the University of South Florida and received a B.S. in biology and a B.S. in chemical engineering. While working as an engineer and living in Japan for two years as a technical liaison for a chemical company, Dan picked up a copy of Turbo C while on a trip to Taiwan for $5, just to keep up his programming skills.

When that job ended, Dan started out on his own and worked as a consultant in the Dallas/Fort Worth area for several years before going to work for NuMega Technologies. While there, Dan was the lead developer for CodeReview and FailSafe, both Visual Basic debugging products. Dan's last position at Compuware (formally NuMega) was that of a technical evangelist, spending 2 years doing nothing but working, learning, teaching, and writing about .NET.

Dan is again an independent consultant who specializes in .NET in general and the .NET Compact Framework in particular.

When not working, Dan spends time with his wife raising their four young boys. In addition to his family, Dan's passion is baseball. As such, he spends the summer coaching and umpiring Little League and high school baseball games.

About the Technical Reviewer

RON MILLER works as a senior engineer at Pitney Bowes developing new shipping systems. He has been in the IT industry for over 20 years and has developed a variety of solutions from distributed asset management systems to those providing daily sales figures to handhelds. He is constantly searching for a better solution to the problem at hand.

In his spare time, Ron takes pleasure in restoring older Lancias and BMWs.

Acknowledgments

THANKS TO KAREN, TRACY, AMI, KARI, and the many other members of the Apress family who made this a great book. Our special thanks to Ron Miller for his often insightful technical evaluation of our writing.

I would like to thank Gary Cornell for finding a writing partner for me to complete my book after I was injured. Additionally, I would like to thank those staff members at Apress for the aid they provided while I struggled through the process of wrapping up this book, for understanding my physical limitations and helping me in any way that they could.

I would also like to thank Dan for becoming a part of my project and picking up the writing load while I recovered.

—Larry Roof

I WOULD LIKE TO THANK GARY CORNELL for asking me to help with the book. Jason Bock and I had almost completed a book on Pocket PC development with the eMbedded tools when the .NET Compact Framework was being released. That project was put on hold in lieu of this book. I'm glad I got the chance to finish a project this time.

Chapter 17, lovingly called the "unmanaged" chapter, almost got out of hand several times. There was just so much to cover and so little time to do it. I appreciate the help that Chris Tacke provided in his review of the material to make sure nothing stupid slipped through.

—Dan Fergus

The .NET Compact Framework

HERE'S THE SCENARIO: You've been stranded on a small deserted island with one small bag of items on which you must survive. Now, here's the question: What do you want in the bag?

Chances are you're going to want the basic items, the items that you've got to have to get by. It's doubtful that you'll take two of anything, for example, two knives. The reason is that the second knife doesn't add any functionality or capabilities, yet it takes up precious space.

Let's complicate the scenario a bit. Let's say there's going to be a second person stranded, but still you're limited to the single bag. The two of you have some common items that you want included, but you also have individual items that are only important to yourself.

Now, take that basic scenario and extrapolate it to mobile application development. The Pocket PC becomes the bag with its limited space. The .NET Framework becomes the item you want to take with you. While you would like to take the whole .NET Framework, it won't fit on the Pocket PC. Enter the .NET Compact Framework, or simply NETCF. It's a subset of the .NET Framework, comprised of just the items that you need to "survive" as a mobile developer. It's a perfect match for the limited space on a Pocket PC.

If you look at the .NET Compact Framework in this light, you'll understand why Microsoft did what they did. While the .NET Compact Framework tops out at a rotund 30 megabytes in size, NETCF is a diminutive 1.5 megabyte. In Disney terms, the .NET Framework is Dumbo, and NETCF is Tinkerbell. Now, it doesn't take a rocket scientist to understand shrinking a framework by a factor of 20-to-1 is going to require that a few things be left out. I'll be honest with you; I'm amazed that NETCF has any functionality at all given the pruning it endured.

So if you're Microsoft, how do you go from 30MB to 1.5MB? For starters, you don't take two knives. In NETCF terms, that is to say you don't include two ways to do the same thing. Microsoft trimmed namespaces. They trimmed methods. They trimmed the number of overloads for each method. They removed functionality that would less likely be useful in developing mobile applications.

What does all this mean to you? That it's unlikely you'll be able to take your .NET experience as it exists today and use it to create mobile applications without experiencing some frustration, heartaches, and despair. You're going to have to adjust your programming style some. You probably will have to learn new ways to do things you already know how to do. You may have to seek therapy.

I'm going to make a prediction. Somewhere along the line, you're going to ask, "Why for the love of all things good did Microsoft leave out that feature?" Trust me, it'll happen. The simple answer is they're just messing with you. Okay, that's not the reason, but it'll probably seem that way. The real reason is that Microsoft made some tough decisions. There were a number of useful, powerful, very cool features and functions that had to be trimmed. For the most part though, they've left an alternative for everything they removed. It might not be the alternative you would like, and it very likely will take a bit more coding, but it's an alternative. In some cases, they haven't provided an alternative. For the most part, these totally abandoned features were either too big in size or considered to be of marginal use to mobile developers.

Understanding the .NET Compact Framework

Microsoft developed the .NET Compact Framework with one intention in mind: to build applications. By applications, I don't mean drivers, COM components, ActiveX controls, Today screen plug-ins, or anything else that might get you called geek by other kids on the tech playground. I'm talking about applications that display, gather, process, and forward information. You know, those applications that give users a reason to carry a device. While they typically will have an interface, they don't have to have one. The data that they are working with might be local, remote, or some combination of the two.

The .NET Compact Framework simplifies application development on smart devices. A *smart device* is Microsoft's generic category name for any device that has, well, smarts. Currently this includes the Pocket PC, Pocket PC 2002, Pocket PC Phone Edition, Smartphone, and other devices running Windows CE .NET 4.1 or later.

 NOTE *Presently, you can't use the .NET Compact Framework to develop applications that target the Smartphone. Microsoft has stated that they will provide a Smartphone SDK in 2003. This SDK, which will install on top of Visual Studio .NET, will include a Smartphone emulator.*

You will need Visual Studio .NET 2003 to build applications that target the .NET Compact Framework. VS .NET 2003 includes Smart Device Extensions, or SDE. It's SDE that enables you to create applications for the .NET Compact

Framework. You can build applications using either Visual C# .NET, Visual Basic .NET, or both.

The .NET Compact Framework has two main components: the common language runtime, or CLR, and the .NET Compact Framework class library.

The CLR is the foundation of the .NET Compact Framework. It's responsible for managing code at execution time, providing core services such as memory management and thread management, while enforcing code safety and accuracy. Code that targets the runtime is known as *managed code;* code that doesn't target the runtime, as is the case with eMbedded Visual C++, is known as *unmanaged,* or *native,* code.

The .NET Compact Framework class library is a collection of reusable classes that you can use to quickly and easily develop applications. This framework was designed with porting in mind, whether that is to Microsoft or other third-party platforms. What does this mean to you? Simply that the coding techniques and the applications you create today to run on a Pocket PC could run on other platforms, such as a cell phone or another vendor's PDA, if a version of the .NET Compact Framework was created for that platform.

Features of the Common Language Runtime

The common language runtime provides a code-execution environment that manages code targeting the .NET Framework. Code management can take the form of memory management, thread management, security management, code verification and compilation, and other system services.

The CLR is designed to enhance performance. It makes use of Just-In-Time (JIT) compiling, which enables managed code to run in the native machine language of the platform on which your application is running. This allows you to create applications that can target a variety of platforms and not have to worry about recompiling or generating executable s that target each specific platform.

Even though your mobile application is written in VB .NET, and as such is managed code, you are still able to incorporate functions and subroutines stored externally in dynamic link libraries (DLLs), including the Windows CE APIs. Unlike eMbedded Visual Basic (eVB), NETCF provides the data types and support for structures to allow you to easily incorporate functions from the Windows CE APIs into your application. At the same time, the need for the use of these functions is far less with NETCF in comparison to eVB. Still, having that functionality available allows you to create robust mobile applications with the .NET Compact Framework. Your only concern as a developer when bridging managed to unmanaged code is garbage collection. If you allocate memory outside managed code, you run the risk of that memory no longer being available to your NETCF application. But all is not lost—Microsoft has built-in mechanisms to handle such eventualities.

NOTE *Accessing the Windows CE API with VB .NET is not without limitations. One glaring absence is that VB .NET doesn't support passing pointers. The workaround for this is to use the Marshall class. More on this subject can be found in Chapter 17. C# .NET doesn't suffer from this same limitation.*

NOTE *For more on leveraging external functions and subroutines from your mobile applications, see Chapter 17.*

.NET Compact Framework Class Library

The .NET Compact Framework class library is a collection of reusable classes that tightly integrate with the common language runtime. Your applications leverage these libraries to derive functionality.

As you would expect from an object-oriented class library, the .NET Compact Framework types enable you to accomplish a range of common programming tasks, including interface design, leveraging XML, database access, thread management, and file I/O.

The following sections describe the common functionality available through NETCF.

Form-Related Classes

NETCF implements a subset of the **System.Windows.Forms** and **System.Drawing** classes, which allow you to construct rich Windows CE–based user interfaces for your device applications. Much of the interaction with these classes is managed for you by the form designer component of Smart Device Extensions operating within Visual Studio .NET.

The implementation of WinForms under the .NET Compact Framework includes support for forms, most controls found in the .NET Framework, hosting third-party controls, bitmaps, and menus. Table 1-1 lists the controls included with the .NET Compact Framework.

Table 1-1. NETCF Controls

CONTROL	DESCRIPTION
Button	Simple command button
CheckBox	Common check box
ComboBox	Drop-down list of times
ContextMenu	Context-sensitive menu for association with another object
DataGrid	Grid that can be bound to a data source
DomainUpDown	Control that provides a list of items the user can navigate using scroll bars
HScrollBar	Horizontal scroll bar
ImageList	Container used to store images, which in turn will be used with other controls such as the ToolBar, ListView, and TreeView
InputPanel	Controls the Soft Input Panel (SIP) on Windows CE devices
Label	Simple control that allows you to display text
ListBox	Control that provides a list of items from which the user can pick
ListView	Control that provides four views for displaying data: large icon, small icon, list, and details
MainMenu	Control that implements a menu with a form
NumericUpDown	Numeric input field that allows both manual entry as well as scroll bars
OpenFileDialog	Interfaces with the standard Windows CE Open File dialog box
Panel	Container used to hold other controls
PictureBox	Control used to display images of a variety of formats
ProgressBar	Visual indicator of a task's progress
RadioButton	Common radio button
SaveFileDialog	Interfaces with the standard Windows CE Save File dialog box
StatusBar	Simple panel for displaying text
TabControl	Control that provides a tabbed interface for an application
TextBox	Standard text input field
Timer	Basic timing component
ToolBar	Control that implements a toolbar on a form
TrackBar	Slider interface used with numeric data
TreeView	Control that presents data in a hierarchical layout
VScrollBar	Vertical scroll bar

NOTE *For more information on the controls included with the .NET Compact Framework, see Chapter 4.*

Like everything else that is part of the .NET Compact Framework, the controls included with NETCF have limited functionality. They're missing properties, methods, and events found in their .NET Framework counterparts. A little coding (well, in some cases a lot of coding) can correct these shortcomings. That's because NETCF allows you to create your own controls by inheriting from the base control class, surprisingly enough named **Control**. From this foundation, you can add your own properties, methods, and events to create just the control you need.

 NOTE *For more on building your own controls, refer to Chapter 5.*

Data and XML Classes

The .NET Compact Framework includes a set of classes that allow you to easily incorporate data, whether that is from a relational or nonrelational data source, and XML content into your mobile applications. These classes are defined under the **System.Data** and **System.Xml** namespaces. The implementation of both data and XML classes under NETCF is a subset of those found in the .NET Framework. More details on both the data and XML classes are included later in this chapter.

Web Services

The .NET Framework is much about Web services. In the .NET Compact Framework **System.Web** namespace, you have a scaled-down version of the capabilities and functionality offered in the corresponding .NET Framework namespace. Most significantly, you can create Web service clients but are not able to host Web services under the .NET Compact Framework.

These Web service clients can be either synchronous or asynchronous. Creating a Web service client that targets the .NET Compact Framework is easy. The Visual Studio .NET IDE does much of the work for you. More on this subject is included later in this chapter.

Visual Basic Support

Visual Basic .NET makes liberal use of helper functions that are located in a VB Helper library. The .NET Compact Framework includes a subset of these functions as well. These functions are considered by VB developers to be a core part of the language, which is the reason for their inclusion.

If you're an existing eVB developer converting over to NETCF, what this means is that many of the VB language functions you are used to working with will be available to you in Visual Basic .NET.

GDI Support

The .NET Compact Framework provides support for the basic GDI drawing elements including bitmaps, brushes, fonts, icons, and pens through the **System.Drawing** namespace.

Base Classes

The .NET Compact Framework provides a robust set of base classes that expose a wide range of functionality for use by developers. This underlying infrastructure enables you to write rich .NET applications by allowing you to create multithreaded applications (System.Threading), leverage networking resources (System.Net), and work with files (System.IO).

IrDA Support

Windows CE devices, such as the Pocket PC and Pocket PC 2002, include infrared (IR) communication capabilities. In support of this, the .NET Compact Framework includes classes that allow you to leverage IR communication from within your application. These classes are part of the **System.Net.IrDA** namespace. You can use IR to communicate to Pocket PCs, printers, and other IR-enabled devices.

NOTE *For more information on working with IR, see Chapter 15.*

Bluetooth Support

The .NET Compact Framework doesn't natively provide support for Bluetooth. You can access most third-party Pocket PC implementations of Bluetooth via either serial port communications or through a provider's API.

A La Carte Features

To conserve resources on the target device, Microsoft divided the .NET Compact Framework into logical components. By delivering components as separate DLLs, or as they are referred to within the .NET Compact Framework, *assemblies*, Microsoft gives you the option of picking and choosing the features you need, and only those features that your target device has the space to hold.

An example of this is the System.SR assembly, which contains error message strings. Including this assembly with your application allows access to detailed descriptions of any errors encountered, which is certainly helpful during a fitful debugging session (like there is any other type of debugging session). Excluding this assembly doesn't affect the performance or functionality of your application; it simply means you won't have access to detailed error messages.

 TIP *Generally speaking, you will only want to include the System.SR assembly while developing your applications.*

The SQL Server CE components, delivered in a set of DLLs totaling slightly over 1MB in size, represent another example of the NETCF a la carte approach. Don't need local database support with your Pocket PC application? Then don't include a reference to the System.Data.SqlServerCe assemblies.

Referencing an Assembly

To add a reference to an assembly to a project, perform the following steps:

1. In the Solutions Explorer window of the VS .NET interface, right-click the **References** folder. Figure 1-1 shows the pop-up window that is displayed.

Figure 1-1. Initiating adding an assembly to a project

2. From the pop-up window, select **Add Reference**. The Add Reference dialog box is displayed, as shown in Figure 1-2. On the .NET tab of the Add Reference dialog box is a list of all of the .NET components.

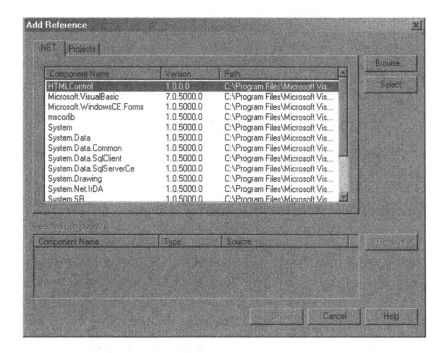

Figure 1-2. The Add Reference dialog box

3. Select the desired component from the list of available components.

4. Click the **Select** button to add the component to the Selected Components list.

5. Click the **OK** button to add the reference to your project.

Viewing Project References

To view the assemblies presently referenced by your project, perform the following steps:

1. In the Solutions Explorer window of the VS .NET interface, click the "+" sign, located to the right of the **References** folder.

2. The References folder will expand to display the current project references. Figure 1-3 provides an example of this.

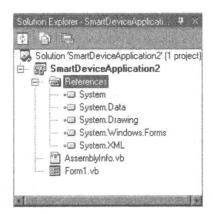

Figure 1-3. Viewing project references

Referencing a Namespace Within a Project

There are two ways to work with namespace elements: either in the full, or qualified form, or in a shortened form. Here is an example of referencing a namespace element, **Microsoft.VisualBasic.Strings.Left**, in its qualified form:

```
Dim mb As MessageBox
mb.Show(Microsoft.VisualBasic.Strings.Left("abcdefg", 3))
```

The second method of referencing an element is to reference a shortened form. This approach is made possible by using the Imports statement. The Imports statement is appropriately named as it imports namespace names from referenced projects and assemblies. You can include any number of Imports statements in a module. The one rule is that you must place all Imports statements before anything else in a code module, including Module or Class statements.

The syntax for the Imports statement is

```
Imports [aliasname = ] namespace
```

The **aliasname** is optional, providing an alternative way to reference the namespace from within your code. Figure 1-4 provides an example of the use of the Imports statement with an **aliasname**. In this case, **vb** has the equivalent value of **Microsoft.VisualBasic**.

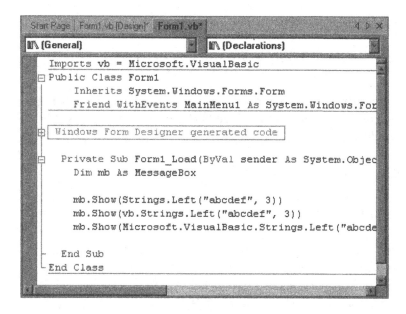

Figure 1-4. Adding an Imports statement

How far you shorten the naming of an element affects how you reference its uniquely named members. For example, if only the namespace is specified, as shown in Figure 1-5, all of the uniquely named members, along with the members of modules within that namespace, are available without having to fully qualify their names. In this example, the Imports statement shortens the naming of members within the **Microsoft.VisualBasic** namespace.

Figure 1-5. An Imports statement that specifies only the namespace

Listing 1-1 demonstrates ways you could subsequently reference the **Strings** module. Any of the options, from fully qualified to abbreviated, provide exactly the same functionality.

Listing 1-1. Working with the Strings Module

```
Imports vb = Microsoft.VisualBasic

Public Class Form1
  Inherits System.Windows.Forms.Form
  Friend WithEvents MainMenu1 As System.Windows.Forms.MainMenu
  Private Sub Form1_Load(ByVal sender As System.Object, _
    ByVal e As System.EventArgs) Handles MyBase.Load
    Dim mb As MessageBox

    mb.Show(Microsoft.VisualBasic.Strings.Left("abcdef", 3))
    mb.Show(vb.Strings.Left("abcdef", 3))
    mb.Show(Strings.Left("abcdef", 3))

  End Sub
End Class
```

As you extend the reference defined by the Imports statement, only the members of that further restricted element are available without qualification. For example, Listing 1-2 shows a further defined reference.

Listing 1-2. Explicitly Referencing the Strings Module

```
Imports vbstr = Microsoft.VisualBasic.Strings

Public Class Form1
   Inherits System.Windows.Forms.Form
   Friend WithEvents MainMenu1 As System.Windows.Forms.MainMenu
   Private Sub Form1_Load(ByVal sender As System.Object, _
     ByVal e As System.EventArgs) Handles MyBase.Load
     Dim mb As MessageBox

     mb.Show(vbstr.Left("abcdef", 3))
     mb.Show(Microsoft.VisualBasic.Strings.Left("abcdef", 3))

   End Sub
End Class
```

Remember, when working with the Imports statement, the key phrase is "uniquely named members." Simply put, this means that to reference a member, *it must be uniquely named.* For example, in Listing 1-2, these two ways of referencing the **Left** method are valid:

```
     mb.Show(vbstr.Left("abcdef", 3))
     mb.Show(Microsoft.VisualBasic.Strings.Left("abcdef", 3))
```

while the following way of referencing the **Left** method is not valid. The reason that it's not valid is because the **Left** method is not a uniquely named member.

```
     mb.Show(Left("abcdef", 3))
```

Now that you have a general understanding of what NETCF is, we'll turn our attention to what it's not.

What's Missing from NETCF?

As I mentioned at the beginning of this chapter, Microsoft had to do some serious trimming to make the .NET Framework fit into the operating constraints of Windows CE. The most notable .NET Framework features that did not make it into NETCF are the subject of this section.

Method Overloads

Overloading a method provides alternative ways to call that method. It also increases the size of a framework. Because of this, the .NET Compact Framework trimmed the overloads from almost all methods.

What this means to you is twofold. First, there is a good chance that a particular method overload you used with a desktop application will not be available under NETCF. Second, when (notice I didn't say if) you read the documentation, pay close attention to whether or not a method is supported by NETCF.

Nonessential Controls

At first, you're led to believe that the list of missing controls is but a few. In fact, the controls that are missing are nearly as many as are included. Now, is that a reason for you to abandon programming with the .NET Compact Framework? Certainly not. Like other missing features, it provides you with an opportunity to demonstrate your programming prowess. How's that for a positive spin.

Table 1-2 lists .NET Framework controls that didn't make it into NETCF. The absence of most of these controls is not going to be of any significance to mobile developers. Since printing has such a limited role in mobile applications, removing the whole family of print-related controls is not an issue. That takes care of the CrystalReportViewer, PageSetupDialog, PrintDialog, PrintDocument, PrintPreviewControl, and PrintPreviewDialog controls. You can replace many of the missing dialog boxes with your own dialog boxes (see Chapter 3) or by accessing system dialog boxes directly using the Windows CE API (see Chapter 17).

Table 1-2. Controls Missing from NETCF

CONTROL	DESCRIPTION
CheckedListBox	Hybrid list box that includes check boxes next to each item; a suitable workaround for this limitation is the ListView control.
ColorDialog	Control that provides access to the operating system's color dialog box.
CrystalReportViewer	Control that links an application to Crystal Reports. No precanned reporting functionality is provided under NETCF, nor for that matter is printing supported.
DateTimePicker	Graphic component for selecting date and time.
ErrorProvider	Graphical indicator to the user as to what fields on a form contain invalid values.
FolderBrowserDialog	Interface to folder hierarchies.
FontDialog	Control that provides access to the operating system's font dialog box.
GroupBox	Control used to group related controls together. The Panel control offers a suitable replacement.
HelpProvider	Control that links an application to a help file.
LinkLabel	Control that combines the functionality of a label with a hyperlink.
MonthCalendar	Pop-up calendar from which the user could select a date.
NotifyIcon	Control that adds a link between a status bar icon and background applications.
PageSetupDialog	Control used to manipulate page, margin, and printing configurations for a document.
PrintDialog	Control that provides access to the operating system's print dialog box.
PrintDocument	Object used to define a print document.
PrintPreviewControl	Preview of how a printed document will appear.
PrintPreviewDialog	Dialog box containing a PrintPreviewControl.
RichTextBox	Text box that supports advanced formatting features.
Splitter	Control that allows the user to resize docked controls.
ToolTip	Pop-up window that provides a brief description of a control.

The missing controls that I'd like most to have added would be the DateTimePicker, MonthCalendar, and RichTextBox. The functionality offered by these controls would be immediately beneficial in developing mobile solutions.

NOTE   *As luck would have it, other developers feel the same way and have done something about it. For a list of third-party controls, see Appendix C.*

XML Functionality

As much as the .NET Compact Framework offers in the way of XML, an equal amount of functionality was trimmed. The key missing XML-related component is the **System.Xml.XPath** namespace. The **XPath** namespace made XML parsing far easier than the methods offered under NETCF. In its absence, you can use a combination of recursive and iterative searches against the Document Object Model (DOM).

The .NET Compact Framework is missing another key XML component: Extensible Stylesheet Language Transformation, or XSLT. With XSLT, you can convert an XML document into different formats. This also means that methods such as the XMLNode object's SelectSingleNode are not supported.

On an XML-related note, NETCF doesn't provide support for developing device-based Web services. Initially this may not seem like much of a limitation for mobile developers. In actuality, it's a serious shortcoming. Device-based Web services would enable you to initiate communication and data transfer from outside of the device.

NETCF doesn't support retrieving typed DataSets from a Web service.

NOTE   *Refer to Chapter 14 for a detailed discussion on the XML functionality offered through the .NET Compact Framework. Chapter 15 demonstrates a way to initiate communication to a device remotely. Chapter 16 shows how to leverage Web services from a mobile application.*

Limited Database Support

While the .NET Compact Framework offers a robust set of data-related tools, it's not without shortcomings. Foremost is its limited support for industry-standard databases. The .NET Compact Framework doesn't provide support for Pocket Access databases, a mainstay of many applications written in eVB. In fact, it doesn't provide support for any device-based database except SQL Server CE.

Things don't get much better on the server end, where NETCF only provides support for SQL Server. What this means is if your enterprise uses Oracle or another relational database, you will need to either turn to a third-party middleware product or develop your own custom interface.

The key missing namespace is **System.Data.OleDb**. Do I expect that third parties will rectify this shortcoming in some way? Yes, certainly they will. The more interesting questions are when and how much more will it cost.

NOTE *There is already a third party that provides the necessary framework for working with Pocket Access databases. For more on this topic, see Appendix C.*

Absence of File Notifications

While NETCF offers a solid subset of input and output functionality, in my opinion it's missing one key component—notifications on changes made to files. This functionality would allow mobile applications to be informed when a file changes, such as when updates are delivered to a device.

Binary Serialization

Both the BinaryFormatter and SoapFormatter classes are absent from the .NET Compact Framework, severely limiting serializing and deserializing objects.

Access to the Windows Registry

The .NET Framework has the **Microsoft.Win32.Registry** namespace, which makes it easy to work with the Windows registry from an application. Obviously, this namespace was not included in NETCF, as it has to do with Win32, not Windows CE. Unfortunately, no Windows CE equivalent of this namespace was included in NETCF. As a result, you're forced to turn to the Windows API if your application requires access to the Windows CE registry.

NOTE *For more information on accessing the Windows CE registry, see Chapter 17.*

Leveraging COM Components

The absence of the COM interop is one of the most loudly debated and complained about limitations of NETCF. This is particularly true for developers who are switching over from eMbedded Visual Basic, where they were accustomed to leveraging COM objects, including ActiveX controls, to extend their development capabilities.

Incorporating COM objects into a NETCF application is a painful two-step process. First, you must write an unmanaged (read eVC++) DLL wrapper that exposes the COM object. Depending upon the complexity of the COM object, this may be anything from a simple to a life-altering challenge. Second, you must use PInvoke to access your DLL wrapper. Luckily, the development community has already begun work on accessing the more commonly used COM components.

 NOTE *For more on accessing DLLs from your mobile applications, see Chapter 17.*

Security

The .NET Compact Framework doesn't secure access to unmanaged code. Any application can call any system or nonsystem API.

There is no role-based security with the .NET Compact Framework. The principal object has no understanding of known identity or known role.

Web Services

The most notable exclusion from the .NET Compact Framework Web service capabilities is the inability to use cookies. Cookies are widely used to maintain state on the server between calls from a client. While the use of cookies in Web services is not as prevalent as their use on Web sites, they are still in use.

The .NET Compact Framework offers limited cryptographic abilities with respect to Web services.

No Support for Printing

NETCF provides as much support for printing as eMbedded Visual Basic provided, that is to say none. There is no easy way to interact with either network printers or external printers via IR.

The workaround for accessing network printers is to build a server-based application that accepts and prints jobs submitted by your mobile application.

You can send output through the IR port directly to IR-enabled printers. You use the **System.Net.IrDA** namespace to access the IR port of your device. The difficult part is that your application needs to control everything sent to the printer, including any control characters that the printer supports.

No Support for GDI+

This is more of a "Windows CE thing" rather than a .NET Compact Framework shortcoming. Windows CE natively doesn't support GDI+, so the GDI+-related functionality was obviously removed from NETCF.

 NOTE *For more on the graphical capabilities offered by NETCF, refer to Chapter 7.*

No Support for Remoting

Remoting, that wonderful feature of the .NET Framework that allows you to easily build distributed applications, is, sad to say, missing from NETCF. Now, one could make the case that mobile applications are ideal candidates for remoting. I'd certainly agree. To make matters worse, there's not a good way to code around this limitation.

Differences Between eVB and VB .NET

If you're migrating from eMbedded Visual Basic to Visual Basic .NET, there are more than a few changes to deal with. In this section, I'll walk you through some of the key differences between these two development tools.

Data Changes

The eMbedded Visual Basic language was built upon VBScript and because of this offered a single data type—**Variant**. In comparison, Visual Basic .NET offers a robust set of data types, which are the subject of this section.

NETCF Data Types

The **Variant** data type, the only data type supported in eMbedded Visual Basic, is not available under Visual Basic .NET. In its place, Visual Basic .NET offers a wide variety of data types to meet your programming needs as shown in Table 1-3.

Table 1-3. Visual Basic .NET Data Types

TYPE	SIZE IN BYTES	USE
Boolean	2	True or False value
Byte	1	Unsigned number from 0 to 255
Char	2	Unicode character
Date	8	Date and time
Decimal	16	Decimal number
Double	8	Double-precision floating point number
Integer	4	32-bit signed integer
Long	8	64-bit signed integer
Object	4	Capable of storing any data type
Short	2	16-bit signed integer
Single	4	Single-precision floating point number
String	n/a	Series of Unicode characters

Declaring Values While Dimensioning a Variable

Visual Basic .NET allows you to declare the value of a variable at the time you are dimensioning the variable. For example:

```
Dim intFactor As Integer = 5
```

Fixed-Length Strings Are Not Supported

Visual Basic .NET doesn't support fixed-length strings. For example, the following eMbedded Visual Basic statement would result in a compilation error under Visual Basic .NET.

```
Dim strDemo As String*50
```

Use Zero-Bound Arrays

eMbedded Visual Basic allowed you to specify the lower and upper bounds for an array. In Visual Basic .NET, you must use zero for the lower bound.

Language Structure Changes

While both eVB and VB .NET are based upon the Visual Basic languages, there are some noticeable differences.

Default Properties

With eMbedded Visual Basic, you could use default properties. When you referenced an object without specifying a property, it would be resolved to the default property for the specific object. For example, the following lines of code operate identically under eMbedded Visual Basic:

```
Text1 = "something"
Text1.Text = "something"
```

Visual Basic .NET in comparison doesn't implement default properties for its controls. In all instances, you must specify the desired property.

Subroutines and Functions Require Parentheses

Under Visual Basic .NET, all calls to subroutines or functions require the use of parentheses. For example, the eMbedded Visual Basic code

```
MsgBox "test..."
```

will need to be written in Visual Basic .NET as

```
MsgBox ("test...")
```

Optional Arguments Are Not Allowed

Visual Basic .NET doesn't support optional arguments. Any calls to methods or procedures must include values for each argument defined by the method or procedure. At the same time VB .NET does support overriding methods, which provide alternate ways of calling a method.

New Assignment Operators

Visual Basic .NET supports a new set of assignment operators borrowed from the C-based languages. Table 1-4 shows these new operators.

Table 1-4. New VB .NET Assignment Operators

TYPE OF OPERATOR	EVB SYNTAX	VB .NET SYNTAX
Addition	intValue = intValue + 1	intValue += 1
Subtraction	intValue = intValue – 1	intValue -= 1
Multiplication	intValue = intValue * 5	intValue *= 5
Division	dblValue = dblValue / 5	dblValue /= 5
String concatenation	strValue = strValue & "demo"	strValue &= "demo"

NOTE *Visual Basic .NET supports these new operators in addition to the operators available in eMbedded Visual Basic.*

Data Access Changes

Visual Basic .NET allows developers to interact with both device and server-based databases. Through the **System.Data** namespace, the .NET Compact Framework provides support for both SQL Server and SQL Server databases. This namespace includes support for disconnected DataSets, which allow developers to work easily with both relational and nonrelational data using the same model used with the .NET Framework. Data is passed as XML, allowing rich, open standards-based communication and interoperability.

The .NET Compact Framework includes two Data Connectors. Each of these connectors is database-specific—that is to say, the Data Connector for SQL Server CE is the SQL Server CE Data Connector.

NOTE *Presently, there are no plans to provide a Data Connector for Pocket Access or the native Windows CE database structure.*

There is no support for ADOCE in Visual Basic .NET, nor will there be any support for ADOCE on Windows CE .NET. In its place, you can use ADO.NET to access DataSets. From your Visual Basic .NET application, you can access data through the **System.Data** classes of the .NET Compact Framework. Listing 1-3 shows an example of this.

Listing 1-3. Working with ADO.NET

```
Dim cmd As System.Data.SqlServerCE.SqlCeCommand
Dim cn As System.Data.SqlServerCe.SqlCeConnection
Dim da As System.Data.SqlServerCe.SqlCeDataAdapter
Dim ds As System.Data.DataSet

' Open the connection.
Try
  cn = New System.Data.SqlServerce.SqlCeConnection("Data Source= " & _
    "\My Documents\NorthwindDemo.sdf")

' Configure the command.
  cmd = New System.Data.SqlServerCE.SqlCeCommand("SELECT * FROM Customers", cn)

' Create the DataAdapter and fill the DataSet.
  da = New System.Data.SqlServerCE.SqlCeDataAdapter(cmd)
  da.Fill(ds)

' Make some changes to the DataSet here.

' Save the DataSet.
  da.Update(ds)

Catch ex As Exception
' Handle errors here.

End Try
```

This example starts by declaring the four variables, which will hold instances of the SqlCeConnection, SqlCeCommand, SqlCeDataAdapter, and DataSet objects. These instances allow us to connect to and retrieve data from a local SQL Server CE database.

The SqlCeConnection object establishes a connection to a SQL Server CE database. The SqlCeCommand object defines the command used to retrieve the desired data from the source. In this case, it's all of the records from the Customers Table. The SqlCeDataAdapter acts as the conduit between the SQL Server CE database and our DataSet. The SqlCeDataAdapter **Fill** method loads the

DataSet. Later in this example, the SqlCeDataAdapter **Update** method saves the DataSet.

As this example demonstrates, you can expect a steep learning curve if you're coming from eMbedded Visual Basic and ADOCE to VB .NET and ADO.NET. Simply stated, everything has changed in the way of dealing with data.

What Are DataSets?

Developers experienced with ADO are accustomed to working with recordsets. The ADO.NET equivalent to a recordset is the DataSet. A DataSet is a disconnected cache that developers can use within their applications. It is essentially an in-memory database (IMDB). It offers a relational view of the database query stored in XML format. Through DataSets, developers can access table, row, and column data. Since DataSets are disconnected, they inherently support a scalable model, since the client application doesn't maintain a database connection for the entire time that the application runs. DataSets can be shuttled between desktop .NET and NETCF. The SQL Data Connector accesses the database to populate a DataSet. You can work with DataSets programmatically, or bind them to controls, such as text boxes, list boxes, and grids.

Recordsets are not included in ADO.NET. DataSets offer a far more flexible approach to working with data sources.

Visual Basic .NET support for DataSets coupled with the capability for binding DataSets to controls will allow developers to quickly build data-enabled applications. This is a great improvement over eMbedded Visual Basic, in which developers were solely responsible for displaying and managing data.

NOTE *For more on ADO.NET and how it can be used to access both local and server-based databases, see Chapters 9 through 14.*

Error Handling Changes

eMbedded Visual Basic lacked adequate error handling. Since eMbedded Visual Basic was built using the VBScript language, it supported only On Error Resume Next. Developers who have worked with this method of error handling are well aware that it often leads to more problems than it solves.

Visual Basic .NET offers a far more robust approach to error handling, if implemented with the Try-Catch-Finally structure. Listing 1-4 shows an example of this structure.

Listing 1-4. The Try-Catch-Finally Error Handling Structure

```
Try

' Your normal application code goes here.

Catch

' This code gets executed if an error occurs.

Finally

' This code would get executed every time. Typically it is used
' as a clean-up area for the error handler.

End Try
```

> **NOTE**   *For details on how to manage runtime errors within your mobile applications, refer to Appendix E.*

Enhanced Support for APIs

The .NET Compact Framework supports calling functions stored in dynamic link libraries written in eMbedded Visual C++, Visual C#, and Visual Basic .NET. Like eMbedded Visual Basic, Visual Basic .NET can use the Declare statement to define these functions. The more preferred approach is to use the DLLImport statement. With its support of structures, Visual Basic .NET can call the Windows CE APIs in a far more robust fashion than was allowed with eMbedded Visual Basic.

Visual Basic .NET support for calling DLLs is limited by the following restrictions:

- American National Standards Institute (ANSI) strings are not supported. Since Windows CE is UNICODE based, only UNICODE strings may be used.

- Simple types are supported, but not nested types.

> **NOTE**   *For more information on working with the Windows CE API, see Chapter 17.*

XML Functionality Included Under NETCF

XML is the universal format for data on the Internet. XML allows developers to easily describe and deliver rich, structured data between applications, varied data sources, and different operating systems in a standard, consistent way.

While eMbedded Visual Basic offered low-level support for XML, the .NET Compact Framework provides Visual Basic .NET with a set of tools that make it simple and straightforward to work with XML structures.

As with other components of the .NET Compact Framework, the XML-related classes offer a subset of the functionality found in the .NET Framework. The support for XML in the .NET Compact Framework

- Adheres to the SOAP standards and provides access to SOAP headers

- Allows developers to create applications that consume DataSets from and post DataSets to Web services

- Enables developers to read an XML document, manipulate the document, post the document to a server, and maintain the document on the device

The .NET Compact Framework provides support for the following XML functionality:

- **XML Reader**—Provides a forward-only, read-only stream of parsed XML tokens

- **XML Writer**—Provides a forward-only, write-only method for generating well-formed XML documents

- **XML Document**—Provides access to the XML Document Object Model (DOM)

Working with Web Services

One of the most powerful new features of Visual Basic .NET is the ability to create applications that access, or consume, a Web service. Web services, running on standard Internet Web servers, expose methods you can call from your Visual Basic .NET–based applications. Developing a Web service client with Visual Basic .NET is simple. It involves adding a reference to the Web service, creating an instance of the Web service, and then calling the methods provided by the Web service. HTTP/S GET/POST (non-SOAP) Web services can also be called but require additional coding. You will need to parse the XML yourself since serialization is not available.

NOTE *For more on Web services and creating a Web service client, see Chapter 16.*

Local Data Storage Using XML

The XML support provided by the .NET Compact Framework, and accessible from Visual Studio .NET, allows developers to keep a persistent XML stream in a serialized manner to a local text file. This provides developers with an alternative to relational databases and standard files as a method of storing data.

Developers can use this technique to store configuration information, as well as for offline caching of small, simple data volumes. This method provides a simple yet effective alternative for situations in which a full-functioned relational database is not required.

The following shows a simple example of reading and writing a DataSet to a file as XML. As you can see, there's really nothing to it.

```
Dim ds As System.Data.DataSet

ds.ReadXml("demo.xml")
ds.WriteXml("demo.xml")
```

NOTE *For more on storing DataSets as XML, refer to Chapter 9.*

Working with Files Under Visual Basic .NET

With eMbedded Visual Basic, file access and directory information was provided by the File System and File Microsoft ActiveX controls. In NETCF, similar functionality is provided by the **System.IO** namespace.

The following code fragment demonstrates opening a text file, writing a line of text to the file, and then closing the file in Visual Basic .NET.

```
Dim sw As System.IO.StreamWriter

' Open the file.
sw = New System.IO.StreamWriter("text.tmp")
```

```
' Add some text to the file.
  sw.Write("This content was written at: ")
  sw.WriteLine(DateTime.Now)

' Close the file.
  sw.Close()
```

CAUTION *The file capabilities provided under the* **Microsoft.VisualBasic** *namespace in the .NET Framework are not supported under the compact version of the framework. Methods such as* **FileOpen**, **FileAttr**, *and* **FileCopy**, *along with many others, are not included.*

NOTE *For more on working with files, see Chapter 8.*

Working Between .NET and .NETCF

For the first time in the history of Windows CE, developers can seriously consider developing code for use with both a desktop and device. This write-once, use-twice approach was not an option with previous versions of Windows CE development tools. Incompatibilities between the eMbedded Visual Tools, which included eMbedded Visual C++ and eMbedded Visual Basic, and Visual Studio did not enable sharing of code to occur easily. With the release of Visual Studio .NET, along with its included Smart Device Extensions, developers now have the ability to reuse code. Well, sort of.

Now, before you run off and tell your management that you have the answer to porting that critical .NET Framework application over to NETCF, carefully consider these points:

- The .NET Compact Framework is a subset of the .NET Framework. Many of the namespaces, elements, modules, overloaded methods, controls, and other items are missing from NETCF.

- The Windows CE and Windows environments differ significantly. Developing an application that works seamlessly under both platforms is at best a challenge.

- There are namespaces within NETCF that are not part of the .NET Framework.

That said, code compiled under the .NET Framework will run under the .NET Compact Framework, as is, as long as it only makes use of functionality found in NETCF. The opposite doesn't hold true though. Code compiled under the .NET Framework will not run under the .NET Compact Framework. The reason for this one-way support is that, while compiled assemblies of both platforms contain the same IL code, the library assemblies for the two platforms are different. In addition, while the assembly loader for the .NET Compact Framework is smart enough to handle these differences, the .NET Framework loader is not.

How NETCF handles this is that the assembly loader maps references to the .NET Framework library assemblies to the appropriate NETCF assemblies. Pretty slick, although I'm not sure that this is something that I'm just dying to be able to do.

In my mind, what is more of an issue is the question of reusing code. Can you write modules for use with both desktop and device applications? The simple answer to this question is yes, with the added qualifier of "if you're careful and have some foresight."

In creating code for use under both .NET and NETCF, you must be selective as to what parts and features of the framework each includes. The way I like to look at this is to "write for the least common denominator," which is almost always NETCF. Another way to look at this is to say that if a piece of code runs under NETCF, it will very likely run under the .NET Framework.

Using Compiler Directives

You may find areas of your code that need to be different between the two platforms, .NET and NETCF. In those situations, you can use *compiler directives*. Compiler directives allow you to substitute pieces of code based upon the target platform.

Listing 1-5 shows a simple example of a compiler directive. At the top of this example is the declaration of the constant **TargetPlatform**. Later in your code, you can reference this constant to conditionally select pieces of code to include in your application. This is implemented with the compiler directive #IF.

Listing 1-5. Using a Compiler Directive

```
#Const TargetPlatform = "device"

Public Class Form1
    Inherits System.Windows.Forms.Form
    Friend WithEvents MainMenu1 As System.Windows.Forms.MainMenu
```

```
Private Sub Form1_Load(ByVal sender As System.Object, _
    ByVal e As System.EventArgs) Handles MyBase.Load

    #If TargetPlatform = "device" Then
' place device-specific code here

    #Else
' place desktop-specific code here

    #End If
  End Sub
End Class
```

To share this code between a desktop and device application, you simply have to change the constant **TargetPlatform**.

Optionally, instead of including a constant definition in code, you can configure a custom directive under your project's properties using the following steps:

1. Select your project's properties from under the Project menu.

2. The Project Properties dialog box displays. From this dialog box, select the **Configuration Properties** folder.

3. Under this folder, select **Build**.

4. On the Build page, enter your custom directive. Figure 1-6 shows an example of defining the **TargetPlatform** directive.

With some careful planning, a bit of foresight, a solid understanding of both the .NET and .NET Compact Frameworks, and the use of some strategically placed compiler directives, you can successfully leverage code between both the desktop and device. For the first time, code written for the device is not restricted to the device, which is a tremendous step forward for the mobile developer.

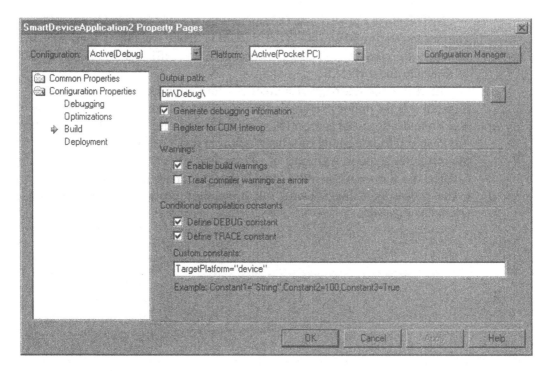

Figure 1-6. Defining a custom directive

Summary

Going from 30 megabytes to 1.5 megabytes is an amazing task. Think about it this way. If you're required to trim (if trim is even the appropriate word—slashing might be better) one of your applications by a factor of 20-to-1, what would you do? More importantly, what degree of functionality would remain after you were done?

The .NET Compact Framework is a subset of the .NET Framework. While similar in appearance and functionality to the .NET Framework, learning how to program under NETCF will take time and effort. Add on top of that limitations imposed by Windows CE devices and the demands associated with creating mobile applications, and I can safely say that you've got your work cut out for you.

Now don't get me wrong. I'm not trying to scare you away from creating mobile solutions. In fact, just the opposite is true. I believe that mobile applications are the next frontier of the tech world. What I'm attempting to do is to keep you from making a mistake, promising your boss or a client that you can build an application in a fraction of the amount of time that it will actually take.

NETCF offers a powerful development environment, but it's not the .NET Framework. Don't underestimate the amount of time it will take to master NETCF. In many cases, the way you do something under the .NET Framework just won't be available under NETCF.

There are a couple of good sources of information for NETCF developers. First, there is the online documentation. It's as good a source as there is available on indicating what is included and what is excluded from NETCF. It might just keep you from bashing your head against a wall. Second, there are the Microsoft newsgroups. A number of newsgroups focus on mobile-related topics. Chances are someone else will be able to give you an idea, a workaround, or even a code sample that helps you out. Appendix C provides a list of NETCF-related newsgroups.

CHAPTER 2

Smart Device Extensions

SMART DEVICE EXTENSIONS (SDE) for Visual Studio .NET provides a robust development environment for creating applications that target the .NET Compact Framework. SDE is a Visual Studio Integration Package, or VSIP, that plugs into Visual Studio .NET. It offers mobile developers a rich, powerful development environment from which to work.

Included as part of the Smart Device Extensions are a set of prebuilt device profiles. A *device profile* contains information necessary to build applications that target specific devices. With SDE, there are profiles that enable you to create applications for the Pocket PC, Pocket PC 2002, and Windows CE .NET 4.1 and later. These profiles allow you to create applications that include WinForms and ADO.NET, and offer the ability to consume XML Web services. In the future, other profiles could be provided that would allow you to create applications targeting cell phones or third-party PDAs.

Profiles may target specific devices, such as the Pocket PC, or platforms, such as the Windows CE platforms in general; generic profiles target any platform to which the .NET Compact Framework has been ported.

SDE supports device kits (formerly known as SDKs). As were earlier versions of the embedded tools, device kits are separate from SDE and may be installed and updated independently.

In addition to all of the features found natively in Visual Studio .NET, Smart Device Extensions offers the following device-specific features:

- **Templates**—Predefined configurations for common project types. Templates are provided for both Pocket PC and Windows CE devices.

- **Device-specific controls**—Controls specifically designed for use with the Pocket PC and Windows CE. The interface, resource consumption, and functionality have been tailored for these environments.

- **Device emulators**—Testing environments that simulate specific devices. Emulators run on the developer's PC, allowing for testing without the presence of a device.

- **Automatic deployment of applications**—Allows you to easily test on either an emulator or a device, providing developers with a seamless testing environment.

- **Remote debugging**—Allows you to leverage the debugging tools offered through the VS .NET IDE with your SDE applications. All of the debugging tools can be used with SDE applications running either in an emulator or on a device.

Languages Supported by SDE

The .NET Compact Framework supports two development languages, C# .NET and VB .NET. While previous versions of Windows CE development tools favored C-based languages, namely eMbedded Visual C++, with NETCF and SDE, it makes little difference with which of these two languages you work, because both are equally powerful and functional.

As a late addition to the .NET development environment, J# is not supported at all under the .NET Compact Framework. Will it be in the future? I expect it will, along with a number of other languages provided by third parties. In the meantime, I would suggest getting started with SDE and C# until J# .NET comes along.

You should also be aware that there is another language limitation under SDE and NETCF that does not exist under .NET. One of the many cool features of .NET is that you can use mixed-language components within a single project. In comparison, NETCF projects are restricted to a single language, either C# .NET or VB .NET. While this isn't a big hurdle, it's an annoying "feature" when the only working example you've got of a particular code trick is in C# and your project is in VB.

TIP *The workaround to this single-language project limitation imposed by NETCF is to create additional projects using the Class template. Add your alternate language code to the template and then simply add references to these classes in your application project.*

SDE Within the VS .NET IDE

This next section provides you with an overview of Smart Device Extensions for Visual Studio .NET. Along the way, I'll give you a fairly high-level overview of the key components and features that are offered by SDE, VS .NET, and the .NET Compact Framework.

When you're working with an SDE project, the VS .NET IDE is extended with SDE-specific features including these:

- **SDE-specific project properties pages** that appear as part of the standard Property Pages dialog box.

- The **Build Cab File** item under the Build menu, which enables you to easily generate Cabinet files, or Cab files, used to deploy your NETCF applications.

- With the **Connect to Device** item located under the Tools menu, you can establish a connection to either a device or the emulator.

- The contents of the Toolbox are modified to contain only **platform-specific controls** that are appropriate for the platform on which your project is built.

SDE-specific help topics are added to the VS .NET help system, providing you with a cohesive source for information on .NET, .NETCF, and other SDE information.

To introduce you to these features and others as well, let's walk through the process of creating and testing a project. In the following section, you will learn about the key components of the Visual Studio .NET IDE as they are used in creating applications that target the .NET Compact Framework.

Creating a New Project

When Visual Studio .NET is launched, it will display the Start Page, as shown in Figure 2-1. The Start Page is used to open existing projects and to create new projects, including projects that target the .NET Compact Framework.

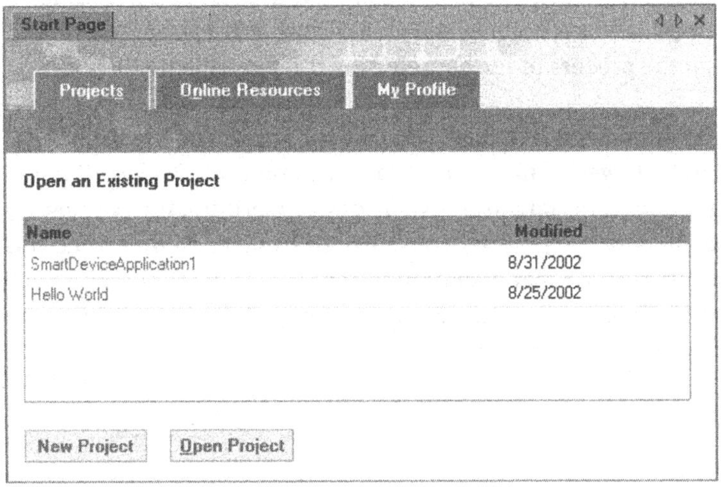

Figure 2-1. The Start Page within the VS .NET IDE

Clicking the **New Project** button causes the New Project dialog box to be displayed, as shown in Figure 2-2. From this dialog box, you can select a template to create a wide variety of project types, including two that target the .NET Compact Framework. Smart Device Extensions installs a project template named Smart Device Application under both the Visual Basic and Visual C# project folders.

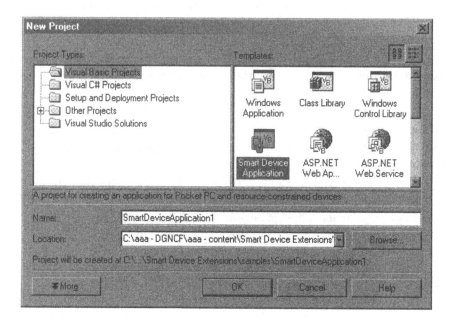

Figure 2-2. The New Project dialog box

Selecting the Smart Device Application template will result in the loading of the Smart Device Application Wizard, as shown in Figure 2-3. This wizard is used to walk you through the process of further selecting the project type for your application.

The interface of this wizard is divided into two list boxes. The top list box allows you to select the target platform. It contains two options, Pocket PC and Windows CE. Where Pocket PC targets a specific device platform, the Windows CE template is used to create a more general-purpose application that could run on a variety of devices running that operating system.

The lower list box displays the project types that are available for the target (Pocket PC or Windows CE) you selected.

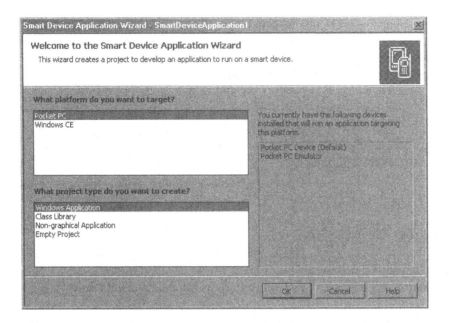

Figure 2-3. Smart Device Application Wizard

Pocket PC Project Types

There are four project types that target the Pocket PC and Pocket PC 2002 platforms as shown in Figure 2-3: Windows Application, Class Library, Non-graphical Application, and Empty Project. A description of each of these project types is provided in Table 2-1.

Table 2-1. Pocket PC Project Types

PROJECT TYPE	DESCRIPTION
Windows Application	WinForm-based project including Pocket PC–specific controls. This is the most commonly used template, as it generates typical Windows-based applications.
Class Library	Class libraries allow you to package related components in a single file. They can be used to develop other applications or as a base for inheritance for other components. This project type is best suited for creating modules of code that will be reused with multiple applications.
Non-graphical Application	This project type is used to create executables that will not have a user interface. Best used for background and maintenance applications that do not require user interaction.
Empty Project	This project type defines a project with no predefined components, allowing you to custom build everything from the ground up.

These project types can be used to create applications that target Pocket PC devices running SH3, MIPS, or ARM processors, and Pocket PC 2002 devices with ARM or XScale processors. Starting with the PPC 2002, Microsoft has restricted PPC CPUs to the ARM architecture.

 TIP *The Pocket PC device does not come with console support. As a workaround you can load console.dll yourself, which is available with Platform Builder.*

Windows CE Project Types

As shown in Figure 2-4, there are four project types that target the Windows CE platform: Windows Application, Class Library, Console Application, and Empty Project.

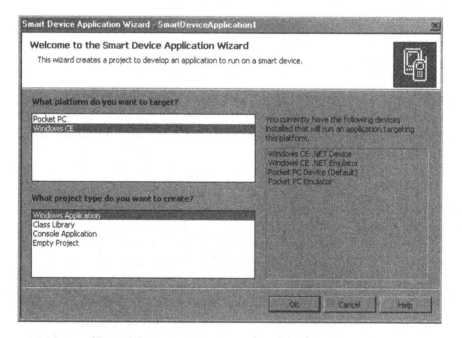

Figure 2-4. Windows CE project types

These project types, which are described in Table 2-2, allow you to create applications that target devices running Windows CE .NET.

Table 2-2. Windows CE Project Types

PROJECT TYPE	DESCRIPTION
Windows Application	WinForm-based project including Windows CE .NET–specific controls. This is the most commonly used template as it generates typical Windows-based applications.
Class Library	Class libraries allow you to package related components in a single file. They can be used to develop other applications or as a base for inheritance for other components. This project type is best suited for creating modules of code that will be reused with multiple applications.
Console Application	This project type is used to create executables that will run within the console window. Best used for background and maintenance applications that may or may not require user interaction. Unlike the Pocket PC, Windows CE natively supports console applications.
Empty Project	This project type defines a project with no predefined components.

Examining Project Contents

Selecting any of these project types will result in the generation of a unique set of project configurations and components. The content of each type of project is the topic of the following section.

Windows Application Project

The Windows Application project is the most commonly used of the project types since it's the starting point for all windows-based applications. Figure 2-5 displays the contents of a Windows Application project in Solutions Explorer, showing the default references and files. Windows Application projects include data, form and XML references, assembly information, and a single form.

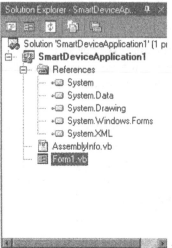

Figure 2-5. A Windows Application project

The form will be appropriately configured for the target platform. A project for the Pocket PC will have a small form and a set of Pocket PC–specific controls with which you can develop your user interface. A project that is targeting Windows CE will have a larger form and a slightly different set of controls.

Class Library Project

The Class Library project is used to create dynamic linked libraries (DLLs). DLLs provide a way to encapsulate functionality that will in turn be used by other applications, such as Windows applications. DLLs are comprised of one or more subroutines and functions. Class libraries serve as the foundation of reusable components, such as wrappers for complex API calls. Figure 2-6 displays the contents of a Class Library project in Solutions Explorer, showing the default references and files. Class Library projects include data and XML references, assembly information, and a single class module.

Note the absence of the **System.Windows.Forms** namespace and any Form module. This project is used to generate a module that will be included in another application. It is not intended to create an application itself, hence the removal of the visual components.

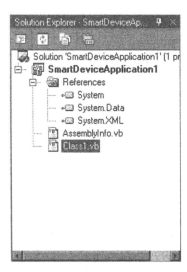

Figure 2-6. A Class Library project

Non-graphical Application Project

The Non-graphical Application project is used in situations where you don't
need an interface to your application. This type of application runs, performing
whatever tasks you program it to do, but without requiring any interaction from
the user. While infrequently used, non-graphical applications offer the capability
to perform a task without the user's knowledge. Figure 2-7 displays the contents
of a Non-graphical Application project in Solutions Explorer, showing the default
references and files. This is a Pocket PC–specific project.

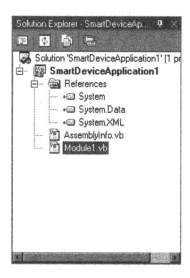

Figure 2-7. Non-graphical Application project

Similar to the Class Library project, the Non-graphical Application project
includes data and XML references along with assembly information. It differs from
a Class Library project in that it has a standard module rather than a class module.

Console Application Project

The Console Application project is used in situations where you don't need the standard Windows interface. The application instead runs in a console window, which is similar to the Command Prompt under Windows. Figure 2-8 displays the contents of a Console Application project in Solutions Explorer, showing the default references and files. This is a Windows CE .NET–specific project.

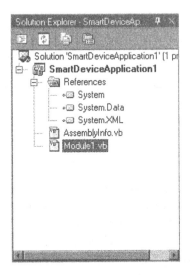

Figure 2-8. Console Application project

This project type is nearly identical to the Non-graphical Application project offered for the Pocket PC platform, but it is configured to make use of the console capabilities offered through the Windows CE operating system.

Empty Project

The Empty Project is just that, a shell of a project sans form and class modules. An Empty Project is shown in Figure 2-9. Empty Projects contain only a single reference. You would use this project type in situations where you want complete control over the contents of your project.

From the bare start, you can add and configure just the combination of references and modules that you need to create a custom project environment.

Now that you have seen how to create new projects and understand what each project type offers, let's turn our attention to configuring project properties.

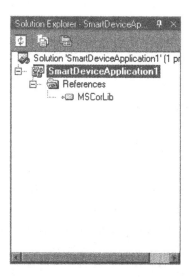

Figure 2-9. An Empty Project

Setting Project Properties

As with all Visual Studio .NET projects, SDE-specific projects are configured using the Property Pages dialog box. Through this dialog box, you can configure namespaces that you want included, what form to use as your startup form, an icon to associate with your application, how your application will be built, where it will be built, how it will be deployed, optimization configurations, and a variety of other settings.

There are two methods for accessing the Property Pages dialog box:

- **Through Solutions Explorer**—Right-click your project; then from the pop-up menu select **Properties**. The Property Pages dialog box will be displayed as shown in Figure 2-10.

- **Through the Project menu**—First select your project in the Solutions Explorer window; then from the Project menu select **Properties**. The Property Pages dialog box will be displayed.

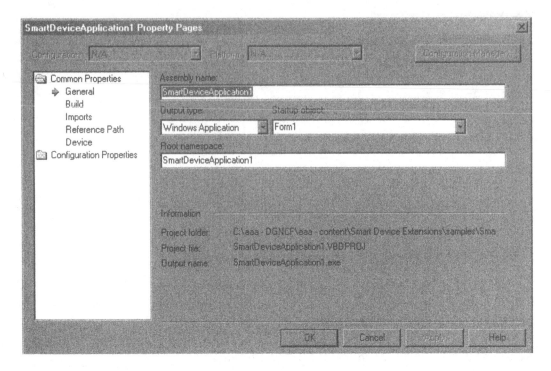

Figure 2-10. The Property Pages dialog box

Next, we'll look in more detail at each page of the Property Pages dialog box and how various settings affect your application.

The Property Pages dialog box is divided into two sections: Common Properties and Configuration Properties. We'll start by looking at the Common Properties section.

Common Properties

The **Common Properties** folder of the Property Pages dialog box contains five groups: General, Build, Imports, Reference Path, and Device. Each of these groups offers settings for and information about your application.

General Properties

The first of the Common Properties groups is the General group. This group is comprised of a combination of settings and information as shown in Figure 2-10.

The contents of the General properties page are described in Table 2-3.

Table 2-3. The General Page Controls

CONTROL	DESCRIPTION
Assembly name	Name of the output file that will hold the assembly manifest.
Output type	Type of application to build. Matches the template used to create a project.
Startup object	Entry point that is called when the application is loaded. You may need to modify this setting if you alter the name of your form or if you add another form, such as a startup form, that needs to be the first form loaded.
Root namespace	Base namespace for all files in the project.
Project folder	Location where the project is stored.
Project file	Name of the .vbproj file that is used to store this project.
Output name	Name of the compiled output.

NOTE *The settings that comprise the General properties page are configured when you specify a project type through SDE. Normally, you do not need to modify these values, with the exception of the Startup object.*

TIP *You can reference the Project folder information to determine where your project is stored on your development PC.*

Build Properties

The Build properties page is used to specify project defaults for compilation, compiler options, and the icon that will represent the application. The icon setting is one of the most frequently modified settings as it defines the icon that will be shown to represent your application under the Start menu and in File Explorer.

NOTE *For more information on the use of the icon setting, see the step-by-step example at the end of this chapter.*

The interface of the Build properties page includes the controls described in Table 2-4.

Table 2-4. The Build Page Controls

CONTROL	DESCRIPTION
Application icon	Defines the icon file (.ico) for use as your application icon. This file should contain both 16×16 and 32×32 versions of your image. Both icon images must be in one file.
Option explicit	Forces declaration of variables. When selected, any variables that are referenced that are not declared will generate a compilation error.
Option strict	Requires explicit narrowing conversions. By default this is turned off. You may want to consider turning it on to better manage conversion-related variances.
Option compare	Defines the compiler default for string comparisons. Valid values are binary (case-sensitive) or text (case-insensitive).

Imports Properties

The third group under the **Common Properties** folder is Imports. Use this dialog box page to specify the namespaces to import for use with your project. The imports you specify in this dialog box are passed directly to the compiler. They apply to all files in your project.

NOTE *You import a namespace so that you can use its elements in your code without having to qualify fully that element. For example, by importing the **System.Data.SqlClient** namespace, you could use a shorter SqlCommand from your code instead of having to use **System.Data.SqlClient.SqlCommand**.*

The primary purpose behind the interface components of the Imports page is to specify, add, update, and remove namespaces. The interface of this page includes the controls described in Table 2-5.

Table 2-5. The Imports Page Controls

CONTROL	DESCRIPTION
Namespace	Specifies the namespace to add to a project
Add import	Adds the specified namespace to your project
Update	Replaces the namespace highlighted in the Project Imports list with the entry from the Namespace field
Project imports	Lists the namespaces referenced by your project
Remove	Removes a namespace from your project

NOTE   *While the SDE templates configure your project with a set of namespaces, you may need to add others depending upon the purpose and needs of your application. For example, most data-related applications will add either the **System.Data.SqlClient** or **System.Data.SqlServerCE** namespace or both.*

Reference Path Properties

The Reference Path page under the Common Properties group is used to specify a directory to search when the project loads to locate references that are used with a project.

NOTE   *As an SDE developer, you shouldn't have to modify this page unless you're working in a multideveloper environment and the location of references differs between each of the individual developer's PCs.*

Device Properties

The last of the groups under the **Common Properties** folder is Device properties. These properties define the deployment device and the location on that device where output, that is to say your application and its related files, are sent. An example of the Device properties page is shown in Figure 2-11.

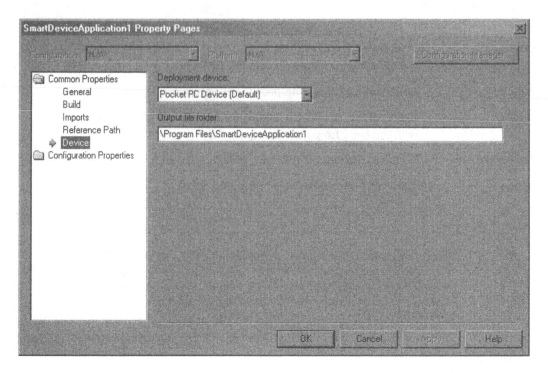

Figure 2-11. Device properties page

The properties contained within this page are some of the most commonly modified for SDE-related projects. The interface of the Device properties page includes the controls described in Table 2-6.

Table 2-6. The Device Page Controls

CONTROL	DESCRIPTION
Deployment device	Device the application is targeting. When you test your application, this is the environment under which it will be tested.
Output file folder	Folder on the target device where your application will be loaded.

TIP   *To add a shortcut to your application to the Start menu change the **Output file folder** setting to \Windows\Start Menu.*

Configuration Properties

The **Configuration Properties** folder makes up the second section of the Property Pages dialog box. This folder is divided into four groups: Debugging, Optimizations, Build, and Deployment.

In general, for SDE projects, the settings under the **Configuration Properties** folder are less frequently modified than those found under the **Common Properties** folder. With that said, let's look at each of these sections in turn.

Debugging Properties

The Debug properties are used to specify actions to be taken when your project is run from within the Visual Studio .NET IDE. The settings under this section have no impact on your application as it is delivered to your end user.

> **NOTE**   *Debugging is covered in more detail later in this chapter.*

The interface of the Debugging properties page includes the controls described in Table 2-7.

Table 2-7. The Debugging Page Controls

CONTROL	DESCRIPTION
Start action	Identifies the item to start when your project is run
Start options	Indicates preferences to use when running your project including command line arguments and the working directory

> **NOTE**   *For the most part, you will not need to modify these settings when constructing an SDE-based project. One configuration of interest is the command line setting, which can be used to test command line argument functionality within your applications.*

> **NOTE**   *For more on debugging, see the "Debugging an Application" section later in this chapter.*

Optimizations Properties

The Optimizations properties are used to streamline or tweak your application. While they are by no means a "fix all" for your application's performance woes, they may provide you with that little boost you are looking for.

The interface of the Optimizations properties page includes the controls described in Table 2-8.

Table 2-8. The Optimizations Page Controls

CONTROL	DESCRIPTION
Remove integer overflow checks	Turns off checking for overflows and dividing by zero. Can make your integer calculations perform faster.
Enable optimizations	Optimizes your output file, making it smaller, faster, and more efficient. It also makes debugging more difficult.
Enable incremental build	Builds only the part of your application that has changed since your last build. Not applicable to SDE.
Base address	Specifies the base address for a DLL.

Build Properties

The third Configuration Properties group is Build properties. These properties are used to configure the attributes that are employed when building your application's executable.

For the most part, the options on this page can be categorized by two functions: setting the Output path and defining various configurations to use when debugging your application.

The interface of the Build properties page includes the controls described in Table 2-9.

Table 2-9. The Build Page Controls

CONTROL	DESCRIPTION
Output path	Defines the path on your development machine to place output generated during the building of your application.
Generate debugging information	Defines whether debugging information should be generated when building your application.
Register for COM interop	Indicates whether an application will expose a COM object. This setting is not applicable to SDE.
Enable build warnings	Indicates to add build warnings to the Task List.
Treat warning as errors	Indicates that all build warnings are to be treated as errors. No output file will be produced if any warnings are encountered during the build process.
Define debug constant	Sets DEBUG=1 for use during compilation. This setting can be queried from code to enable you to program in additional functionality while debugging your application.
Define trace constant	Sets TRACE=1 for use during compilation. Similar to DEBUG, this setting can be queried from your code to control debugging functionality.
Custom constants	Allows you to define custom constants that can be accessed programmatically.

Deployment Properties

The last of the groups under the **Configuration Properties** folder is Deployment properties. The page for this group has a single setting, which defines the configuration file to use when building your application's executable. Configuration files have the extension .config. With configuration files, you can define alternate sets of build settings to fit your various needs. Use the **Override file** setting to specify the file containing the configurations to use when building your application.

Designing a Form

So, we've created and configured a project. Now, we're ready to take the next step and look at how you design the interface of an SDE-based application.

If you are already an experienced Visual Studio .NET developer, you will require little orientation to begin creating user interfaces for Smart Device

Extensions applications. For those who are new to the VS .NET IDE, new projects based upon the Windows Application template will automatically display a default form as shown in Figure 2-12.

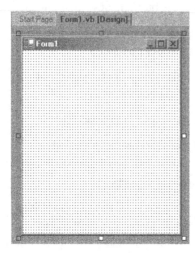

Figure 2-12. An empty Pocket PC form

In this example, the project type is a Windows Application that will target the Pocket PC. The template for this type of application includes a form that is correctly sized for the Pocket PC platform. A menu control, shown below the form, is included with the form, as most Pocket PC applications include menus.

The Toolbox in the Visual Studio .NET IDE is located to the left of the form shown in Figure 2-12. Initially the Toolbox is hidden. The Visual Studio .NET IDE supports panels that automatically hide themselves when not in use. This feature provides you with more available screen space when designing forms and writing code.

Placing your mouse over the **Toolbox** tab will cause the Toolbox to be displayed as shown in Figure 2-13.

Figure 2-13. The Toolbox

TIP *If you would like the Toolbox to remain displayed, click the small pushpin located in the top-right corner of the Toolbox.*

To add a control to your user interface, simply select the control in the Toolbox, then draw the control on your form. To aid in the adjustment of your user interface, Visual Studio .NET offers a complete set of configuration tools under the Format menu. These tools allow you to align, size, space, center, and lock control position.

NOTE *Some controls, such as the MainMenu and Timer, do not have a runtime interface. That is to say, they will not appear graphically to the user of your application. As you add these types of controls to your application, they will be placed on the panel below your form.*

Controls Provided with SDE

Smart Device Extensions includes a subset of the controls that can be used to construct a desktop Windows application. For the most part, you will find that these controls offer a subset of equivalent controls found under the .NET Framework. This difference has to do with resource limitations imposed by the target platforms.

The controls provided through SDE are shown in Table 2-10.

Table 2-10. The SDE Controls

Button	CheckBox	ComboBox	ContextMenu
DomainUpDown	HScrollBar	ImageList	InputPanel
Label	ListBox	ListView	MainMenu
NumericUpDown	OpenFileDialog	Panel	PictureBox
ProgressBar	RadioButton	SaveFileDialog	StatusBar
TabControl	TextBox	Timer	ToolBar
TrackBar	TreeView	VScrollBar	

NOTE *For more information on the controls offered with Smart Device Extensions, see Chapter 4.*

Adding Code to an Application

Now that you've seen the basics of constructing an interface, we're ready to turn our attention to how you add code to your application. As with any applications developed within the VS .NET IDE, code is added through the Code window as shown in Figure 2-14.

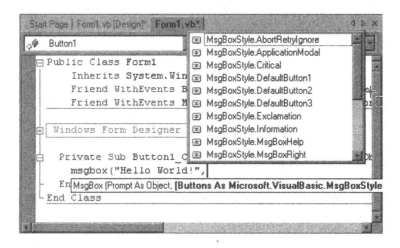

Figure 2-14. The VS .NET Code window displaying some of its functionality

If you are new to the VS .NET environment, you are in for a treat. The Code window provides a plethora of functionality, everything from statement completion to auto-Listing members, providing parameter information and collapsible regions of code, just to name a few features.

The easiest way to navigate about your code is by using the two combo boxes located at the top of the window. The combo box at the top left of the Code window allows you to select a class within a module. The combo box at the top right of the window allows you to select a method from within that class.

NOTE *The .NET Compact Framework supports overloading methods. For the typical eVB developer, overloading is a new concept. Simply stated, overloading allows you to declare a method multiple times, each time with a different parameter list. In Figure 2-14, you can see the addition of a navigational feature at the left end of the method description window. This navigational tool allows you to select the method description that best suits your development needs.*

The Code Behind a Windows Form

When you create a form with the Windows Form Designer, you are in fact creating the code used to define your form's interface. This is unlike eVB, where form definitions were described separately from the form's code.

The Windows Form Designer automatically generates this code and adds it to the form's code module as shown in Figure 2-15. This code is normally hidden from the developer's view in what is referred to as a *region*. The region, which defines your form, has the label "Windows Form Designer generated code".

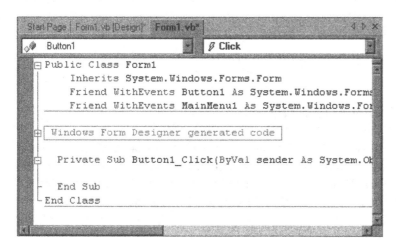

Figure 2-15. The Windows Form Designer code region

CAUTION *You should not modify code within the Windows Form Designer generated code section. Doing so could produce unpredictable results, and the Form Designer may overwrite your code.*

Regions can be expanded and collapsed by clicking the plus (+) and minus (–) symbols at the far left of the Code window. Expanding the code generated by the Windows Form Designer reveals the code used to define the form's interface as shown in Figure 2-16.

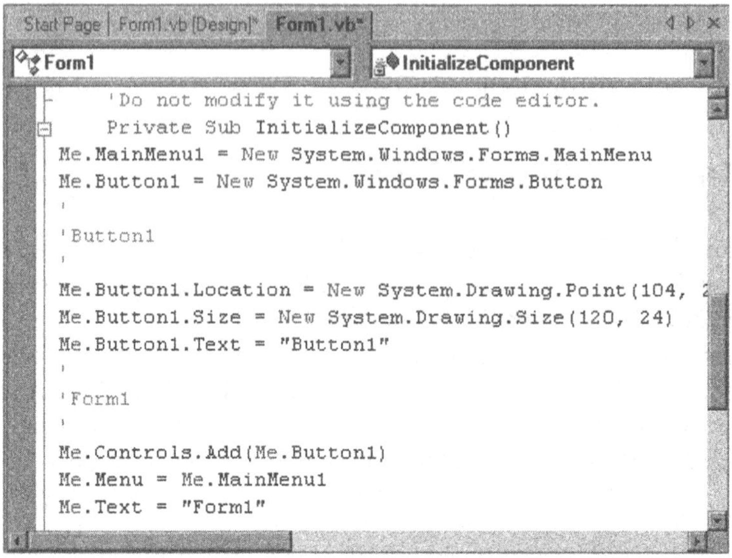

```
Start Page | Form1.vb [Design]*   Form1.vb*                          ◁ ▷ ×
Form1                          ▾    InitializeComponent               ▾
        'Do not modify it using the code editor.
        Private Sub InitializeComponent()
    Me.MainMenu1 = New System.Windows.Forms.MainMenu
    Me.Button1 = New System.Windows.Forms.Button
    '
    'Button1
    '
    Me.Button1.Location = New System.Drawing.Point(104,
    Me.Button1.Size = New System.Drawing.Size(120, 24)
    Me.Button1.Text = "Button1"
    '
    'Form1
    '
    Me.Controls.Add(Me.Button1)
    Me.Menu = Me.MainMenu1
    Me.Text = "Form1"
```

Figure 2-16. Code generated by the Form Designer

Accessing Event Procedures

As with earlier versions of Visual Basic and eMbedded Visual Basic, the quickest way to access the event procedures for a particular control is to double-click that control in the Form Designer window. The Code window will automatically be displayed, and you will be placed in the default event for that control.

Adding Other Files

Depending upon your needs, you may want to include images, text, configuration, or other files with your application. By adding files to your project, you can cause those files to be deployed with your application.

You can add a file to your application with any of the following methods:

- In Solutions Explorer, right-click your project. From the pop-up menu, select **Add** and then **Add Existing Item**.

- From the Project menu, select **Add Existing Item**.

- Drag a file from Windows Explorer and drop it on your project in Solutions Explorer.

Files that you include in your project can be configured to meet your specific build and output needs. The **BuildAction** property for each file determines how the file will be handled when your application is built. The valid settings for the **BuildAction** property are shown in Table 2-11.

Table 2-11. BuildAction Property Settings

SETTING	DESCRIPTION
None	Used with files that you want to include with a project but do not want to be part of the project output group. Will not be compiled in the build process.
Compile	Used with code files. Will be compiled as part of the build process.
Content	Used with files that will be employed by your application. Will not be compiled, but will be part of the project output group. For example, you would use this setting to include a ReadMe file.
Embedded Resource	Embeds the file in the executable. Typically used for resources such as images where you want the file to be part of the executable rather than be delivered as a separate file.

Testing Your Application

With the user interface completed and the code written, it is time to turn our attention to testing your application. Smart Device Extensions offers two methods for testing: through an emulator and on a device. With either the emulator or a device, SDE handles deploying both your application and all of the components your application requires, including the .NET Compact Framework and SQL Server CE.

Here is how all this is handled: When you test a .NET Compact Framework application from within Visual Studio .NET, a check is made of the target platform to confirm that the .NET Compact Framework is installed. If SDE finds the framework missing, it will automatically copy and install the framework before attempting to run your application. This installation process will occur the first time you test to a device or the emulator and if you hard reset either the device or emulator.

A similar process applies if your application uses SQL Server CE. SDE will check the target platform to confirm that the SQL Server CE components are installed. If SDE does not find them, it will automatically copy and install the required SQL Server CE components before running your application.

After SDE confirms that all of the components required by your application are present, it will copy your application to the target platform, place it in the directory you specified in your project configurations, and finally launch your application.

Running a Test

There are several ways to run a test of your application:

- From the SDE toolbar, click the **Start** button.

- From the Debug menu, select **Start** or **Start without Debugging**.

- Press the F5 key (start with debugging) or Ctrl+F5 (start without debugging).

Testing in the Emulator

The emulator provides an environment within your desktop PC that mimics the functionality and operation of the device platform you are targeting with your application. The emulator is useful in situations where you do not have a device or when your device is not available.

Be forewarned: Testing in the emulator has its shortcomings. First and foremost is that the emulator runs on a desktop PC, which has far more processing resources than the target device. This can give you a false sense of how well your application performs. In addition, input for the emulator is provided through a keyboard and a mouse rather than the stylus the end user will be forced to use. If you are not consciously aware of this difference, you can create an application that is easy to use in the emulator and a pain to use on the device. Finally, the emulator offers a "close" representation of a device, not an exact match. There are subtle differences in all emulators.

TIP *Always do final testing on a device, not in the emulator. The rule of thumb is to test your application on every brand of device on which it will be used. Beta programs work well for this. Pick participants so that you have a test group for each of the brands of devices available.*

NOTE *For detailed information on the emulator, and its use and configuration, see Appendix B.*

There can be several different types of emulators on a development PC, each of which represents a specific device. When you choose to test your application in the emulator, Smart Device Extensions uses your project configurations to determine the appropriate emulator.

NOTE *You must have a network connection on your development PC to test your application in an emulator. If you do not have a network connection, refer to Appendix B for instructions on how you can use a loopback connection in place of a network connection.*

Deploying to the Emulator

You can elect to deploy to the emulator using any of the following methods:

- On the Smart Device Extensions toolbar, select **Pocket PC Emulator** from the Deployment Device combo box as shown in Figure 2-17.

Figure 2-17. Selecting the emulator for deployment

- Under the Device page of the Property Pages dialog box, select **Pocket PC Emulator** from the Deployment Device combo box.

- From the Properties window, set the **Deployment Device** property of your project to **Pocket PC Emulator**.

Testing on a Device

Testing on a device allows you to get first-hand experience for how your applications perform. With Smart Device Extensions you can test on devices connected to your development PC via USB, serial, or Ethernet.

 TIP *Use Ethernet to connect your device to your development PC. This is by far the quickest and easiest method for testing and debugging. For further details, see Appendix A.*

Deploying to a Device

You can deploy to a device using any of the following ways:

- On the Smart Device Extensions toolbar, select **Pocket PC Device** from the Deployment Device combo box as shown in Figure 2-18.

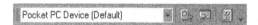

Figure 2-18. Selecting the device for deployment

- Under the Device page of the Property Pages dialog box, select **Pocket PC Device** from the Deployment Device combo box.

- From the Properties window set the **Deployment Device** property of your project to **Pocket PC Device**.

Debugging an Application

First and foremost, let me state the obvious: If you build your application correctly the first time, you can save yourself the time and headache of having to go through the process of debugging. That said, assuming you are a typical developer, your development process hinges on at least a bit of debugging. Well, this is one area where SDE can help you out tremendously. The debugging environment provided through the SDE and the VS .NET IDE is robust. It allows you to pause your application, look about its inner workings, modify code, examine values, and step through your application in a systematic manner.

The core of the debugging functionality can be found under the Debug menu in the VS .NET IDE. From this menu, you can start and stop a debugging session, set breakpoints, and navigate about your application while in debug mode.

NOTE *Breakpoints identify a line of code within your application where you want to pause or interrupt the execution of your application when encountered.*

The combination of SDE and VS .NET enables you to debug remotely applications that are running on a device or in an emulator from the comfort of your development PC. You can use the Command window to enter statements, query and set variables, execute lines of code, and other similar tasks.

TIP *For the optimal debugging environment, use an Ethernet card to connect your device to your PC.*

Now that you have a general understanding of Smart Device Extensions, and how they can be used to create applications that target the .NET Compact Framework, we'll walk through an example application from creation to deployment.

Step-by-Step Tutorial: Hello World.NET

In this step-by-step exercise, you will create a NETCF version of the vastly over-exposed Hello World application. As part of this exercise, you will learn how to

- Create a project.

- Configure project settings.

- Add an icon to your application.

- Construct a user interface.

- Add some code to event procedures.

- Test an application in the emulator.

- Test an application on a device.

- Deploy your application with a Cab file.

Step 1: Creating the Project

The first step in the development of the Hello World application is to create
a project. To create a project for this application, follow these steps:

1. Start Visual Studio .NET.

2. From the File menu select **New** and then **Project**, or click the New
    Project icon on the Visual Studio .NET toolbar. This icon is shown at the
    far left of Figure 2-19.

Figure 2-19. The New Project icon

3. The New Project dialog box will be displayed. Select **Visual Basic
    Projects** from the Project Types window.

4. Select **Smart Device Application** from the Templates window.

5. In the Name field, enter **Hello World**.

6. In the Locate field, enter the path where you would like to create the
    Hello World project.

7. Click the **OK** button. The Smart Device Application will be displayed.

8. From the "What platform do you want to target?" list, select **Pocket PC**.

9. From the "What project type do you want to create?" list, select
    Windows Application.

After a short pause, your project will be created and displayed within the
Visual Studio .NET development environment.

Step 2: Setting Project Properties

Before beginning the construction of the Hello World application itself, let's set
a couple of project properties to specify where your application will be created
and to define an icon to associate with your application.

Defining the Output Folder

By default, Pocket PC applications will be deployed to and run from the directory \Program Files*your application name*. In our example, that would be \Program Files\Hello World. With this configuration, if you wanted to manually start your application at a later time, you would need to open File Explorer, navigate to \Program Files\Hello World, and click the Hello World executable. That's way too much work for me, so let's change it.

I find it much easier to launch an application from the Start menu. This allows you to quick-start the application, making it easier to show it to your significant other, friends, boss, clients, or coworkers.

This is accomplished by setting the output file folder property. To deploy the Hello World application to the Start menu, perform the following steps:

1. From the Project menu select **Hello World Properties**. The Hello World Properties dialog box will be displayed.

2. Select the **Common Properties** folder. Five items will be displayed under the folder: General, Build, Imports, Reference Path, and Device.

3. From under the **Common Properties** folder select **Device**. The Device properties page will be displayed in the dialog box.

4. In the Output file folder field, enter **\Windows\Start Menu**.

5. Click the **OK** button on the Hello World Property Pages dialog box.

The next time you build your Hello World application, it will be deployed to the **\Windows\Start Menu** folder and will appear on the Start menu on your device.

 NOTE *Changing this setting does not affect where the application will be installed when you create a Cab file to deploy your application. It only impacts deployment during testing from within the VS .NET IDE.*

Adding an Icon

All of the applications that you create with Smart Device Extensions will have the same program icon unless you specify otherwise. By program icon, I'm referring to the icon that is displayed when you browse a folder with File Explorer or when the application appears in either the Start menu or under Programs. From my standpoint, this is in no way a feature, so let's look at how you specify a custom icon to use with this Hello World application.

To specify a custom icon, follow these steps:

1. From the Project menu, select **Hello World Properties**. The Hello World Properties dialog box will be displayed.

2. Select the **Common Properties** folder. Five items will be displayed under the folder: General, Build, Imports, Reference Path, and Device.

3. From under the **Common Properties** folder, select **Build**; the Build properties page will be displayed in the dialog box.

4. Click the ellipse button (...) to the right of the Application icon field; the Add Existing File to Project dialog box will be displayed.

5. Navigate to and select an icon to associate with your Hello World application. There is a selection of icons included with Visual Studio .NET. They are located under \Program Files\Microsoft Visual Studio .NET\Common7\Graphics\Icons. For this example, I've selected the **Sun** icon from the **Weather** folder.

6. Click the **OK** button on the Hello World Property Pages dialog box.

The icon you specified will be added to your project and will appear in the Solutions Explorer window as shown in Figure 2-20.

Figure 2-20. The custom icon file as part of the project

At this point, if you were to build your Hello World application, it would include the icon you selected, but with an undesirable side effect. As part of deploying your application, the icon file itself would be copied to the device. That's not what you want. You want the icon file embedded in the executable itself, rather than have it in a separate file. That can be easily accomplished by setting a single property.

To configure your icon to be included in the executable, perform the following steps:

1. In Solutions Explorer, select the icon; an example of this is shown in Figure 2-20.

2. In the Properties window, select **Build Action**.

3. Set the **Build Action** property to **Embedded Resource**.

This additional configuration will cause your icon to be embedded into the Hello World executable instead of being deployed as a separate file.

Correctly Configuring an Icon

The icon you include in your project must have both 32×32 and 16×16 versions. The 16×16 version is used for the Start menu and the previously run application section of the Start menu. The 32×32 version will be displayed if your application appears under the Programs section.

Both versions of the icon must be placed in the same icon file. You can use the image editor within the VS .NET IDE to build this type of dual-purpose icon. Simply follow these steps:

1. Double-click your icon in Solutions Explorer. The icon will be loaded into the image editor.

2. Right-click the left panel of the image editor, where the small version of your image is displayed.

3. From the pop-up menu, select **Current Image Types**. If you are missing either the 16×16 or 32×32 version of your icon, use the **Add image type** option to add the missing type.

4. Construct an image for each size icon.

5. Close the image editor window.

NOTE *In this example, the Sun icon already contains both 16×16 and 32×32 versions.*

Step 3: Building the Interface

Next up, we'll build the interface. The interface to the Hello World application is comprised of three components: a TextBox that is used to display a message, a Button that controls how the message is displayed, and a Timer that handles updating the display. An example of this interface is shown in Figure 2-21.

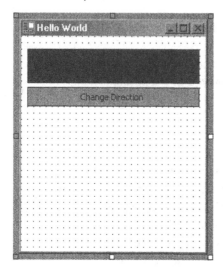

Figure 2-21. The Hello World interface design

To add the TextBox to your Hello World interface, follow these steps:

1. Select the **Form1.vb [Design]** tab in the Visual Studio .NET IDE.

2. From the Toolbox, select a TextBox.

3. Draw a TextBox on the top of Form1 as shown in Figure 2-21.

Next, you need to configure some properties for the TextBox. These properties are set through the Properties window.

1. Select the TextBox on your form.

2. In the Properties window, set the **Text** property to an empty string.

3. Set the **Name** property to **txtMessage**.

4. Set the **Font** property to **Tahoma, 22pt**.

5. Set the **BackColor** property to **Black**.

6.   Set the **ForeColor** property to **Lime**.

7.   Set the **Locked** property to **True**.

To add the Button to your Hello World interface, follow these steps:

1.   From the Toolbox, select a Button.

2.   Draw the Button below your TextBox on Form1 as shown in Figure 2-21.

Use the Properties window to set the following properties for the Button:

1.   Select the Button on your form.

2.   In the Properties window, set the **Text** property to **Change Direction**.

3.   Set the **Name** property to **btnChange**.

4.   Set the **Font** property to **Tahoma, 8pt**.

To add the Timer to your Hello World Interface, do the following:

1.   From the Toolbox, select a **Timer**.

2.   Draw the Timer on Form1. Where you draw it doesn't matter as it won't be (and can't be) part of the visual interface; it will instead appear on a panel below your form.

Use the Properties window to set the following properties for the Timer:

1.   Select the Timer from the panel below your form.

2.   In the Properties window, set the **Name** property to **timMain**.

3.   Set the **Interval** property to **200**.

All that remains to complete the interface are two configurations on the form:

1.   Select the form to display the form properties in the Properties window.

2.   Set the **Text** property to **Hello World**.

3.   Set the **Name** property to **frmHelloWorld**.

Step 4: Adding the Code

With the user interface complete, we're ready to turn our attention to the code behind the Hello World application.

At the heart of this Hello World application is a scrolling message, a marquee that displays whatever message you choose to provide. The scrolling effect is created with some simple string manipulation that rearranges the order of the message within a working variable.

In this section, you will add code to

- Dimension three variables that are used throughout the Hello World application.

- Perform some initializations when the Hello World application begins.

- Cause the message to scroll.

- Control the direction of the scrolling.

Dimensioning the Variables

Three variables are used throughout the Hello World example. The variable **strDirection** stores the direction that the message is scrolling. The variable **strMessage** contains the message that will be displayed. The variable **strTemp** is a working variable.

Add the three variables to the **Declaration** section of the class **frmHelloWorld** as shown in the following code. This will allow them to be used throughout the class.

```
Dim strDirection As String
Dim strMessage As String
Dim strTemp As String
```

Performing Some Initializations

The **Load** event procedure of the form is used to perform some initializations for the Hello World application. Here the three module-level variables will be set and then the timer will be enabled, which will begin the scrolling process.

Place the code in Listing 2-1 in the **Load** event procedure of **frmHelloWorld**.

Listing 2-1. Initializing the Variables and Starting the Timer

```
   Private Sub frmHelloWorld_Load(ByVal sender As _
      System.Object, ByVal e As System.EventArgs) _
      Handles MyBase.Load
' Initialize the operating variables.
      strDirection = "forwards"
      strMessage = "Hello World from the DGNCF"
      strTemp = New String(Chr(Asc(" ")), 30) & strMessage

' Start the marquee.
      timMain.Enabled = True

   End Sub
```

Scrolling the Message

The scrolling marquee effect is implemented through the Timer control's **Tick** event procedure. This event fires every 200 milliseconds, as set by the control's **Interval** property. In this event procedure, the message is manipulated by taking a character off one end of the string and appending it to the other end. The message is then redisplayed in the TextBox, giving the effect that the text is scrolling.

Place the code in Listing 2-2 in the **Tick** event procedure of the Timer control.

Listing 2-2. Controlling the Marquee

```
   Private Sub timMain_Tick(ByVal sender As System.Object, _
      ByVal e As System.EventArgs) Handles timMain.Tick

' Depending upon what direction we are scrolling, take
' either the left or right-most character off of the
' string and append it to the opposite end.
      If (strDirection = "forwards") Then
        strTemp = strTemp.Substring(1, strTemp.Length - 1) & _
          Mid(strTemp, 1, 1)
      Else
        strTemp = strTemp.Substring(strTemp.Length - 1, 1) & _
          Mid(strTemp, 1, Len(strTemp) - 1)
      End If
```

```
' Display the string, giving the feeling that the
' text is scrolling.
    txtMessage.Text = strTemp
  End Sub
```

Changing the Scrolling Direction

The direction that the marquee scrolls, either left or right, is controlled through the **Click** event procedure of **btnChange**. In this procedure, the variable **strDirection** is toggled between the values of "forwards" and "backwards".

The **strDirection** variable is subsequently referenced in the Timer event to decide how to scroll the message.

Place the code shown in Listing 2-3 in the **Click** event procedure of **btnChange**.

Listing 2-3. Changing the Direction of the Marquee

```
Private Sub btnChange_Click(ByVal sender As _
  System.Object, ByVal e As System.EventArgs) _
  Handles btnChange.Click
Toggle the directional flag.
  Select Case strDirection
    Case "forwards"
      strDirection = "backwards"
    Case "backwards"
      strDirection = "forwards"
  End Select
End Sub
```

Step 5: Testing Hello World

With the interface design and coding complete, you are ready to test the Hello World application. As I stated earlier in this chapter, Smart Device Extensions provides two methods for testing your applications: in an emulator or on a device. We'll test in the emulator first.

Testing in the Emulator

To test the Hello World application in the Pocket PC emulator, perform the following steps:

1. On the Visual Studio .NET toolbar, select **Pocket PC Emulator** from the Deployment Device combo box as shown in Figure 2-22.

2. On the toolbar, click the **Start** button.

Figure 2-22. Deploying to the emulator

After a brief pause the emulator will be started. Next, any required components will be copied and installed on the device. This will include the .NET Compact Framework the first time you test an application in the Pocket PC emulator. Finally, your Hello World application is copied to the emulator and launched. An example of Hello World running in the Pocket PC emulator is shown in Figure 2-23.

TIP *It takes some time to launch, configure, and start the Pocket PC emulator. You can streamline your testing process by leaving the emulator running between each test.*

Figure 2-23. Hello World running in the Pocket PC emulator

Testing on the Device

Now, let's switch our testing to your device. To test the Hello World application on a Pocket PC device, perform the following steps:

1. Connect your device to your development PC.

2. On the Visual Studio .NET toolbar, select **Pocket PC Device** from the Deployment Device combo box as shown in Figure 2-24.

Figure 2-24. Deploying to a device

3. On the toolbar, click the **Start** button.

As was the case with the emulator, SDE will first verify that all of the necessary components are on the target device. Any missing components will be copied to the device and installed. With everything in place, your Hello World application is copied to the device and launched. An example of Hello World running on a Pocket PC device is shown in Figure 2-25.

Figure 2-25. Hello World running on a device

Since you configured your Hello World application to deploy to the \Windows\Start Menu directory, it will appear in the Start menu of your device as shown in Figure 2-26. This configuration allows you to directly run your application on your device.

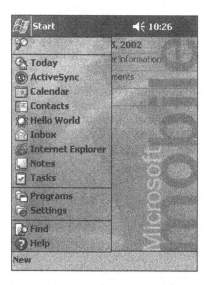

Figure 2-26. Hello World in the Pocket PC Start menu

Step 6: Deploying Hello World

With the application complete, we're ready to deploy Hello World. While deploying is a fairly involved topic, the addition of Smart Device Extensions to Visual Studio .NET does provide a simple way to create the most basic Cab file.

To create a Cab file for your Hello World application, perform the following step:

Under the Build menu, select **Build Cab File**; several Command windows will appear and be removed as the Cab is generated.

NOTE *For more information on deploying applications, refer to Chapter 21.*

That's it—steps for a complete application from selecting the template to deploying an application. You should now have a fair understanding of what SDE provides and how it can be used to create applications that target the .NET Compact Framework.

HOMEWORK *Create a Windows Application project of your own from scratch. Build an interface consisting of a single button. Add some simple code to the Click event of the button to display a message box. Test your application in both the emulator and on a device.*

HOMEWORK *There are a number of sample projects included with the .NET Compact Framework. These samples are by default located under C:\Program Files\Microsoft Visual Studio .NET 2003\CompactFrameworkSDK\v1.0.XXXX\Windows CE\Samples, where XXXX is the version of NETCF you have installed. Load, run, and examine these projects to get a better feeling of what the .NET Compact Framework has to offer.*

Summary

Smart Device Extensions for Visual Studio .NET allows you to leverage your .NET development skills to create mobile solutions. SDE integrates with the VS .NET IDE, providing you with a single development environment for both your desktop and device applications.

SDE can be used to create projects that target either Pocket PC or Windows CE devices. These projects have their own set of controls from which you can construct user interfaces.

With Smart Device Extensions, you can test your applications either in a device or in an emulator that runs on your development PC.

This completes the first part of this book, which was designed to provide you with a basic understanding of the .NET Compact Framework and Smart Device Extensions. In the next part, you will learn how to construct effective user interfaces using Windows Forms, the controls provided through NETCF, ways to create your own controls, adding menus to an application, and how to kick up your application with graphics.

CHAPTER 3

Designing an Effective Interface

So, you're ready to start developing applications for the Pocket PC. Now, odds are that you're already experienced in creating programs for some Windows operating system. In addition, you probably are comfortable with developing application interfaces. As Dorothy said to the Scarecrow, Tin Man, and Cowardly Lion, "Developing a Pocket PC application isn't the same as creating a Windows application in Kansas now, is it?" Well, she said something like that.

My point is that it would be a serious mistake on your part to skip this chapter. While you could make the case that a program is a program, regardless of its target operating system or platform, I will tell you plainly that developing mobile applications is an acquired skill. It requires you to understand the limitations of the OS. It requires you to understand the differences between developing an application that will be used in the comfortable confines of a business office and one that may be used anywhere, anytime.

In this chapter, I'm going to show you how to build effective interfaces. I'll

- **Introduce you to the Pocket PC interface standards.** These guidelines will help you create effective applications for the Pocket PC.

- **Give you some "rules of thumb,"** based upon my personal experiences in developing mobile solutions.

- **Show you how forms serve as the foundation to successful interface design.**

- **Define the Form namespace.** You'll learn about its key classes, properties, methods, and events.

- **Provide you with examples of how to perform common form-related tasks.**

Pocket PC Design Standards

The Pocket PC, like other operating systems, has interface standards. These standards lay out guidelines for how applications should look, feel, and act. Now, do you have to adhere to these guidelines? Certainly not. You can be one of those rogue developers who walks your own path, creating applications in the spirit of Pablo Picasso and Salvador Dali. Your users will hate you for it, but you can do it.

Remember, interface standards are created for a purpose—to make it easier for the end user to effectively use a tool. In this case, the tool is a Pocket PC, on which you want your application to run. No matter how much time and energy you put into your application, if in the end it doesn't help the user be more productive, you've failed. Moreover, here is the shocking truth—it's never the user's fault. The user is the user. You can't swap a user out for a better user, say User version 2.0. You can't make users more knowledgeable than they already are. You have to design your application with this limitation in mind.

This is where interface standards come into play. They provide an environment where users can expect applications to perform similarly to each other. Applications will have similar menu structures, button layouts, and terminology. In the case of Pocket PC applications, they will support such functionality as tap-and-hold context-sensitive menus and IR beaming.

The Microsoft document, "Designed for Windows for Pocket PC—Handbook for Software Applications," provides guidelines that you can use when developing your applications. This document is included under **Reference** in the **Samples** folder for this book. I've included key design criteria taken from this document in the following sections.

Displaying the Title of Your Application

Your application must display its title on the NavBar of each window and dialog box. This differs from desktop applications, such as Microsoft Notepad, that modify the title bar to include the name of the current file. Under the Pocket PC guidelines, you can't modify the title. Any additional information, such as the file that is open or the mode that you're in, must be displayed in the client portion, the body of your application. Furthermore, the title that is displayed in the NavBar must not be truncated or abbreviated. So, if you were thinking about naming your application the Pocket Guide for Wine Lovers, you might want to reconsider.

Use of the NavBar

Your application can't use the NavBar for anything else other than displaying the title. Don't add buttons, icons, status displays, or whatever other cool feature that you've dreamed up. I know, you're giving up a whole piece of what is already a small interface to just a title. Pocket PC users don't expect that there will be anything else there though, so don't confuse them. They get confused easily enough on their own.

Hide the NavBar the Right Way

There may be situations when you want to hide the system NavBar completely, including the Start menu icon. Hiding the system NavBar is commonly used in situations where the only reason that the user has a device is to run your application. An example of this is a barcode scanning application in a warehouse. In this situation, you wouldn't expect the user to need to access Contacts, Tasks, Pocket Word, and certainly not Solitaire. So, you make your application full screen. You hide the Start menu so that the user can't access anything else.

To hide the NavBar, use the Windows CE API function SHFullScreen. Calling this API will place the NavBar directly behind your application in the Z-order. If your application were to close, the NavBar will be displayed. The Z-order specifies the order in which interface components are stacked on top of each other.

NOTE *For more information on working with the Windows CE API, see Chapter 17.*

Display the New Button

The Pocket PC uses the menu item **New** to specify creating a new item in an application. What that item is depends upon the application itself. In Pocket Word, tapping **New** creates a new document. In Tasks, **New** creates a new task. In both of these applications and other applications that follow the Pocket PC guidelines, you'll find **New** at the far left end of the menu bar.

Taking this a step further, if you're used to creating desktop applications that use the standard File | Open menu design, don't try to carry that over to the Pocket PC. There shouldn't be a File | Open menu in your mobile applications. Instead, have a New menu by itself to create new items. To open items, use the Pocket Word approach with all of the available documents on a separate form.

Display the SIP Button

The Soft Input Panel, or SIP, is that little graphical keyboard provided with the Pocket PC. Your application should display the SIP at the far-right end of the menu bar. The user expects it to be there. The only time you can hide the SIP button is if your application doesn't require any user input.

Order of Menus and Buttons

Menus must be at the far-left end of the menu bar. Buttons should be immediately to the right of any menus on the menu bar. Figure 3-1 shows an example of this.

Figure 3-1. The correct order of menus and buttons

Use the Same Menu Order as Other Pocket PC Applications

If your application includes any of the following menus, they must appear in the order presented here: Edit, View, Insert, Format, or Tools.

Use the Same Button Order as Other Pocket PC Applications

If your application includes any of the following buttons, they must appear in the order presented here: New, Open, Save, or Print.

Use the Same Common Control Order as Other Pocket PC Applications

If your application includes any controls on the menu bar, such as buttons or drop-down boxes, for configuring Style, Font, Font Size, Bold, Italic, or Underline, they must appear in this order.

Don't Provide a Method for the User to Close Your Application

This is a hard one for the desktop developer to accept. You're so used to having a File | Exit menu item that it may take serious therapy to get you past this issue. The simple fact is that the Pocket PC interface is designed to take the worry about closing applications away from the user. Your applications shouldn't offer a way to exit. Hey, look at it in a positive way, it's one less thing you have to code.

NOTE *The "X" in the upper-left corner of your application effectively hides your application, returning the user to the last application that they were using. It doesn't halt the application. Also, realize that since your application isn't closing, no events fire when the user taps the "X".*

Provide Both 16×16 and 32×32 Pixel Icons for Your Application

The 16×16-pixel icon is used in the Start menu. File Manager uses the 32×32-pixel icon to display your application. Refer to Chapter 2 for more information on incorporating icons into your application.

Don't Duplicate Pocket Outlook Data

There's already a Personal Information Manager (PIM) on Pocket PCs. It's Pocket Outlook. If your application includes some type of PIM functionality, the data used with this functionality should be stored within the Pocket Outlook data structure. For example, if you create an application for a sales route, and as part of that application you have contact information, you should store that inside of the Pocket Outlook data structure.

The Pocket Outlook Object Model, or POOM, provides access to Pocket Outlook data. For more information on incorporating POOM functionality into your NETCF applications, see Chapter 18.

NOTE *The Pocket Outlook data store experiences significant performance issues as the size of a Pocket Outlook data store increases. You should consider other alternatives for applications that make use of thousands of records.*

If Your Application Sends E-Mail, Use the Inbox

The Message API (MAPI) provides access to the Pocket PC Inbox. Your application should use MAPI to send e-mail.

Display the Standard Wait Cursor

Display a wait cursor when your application is going to occupy the system for a while and restrict user input. The Pocket PC wait cursor is a spinning color wheel. Refer to Chapter 17 for an example of how to display the wait cursor from within your application.

Correctly Handle the Displaying of the SIP

The Soft Input Panel (SIP) when displayed occupies an 80-pixel area just above the menu bar. Design your interface with this in mind. This means that either you have to keep input fields out of this area or you have to slide your form up when working with these fields.

Don't Have Any Access to Help from Within Your Application

The Pocket PC makes use of a System-level help design, where all help is accessible under the **Help** menu item of the Start menu. Under this design, your application should not have either a help menu or a help item.

Taking this a step farther, when the user is running an application and taps Start | Help, the help for that particular application is displayed. You can try this with Pocket Word. Start Pocket Word, and then tap Start | Help. The help for Pocket Word is displayed. Cool. Attempting to do this with one of your NETCF applications though will produce different results. Instead of displaying the help for your application, it will display the Help Contents. Why the difference?

The answer is what is going on behind the scenes. When an application is running and the user taps Start | Help, the operating system sends a WM_HELP message to that application. It's the responsibility of the application to receive and process that message, and to launch its help feature. If the application doesn't process the WM_HELP message, it is passed on to the operating system itself, which in turn displays the default Help Contents.

So how does your NETCF application receive and process the WM_HELP message? The answer is that it can't. Windows messages, like this WM_HELP message, are not passed on to NETCF applications. What you need is some sort of message hook, much like what was used by Visual Basic developers for years.

TIP *I have to tell you, of all the Pocket PC design requirements, this is not one of which I'm fond or usually follow. My feeling is that when users have a question about my application, I don't want to make them go off looking elsewhere for the answer. Along those lines, in Chapter 19 I show you how to incorporate help into your application.*

Integrate Your Help into the System Help

This is a continuation of the previous item. Since Pocket PC users are used to having a central repository for help, you need to add your application's help to the System help. Chapter 19 provides an example of adding your help to the System help.

Use the Common Dialog Boxes

The Pocket PC provides dialog boxes for opening and saving files. Don't create your own versions of these dialog boxes. Chapter 4 provides more information on working with both the OpenFileDialog and the SaveFileDialog controls.

Don't Allow Multiple Instances of Your Application to Run

The Pocket PC environment is limited in resources. To help minimize the use of these resources, there should never be more than a single instance of any application running at one time. Chapter 17 includes an example of how you can limit multiple instances of your application from running.

Provide a Graceful Method for Application Shutdown

Under the Pocket PC environment, applications are shut down by the operating system itself, not the user. Your application must plan for this occurrence. Automatically save data either to a permanent or cached location, depending upon what is appropriate for your application. Don't display any dialog boxes or modal windows as part of your application's exit process.

Restore Everything to How the User Left It

Pocket PC users are relieved of the concern of whether an application is running or not running. You can see an example of this in Pocket Word. If you start working with a document, go off to do something else, and then come back, you'll be working with the same document. Your applications should do the same. Chapter 20 shows how to incorporate this functionality into your applications.

Larry Roof's Design Rules

Okay, so now that you have some Pocket PC design requirements to work from, you're good to go, right? Well, not quite. As I mentioned at the start of this chapter, designing applications for the Pocket PC is different from what you might do for a desktop application. There are interface and input restrictions to deal with. Data connectivity, along with its associated data transfer issues, is another matter.

In the following section, I'm going to give you some rules of thumb to use when developing your applications. I've compiled these rules over the years while developing mobile solutions. Many of them came through trial and error, which in my opinion is the worst and slowest method of learning. Now I'm going to pass them on to you, as I'm sure you have better things to do with your time than stumble upon them on your own. I've divided these rules into four categories:

- **Interface rules** that address how to create effective user interfaces on the limited Pocket PC screen

- **Input rules** that show you how to best handle user input on a device that doesn't offer much in the way of user input

- **Usage rules** that help you understand how and where your application is going to be used, so that you can create a solution that will be effective in the target location

- **Porting rules** that address issues to consider before attempting to port an application from a desktop PC to a device

My Interface Rules

Constructing a usable interface is always a key step in creating an effective application, whether that is for a desktop PC or a device. The interface is after all what users will be working with. They don't care about all of that cool code you wrote that makes everything happen behind the interface.

While a good interface can help a marginal application, a bad interface can kill an otherwise great application. Now here's the tough question: If you're new to the world of Pocket PCs, how do you know a good interface? After all, what worked well for a desktop application might not work at all on a device. The way you learn what a good interface is, what works and doesn't work, is to try as many Pocket PC applications as you can. Work through all of the applications that come with your Pocket PC, and then ask yourself these questions:

- How do they lay out their screens?

- What menus do they offer?

- How do they handle input?

- How do they keep the user informed?

- How many different screens/forms do they use?

- What is the purpose of each screen?

- How do they interact with desktop and server components?

TIP   *Here's a story that might help you understand the importance of this point. When I hire young developers, the first day I give them a Pocket PC. As I'm handing it to them, I tell them that if I ever run into them outside of the office and they don't have the device with them, they're fired. My point here is that the only way you can understand what works on a Pocket PC is by using a Pocket PC a lot.*

Interface Rule #1: Bigger Is Better

One mistake that desktop developers commonly make when switching over to device development is that they want to make everything smaller. I understand their thought process. The screen is smaller, so therefore everything should be smaller. Where on the desktop they might have used a 10- or 12-point font, on the device they'll use an 8-point font. This approach will only work if you don't mind seeing your users walking around with their noses pressed against their Pocket PCs.

What I've found is that with Pocket PC applications you need to make the interface components at least as big as you would for the desktop, if not bigger. Take for example the interface shown in Figure 3-2. This interface demonstrates the default appearance of the TextBox and Label controls. Is this a workable interface? Certainly it is. Is it the best we can do? No, it's too small and about as interesting as those black-and-white generic food boxes from the 1980s.

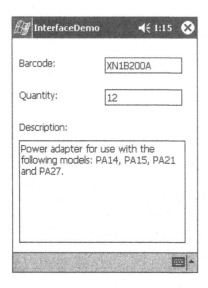

Figure 3-2. The default appearance of TextBox and Label controls

Now, let's look at a revision of this. Figure 3-3 shows an improved version of this interface. It's key to note here that nothing has changed in the way of the content. You still have three text input fields. What I've done is increased the font size of the import elements, that being the barcode and quantity, and at the same time decreased the font size of the unimportant elements, in this case the labels. Looking between these two examples, can you see the difference? Fact is, I would probably make both the barcode and quantity fields even bigger.

Figure 3-3. The new and improved user interface

Interface Rule #2: There Are Colors Other Than Black and White

One of the cool features that set the Pocket PC apart from other handheld devices is the color screen. It just rocks. Why is it then that Pocket PC developers seem bound and determined to create applications that are in black and white, like Dorothy's world was before she got to Oz? Leverage the power of color in your applications. Use color images on your toolbars. Throw a splash of color on your forms. Interject color elements to spice up your interface.

Take for example Figure 3-3, our "improved" interface. Yes, it's easier to read than the original version. Nevertheless, it's still pretty boring. Now, look at the revised version shown in Figure 3-4. Granted, you're looking at a black-and-white replication of a color screenshot, but grab your crayons and follow along with me. Color the form background a color you like and the description TextBox gray, and add a dash of color to each of the graphics on the toolbar. See, isn't that better?

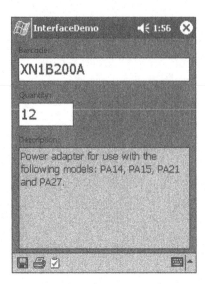

Barcode:

XN1B200A

Quantity:

12

Description:

Power adapter for use with the following models: PA14, PA15, PA21 and PA27.

Figure 3-4. The further refined user interface

 TIP *Try changing the color of a font, rather than bolding the font. Not only will your interface be more appealing, it will also make better use of limited screen real estate.*

My point here is that you have a multitude of colors at your disposal, so use them. Consider allowing your user to customize the appearance, to define the colors of the various elements. Consider adding skins to your application. They're a wonderful way of kicking up an interface, building a user community, and enhancing the appearance of your application.

Interface Rule #3: Less Is More

This seems to be a common mistake made by developers porting applications from the desktop to a device. Their thought process goes something like this: The desktop form had 10 fields, so I should just squash 10 fields onto a device form.

Following this line of logic is a sure way to get your users to hate you. Well, it's not as if you're on their Christmas card list anyway, but you know what I mean. When it comes to designing an interface for Pocket PC applications, remember the simple phrase "less is more."

What I mean by this is that it's better to spread a set of fields out between several input forms rather than cramming them all into a single form. Take the interface shown in Figure 3-5. This is a perfect example of how not to design a form. Yes, all of the fields fit. Yes, it's readable, but is it ever annoying to look at.

Figure 3-5. An example of an overcrowded form

Now, let's look at a revised version of this application. Figure 3-6 shows how I've taken the fields and spread them out over several tabs of a form. This simplifies the interface and makes it easier to read, even though I haven't applied any of the font sizing tips that were shown earlier in this section.

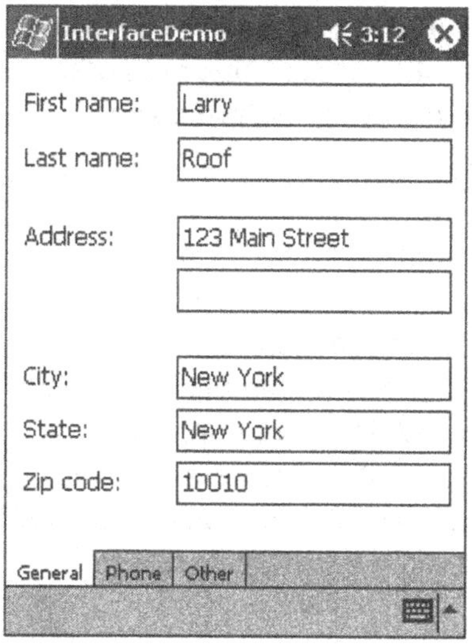

Figure 3-6. An improved form where some of the controls have moved to the suburbs

TIP *Infrequently modified input fields are better suited for separate forms, tabs, or panels. Design your interface such that users don't have to deal with them unless they desire.*

My Input Rules

I'm telling you right here and now, how you handle user input will make or break your application. "Why?" you might ask. Simply because input is such a pain to users of Pocket PCs. You don't have a mouse, you don't have a keyboard (please don't say to me, "What about the SIP?"), and yet you still need to be able to gather data. Who said mobile application development was going to be easy?

Not only is your method of input limited and, generally speaking, a pain, add to the mix the fact that your user might be standing, walking, riding in a car or performing some other activity that will make tapping a small screen hard to do.

Now if that isn't enough for you to think about, consider this: Often your application will be solely responsible for verifying the quality of the data. Applications developed for the Pocket PC are commonly used "out in the field," which is a poetic way of saying a long way from you. The application probably won't have a connection to your server, and as such your application will need to make sure that the data is good while it is being gathered. The worst thing that could happen is a user is out gathering data all day long only to have all of that data thrown out when it's processed. Don't even think that you can send a user back out to gather exactly the same information again without expecting to have the imprint of a Pocket PC on your forehead the next time you look in a mirror.

Input Rule #1: Bigger Is Better

First, this isn't a mistake on my part. Yes, I know that the first interface rule was "bigger is better." Well, so is the first input rule. It's pretty simple when you think about it. Bigger objects are easier to tap. Enough said. Take for example the interface shown in Figure 3-7. The buttons on this interface are too small. You may be able to tap them if you're sitting and the device is in the cradle. I doubt if it will be an easy task to tap these buttons as you walk about a grocery store.

Figure 3-7. Hard-to-tap buttons

 TIP *Often it's more convenient for the user to tap a screen with a finger than with the stylus. You should consider this when you are designing your applications.*

Now, look at Figure 3-8. I've increased the size of the buttons. This is what I like to refer to as my *Sesame Street* approach to interface design. Most desktop developers won't be comfortable with this design. It's out of proportion to what they're accustomed. All that I can say to that is, this isn't a desktop application anymore, Dorothy, and you have to do what you have to do to make an application work for the user.

Figure 3-8. Real big buttons are easy to push.

Input Rule #2: Do It for Them

This isn't a mobile input rule as much as it's just a good general-purpose development technique. If you don't want users to have to deal with the frustrations of the limited input capabilities offered by the Pocket PC, don't have them do any more input than is necessary. To accomplish this you should

- Use default values wherever possible.

- Provide combo and list boxes from which users can pick items, rather than making them type something in.

- Lead users through the input process. Only require them to provide input as it applies to their previous entries. If they have already checked that they don't have any kids, please don't take them to a screen where they enter the names of their kids.

- Make it easy to move through a form. If users are entering five text fields in a row, write some code so that you automatically move the focus to the next input field when the user taps the Enter key. Listing 3-1 shows an example of how this is accomplished.

- Provide predefined strings of text from which users can select rather than requiring them to type in frequently used word combinations repeatedly.

Listing 3-1. Moving Between Fields with the Enter Key

```
Private Sub TextBox1_KeyUp(ByVal sender As Object, _
  ByVal e As System.Windows.Forms.KeyEventArgs) Handles TextBox1.KeyUp

' Was the [Enter] key pressed? If so, move to the next field.
  If (e.KeyCode = System.Windows.Forms.Keys.Enter) Then
    TextBox2.Focus()
  End If

End Sub
```

Input Rule #3: Keep Users Away from the Dangerous Buttons

This rule falls into the same category as not letting your kids play with chainsaws or letting your dog borrow your SUV for the evening. I almost freak out when

I see an interface that has relatively harmless buttons nestled right up against real nasty buttons with serious ramifications. Figure 3-9 demonstrates just such a poorly designed interface.

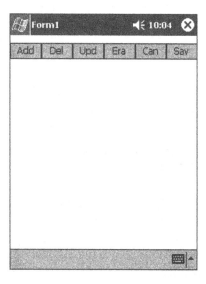

Figure 3-9. Dangerously placed buttons

The buttons shown in Figure 3-9 are, from left to right, **Add**, **Del** (Delete), **Upd** (Update), **Era** (Erase), **Can** (Cancel), and **Sav** (Save). For the purpose of our example, let's assume this is a general-purpose database application. The **Add** button adds a record to the database. The **Del** button deletes the current record from the database. The **Upd** button updates the current record with the new values you entered. The **Era** button is the Death Star of buttons; it erases the database completely. The **Can** button throws away any changes you've made to the database. Finally, the **Sav** button saves all changes back to the database.

None of these buttons has confirmations. That's to say, you won't get one of those "Do you really want to do that?" safety messages that keep you from doing real harm by accident. This is a serious application for serious users. If you tap the **Era** button, the database is toast, no questions asked.

Granted, I've created an extreme example here, but I have to tell you I've seen some in-production mobile applications that weren't far from this. My point to this example is that the combination of the size and placement of the buttons makes it more likely the user will have an accident. Tapping a button is not as precise a task as clicking an item with a mouse. If a user is moving about while using your application, the likelihood of error increases. When you're developing your interface, you should do the following things.

- Make buttons as big as you possibly can.

- Keep serious buttons away from general-purpose buttons.

- Always ask your users if they really want to perform a serious action before performing that action.

Input Rule #4: Stay Away from the SIP

For the love of all that is just and right in the world, keep your applications as far away from the Soft Input Panel as humanly possible. The way I look at it, forcing someone to use the SIP borders on cruel and inhuman punishment. The only thing worse than using the SIP is using the SIP with the input field parked directly underneath the SIP.

Okay, I'm done ranting. You get the point. Now, you're probably thinking to yourself, "Okay Mr. Wizard, how do I do text input if I don't use the SIP?" Well, I have to say that this is more of a guideline than a rule.

There are times when you've no other alternative than to use the SIP. Just be aware that there are options, including the following:

- **Hardware keyboards** are a great way to get away from using the SIP. There are fold-up keyboards, like the one from Targus, that give the user a full-size keyboard. There are micro keyboards that snap onto the bottom of devices, like the Compaq iPAQ Micro Keyboard and the Snap'N'Type keyboard. Some specialty Pocket PC devices, like those offered by Symbol, include a small hardware keyboard.

- **Combo and list boxes** are always better choices than the SIP. If users need to enter a value, and that value has to be from a predefined list of values, use a combo or list box. Don't make them type it. First, they'll have to use the SIP. Second, they're liable to screw it up.

- **Provide predefined fragments** to users. Users can select these commonly used sentence fragments in lieu of typing them in. Let's say you're creating a medical record system that will be used by doctors as they see patients. You could create a set of phrases that are applicable to this environment, for example, "See me in," followed by "days," "weeks," or "months." Your interface provides these options to the user in a timely fashion, allowing the doctor to simply tap and build sentences from the phrases.

My point with this rule: Don't make the mistake of just assuming that the SIP will be fine. It's not. It's a pain to use and error prone to boot. Look for alternatives.

Usage Rules

For some reason this is an area where mobile developers frequently fall on their faces. When you're developing mobile applications, always ask yourself, "Where is the user going to be when running my software?" The answer usually will not be "at home, with the device in its docking cradle."

Surprisingly, most mobile developers never test their applications on devices anywhere other than in their cradles. The problem with this approach is that your docking cradle usually doesn't provide a good representation of the target use of your application for the following reasons:

- The power never runs out.

- Working with the interface is easy since both you and the device are stable.

- You don't have to hold a device and work with it at the same time.

- The lighting and weather in your office is controlled by you; there's no sunshine, clouds, reflections, or rain to deal with.

 CAUTION *Don't take this topic lightly. It's paramount to the success of your application that you consider the user environment during the design phase and test your application in the target environment.*

Usage Rule #1: Does It Work There?

I mentioned the following point earlier in this chapter, but it's worth repeating: If you want to be a mobile application developer, get in the habit of carrying your device with you wherever you go. That's the only way you're going to know how well a device, and subsequently your application, works in various locations and situations.

Here's an example: You've created an e-book application, because, well, the world can never have too many of them. When designing and testing your application, did you considered all of the possible places that a user may be? Will it work well when the user is standing on a subway train holding onto a cell phone, or a briefcase, or a cup of coffee, at the same time? It won't if you require users to tap on the screen to move from page to page in the book. The same holds true if they're using your application to read a book at lunch. Are you going to make them set down their sandwich, pick up the stylus, tap to move a page, put down the stylus, and finally resume eating?

Usage Rule #2: It Has to Work Here

Certain applications have specific location restrictions—places where they have to work. For example, take an application for reading gas meters. This application has to work outside. It has to work under a variety of weather conditions and levels of light. It has to run for 6 to 8 hours. Your application will fail unless you designed for all of these requirements.

Designing mobile applications often involves taking field trips so that you can fully understand the target site and conditions. Think of it as an adventure, that leaving your office is a good thing. This is truly one of those walk the walk things, where you gain an understanding of the work life of your user.

To further my point, I'll provide an example from my development experiences. In the early days of Windows CE, I created an application to provide real estate agents with a mobile Listing service. Early on, I ran into a design issues. At that time, Casio had a device that had a gorgeous screen. The real estate agents loved it. They wouldn't accept any other device. Sounds like a simple decision—just give them the device. The problem was, while the Casio screen was beautiful indoors, it was useless outdoors. In the direct sun, or even in a car, it was as if the device wasn't even on. My application would've been a dismal failure had I not tested it where it would most likely be used—in the car and standing outside a house talking to a potential buyer.

Usage Rule #3: Will It Work for as Long as I Need It?

Here's a news flash: Pocket PCs run on batteries. The follow-up to this scientific bulletin is that when the battery runs out, your application stops. When you're selecting the device on which your application will be run, you need to consider this fact. Some Pocket PC devices offer replaceable batteries, others don't. Finding that out after the fact can be a career ender. You should consider the user's time between charges when you're selecting hardware.

Usage Rule #4: Does It Work on All Devices?

If you're developing a general-purpose consumer application that is expected to run on any version of Pocket PC device, you had better test on each and every one of these devices. Chances are good that you don't have one of each—a scenario I like to call the introvert's view of Noah's Ark device plan. The way to work around this limitation is to run an extensive beta program where you solicit testers who have each of the various devices.

Usage Rule #5: Does It Work Everywhere in the World?

Will individuals who speak different languages use your application? If so, then you need to incorporate localization functionality into your design. Simply stated, this means your application's interface, data sources, and messages need to automatically adjust to the appropriate language of the end user. In Chapter 20, we will look at this topic in detail.

Porting Rules

In my vocabulary, port is a four-letter word. If you've ever tried porting a complex desktop application to a Pocket PC, you'll understand.

Now don't get me wrong. Porting is not inherently an evil thing, as long as you go about it correctly. By correctly, I mean understanding the limitations of the device and adjusting your port accordingly.

The key to any port is to understand you are going to have to rewrite. There are just too many differences between the desktop and device environments to address to simply run the same code in both places.

Porting Rule #1: Jim, Is It Just Me or Is the Screen Smaller?

Unless the desktop version of your application uses forms that are 240×320 pixels in size, you had better plan on reworking the interface. The first mistake you can make here is to think that you'll just squash it all in (see "Interface Rule #1: Bigger Is Better" and "Interface Rule #3: Less Is More").

Your best bet is to build the interface from scratch. Forget what you do on the desktop, there are too many differences between the desktop and device environments. If you try to carry your desktop design over, what you're going to end up with is an interface that looks and acts like a desktop application, which is a certain formula for failure on a device.

Porting Rule #2: Hey, This Isn't a PC

In case you've yet to buy a Pocket PC, let me fill you in on a few things. They have smaller screens, no mouse, slower processors, no hard drive, less memory, and they run on batteries. Unless your desktop application was running on a similar hardware environment, chances are you will have to change more than a few things.

Porting Rule #3: Operator, I've Been Disconnected

In most cases, desktop applications are designed with the assumption that the client's PC will always be connected to the network. Pocket PC applications are just the opposite when it comes to connectivity. They rarely are connected. Even when they are connected, there is a good chance that the user will wander out of a coverage area. What all of this means is that you'll have to adjust your application accordingly during the porting process.

Porting Rule #4: NETCF, the Mini Me of .NET Framework

Okay, the interface is different, the hardware is different, and connectivity is different, but you should be able to take basic .NET desktop code and just use it as is on a device, right? Well, probably not. The .NET Compact Framework is a subset of the .NET Framework. To make NETCF fit on a Pocket PC, .NET Framework had to be significantly trimmed. As a result, coding techniques you use under the .NET Framework may not be supported under NETCF.

Am I saying that it's impossible to write code for use with both desktop and device applications? No, I'm not. I am suggesting that it would be easier to write the code for the limited framework of the device and then port it to the desktop, rather than the other way around.

Step-by-Step Tutorial: Panel-Based Interface

This tutorial provides an example of how you can simplify an interface by dividing input fields between several virtual forms. By virtual, what I mean is that the "forms" are in actuality individual panels that are moved in and out of the user's view as needed, so that the panels appear to be separate forms to the user.

As part of this exercise, you'll do the following:

- Create a multipart interface with panels.

- Learn how to move panels in and out of view.

NOTE *A completed version of this application, titled PanelDemo, is provided under the **Chapter 3** folder of this book's **Samples** folder. See Appendix D for more information on accessing and loading the sample applications.*

Step 1: Start a New Project

Begin this step-by-step exercise by creating a new project using the following steps:

1. Start Visual Studio .NET if necessary.

2. From the Start Page, select **New Project.**

3. From the New Project dialog box, select **Smart Device Application.**

4. Specify a project name of **PanelDemo.**

5. Select a location to create the project and click the **OK** button.

Step 2: Configuring the Project

To configure the target output folder for this project, perform the following steps:

1. Under the Project menu, select **PanelDemo Properties.**

2. Under the Device page of the Text File Property Pages dialog box, set the output file folder to **\Windows\Start Menu\Programs\Apress.**

Step 3: Constructing the Interface

The interface for the PanelDemo application is comprised of three Panel controls, a simple menu, and a number of TextBox and Label controls. You'll start by adding and configuring the first panel:

1. Set the **Text** property of the Form to **PanelDemo.**

2. Add a Panel control to your form.

3. Set the **Name** property of the Panel control to **pnlGeneral.**

4. Resize the Panel control so that it's **236, 268.**

5. Add a Label and TextBox control to the Panel. Set the Label's **Text** property to **Company:** and the **TextBox Text** property to an empty string. Align the controls so that they appear as shown in Figure 3-10.

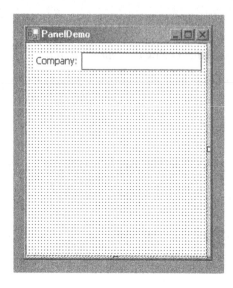

Figure 3-10. The first panel of the PanelDemo interface

6. Set the **Location** property of the Panel control to **300,0**. This will move the panel out of view, off the right side of the form's view area.

Perform the following steps to add and configure the second panel:

1. Add a Panel control to your form.

2. Set the **Name** property of the Panel control to **pnlContact**.

3. Resize the Panel control so that it's **236, 268**.

4. Add a Label and TextBox control to the Panel. Set the Label's **Text** property to **Contact:** and the **TextBox Text** property to an empty string. Align the controls so that they appear as shown in Figure 3-11.

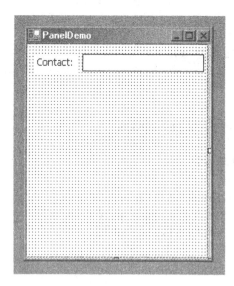

Figure 3-11. The second panel of the PanelDemo interface

5. Set the **Location** property of the Panel control to **300,0**. This will move the panel out of view, out with the first panel you created.

The following steps will add the third and final panel to your application:

1. Add a Panel control to your form.

2. Set the **Name** property of the Panel control to **pnlOrders**.

3. Resize the Panel control so that it's **236, 268**.

4. Add a DataGrid control to the panel. Size and align the DataGrid so that it appears as shown in Figure 3-12.

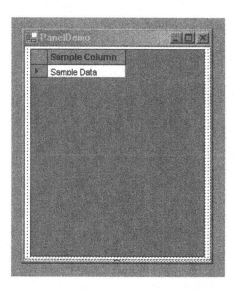

Figure 3-12. The third panel of the PanelDemo interface

5. Set the **Location** property of the Panel control to **300,0**. This will move the panel out of view, out with the other two panels.

All that is left is to create the menu that will allow the user to move between panels. To create the menu, perform the following steps:

1. Using the menu editor create a Panel menu.

2. Add a **General** menu item to the Panel menu. Name this item **mnuPanelGeneral**.

3. Add a **Contact** menu item to the Panel menu. Name this item **mnuPanelContact**.

4. Add an **Orders** menu item to the Panel menu. Name this item **mnuPanelOrders**. Your menu should appear as shown in Figure 3-13.

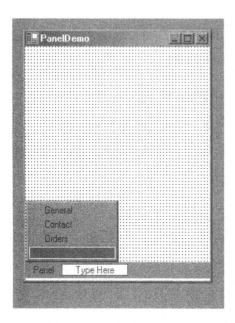

Figure 3-13. The Panel menu

Step 4: Adding the Code

With the interface completed, you're ready to add the code that will control the hiding and displaying of panels. Start by creating a general-purpose routine that will display the specified panel. Add the code shown in Listing 3-2 to your form module.

Listing 3-2. The ShowPanel Routine Handles Hiding and Displaying Panels

```
Sub ShowPanel(ByVal PanelToShow As Panel)

   Hide all of the panels.
   pnlGeneral.Left = 300
   pnlContact.Left = 300
   pnlOrders.Left = 300
```

```
' Display the selected panel.
  PanelToShow.Left = 0

End Sub
```

This routine accepts a single argument, the panel to display. It starts by hiding all of the panels by moving them off to the right of the viewable area of the form. It then displays the selected panel by moving it back into the viewable area.

Displaying a Panel at Startup

Next, you'll add code to display the General panel when the application starts. Add the code shown in Listing 3-3 to the **Load** event of the form.

Listing 3-3. The Form's Click Event for Displaying the First Panel

```
Private Sub Form1_Load(ByVal sender As System.Object, _
  ByVal e As System.EventArgs) Handles MyBase.Load

' When we start show the general panel.
  ShowPanel(pnlGeneral)

End Sub
```

Wiring the Menu

Add the code shown in Listing 3-4 to the **Click** events of the three menu items, **mnuPanelGeneral**, **mnuPanelContact**, and **mnuPanelOrders**. In each of these event procedures, the ShowPanel routine is called to display the appropriate panel.

Listing 3-4. The Code Behind the Click Event of the Three Menu Items

```
Private Sub mnuPanelGeneral_Click(ByVal sender As System.Object, _
  ByVal e As System.EventArgs) Handles mnuPanelGeneral.Click

' Show the General panel.
  ShowPanel(pnlGeneral)

End Sub
```

```
Private Sub mnuPanelContact_Click(ByVal sender As System.Object, _
  ByVal e As System.EventArgs) Handles mnuPanelContact.Click

' Show the Contact panel.
  ShowPanel(pnlContact)

End Sub

Private Sub mnuPanelOrders_Click(ByVal sender As System.Object, _
  ByVal e As System.EventArgs) Handles mnuPanelOrders.Click

' Show the Orders panel.
  ShowPanel(pnlOrders)

End Sub
```

Step 5: Testing Your Application

To test your application, perform the following steps:

1. Select either **Pocket PC Device** or **Pocket PC Emulator** from the Deployment Device combo box.

2. Select **Release** from the Solution Configurations combo box.

3. Click the **Start** button.

Your application will be copied to the target device and run. It should appear as shown in Figure 3-14. Perform the following steps to verify your application is running correctly:

1. Verify that the **General** tab is displayed when the application starts.

2. From the Panel menu, select the **Contact** menu item. Verify that the Contact panel is displayed.

3. From the Panel menu, select the **Orders** menu item. Verify that the Orders panel is displayed.

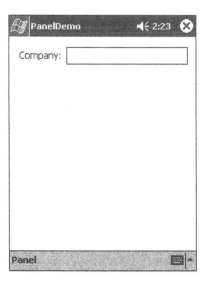

Figure 3-14. The PanelDemo application

HOMEWORK *Add a fourth panel, Order Details, to the application. Add a menu item for selecting this panel and the code necessary for hiding and displaying this panel.*

NOTE *You could do something very similar to this panel demo with the TabControl control. Chapter 4 provides additional information on this control.*

Windows Forms

Now that you have a general understanding of application design, let's turn our attention to the foundation of NETCF interfaces—forms.

Forms, as you're probably already aware of, are the whiteboard on which you draw an application's interface. Using controls, you construct that interface. As you will see in Chapter 4, there are nearly thirty controls provided with the .NET Compact Framework.

Forms, like all other objects in the .NET Compact Framework, are instances of classes. The **Form** class is part of the **System.Windows.Forms** namespace, which also includes

- **Controls**—The classes that define the controls available for use under the .NET Compact Framework

- **Components**—Such as the Menu, MenuItem, and ContextMenu

- **Common dialog boxes**—Including OpenFileDialog and the SaveFileDialog

As we'll see in Chapter 5, the .NET Compact Framework allows you to inherit from existing forms and controls. These objects can then be modified by adding or removing functionality. For the remainder of this chapter, we'll be focusing on forms alone, and the **System.Windows.Forms.Form** class.

Form Properties

As with everything else in NETCF, forms offer a subset of the properties and methods found in their .NET Framework counterpart. Table 3-1 shows commonly used properties of the **Form** class.

Table 3-1. Commonly Used Properties of the Form Class

PROPERTY	DESCRIPTION
BackColor	Specifies the background color of the form.
ContextMenu	Specifies the context menu associated with a form. For more on context menus, see Chapter 6.
Controls	Defines a collection of controls on a form.
DialogResult	Indicates the dialog box result for a form.
Enabled	Enables or disables a form, along with all of its contents.
MaximizeBox	Controls whether the maximize button is displayed.
Menu	Specifies the main menu that will be displayed with a form.
MinimizeBox	Controls whether an "X" or "OK" is displayed in the upper-right corner of a form. Tapping the "X" will hide your application; tapping the "OK" will close your application.
Text	Defines the caption that will appear on a form.
Visible	Controls whether a form is visible.

NOTE *There is no windows handle available, which used to be provided in VB and eVB through the **hWnd** property of the form. This shortcoming limits working with a variety of Windows CE API functions that require a handle. This shortcoming can be worked around through the Windows API. See Chapter 17 for more details.*

Form Methods

The list of **Form** methods that a mobile developer frequently utilizes is small. Table 3-2 lists the commonly used methods of the **Form** class.

Table 3-2. Commonly Used Methods of the Form Class

METHOD	DESCRIPTION
Close	Closes a form
Hide	Hides a form
Show	Shows a form

Form Events

The Form events that you'll work with when developing mobile applications are very similar to those commonly utilized with desktop applications. Table 3-3 provides a list of commonly used events of the **Form** class.

Table 3-3. Commonly Used Events of the Form Class

EVENT	DESCRIPTION
Activated	Fires when the form is activated.
Click	Fires when the user taps the surface of a form.
Closing	Fires as a form is closing. This event can be used to perform functions, such as saving data, before the application exits.
Load	Fires when the form loads. This event is frequently used to perform initialization tasks.

The Code Behind a Form

Chances are if you're an experienced Visual Basic or eMbedded Visual Basic developer, you've never given much thought to how a form is created. For the most part, that's because there was no good way to know what was going on behind the scenes, and even less control over what was happening. All of that has changed with the .NET Compact Framework. Now, all of the construction and configuration used to create a form is readily available to you as code that is part of every form you create. In this section, I'll walk you through that code, providing you with an overview of how forms are built.

For the purpose of this example, I'm going to show you the code behind the form shown in Figure 3-15. This is a simple form. It consists of two Label controls, two TextBox controls, and a three-item menu.

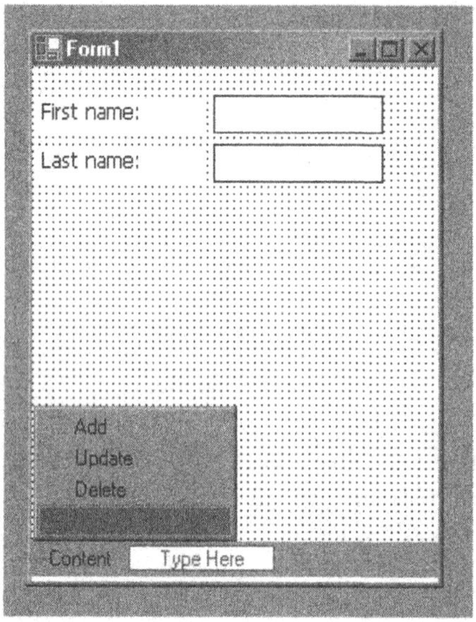

Figure 3-15. The example form

As you work with the Windows Form Designer within Visual Studio .NET to construct your application's interface, behind the scenes the code that will be used to re-create your interface is being automatically generated. This code is part of a form's module. It's located in the Windows Form Designer generated code region, as shown in Figure 3-16.

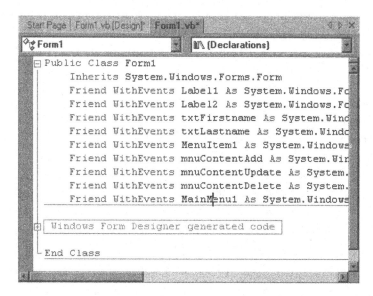

Figure 3-16. The region containing the Windows Form Designer–generated code

Expanding this region shows us all of the code used to define and configure the interface of this example interface. Listing 3-5 shows this code. Following this Listing , I'll walk you through the various bits, explaining the various parts of this Form Designer–generated code.

Listing 3-5. The Code Used to Create the Example Interface

```
#Region " Windows Form Designer generated code "

    Public Sub New()
        MyBase.New()

        'This call is required by the Windows Form Designer.
        InitializeComponent()

        'Add any initialization after the InitializeComponent() call

    End Sub

    'Form overrides dispose to clean up the component list.
    Protected Overloads Overrides Sub Dispose(ByVal disposing As Boolean)
        MyBase.Dispose(disposing)
    End Sub
```

```
'NOTE: The following procedure is required by the Windows Form Designer
'It can be modified using the Windows Form Designer.
'Do not modify it using the code editor.
Private Sub InitializeComponent()
Me.MainMenu1 = New System.Windows.Forms.MainMenu
Me.Label1 = New System.Windows.Forms.Label
Me.Label2 = New System.Windows.Forms.Label
Me.txtFirstname = New System.Windows.Forms.TextBox
Me.txtLastname = New System.Windows.Forms.TextBox
Me.MenuItem1 = New System.Windows.Forms.MenuItem
Me.mnuContentAdd = New System.Windows.Forms.MenuItem
Me.mnuContentUpdate = New System.Windows.Forms.MenuItem
Me.mnuContentDelete = New System.Windows.Forms.MenuItem
'
'MainMenu1
'
Me.MainMenu1.MenuItems.Add(Me.MenuItem1)
'
'Label1
'
Me.Label1.Location = New System.Drawing.Point(4, 18)
Me.Label1.Text = "First name:"
'
'Label2
'
Me.Label2.Location = New System.Drawing.Point(4, 46)
Me.Label2.Text = "Last name:"
'
'txtFirstname
'
Me.txtFirstname.Location = New System.Drawing.Point(108, 16)
Me.txtFirstname.Text = ""
'
'txtLastname
'
Me.txtLastname.Location = New System.Drawing.Point(108, 44)
Me.txtLastname.Text = ""
'
'MenuItem1
'
Me.MenuItem1.MenuItems.Add(Me.mnuContentAdd)
Me.MenuItem1.MenuItems.Add(Me.mnuContentUpdate)
Me.MenuItem1.MenuItems.Add(Me.mnuContentDelete)
Me.MenuItem1.Text = "Content"
'
```

```
'mnuContentAdd
'
Me.mnuContentAdd.Text = "Add"
'
'mnuContentUpdate
'
Me.mnuContentUpdate.Text = "Update"
'
'mnuContentDelete
'
Me.mnuContentDelete.Text = "Delete"
'
'Form1
'
Me.Controls.Add(Me.txtLastname)
Me.Controls.Add(Me.txtFirstname)
Me.Controls.Add(Me.Label2)
Me.Controls.Add(Me.Label1)
Me.Menu = Me.MainMenu1
Me.Text = "Form1"

    End Sub

#End Region
```

CAUTION *Do not modify the code within the InitializeComponent routine, located within this region. The Form Designer generates this code. Modifications you make to this section may cause problems for the Form Designer or may be disposed of by the Form Designer.*

TIP *Create your own initialization routine where you perform specific startup activities. Call your initialization routine after the InitializeComponent call.*

Handling the Creation of a Form

At the top of the Windows Form Designer generated code region is the public procedure **New**. This procedure executes every time you create an instance of this form. The **New** procedure in turn calls the **InitializeComponent** procedure, which defines the rest of the interface.

```
Public Sub New()
    MyBase.New()

    'This call is required by the Windows Form Designer.
    InitializeComponent()

    'Add any initialization after the InitializeComponent() call

End Sub
```

Handling the Disposal of a Form

Immediately after the **New** procedure is the **Dispose** procedure. This procedure handles the cleaning up of all of the components and system resources used within a form.

```
'Form overrides dispose to clean up the component list.
Protected Overloads Overrides Sub Dispose(ByVal disposing As Boolean)
    MyBase.Dispose(disposing)
End Sub
```

 NOTE *Any other system resources used within the form's code should be disposed here. That includes files, database connections, and GUI resources such as fonts and pens.*

Building the Form's Interface

The InitializeComponent routine handles the construction of the form's interface. This routine starts by defining all of the components that are part of the interface. For our example application, those components are a MainMenu, two Labels, two TextBoxes, and four MenuItems (one for the Content menu and three for its items).

```
    Private Sub InitializeComponent()
Me.MainMenu1 = New System.Windows.Forms.MainMenu
Me.Label1 = New System.Windows.Forms.Label
Me.Label2 = New System.Windows.Forms.Label
Me.txtFirstname = New System.Windows.Forms.TextBox
Me.txtLastname = New System.Windows.Forms.TextBox
Me.MenuItem1 = New System.Windows.Forms.MenuItem
Me.mnuContentAdd = New System.Windows.Forms.MenuItem
Me.mnuContentUpdate = New System.Windows.Forms.MenuItem
Me.mnuContentDelete = New System.Windows.Forms.MenuItem
```

NOTE *The type of control, and the name of that control, are defined in this section of the Form Designer–generated code.*

Next, the Content menu (MenuItem1) is added to the MainMenu. If you were to have additional menus, they would be added here as well.

```
'
'MainMenu1
'
Me.MainMenu1.MenuItems.Add(Me.MenuItem1)
```

Next is the configuration of controls. Any property settings that you configured through the Form Designer will show up here.

```
'
'Label1
'
Me.Label1.Location = New System.Drawing.Point(4, 18)
Me.Label1.Text = "First name:"
'
'Label2
'
Me.Label2.Location = New System.Drawing.Point(4, 46)
Me.Label2.Text = "Last name:"
'
'txtFirstname
'
Me.txtFirstname.Location = New System.Drawing.Point(108, 16)
Me.txtFirstname.Text = ""
'
'txtLastname
'
Me.txtLastname.Location = New System.Drawing.Point(108, 44)
Me.txtLastname.Text = ""
'
'MenuItem1
'
Me.MenuItem1.MenuItems.Add(Me.mnuContentAdd)
Me.MenuItem1.MenuItems.Add(Me.mnuContentUpdate)
Me.MenuItem1.MenuItems.Add(Me.mnuContentDelete)
Me.MenuItem1.Text = "Content"
```

```
'
'mnuContentAdd
'
Me.mnuContentAdd.Text = "Add"
'
'mnuContentUpdate
'
Me.mnuContentUpdate.Text = "Update"
'
'mnuContentDelete
'
Me.mnuContentDelete.Text = "Delete"
```

Finally, the individual controls are added to the form. The InitializeComponent routine completes with configurations to the form itself.

```
'
'Form1
'
Me.Controls.Add(Me.txtLastname)
Me.Controls.Add(Me.txtFirstname)
Me.Controls.Add(Me.Label2)
Me.Controls.Add(Me.Label1)
Me.Menu = Me.MainMenu1
Me.Text = "Form1"

End Sub
```

> **NOTE**   *Controls are added to the controls list associated with the window. The **Dispose** method uses this control array to dispose of all controls when the window is destroyed. If you add controls to the window yourself outside InitializeComponent, you should follow this technique of adding the controls to the controls collection of the window. This will ensure that your controls are also disposed of properly.*

Now at this point you might be thinking to yourself, "And this means what to me?" I understand your puzzlement. After all, the Form Designer takes care of all of this, so why worry? The answer is that understanding how an interface is constructed allows you to do the same from code. With this knowledge, you can create menus at runtime or add controls to an interface, as needed. Granted, this is not something that you'll be doing with every application. Still, it's a powerful capability offered with the .NET Compact Framework, and a handy programming skill.

Working with Forms

Now that you have a general understanding of building forms, let's turn our attention to some common form-related tasks that are performed when developing applications with the .NET Compact Framework.

Renaming a Form

Commonly a developer will rename a form, changing its name from the default "Form1" to something more appropriate. With NETCF, renaming your default form takes on an extra step. That step is the topic of this section.

First, let me point out the difference between renaming a form and changing the filename under which a form is saved. These are two different configurations, and while I would recommend that for clarity you use the same name for each, you may choose differently.

Configuring the Filename for a Form

To configure the filename for a form, perform the following steps:

1. In the Solutions Explorer window, right-click the form.

2. From the pop-up menu, select **Rename**.

3. Type in the new name for the form.

Configuring the Object Name for a Form

To configure the object name for a form, perform the following steps:

1. Open the form in the Form Designer.

2. In the Form Designer, click the form itself.

3. In the Properties Windows, select the **Name** property.

4. Type in the new name for the form.

NOTE *If the form that you're renaming is the startup form for your application, you will need to reconfigure your project with the new form name. See the next section, "Configuring the Startup Form," for details on how to perform this task.*

Configuring the Startup Form

The startup form is the first form displayed when your application runs. By default, when you create a new project, the first form, Form1, is set as the startup form. The fact is, you never have to worry about this project setting if all you create are single-form applications.

There may be situations though when you want, or need, to add additional forms to a project. Again, as long as the first project form, Form1, remains the first form shown by your application, there is still nothing for you to do in the way of configuring the startup form.

When might you want to change your startup form? One common situation is to add a splash form to your application. If you're not familiar with them, splash forms are used for two general purposes: 1) to keep the user's attention while a more laborious task is performed in the background, and 2) to display licensing information, particularly with shareware products. Splash forms themselves are by definition lean. They have little code and use minimal resources, all with the intent that they will load and display quickly.

To configure the startup form for your application, perform the following steps:

1. Right-click your project in the Solutions Explorer window.

2. From the pop-up menu, select **Properties**. The Property Pages dialog box will be displayed.

3. Under the **Common Properties** folder, select **General**.

4. Use the **Startup Object** combo box to configure the startup form for your application.

Showing a Form

Displaying a form is only slightly more complicated under NETCF and VB .NET than it was from Visual Basic and eMbedded Visual Basic. Listing 3-6 demonstrates how to display a form.

It's a simple two-step process. First, you create an instance of the form. In this case, it's Form2. Second, you use the **Show** method of the **Form** class to display the form. That's all there is to it.

Listing 3-6. Displaying a Form

```
' Create an instance of the form.
  Dim secondForm As New Form2

' Display the form.
  secondForm.Show()
```

Getting Rid of a Form

There are two options when it comes to getting rid of a form: You can close the form, or you can hide the form. Closing a form releases all of its resources and disposes the form. Hiding a form does just that, it hides the form from the user's view, but maintains all of its resources and values. Which option you use, close or hide, depends upon the needs of your application.

Closing a Form

There are two ways to close a form. Listing 3-7 shows the first way, closing a form from another form.

Listing 3-7. Closing from Another Form

```
' Create an instance of the form.
  Dim secondForm As New Form2

' Display the form.
  secondForm.Show()

' Close the form.
  secondForm.Close()
```

Listing 3-8 shows the second way to close a form. You use this approach from within the closing form itself. This second approach makes use of the

Me keyword. **Me** refers to the object, in this case the form, in which the code is currently executing.

Listing 3-8. Closing from Within a Form

```
Close myself.
Me.Close()
```

Scrolling Forms

Earlier in this chapter, I showed you how to use multiple panels to limit the number of fields visible at one time on a form. Chapter 4 demonstrates how you can use the TabControl for this same purpose.

Another way to accomplish this is with scrolling forms, where the contents of the form are greater than the view port for that form. Take for example Figure 3-17. In this form, you can see a panel that is longer than the form itself.

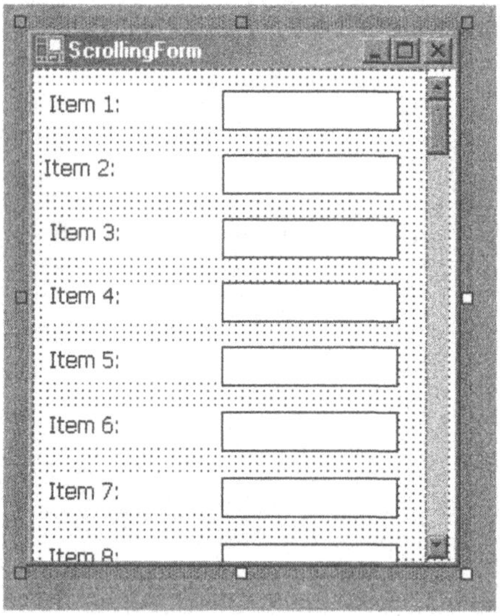

Figure 3-17. The top of the panel

Now look at Figure 3-18. I've pushed the panel off the top of the form so that you can see the bottom of the panel. I scrolled the panel up by setting its **Top** property to a negative value, effectively pushing it off the top of the form.

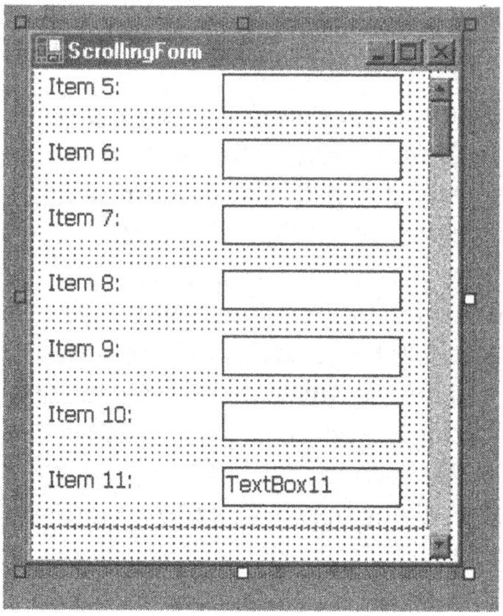

Figure 3-18. The bottom of the panel

All that you need is a way for the user to scroll the panel. I like to add two methods, one automatic and one manual. The automatic method involves trapping the Enter key as the user enters information. When the user taps the Enter key on the SIP, simply move the focus to the next field and at the same time scroll the form up.

The manual method makes use of a VerticalScrollBar control. Place the scroll bar next to the panel, as shown in Figures 3-17 and 3-18. When the user adjusts the scroll bar, you adjust the position of the panel. Listing 3-9 shows the simple code used to implement this functionality.

Listing 3-9. Linking a Scroll Bar to a Panel

```
Private Sub vscPanel_ValueChanged(ByVal sender As System.Object, _
  ByVal e As System.EventArgs) Handles vscPanel.ValueChanged

' Reposition the panel.
  Panel1.Top = -1 * (vscPanel.Value * 2)

End Sub
```

NOTE   *The sample ScrollingForm is included under the **Chapter 3** folder of the **Samples** folder. See Appendix D for more information on working with the sample applications for this book.*

Working with Dialog Boxes

No discussion of forms would be complete without mentioning dialog boxes. Dialog boxes are special-purpose forms. The key difference between forms and dialog boxes is that dialog boxes are generally used to gather and return values. There are special-purpose dialog boxes, such as OpenFileDialog and SaveFileDialog, as well as more general-purpose dialog boxes, such as MessageBox and InputBox. Finally, there are completely custom dialog boxes that can look, act, and respond in the manner that best suits your application.

Understanding what dialog boxes are and how to utilize them in an application is paramount for a mobile developer. Dialog boxes provide a structured control for gathering input from the user. In this section, I'll show you how to work with both the MessageBox and InputBox dialog boxes plus, how to create a custom dialog box from scratch.

NOTE   *See Chapter 4 for more information on the OpenFileDialog and SaveFileDialog controls.*

Working with the MessageBox Dialog Boxes

The MessageBox dialog box provides an easy way to display information to the user and obtain simple responses from the user. The dialog box can include text, symbols, and a combination of buttons. The class **System.Windows.Forms.MessageBox** implements the MessageBox dialog box. This is an easy class to work with because only a single method of this class, the **Show** method, is commonly used.

The **Show** method is overloaded, providing three ways in which it can be called to display the following items:

- Simple text message

- Message and caption

- Message, caption, combination of buttons, and symbol

NOTE   *In addition to the **MessageBox** class, VB .NET developers can use the MsgBox function, a holdover from Visual Basic.*

TIP   *Remember, screen real estate is minimal on the Pocket PC. Keep your messages short and sweet.*

Displaying a MessageBox with Simple Text

In its easiest form, the MessageBox dialog box contains only text. The following line of code demonstrates this approach. The message either can be a static text string as shown, or can be a combination of strings that are built at runtime.

```
MessageBox.Show("This is a simple text message.")
```

Figure 3-19 shows the resulting MessageBox. I rarely use this simplest of MessageBox dialog box forms. I find that it's only suited for debugging purposes.

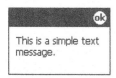

Figure 3-19. A simple MessageBox dialog box

Displaying a MessageBox with Text and a Caption

The second way to call the **Show** method includes both a text message and a caption. The following code demonstrates this approach. The second argument to the **Show** method specifies the caption for the dialog box.

```
Dim mb As System.Windows.Forms.MessageBox
mb.Show("This is a simple text message.", _
   "My Caption")
```

Figure 3-20 shows the dialog box that results from this code. I use this form of the MessageBox dialog box in situations where I want to inform the user that an event occurred or an action completed.

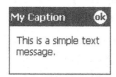

Figure 3-20. A MessageBox dialog box with text and a caption

Displaying a MessageBox with Text, Caption, Buttons, and Symbol

The third way for calling the **Show** method allows you to include a text message, a caption, a combination of buttons, and a symbol. It's this form of the MessageBox dialog box that I use most. Listing 3-10 demonstrates this approach.

Listing 3-10. A MessageBox with Text, Caption, Buttons, and Symbol

```
Dim mb As System.Windows.Forms.MessageBox
mb.Show("This is a simple text message.", _
  "My Caption", _
  MessageBoxButtons.AbortRetryIgnore, _
  MessageBoxIcon.Asterisk, _
  MessageBoxDefaultButton.Button1)
```

Figure 3-21 shows the dialog box that results from Listing 3-10. I use this form of the MessageBox dialog box in situations where I need to acquire a specific answer from the user.

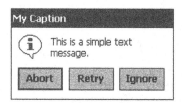

Figure 3-21. A MessageBox dialog box with buttons

In this form, the **Show** method accepts five arguments. Table 3-4 lists those arguments.

Table 3-4. MessageBox Show Method Arguments

ARGUMENT	VALUE	DESCRIPTION
Text	string	Text to display in the body of the dialog box.
Caption	string	Caption to apply to the dialog box.
Buttons	MessageBox Buttons	Combination of buttons to display with the dialog box. Refer to Table 3-5 for the values to use with this argument.
Icon	MessageBoxIcons	Symbol to display with the dialog box. Refer to Table 3-6 for the values to use with this argument.
DefaultButton	MessageBox DefaultButtons	Default button of the buttons displayed. Refer to Table 3-7 for the values to use with this argument.

Table 3-5 lists the enumerated values to use with the **Buttons** argument of the **Show** method.

Table 3-5. Buttons Argument Values

VALUE	DESCRIPTION
AbortRetryIgnore	Adds Abort, Retry, and Ignore buttons to the dialog box
OK	Adds an OK button to the dialog box
OKCancel	Adds OK and Cancel buttons to the dialog box
RetryCancel	Adds Retry and Cancel buttons to the dialog box
YesNo	Adds Yes and No buttons to the dialog box
YesNoCancel	Adds Yes, No, and Cancel buttons to the dialog box

Table 3-6 lists the enumerated values to use with the **Icon** argument of the **Show** method.

Table 3-6. Icon Argument Values

VALUE	DESCRIPTION
Asterisk	Adds an image of a lowercase letter "i" in a blue circle to the dialog box. Use this icon when you want to display information to the user, such as when a process completes.
Exclamation	Adds an image of an exclamation point in a yellow triangle to the dialog box. Use this icon to highlight the importance of a message.
Hand	Adds an image of a white "X" in a red circle to the dialog box. Use this icon when displaying errors.
None	Specifies that no icon is displayed.
Question	Adds the image of a question mark in a circle to the dialog box. Use this icon when you are asking the user a question, such as "File exists. Do you want to overwrite it?"

Table 3-7 lists the enumerated values to use with the **DefaultButton** argument of the **Show** method.

Table 3-7. DefaultButton Argument Values

VALUE	DESCRIPTION
Button1	Defines the first button as the default button
Button2	Defines the second button as the default button
Button3	Defines the third button as the default button

Handling the User's Response to a MessageBox

You can use the MessageBox dialog box in two ways. The first way is to simply use the dialog box to display a message. The second way displays a message and returns a value that's based upon the dialog box button that was tapped by the user.

We've already looked at the various ways to display a MessageBox dialog box. Listing 3-11 shows how to handle the response returned from this dialog box. At the top of this example, you'll see the declaration of the variable that will hold the response. Use a Select Case statement to compare the value returned against a list of possible values. In this example, I've configured the MessageBox with **Abort**, **Retry**, and **Ignore** buttons. Subsequently the check made is against those values.

Listing 3-11. Handling a MessageBox Response

```
Dim intResponse As DialogResult
Dim mb As System.Windows.Forms.MessageBox
intResponse = mb.Show("This is a simple text message.", _
  "My Caption", _
  MessageBoxButtons.AbortRetryIgnore, _
  MessageBoxIcon.Asterisk, _
  MessageBoxDefaultButton.Button1)

Select Case intResponse
  Case DialogResult.Abort    ' Handle the request to abort.
  Case DialogResult.Ignore   ' Handle the request to ignore.
  Case DialogResult.Retry    ' Handle the request to retry.
End Select
```

Working with the InputBox Dialog Box

You access the InputBox dialog box through the InputBox function. Table 3-8 lists the arguments for this function.

Table 3-8. InputBox Function Arguments

ARGUMENT	REQUIRED	DESCRIPTION
Prompt	Required	Message displayed in the body of the dialog box
Title	Required	Caption displayed on the dialog box
DefaultResponse	Optional	Default response if no user input is provided
XPos	Optional	Distance from the left edge of the screen
YPos	Optional	Distance from the top edge of the screen

Following is an example of calling the InputBox function. The InputBox always returns a string value. The value returned would then need to be converted to the appropriate data type for your application's needs.

```
Dim strResponse As String

strResponse = InputBox("Enter a value: ", "Specify Count", "10")
```

Figure 3-22 shows the InputBox as it appears to the user.

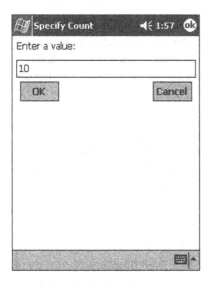

Figure 3-22. An InputBox

TIP   *The InputBox dialog box is an excellent way to obtain a single value from the user. It saves you the hassle of having to create and display your own custom dialog box for gathering simple information from the user.*

Working with Custom Dialog Boxes

While the MessageBox and InputBox dialog boxes are useful, sometimes you need additional functionality, the ability to have complete control over how the dialog boxes appear, and what they contain. That's where custom dialog boxes come in.

Constructing a Custom Dialog Box

Custom dialog boxes are nothing more than regular forms that are configured and displayed in a specific manner. To configure a form as a dialog box, perform the following steps:

1. Add a new form to your project.

2. Set the new form's **FormBorderStyle** property to **FixedDialog**.

3. Configure the interface of the form as desired. Remember, all of the controls that you add to your dialog box's interface are accessible from your application. That's to say, once the user responds to and closes the dialog box, your application will be able to query the values from the dialog box.

NOTE   *While you can certainly adorn your custom dialog box with any of a variety of interface elements, Pocket PC standards recommend that your dialog boxes do not include menus, scroll bars, or sizable borders.*

Using this configuration, your dialog box will have an **OK** button in the upper-right corner. Tapping this button sets the form's **DialogResult** property to DialogResponse.OK. For more on this topic, refer to the "Processing the Dialog Box's Response" section later in this chapter.

Displaying a Custom Dialog Box

At this point, you're done with the hard work. Displaying a custom dialog box is no more difficult than displaying a regular form. To display a custom dialog box, perform the following steps:

1. Open the event procedure where you'll be opening the dialog box.

2. In that procedure, you'll need to add two lines of code. The first line declares a variable that holds an instance of your dialog box form. The second line displays the dialog box. The code that follows provides an example of these steps:

```
Dim dlg As New frmDialog()

' Display the dialog.
  dlg.ShowDialog()
```

Processing the Dialog Box's Response

Now, chances are that if you went to all of the trouble to create your own custom dialog box, you're going to want to retrieve data, that's to say the user's responses, from that dialog box. If that's not the case, then you would have been better off using the standard MessageBox and InputBox dialog boxes.

There are some nuances specific to a dialog box that you'll need to consider from within your application. Dialog boxes typically include a **Cancel** button, which enables the user to terminate whatever process your dialog box is part of. In the event that the user taps this button, you dispose any data entered, rather than processing the data. To determine how a form was closed, check the form's **DialogResult** property. Listing 3-12 shows an example of first displaying a dialog box and then checking the **DialogResult** property once the dialog box closes.

Listing 3-12. Checking How a Dialog Box Was Closed

```
Dim dlg As New frmDialog()

' Display the dialog.
  dlg.ShowDialog()
```

```
' Check the state returned by the dialog. Did the user tap OK?
  If dlg.DialogResult = DialogResult.OK Then

' They tapped OK, so retrieve the values they entered.
' Retrieve the values here...
  End If
```

Within the dialog box, you'll need to add a bit of code to configure your **Cancel** button to cancel the dialog. Listing 3-13 shows the single line of code required to perform this configuration. In this example, the **DialogResult** property of the button **btnCancel** is set to Dialog.Cancel. This configuration will cause the dialog box to close if and when the **Cancel** button is tapped, and more importantly to set the **DialogResult** property of the form to Dialog.Cancel.

Listing 3-13. Configuring a Cancel Button

```
Private Sub frmDialog_Load(ByVal sender As System.Object, _
  ByVal e As System.EventArgs) Handles MyBase.Load

' Link the Cancel button to the cancel result.
  btnCancel.DialogResult = DialogResult.Cancel

End Sub
```

Forms displayed as dialog boxes respond differently when they are closed. Tapping the **OK** button doesn't close the form; it merely hides the form. It's because of this behavior that you're able to query the values of the various elements of the dialog box. To facilitate the querying of the dialog box's controls from the calling form, you add a single read-only **Property** procedure to our dialog box. This **Property** procedure will return the values to the dialog box's controls in a structure.

Let's look at an example dialog box to help clarify this concept. Figure 3-23 shows a simple dialog box containing two input fields (name and phone number) and a **Cancel** button.

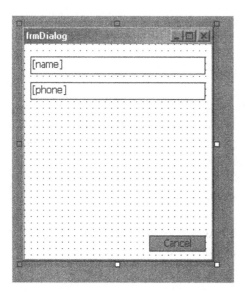

Figure 3-23. A simple dialog box example

To expose the dialog box's two input fields, we add two small code fragments to the dialog box. Listing 3-14 shows the first fragment, which defines the structure used to return the input values. This structure contains two values, one for the name and the other for the phone number.

Listing 3-14. Defining the Structure

```
Public Class CustomerInfo
   Public Name As String
   Public Phone As String
End Class
```

The second fragment of code defines the **Property** procedure that returns the input field values. Listing 3-15 shows this code.

Listing 3-15. Returning the Values

```
Public ReadOnly Property CustomersInfo() As CustomerInfo
' Create an instance of the CustomerInfo object to use to pass values.
   Get
      Dim ci As New CustomerInfo
      ci.Name = Me.txtName.Text
```

```
            ci.Phone = Me.txtPhone.Text
            Return ci
        End Get
    End Property
```

With this code in place, the calling form is now able to query the values from the dialog box. Listing 3-16 shows how this is accomplished. By calling the **CustomerInfo Property** procedure, the form receives the structure containing both the name and phone number entered by the user.

Listing 3-16. Retrieving the Values from the Dialog Box

```
Private Sub btnShowDialog_Click(ByVal sender As System.Object, _
    ByVal e As System.EventArgs) Handles btnShowDialog.Click
    Dim ci As CustomerInfo
    Dim dlg As New frmDialog

' Display the dialog.
    dlg.ShowDialog()

' Check the state returned by the dialog. Did the user tap OK?
    If dlg.DialogResult = DialogResult.OK Then

' They tapped OK, so retrieve the values they entered.
        ci = dlg.CustomersInfo
        MessageBox.Show(ci.Name.ToString())
        MessageBox.Show(ci.Phone.ToString())
    End If

' Get rid of the dialog.
    dlg.Dispose()

End Sub
```

Disposing of a Dialog Box

Since dialog boxes aren't actually closed, but rather hidden when they return, it's up to your application to clean up the resources after you're done with the dialog box. You use the **Dispose** method of the dialog box form for this. There's an example of disposing of a dialog box near the bottom of Listing 3-16.

There you have it, the complete process of creating and using a custom dialog box. It's pretty straightforward once you work through one. If you still have any questions, I'd recommend that you work through the following tutorial.

Step-by-Step Tutorial: Building a Custom Dialog Box

In this step-by-step exercise, you'll create an application that demonstrates incorporating a custom dialog box into a Pocket PC application. As part of this exercise, you'll

- Construct the interface for a custom dialog box.

- Add code to expose the values gathered by the dialog box.

- Display the dialog box.

- Retrieve values from the dialog box.

 NOTE *A completed version of this application is provided under the **Chapter 3** folder of the **Samples** folder for this book. It's titled DialogDemo. See Appendix D for more information on accessing and loading the sample applications.*

Step 1: Creating the Project

Begin this tutorial exercise by creating a new project using the following steps:

1. Start Visual Studio .NET if necessary.

2. From the Start Page, select **New Project**.

3. From the New Project dialog box, select **Smart Device Application**.

4. Specify a project name of **DialogDemo**.

5. Select a location to create the project and click the **OK** button.

Step 2: Configuring the Project

To configure the target output folder for this project, perform the following steps:

1. Under the Project menu, select **DialogDemo Properties**.

2. Under the Device page of the Text File Property Pages dialog box, set the output file folder to **\Windows\Start Menu\Programs\Apress**.

Step 3: Configuring the Main Form

Figure 3-24 shows the interface to the main form of this sample application. Perform the following steps to construct this interface:

1. Add a button to the lower-right corner of the form.

2. Set the **Name** property of the button to **btnShowDialog**.

3. Set the **Text** property of the button to **Show Dialog**.

4. Set the **Text** property of the form to **DialogDemo**.

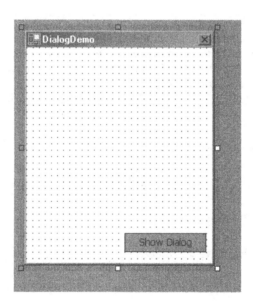

Figure 3-24. The interface to the main form

Step 4: Adding the Dialog Box Form

Perform the following steps to add the form for your custom dialog box:

1. Under the Project menu, select **Add Windows Form**.

2. The Add New Item dialog box will be displayed. Enter **frmDialog.vb** in the Name field of this dialog box.

3. Click the **Open** button to add the form.

Step 5: Configuring the Dialog Box Form

Figure 3-25 shows the interface to the dialog box form. Perform the following steps to construct this interface:

1. Add a button to the lower-right corner of the dialog box form.

2. Set the **Name** property of the button to **btnCancel**.

3. Set the **Text** property of the button to **Cancel**.

4. Add the first TextBox (upper) to the form.

5. Set the **Name** property of the TextBox to **txtName**.

6. Set the **Text** property of the TextBox to **[name]**.

7. Add the second TextBox (lower) to the form.

8. Set the **Name** property of the TextBox to **txtPhone**.

9. Set the **Text** property of the TextBox to **[phone]**.

10. Set the **FormBorderStyle** of the form to **FixedDialog**.

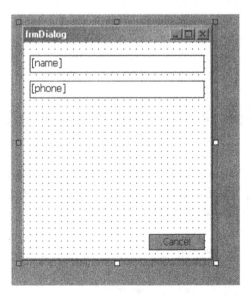

Figure 3-25. The interface to the dialog box form

Step 6: Configuring the Cancel Button at Runtime

With the interface complete, you're ready to turn your attention to the code. First, you'll configure the dialog box form's **Cancel** button so that it acts as a **Cancel** button for the dialog box. Add the code from Listing 3-17 to the **Load** event procedure of the dialog box form.

Listing 3-17. Configuring the Cancel Button

```
Private Sub frmDialog_Load(ByVal sender As System.Object, _
  ByVal e As System.EventArgs) Handles MyBase.Load

' Link the Cancel button to the cancel result.
  btnCancel.DialogResult = DialogResult.Cancel

End Sub
```

Step 7: Defining the CustomerInfo Class

Next, you'll define the structure that will be used to return the values from the dialog box. Add the code shown here directly below the End Class statement for the dialog box form:

```
Public Class CustomerInfo
   Public Name As String
   Public Phone As String
End Class
```

Step 8: Adding a Property Procedure to the Dialog Box Form

With the structure in place, you're ready to add the **Property** procedure that will expose the values of the dialog box's two TextBox controls. Add the code shown in Listing 3-18 to the dialog box form's class.

Listing 3-18. Defining the Property Procedure

```
Public ReadOnly Property CustomersInfo() As CustomerInfo
' Create an instance of the CustomerInfo object to use to pass values.
```

```
Get
    Dim ci As New CustomerInfo
    ci.Name = Me.txtName.Text
    ci.Phone = Me.txtPhone.Text
    Return ci
End Get
End Property
```

That completes the code behind the dialog box. Next, you'll turn your attention to coding the parent form.

Step 9: Showing the Dialog Box and Displaying the Response

The final bit of coding happens in the **Click** event of the button **btnShowDialog** on the parent form. Add the code shown in Listing 3-19 to the **Click** event procedure of this button.

Listing 3-19. Displaying the Dialog Box and Its Response

```
Private Sub btnShowDialog_Click(ByVal sender As System.Object, _
    ByVal e As System.EventArgs) Handles btnShowDialog.Click
    Dim ci As CustomerInfo
    Dim dlg As New frmDialog

' Display the dialog.
    dlg.ShowDialog()

' Check the state returned by the dialog. Did the user tap OK?
    If dlg.DialogResult = DialogResult.OK Then

' They tapped OK, so retrieve the values they entered.
        ci = dlg.CustomersInfo
        MessageBox.Show(ci.Name.ToString())
        MessageBox.Show(ci.Phone.ToString())
    End If

' Get rid of the dialog.
    dlg.Dispose()

End Sub
```

The three parts that make up this event procedure merit mentioning. The first is near the top of the procedure where an instance of the dialog box form is created and then displayed. The second is in the middle of the procedure where the dialog box's response is processed. The third is at the bottom of the procedure where the instance of the dialog box in disposed.

Step 10: Testing Your Application

To test your application, perform the following steps:

1. Select either **Pocket PC Device** or **Pocket PC Emulator** from the Deployment Device combo box.

2. Select **Release** from the Solution Configurations combo box.

3. Click the **Start** button. Your application copies to the target device and runs.

4. Tap the **Show Dialog** button. Your custom dialog box will displayed.

5. Enter a name and phone number.

6. Tap the **OK** button. The dialog box will close. The main form will reappear. Two message box dialog boxes will display. The first shows the name you entered. The second shows the phone number you entered.

 HOMEWORK   Add a third field to the dialog box for entering the customer's zip code. Display the zip code returned from the dialog box along with the customer name and phone number.

Summary

Interface design is the key behind every successful Pocket PC application. Building a successful interface isn't always a simple process, especially if you've spent all of your development years working on desktop applications.

Building applications for Pocket PCs requires you to understand how to use Pocket PCs. The limitations imposed by the device and the environment where your application is used require you to develop new skills, new ways of constructing interfaces.

Two good places to start are the "Pocket PC Design Standards" and "Larry Roof's Design Rules" sections. The Pocket PC design standards presented in this chapter are helpful because they will aid you in creating interfaces that look and act like other Pocket PC applications. This will allow your user to leverage existing experiences and knowledge with your application. I feel that making it easier for the user is always a good thing.

Referencing my design rules will help you get up and running quickly in creating highly effective Pocket PC applications. After all, you probably have better things to do with your time than bumping about trying to figure out what works well on a device.

NETCF Controls

HAVING WORKED WITH the Windows CE development tools since the beginning, I've got to tell you that I'm *really* excited about the control offerings provided by the .NET Compact Framework. NETCF includes nearly thirty controls offering developers a wide variety of options when it comes to designing user interfaces.

Think of this chapter as a "sampler" of those controls. It presents each of them, highlighting the key properties, methods, and events, and demonstrating commonly performed programming techniques that relate to specific controls. I recommend that you work through this chapter from start to finish, trying out the numerous sample programs and enhancing your understanding of what controls are available and just what they can do.

I like to think of controls as tools in a developer's toolbox. Having a toolbox full of tools does you little good if all you use is the hammer, which in this case would probably be the TextBox. Developing an effective interface for a mobile application is hard enough as it is, let alone if your knowledge level limits your design to a subset of the possibilities.

If you haven't already done so, I'd urge you to take a look at Chapter 3. (I know it's the kind of chapter programmers are apt to skip—but in it I've tried to encapsulate some hard-earned lessons, so I hope you'll read it.) Without a solid understanding of the requirements and limitations imposed by the Pocket PC environment, you're going to have a hard time selecting the appropriate controls from which to build your interface.

Finally, remember this *isn't* .NET, it's NETCF. Almost all of the controls provided with NETCF are—let's be honest—watered-down versions of those found in .NET. They have fewer properties, methods, and events. While most of the key features will be there, many less-used features and functionalities aren't included. You'll need to adjust accordingly, unless you like banging your head against your monitor. Without further adieu, let's begin our journey through the controls of NETCF.

The Button Control

The NETCF implementation of the Button control provides a simple command button as shown in Figure 4-1. This control is a mainstay of mobile applications.

Figure 4-1. The Button control

Table 4-1 lists Button control properties frequently leveraged in NETCF applications.

Table 4-1. Key Button Properties

PROPERTY	DESCRIPTION
Enabled	Specifies whether the control responds to the user's taps. Set this property to False when you want to temporarily disable the button.
Font	Defines the font used with the Text property. See Chapter 3 for more on the importance of font size in mobile applications.
Text	Text that appears on the face of the button.

The Button control has a single event that's of any importance to mobile developers—the **Click** event. This event fires when the user taps a button.

Coding the Button Control's Click Event

As pointed out in the preceding section, the Button control has a single event that is frequently used. That event is the **Click** event. The **Click** event fires when the user taps a button. Listing 4-1 demonstrates coding a simple procedure for this event.

Listing 4-1. Coding a Button Control Click Event

```
Private Sub Button1_Click(ByVal sender As System.Object, _
  ByVal e As System.EventArgs) Handles Button1.Click
  Dim mb As MessageBox
  mb.Show("button clicked...")
End Sub
```

NOTE *The ButtonDemo application included under **Chapter 4** of the **Samples** folder demonstrates working with the Button control. See Appendix D for information on obtaining and working with the sample applications.*

CAUTION *If you are a VB or eVB developer switching over to programming with NETCF, you should note a subtle difference in the format of event procedures. Under .NET (and NETCF) the definition of an event procedure includes the keyword **Handles**. It's in fact the **Handles** portion of the statement that causes the event to be captured.*

The CheckBox Control

The NETCF CheckBox control provides a Windows check box. As shown in Figure 4-2, the CheckBox control is comprised of two elements: the check box itself and a text string that appears next to the check box.

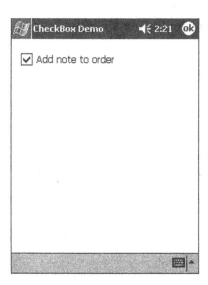

Figure 4-2. The CheckBox control

Table 4-2 lists commonly used CheckBox properties. There are rare instances where you won't use the **Text** property, as it defines the text that appears next to the check box. From code, you can query the **Checked** property to determine the status of the CheckBox, that's to say whether it's checked or not.

Table 4-2. Key CheckBox Properties

PROPERTY	DESCRIPTION
AutoCheck	Defines whether a CheckBox automatically toggles on and off when tapped by the user. Set this property to false if you want control over how the CheckBox is toggled.
Checked	Indicates whether a CheckBox is checked or unchecked.
CheckState	Indicates the state of a CheckBox—checked, unchecked, or indeterminate.
Enabled	Specifies whether the control responds to the user's taps.
Font	Defines the font used with the Text property.
Locked	Prohibits the user from altering the value displayed by the control.
Text	Indicates the text that is displayed with the CheckBox.
ThreeState	Specifies whether the indeterminate state is available.

The NETCF implementation of the CheckBox supports three states: checked, unchecked, and indeterminate. Use a CheckBox in this configuration when you want to provide a setting that has three states: The user has selected it, the user doesn't want it, and the user has yet to specify a preference.

Table 4-3 lists the two CheckBox events that are commonly leveraged within mobile applications.

Table 4-3. Key CheckBox Events

EVENT	DESCRIPTION
CheckStateChanged	Fires when the state of the control changes, commonly when the user taps the control
Click	Fires when the user taps the control

Coding the CheckBox Control's CheckStateChanged Event

The CheckBox control has a single event that is frequently used: **CheckStateChanged**. This event fires in two situations: when the user taps the control (with the **AutoCheck** property enabled) and if you set the value of the control from code. Listing 4-2 demonstrates coding a simple event procedure for this event.

Listing 4-2. Coding a CheckBox Control CheckStateChanged Event

```
Private Sub CheckBox1_CheckStateChanged(ByVal sender As System.Object, _
  ByVal e As System.EventArgs) Handles CheckBox1.CheckStateChanged
  Dim mb As MessageBox
  mb.Show("checkbox state changed...")
End Sub
```

> **NOTE** *The CheckBoxDemo application included under* **Chapter 4** *of the* **Samples** *folder demonstrates working with the CheckBox control. See Appendix D for information on obtaining and working with the sample applications.*

The ComboBox Control

The NETCF ComboBox control provides a Windows combo box. As shown in Figure 4-3, the NETCF ComboBox provides a drop-down list from which users can select a value. This is an incredibly useful component in mobile applications as it 1) makes very good use of screen real estate, and 2) provides an easy way for users to specify input values.

Figure 4-3. The ComboBox control

Table 4-4 lists commonly used ComboBox properties. If you're an experienced Visual Basic or .NET programmer, the most noTable absence from this list
is the **Style** (for VB) or **DropDownStyle** (for .NET) property. The NETCF implementation of the ComboBox limits you to a single style, a drop-down list.

Table 4-4. Key ComboBox Properties

PROPERTY	DESCRIPTION
DataBindings	Used to bind data to the control.
Enabled	Specifies whether the control responds to the user's taps.
Font	Defines the font used with the Text property.
Items	Specifies the collection of items contained within this control.
SelectedIndex	Indicates the index number of the item presently selected. You can set this property to select an item from code.
Text	Specifies the text that is displayed with the ComboBox.

The Items collection contains the items displayed by the control. Listing 4-3,
4-4, and 4-5, shown later in this chapter, demonstrate working with this collection.

Use the **SelectedIndex** property to determine which item the user has
selected from a ComboBox.

The single commonly used ComboBox event, **SelectedIndexChanged**, fires
when the **SelectedIndex** property changes, and that occurs in two situations: when
the user taps the control, and when you select an item from code.

The following section demonstrates several commonly performed operations involving a ComboBox.

Loading a ComboBox from Code

Listing 4-3 demonstrates loading a ComboBox with four items. Use the Items collection **Add** method for this purpose. Unlike the .NET version of the ComboBox, the .NET CF incarnation of this control does not support the **AddRange** method for loading an array of items. The **Clear** method of the Items collection removes any existing items.

Listing 4-3. Loading a ComboBox

```
Private Sub btnLoad_Click(ByVal sender As System.Object, _
  ByVal e As System.EventArgs) Handles btnLoad.Click
  ComboBox1.Items.Clear()
  ComboBox1.Items.Add("Senior")
  ComboBox1.Items.Add("Junior")
  ComboBox1.Items.Add("Sophomore")
  ComboBox1.Items.Add("Freshman")
End Sub
```

NOTE *You can also define the ComboBox items at design time through the Properties window.*

Deleting an Item from a ComboBox

Use the Items collection **Remove** method to delete an item from a ComboBox. Listing 4-4 demonstrates removing the presently selected item.

Listing 4-4. Deleting an Item from a ComboBox

```
Private Sub btnDelete_Click(ByVal sender As System.Object, _
  ByVal e As System.EventArgs) Handles btnDelete.Click
  ComboBox1.Items.Remove(ComboBox1.Items.Item(ComboBox1.SelectedIndex))
End Sub
```

Accessing the Selected Item in a ComboBox

A commonly performed programming task employed with ComboBox controls involves determining the item presently selected within the control. As shown in Listing 4-5, the **SelectedIndex** property provides this information.

Listing 4-5. Accessing the Selected Item in a ComboBox

```
Private Sub btnDisplay_Click(ByVal sender As System.Object, _
  ByVal e As System.EventArgs) Handles btnDisplay.Click
  Dim mb As MessageBox
  mb.Show("The selected item is " & _
    ComboBox1.SelectedIndex.ToString & _
    " with the value of " & _
    ComboBox1.SelectedItem)
End Sub
```

 NOTE *The ComboBoxDemo application included under **Chapter 4** of the **Samples** folder demonstrates working with the ComboBox control. See Appendix D for information on obtaining and working with the sample applications.*

The ContextMenu Control

If you're not already familiar with them, context-sensitive menus are the pop-up menus displayed when you hold your stylus on an object or item within a Pocket PC. Figure 4-4 shows an example of such a menu. These menus provide easy access to tasks commonly performed with an object. The menu in Figure 4-4 provides appointment-related items.

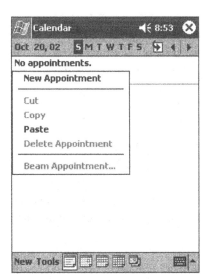

Figure 4-4. A context-sensitive menu

You build context menus just as you would regular menus. First, you add the ContextMenu control to a form. Then, you define the menu items with the Form Designer. Figure 4-5 demonstrates a simple use of the ContextMenu control.

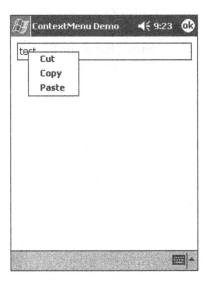

Figure 4-5. A ContextMenu as it's displayed to the user

NOTE *The ContextMenuDemo application included under **Chapter 4** of the **Samples** folder demonstrates working with the ComboBox control. See Appendix D for information on obtaining and working with the sample applications.*

The most commonly used ContextMenu property is **MenuItems**, which represents a collection of the items that comprise a context-sensitive menu. These items can be defined at design time or runtime.

Popup is a commonly used ContextMenu event that fires just before displaying the context menu. You can use this event procedure to customize the menu at runtime.

 NOTE *For a detailed example of working with the ContextMenu control, refer to Chapter 6.*

The DataGrid Control

The NETCF DataGrid control provides an easy way to display data taken from an ADO.NET source in a grid. The DataGrid control displays data from a DataSet, DataTable , or DataView. Figure 4-6 shows a DataGrid control displaying the Customers Table of a SQL Server CE version of the Northwind database.

Figure 4-6. The DataGrid control

Table 4-5 lists commonly used DataGrid properties.

Table 4-5. Key DataGrid Properties

PROPERTY	DESCRIPTION
BackColor	Defines the cell color for even-numbered rows in the grid.
ColumnHeadersVisible	Specifies whether to show column headers.
ContextMenu	Defines a context menu for the grid. Useful in adding editing functionality to the grid.
CurrentCell	Indicates the active cell, the cell that has focus. Useful when adding editing functionality.
CurrentRowIndex	Specifies the selected row.
DataSource	Specifies the ADO.NET source for the grid.
Font	Defines the font used with the data displayed.
ForeColor	Specifies the color of the text within the grid.
GridLineColor	Specifies the color of the grid lines.
HeaderBackColor	Specifies the background color of the header cells.
RowHeadersVisible	Indicates whether row headers are visible.
SelectionBackColor	Defines the background color of selected rows.
SelectionForeColor	Defines the foreground color of selected rows.
Text	Specifies the value contained within the cell having focus.
VisibleColumnCount	Indicates the number of visible columns; useful in controlling paging between columns from code.
VisibleRowCount	Specifies the number of visible rows. Useful in controlling paging between rows from code.

GetCurrentCellBounds is a commonly used method of the DataGrid control that returns four points identifying the four corners of a specified cell. This proves useful in implementing editing functionality for a DataGrid, as these points allow you to place an edit control directly over a cell.

In addition, there is a commonly used event of the DataGrid control, called **Click**, that fires when the user taps the grid.

Displaying a Table in a DataGrid

Listing 4-6 demonstrates displaying a Table in a DataGrid. This example uses data from the SQL Server CE version of the Northwind database. The Customers Table of the Northwind database is first loaded into a DataTable, then added to a DataSet, and finally displayed in the DataGrid.

Listing 4-6. Displaying a Table in a DataGrid

```
Private Sub btnLoad_Click(ByVal sender As System.Object, _
  ByVal e As System.EventArgs) Handles btnLoad.Click
  Dim cmd As System.Data.SqlServerCE.SqlCeCommand
  Dim cn As System.Data.SqlServerCe.SqlCeConnection
  Dim da As System.Data.SqlServerCe.SqlCeDataAdapter
  Dim ds As New System.Data.DataSet

' Establish a connection to the SQL Server CE database.
  cn = New System.Data.SqlServerce.SqlCeConnection("Data Source= " & _
    ApplicationLocation() & "\NorthwindDemo.sdf")
  cmd = New System.Data.SqlServerCE.SqlCeCommand("SELECT * FROM Customers", cn)
  da = New System.Data.SqlServerCE.SqlCeDataAdapter(cmd)

' Add the new Table to the DataSet.
  Dim dt As System.Data.DataTable = New System.Data.DataTable ("Customers")
  da.Fill(dt)
  ds.Table s.Add(dt)

' Display the Table .
  DataGrid1.DataSource = ds.Table s("Customers")
End Sub

Private Function ApplicationLocation() As String
' Fetch and return the location where the application was launched.
  ApplicationLocation = _
    System.IO.Path.GetDirectoryName(Reflection.Assembly. _
    GetExecutingAssembly().GetName().CodeBase.ToString())
End Function
```

 NOTE *For more information on working with DataAdapters, DataSets, and DataTables, see Chapter 9.*

NOTE *The DataGridDemo application included under* **Chapter 4** *of the* **Samples** *folder demonstrates working with the DataGrid control. See Appendix D for information on obtaining and working with the sample applications.*

The DomainUpDown Control

For developers new to the .NET world, the DomainUpDown control is a cross between a combo or list box and a vertical scroll bar. It stores a series of strings that the user can select from using the up and down buttons. Figure 4-7 shows an example of the DomainUpDown control with a selected item.

Figure 4-7. A DomainUpDown control

Table 4-6 lists commonly used DomainUpDown properties.

Table 4-6. Key DomainUpDown Properties

PROPERTY	DESCRIPTION
ContextMenu	Defines a context menu for the control.
DataBindings	Used to bind data to the control.
Enabled	Indicates whether the control can be manipulated by the user.
Items	Specifies the collection of text strings contained within the control. This collection can be built at design time or runtime.
ReadOnly	Defines whether the user can enter values into the control or only select items using the up and down arrows.
Text	Specifies the value of the control.

Loading the DomainUpDown Control

The most commonly performed task for the DomainUpDown control is defining the list of items that the control displays. There are two ways to load the control, at design time and at runtime.

At design time, use the following steps to define the contents of a DomainUpDown control:

1. Select the DomainUpDown control on your form.

2. In the Properties window, select the **Items** property.

3. Click the ellipse button (...) at the right end of the **Items** property line to access the String Collection Editor dialog box; Figure 4-8 shows an example of this dialog box.

4. Define the strings for your application.

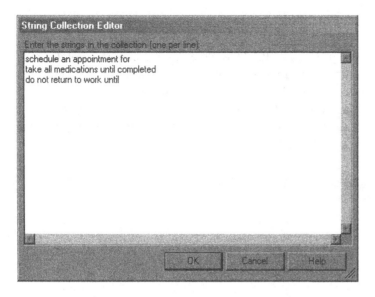

Figure 4-8. The String Collection Editor dialog box

Listing 4-7 demonstrates how to define the DomainUpDown control's Items collection at runtime.

Listing 4-7. Defining the DomainUpDown Items from Code

```
Private Sub Form1_Load(ByVal sender As System.Object, _
  ByVal e As System.EventArgs) Handles MyBase.Load

  Define the items for the DomainUpDown control.
  domComments.Items.Add("schedule an appointment for")
  domComments.Items.Add("take all medications until complete")
  domComments.Items.Add("do not return to work until")
End Sub
```

NOTE *The DomainUpDownDemo application included under **Chapter 4** of the **Samples** folder demonstrates working with the DomainUpDown control. See Appendix D for information on obtaining and working with the sample applications.*

The HScrollBar Control

The HScrollBar control provides a simple implementation of a horizontal scroll bar. I think of this control as a supporting control. That's to say, it's generally used to augment another control. In the example shown in Figure 4-9, the HScrollBar control is an alternate form of input. Rather than use the Soft Input Panel (SIP) to enter a value, the user can simply tap the left or right arrows of the HScrollBar control to specify a value.

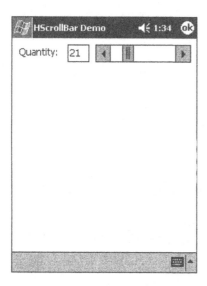

Figure 4-9. A HScrollBar control

 NOTE *The HScrollBar control is frequently used to implement scrollable forms. Unlike under .NET, forms don't support scrolling under NETCF. The workaround for this shortcoming is to implement your own scrolling using a Panel and a HScrollBar. For more information on this topic, see the "Scrolling Forms" section in Chapter 3.*

Table 4-7 shows commonly used properties of this control. Two properties that you'll always want to set are **Maximum** and **Minimum**. These properties specify the numeric range for the control.

Table 4-7. Key HScrollBar Properties

PROPERTY	DESCRIPTION
Enabled	Specifies whether the control can be manipulated by the user
LargeChange	Indicates the amount to add or subtract from the scroll bar's Value property when the scroll box is moved in large increments
Maximum	Sets the upper limit for the Value property
Minimum	Specifies the lower value the control can be set
SmallChange	Indicates the amount to add or subtract from the scroll bar's Value when the scroll box is moved in small increments
Value	Defines the numeric value of the control

The single commonly used HScrollBar event, **ValueChanged**, fires anytime the **Value** property changes, whether that is by the user or from your code.

Linking a HScrollBar Control to Another Control

Listing 4-8 demonstrates how simple it is to link a HScrollBar control to another control. In this example, the scroll bar is tied to a TextBox control. As the user taps on the left and right arrows of the scroll bar, the value displayed by the TextBox changes.

Listing 4-8. Linking a HScrollBar to a TextBox

```
Private Sub HScrollBar1_ValueChanged(ByVal sender As System.Object, _
  ByVal e As System.EventArgs) Handles HScrollBar1.ValueChanged
  txtQuantity.Text = HScrollBar1.Value.ToString
End Sub
```

NOTE *The HScrollBarDemo application included under* **Chapter 4** *of the* **Samples** *folder demonstrates working with the HScrollBar control. See Appendix D for information on obtaining and working with the sample applications.*

The ImageList Control

The ImageList control is a supporting control. It holds and provides images to the ListView, TreeView, and ToolBar controls. By itself, the ImageList control has little purpose. It does not have a runtime interface, which means that users never see the actual control. They only see the images that the control contains and provides to other controls. This control is all about performance. Instead of loading the images in memory on the device for various display places, you load them all once and reference them.

Table 4-8 lists commonly used properties of the ImageList control.

Table 4-8. Key ImageList Properties

PROPERTY	DESCRIPTION
Images	Collection of images contained within a control
ImageSize	Size of the images within a control

You can define the Images collection at either design time or runtime, although you'll usually do so at design time. Use the following steps to define the collection at design time:

1. Select the ImageList control on the panel below your form.

2. In the Properties window, select the **Images** property.

3. Click the ellipse button (...) at the right end of the **Images** property line to access the Image Collection Editor dialog box; Figure 4-10 shows an example of this dialog box.

4. Use the **Add**, **Remove**, **Promote**, and **Demote** buttons to configure the collection of images.

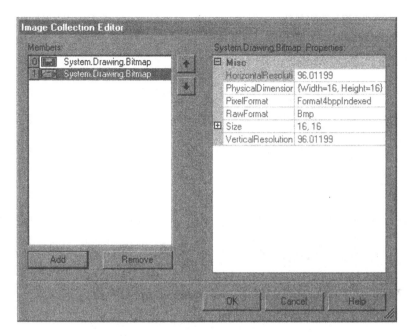

Figure 4-10. Configuring the images used with an ImageList control

 NOTE *For examples of working with the ImageList control, see the sections "The ListView Control," "The ToolBar Control," and "The TreeView Control" in this chapter.*

The InputPanel Control

The InputPanel control controls the Soft Input Panel on the Pocket PC. Through this control, you can display and hide the SIP automatically as required for your application. The InputPanel control does not have a runtime interface.

Figure 4-11 shows an example of this in use. In this demonstration application, there are two TextBox controls. The upper TextBox does not use the SIP for input. It's tied to the HScrollBar control at its left. The lower TextBox is a general-purpose text field that does make use of the SIP. Code added to this application displays and hides the SIP as the user enters and leaves this field.

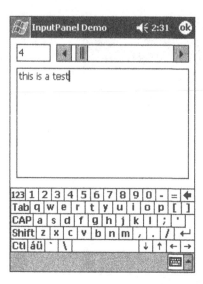

Figure 4-11. The InputPanel control being used to display the SIP

Table 4-9 lists commonly used properties of the InputPanel control.

Table 4-9. Key InputPanel Properties

PROPERTY	DESCRIPTION
Enabled	Shows and hides the SIP.
VisibleDesktop	Specifies the area not obscured by the SIP. You can use this value to resize or reposition your input fields so that they aren't located beneath the SIP.

Displaying the SIP

Listing 4-9 demonstrates how to show the SIP. In this example, the **GotFocus** event of a TextBox control triggers displaying the input panel.

Listing 4-9. Displaying the SIP

```
Private Sub TextBox2_GotFocus(ByVal sender As Object, _
  ByVal e As System.EventArgs) Handles TextBox2.GotFocus
  InputPanel1.Enabled = True
End Sub
```

Hiding the SIP

Listing 4-10 demonstrates how to hide the SIP. In this example, the **LostFocus** event of a TextBox control triggers hiding the input panel.

Listing 4-10. Hiding the SIP

```
Private Sub TextBox2_LostFocus(ByVal sender As Object, _
  ByVal e As System.EventArgs) Handles TextBox2.LostFocus
  InputPanel1.Enabled = False
End Sub
```

 NOTE *The InputPanelDemo application included under **Chapter 4** of the **Samples** folder demonstrates working with the InputPanel control. See Appendix D for information on obtaining and working with the sample applications.*

The Label Control

The Label control is a general-purpose control whose whole existence is to display text. I like to refer to labels as the "Vanna White control." I gave them that name because for the most part they just sit on a form and point to the control next to them, which usually is a TextBox. Labels are well suited for situations where you need to display text that you don't want the user to modify. Figure 4-12 demonstrates these two uses for the Label control.

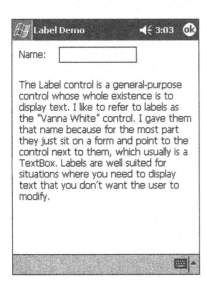

Figure 4-12. The Label control

Table 4-10 lists commonly used properties of the Label control.

Table 4-10. Key Label Control Properties

PROPERTY	DESCRIPTION
DataBindings	Used to bind data to the control
Font	Defines the font used to display text
ForeColor	Specifies the color of the text
Text	Specifies the text displayed within the control
TextAlign	Dictates how the text is aligned within the control

 NOTE *The LabelDemo application included under **Chapter 4** of the **Samples** folder demonstrates working with the Label control. See Appendix D for information on obtaining and working with the sample applications.*

The ListBox Control

The NETCF ListBox control includes a Windows list box. As shown in Figure 4-13, the ListBox provides a list of items from which users can select a value. The ListBox control serves the same general purpose as the ComboBox control; it provides a list of items from which the user can pick. Which one you use depends upon the availability of screen real estate.

Figure 4-13. The ListBox control

Table 4-11 lists commonly used ListBox properties. The Items collection contains the items displayed by the control. Listings 4-11, 4-12 and 4-13, shown later in this chapter, demonstrate working with this collection.

Table 4-11. Key ListBox Properties

PROPERTY	DESCRIPTION
ContextMenu	Defines a context menu for the ListBox.
DataBindings	Used to bind data to the control.
DataSource	Specifies the ADO.NET source for the control.
DisplayMember	Specifies the property of the data source to display.
Enabled	Specifies whether the control responds to the user's taps.
Font	Defines the font used with the control.
Items	Specifies the collection of items contained within this control.
SelectedIndex	Indicates the index number of the item that is presently selected. You can set this property to select an item from code.
Text	Specifies the text of the selected item.

Use the **SelectedIndex** property to determine which item the user has selected from a ListBox.

The single commonly used ListBox event, **SelectedIndexChanged**, fires when the SelectedIndex property changes, which occurs in two situations: when the user taps the control, and when you select an item from code.

The following section demonstrates several commonly performed operations involving a ListBox.

Loading a ListBox from Code

Listing 4-11 demonstrates loading a ListBox with four items. Use the Items collection **Add** method for this purpose. The **Clear** method of the Items collection removes any existing items.

Listing 4-11. Loading a ListBox

```
Private Sub btnLoad_Click(ByVal sender As System.Object, _
  ByVal e As System.EventArgs) Handles btnLoad.Click
  ListBox1.Items.Add("Senior")
```

```
ListBox1.Items.Add("Junior")
ListBox1.Items.Add("Sophomore")
ListBox1.Items.Add("Freshman")
End Sub
```

 NOTE *You can also define the ListBox items at design time through the Properties window.*

Deleting an Item from a ListBox

Use the Items collection **Remove** method to delete an item from a ListBox. Listing 4-12 demonstrates removing the presently selected item.

Listing 4-12. Deleting an Item from a ListBox

```
Private Sub btnDelete_Click(ByVal sender As System.Object, _
  ByVal e As System.EventArgs) Handles btnDelete.Click
  ListBox1.Items.Remove(ListBox1.Items.Item(ListBox1.SelectedIndex))
End Sub
```

Accessing the Selected Item in a ListBox

Frequently you'll want to access the selected item within a ListBox. Listing 4-13 demonstrates how to accomplish this.

Listing 4-13. Accessing the Selected Item in a ListBox

```
Private Sub btnDisplay_Click(ByVal sender As System.Object, _
  ByVal e As System.EventArgs) Handles btnDisplay.Click
  Dim mb As MessageBox
  mb.Show("The selected item is " & _
    ListBox1.SelectedIndex.ToString & _
    " with the value of " & _
    ListBox1.SelectedItem)
End Sub
```

 NOTE *The ListBoxDemo application included under **Chapter 4** of the **Samples** folder demonstrates working with the ListBox control. See Appendix D for information on obtaining and working with the sample applications.*

The ListView Control

The ListView control is a mainstay of mobile developers. With its four views (large icon, small icon, list, and details), this control packs a powerful interface punch. If you've not had any previous experience with a ListView control, think of the right panel of a Windows Explorer window. That's a ListView.

In the mobile arena, most of the use for this control comes down to the fourth view, details, because in that configuration the ListView acts and appears much like a grid.

The major drawback of this control is that, compared to other controls, it's fairly complicated to program. While we're not talking space shuttle navigation type of complexity here, it still can be a daunting task for a novice developer. I'll show you some of the commonly performed ListView-related programming techniques later in this section.

Figure 4-14 shows an example of the ListView control. This example demonstrates the details view of the control.

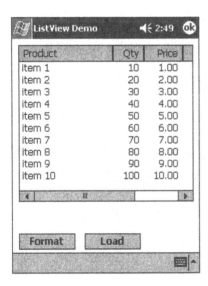

Figure 4-14. A ListView control

Table 4-12 lists commonly used ListView properties. Some of these properties are view specific, such as **LargeImageList** and **SmallImageList**, which pertain to the LargeIcon and SmallIcon views, respectively. Some are used in combination, such as the **CheckBoxes** and **SelectedIndicies** properties.

Table 4-12. Key ListView Properties

PROPERTY	DESCRIPTION
CheckBoxes	Indicates whether a check box appears next to each item displayed in a ListBox
Columns	Specifies the collection of column headers
ContextMenu	Defines a context menu for the control
Enabled	Specifies whether the control can be manipulated by the user
FullRowSelect	Specifies whether tapping an item selects the whole row or just a cell
HeaderStyle	Defines the style to apply to the header row
Items	Specifies the collection of items within the control
LargeImageList	Indicates the ImageList control that contains the large icons to use with the control
SelectedIndicies	Specifies the list of items selected within the control
SmallImageList	Indicates the ImageList control that contains the small icons to use with the control
View	Specifies the view to use with the control

You propagate the ListView control through its Items collection, much like the ComboBox and ListBox controls, only in this case the process is slightly more complicated.

Table 4-13 lists commonly used ListView events.

Table 4-13. Key ListView Events

EVENT	DESCRIPTION
ColumnClick	Occurs when the user taps a column header
ItemCheck	Triggered when the check state for an item changes
SelectIndexChanged	Fires when the index of the control changes

The following section demonstrates several commonly performed operations involving a ListView.

Configuring a ListView in Details View

Listing 4-14 shows how to configure a ListView control for the details view. The procedure starts by setting the View to details. Next, five columns are added, specifying the header, the column width, and alignment.

Listing 4-14. Configuring a Details View

```
Private Sub btnFormat_Click(ByVal sender As System.Object, _
  ByVal e As System.EventArgs) Handles btnFormat.Click

' Define the view.
  ListView1.View = View.Details

' Configure the columns.
  ListView1.Columns.Add("Product", 120, HorizontalAlignment.Left)
  ListView1.Columns.Add("Qty", 40, HorizontalAlignment.Right)
  ListView1.Columns.Add("Price", 50, HorizontalAlignment.Right)
  ListView1.Columns.Add("Disc", 50, HorizontalAlignment.Right)
  ListView1.Columns.Add("Total", 60, HorizontalAlignment.Right)

End Sub
```

TIP *To hide a value within a ListView, simply set its column width to 0. You'll still be able to reference the value from your code, but the user won't know it is there.*

Loading Data into a ListView

The process of loading data into a ListView isn't too bad once you understand the basic procedure. Listing 4-15 shows how to load a ListView.

Listing 4-15. Loading a ListView Control

```
Private Sub btnLoad_Click(ByVal sender As System.Object, _
  ByVal e As System.EventArgs) Handles btnLoad.Click
  Dim Discount As Single
  Dim intCounter As Integer
  Dim ItemTotal As Single
  Dim Quantity As Integer
  Dim UnitPrice As Integer
  Dim LVItem As ListViewItem
```

```
' Load the order details into the ListView control.
  ListView1.Items.Clear()

  For intCounter = 1 To 10

' Build the contents.
    LVItem = New ListViewItem
    LVItem.Text = "item " & intCounter.ToString
    Quantity = intCounter * 10
    LVItem.SubItems.Add(Quantity.ToString)
    UnitPrice = intCounter
    LVItem.SubItems.Add(UnitPrice.ToString("N2"))
    Discount = intCounter * 0.01
    LVItem.SubItems.Add(Discount.ToString("N2"))

    ItemTotal = Quantity * (UnitPrice * (1 - Discount))
    LVItem.SubItems.Add(ItemTotal.ToString("N2"))

' Add the new row to the ListView.
    ListView1.Items.Add(LVItem)
  Next intCounter
End Sub
```

The load process begins by first emptying the control using the **Clear** method of the Items collection. Next, I add a series of items. The process for adding a new item is as follows:

1. Create a new instance of a ListViewItem.

2. Define the **Text** property of the new item; this is the first column within the control.

3. Use the **SubItems** collection of the ListViewItem to add each additional column value.

4. Finally, add the ListViewItem to the Items collection of the ListView control.

NOTE *The two examples shown in Listings 4-14 and 4-15 were taken from the ListViewDemo application. This application is included under **Chapter 4** of the **Samples** folder. See Appendix D for information on obtaining and working with the sample applications.*

Using Images with a ListView Control

One of the cool features about the ListView control is its support of images. All four of the views—large icon, small icon, list, and details—will display images if provided. You provide images to the ListView through two ImageList controls, one for the larger images and the other for the smaller images.

Listing 4-16 demonstrates defining an associated image as you add an item to a ListView control. The **ImageIndex** property is set to the index value corresponding to the image location within an ImageList control.

Listing 4-16. Defining Images for ListView Items

```
Private Sub btnLoad_Click(ByVal sender As System.Object, _
  ByVal e As System.EventArgs) Handles btnLoad.Click
  Dim intCounter As Integer
  Dim LVItem As ListViewItem

' Load the file info into the ListView.
  ListView1.Items.Clear()

' Define the first item.
  LVItem = New ListViewItem
  LVItem.Text = "Expenses.pxl"
  LVItem.SubItems.Add("3.11KB")
  LVItem.SubItems.Add("Pocket Excel Workbook")
  LVItem.SubItems.Add("9/18/2002 10:10:10 AM")
  LVItem.ImageIndex = 0
  ListView1.Items.Add(LVItem)

' Define the second item.
  LVItem = New ListViewItem
  LVItem.Text = "My Lists.clf"
  LVItem.SubItems.Add("9.50KB")
  LVItem.SubItems.Add("ListPro Document")
  LVItem.SubItems.Add("10/19/2002 11:11:11 AM")
  LVItem.ImageIndex = 1
  ListView1.Items.Add(LVItem)

' Define the third item.
  LVItem = New ListViewItem
  LVItem.Text = "My Wallet.wlt"
  LVItem.SubItems.Add("62.5KB")
```

```
        LVItem.SubItems.Add("eWallet Document")
        LVItem.SubItems.Add("11/20/2002 12:12:12 PM")
        LVItem.ImageIndex = 2
        ListView1.Items.Add(LVItem)
    End Sub
```

> **NOTE** *When you're using both large and small images, you must place the images in two separate ImageList controls. In addition, the order in which you place the images in each ImageList must be identical.*

> **NOTE** *This example was taken from the ListViewDemo2 application. Figure 4-15 shows the resulting display. This application is included under **Chapter 4** of the **Samples** folder. See Appendix D for information on obtaining and working with the sample applications.*

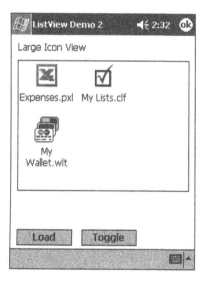

Figure 4-15. The large icon view of the ListView control

The MainMenu Control

The MainMenu control adds a menu to a form. By default, this control is added to the form created with every new project. Typically, you'll define your menu structure at design time using the Menu Designer. You configure menus at runtime through the menu's MenuItems.

The process of incorporating a MainMenu control into an application is involved and exceeds the constraints of this overview chapter. For more information on the MainMenu control, configuring menus, and responding to menu events, see Chapter 6.

The NumericUpDown Control

The NumericUpDown control provides a combination of a text box and a vertical scroll bar. It's well suited for numeric input, as it does not require users to make use of the SIP; they simply tap the up and down arrows to enter a value. That's not to say that users can't use the SIP if they so choose, because the NumericUpDown control features an ediTable text box as well.

Figure 4-16 shows an example of the NumericUpDown control in use.

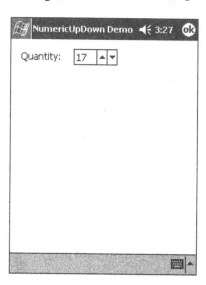

Figure 4-16. A NumericUpDown control

Table 4-14 lists commonly used NumericUpDown properties. Of particular interest are the **Value** and **ReadOnly** properties. The **Value** property contains the numeric value held by a NumericUpDown control. The **ReadOnly** property disables manual entry into the text box portion of this control, limiting entry to the up and down arrows. This is useful in situations where you're making every attempt not to require the use of the SIP.

Table 4-14. Key NumericUpDown Properties

PROPERTY	DESCRIPTION
DataBindings	Used to bind data to the control
Enabled	Specifies whether the control can be manipulated by the user
Increment	Sets the amount that the control increments or decrements the value as the user taps the buttons
Maximum	Defines the maximum value allowed by the control
Minimum	Defines the minimum value allowed by the control
ReadOnly	Disables the text box portion of this control, limiting entry to the buttons
Value	Indicates the numeric value contained within the control

 NOTE *The NumericUpDownDemo application included under* **Chapter 4** *of the* **Samples** *folder demonstrates working with the NumericUpDown control. See Appendix D for information on obtaining and working with the sample applications.*

The OpenFileDialog Control

The OpenFileDialog control provides access to the standard Pocket PC Open File dialog box. This control does not have a runtime interface of its own. Figure 4-17 shows an example of how the Open File dialog box appears to the end user.

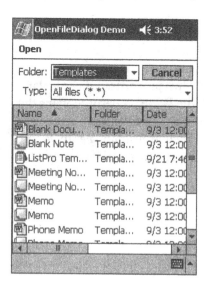

Figure 4-17. The Pocket PC Open File dialog box

The properties of the OpenFileDialog control configure the appearance of the Open File dialog box. Table 4-15 lists commonly used properties of this control.

Table 4-15. Key OpenFileDialog Properties

PROPERTY	DESCRIPTION
Filename	Indicates the complete path to the file selected by the user
Filter	Defines the choices of files that appear in the dialog box
InitialDirectory	Specifies the initial directory shown in the dialog box

NOTE *The **InitialDirectory** property is nonfunctional on Pocket PCs. The Open File dialog box will always display the **My Documents** folder.*

The single method commonly used with the OpenFileDialog control, **Show**, displays the Open File dialog box.

Configuring, Displaying, and Responding to an Open File Dialog Box

Listing 4-17 shows the basics of working with the OpenFileDialog control. As you can see, it's a simple process.

Listing 4-17. Working with the OpenFileDialog Control

```
Private Sub btnOpen_Click(ByVal sender As System.Object, _
  ByVal e As System.EventArgs) Handles btnOpen.Click
  Dim diaResult As DialogResult
  Dim mb As MessageBox

' Configure the dialog.
  OpenFileDialog1.Filter = txtFilter.Text

' Display the dialog.
  diaResult = OpenFileDialog1.ShowDialog()
```

```
' Respond to the dialog.
  If (diaResult = DialogResult.OK) Then
    mb.Show(OpenFileDialog1.FileName)
  End If

End Sub
```

The syntax for the **Filter** property deserves some discussion. For each filtering option your application requires, you define a string of that filter followed by a vertical bar and the filter pattern. For example, if your application works with XML files, you would use the following filter:

```
"XML files (*.xml)|*.xml"
```

If you wanted to allow the user to select any other file, extend the filter string using the *.* pattern. The following string shows an example of this:

```
"XML files (*.xml)|*.xml|All files (*.*)|*.*"
```

TIP *Make it a habit to check the result returned from the Open File dialog box. That way you'll be aware if the user taps the **Cancel** button.*

NOTE *The OpenFileDialogDemo application included under **Chapter 4** of the **Samples** folder demonstrates working with the OpenFileDialog control. See Appendix D for information on obtaining and working with the sample applications.*

The Panel Control

The Panel control is a supporting control, serving as a container for other controls. As a container, it groups together all of the controls placed within its boundaries. Moving the Panel control will move the controls it contains. Disabling the Panel control will disable the controls it contains.

Table 4-16 lists commonly used properties of the Panel control. Two key properties used with this control are **Left** and **Top**. These properties define the position of the panel. In mobile applications, they are frequently used to move a panel, and the controls it contains, in and out of the user's view.

Table 4-16. Key Panel Properties

PROPERTY	DESCRIPTION
BackColor	Specifies the background color for the panel.
ContextMenu	Defines a context menu for the control.
Controls	Specifies the collection of controls contained within a panel.
Enabled	Specifies whether all of the controls contained within the panel are available to the user.
Left	Indicates the location of the left edge of the panel. This location is in pixels, calculated from the left side of the container in which the panel is placed, which is commonly a form.
Top	Indicates the location of the top edge of the panel. This location is in pixels, calculated from the top edge of the container in which the panel is placed, which is commonly a form.
Visible	Controls whether the panel is visible to the user.

Another use of the **Left** and **Top** properties is to create a scrolling form. You start by creating a panel larger than the form. Then by modifying the **Left** and **Top** properties, you can give the illusion that the form itself is scrolling. Chapter 3 discusses this technique is detail.

 NOTE *Unlike the .NET Framework version of a Panel, the NETCF implementation does not support borders. The only way to give a Panel a similar type of appearance is to define its background color.*

Creating a Complex Interface with Panels

You can create manageable complex interfaces easily with Panels. The process is simple. Divide the interface between a set of panels. Each panel contains a set of controls. You then move the panels out of the user's view by setting the Panel control's **Left** and **Top** properties to large and/or negative values. You can see a detailed demonstration of this technique in the "Step-by-Step Tutorial: Panel-Based Interface" section in Chapter 3.

The PictureBox Control

The PictureBox control displays images. The PictureBox control will display images in their original size, resized to fit the control, or cropped.

This is a powerful control for allowing mobile applications to display photos, maps, and other graphical images. Figure 4-18 shows an example of a PictureBox control displaying a map.

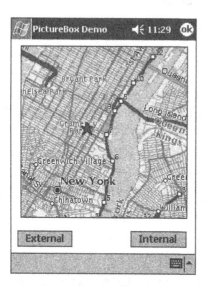

Figure 4-18. A PictureBox control

Table 4-17 lists the few commonly used PictureBox properties. The **Image** property specifies the bitmap to display. The bitmap can be loaded from an external file, an embedded resource, passed from a Web service, or created entirely from code.

Table 4-17. Key PictureBox Properties

PROPERTY	DESCRIPTION
ContextMenu	Defines a context menu for the control.
DataBindings	Used to bind data to the control.
Enabled	Specifies whether the control can be manipulated by the user.
Image	Specifies the image displayed by the control.
SizeMode	Defines how to display the picture. See Table 4-18 for a list of valid values.

Table 4-18 shows values for the **SizeMode** property. The value Normal is the default for this property.

Table 4-18. SizeMode Property Values

VALUE	DESCRIPTION
AutoSize	Control's size matches the image it contains.
CenterImage	Image is centered in the PictureBox. If the image is larger than the control, the image is centered and its edges trimmed.
Normal	Image is placed in the upper-left corner of the control.
StretchImage	Image is resized to fit the control.

Table 4-19 lists PictureBox events commonly used with mobile applications.

Table 4-19. Key PictureBox Events

EVENT	DESCRIPTION
Click	Fires when the user taps on the control. This event is useful in situations where you're using a PictureBox in place of a button (for the reason that the PictureBox can display an image where the button can't).
MouseDown	Fires when the user touches the PictureBox with the stylus.
MouseMove	Fires when the user drags the stylus across the PictureBox.
MouseUp	Fires when the user lifts the stylus from the PictureBox.

The mouse-related events frequently are used in mobile applications to implement drawing. Refer to Chapter 7 for additional information on this topic.

Displaying an Image in a PictureBox

The process of displaying an image in a PictureBox is simple. Listing 4-18 demonstrates loading an image from a file. In this example, the file resides in the application's directory.

Listing 4-18. Displaying an Image

```
Private Sub btnDisplay_Click(ByVal sender As System.Object, _
   ByVal e As System.EventArgs) Handles btnDisplay.Click
' Display the external image.
   PictureBox1.Image = New Bitmap(ApplicationLocation() & "\map.jpg")
End Sub

Private Function ApplicationLocation() As String
' Fetch and return the location where the application was launched.
   ApplicationLocation = _
     System.IO.Path.GetDirectoryName(Reflection.Assembly. _
     GetExecutingAssembly().GetName().CodeBase.ToString())
End Function
```

Sometimes, you may choose to store the image within your application. This approach prohibits the user from deleting or altering the image. Listing 4-19 shows an example of how to load an image from an embedded resource.

Listing 4-19. Displaying an Embedded Image

```
Private Sub btnInternal_Click(ByVal sender As System.Object, _
   ByVal e As System.EventArgs) Handles btnInternal.Click
' Display the embedded image.
   PictureBox1.Image = New Bitmap( _
System.Reflection.Assembly.GetExecutingAssembly.GetManifestResourceStream( _
"PictureBoxDemo.map2.jpg"))
End Sub
```

 NOTE *The PictureBoxDemo application included under* **Chapter 4** *of the* **Samples** *folder demonstrates loading an image from both an external file and an embedded resource. See Appendix D for information on obtaining and working with the sample applications.*

The ProgressBar Control

The ProgressBar control provides your user with a visual indicator of the progress of a task. Use this control when a task is going to take an extensive amount of time. That task may be loading a database, retrieving data from an enterprise server, querying a database, or any other operation that takes a bit of time to perform.

A progress bar can greatly improve the usability of your application. It keeps your user occupied while a task performs. Informed users are less likely to do something bad, such as rebooting their device or calling you. Figure 4-19 shows an example of a ProgressBar.

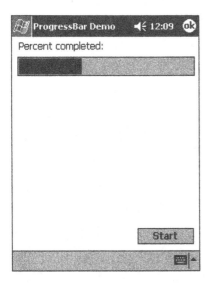

Figure 4-19. A ProgressBar control

Table 4-20 lists commonly used ProgressBar properties. It's rare that you won't use all of these properties every time you use a ProgressBar control.

Table 4-20. Key ProgressBar Properties

PROPERTY	DESCRIPTION
Maximum	Maximum value allowed for the control.
Minimum	Minimum value allowed for the control.
Value	Present value of the ProgressBar. The Value property controls the display, that is to say, how much of the bar is filled.

 CAUTION *Increasing the **Value** property past the Maximum value will generate an exception. Always check the Maximum value before incrementing the **Value** property. An example of this is shown in Listing 4-20 in the following section.*

Updating a ProgressBar

Listing 4-20 provides a simple example of how to update a ProgressBar. In this example, a Timer control updates the ProgressBar every 1/10th of a second.

Listing 4-20. Working with a ProgressBar

```
Private Sub Timer1_Tick(ByVal sender As System.Object, _
  ByVal e As System.EventArgs) Handles Timer1.Tick
  Dim mb As MessageBox

' If the ProgressBar has not reached its maximum value update its value.
  If (ProgressBar1.Value <> ProgressBar1.Maximum) Then
    ProgressBar1.Value = ProgressBar1.Value + 1

' The ProgressBar has reached its maximum so terminate the process.
  Else
    Timer1.Enabled = False
    mb.Show("Task completed.", _
      "ProgressBar Demo", _
      MessageBoxButtons.OK, _
      MessageBoxIcon.Asterisk, _
      MessageBoxDefaultButton.Button1)
  End If
End Sub
```

NOTE *This example was taken from the ProgressBarDemo application included under **Chapter 4** of the **Samples** folder. See Appendix D for information on obtaining and working with the sample applications.*

The RadioButton Control

The RadioButton control is comprised of two elements: a graphical button and a text descriptor. Usually used in groups, radio buttons have the unique characteristic that only a single button can be selected at one time. Radio buttons become part of a group when placed in a container together. In mobile development, radio buttons are commonly grouped together in either a form or a Panel control.

Figure 4-20 shows an example of a group of RadioButtons. The user is limited to selecting a single button from this group.

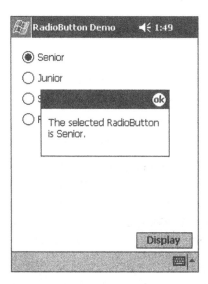

Figure 4-20. A group of RadioButtons

Table 4-21 lists the commonly used RadioButton properties.

Table 4-21. Key RadioButton Properties

PROPERTY	DESCRIPTION
Checked	Indicates whether the control is checked
Font	Defines the font used with the text portion of the control
Text	Specifies the text displayed with the control

The single event that is commonly used with the RadioButton control, **CheckedChanged**, fires when the user taps the control.

Handling Multiple RadioButtons

Typically, RadioButtons are deployed in groups of two or more buttons. The programming trick is to determine the selected button in the group. An easy way to perform this is to use a single, shared procedure to handle the **CheckedChanged** event for each of the individual buttons. Listing 4-21 demonstrates this technique.

Listing 4-21. Handling Multiple RadioButtons

```
Dim ButtonSelected As String

Private Sub RadioButtonHandler(ByVal sender As System.Object, _
  ByVal e As System.EventArgs) Handles _
  RadioButton1.CheckedChanged, _
  RadioButton2.CheckedChanged, _
  RadioButton3.CheckedChanged, _
  RadioButton4.CheckedChanged

' Determine which button was selected.
  ButtonSelected = CType(sender, System.Windows.Forms.RadioButton).Text
End Sub

Private Sub btnDisplay_Click(ByVal sender As System.Object, _
  ByVal e As System.EventArgs) Handles btnDisplay.Click

' Display the button selected.
  Dim mb As MessageBox
  mb.Show("The selected RadioButton is " & ButtonSelected & ".")
End Sub
```

The RadioButtonHandler routine handles the **CheckedChanged** event for four RadioButtons. A check to the **Text** property of the Sender object allows us to identify which of the buttons called the procedure.

 NOTE *The RadioButtonDemo application included under* **Chapter 4** *of the* **Samples** *folder demonstrates working with a group of RadioButtons. See Appendix D for information on obtaining and working with the sample applications.*

The SaveFileDialog Control

The SaveFileDialog control provides access to the Pocket PC Save File dialog box. This control doesn't have a runtime interface of its own. Figure 4-21 shows an example of the dialog box as it appears to the user.

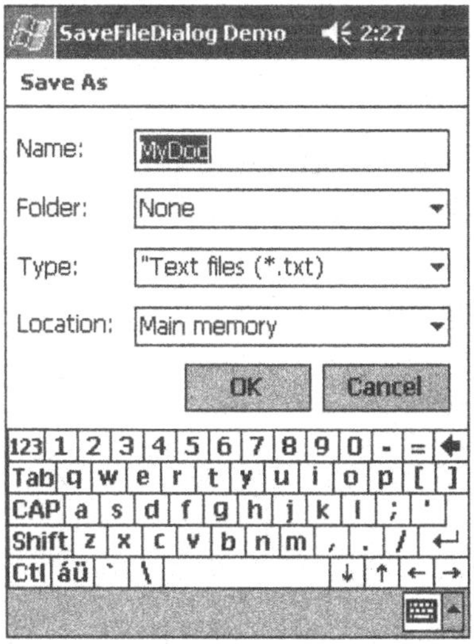

Figure 4-21. The Pocket PC Save File dialog box

The properties of the SaveFileDialog control configure the appearance of the Save File dialog box. Table 4-22 lists commonly used properties of this control.

Table 4-22. Key SaveFileDialog Properties

PROPERTY	DESCRIPTION
Filename	Indicates the complete path to the file specified by the user.
Filter	Defines the choices of files that appear for the user. This translates to the extension applied to the filename as returned to your application.
InitialDirectory	Specifies the initial directory shown in the dialog box.

NOTE *The **InitialDirectory** property is nonfunctional on Pocket PCs. The Save File dialog box will always display the **My Documents** folder.*

The single method commonly used with the SaveFileDialog control, **Show**, displays the Save File dialog box.

Configuring, Displaying, and Responding to a Save File Dialog Box

Listing 4-22 shows the basics of working with the SaveFileDialog control. It's a simple process for the functionality the Save File dialog box provides.

Listing 4-22. Working with the SaveFileDialog Control

```
Private Sub btnSave_Click(ByVal sender As System.Object, _
  ByVal e As System.EventArgs) Handles btnSave.Click
  Dim diaResult As DialogResult
  Dim mb As MessageBox

' Configure the dialog.
  SaveFileDialog1.Filter = txtFilter.Text

' Display the dialog.
  diaResult = SaveFileDialog1.ShowDialog()

' Respond to the dialog.
  If (diaResult = DialogResult.OK) Then
    mb.Show(SaveFileDialog1.FileName)
  End If
End Sub
```

The syntax for the **Filter** property is identical to that used with the OpenFileDialog. For each filtering option, you define a string. That string is comprised of the filter followed by a vertical bar and the filter pattern. For example, if your application works with XML files, you would use the following filter:

```
"XML files (*.xml)|*.xml"
```

If you want to allow the user to select any other file, extend the filter string using the *.* pattern as follows:

```
"XML files (*.xml)|*.xml|All files (*.*)|*.*"
```

TIP *You should always check the result returned from the Save File dialog box. It will tell you whether the user tapped the OK or Cancel button. After all, you don't want to perform a save operation if users change their mind.*

NOTE *The SaveFileDialogDemo application included under* ***Chapter 4*** *of the* ***Samples*** *folder demonstrates the basics of working with the SaveFileDialog control. See Appendix D for information on obtaining and working with the sample applications.*

The StatusBar Control

The StatusBar control adds a status bar to a form. As with all of the other NETCF controls, the StatusBar offers a subset of the full functionality found under the .NET Framework. In the case of the NETCF StatusBar, that subset is minimal.

The StatusBar control is limited to a single text panel. Figure 4-22 shows an example of this.

Figure 4-22. A StatusBar control

Table 4-23 lists the commonly used StatusBar properties.

Table 4-23. Key StatusBar Properties

PROPERTY	DESCRIPTION
Font	Defines the font used with the text portion of the control
Text	Specifies the text displayed with the control

Displaying Text on a StatusBar

Listing 4-23 demonstrates how to modify the contents of a StatusBar from code. In this example, a Timer control displays the current date and time on the StatusBar.

Listing 4-23. Updating a StatusBar

```
Private Sub Timer1_Tick(ByVal sender As System.Object, _
    ByVal e As System.EventArgs) Handles Timer1.Tick
    StatusBar1.Text = System.DateTime.Now.ToString
End Sub
```

> **NOTE** *This example was taken from the StatusBarDemo application included under **Chapter 4** of the **Samples** folder. See Appendix D for more information on obtaining and working with the sample applications. For more information on the StatusBar control, see Chapter 6.*

The TabControl Control

The TabControl provides a tabbed interface for an application. It's a powerful tool for mobile developers, and it's used to manage complex interfaces. TabControls are comprised of one or more TabPages. Each TabPage defines a separate interface, much as if it was its own form.

Figure 4-23 shows an example of a TabControl with four pages. You define the pages of a TabControl through its TabPages collection. The process for adding tab pages is as follows:

1. Add a TabControl to your form.

2. Select the TabControl.

3. In the Properties Window, select the **TabPages** property.

4. At the right end of the **TabPages** property line, click the ellipse button (...) to access the TabPage Collection Editor.

5. Add and order pages as required.

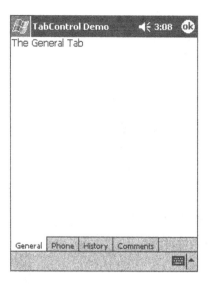

Figure 4-23. A TabControl

After defining the pages of a TabControl, you would next build the interfaces for each tab, just as you would a form.

That's pretty much all there is to TabControls. There is one commonly used TabControl property, **SelectedIndex**, that you use to redirect the user to a particular tab page.

The commonly used TabControl event, **SelectedIndexChanged**, lets you implement functionality as the user moves between tab pages. It fires when the **SelectedIndex** property changes, typically when the user taps on a tab.

> **NOTE** *The TabControlDemo application included under **Chapter 4** of the **Samples** folder provides a simple demonstration of working with the TabControl. See Appendix D for more information on obtaining and working with the sample applications.*

The TextBox Control

The TextBox control provides your basic text input field. It's rare that you'll find a mobile application that doesn't make use of this control. Its broad set of properties, methods, and events provides you with an abundance of functionality to meet a wide variety of programming needs.

Table 4-24 lists the commonly used TextBox properties. As you can see by this list, the TextBox offers a broad set of useful properties.

Table 4-24. Key TextBox Properties

PROPERTY	DESCRIPTION
AcceptsReturn	Indicates whether the Enter key will start a new line in a multiline text box.
AcceptsTab	Indicates whether a Tab key will be entered as a tab in a multiline text box.
BackColor	Specifies the background color of the control.
ContextMenu	Defines a context menu for the control.
DataBindings	Used to bind data to the control.
Enabled	Indicates whether the control can be manipulated by the user.
Font	Defines the font used with the Text property.
ForeColor	Specifies the foreground color of the control.
MaxLength	Specifies the maximum number of characters that the user can enter.
Modified	Indicates whether the contents of the control have been modified by the user.
Multiline	Configures the control to allow for multiple lines of input.
PasswordChar	Defines a character to be displayed in place of the actual text contents of the control. Used for security purposes to hide input values.
ReadOnly	Prohibits the user from entering values into the control.
ScrollBars	Adds vertical and horizontal scroll bars to a multiline text box.
SelectedText	Indicates the text presently selected within the control.
SelectedLength	Specifies the length of the text selected within the control.
SelectedStart	Indicates the position within the text where the selection starts.
TextAlign	Specifies the alignment of text within the control.
TextLength	Returns the length of the text held within the control.
WordWrap	Specifies whether text should be wrapped within the control.

Table 4-25 lists the commonly used TextBox events. The key-related events (**KeyDown**, **KeyPress**, and **KeyUp**) are useful in examining, restricting, and rejecting text entered by the user. The **GotFocus** and **LostFocus** events are useful in automatically displaying the soft input panel.

Table 4-25. Key TextBox Events

EVENT	DESCRIPTION
GotFocus	Fires when the control receives focus.
KeyDown	Fires when the user taps a key. Provides KeyEventArgs.
KeyPress	Fires immediately after the KeyDown event. Provides KeyPressEventArgs.
KeyUp	Fires immediately after the user lifts the stylus from a SIP key.
TextChanged	Fires when the text value changes.

NOTE *There is an example earlier in this chapter of using the* **Focus** *events to display the SIP. Refer to the "Displaying the SIP" and "Hiding the SIP" sections.*

There is only one commonly used TextBox method, **Focus,** and it allows you to position the input in the desired field of your form, directing the user's attention to the appropriate location.

The Timer Control

The Timer control offers simple timer functionality. The premise behind this control is that you configure how often you want the timer to go off, or fire, and then write code that executes every time it does.

The Timer control does not have a runtime interface. Table 4-26 lists its two commonly used properties: Enabled and Interval.

Table 4-26. Key Timer Properties

PROPERTY	DESCRIPTION
Enabled	Controls whether the timer is running.
Interval	Specifies the frequency in which the timer fires. This value is in milliseconds.

The single commonly used Timer event is **Tick**, and it fires every time that the timer expires.

TIP *The key concept behind the **Tick** event is that it will continue to fire at the interval you define until you disable the Timer. Because of this, you should not place any user interaction (for example, a MessageBox) within the **Tick** event.*

NOTE *The StatusBarDemo application included under **Chapter 4** of the **Samples** folder provides a demonstration of working with the Timer control. See Appendix D for information on obtaining and working with the sample applications.*

The ToolBar Control

The ToolBar control adds a toolbar to a form. ToolBars offer two benefits to a mobile application. First, they enhance the appearance of your application by adding a splash of graphics. Second, they simplify user input by providing single-tap access to commonly performed tasks.

As with the MainMenu control, the process of incorporating a ToolBar into an application is involved and outside the scope of this chapter. For more information on the ToolBar control, configuring buttons, adding images, and responding to toolbar events, see Chapter 6.

The TrackBar Control

The TrackBar control provides an interface similar to the two scroll bar controls, HScrollBar and VScrollBar. This control is commonly used where you need to obtain numeric input but don't want to have the user type in a value.

Figure 4-24 shows an example of the TrackBar control. Here, it's being used horizontally. Optionally, you can configure it to display vertically. A common use of this control is to implement graphical control over settings, such as a volume control on an audio application.

The commonly used properties of the TrackBar control are similar to the other scroll bar controls. The **Value** property contains the current numeric value of the control. The **Maximum** and **Minimum** properties limit the range of the control. Table 4-27 provides a list of commonly used properties for the TrackBar control.

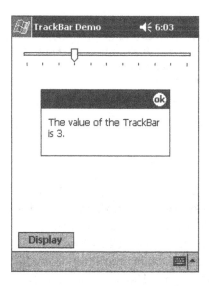

Figure 4-24. The TrackBar control

Table 4-27. Key TrackBar Properties

PROPERTY	DESCRIPTION
Enabled	Specifies whether the control responds to the user's taps
LargeChange	Specifies the amount to add or subtract from the control's Value property when the user taps the control's background
Maximum	Indicates the upper limit for the Value property
Minimum	Indicates the lower limit for the Value property
Orientation	Specifies whether the control is placed horizontally or vertically
SmallChange	Specifies the amount to add or subtract from the control's Value property when the slider is moved a small distance
TickFrequency	Indicates the numeric spacing between ticks
Value	Indicates the numeric value of the control

There is a single event commonly used with the TrackBar control, and that is **ValueChanged**. The **ValueChanged** event fires upon modification of the numeric value either by the user or from code. In the case of our audio application example, you would place code inside this event procedure to implement the adjustment of the sound level.

NOTE *The TrackBarDemo application included under* **Chapter 4** *of the* **Samples** *folder provides a simple demonstration of working with the TrackBar control. See Appendix D for information on obtaining and working with the sample applications.*

The TreeView Control

Like the ListView, the TreeView is a key control for mobile developers. The reason is simple: It packs a ton of interface functionality into a small area—an ideal trait for mobile applications. If you're not familiar with the TreeView control, think of the left panel of a Windows Explorer window. That's a TreeView.

The drawback of this control is that compared to other controls it's complicated to configure and program. Not to worry though, I'll lead you through the process used to configure the hierarchical relationship within a TreeView later in this section.

Figure 4-25 shows an example of the TreeView control. The mainstay of this control is that it presents information in a hierarchy that can be expanded, collapsed, and navigated.

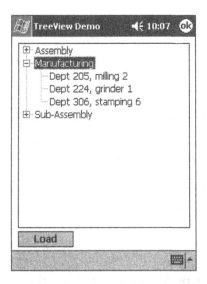

Figure 4-25. The TreeView control

You define the contents of a TreeView control with *nodes*. Nodes can be added directly to the Nodes collection, in which case they're referred to as *root nodes*, or added to existing nodes, where they're referred to as *child nodes*. Your application defines these relationships during the adding of the nodes.

The TreeView control supports the use of images. You can apply images for either all nodes or only specific individual nodes. To configure images for all nodes, set the **ImageIndex** and **SelectedImageIndex** properties of the TreeView control. To configure images for a specific node, set the **ImageIndex** and **SelectedImageIndex** for that node.

Table 4-28 lists other commonly used TreeView properties.

Table 4-28. Key TreeView Properties

PROPERTY	DESCRIPTION
CheckBoxes	Adds check boxes next to each node.
ContextMenu	Defines a context menu for the control.
ImageIndex	Specifies the default image to use with nodes.
ImageList	Specifies the control containing the images.
Indent	Defines the amount to indent for each node.
PathSeparator	Indicates the delimiter string used to building node paths.
SelectedImageIndex	Specifies the image to use with selected nodes.
SelectedNode	Indicates the node presently selected.
ShowLines	Specifies whether lines are shown between nodes.
ShowPlusMinus	Specifies whether plus and minus signs are shown with nodes. These are used to signify expanded and collapsed nodes.

Table 4-29 lists commonly used TreeView events. There are two key events, **AfterCheck** and **AfterSelect**. The **AfterCheck** event is applicable only if you have the TreeView configured to use check boxes.

Table 4-29. Key TreeView Events

EVENT	DESCRIPTION
AfterCheck	Occurs when the user checks a node
AfterSelect	Occurs when a node is selected

Table 4-30 lists commonly used TreeView methods. Two of these methods, **BeginUpdate** and **EndUpdate**, improve the visual appearance of your application when loading a TreeView with a large number of items.

Table 4-30. Key TreeView Methods

METHOD	DESCRIPTION
BeginUpdate	Suppresses the redrawing of the control
CollapseAll	Collapses all nodes
EndUpdate	Enables the redrawing of the control
ExpandAll	Expands all nodes
GetNodeCount	Retrieves the count of nodes

Loading Items into a TreeView

The process of loading items into a TreeView involves defining parent and children nodes. Listing 4-24 shows an example of loading three parent nodes and a number of children nodes into a TreeView.

Listing 4-24. Loading a TreeView

```
Private Sub btnLoad_Click(ByVal sender As System.Object, _
  ByVal e As System.EventArgs) Handles btnLoad.Click

' Suppress repainting the TreeView.
  TreeView1.BeginUpdate()

' Clear the TreeView.
  TreeView1.Nodes.Clear()

' Add the Assembly department.
  TreeView1.Nodes.Add(New TreeNode("Assembly"))

' Add a few maintenance calls to Assembly.
  TreeView1.Nodes(0).Nodes.Add(New TreeNode("North, part feeder 5"))
  TreeView1.Nodes(0).Nodes.Add(New TreeNode("North, test stand 2"))
  TreeView1.Nodes(0).Nodes.Add(New TreeNode("South, torq gun 4"))

' Add the Manufacturing department.
  TreeView1.Nodes.Add(New TreeNode("Manufacturing"))

' Add a few maintenance calls to Assembly.
  TreeView1.Nodes(1).Nodes.Add(New TreeNode("Dept 205, milling 2"))
  TreeView1.Nodes(1).Nodes.Add(New TreeNode("Dept 224, grinder 1"))
  TreeView1.Nodes(1).Nodes.Add(New TreeNode("Dept 306, stamping 6"))
```

```
' Add the Sub-Assembly department.
  TreeView1.Nodes.Add(New TreeNode("Sub-Assembly"))

  TreeView1.Nodes(2).Nodes.Add(New TreeNode("South conveyor"))
  TreeView1.Nodes(2).Nodes.Add(New TreeNode("welder 4"))

' Begin repainting the TreeView.
  TreeView1.EndUpdate()

End Sub
```

This example starts by first suppressing the repainting of the TreeView. You should use this approach anytime that you're bulk loading a TreeView. Next, you remove any existing nodes using the **Clear** method of the Nodes collection.

The process of adding nodes is next. You define the parent/child hierarchy during this process. Nodes added without specifying a parent are root nodes. For example:

```
TreeView1.Nodes.Add(New TreeNode("Assembly"))
```

Nodes added that specify a parent become children of that parent. For example:

```
TreeView1.Nodes(0).Nodes.Add(New TreeNode("North, part feeder 5"))
```

This node references Node(0), its parent. By referencing the index of a parent node when adding a node, you establish a relationship between those nodes.

 NOTE *The TreeViewDemo application included under **Chapter 4** of the **Samples** folder demonstrates loading a TreeView control. See Appendix D for information on obtaining and working with the sample applications.*

The VScrollBar Control

The VScrollBar control provides a simple implementation of a vertical scroll bar. This control, like the HScrollBar control, is a supporting control. It's typically used to control or configure other controls. Figure 4-26 shows an example of this. In this example, the VScrollBar control provides a way for the user to scroll up and down what appears to be a long form. In fact, it's nothing more than a Panel control that is slid up and down on a form to give this appearance.

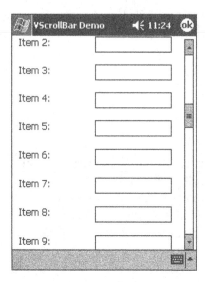

Figure 4-26. A VScrollBar control

Table 4-31 shows commonly used properties of this control. Two properties that you'll always set are **Maximum** and **Minimum**. These properties specify the numeric range of the control.

Table 4-31. Key VScrollBar Properties

PROPERTY	DESCRIPTION
Enabled	Specifies whether the control can be manipulated by the user
LargeChange	Specifies the value to add or subtract from the Value property when the scroll box is moved in large increments
Maximum	Defines the upper limit for the Value property
Minimum	Defines the lower limit for the Value property
SmallChange	Specifies the value to add or subtract from the Value property when the scroll box is moved in small increments
Value	Defines the numeric value of the control

The single commonly used VScrollBar event, **ValueChanged**, fires anytime the **Value** property changes, whether that is by the user or from your code.

Using a VScrollBar to Simulate a Scrolling Form

It's easy to use a VScrollBar control to simulate a scrolling form. Listing 4-25 demonstrates the miniscule amount of code required to implement this functionality.

TIP *You'll need to perform a bit of tweaking to get the sliding ratio right. In this example, I'm using a 2-for-1 ratio of the VScrollBar **Value** to pixels. The easiest way to calibrate your form is to run it, try your slider, adjust the ratio, and repeat until you find the desired effect.*

Listing 4-25. Using a VScrollBar to Control a Scrolling Form

```
Private Sub vscPanel_ValueChanged(ByVal sender As System.Object, _
  ByVal e As System.EventArgs) Handles vscPanel.ValueChanged
' Adjust the panel.
  Panel1.Top = -1 * (vscPanel.Value * 2)
End Sub
```

TIP *Want to make your left-handed users happy? Here's a simple way: Add a configuration feature that allows them to swap scroll bars from the right side of an application to the left side. A perfect use for this technique would be in the scrolling form demo. With the scroll bar on the right, left-handed users have to place their hand over the screen to control the scroll bar, which is truly an exercise of driving your Pocket PC while your vision is impaired.*

NOTE *The VScrollBarDemo application included under **Chapter 4** of the **Samples** folder demonstrates this scrolling form example. See Appendix D for information on obtaining and working with the sample applications.*

Summary

Controls are the building blocks of your application's interface. Knowing what controls are available and what they're able to do is paramount. As I said at the start of this chapter, knowing how to use the NETCF controls is like knowing how to use all of the tools in a toolbox. They don't do anybody any good if you don't know what they can do.

This chapter provided a sampler plate of controls. NETCF controls range from the very simple, such as Label and Timer, to complex, in the case of TreeView, ListView, and DataGrid. I hope that you'll take the time to look through the sample applications included with this chapter to develop a feeling of the control basics.

If you're disappointed in the limited functionality or missing features of any of the NETCF controls, you'll want to read the next chapter. I'll show you how the .NET Compact Framework enables you to extend the capabilities of controls. Also, see Appendix C, which provides links to a number of third-party controls.

CHAPTER 5

Creating Controls

ONE OF THE FIRST THINGS that I hear developers complain about with the .NET Compact Framework is that something crucial to their development style is missing. That "something" could be any number of things, from an item that is seriously significant, meaning it affects me as well, to the mundane, which is another way of saying some feature that I had never intended to use in the first place. I think they (Microsoft) have done a good job of taking a 400-pound gorilla of a product (the .NET Framework) and shrinking it to a mere Chihuahua in size (the .NET Compact Framework).

One of the coolest features about the .NET Compact Framework is how it enables you to code around limitations. Take controls, for example. All of the controls delivered with the .NET Compact Framework are limited in comparison to their full-framework counterparts. They are missing properties, methods, and events. Through the .NET Compact Framework, you can modify the functionality of the standard controls to fit just your needs. In this chapter, I will walk you through the processes used to alter a control.

This is a very "hands-on" type of chapter, as it introduces a number of topics that are new to most developers. In this chapter you'll learn

- **About the three types of custom controls,** user, inherited, and custom

- **The basics of control manipulation,** including altering and augmenting properties, methods, and events

- **Techniques for controlling property values**

- **How to override underlying properties, methods, and events**

- **To incorporate exception handling into your controls**

My focus with this chapter is to demystify what to many developers is a "black art." By the end of this chapter, you'll see how easy it is to tweak controls so that they fit your every need.

Types of Custom Controls

You can divide .NET-based custom controls into three categories: user, inherited, and owner-drawn. User controls are the simplest to create. They typically offer a standard, predefined interface comprised of one or more common .NET controls. Inherited controls start with a .NET control. They then add, remove, or modify the properties, methods, and events of that base control as desired. As complexity of a control goes, inherited controls tend to fall between user and owner-drawn controls. Owner-drawn controls offer the most flexibility in the way of their interface. They also require the greatest amount of work.

In this section, I'll discuss each of these types of controls in greater detail.

User Controls

I like to refer to user controls as compilation controls, because generally that's how they are created. Usually, they will have a preconfigured interface, one set to a particular size and appearance. User controls are comprised of two elements: the interface and supporting logic that resides behind the control. Normally, they are built from one or more standard controls.

You build the interface for this type of custom control upon a user control, which from the design standpoint is similar to a form. Figure 5-1 shows an empty user control as it appears within the Visual Studio .NET design environment. As you can see, it has a very form-like look to it.

This background defines the basic size of your user control. You can shrink or enlarge the user control as required by your particular needs.

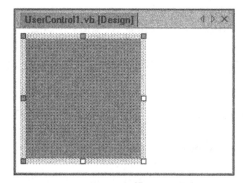

Figure 5-1. An empty user control

By selecting and placing common controls on the user control, you define its appearance. Take for example Figure 5-2, which demonstrates a typical login interface defined on a user control.

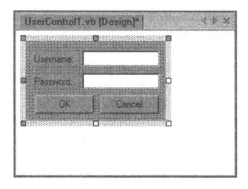

Figure 5-2. A login user control

As I wrote at the beginning of this section, I like to refer to user controls as compilation controls. Figure 5-2 shows a perfect example of this. The login control is comprised of two Labels, two TextBoxes, and two Button controls. When added to a form, the user control will appear just as it does in the Form Designer.

The second part of a user control is the logic behind the control. The logic can be anything from the simple to the complex, depending upon your specific needs. In the case of this login example, you could add logic to process the login to allow or deny access. This might include querying a database, encrypting the password, limiting login attempts to a certain number, or performing other functions.

While user controls are often the easiest type of custom control to build and understand, I've chosen not to discuss them in any further detail. My reasoning for this is simple: There is no support for user controls provided by the .NET Compact Framework. That's right—they're another casualty of the long list of features pruned from the .NET Framework.

NOTE   *The .NET Compact Framework does not support user controls. For your custom control needs, you will have to use either inherited or owner-drawn controls.*

Inherited Controls

The second type of custom control we are going to look at is the inherited control. I have to tell you, inherited controls are my personal favorite for two reasons: First, they're the easiest form of custom control you can create, which in my opinion is always a good thing. Second, they offer a ton of functionality for a bit of effort.

Inherited controls are exactly as their name implies. They're inherited from other controls. You can create inherited controls either from the generic base **Control**, or from a specific control type, such as a TextBox, ListBox, or Label.

Custom controls built by inheriting an existing control by default contain all of the properties, methods, and events of their base control. This is the great advantage of creating controls in this manner. Much of the functionality of your custom control already exists. You only need to add, modify, or remove functionality to create what you need.

If you build an inherited control on a specific control type, your custom control has the interface of its base control. For example, if you built a custom control by inheriting a TextBox control, your custom control would look like a TextBox.

 NOTE *Custom controls that inherit the **Control** class are responsible for drawing their own interface. See the sections on owner-drawn controls later in this section for more details on this topic.*

Owner-Drawn Controls

If you need complete control over the interface of your custom control, then you'll want to create an owner-drawn control. Owner-drawn controls are exactly as their name implies—you are responsible for drawing their interface. You draw the control interface with the Graphics Device Interface, or GDI. The good part of this process is that you have total control over every part of the interface. It can look any way you desire. The bad part of this process is that you have total control over every part of the interface. I know; I used the same point twice. Let me clarify. Having total control over the interface means that you have to handle every little issue of how the interface is drawn, maintained, and refreshed. Simply stated, this usually means laborious coding.

Owner-drawn controls frequently require more behind the scene coding as well. Since they are built using the base **Control** class, they don't provide as many predefined properties, methods, and events as custom controls that start with a specific control type.

Now that you have a general understanding of each of these individual types of controls, we can turn our attention to the specifics of constructing custom controls. We'll start with inherited controls, and then move on to owner-drawn controls.

Creating an Inherited Control

Inherited controls start with either the generic **Control** class, or a more specific control class, such as a **TextBox**, **ListBox**, or **Button**. Your selection of the starting point for your control dictates what inherited properties, methods, and events that your control will natively have.

TIP *The rule of thumb when it comes to selecting the base class is that if your custom control is going to be a hybrid of an existing control, then you should use that specific control type as the base. For example, let's say you want a TextBox that has a **Locked** property. It makes far more sense to start with a TextBox and add a single property, than to start with the **Control** class and add all of the properties, methods, and events found in a standard TextBox.*

Creating inherited controls can be everything from simplistic to complex, depending upon how much functionality you want to add to, modify, or remove from the base control.

Starting the Control

All inherited controls start in the same manner, with a single line of code within a **Class** module that defines the base class of the control. As I have already mentioned, this base class can be either a generic **Control** class or more specific to a particular control.

Adding a Class Module

You build custom controls inside a **Class** module. You can create this module as a stand-alone solution or as part of a Pocket PC application.

The most important step in adding a **Class** module is defining its name. The name you give to the module is the name by which you will refer to your custom control. By default, **Class** modules will have cool names like Class1 and Class2. Now, I'm not saying that you can't have a control called Class1; I just think that the likelihood of this is pretty thin.

TIP *Name your **Class** module when you first create it. Remember, the name you give to the module is how you will have to refer to your control.*

NOTE *You should consider prefixing the name of your controls with a unique identifier. Microsoft recommends the use of your company name for the namespace of your control, for example, **LarryRoof.TextBox**. This limits the possibility of conflicting names between control vendors.*

Listing 5-1 shows an example of an empty **Class** module, which is the starting point for a TextBox hybrid control. Note the class name, **TextBoxPlus**.

Listing 5-1. A Basic Class Module

```
Public Class TextBoxPlus

End Class
```

It's by this class name that you will refer to this control when using it within an application. For example, the following code line shows how to declare and refer to this control from an application:

```
Dim WithEvents txtDemo As New TextBoxPlus
```

TIP *I like to give my controls names that provide some insight into their purpose and functionality. I happen to think that TextBoxPlus is a good name, as it implies that this control has everything that a normal TextBox has, plus some additional functionality.*

Defining the Base Control

As I've previously mentioned, you can start your control from either the generic **Control** class, or a more specific type of control. Listing 5-2 demonstrates starting with the **Control** class.

Listing 5-2. Starting with the Control Class

```
Public Class TextBoxPlus
  Inherits Control
End Class
```

The **Control** class is the base class from which all of the .NET Compact Framework controls are derived. As you expect, it includes a set of properties, methods, and events that are apparent in all controls. These properties, methods, and events will be automatically included in any control that you create from the **Control** class.

Table 5-1 lists key properties of the **Control** class. Any custom control you create that you derive from the **Control** class automatically has all of these properties.

Table 5-1. Key Properties of the Control Class

PROPERTY	DESCRIPTION
BackColor	Background color of the control
ContextMenu	Context menu to use with the control
Enabled	Property that controls whether the user can interact with the control
Font	Font to use with the control
ForeColor	Foreground color of the control
Height	Height of the control
Left	Distance from the left side of the container in which the control is placed
Size	Size of the control
Text	Text associated with the control
Top	Distance from the top side of the container in which the control is placed
Visible	Property that defines whether the control appears to the user
Width	Width of the control

Table 5-2 lists key methods provided through the **Control** class. All of these methods are included in any control that you create from the **Control** class.

Table 5-2. Key Methods of the Control Class

METHOD	DESCRIPTION
CreateGraphics	Creates a graphics object for the control
Dispose	Releases all resources used by the control
Focus	Sets the user focus to the control
Refresh	Causes the control to redraw its interface

Table 5-3 lists key events made available through the base **Control** class. As with properties and methods of this class, all controls derived from the **Control** class will include these events.

Table 5-3. Key Events of the Control Class

EVENT	DESCRIPTION
Click	Occurs when the user taps on the control
GotFocus	Occurs when the user moves to a control
LostFocus	Occurs when the user moves away from a control
KeyDown	Occurs when a key is pressed
KeyPressed	Occurs when a key is pressed
KeyUp	Occurs when a key is released
MouseDown	Occurs when the user presses down the stylus on a control
MouseMove	Occurs when the user drags the stylus across a control
MouseUp	Occurs when the user lifts the stylus from a control
TextChanged	Occurs when the contents of the Text property are altered

As you can see, the simple statement of Inherits Control provides a tremendous amount of functionality to your control, without your having to write a single line of code.

I mentioned at the beginning of this section how controls can be made based either on the generic **Control** class or on more specific types of controls, such as the TextBox, ListBox, or Button. Listing 5-3 shows an example of creating a control based on a TextBox.

Listing 5-3. Starting with a TextBox Control

```
Public Class TextBoxPlus
  Inherits TextBox
End Class
```

Custom controls created from a specific type of control have by default all of the properties, methods, and events of the base control. Figure 5-3 shows an example of how all of these items pass through from the base class.

Again, without having to do anything else but adding the single line, **Inherits TextBox**, you've gained all of the functionality of the base TextBox control.

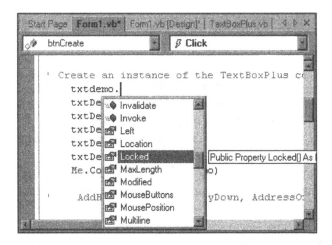

Figure 5-3. Default properties and methods provided by the TextBox class

Remember, the main difference between selecting the generic **Control** class or a more specific class, such as **TextBox** or **Button**, is that with the **Control** class you have the additional responsibility of constructing an interface. Starting from the more specific control classes allows you to leverage the interface provided through those controls.

Now that we have the foundation of a custom control, we'll turn our attention to tweaking the control through the addition of properties, methods, and events.

Adding Properties to Your Control

The process of adding properties can be anything from simple to complex, depending upon what functionality you want to have associated with a property.

You add a property to a **Class** module, which in turn adds it to your control. Properties are added through **Property** procedures. Listing 5-4 shows the basic structure of a **Property** procedure.

Listing 5-4. An Empty Property Procedure Structure

```
Public Class TextBoxPlus
  Inherits TextBox

  Public Property Tag() As String
  Get

  End Get
  Set(ByVal Value As String)
```

```
    End Set
  End Property
End Class
```

There are several key points shown in Listing 5-4. First is the name of the property. In this example, the property name is **Tag**.

Second is the property's data type. The **Tag** property is a **String**, and it appears in two places, on the property definition line and with the **Set** component of the procedure.

Third, there are two distinct parts to a **Property** procedure, the **Get** and **Set** procedures. The **Get** procedure executes when an application requests the value of a property.

```
Dim WithEvents txtDemo As New TextBoxPlus
MsgBox(txtDemo.Tag)
```

The **Set** procedure executes when an application defines the value of a property.

```
Dim WithEvents txtDemo As New TextBoxPlus
txtDemo.Tag = "some value"
```

Within these two procedures, **Get** and **Set**, you place code for storing and returning a property. Listing 5-5 shows a more complete version of the **Tag** property introduced earlier in this section.

Listing 5-5. Saving and Returning a Property

```
Public Class TextBoxPlus
  Inherits TextBox

  Private mTag As String
  Public Property Tag() As String
  Get
    Tag = mTag
  End Get
  Set(ByVal Value As String)
    mTag = Value
  End Set
  End Property
End Class
```

I want to point out three details in this listing. First is the definition of the private variable **mTag**. This variable is not visible to the application using this control. It's used internal to the control to store the current value of the **Tag** property.

TIP *I like to preface my internal variables for properties with the letter **m**, followed by the name of the property. For the **Tag** property, that results in the **mTag** variable.*

Second is the code added to the **Get** procedure. The **Get** procedure works just like a function, so setting

```
Tag = mTag
```

effectively takes the value stored in **mTag** and returns it to the application.

 NOTE *VB .NET supports two ways to return a value from a function. The first is the method just demonstrated, where you set the name of the function to the desired value. The second is to use the Return statement.*

Third is the code added to the **Set** procedure. Note that the **Set** procedure receives an argument that is the property value set by the application. The single line of code

```
mTag = Value
```

handles storing the property value in the internal variable.

Now admittedly, this demonstration is the simplest example of property **Get** and **Set** procedures. Still, it gives you a good foundation of what **Property** procedures are and how they are used.

Let's continue with our discussion of properties, stepping from this plain-vanilla implementation to some specific variations.

Adding Read-Only Properties

Simply stated, read-only properties are properties that can't be set from the application. Commonly, they are used in situations where it wouldn't make any sense for them to be altered by the application. Properties that are counters or provide a current status are perfect examples of read-only properties.

You implement read-only properties by making two alterations to a **Property** procedure. First, you add the keyword **ReadOnly** to the **Property** procedure description. Second, you remove the **Set** procedure component of the procedure. Listing 5-6 shows an example of a read-only **Property** procedure.

Listing 5-6. A Read-Only Property Procedure

```
Public Class TextBoxPlus
  Inherits TextBox

  Private mCount As Integer
  Public ReadOnly Property Count() As Integer
  Get
    Count = mCount
  End Get
  End Property
End Class
```

NOTE *You must include the keyword **ReadOnly** in addition to removing the **Set** procedure from your **Property** procedure.*

TIP *If you create the **Property** procedure using the **ReadOnly** clause, VB .NET will leave out the **Set** procedure component for you.*

Adding Write-Only Properties

While creating read-only properties is common, write-only properties are rare. A write-only property is one that can be written to, but not read from.

Write-only properties are commonly used to store information that you don't want to redisplay, such as a password. You implement write-only properties by making two modifications to a **Property** procedure. First, add the keyword **WriteOnly** to the **Property** procedure description. Second, remove the **Get** procedure component of the procedure. Listing 5-7 shows an example of a write-only **Property** procedure.

Listing 5-7. A Write-Only Property Procedure

```
Public Class TextBoxPlus
  Inherits TextBox
```

```
   Private mPassword As String
   Public WriteOnly Property Password() As String
   Set(ByVal Value As String)
     mPassword = Value
   End Get
   End Property
End Class
```

 NOTE *You must include the keyword **WriteOnly** in addition to removing the **Get** procedure from your **Property** procedure.*

Adding Collection Properties

Up to this point, we've been focusing on fairly standard and straightforward properties. But what if you wanted to add a collection property to your control? An example of this is the **Items** property of the ListBox control. This property is not a single value, but a collection of values. You can add and remove items just as you would with any collection. Well, the .NET Compact Framework allows you to create properties based on collections.

In this section, I'll show you two ways to implement this type of functionality: a simple, minimal control approach, and a significantly more complicated method that offers complete control over the underlying collection.

The Simple Way to Implement Collection Properties

As I already mentioned, there are two ways to implement collection properties. One way is simple, and that's the topic of this section.

Listing 5-8 shows an example of a simple implementation of a collection property. At first glance, you will notice that it's structured exactly like any other simple property.

Listing 5-8. Implementing a Collection Property the Easy Way

```
Public Class Scheduler
   Inherits Control

   Private mItems As New Collection
   Public Property Items() As Collection
```

```
Get
   Items = mItems
End Get
Set(ByVal Value As Collection)
   mItems = Value
End Set
End Property


End Class
```

This method of implementation works for the following reasons:

- The internal variable used to store the property is a collection.

- The data type of the property is a collection.

- The data type of the argument received by the **Set** procedure is a collection.

From the application working with your control and its collection property, this simple implementation offers everything that you would expect in the way of IntelliSense support. Figure 5-4 shows an example of how this simple implementation of a collection property appears when it's inserted into an application.

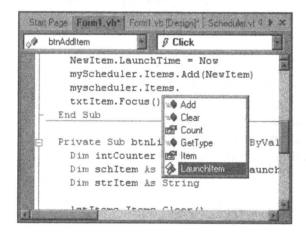

Figure 5-4. IntelliSense support offered by the simple collection property

While this approach of creating a collection property is simple, it at the same time offers no control over the values added to the collection. Simply stated, the application using this control could add anything to the collection—a string, an integer, a structure, or an object. Usually, that is not a desirable feature for a control to have. Now, don't get me wrong. If you're creating a control for your own use, this approach is fine. You can make sure that you don't put anything into the collection that is incorrect. On the other hand, if you're preparing this control for commercial release, you should consider making use of a more controlled implementation of a collection property.

A Controlled Way to Implement a Collection Property

Taking control over your collection property involves a bit of coding. To implement this type of property, you first need to create a separate class that defines the functionality of the collection. Next, you create the property using your new class as the property's data type.

Listing 5-9 shows an example of this process. At the top of this Listing is a single line that defines the **Items** property. I've defined this property with the data type of **ScheduleItem**. I've defined **ScheduleItem** in a separate class, immediately below the control's class.

Listing 5-9. A Controlled Method of Implementing a Collection Property

```
Public Class Scheduler
   Inherits Control

   Public Items As New ScheduleItem

End Class

Public Class ScheduleItem

   The layout of each item.
   Structure LaunchItem
     Dim Application As String
     Dim Arguments As String
     Dim LaunchTime As Date
   End Structure

   Used to store the items.
   Private mItems As New Collection

Public ReadOnly Property Count() As Integer
   Return the count of the number of items in the collection.
Get
   Count = mItems.Count
End Get
End Property
```

```
Public ReadOnly Property Item(ByVal Index As Integer) As LaunchItem
' Return the specified item from the collection.
Get
  Item = mItems.Item(Index)
End Get
End Property

Public Sub Add(ByVal Item As LaunchItem)
' Add the specified item to the collection.
  mItems.Add(Item)
End Sub

Public Sub Clear()
' Remove all of the items from the collection.
  While mItems.Count > 0
    mItems.Remove(1)
  End While
End Sub
End Class
```

In this class, I've re-created the methods and properties that you would expect to find in a normal collection. There are **Add** and **Clear** methods and the **Count** and **Item** properties. I've defined a structure used by the collection. All items placed into the collection are required to use this structure, which in turn enables me to control the content of the items within the collection. Both the **Count** and **Item** properties are read-only.

Within the second class, I use a private collection for storing the items. Still, to the developer, the interface to this control appears identical between each of these versions.

Which method of implementing collections should you choose? It depends upon how your control is used. If you're creating the control for only your own use, then by all means go with the simple approach. It's quick and easy. On the other hand, if your control is going to be used by other members of your development group, sold, or distributed commercially, or even shared free with the developer community, then you need to use the controlled method of implementing collections.

Restricting Property Values

Up to this point, all of the **Property** procedures shown have accepted any data as long as it was of the appropriate type. For many cases that will be good enough. Take for example a **Tag** property. It holds a string, any string, regardless of its value. This works because the property is designed for no particular purpose other than offering a convenient place to store a bit of data.

What if the value of a property needs to be limited? How do you control the value of a property with a **Property** procedure? That's the topic of this section.

There are two key ways to limit or control property values. One way is to restrict the value through the property's data type. The other way is to write code within the **Set** portion of the **Property** procedure to validate the new property value.

Restricting a Property Value Through Enumerations

An easy way to limit property values is through the use of an enumerated data type. Listing 5-10 shows an example of this approach. At the top of this **Class** module is an Enum structure that defines the five values that in turn will be used with the **Rating** property. Later in this same **Class** module is the definition of the **Rating** property. The key point here is the use of the enumerated type as the data type for the property.

Listing 5-10. Using an Enumerated Data Type

```
Public Class Demo
   Inherits Control

' Define the acceptable values for the Rating property.
   Enum Values
     Excellent = 5
     Good = 4
     Average = 3
     BelowAverage = 2
     Poor = 1
   End Enum

' Define the Rating property.
   Dim mRating As Values
   Public Property Rating() As Values
   Get
     Rating = mRating
   End Get
   Set(ByVal Value As Values)
     mRating = Value
   End Set
   End Property

End Class
```

Figure 5-5 shows how all of this appears to the developer working with this control. Note how the IntelliSense feature automatically presents the acceptable values.

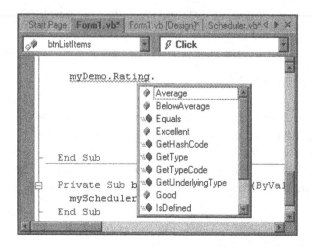

Figure 5-5. Working with an enumerated type property

Restricting Property Values Through Code

The second way of limiting property values is by adding validation code to the **Set** procedure. Listing 5-11 shows an example of how to enhance a **Set** procedure. In this case, a simple check made against the new property value does the trick. Valid values are stored, invalid values are rejected.

Listing 5-11. Checking the Value of a Property

```
Public Class Demo
  Inherits Control

  Define the Rating property.
Dim mRating As Integer
Public Property Rating() As Integer
Get
  Rating = mRating
End Get
```

```
Set(ByVal Value As Integer)
  If (Value > 5) Or (Value < 1) Then
    Err.Raise(vbObjectError + 1234, "scheduler.rating", _
      "An invalid property value was provided")
  Else
    mRating = Value
  End If
End Set
End Property


End Class
```

The validation process you employ within your **Property** procedures can be anything from simple, as is the case with Listing 5-11, to complex, depending upon your needs.

Error Handling Within Property Procedures

Listing 5-11 introduced you to the subject of error handling within a **Property** procedure. I want to emphasize the importance of this.

When you're developing an application, you have to take into consideration how to deal·with and handle the actions of a single person—the end user. When you are developing controls, you have another individual to deal with—the developer using your control. Now, that developer might be you, in which case you can ignore the rest of this. If the developer is someone else, you need to make sure that your control is solid and without fault. That typically requires the addition of error handling.

Adding error handling to **Property** procedures allows you to provide feed-back to the developer using your control. Like all error handling, while it's not difficult to do, it's frequently overlooked.

When I talk about error handling, I'm not focusing on the capturing of errors using the Try-Catch structure, as much as I'm talking about raising errors. Raising errors enables you to inform developers that they have violated the use of your control. The syntax for raising an error is

```
Err.Raise(number, source, description, helpfile, helpcontent)
```

Table 5-4 describes each of these parameters in further detail.

Table 5-4. Raise Method Parameters

PARAMETER	DESCRIPTION
Number	Integer value between 0 and 65535. The range between 0 and 512 is reserved. This will be accessible to the developer through Err.Number.
Source	Parameter that defines the source of the error. I like to set this to a combination of the control and property names. This will be accessible to the developer through Err.Source.
Description	Description of the error. This will be accessible to the developer through Err.Description.
HelpFile	Path to a help file that provides additional information on this error. This parameter is of no use with mobile applications.
HelpContent	Context ID that defines a topic within the help file. This parameter is of no use with mobile applications.

NOTE *For more on error handling under Visual Basic .NET, see Appendix E.*

Adding Object Properties

The properties that you add to your controls can accept a wide variety of data types, including objects such as other controls. The .NET Compact Framework employs this technique with several of its standard controls. The ListView control has two properties, **LargeImageList** and **SmallImageList**. The Toolbox control has the **ImageList** property. Both of these examples accept an ImageList control, but in fact, you can have a property that accepts any type of control, or more generally, any type of object.

Listing 5-12 shows an example of this technique. In this example, I've added the property **InputPanel**, which is of type **Microsoft.WindowsCE.Forms. InputPanel**. Note that with all of the earlier **Property** procedure examples, this property type is carried throughout. The internal variable used to store the property and the arguments received by the **Set** procedure are both of the type **Microsoft.WindowsCE.Forms.InputPanel**.

Listing 5-12. Working with Object Properties

```
Public Class TextBoxPlus
  Inherits TextBox

  Implement the InputPanel property.
  Private mInputPanel As Microsoft.WindowsCE.Forms.InputPanel
  Public Property InputPanel() As Microsoft.WindowsCE.Forms.InputPanel
  Get
    InputPanel = mInputPanel
  End Get
  Set(ByVal Value As Microsoft.WindowsCE.Forms.InputPanel)
    mInputPanel = Value
  End Set
  End Property

End Class
```

You can manipulate, reference, and control these objects passed to
a **Property** procedure just as if you were working with the control directly,
which is the beauty behind this approach. You'll see a comprehensive example
of this technique later in this chapter in the step-by-step tutorial on creating
a hybrid TextBox.

Overriding Underlying Properties

Everything up to this point has dealt with adding new properties. You can also
modify properties provided through the inherited control. For example, every
inherited control has the **Text** property. Well, if for some bizarre reason you want
to modify this property, you can. Simply add the keyword **Overrides** to the property declaration. Listing 5-13 shows an example of this technique.

Listing 5-13. Overriding an Existing Property

```
Public Overrides Property Text() As String
Get

End Get
Set(ByVal Value As String)

End Set
End Property
```

Overriding properties enables you to implement all of the functionality and features covered in this section for existing properties. While it won't be the most common technique you'll employ with your custom controls, in the right situation it can be a savior.

Adding Methods to Your Control

To add a method to a control, you simply have to define a public subprocedure or function within the **Control** class. Adding the keyword **Public** exposes the procedure to the application using your control.

Listing 5-14 shows an example of adding a method to a control. The **PerformSomething** method accepts two arguments and performs, well, absolutely nothing. But it could perform any functionality that you desired.

Listing 5-14. A Simple Method Implemented with a Subprocedure

```
Public Class TextBoxPlus
  Inherits TextBox

  Public Sub PerformSomething(ByVal intValue As Integer, _
    ByVal strValue As String)
  Insert some functionality here.
  End Sub

End Class
```

Listing 5-15 shows an example of another method, **CalcValue**. In this example, I've used a function to implement the method.

Listing 5-15. A Simple Method Implemented with a Function

```
Public Class TextBoxPlus
  Inherits TextBox

  Public Function CalcValue(ByVal SomeValue As Integer) As Integer
    Dim Result As Integer

  Insert some functionality here.
    Result = SomeValue * 3
```

```
' Return the result.
   PerformSomething = Result


   End Function

End Class
```

 NOTE *The key difference between a method implemented with a subprocedure and one implemented with a function is that the function returns a value.*

Overriding Underlying Methods

Just as you can override underlying properties from the inherited control, you can also override underlying methods. Well, sort of.

To be able to override a method provided through the base control, that method must have been defined to allow it to be overridden. The problem is that few underlying methods have this configuration.

The following shows an example of adding the **Override** keyword to the method declaration:

```
Public Override Sub Add(ByVal Item As String)
' Insert some functionality here.
End Sub
```

Shadowing Underlying Methods

In situations where you want to replace a method provided through the base class of your control, and that method can't be overridden, you can instead shadow the method.

Adding the keyword **Shadows** to a method declaration instructs a program to ignore the underlying method provided through the base class and use this one instead.

Listing 5-16 displays an example of this technique. Here, I've replaced the **Show** method provided through the **TextBox** class with my own custom **Show** method.

Listing 5-16 Shadowing a Method

```
Public Class TextBoxPlus
   Inherits TextBox

   Public Shadows Sub Show()
' Insert some functionality here.
   End Sub

End Class
```

Adding Events

Adding events to a control is a two-step process. First, you need to declare the event. Second, you need to raise the event.

You define events with the Public Event statement. The syntax of this statement is

```
Public Event EventName(ByVal EventArgument)
```

You raise an event with the RaiseEvent statement. The syntax of this statement is

```
RaiseEvent EventName(EventArgumentValue)
```

Listing 5-17 shows an example of implementing a simple event. At the top of this **Class** module is the declaration of the event. The statement

```
   Public Event NetCheck(ByVal Available As Boolean)
```

defines the event **NetCheck**. This event has a single argument, **Available**. Near the bottom of Listing 5-17 is the RaiseEvent statement, where the **NetCheck** event is fired.

Listing 5-17. Adding an Event

```
Public Class NetworkConnection
   Inherits Control

' Add an event
   Public Event NetCheck(ByVal Available As Boolean)
```

```
' My internal timer.
  Dim WithEvents myTimer As New Timer

' Use the native Tick event of the Timer control to perform the network check.
  Private Sub myTimer_Tick(ByVal sender As Object, _
    ByVal e As System.EventArgs) Handles myTimer.Tick
    RaiseEvent NetCheck(IsNodeAccessible)
    Me.Refresh()
  End Sub

End Class
```

 NOTE *Frequently, you will use the event of another object as the trigger of your custom event. In Listing 5-17 I've used the* **Tick** *event of a Timer control to raise my own event.*

Overriding Events

The process of overriding events allows you to supplement or replace events provided through the base class. This powerful technique requires exactness in matching existing event arguments.

You use the following syntax to override a base class event:

```
Protected Overrides Sub EventName(By Vale EventArguments)
```

There are two key points to this declaration. First, **EventName** will be the actual name of the event (**KeyDown**, **GotFocus**, etc.) prefixed with the word **On**. For example, to override the **KeyDown** event of a TextBox control you would use **OnKeyDown** as the event name. To override the **GotFocus** event of a TextBox, you would use **OnGotFocus** as the event name.

The second key point to this declaration is the argument list. This list must match exactly the definition of the underlying base event but without the **sender** argument. For example, the following code shows the event declaration for a TextBox **KeyDown** event:

```
Private Sub TextBox1_KeyDown(ByVal sender As Object, _
  ByVal e As System.Windows.Forms.KeyEventArgs) Handles TextBox1.KeyDown

End Sub
```

The next example shows how I converted this into an overridden event declaration. The key to this is to define identically the argument **e** in both versions.

```
Protected Overrides Sub OnKeyDown(ByVal e As System.Windows.Forms.KeyEventArgs)
End Sub
```

 TIP *The easiest way to define the argument(s) for an overridden event is to take the original event procedure declaration and simply remove the **sender** argument.*

Allowing an Event to Fire Through

Many times, you will want to alter an existing event only under certain conditions. If that condition is met, you control the event. If the condition isn't met, you let the event fire through as it would in the underlying base control.

Listing 5-18 provides a demonstration of this technique. In this example, a check made against an internal variable controls whether the underlying event fires or is ignored. You pass an event through to the base control by referencing **MyBase**. This keyword refers to the object on which you built your custom control.

Listing 5-18. Allowing an Event to Fire Through

```
Protected Overrides Sub OnKeyDown(ByVal e As System.Windows.Forms.KeyEventArgs)
  If (mLocked = False) Then
    MyBase.OnKeyDown(e)
  Else
  End If
End Sub
```

In this example, if **mLocked** is False, the **KeyDown** event of the underlying control will fire. If **mLocked** is True, no code is provided, effectively discarding the event.

Use this technique to circumvent or augment underlying events as needed with your custom control. It's a powerful capability that takes a bit of effort to fully understand.

Using a Custom Control in an Application

To use a custom control that you created from a **Class** module, perform the following steps:

1. Add the **Class** module to your application project.

2. In the declaration section of a **Form** module, create an instance of your control. For example:

```
Dim WithEvents txtDemo As New TextBoxPlus
```

3. In the **Form Load** event, first configure the instance of the control and then add that instance to the Controls collection of the form. For example:

```
txtDemo.Left = 10
txtDemo.Top = 10
txtDemo.Width = 100
txtDemo.Height = 20
Me.Controls.Add(txtDemo)
```

At this point, you have a fully functional version of your custom control on your form. It appears to the user like any other control. Your new control reacts and responds like any other control.

NOTE   *We have yet to discuss creating a design-time version of a control that would allow the control to be added to the VS .NET Toolbox and subsequently dropped on a form. For more on this topic, see the section "Adding Design-Time Support" later in this chapter.*

A Word About the Construction Process

The process of constructing a control can range from simple to complex. Like any other programming task, it's detailed by nature. At the same time, this process has an added twist. In developing a control, you're not creating an application for an end user. Instead, you're creating a tool for fellow developers. This subtle difference brings with it a set of its own issues.

The following set of simple rules can help you throughout the process of creating custom controls. These rules ease the development process while adding structure.

- **Plan before you build**—I know that this is against most developers' nature, but trust me; it will help. Before you write a single line of code, you should draw up an object model for your new control. This doesn't need to be one of those roadmap posters that Microsoft produces. A simple drawing or document will suffice. At minimum, it should define all of the properties, methods, and events that your new control will provide. Ideally, you would include more detail in the form of arguments and definitions.

- **Build small**—The best way to build custom controls is in increments. It's the baby-step approach, where you add a small feature and immediately test that feature. Continue this process as you add properties, methods, and events. The worst thing that you could do is to create a control, add a number of properties, methods, and events, and finally try to test it at the end.

- **Use appropriate names**—Often the names of your properties, methods, and events are all that the end developer has when using your control. Because of this, you should carefully consider your naming practices. Use names that describe the items. Select names that aren't ambiguous, confusing, or contradictory.

- **Handle versioning**—Be careful when you release new versions of your control that you don't break previous versions. As you are well aware, nothing ticks off a developer more than having to change a couple hundred lines of code because a control vendor altered the definition of a commonly used component. You're pretty safe adding new properties, methods, and events. It's the process of altering existing items that can get you into trouble.

- **Test everything**—You need to test your control in every possible use and condition. This is a painstaking process. You must verify that all of the properties, methods, and events work as desired, both independently and in conjunction with each other.

Step-by-Step Tutorial: Creating a Hybrid TextBox

Okay, it's time to pull all of this new control development knowledge together. In this tutorial, you will create a hybrid TextBox control, which I have conveniently named TextBoxPlus. You will augment the standard TextBox control by adding two key features: a **Locked** property and automatic display of the Soft Input Panel, or SIP, when the control receives focus.

The **Locked** property allows the developer to restrict input to a TextBox. This property is part of a TextBox control under the .NET Framework, but doesn't appear in the .NET Compact Framework version.

Having the SIP automatically displayed when the user moves to a TextBox is a tremendous feature. The hybrid control provides this functionality rather than making the end user or the developer responsible for showing the SIP.

This tutorial demonstrates adding properties and modifying underlying events.

NOTE *I provide a completed version of this application under the* **Chapter 5** *folder of the* **Samples** *folder for this book, titled TextBoxPlus Demo-Complete. See Appendix D for more information on accessing and loading the sample applications.*

Step 1: Opening the Project

To simplify this tutorial, I've already created the project and the user interface for the TextBoxPlus Demo application. You will add your custom control to this project. Subsequently you will test your control with this project.

This template project is included under the **Chapter 5** folder of the **Samples** folder. To load this project, follow these steps:

1. From the VS .NET IDE Start Page, open a project. The Open Project dialog box will be displayed.

2. Use the dialog box to navigate to the **Chapter 5** folder under the **Samples** folder for this book.

3. Select and open the project **TextBoxPlus Demo - Starting**. The project will be loaded.

Step 2: Examining the User Interface

The user interface of the TextBoxPlus Demo application is comprised of three Buttons, four Labels, one TextBox, and an InputPanel. Figure 5-6 shows the pre-configured interface.

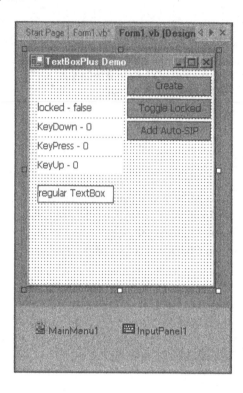

Figure 5-6. The TextBoxPlus Demo application interface

Presently, there is no code behind this application. We'll add that later in this tutorial.

Step 3: Adding a Class Module

You build the TextBoxPlus control using a standard **Class** module. In this demo application, you simply add a **Class** module to a Pocket PC application project.

Perform the following steps to add a **Class** module to your project:

1. Under the Project menu, select **Add Class**.

2. From the Templates window of the Add New Item dialog box, select the **Class** template.

3. In the Name field of the dialog box, enter **TextBoxPro.vb**.

At this point, there is nothing to this "new" TextBoxPlus control except the basic Class structure shown in Listing 5-19. The key point to note here is that the Class name has been set to **TextBoxPro**, which defines the name of the new control.

Listing 5-19. An Empty Class Structure

```
Public Class TextBoxPro

End Class
```

Step 4: Inheriting the TextBox Class

As I stated earlier, the TextBoxPlus control is a hybrid control. It's derived from a **TextBox** class. You accomplish this by adding a single line of code to your **Class** module, which specifies that you are inheriting your new control from a TextBox.

Perform the following steps to add the line of code to inherit the **TextBox** class:

1. Open the **TextBoxPlus Class** module.

2. Insert **Inherits TextBox** in the **Class** module as shown here:

```
Public Class TextBoxPlus
  Inherits TextBox
End Class
```

At this point, if you were to do absolutely nothing else, you would have an exact replica of a TextBox control. Your new and not at all improved control would act and respond just like a standard TextBox control. It would have the same properties, methods, and events.

That is the beauty behind developing hybrid controls; you get all of the functionality of the original control along with any additional features you want to throw into the mix.

Step 5: Adding the Locked Property

Now you are ready to begin with the customization of this control. The first feature that I want to show you how to add is a **Locked** property. The standard .NET Compact Framework TextBox control does not include this property.

There are two steps to adding the **Locked** property. First, you need to add the property itself. Second, you need to provide the functionality behind the property, which will prohibit the user from modifying the contents of a TextBox.

As you learned earlier in this chapter, you add properties to a control by defining a **Property** procedure within the **Class** module.

Perform the following steps to add the **Locked** property to your control:

1. Open the **TextBoxPlus Class** module.

2. Add the new code shown in Listing 5-20 to the **Class** module.

Listing 5-20. Adding the Locked Property

```
' Implement the Locked property.
  Private mLocked As Boolean
  Public Property Locked() As Boolean
  Get
     Locked = mLocked
  End Get
  Set(ByVal Value As Boolean)
     mLocked = Value
  End Set
  End Property
```

I want to point out four parts of this definition.

First, you define the private variable, **mLocked**. You use this variable to store the value of the **Locked** property internal to your control. You define this variable as private, because you don't want it to appear to the application using your control.

Second, you define the **Locked** property through a **Property** procedure. This procedure specifies the property name, **Locked**, and the property type, **Boolean**. Notice that there are two parts to this procedure, the **Get** and **Set** sections. Remember, the **Get** section of this procedure fires when the calling application requests the value of a property. The **Set** section runs when the calling application sets the value of a property.

Third, under the **Get** section is a single line of code that returns the current value of the **Locked** property. The internal variable **mLocked** contains this value, so all that is required is to return its contents.

Fourth, under the **Set** section is another single line of code that saves the new value provided by the hosting application. Notice that the **Set** structure receives a single argument, **Value**, which is the new property setting. All that you need to do is store that away in your internal variable.

Step 6: Adding the Locked Functionality

At this point, your TextBoxPlus control has a new **Locked** property. You could set and retrieve the value of this property from within an application. The only problem is that the control still would not prohibit the user from modifying the contents of the control.

To restrict user input, you need to add some code to your control. What you are going to do is circumvent three event procedures that are part of the underlying TextBox control.

When a user enters a character into a TextBox, three events fire: **KeyDown**, **KeyPress**, and **KeyUp**. It's through these events that we are going to implement the functionality for the **Locked** property.

Each of these events receives as an argument a value representing the character being entered. The trick here is to make the control think that nothing was entered.

Perform the following steps to limit data entry when the **Locked** property is set:

1.   Open the **TextBoxPlus Class** module.

2.   Add the new code shown in Listing 5-21 to the **Class** module.

Listing 5-21. Adding the Locked Functionality

```
' Tweak the OnKeyDown event of the underlying control, to circumvent the
' event when the control is locked.
  Protected Overrides Sub OnKeyDown(ByVal e As System.Windows.Forms.KeyEventArgs)
    If (mLocked = False) Then
      MyBase.OnKeyDown(e)
    Else
    End If
  End Sub


' Tweak the OnKeyPress event of the underlying control, to circumvent the
' event and throw away the key value when the control is locked.
  Protected Overrides Sub OnKeyPress( _
    ByVal e As System.Windows.Forms.KeyPressEventArgs)
    If (mLocked = False) Then
      MyBase.OnKeyPress(e)
    Else
      e.Handled = True
    End If
  End Sub


' Tweak the OnKeyUp event of the underlying control, to circumvent the
' event when the control is locked.
  Protected Overrides Sub OnKeyUp(ByVal e As System.Windows.Forms.KeyEventArgs)
    If (mLocked = False) Then
      MyBase.OnKeyUp(e)
    Else
    End If
  End Sub
```

Three procedures have been added, one for each of the key events. The **OnKeyDown** procedure corresponds to the **KeyPress** event, **OnKeyPress** matches the **KeyPress** event, and **OnKeyUp** handles the **KeyUp** event.

In each of these events, you check the value of the **Locked** property. Remember, the current value of this property is stored in the variable **mLocked**. If the **Locked** property is set to the value of False, you simply pass the event on to the underlying TextBox control, where it will be handled. You accomplish this with the following line of code:

```
MyBase.OnKeyPress(e)
```

This line of code doesn't execute when the value of the **Locked** property is True, effectively causing the event not to fire.

The last thing that we need to do is to add a single line of code in the **OnKeyPress** procedure, which says to the operating system, "Ignore what the user just entered, I'm taking care of it." You accomplish this task by setting the **Handled** property to True, as shown in the following line of code:

```
e.Handled = True
```

That's it. At this point, your hybrid control now includes a **Locked** property. When set, the user will not be able to enter any characters via the Soft Input Panel.

Step 7: Adding the InputPanel Property

The second feature to add to the TextBoxPlus control is to display automatically the Soft Input Panel, or SIP, whenever the control receives focus. As with the **Locked** property, there are two parts to adding the **InputPanel** property. First, you need to add the property itself. Then you need to add the functionality that goes with the property.

The approach used to implement the **InputPanel** property is similar to that used with the **Locked** property, with a few key differences. Most notable is the fact that where the **Locked** property type was **Boolean**, this property type is **Microsoft.WindowsCE.Forms.InputPanel**. That's right, the new property will hold an InputPanel control. What I have chosen to demonstrate is creating the **InputPanel** property in a fashion similar to the **ImageList** property of the Toolbar control. Each of these properties, **InputPanel** and **ImageList**, hold a specific type of control, an InputPanel and ImageList control, respectively.

Perform the following steps to define the **InputPanel** property:

1. Open the **TextBoxPlus Class** module.

2. Add the new code shown in Listing 5-22 to the **Class** module.

Listing 5-22. Adding the InputPanel property

```
' Implement the InputPanel property.
Private mInputPanel As Microsoft.WindowsCE.Forms.InputPanel
Private mSipDefined As Boolean
Public Property InputPanel() As Microsoft.WindowsCE.Forms.InputPanel
Get
  InputPanel = mInputPanel
End Get
Set(ByVal Value As Microsoft.WindowsCE.Forms.InputPanel)
  mInputPanel = Value
  mSipDefined = True
End Set
End Property
```

There are two private variables used with this procedure. The first, **mInputPanel**, will hold the InputPanel control. The second, **mSipDefined**, flags whether the **InputPanel** property has been set.

Note the data types used match throughout the procedure. The private variable **mInputPanel**, the argument to the **Property** procedure, and the argument to the **Set** procedure are all **Microsoft.WindowsCE.Forms.InputPanel**.

Step 8: Adding the InputPanel Functionality

As with the **Locked** property, at this point your TextBoxPlus control has a new **InputPanel** property. Also like the early version of the **Locked** property, it offers no actual functionality. The SIP isn't displayed when you move to the control, as you would like.

To implement this functionality, you need to add a bit more code to your control. While for the **Locked** property you circumvented three event procedures, here you are instead going to augment two event procedures.

When the user moves to a TextBox control, the **GotFocus** event fires. When the user moves away from that control, the **LostFocus** event fires. You are going to modify these two controls to add the desired functionality.

Perform the following steps to add the InputPanel functionality:

1. Open the **TextBoxPlus Class** module.

2. Add the new code shown in Listing 5-23 to the **Class** module.

Listing 5-23. Adding the InputPanel Functionality

```
' Augment the OnGotFocus event to include showing the SIP, if 1) the
' control is not locked and 2) an InputPanel control has been defined.
  Protected Overrides Sub OnGotFocus(ByVal e As System.EventArgs)
    If (mLocked = False) Then
      If (mSipDefined) Then
        mInputPanel.Enabled = True
      End If
    End If
    MyBase.OnGotFocus(e)
  End Sub

' Augment the OnLostFocus event to include hiding the SIP, if 1) the
' control is not locked and 2) an InputPanel control has been defined.
  Protected Overrides Sub OnLostFocus(ByVal e As System.EventArgs)
    If (mLocked = False) Then
      If (mSipDefined) Then
        mInputPanel.Enabled = False
      End If
    End If      MyBase.OnLostFocus(e)
  End Sub
```

You add two procedures to augment the functionality, **OnGotFocus** and **OnLostFocus**. These two procedures will fire as the user moves to and from the TextBoxPlus control.

In the **OnGotFocus** procedure, you first check to make sure that the TextBoxPlus control isn't locked. After all, there is no sense displaying the SIP when the user can't enter data. If the control isn't locked, you simply have to set the **Enabled** property of the InputPanel control to True, which causes the SIP to be displayed. At the end of this procedure, you will find **MyBase.OnGotFocus**. By calling the underlying event procedure, you allow the developer using your control access to the event.

NOTE *In this example you display the SIP before calling the underlying event. That way you can be sure that the desired functionality occurs first.*

The **OnLostFocus** procedure is similar. It uses the **Enabled** property of the InputPanel control to hide the SIP.

One key point to note is that both procedures finish by calling the corresponding event in the underlying control, ensuring that the **GotFocus** and **LostFocus** events will still fire. This will enable the application developer using your TextBoxPlus control to write code for the events.

Step 9: Creating an Instance of Your Control

At this point, you have completed the TextBoxPlus control. Now, you can turn your attention to testing the control.

First, you have to add the control to your form. Since you haven't developed a design-time version of the control, you'll have to do that from code.

Perform the following steps to create an instance of your control:

1. Open the **Form** module.

2. In the Declarations section of this module, declare an instance of your control.

    ```
    Dim WithEvents txtDemo As New TextBoxPlus
    ```

3. Listing 5-24 shows how the **Form** module should appear with this additional declaration.

Listing 5-24. Defining an Instance of Your Control

```
Public Class Form1
    Inherits System.Windows.Forms.Form
    Friend WithEvents btnCreate As System.Windows.Forms.Button
    Friend WithEvents MainMenu1 As System.Windows.Forms.MainMenu

    Dim WithEvents txtDemo As New TextBoxPlus
```

While you're here, add three variable declarations to the Declarations section of the form. These variables are used to track the number of times that the key-related events fire.

```
Dim intKeyDownCounter As Integer
Dim intKeyPressCounter As Integer
Dim intKeyUpCounter As Integer
```

Step 10: Configuring the Control

At this point, you have an instance of your custom control. Next, you'll configure the control and add it to your test form.

All of this occurs inside the **Click** event of the **Create** button. Add the code shown in Listing 5-25 to the **btnCreate_Click** event procedure.

Listing 5-25. Configuring Your Custom Control

```
Private Sub btnCreate_Click(ByVal sender As System.Object, _
  ByVal e As System.EventArgs) Handles btnCreate.Click

' Create an instance of the TextBoxPlus control.
  txtDemo.Left = 10
  txtDemo.Top = 10
  txtDemo.Width = 100
  txtDemo.Height = 20
  txtDemo.Locked = False
  Me.Controls.Add(txtDemo)

' Display the initial status of the Locked property.
  lblStatus.Text = "locked - " & txtDemo.Locked.ToString

' Disable the button so that the user can't tap it again.
  btnCreate.Enabled = False

End Sub
```

This code configures the size and location of the control. It also displays the status of the **Locked** property.

Step 11: Toggling the Locked Property

To be able to test the **Locked** property, you need a method to toggle the property on and off. You'll add this functionality through the **Click** event of the **Toggle Locked** button. Every time the button is tapped, you'll toggle the **Locked** property of the control.

Add the code from Listing 5-26 to the **btnLocked_Click** event procedure.

Listing 5-26. Toggling the Locked Property

```vb
Private Sub btnLocked_Click(ByVal sender As System.Object, _
  ByVal e As System.EventArgs) Handles btnLocked.Click

' Toggle the TextBoxPlus control's Locked property.
  txtDemo.Locked = Not txtDemo.Locked

' Update the display.
  lblStatus.Text = "locked - " & txtDemo.Locked.ToString
  txtDemo.Focus()

End Sub
```

Step 12: Displaying Key-Related Counters

To demonstrate that the **Click** event procedures of the underlying TextBox control still function, you'll add a piece of code to the **KeyDown**, **KeyPress**, and **KeyUp** event procedures. These events should only fire when the control isn't locked.

Add the code shown in Listing 5-27 to the **txtDemo_KeyDown** event procedure.

Listing 5-27. Tracking the KeyDown Event

```vb
Private Sub txtDemo_KeyDown(ByVal sender As Object, _
  ByVal e As System.Windows.Forms.KeyEventArgs) Handles txtDemo.KeyDown
' Increment the event counter.
  intKeyDownCounter += 1
  lblKeyDown.Text = "KeyDown - " & intKeyDownCounter.ToString
End Sub
```

Add the code shown in Listing 5-28 to the **txtDemo_KeyPress** event procedure.

Listing 5-28. Tracking the KeyPress Event

```vb
Private Sub txtDemo_KeyPress(ByVal sender As Object, _
  ByVal e As System.Windows.Forms.KeyPressEventArgs) Handles txtDemo.KeyPress
' Increment the event counter.
  intKeyPressCounter += 1
  lblKeyPress.Text = "KeyPress - " & intKeyPressCounter.ToString
End Sub
```

Add the code shown in Listing 5-29 to the **txtDemo_KeyUp** event procedure.

Listing 5-29. Tracking the KeyUp Event

```
Private Sub txtDemo_KeyUp(ByVal sender As Object, _
  ByVal e As System.Windows.Forms.KeyEventArgs) Handles txtDemo.KeyUp
' Increment the event counter.
  intKeyUpCounter += 1
  lblKeyUp.Text = "KeyUp - " & intKeyUpCounter.ToString
End Sub
```

All of these procedures are similar. They simply update and display a counter showing how many times the event procedure has fired.

Step 13: Assigning an InputPanel to Your Control

To test the feature where the SIP automatically displays, you need to configure the **InputPanel** property of your custom control. You'll add this functionality to the click event of the **Add Auto-SIP** button.

Add the code shown in Listing 5-30 to perform this configuration.

Listing 5-30. Configuring the InputPanel Property

```
Private Sub btnAutoSip_Click(ByVal sender As System.Object, _
  ByVal e As System.EventArgs) Handles btnAutoSip.Click
  txtDemo.InputPanel = InputPanel1
  btnAutoSip.Enabled = False
End Sub
```

 NOTE *The InputPanel, InputPanel1, was already part of the project from the point you started.*

Step 14: Testing Your Control

Finally, you're ready to test the functionality of your control. To run the demo application, perform the following steps:

1. Select either **Pocket PC Device** or **Pocket PC Emulator** from the Deployment Device combo box.

2. Select **Release** from the Solution Configurations combo box.

3. Click the **Start** button.

The demo application copies to the target device and runs. When the application starts, your custom control isn't visible. To test out your new control, perform the following steps:

- **To add your control to the demo form**—Tap the **Create** button. An instance of your TextBoxPlus control appears in the top-left corner of the form.

- **To test the Locked property**—Try typing something into the new TextBoxPlus control. You should be able to enter text because the control isn't locked. Next, tap the **Toggle Locked** button. Now try entering text into the TextBoxPlus control. You should be restricted.

- **To test the automatic display of the SIP**—First, turn off the **Locked** property and hide the SIP. Move between the TextBoxPlus control and the standard TextBox control that's lower on the form. Did the SIP appear? It shouldn't. Tap the **Add Auto-SIP** button. Now, try moving between the two text controls. When you move to the TextBoxPlus control, the SIP should be displayed.

 HOMEWORK *Add a* **Tag** *property to your TextBoxPlus control. This property stores a text string. Test setting and retrieving this property from the demo application.*

Creating an Owner-Drawn Control

At the beginning of this chapter, I mentioned that there were three types of custom controls. The first type was user controls, which the .NET Compact Framework doesn't support. The second type was inherited controls, which we just covered in detail. The third type is owner-drawn controls, which is the topic of this section.

Owner-drawn controls provide you, the developer, with complete command over the runtime interface of the control. Unlike inherited controls, which assume the interface of their base control, owner-drawn controls leave the interface completely up to you.

Owner-drawn controls are the most difficult type of control to develop. This is because in addition to all of the property-, method-, and event-related items that you have with any type of control, with owner-drawn controls you have the additional burden of creating and maintaining the interface.

Now, that's not to say that creating owner-drawn controls is a "space shuttle landing on Mars" type of thing. The complexity of the interface component can in fact range from simplistic to complex.

You construct the interface of an owner-drawn control using the Graphics Device Interface, or GDI. The focus of this chapter is custom controls, not GDI, so I won't go into great depth here on specific drawing techniques. In rendering your control interface, you can use any graphical technique provided through the .NET Compact Framework implementation of GDI.

 NOTE *For more information on working with the Graphics Device Interface, see Chapter 7.*

Starting the Owner-Drawn Control

Owner-drawn controls are started just like inherited controls. You first add a **Class** module that hosts the control. Next, you add an Inherits Control statement to the **Class** module. Starting from the **Control** class rather than a specific control type means that you won't have any predefined interface.

Just as you would with inherited controls, you can add properties, methods, and events to this base control. In fact, everything presented up to this point on control development applies to owner-drawn controls as well.

Constructing the Interface

You draw the interface for a custom control by overriding the **OnPaint** event of the base control. This event fires when the control is redrawn. You can also trigger this event manually to cause the interface of your control to refresh.

The **OnPaint** event receives a single argument of type **System.Windows.Forms.PaintEventArgs**. Within these paint arguments are two key pieces of information: **ClipRectangle** and **Graphics**. **ClipRectangle** is the rectangle that requires painting. **Graphics** are the graphics used to paint.

Listing 5-31 shows an example of an **OnPaint** procedure that draws a simple rectangular interface. The interface is comprised of a rectangle bordered in black and filled with red, yellow, or green. Note how the graphics object passed to the event procedure is used with the drawing statements.

Listing 5-31. Drawing an Interface

```
' Draw the control interface.
Protected Overrides Sub onPaint(ByVal e As System.Windows.Forms.PaintEventArgs)
  Dim ControlInterface As Graphics = e.Graphics
  Dim myPen As New Pen(Color.Black)

' Draw the outline of the control.
  ControlInterface.DrawRectangle(myPen, 0, 0, Me.Width - 1, Me.Height - 1)

' Add the status color.
  Select Case LastStatus
    Case NetworkStatus.Available
      Dim myBrush As New SolidBrush(Color.Lime)
      ControlInterface.FillRectangle(myBrush, 1, 1, Me.Width - 2, Me.Height - 2)
    Case NetworkStatus.Unavailable
      Dim myBrush As New SolidBrush(Color.Red)
      ControlInterface.FillRectangle(myBrush, 1, 1, Me.Width - 2, Me.Height - 2)
    Case NetworkStatus.Unknown
      Dim myBrush As New SolidBrush(Color.Yellow)
      ControlInterface.FillRectangle(myBrush, 1, 1, Me.Width - 2, Me.Height - 2)
  End Select

End Sub
```

This is a simple example of an owner-drawn interface. A control's interface can be far more complex.

Managing the Interface

The easiest way to manually update your control's interface is to trigger the **OnPaint** event. You accomplish this by calling the **Refresh** method of your control. The base **Control** class provides this method.

The following is an example of this technique:

```
Me.Refresh
```

Step-by-Step Tutorial: Creating an Owner-Drawn Control

In this tutorial, you'll create a simple owner-drawn control. This control has a single property, **Mode**, which controls its interface. Other than that, it has no useful purpose.

 NOTE   *I provide a completed version of this application under the **Chapter 5** folder of the **Samples** folder for this book, titled Owner-drawn Demo. See Appendix D for more information on accessing and loading the sample applications.*

Step 1: Starting a New Project

As part of this tutorial, you will create both the owner-drawn control as well as a demo application. Begin this step-by-step exercise by creating a new project using the following steps:

1. Start Visual Studio .NET if necessary.

2. From the Start Page, select **New Project**.

3. From the New Project dialog box, select **Smart Device Application**.

4. Specify the project name as **Owner-drawn Demo**.

5. Select a location to create the project and click the **OK** button.

Step 2: Configuring the Project

To configure the target output folder for your project, perform the following steps:

1. Under the Project menu, select **Owner-drawn Demo Properties**.

2. Under the Device page of the Text File Property Pages dialog box, set the output file folder to **\Windows\Start Menu\Programs\Apress**.

 NOTE   *If you are unsure of the purpose of project properties or how to set them, refer to Chapter 3, which provides a detailed overview of this topic.*

Step 3: Constructing the Interface

The interface for this demo application consists of a single button. Figure 5-7
provides an example of how the interface should appear when completed.

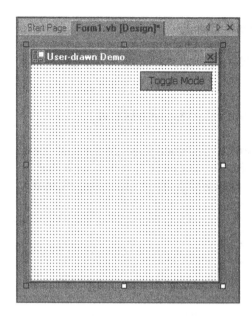

Figure 5-7. The completed interface for the Owner-drawn Demo application

Step 4: Setting Properties

Use Table 5-5 to configure the properties for the form and controls.

Table 5-5. Form and Control Properties

OBJECT	PROPERTY	VALUE
Form1	Text	Owner-drawn Demo
Form1	MaximizeBox	False
Form1	MinimizeBox	False
Button1	Name	btnToggleMode
Button1	Text	Toggle Mode

Step 5: Adding a Class Module

You build the owner-drawn control using a standard **Class** module. In this demo application, you simply add a **Class** module to a Pocket PC application project.

Perform the following steps to add a **Class** module to your project:

1. Under the Project menu, select **Add Class**.

2. From the Templates window of the Add New Item dialog box, select the **Class** template.

3. In the Name field of the dialog box, enter **OwnerDrawn.vb**.

At this point, there is nothing to your "new" OwnerDrawn control but the basic Class structure shown in Listing 5-32. The key point to note here is that the class name has been set to **OwnerDrawn**, which defines the name of your new control.

Listing 5-32. An Empty Class Structure

```
Public Class OwnerDrawn

End Class
```

Step 6: Inheriting the Control Class

The OwnerDrawn control will be based upon the **Control** class. You accomplish this by adding a single line of code to your **Class** module.

Perform the following steps to add the line of code to inherit the **Control** class:

1. Open the **OwnerDrawn Class** module.

2. Insert **Inherits Control** in the **Class** module as shown here:

```
Public Class OwnerDrawn
  Inherits Control
End Class
```

Step 7: Adding the Locked Property

Now you are ready to begin with the customization of your control. The first feature you'll add is a **Mode** property.

Perform the following steps to add the **Mode** property to your control:

1. Open the OwnerDrawn **Class** module.

2. Add the code shown in Listing 5-33 to the **Class** module.

Listing 5-33. Adding the Mode Property

```
' The Mode property.
  Private mMode As ModeTypes = ModeTypes.Operational
  Public Property Mode() As ModeTypes
  Get
    Mode = mMode
  End Get
  Set(ByVal Value As ModeTypes)
    mMode = Value
    Me.Refresh()
  End Set
  End Property
```

This is a standard **Property** procedure. It saves the property in an internal variable and subsequently returns that property value when it's requested.

The only interesting element in this routine is the line that causes the control to refresh its interface. That line is

```
Me.Refresh()
```

This statement is executed every time the **Mode** property changes. Issuing the **Refresh** method causes the **OnPaint** event to fire, which in turn redraws the control's interface.

Step 8: Add the OnPaint Event

You draw the interface of the control within the **OnPaint** event. Perform the following steps to add this procedure:

1. Open the **OwnerDrawn Class** module.

2. Add the code shown in Listing 5-34 to the **Class** module.

Listing 5-34. Adding the OnPaint Event Procedure

```
' Draw the control interface.
  Protected Overrides Sub onPaint(ByVal e As _
    System.Windows.Forms.PaintEventArgs)
    Dim ControlInterface As Graphics = e.Graphics
    Dim myPen As New Pen(Color.Black)

' Draw the outline of the control.
    ControlInterface.DrawRectangle(myPen, 0, 0, Me.Width - 1, Me.Height - 1)

' Add the status color.
    Select Case mMode
      Case ModeTypes.Operational
        Dim myBrush As New SolidBrush(Color.Lime)
        ControlInterface.FillRectangle(myBrush, 1, 1, Me.Width - 2, _
          Me.Height - 2)
      Case ModeTypes.Stopped
        Dim myBrush As New SolidBrush(Color.Red)
        ControlInterface.FillRectangle(myBrush, 1, 1, Me.Width - 2, _
          Me.Height - 2)
      Case ModeTypes.Warning
        Dim myBrush As New SolidBrush(Color.Yellow)
        ControlInterface.FillRectangle(myBrush, 1, 1, Me.Width - 2, _
          Me.Height - 2)
    End Select

  End Sub
```

This procedure draws the control interface in two steps. First, it draws a black rectangle around the interface. Second, depending upon the current Mode setting, it fills the rectangle with green, yellow, or red. Obviously, this control is not going to win any graphical design awards. Still, it does demonstrate the basics of an owner-drawn control.

 NOTE *You will notice that I did not have you call the underlying* ***Paint*** *event procedure. The reason for this is that this demo takes complete control of the control's interface.*

Step 9: Creating an Instance of Your Control

At this stage, you have completed the OwnerDrawn control. Now, you're ready to test the control. The first step is to add an instance of your control to your test form.

Perform the following steps to create an instance of your control:

1. Open the **Form** module.

2. In the Declarations section of this module, declare an instance of your control.

    ```
    Dim WithEvents udControl As New OwnerDrawn
    ```

3. Listing 5-35 shows how the **Form** module should appear with this additional declaration.

Listing 5-35. Defining an Instance of Your Control

```
Public Class Form1
    Inherits System.Windows.Forms.Form
    Friend WithEvents btnToggleMode As System.Windows.Forms.Button
    Friend WithEvents MainMenu1 As System.Windows.Forms.MainMenu

    Dim WithEvents udControl As New OwnerDrawn
```

Step 10: Configuring the Control

You'll use the form's **Load** event to configure the instance of the OwnerDrawn control. Add the code shown in Listing 5-36 to the **Form_Load** event procedure.

Listing 5-36. Configuring Your Custom Control

```
Private Sub Form1_Load(ByVal sender As Object, _
  ByVal e As System.EventArgs) Handles MyBase.Load
' Configure and display the custom control.
  udControl.Left = 10
  udControl.Top = 10
  udControl.Width = 20
  udControl.Height = 20
  Me.Controls.Add(udControl)
End Sub
```

Step 11: Toggling the Mode Property

To test the drawing capabilities of your control, you need only to toggle the **Mode** property. You accomplish this through the **Click** event procedure of the **Toggle Mode** button.

Add the code from Listing 5-37 to the **btnToggle_Click** event procedure.

Listing 5-37. Toggling the Mode Property

```
Private Sub btnToggleMode_Click(ByVal sender As System.Object, _
  ByVal e As System.EventArgs) Handles btnToggleMode.Click
' Rotate through the various modes.
  Select Case udControl.Mode
    Case OwnerDrawn.ModeTypes.Operational
      udControl.Mode = OwnerDrawn.ModeTypes.Stopped
    Case OwnerDrawn.ModeTypes.Stopped
      udControl.Mode = OwnerDrawn.ModeTypes.Warning
    Case OwnerDrawn.ModeTypes.Warning
      udControl.Mode = OwnerDrawn.ModeTypes.Operational
  End Select
End Sub
```

This event procedure uses a simple process to rotate through the available modes.

Step 12: Testing Your Control

You're ready to test the functionality of your control. To run the demo application, perform the following steps:

1. Select either **Pocket PC Device** or **Pocket PC Emulator** from the Deployment Device combo box.

2. Select **Release** from the Solution Configurations combo box.

3. Click the **Start** button.

The demo application copies to the target device and runs. Tap the **Toggle Mode** button. You should see the color of your OwnerDrawn control change between green, red, and yellow.

HOMEWORK *Modify the appearance of the control. Change the shape of the interface. Add some text to the left of the graphical element, much like the CheckBox control. Refer to Chapter 7 for information on working with GDI.*

Creating a Component

Let's say that you want to create a custom control but you don't want to inherit any underlying properties, methods, and events that are provided through the base control. One approach would be to override or shadow everything passed on by the base control. While this is certainly doable, on a good day it's going to be a serious pain.

Instead, what if you could start with an empty slate that provided nothing more than the foundation on which you could build your custom control? The .NET Compact Framework provides just such an item in the form of a component.

The **System.ComponentModel.Component** class provides a base implementation that allows object sharing. In addition, a container, such as a form, can host the **Component** class.

Components don't have runtime interfaces. The perfect example of a component is the Timer. Components provide you with total control over the object structure. They carry none of the inherited "baggage" found in inherited controls.

Starting a Component

Components are initiated and constructed in a manner similar to the custom controls we've been examining within this chapter. The steps to creating a component are as follows:

1. Under the Project menu, select **Add Component**.

2. From the Templates window of the Add New Item dialog box, select **Component Class**.

3. In the Name field of the Add New Item dialog box, enter the name of your component. Just as it was with **Class** modules, this name is how you will refer to the component.

4. Click the **OK** button to create the component. A **Class** module is created that defines the shell of your component.

5. Within this module add the line:

```
Inherits System.ComponentModel.Component
```

The following code shows an example of the **Component Class** module at this point:

```
Public Class MyComponent
  Inherits System.ComponentModel.Component
End Class
```

NOTE *You will notice that there is a region of component designer—generated code within your **Component** module. Obviously, you didn't run any designer. You can simply ignore this region. It doesn't figure into either the design or use of a component.*

From here, you can augment and accessorize your component just as you would a custom control. You can add properties, methods, and events. Listing 5 38 shows a **Component** module that defines a property and a method.

Listing 5-38. A Simple Component

```
Public Class Component1
  Inherits System.ComponentModel.Component

' Add a property.
  Private mTest As Boolean
  Public Property Test() As Boolean
  Get
    Test = mTest
  End Get
  Set(ByVal Value As Boolean)
    mTest = Value
  End Set
  End Property

' Add a method.
  Public Function calc(ByVal value1 As Int16, ByVal value2 As Int16) As Int16
    calc = value1 * value2
  End Function

End Class
```

Adding Design-Time Support

The last topic that I want to discuss is adding design-time support for your custom controls. Adding design-time support to a custom control allows the control to be used within the Visual Studio .NET design environment. You will be able to add the control to the Toolbox and subsequently draw it on a form.

Without design-time support, you're forced to create and configure the control from code, as was shown in the two tutorials in this chapter. You completely lose the GUI design capability that has made Visual Basic what it is today.

Design-time support for a custom control requires that you create a second version of your control, one compiled for use under Windows, rather than under Windows CE. The only purpose behind this second version of your control is to provide a visual design experience. It allows the developer to visually configure a control through the Windows Form Designer and the Properties window.

Now the bad news: You can't create a design-time version of a control that targets the .NET Compact Framework and is written using Visual Basic .NET. You have to use C# .NET. The reason behind this shortcoming is that to create the design-time version of the control you need to add references to a set of NETCF-specific namespaces. Adding these namespaces introduces ambiguities between existing referenced namespaces.

In C# .NET, these ambiguities manifest themselves as warnings during a compile. The C# .NET compiler allows you to ignore these warnings to produce the desktop version of your control.

In Visual Basic .NET these same ambiguities appear as compiler errors: errors that can't be overridden, which in turn prohibits you from producing a desktop version of your control.

The bottom line is that if your control has to have a design-time version, you had better learn C# .NET.

Summary

Being able to create custom controls is just another of the many ways in which the .NET Compact Framework outperforms eMbedded Visual Basic.

Custom controls allow you to work around the limitations of the controls provided with the .NET Compact Framework. As this chapter demonstrated, they can be anything from the incredibly simplistic, to complicated, depending upon your needs.

NETCF supports two types of custom controls, inherited and owner-drawn. Inherited controls allow you to easily create hybrid versions of existing controls. Owner-drawn controls allow you to graphically create custom interfaces for controls.

Components provide a third alternative. They provide a foundation on which you can build a custom object. They are best suited for situations where you 1) do not require a visual element, and 2) want complete control over the properties, methods, and events provided by your object.

Remember, controls that target the .NET Compact Framework and require a design-time interface can't be written in Visual Basic .NET. A compiler limitation prohibits the generation of a desktop version of your controls. If you absolutely need a design-time version of a custom control, you need to create that control using C# .NET.

CHAPTER 6

Menus, Toolbars, and Status Bars

IN CHAPTER 5, WE looked at controls. You learned what controls are, which ones are available with SDE, and how they work. In this chapter, we're going to turn our attention to three controls that can give your applications that professional look and feel—the MainMenu, the ToolBar, and the StatusBar.

The use of these three controls can be seen in the most successful commercial Pocket PC applications. The MainMenu control is a staple, providing users with a graphical menu hierarchy. At first glance, the ToolBar control is slightly different from what a desktop developer has come to expect from a toolbar. The Pocket PC version enables you to add buttons to the menubar, providing direct access to the most frequently used tasks that an application offers. The NETCF version of the StatusBar control is pretty limited in comparison to the .NET version. Even in its limited state, this control can be highly effective when appropriately used.

In this chapter, I'm going to walk you through the configuration and use of each of these controls. Along the way you will learn how to

- **Design menus at design time** using the menu editor that is part of the Form Designer.

- **Construct menus in code.** In some situations, you will need to build menus from code. Most commonly this technique is used to extend a menu at runtime or to be able to reuse a common menu structure between applications.

- **Tweak menu properties at runtime,** enabling you to alter the appearance of a menu depending upon the needs of your application or in response to a user's actions.

- **Build context-sensitive menus.** Pop-up menus are one of the pivotal elements of the Pocket PC interface. NETCF and SDE make creating and responding to pop-up menus a snap.

- **Create toolbars.** Toolbars are a key element of effective Pocket PC interface design. They allow you to add single-tap access to key functionality of your applications.

- **Add StatusBars.** While the NETCF implementation of StatusBars may be limited, when used appropriately StatusBars can still be highly effective.

At the end of this chapter, you will find a comprehensive step-by-step project that walks you through a practical implementation of the key topics that are contained within this chapter. But enough about that—let's get on to the topics at hand starting with menus.

Building Menus

Look at any commercially successful Pocket PC application, and you will find a menubar. Almost without exception, to build a highly effective Pocket PC application with a fair set of functionality requires the use of a menubar.

The use of menubars is so common that the default Pocket PC Windows Application template automatically attaches a menubar to the initial form it creates. The template figures that, chances are, you are going to need one anyway, so why not add it for you.

The physical process of building menus and responding to taps on menu items is far easier than it was in eMbedded Visual Basic (eVB). With eVB, you had to create menus completely from code. While this wasn't an extremely difficult programming task, it was by no means intuitively obvious to the most casual observer, that being the novice mobile developer. With SDE and the NETCF, building menus has become a snap. You simply build a menu hierarchy with a graphical tool provided through the Form Designer. It's quick and easy to do.

While constructing menus with the design-time tool is the easiest approach, it's not the only approach. Menus can also be constructed with code. While slightly more complicated, there are situations where you will want to create your menus on the fly while your application is running.

For example, let's say you have a common menu that you want to use with a series of applications. Instead of manually re-creating this same menu for every application using the design-time tool, you could instead create the menu completely from code. By placing your menu declaration within a **Class** module, you could easily reuse your common menu in all of your applications.

We'll start our examination of menus with the simplest approach—building menus at design time.

Building Menus at Design Time

If you are an eVB developer switching over to SDE, one new feature you are going to love is the Menu Designer, which enables you to graphically construct menus. The designer makes creating and modifying menus quick and painless. In actuality, the Menu Designer offers a graphical interface for configuring a MainMenu control. The MainMenu control physically implements a menubar on a form.

In this section, you will learn how to add a MainMenu control to a form, build a menu interface with the Menu Designer, and configure the most commonly utilized properties of the MainMenu control.

The MainMenu Control

The MainMenu control carries the honor of being the most commonly used control that is seldom added to a form. This abnormality occurs because the template used to create Pocket PC applications, the Windows Application template, is configured to add a MainMenu control with the default form. It's there for you from the start. All you need to do is configure it.

Adding a MainMenu Control to a Form

While the general rule of thumb is just to use the menubar that is automatically added to the default form, there may be situations where you need to add one yourself. The process is simple and is detailed next.

To add a MainMenu control to a form, perform the following steps:

1. In the VS .NET IDE, bring up the form for which you will be adding a menu.

2. From the Toolbox, double-click the MainMenu control as shown in Figure 6-1.

Figure 6-1. The MainMenu control in the Toolbox

This adds a MainMenu control to the icon tray located below your form. Figure 6-2 shows an example of this. Adding the MainMenu control sets the **Menu** property of the form automatically.

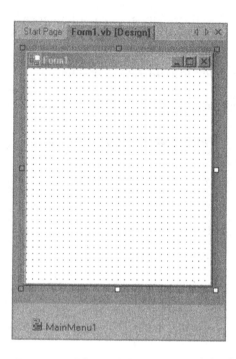

Figure 6-2. The MainMenu control displayed in the icon tray

NOTE *Controls that do not have a graphical interface at runtime, such as MainMenu, ContextMenu, ImageList, and Timer, are shown as being part of a form by placing the icon in the icon tray.*

Normally, after adding any control, I always recommend that you code the key, or most commonly utilized properties, of that control before doing anything else. Well, with the MainMenu control this is a pretty sparse task because there is only one property that you will regularly configure—the **Name** property.

Understanding Menu Terminology

Before showing you how to create a menu with the designer, let's define some menu-related terms.

Menus are a collection of individual items that are displayed under a single menubar item. For example, take the menubar that is shown in Figure 6-3. This menubar has three menus: New, Edit, and Tools.

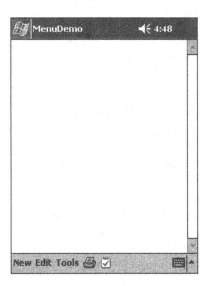

Figure 6-3. An example menubar that includes three menus

Menus are comprised of *menu items*, which are the options, or choices, listed in a menu. Figure 6-4 shows an Edit menu that contains the menu items **Cut, Copy, Paste, Clear, Select All**, and **Find/Replace**.

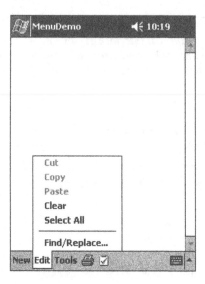

Figure 6-4. An example menu with its menu items

Configuring a Menu with the Designer

After adding a MainMenu control to a form, you then use the Menu Designer to construct the menus and menu items that will comprise your overall menubar.
To activate the Menu Designer, perform the following steps:

1. From within the VS .NET IDE, open the form on which you will be adding the menu. If your form does not already contain a MainMenu control, add one at this time.

2. Click the MainMenu icon in the icon tray. The menubar on your form will become activated.

3. Click the menubar on the form. This activates the Menu Designer. The space for the first menu will be highlighted as shown in Figure 6-5.

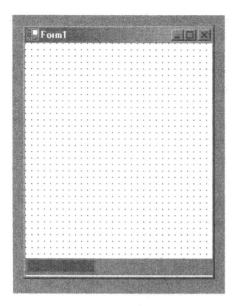

Figure 6-5. An empty menu in the Menu Designer

4. Enter the name of your first (left-most) menu in the highlighted area. In the example shown in Figure 6-6, the menu New is defined.

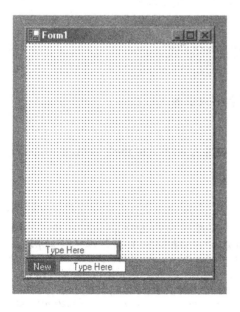

Figure 6-6. Adding the first menu

5. At this point, you could either add additional menus or define the items that will appear under the New menu. To add additional menus, simply enter the name of the next menu in the **Type Here** box immediately to the right of the first menu defined. In Figure 6-6, this would be just to the right of New. For our example, we'll add an Edit menu.

6. To define a menu item for the Edit menu, click the Type Here box immediately above Edit and enter the name of the menu item. Figure 6-7 demonstrates adding the menu item **Cut** to the Edit menu.

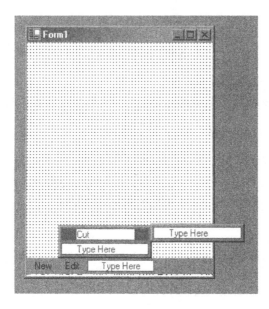

Figure 6-7. Adding a menu item to a menu

7. Continue this process of creating menus and their items until you complete your menu.

TIP *Think long and hard before you create submenus. Remember, when you are developing the interface for your Pocket PC applications, it's all about taps, that is to say, the number of taps it takes to perform some function or feature of your application. Ideally, this should always be a single tap. Menu items take at least two taps— one for the menu and the second for the item. Items in submenus take an additional tap.*

Configuring Menu Item Properties at Design Time

Inevitably, you will want to configure some properties of menu items at design time. Most notable is the **Name** property, although you might consider setting the **Checked** or **Enabled** properties.

As presented in Chapter 4, the **Name** property plays an important role in that it's used when referring to a control from code.

 TIP *When naming menu items, I like to use the prefix **mnu** followed by the name of the menu and then the name of the item. For example, the menu item **Open**, which is located under the File menu, would be named **mnuFileOpen**.*

The **Checked** property controls the display of a checked mark next to a menu item. Check marks are used for menu items that can be toggled on and off. For example, let's say you've built a simple network chat client. A feature of this application is the ability to automatically spell check a message before it's sent. Well, you may want to give users control over this feature, allowing them to enable or disable the auto spell-check functionality. That is easy to do using the **Checked** property of a menu item.

Typically, you would set the **Checked** property of a menu item to a default value, either checked or unchecked, while in design mode. The **Checked** property of a menu item can be set by first selecting the menu item on your form and then using the Properties window to set the desired value.

 NOTE *You will see an example of toggling the **Checked** property for a menu item later in this chapter.*

Another commonly used menu item property is the **Enabled** property. By toggling this property between True and False, you can control whether a menu item can be tapped by the user. This allows you to limit access to particular functions and features based upon the current situation within your application. For example, going back to our simple text editor application, let's say this application has **Cut**, **Copy**, and **Paste** menu items that are used to manipulate text. These menu items shouldn't be enabled except in situations where they can be used. Take the **Paste** menu item. It shouldn't be enabled unless there is some text in the Clipboard. The same with the **Cut** and **Copy** items; they should not be enabled unless some text is selected.

Usually you would set the **Enabled** property of a menu item to a default value, either checked or unchecked, while in design mode. The **Enabled** property of a menu item can be set by first selecting the menu item on your form and then using the Properties window to set the desired value.

NOTE   *You will see an example of toggling the **Enabled** property for a menu item later in this chapter.*

TIP   *In the following section you will learn how to dynamically construct menus at runtime. While this is a viable option, I would suggest using enabling and disabling instead. Users become confused and concerned when menu items appear and disappear.*

Building Menus from Code

Whether you use the Menu Designer or build a menu on your own, in the end all menus are constructed in code. In addition, while the Menu Designer makes easy work of constructing a menu at design time, there are situations where you may want to create menus on your own. For example, you may want to reuse a common menu between several applications. Rather than having to re-create the menu manually for each application, you could instead create a **Class** module that contains the menu and then simply add it each project.

Another common situation where you may want to build menus from code is when a menu or its items will be constructed from information that is not available *until* runtime. An example of this might be a menu that contains items gathered from either a file, the contents of a directory, or settings retrieved from the registry.

While building menus from code is slightly more detailed and involved than the graphical method offered by the Menu Designer, it's by no means a difficult task. To give you a better understanding of the steps involved in implementing a menu from code, I'm going to walk you through the code generated by the Menu Designer to create a simple menu.

In this example, I've used the Menu Designer to create the menu shown in Figure 6-8. While this is a simple example, it will demonstrate many of the steps required to create a menu from code. In this example there is a single menu, Edit, along with three menu items **Cut**, **Copy**, and **Paste**.

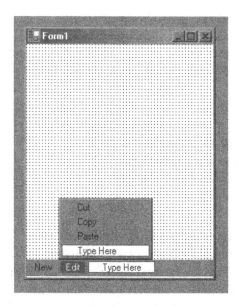

Figure 6-8. The example menu

The names for each of the menu objects is shown in Table 6-1.

Table 6-1. Menu Object Names

NAME	OBJECT
mnuEdit	The Edit menu
mnuEditCut	The Cut menu item under the Edit menu
mnuEditSave	The Save menu item under the Edit menu
mnuEditSaveAs	The Save As menu item under the Edit menu

Let's look at the code that was generated to define the Edit menu. Listing 6-1 shows the first few lines of this form's module. On the third line of this code sample is where the MainMenu control is defined.

Listing 6-1. The Definition of the MainMenu Control

```
Public Class Form1
  Inherits System.Windows.Forms.Form
  Friend WithEvents MainMenu1 As System.Windows.Forms.MainMenu
```

Next, we'll look in the section of code that is generated by the Form Designer. I'm not going to cover all of the code that comprises this section but instead will focus on the lines that are used to define and configure the example menu. Listing 6-2 contains the definition of the Edit menu and its three items.

Listing 6-2. The Definition of the Edit Menu Items

```
Friend WithEvents mnuEdit As System.Windows.Forms.MenuItem
Friend WithEvents mnuEditCut As System.Windows.Forms.MenuItem
Friend WithEvents mnuEditCopy As System.Windows.Forms.MenuItem
Friend WithEvents mnuEditPaste As System.Windows.Forms.MenuItem
```

You should note three key points from Listing 6-2. First, when these menu items are created, they include WithEvents. This will allow each menu item to respond to events, such as when the user taps on the item. Second, the names of the controls, taken from Table 6-1, are defined here. Third, each is defined as System.Windows.Forms.MenuItem, even though one item is our menu, Edit, and the three other items are our menu items.

 NOTE *The Edit menu is a menu item of the MainMenu control, while **Cut**, **Copy**, and **Paste** are menu items of Edit.*

The InitializeComponent routine, shown in Listing 6-3, handles adding the MainMenu control and the menu items first to this form.

Listing 6-3. Adding the MainMenu Control and the Menu Items to the Form

```
Private Sub InitializeComponent()
    Me.MainMenu1 = New System.Windows.Forms.MainMenu
    Me.mnuNew = New System.Windows.Forms.MenuItem
    Me.mnuEdit = New System.Windows.Forms.MenuItem
    Me.mnuEditCut = New System.Windows.Forms.MenuItem
    Me.mnuEditCopy = New System.Windows.Forms.MenuItem
    Me.mnuEditPaste = New System.Windows.Forms.MenuItem
```

Next, Listing 6-4 shows the Edit menu item being added to the MainMenu control.

Listing 6-4. Adding the Edit Menu to the MainMenu Control

```
'
'MainMenu1
'
Me.MainMenu1.MenuItems.Add(Me.mnuEdit)
```

In Listing 6-5, the Edit menu is further defined by first adding the three menu items for **Cut**, **Copy**, and **Paste**. The **Text** property of the Edit menu item is then defined. This is what the user will see when this application runs.

Listing 6-5. Configuring the Edit Menu

```
'
'mnuEdit
'
Me.mnuEdit.MenuItems.Add(Me.mnuEditCut)
Me.mnuEdit.MenuItems.Add(Me.mnuEditCopy)
Me.mnuEdit.MenuItems.Add(Me.mnuEditPaste)
Me.mnuEdit.Text = "Edit"
```

The individual menu items are then configured as shown in Listing 6-6. In this case, only the **Text** properties are being configured.

Listing 6-6. Configuring the Items That Comprise the Edit Menu

```
'
'mnuEditCut
'
Me.mnuEditCut.Text = "Cut"
'
'mnuEditCopy
'
Me.mnuEditCopy.Text = "Copy"
'
'mnuEditPaste
'
Me.mnuEditPaste.Text = "Paste"
```

Finally, in Listing 6-7, the **menu** property of the form itself is set to the MainMenu just defined.

Listing 6-7. Adding the MainMenu to the Form

```
'
'Form1
'
Me.Menu = Me.MainMenu1
Me.Text = "Form1"
```

Now that you have a general understanding of how menus are defined, configured, and associated to a form, let's turn our attention to specific menu-related coding techniques.

Toggling Menu Item Checkmarks

One commonly used code technique involves toggling checkmarks on a menu. This allows you to implement a visual indicator to the user as to whether a feature is turned on or off, selected or not selected. Toggling the **Checked** property of a menu item is simple. An example is shown in Listing 6-8. The toggle is carried out by using the **Not** operator, which in this case says take the opposite value of whatever is the current **Checked** property, and assign it back to the **Checked** property. If it was on, it will be turned off. If it was off, it will be turned on.

Listing 6-8. Toggling the Checkmark Property of a Menu Item

```
Private Sub mnuToolsSpellCheck_Click(ByVal sender As System.Object, _
    ByVal e As System.EventArgs) Handles mnuToolsSpellCheck.Click
        mnuToolsSpellCheck.Checked = Not mnuToolsSpellCheck.Checked
End Sub
```

NOTE *Obviously, toggling the **Checked** property only takes care of the visual side of this feature. Elsewhere in your code, you would need to add code to implement the appropriate functionality for this menu item.*

An example of how a menu item that has its **Checked** property set to True is shown in Figure 6-9.

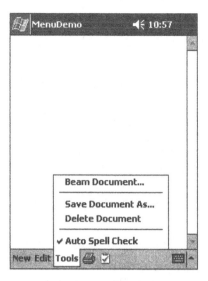

Figure 6-9. Checking a menu item

Enabling and Disabling Menu Items

Another common programming technique involves enabling or disabling menu items while an application is running. To understand better the use of this technique, let's take a look at a simple example of a text editor application. Part of the interface for this application is an Edit menu containing three items: **Cut**, **Copy**, and **Paste**. In building an effective interface, you only want these menu items to be enabled when the functionality they provide is applicable. For the **Cut** and **Copy** items, that would be when text is selected in the editing area. The **Paste** menu item would be enabled when the Clipboard contains text.

An example of enabling and disabling a menu item is shown in Listing 6-9 where a Timer control is used to monitor the TextBox control txtContent. When there is text selected in txtContent, the **Cut** and **Copy** menu items are enabled. If no text is selected, the two menu items are disabled.

Listing 6-9. Enabling Menu Items

```
Private Sub timCheckText_Tick(ByVal sender As System.Object, _
  ByVal e As System.EventArgs) Handles timCheckText.Tick
    If (txtContent.SelectionLength <> 0) Then
      mnuEditCut.Enabled = True
      mnuEditCopy.Enabled = True
```

```
    Else
      mnuEditCut.Enabled = False
      mnuEditCopy.Enabled = False
    End If
  End Sub
```

 NOTE   *Ideally, this check would be better placed in a TextBox-related event, but no TextBox events fire when the user is selecting text. That is why I used a Timer control for this example.*

Responding to Menu Click Events

If you are building a menu, you are most certainly going to want to respond to the user tapping, or clicking, a menu item. All menu items have a **Click** event that fires when the user taps the item. Listing 6-10 shows an example of such a procedure.

Listing 6-10. The Click Event Procedure for a Menu Item

```
Private Sub mnuEditCut_Click(ByVal sender As System.Object, _
  ByVal e As System.EventArgs) Handles mnuEditCut.Click
  MsgBox("cut...")
End Sub
```

Generating Menus

One good reason for understanding the code that is generated by the Menu Designer is that you can construct menus on the fly while your application is running. For example, you may want to add the names of the four most recently edited files to the File menu of a text editor, providing users with an easy way to access those files. This is easily accomplished through code as shown in Listing 6-11.

Listing 6-11. Adding a List of Recently Accessed Files to a Edit Menu

```
Private Sub Form1_Load(ByVal sender As System.Object, _
  ByVal e As System.EventArgs) Handles MyBase.Load

' Define the menu items.
    Me.mnuEditFile1 = New System.Windows.Forms.MenuItem
    Me.mnuEditFile2 = New System.Windows.Forms.MenuItem
    Me.mnuEditFile3 = New System.Windows.Forms.MenuItem
    Me.mnuEditFile4 = New System.Windows.Forms.MenuItem
```

```
' Add them to the Edit menu.
    Me.mnuEdit.MenuItems.Add(Me.mnuFileFile1)
    Me.mnuEdit.MenuItems.Add(Me.mnuFileFile2)
    Me.mnuEdit.MenuItems.Add(Me.mnuFileFile3)
    Me.mnuEdit.MenuItems.Add(Me.mnuFileFile4)

' Configure the filenames.
    Me.mnuEditFile1.Text = strFilename1
    Me.mnuEditFile2.Text = strFilename2
    Me.mnuEditFile3.Text = strFilename3
    Me.mnuEditFile4.Text = strFilename4
End Sub
```

This code sample starts by defining four menu items. It then adds the items to the Edit menu. Finally, it configures the items with the names of the four most recently edited files. In this example, those names are stored in four variables that would presumably be loaded from values retrieved from registry settings or a configuration file.

Now, at this point you might be wondering why you don't just create slots for the four menu items using the Menu Designer and then modify their **Text** properties at runtime. The reason is that by using that approach you would always have four slots reserved for filenames. When you don't have four previous files, you would have too many items. You would also have a problem if you wanted to allow the user to configure the number of previous files to show. So as you can see, knowing how to add menu items at runtime is a good thing.

Building Context-Sensitive Menus

One of the cornerstone features of the Pocket PC environment are context-sensitive menus, or as they are also known, pop-up menus. Context-sensitive menus play such a pivotal role with Pocket PC users because they simplify interfaces and place functionality at the point at where it's needed.

Context-sensitive menus are activated in the Pocket PC environment when the user taps and holds on an object for which a menu has been defined. As the user holds the stylus against the screen of the device, a series of dots are displayed in a circle pattern as shown in Figure 6-10. Continuing to hold down the stylus until the circle is completed will result in the context-sensitive menu being displayed.

Figure 6-10. A series of red dots are displayed just before showing the menu

---

NOTE *Within the Pocket PC emulator, the process of displaying context-sensitive menus is significantly delayed. All that I can tell you is be patient and continue to hold your mouse button down; your menu will eventually be displayed.*

To implement context-sensitive menus with Smart Device Extensions and the .NET Compact Framework requires several steps, which are fairly straightforward once you know what they are. That is the topic of this section—showing you how to create and implement context-sensitive menus in your Pocket PC applications.

Adding a ContextMenu Control

Like regular menus, context-sensitive menus based upon the ContextMenu control are built either with the Menu Designer or completely through code. In this section, we'll walk through the complete process of constructing a context-sensitive menu. Since we've already examined the Menu Designer in detail, I'll focus on the code approach.

The first step in constructing a context-sensitive menu is to add a ContextMenu control to your form. To add a ContextMenu, perform the following steps:

1. In the VS .NET IDE, bring up the form to which you will be adding the ContextMenu.

2. From the Toolbox, double-click the ContextMenu control as shown in Figure 6-11.

Figure 6-11. The ContextMenu control in the Toolbox

A ContextMenu control will be added to the icon tray located below your form. An example of this is shown in Figure 6-12.

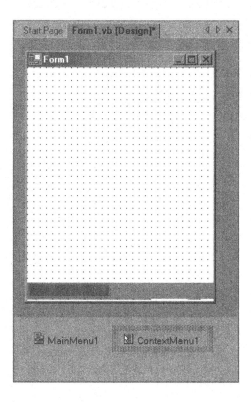

Figure 6-12. The ContextMenu control displayed in the icon tray

This is a good time to set the **Name** property of the ContextMenu control. I like to use the prefix **mnu** (just like regular menus) followed by the name **Context** to identify that this particular menu is a context-sensitive menu.

Configuring the Responding Controls

When you are talking about implementing context-sensitive menus, there are always at least two controls involved, the ContextMenu control and the target control. The target control is the control for which the context-sensitive menu will be displayed. Understand there may be more than a single target control. You can create and associate context-sensitive menus for as many controls on your application's interface as you like.

To associate a ContextMenu control with another control, perform the following steps:

1. From the VS .NET IDE, open the form on which you have added the ContextMenu control.

2. On the form, click the target control.

3. In the Properties window, select the name of your ContextMenu control for the **ContextMenu** property of the target control. An example of this is shown in Figure 6-13.

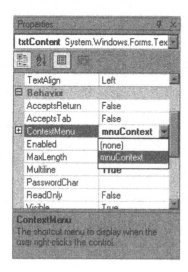

Figure 6-13. Configuring a control to use a ContextMenu control

At this point, you have made the association between your target control and a ContextMenu control, but we've yet to define the pop-up menu to display. That's the topic of the next section.

Coding a Context-Sensitive Menu

As you saw earlier in this chapter, all menus, even those created with the Menu Designer, are in the end implemented through code. Context-sensitive menus are included.

Listing 6-12 shows some simple code that implements a context-sensitive menu that contains three menu items: **Cut**, **Copy**, and **Paste**. We'll walk through this code so that you understand the steps required to construct context-sensitive menus.

Listing 6-12. A Simple Example of Defining a Context-Sensitive Menu

```
Private Sub mnuContext_Popup(ByVal sender As System.Object, _
  ByVal e As System.EventArgs) Handles mnuContext.Popup
    Dim mnuContextCut As New MenuItem
    Dim mnuContextCopy As New MenuItem
    Dim mnuContextPaste As New MenuItem

' Define the menu items.
    mnuContextCut.Text = "Cut"
    mnuContextCopy.Text = "Copy"
    mnuContextPaste.Text = "Paste"

' Clear the contents of the context menu.
    mnuContext.MenuItems.Clear()

' Add the menu items to the context menu.
    mnuContext.MenuItems.Add(mnuContextCut)
    mnuContext.MenuItems.Add(mnuContextCopy)
    mnuContext.MenuItems.Add(mnuContextPaste)

' Add the event handlers for the individual menu items.
    AddHandler mnuContextCut.Click, AddressOf Me.mnuContextCut_OnClick
    AddHandler mnuContextCopy.Click, AddressOf Me.mnuContextCopy_OnClick
    AddHandler mnuContextPaste.Click, AddressOf Me.mnuContextPaste_OnClick

End Sub
```

The first thing to note about this example is that it's contained within the **Popup** event of the ContextMenu control. This event is fired when the user taps and holds the stylus over a control that has been configured to use the ContextMenu control.

The first argument for the **Popup** event procedure is the object that triggered, or caused, the event to fire. In this case, that is the control on which the user is holding the stylus. You can use the information provided by this first argument to create different menus for different target controls. You simply need to check the sending argument and then create the appropriate context-sensitive menu for that target control.

The example shown in Listing 6-12 is simple. It supports a single context-sensitive menu. The event procedure begins by defining three menu items, one for each of the corresponding menu entries of **Cut**, **Copy**, and **Paste**. Next, the **Text** properties for these three items are set. These names are what will appear to the user.

Before you begin to build the menu, you first make sure that the ContextMenu is empty by issuing the **Clear** method of the MenuItems collection. This empties the menu of any existing menu items.

With the menu empty, you're ready to add your three menu items. This is accomplished by using the **Add** method of the MenuItems collection.

Finally, you define three event procedures, one for each menu item that will be called when the user taps on an entry within the context-sensitive menu. The AddHandler statement is used for this. With this statement, you first specify the event to which you are responding as the first argument. The second argument is the event procedure that will be executed when the event occurs.

 NOTE *In situations where you have a single context-sensitive menu within an application, you have the option of configuring the menu a single time, rather than repetitively as shown in Listing 6-12. Simply add a procedure to define the menu to your startup activities. I chose to show you the method demonstrated in Listing 6-12 because you typically will have several context-sensitive menus within an application; in those cases, you would need to use the **Popup** event of the ContextMenu control to define selectively the appropriate menu for the target control.*

 TIP *Instead of using three separate event procedures to handle the individual menu items, you could instead use a single event procedure. To do this, simply define the same event procedure with each of the AddHandler statements in the Listing 6-12 example.*

Responding to Context-Sensitive Menu Events

Building the menus themselves is only half of the task. The other half involves creating the event procedures that will respond to the user selecting an item from the pop-up menu. As shown in Listing 6-13, these types of event procedures are no different than any **Click** event procedures.

Listing 6-13. Example Click Event Procedures for a Context-Sensitive Menu Items

```
Private Sub mnuContextCut_OnClick(ByVal sender As Object, _
  ByVal e As System.EventArgs)
    MsgBox("cut...")
End Sub


Private Sub mnuContextCopy_OnClick(ByVal sender As System.Object, _
  ByVal e As System.EventArgs)
    MsgBox("copy...")
End Sub


Private Sub mnuContextPaste_OnClick(ByVal sender As System.Object, _
  ByVal e As System.EventArgs)
    MsgBox("paste...")
End Sub
```

NOTE *The **Click** event procedure receives the control that triggered the event as the first argument. You can use this to identify the target control in situations where you are sharing a single event procedure between multiple menu items.*

That's everything that you need to know to implement context-sensitive menus for your applications. It's a simple four-step process. First, add a ContextMenu control to your form. Second, configure each of the target controls (the controls that you want to have context-sensitive menus) to use the ContextMenu control by setting their **ContextMenu** property. Third, construct the context-sensitive menu through code. Typically, this is done in the **Popup** event of the ContextMenu control. Finally, code the event procedures that will be fired when the user taps a menu item within your context-sensitive menu.

NOTE *Remember, you could have configured the context-sensitive menu using the Menu Designer. I highly recommend using the designer except in situations where the contents of the context-sensitive menu will vary at runtime.*

That wraps up our discussion of menus. Next, we'll look at another user interface staple—toolbars.

Building ToolBars

The second component to our trifecta of user interface components is the toolbar. Desktop developers should note, when discussing toolbars, that toolbars as they exist in the Pocket PC environment are different from those deployed with a standard desktop application. Most notably, Pocket PC toolbars appear at the bottom of an interface, rather than the top. In addition, they are always limited to a small number of buttons, a restriction that is enforced by the minimal screen real estate offered on the Pocket PC. Both of these traits can be seen in Figure 6-14.

Figure 6-14. A Pocket PC toolbar consisting of two buttons

Why Use ToolBars?

Before we jump into the process of creating a toolbar, let's look first at the why and where for toolbars within an application. Toolbars serve two important roles in an application:

First, they add some spice to your application. Pocket PC applications in general, because of the limited size, tend to be plain in appearance. Toolbars, and the buttons they contain, can give your application's interface visual "punch."

Second, toolbars simplify user interaction. Commonly used functions and features can be placed on a toolbar instead of nested in a menu. The advantage of this is that accessing a toolbar button requires only a single tap. In comparison, a menu item requires at least two taps, and possibly a third if the item is part of a submenu.

 TIP *Try to follow these rules of thumb with toolbars: 1) Use them whenever possible to improve your GUI. 2) Create buttons for the most commonly used features of your application. 3) The purpose of buttons has to be intuitively obvious to the user for them to be effective.*

Constructing a Toolbar

In the following sections, I'm going to show you how to construct a toolbar, from design through to responding to button taps within your code. This process is divided into three steps:

1. **Add and configure an ImageList control.** The ImageList control provides the images that will ultimately be displayed on the buttons of your menu.

2. **Add and configure a ToolBar control.** The ToolBar control defines the buttons that will comprise the physical toolbar as it is displayed to the end user.

3. **Write an event procedure to respond to button taps.** The ToolBar control uses a single event procedure to respond to taps on any of its buttons.

Let's get started with the first step, adding and configuring an ImageList control.

Step 1: The ImageList Control

Using a ToolBar control without an ImageList control is, well, quite bland. It's the ImageList control that provides the splash of graphical excitement found in a toolbar. It's the vessel that holds the images for each of the buttons displayed as part of a toolbar.

Preparing an ImageList control for use with a toolbar requires two steps: adding the ImageList and configuring the ImageList.

Adding an ImageList Control

To add an ImageList control to your application, perform the following steps:

1. In the VS .NET IDE, bring up the form on which you will be adding the ImageList.

2. From the Toolbox, double-click the ImageList control as shown in Figure 6-15.

Figure 6-15. The ImageList control in the Toolbox

An ImageList control will be added to the icon tray located below your form. An example of this is shown in Figure 6-16.

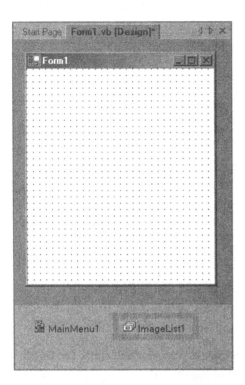

Figure 6-16. The ImageList control displayed in the icon tray

Configuring an ImageList Control

First, set the **Name** property for your ImageList control. While you will rarely refer to the ImageList from within your code, providing a friendly name makes for a cleaner design. I like to use the prefix **img** with ImageList controls.

The only other configuration task is to define the images that will be used with your toolbar. These images are defined through the **Images** property of the ImageList control. This property is comprised of a collection of images. To access the dialog box that enables you to select images, click the ellipse button (...) located at the far right of the **Images** property in the Properties window, as shown in Figure 6-17.

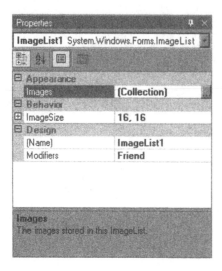

Figure 6-17. The Images property defines the images that will appear on your toolbar.

Clicking the ellipse button (...) for the Images property will cause the Image Collection Editor to be displayed as shown in Figure 6-18.

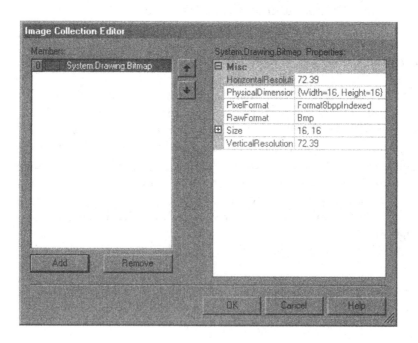

Figure 6-18. The Image Collection Editor

With this editor, you can select, configure, order, and remove images that will be used with your toolbar. Clicking the **Add** button will display an Open dialog box from which you can select the images to include in the ImageList.

NOTE *Images should be 16×16 in size and be at least 256 colors. Be sure to correctly design your images so that they blend in with the toolbar on which they will be displayed.*

The order in which you add images to the ImageList control is how you will need to refer to each image (0, 1, 2, etc.) from the ToolBar control.

TIP *Place the images in the ImageList in the order that they will appear in your ToolBar, from left to right. This makes it much easier to assign the images to the individual buttons.*

Step 2: The ToolBar Control

The next step of this process involves first adding and then configuring a ToolBar control. This process is fairly straightforward. The only slightly difficult task is assigning the individual images from the ImageList control to the buttons offered by the ToolBar.

Adding a ToolBar Control

To add a ToolBar control to your application, perform the following steps:

1. In the VS .NET IDE, bring up the form to which you will be adding the ToolBar.

2. From the Toolbox, double-click the ToolBar control as shown in Figure 6-19.

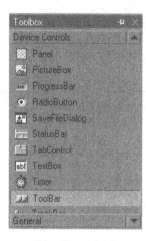

Figure 6-19. The ToolBar control in the Toolbox

A ToolBar control will be added to your form. The tricky part here is that it won't appear anywhere—not on the form nor in the icon tray. So how do you know it was even added? Look in the Properties window. You will see that it's the active object. Don't worry, once you've added a button you'll see that the ToolBar is in fact sitting at the right-end of the menubar.

Configuring a Toolbar Control

As with any process of configuring a control, I recommend starting by setting the **Name** property. For ToolBar controls, I use the prefix **tlb**.

Next, set the **ImageList** property by selecting the name of your ImageList from the drop-down combo box provided with this property.

Finally, we need to define the buttons that will comprise our toolbar. As with the ImageList, the ToolBar control provides a designer to simplify this process. To access this designer, click the ellipse button (...) that is located at the far right of the **Buttons** property line in the Properties window. The ToolBarButton Collection Editor displays as shown in Figure 6-20.

Use the **Add** button to add buttons to your toolbar. The ToolBarButton Collection Editor also allows you to configure the properties for each button. For the purposes of this example, you will want to configure two properties: **Name** and **ImageIndex**. The **ImageIndex** property corresponds to the index (order) that you assigned each of your toolbar images within the ImageList control. Figure 6-21 shows an example of configuring button properties.

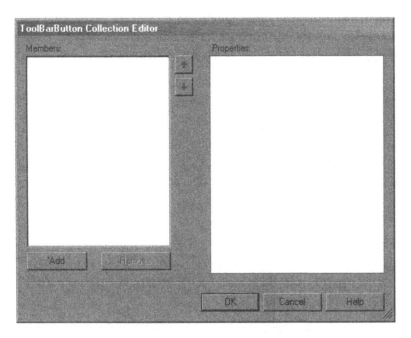

Figure 6-20. The ToolBarButton Collection Editor

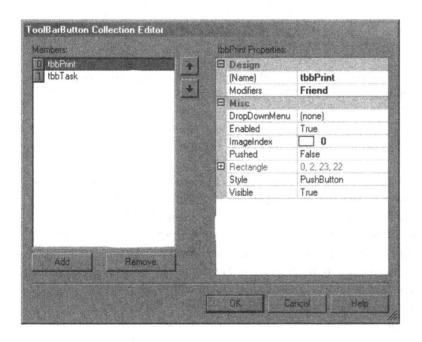

Figure 6-21. Configuring button properties

After adding two buttons, one corresponding to each of the images that you added to the ImageList control, the interface for your toolbar is complete. Finally you can see how it will appear to the user as shown in Figure 6-22.

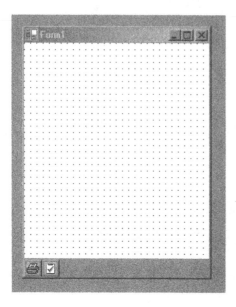

Figure 6-22. The completed interface to the example toolbar

With the interface completed, we're ready to turn our attention to the final step in implementing a toolbar—responding to button taps.

Step 3: Responding to Button Taps

With toolbars, you are only concerned about a single event, the event that fires when the user taps on a button. That event is the **ButtonClick** event. The event procedure for the **ButtonClick** event is shared between all of the buttons.

The only issue when working with this event procedure is determining which button was tapped. This can be easily accomplished by referencing the event arguments passed to the procedure. By referencing **e.Button.ImageIndex**, you can determine the image that was associated with the button that was tapped. This index is the one you originally assigned to the images as you stored them within the ImageList control. Listing 6-14 provides a demonstration of handling the button taps.

Listing 6-14. Handling Button Taps

```
Private Sub tlbMain_ButtonClick(ByVal sender As System.Object, _
    ByVal e As System.Windows.Forms.ToolBarButtonClickEventArgs) _
    Handles tlbMain.ButtonClick
        Select Case e.Button.ImageIndex
          Case 0
            MsgBox("print...")
          Case 1
            MsgBox("task...")
        End Select
End Sub
```

That's all there is to toolbars. Once you know the sequence of steps that you need to go through, they are fairly simple to implement. Next, we'll look at the final piece of our interface trilogy—status bars.

Building Status Bars

Of the three interface components—menus, toolbars, and status bars—status bars are by far the easiest to implement. The reason is simple: They don't offer much in the way of functionality. That doesn't mean that they aren't useful. They are just significantly more limited in their NETCF incarnation than they are under .NET.

Adding status bars to your application involves two steps: adding the control and configuring the properties of the control.

Adding a StatusBar Control

To add a StatusBar control to your application, perform the following steps:

1. In the VS .NET IDE, bring up the form to which you will be adding the StatusBar.

2. From the Toolbox, double-click the StatusBar control as shown in Figure 6-23.

Figure 6-23. The StatusBar control in the Toolbox

A StatusBar control will be added to your form as shown in Figure 6-24. Notice how it's aligned automatically with the bottom of your form, and that it's automatically sized to the width of your form.

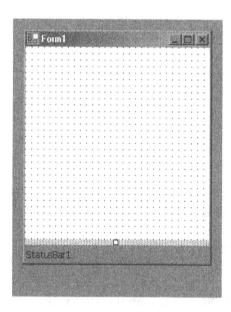

Figure 6-24. The StatusBar control as it appears on a form

Configuring StatusBar Properties

As with every other control that you add, I recommend starting by setting the **Name** property for the StatusBar. For StatusBars, I use the naming prefix **stb**.

The only other property that I usually configure at design time is the **Text** property. The **Text** property defines what displays in the StatusBar. I typically set this to a blank string.

Coding the StatusBar

Working with the StatusBar control in code is simple. Coding activities that involve the StatusBar control generally involve setting the value of the control's **Text** property. An example of this is shown in Listing 6-15.

Listing 6-15. Setting the Text Property of the StatusBar Control

```
Private Sub Button1_Click(ByVal sender As System.Object, _
  ByVal e As System.EventArgs) Handles Button1.Click
    stbMain.Text = "status message..."
End Sub
```

That's it for status bars. That also concludes our overview of three key components of interface design for the Pocket PC—menus, toolbars, and status bars. The remainder of this chapter is comprised of a step-by-step tutorial that pulls together many of the techniques presented in this chapter into a single application.

Step-by-Step Tutorial: Menus and Toolbars

In this step-by-step tutorial, you'll create a Pocket PC project that provides a practical demonstration of various techniques presented in this chapter. As part of this exercise, you will

- Construct a menu at design time.

- Construct a toolbar at design time.

- Add code to respond to menu events.

- Implement a context-sensitive menu.

- Add code to respond to toolbar events.

This simple application provides the foundation for a text editor, much like Microsoft Notepad. Please note that none of the functionality that you would expect to find with a text editor—opening files, saving files, etc.—is provided with this application.

NOTE *If you are really in need of another Notepad knockoff, see Chapter 8, where you learn how to write text to and read text from a file.*

 NOTE *A completed version of this application, titled MenuDemo, is provided under **Chapter 6** of the **Samples** folder containing the sample applications for this book. See Appendix D for more information on accessing and loading samples.*

The complete interface of this step-by-step project is shown in Figure 6-25.

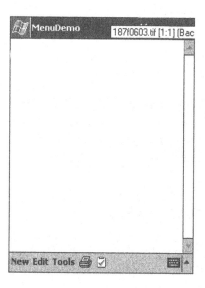

Figure 6-25. The MenuDemo application in its completed form

Step 1: Starting a New Project

Begin this step-by-step exercise by creating a new project using the following steps:

1. Start Visual Studio .NET if necessary.

2. From the Start Page, select **New Project**.

3. From the New Project dialog box, select **Smart Device Application**.

4. Specify a project name of **MenuDemo**.

5. Select a location to create the project and click the **OK** button.

Step 2: Configuring the Project

Before jumping into building the application, you need to define the output file folder for the project. Perform the following steps to set this property:

1. Under the Project menu, select **MenuDemo Properties**.

2. Under the Device page of the MenuDemo Property Pages dialog box, set the output file folder to **\Windows\Start Menu\Programs\Apress**.

TIP   *Using **\Windows\Start Menu\Programs** as the output folder will add your application under the **Programs** folder that can be accessed from the Start menu on your Pocket PC device. This is a good way to organize your test applications and make them easy to access.*

NOTE   *If you are unsure of the purpose of project properties, or how to set them, refer to Chapter 3, which provides a detailed overview of this topic.*

Step 3: Constructing the Interface

Now we get into the fun stuff. After all, that is what this chapter is all about, making cool Pocket PC interfaces. For this sample application you need to add four controls:

-   TextBox

-   ContextMenu

-   ImageList

-   ToolBar

The Pocket PC Windows Application template has already added the fifth control that is part of this interface, the MainMenu control.

Step 4: Setting Properties

Table 6-2 details the handful of properties that need to be defined.

Table 6-2. Properties to Set for the Controls

OBJECT	PROPERTY	VALUE
Form1	Text	MenuDemo
TextBox	Name	txtContent
TextBox	Multiline	True
TextBox	ScrollBars	Vertical
TxtBox	Text	(empty)
MainMenu	Name	mnuMain
ContextMenu	Name	mnuContext
TextBox	ContextMenu	mnuContext
ImageList	Name	imgToolbar
ToolBar	Name	tlbMain
ToolBar	ImageList	imgToolbar

Resize the TextBox control so that it consumes the body of your form, everything between the title and menubars.

Step 5: Building the Menu

The MenuDemo application has three menus: New, Edit, and Tools. To build the New and Edit menus, perform the following steps:

1. If it's not already open, open Form1.

2. Form1 should already have a MainMenu control. Click this control.

3. Let's begin by renaming the MainMenu control to something less generic. In the Properties window, rename the MainMenu control to **mnuMain**.

4. We're now ready to start constructing the menu. Click the dark box located in the lower-left corner of the form. This will activate the Menu Designer.

5. Enter **New** for the first menu name. In the Properties window, set the **Name** property of this menu to **mnuNew**.

6. Add a second menu, **Edit**. In the Properties window, set its **Name** property to **mnuEdit**.

7. Build the rest of the Edit menu using the values specified in Table 6-3. The menu items are presented in the table in the order that they should be created.

Table 6-3. File Menu Item Properties

TEXT	NAME	ENABLED
Cut	mnuEditCut	False
Copy	mnuEditCopy	False
Paste	mnuEditPaste	False
Clear	mnuEditClear	True
Select All	mnuEditSelectAll	True
	mnuEditBar1	True
Find/Replace	mnuEditFind	True

Figure 6-26 shows the finished Edit menu.

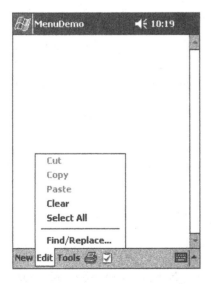

Figure 6-26. The Edit menu

With the Edit menu complete, we can turn our attention to the Tools menu. To build this menu, perform the following steps:

1. Click the box next to the Edit menu.

2. Enter **Tools** for the third menu name. In the Properties window, set the **Name** property of this menu to **mnuTools**.

3. Build the rest of the Tools menu using the values specified in Table 6-4.

Table 6-4. Tools Menu Item Properties

TEXT	NAME	ENABLED
Beam Document...	mnuToolsBeam	True
	mnuToolsBar1	True
Save Document As...	mnuToolsSaveAs	True
Delete Document	mnuToolsDelete	True

Figure 6-27 shows the finished Tools menu.

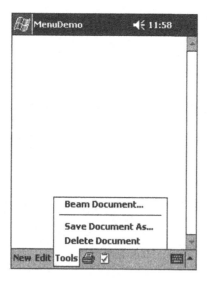

Figure 6-27. The Tools menu

That completes the menu for your application. Next, we'll turn our attention to building the toolbar.

Step 6: Loading the ImageList

Start the process of building the toolbar by first configuring the ImageList that will provide the graphics that will be displayed on the toolbar.

To load the ImageList control with the images that will be used with the ToolBar, perform the following steps:

1. With your form displayed, click the ImageList control icon in the icon tray.

2. In the Properties window, click the ellipse button (...) located at the right end of the **Images** property row. The Image Collection Editor will be displayed.

3. Add the two images defined in Table 6-5. These images are located under **Chapter 6** of the **Samples** folder.

Table 6-5. Images to Add to the ImageList Control

IMAGE	FILENAME
Print	print.bmp
Task	task.bmp

You have completed configuration of the ImageList control. Close the Image Collection Editor and proceed to the next step.

Step 7: Defining the ToolBar Buttons

With the ImageList loaded, you're ready to define the ToolBar buttons. There will be two buttons on your toolbar, one corresponding to each of the images that you loaded into the ImageList.

To define the buttons for the ToolBar, perform the following steps:

1. With your form displayed, click the ToolBar control. Even though you can't see it, the ToolBar control is located at the right end of the menubar on your form.

2. In the Properties window, click the ellipse button (...) located at the right end of the **Buttons** property row. The ToolBarButton Collection Editor will be displayed.

3. Add the buttons defined in Table 6-6.

Table 6-6. Buttons to Add to the ToolBar Control

BUTTON	NAME	IMAGEINDEX
Print	tbbPrint	0
Task	tbbTask	1

That's it for the ToolBar and for that matter the graphical component of this application. You can close the ToolBarButton Collection Editor. At this point, if you've done everything right, your application should appear as shown in Figure 6-28.

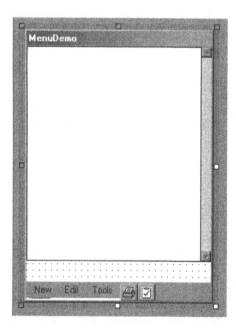

Figure 6-28. The completed interface to the MenuDemo application

Next, we'll turn our attention to the code behind this demonstration application.

Step 8: Coding the Menu

Let me tell you from the outset that the code behind this demonstration app is provided just to verify that the program is working and that everything is wired correctly. It's not in any way intended to implement actual functionality. This is a shell of a text editor, not an actual text editor.

With that said, let's look at the code required to respond to each of the menu items that you created earlier in this exercise. For the New menu you need a single event procedure. Add the code shown in Listing 6-16 to your application to handle this item.

Listing 6-16. Implementing the New Menu

```
Private Sub mnuNew_Click(ByVal sender As System.Object, _
  ByVal e As System.EventArgs) Handles mnuNew.Click
    MsgBox("new...")
End Sub
```

For the Edit menu you need six event procedures: **Cut**, **Copy**, **Paste**, **Clear**, **Select All**, and **Find/Replace**. The code for each of these items is shown in Listing 6-17.

Listing 6-17. Implementing the Edit Menu Items

```
' *** the Cut menu item ***
Private Sub mnuEditCut_Click(ByVal sender As System.Object, _
  ByVal e As System.EventArgs) Handles mnuEditCut.Click
    MsgBox("cut...")
End Sub


' *** the Copy menu item ***
Private Sub mnuEditCopy_Click(ByVal sender As System.Object, _
  ByVal e As System.EventArgs) Handles mnuEditCopy.Click
    MsgBox("copy...")
End Sub


' *** the Paste menu item ***
Private Sub mnuEditPaste_Click(ByVal sender As System.Object, _
  ByVal e As System.EventArgs) Handles mnuEditPaste.Click
    MsgBox("paste...")
End Sub


' *** the Clear menu item ***
Private Sub mnuEditClear_Click(ByVal sender As System.Object, _
  ByVal e As System.EventArgs) Handles mnuEditClear.Click
    MsgBox("clear...")
End Sub
```

```
' *** the Select All menu item ***
Private Sub mnuEditSelectAll_Click(ByVal sender As System.Object, _
  ByVal e As System.EventArgs) Handles mnuEditSelectAll.Click
    MsgBox("select all...")
End Sub


' *** the Find/Replace menu item ***
Private Sub mnuEditFind_Click(ByVal sender As System.Object, _
  ByVal e As System.EventArgs) Handles mnuEditFind.Click
    MsgBox("find/replace...")
End Sub
```

Listing 6-18 shows the **Click** event procedures for this ToolBar's menu items.

Listing 6-18. Toggling the Auto Save Feature

```
' *** the Beam menu item ***
Private Sub mnuToolsBeam_Click(ByVal sender As System.Object, _
  ByVal e As System.EventArgs) Handles mnuToolsBeam.Click
    MsgBox("beam...")
End Sub


' *** the Save As menu item ***
Private Sub mnuToolsSaveAs_Click(ByVal sender As System.Object, _
    ByVal e As System.EventArgs) Handles mnuToolsSaveAs.Click
    MsgBox("save as...")
End Sub


' *** the Delete menu item ***
Private Sub mnuToolsDelete_Click(ByVal sender As System.Object, _
  ByVal e As System.EventArgs) Handles mnuToolsDelete.Click
    MsgBox("delete...")
End Sub
```

That takes care of the menu and related items. Next you'll build the code to implement the context-sensitive menu.

Step 9: Coding the Context-Sensitive Menu

The coding behind implementing a context-sensitive menu can be divided into two parts: 1) implementing the menu, and 2) responding to the user tapping on the menu items. We'll start by looking at how the menu is implemented.

The context-sensitive menu that we're adding to this demonstration application will pop up in response to the user tapping and holding the stylus over the TextBox control. The ContextMenu control was added earlier in this exercise. The TextBox control has already been configured to use this control. All that remains is for you to include a bit of code that will create the menu. That code is shown in Listing 6-19.

Listing 6-19. Creating the Context-Sensitive Menu

```
Private Sub mnuContext_Popup(ByVal sender As System.Object, _
  ByVal e As System.EventArgs) Handles mnuContext.Popup
    Dim mnuContextCut As New MenuItem
    Dim mnuContextCopy As New MenuItem
    Dim mnuContextPaste As New MenuItem

' Define the menu items.
    mnuContextCut.Text = "Cut"
    mnuContextCopy.Text = "Copy"
    mnuContextPaste.Text = "Paste"

' Clear the contents of the context menu.
    mnuContext.MenuItems.Clear()

' Add the menu items to the context menu.
    mnuContext.MenuItems.Add(mnuContextCut)
    mnuContext.MenuItems.Add(mnuContextCopy)
    mnuContext.MenuItems.Add(mnuContextPaste)

' Add the event handlers for the individual menu items.
    AddHandler mnuContextCut.Click, AddressOf Me.mnuContextCut_OnClick
    AddHandler mnuContextCopy.Click, AddressOf Me.mnuContextCopy_OnClick
    AddHandler mnuContextPaste.Click, AddressOf Me.mnuContextPaste_OnClick

End Sub
```

This code is placed in the **Popup** event of the ContextMenu control. In this procedure you first create three new menu items. Next, you set the **Text** properties for each item. As you can see from the code, the three menu items will be **Cut**, **Copy**, and **Paste**. You then clear the context menu. Following that you add the three items to the menu. Finally, you define the three event procedures that will be called when the user taps on a menu item.

All that you need to do to complete the context-sensitive menu is to create the three **Click** event procedures for the menu items. These procedures are shown in Listing 6-20.

Listing 6-20. The Click Event Procedures for the Cut, Copy, and Paste Menu Items

```
Private Sub mnuContextCut_OnClick(ByVal sender As Object, _
  ByVal e As System.EventArgs)
    MsgBox("cut...")
End Sub


Private Sub mnuContextCopy_OnClick(ByVal sender As System.Object, _
  ByVal e As System.EventArgs)
    MsgBox("copy...")
End Sub


Private Sub mnuContextPaste_OnClick(ByVal sender As System.Object, _
  ByVal e As System.EventArgs)
    MsgBox("paste...")
End Sub
```

That's all of the code required to implement and respond to the context-sensitive menu. That leaves one item to code, the ToolBar.

Step 10: Coding the ToolBar

As I explained earlier in this chapter, the ToolBar uses a single event procedure, **ButtonClick**, to handle taps on any buttons it contains. In this example application, you have two buttons. Handling each of these buttons is shown in Listing 6-21, where a check is made against the **ImageIndex** property to determine which button was tapped.

Listing 6-21. Responding to Button Taps

```
Private Sub tlbMain_ButtonClick(ByVal sender As Object, _
  ByVal e As System.Windows.Forms.ToolBarButtonClickEventArgs) _
  Handles tlbMain.ButtonClick
    Select Case e.Button.ImageIndex
      Case 0
        MsgBox("print...")
      Case 1
        MsgBox("task...")
    End Select
End Sub
```

That completes the construction of the application. All that remains is to test your work.

Step 11: Testing Your Application

To test your application, perform the following steps:

1. Select either **Pocket PC Device** or **Pocket PC Emulator** from the Deployment Device combo box.

2. Select **Release** from the Solution Configurations combo box.

3. Click the **Start** button.

Your application copies to the target device and runs. It should appear as shown in Figure 6-29.

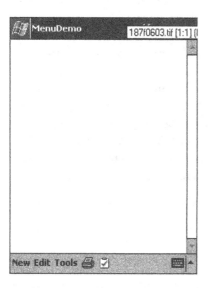

Figure 6-29. The MenuDemo application

 Homework   *Enhance your simple text editor shell by adding code to generate menu items for the four most recently added files under the Edit menu.*

Homework *Modify the code that creates the context menu used with the TextBox so that its menu items, **Cut**, **Copy**, and **Paste**, are only enabled when applicable. For example, the **Cut** and **Copy** menu items won't be enabled unless some text is selected.*

Summary

Menus, toolbars, and status bars, oh my! Certainly, you can develop successful Pocket PC applications without these controls. The question is why would you want to? These three controls offer so much in the way of appearance and functionality that they should be considered long and hard for every application you build.

Menus are a staple of Pocket PC applications. Construction of menus is simple using the Menu Designer. Coding of menus is only slightly harder.

Context-sensitive menus, while slightly more complicated than menus to implement, are another interface feature that should be part of most, if not all, of your applications. There are two reasons for this: First, Pocket PC users have come to expect pop-up menus. Second, they place functionality at the point it's needed.

Toolbars offer a powerful one-two combo: cool appearance and end-user ease. Graphics on buttons offer just the right amount of visual spice to make a user interface exciting. More importantly, anytime you can cut down on the number of taps required from the user, you are going to have a better application.

The final member of this trio of controls is the status bar. Yes, it's limited in the incarnation provided through the .NET Compact Framework. Stop your whining and use them anyway. They offer a wonderful means to keep your user informed as to what is going on in your application. That is always a good thing.

CHAPTER 7

Graphics

IF YOU LOOK AT ANY APPLICATION on the Pocket PC, you'll notice right away that the developers weren't using your standard set of controls. There are three basic areas where you'll find yourself using the graphics provided by the .NET Compact Framework. You can write your own custom controls and change their look at the same time. A second opportunity is when you want to show some data to the user in a report form. Perhaps you want to generate a pie chart, or bar graph, or line graph. You have almost as much power drawing on a Pocket PC as you do on the desktop. The third area has to do with displaying graphic images. You can load and display bitmaps, icons, and more onto just about any surface.

I want to make a point about something here that you may see referenced incorrectly in papers or articles (I made the mistake myself for a while). In the desktop .NET Framework, the graphics namespace and the functionality it provides is referred to as GDI+. (For more information on developing GDI+ applications on the desktop, you can read *GDI+ Programming in C# and VB .NET* by Nick Symmonds [Apress. ISBN: 1-59059-035-X]). On the NETCF platform, the graphics engine is only referred to as GDI (which stands for Graphics Device Interface). The plus (+) stuff was left on the desktop.

This chapter will cover each of the areas just discussed. And as in Chapter 5, I'll show you how to create a custom control, but unlike in Chapter 5, I'll focus more extensively on the GDI side of the control. I'll also show how you can create colored and transparent backgrounds in labels, which aren't provided by the CF.

Some Basic Knowledge

There are some basic terms to define and introductions to make before we can get into the hard-core graphics manipulation. You need to understand the classes that are integral to doing even the simplest drawing with GDI. Anytime you draw something other than a bitmap, you'll need to specify a color for the object.

NOTE *By bitmap, I mean any of the group of images supported by NETCF. The types currently supported by the .NET Compact Framework are bitmaps, icons, JPEGs, TIF files, etc.*

297

Colors are represented by a Color structure. This structure has standard colors defined as static properties. The following sets a Color structure to a pre-defined color:

```
Dim _activeColor  As Color = Color.LightGreen
Dim _disabledColor As Color = Color.DarkGreen
```

You can also create your own colors by using the **FromArgb** method of the Color structure. There are four overloads in the desktop, but only two of them are supported in the .NET Compact Framework.

```
Dim _activeColor As Color = Color.FromArgb(155, 155, 155)
Dim _disabledColor As Color = Color.FromArgb(&H7800FF00)
```

The first overload takes the Red, Green, Blue values as individual values, while the second overload takes the alpha blending value. But before you get excited, the alpha component value is ignored in NETCF. While the documentation is usually good about what is and what isn't supported in the .NET Compact Framework, this is one of the few places that it leads you down the proverbial primrose path. The examples say you can do transparent colors, but those examples were actually written for the desktop framework.

 NOTE *Colors are structures, meaning that they are **Value** types. As such, you don't need to worry about releasing them or disposing of them. They're created on the stack and are destroyed by the system when they go out of scope.*

Once you have defined a color, you'll naturally want to use it to do something. There are two classes that you'll use in drawing graphics in NETCF: **SolidBrush** and **Pen**. Speaking of brushes, this would be a good time to mention that although you may be familiar with the five different brushes available on the desktop, guess what, only one is supported on in the .NET Compact Framework. A SolidBrush is used to draw filled objects, while a Pen is used to draw lines.

```
Dim activeBrush As SolidBrush =  New SolidBrush(Color.Blue)
Dim activePen As Pen = New Pen(Color.Red)
...
activeBrush.Dispose
activePen.Dispose
```

Constructing a Pen or a Brush is pretty simple and straightforward. You specify a color and the object is ready to use.

NOTE   *Both Pen and SolidBrush objects are classes, meaning that they are **Reference** types. As such, you must be sure to call the **Dispose** method on them before leaving scope.*

TIP   *Since Pen and SolidBrush objects require some construction to allocate space for them on the heap, I often create them in the class's constructor. This technique keeps me from creating and destroying them repeatedly as various methods of my class are called. This technique also requires that I implement the IDisposable interface on my class so that when the class's **Dispose** method is called, the resources get cleaned up in a timely manner.*

I know that I'm getting antsy to do some drawing—maybe you are too?—but we still have a little foundation work to do. As mentioned a little earlier, you can draw lines or shapes. When drawing shapes, you have several ways of determining the shape that the drawing will take. Based on the method you've decided to use, you might need an array of Point objects or just a Rectangle object.

```
Dim rect As Rectangle = New Rectangle(0, 0, 100, 100)
Dim pnt As Point = New Point(10, 10)
Dim arrayPoints() As Point = New Point(3) _
    {New Point(0, 0), New Point(10, 0), New Point(10, 10), New Point(0, 10)}
```

The last line of the preceding code snippet builds an array of points that can be used to draw a shape that is *not* defined as a simple rectangle or ellipse. In order to do the actual drawing, you need a Graphics object. You can get a Graphics object two ways: Create one yourself or use the one passed to you in the **Paint** or **OnPaint** events.

```
Private Sub Button_Paint(ByVal sender As Object, _
    ByVal e As System.Windows.Forms.PaintEventArgs) _
    Handles btnTest.Paint
End Sub
```

Okay, where is it? I told you that you were passed a Graphics object, but you don't see one, right? Well, it's actually one of the properties of the **PaintEventArgs** parameter. The Graphics object is what is used to draw on the form surface. If you've ever written Win32 apps, in Win32 parlance this would be analogous to a forms device context. If you use the Graphics object supplied through the **PaintEventArgs** parameter, you don't need to worry about disposing of the object. However, if you create your own, you *do* need to call its **Dispose** method.

NOTE *I have made a couple of points so far about the difference between value types and reference types. I have also talked about the need to dispose of reference objects when you are finished with them. Let me reiterate this point again.* When you create a reference object, you MUST dispose of it when you are finished using the object. *One of the biggest problems that C++ developers have encountered over the years is memory leaks. Before .NET, Visual Basic developers had been pretty well insulated from those problems. Now, in the .NET world, you have to contend with memory leaks. That is what you'll get if you fail to properly dispose of your objects. Failing to close and dispose of an open file handle will make it impossible to reopen the same file until the garbage collector has cleaned up. Forgetting to dispose of a Font object can cause nasty problems that are very difficult to debug.*

The other property of **PaintEventArgs** is **ClipRectangle**. This rectangle is the area of the graphics context that requires painting. Where does this clipped area come from? When you want to force an **OnPaint** event, you can invalidate an entire form or only a portion of that form. There are two overloaded methods for **Invalidate** on the **Control** class (from which a form is derived) in the .NET Compact Framework.

```
Me.Invalidate( New Rectangle(0, 0, 100, 100) )
Me.Invalidate()
```

When you get **OnPaint**, you can look at the clipped region to see which area of the control actually needs repainting. This can be beneficial for several reasons, the biggest of which is related to speed. To increase the speed that the control is repainted, you only need to redraw a portion of the control. This may or may not be important to you, and if it isn't, just ignore the clipped region and repaint the entire control. We'll look at some examples later in the chapter. I can hear you now, "When are we ever going to actually *draw* something?" Well, the wait is over.

Okay, Let's Draw Something

I'll start this section with an example, shown in Listing 7-1, that uses the basic graphics methods that draw shapes on the device.

Listing 7-1. Using FillRectangle

```
Protected Overrides Sub OnPaint(ByVal e As System.Windows.Forms.PaintEventArgs)
    Dim g As Drawing.Graphics = e.Graphics
    Dim bshRectFill As SolidBrush = New SolidBrush(Color.LightBlue)
    g.FillRectangle(bshRectFill , Me.ClientRectangle)
    bshRectFill.Dispose()
End Sub
```

This simple code creates a local reference to the Graphics object and uses that instance to call the **FillRectangle** method. **FillRectangle** has two overloads in the .NET Compact Framework; one takes a rectangle that defines the boundaries of the filled area, while the other takes coordinates to the upper left of the rectangle and its width and height. Both methods require a System.Drawing.Brush object, which you create with the New statement and then dispose of when you are finished.

If you use the **DrawRectangle** method, then instead of a Brush object you use a Pen object. In Listing 7-2, you can see how to alter the color of a Pen without causing additional object creation.

Listing 7-2. Using DrawRectangle

```
Protected Overrides Sub OnPaint(ByVal e As System.Windows.Forms.PaintEventArgs)
    Dim g As Drawing.Graphics = e.Graphics
    Dim penRect As Pen = New Pen(Color.Black)
    g.DrawRectangle(penRect, Me.ClientRectangle)
    penRect.Dispose()
End Sub
```

If your routine requires that you create several Pen objects, you might want to look at creating a single Pen and changing its color as needed. You can change a Pen's color by changing its **Color** property, as shown in the example in Listing 7-3.

Listing 7-3. Drawing Rectangles with Different Colors

```
Dim penRect As Pen = New Pen(Color.Black)
g.DrawRectangle(penRect, Me.ClientRectangle)
penRect.Color = Color.Red
```

```
g.DrawRectangle(penRect, Me.ClientRectangle.Left + 15, _
    Me.ClientRectangle.Top + 15, _
    Me.ClientRectangle.Width - 30, _
    Me.ClientRectangle.Height - 30)
penRect.Color = Color.Green
g.DrawRectangle(penRect, Me.ClientRectangle.Left + 10, _
    Me.ClientRectangle.Top + 10, _
    Me.ClientRectangle.Width - 20, _
    Me.ClientRectangle.Height - 20)
penRect.Dispose()
```

This technique can be useful if the speed of your graphics routines is important. Again, it gets down to whether it's faster to change a property or to create and destroy additional objects. The **FillRectangle** and **DrawRectangle** method are good for drawing four-sided shapes that are bounded by the defining points. And guess what? To draw circles, and more generally ellipses, you use the **DrawEllipse** and **FillEllipse** methods, as shown in Listing 7-4.

Listing 7-4. Drawing Ellipses

```
Try
    Dim g As System.Drawing.Graphics = e.Graphics
    Dim myColor = Color.FromArgb(155, 155, 155)
    Dim myColor2 = Color.FromArgb(&H7800FF00)

    g.FillEllipse(New SolidBrush(myColor), 75, 25, 100, 100)
    g.FillEllipse(New SolidBrush(myColor2), 125, 100, 100, 100)
    g.FillEllipse(New SolidBrush(Color.FromArgb(75, 0, 75)), 25, 100, 100, 100)
Catch ex As Exception
    MessageBox.Show("An error occurred creating the images")
Finally
    g.Dispose()
End Try
```

These four methods take care of the simple drawing functions that create either ellipses or rectangles within a bounding area. Figure 7-1 shows the output from the code in Listing 7-4.

Figure 7-1. Drawing ellipses

To draw more complex shapes, you need to look to the next set of methods, **Regions** and **Polygons**. Polygons are multisided shapes that include the equilateral shapes we know as pentagons, octagons, and so-forth-agons. While the rectangle drawing was done by specifying the bounds within which the rectangle was to be drawn, polygons require you to specify the points that define the end of each of the connecting lines that create the outside of the shape. Listing 7-5 shows how you would draw an eight-sided shape.

Listing 7-5. Drawing an Eight-Sided Polygon

```
Dim g As Drawing.Graphics = Me.CreateGraphics()
Dim arrayPoints() As Point = New Point(7) {
    New Point(100, 50), New Point(150, 50), New Point(200, 100), _
    New Point(200, 150), New Point(150, 200), New Point(100, 200), _
    New Point(50, 150), New Point(50, 100)}
Dim penLine As Pen = New Pen(Color.Red)
g.DrawPolygon(penLine, arrayPoints)
penLine.Dispose()
```

The **FillPolygon** method is the same, except, of course, it requires SolidBrush instead of a Pen as the first parameter. Notice that you don't need to close the shape by specifying the first and last point to be the same. The class automatically connects your last point to the first point to compete the shape.

The last method to cover is **FillRegion**. This method can be employed to make some rather unusual shapes by using methods on the Region object. The following example shows how you can use the **Region** class to create some rather odd shapes. The output of the code can be seen in Figure 7-2.

Figure 7-2. Complex shapes with regions

```
Dim regionBrush As SolidBrush = New SolidBrush(Color.Red)
Dim excludeRegion As Region = New Region(New Rectangle(75, 75, 100, 100))
excludeRegion.Xor(New Rectangle(50, 50, 75, 150))
excludeRegion.Intersect(New Rectangle(50, 50, 100, 100))
g.FillRegion(regionBrush, excludeRegion)
excludeRegion.Dispose()
```

Table 7-1 shows a summary of the methods of the Graphics object used to draw shapes and (the as of yet undiscussed) lines and text.

Table 7-1. Key Properties of the Graphics Class

METHOD	DESCRIPTION
DrawEllipse	Draws an ellipse using a bounded area
DrawIcon	Draws an icon
DrawImage	Draws an image
DrawLine	Draws a line using end points
DrawPolygon	Draws a polygon using end points
DrawRectangle	Draws a rectangle using a bounded area
DrawString	Draws a text string using a bounded area
FillEllipse	Fills an ellipse using a bounded area
FillPolygon	Fills a polygon-shaped area using end points
FillRectangle	Fills a rectangle using a bounded area
FillRegion	Fills the inside of an irregular rectangular shape composed by the union, intersection, or exclusion of various other rectangles

The last drawing method we need to look at quickly is the **DrawLine** method. To create a line, you specify a Pen object and the end points of the line to draw as follows:

```
Dim penLine As Pen = New Pen(Color.DodgerBlue)
g.DrawLine(penLine, 0, 0, Me.ClientRectangle.Width, Me.ClientRectangle.Height)
```

That's it for a line. And that's it for this section about drawing simple shapes. Before we move on to tackling a large-scale project, I want to cover one more item: drawing strings.

HOMEWORK   *Create some of your own shapes using the* ***DrawPolygon***. *Create the array of points for a pentagon, hexagon, or any multisided shape that you want to experiment with. Speaking of experimenting, write some code to try out different combinations of the* ***Exclude***, ***Intersect***, ***Complement***, ***Union***, *and* ***Xor*** *methods of the* ***Region*** *class.*

Drawing Strings

Table 7-1 mentions the method **DrawString**, which we'll take a closer look at here. You can see an example of using this method in the following code snippet:

```
Dim fnt as Font = New Font("Arial", 8, FontStyle.Bold)
Dim brush As SolidBrush = New SolidBrush(Color.Red)
g.DrawString("This is a string", fnt, brush, 0, 50)
brush.Dispose()
fnt.Dispose()
```

DrawString requires the text string to draw, a Font object, a SolidBrush object, and either the coordinates of the upper-left corner to place the text or a bounding rectangle into which the text will be drawn. If the string doesn't fit in the bounding rectangle, then it's wrapped to multiple lines, if the rectangle has enough height. Any text that doesn't fit is simply cut off.

If you need the entire string to fit into a specified rectangle, then you have a few more steps to do. The Graphics object exposes a method called **MeasureString**. When you call this method, you specify the text string to be displayed and the Font object describing the requested appearance.

```
Dim fnt As Font = new Font("Arial", 12, FontStyle.Bold)
Dim brush As SolidBrush = New SolidBrush(Color.Red)
Dim siz As SizeF = g.MeasureString(this.Text, fnt)
g.DrawString("This is a Test String", _
    fnt, _
    brush, _
New RectangleF(0, 0, siz.Width, siz.Height))
```

The two important properties of the SizeF structure are the **Height** and **Width**. You can use these properties to calculate the size of the rectangle that is required to hold the entire string as I show in the preceding code snippet.

Step-by-Step Tutorial: Creating a New Button

In this tutorial, you'll create a new command button that has rounded edges and a colored button surface. This control will have multiple properties related to its visual appearance (i.e., colors, enabled state, and so on) and will also handle various events. This tutorial won't go into detail about portions of control development that were covered in Chapter 5. Any new features of control development will be covered, but this tutorial is meant as a graphics tutorial.

NOTE   *I provide a completed version of this application, titled RoundButton Demo, under the **Chapter 7** folder of the **Samples** folder for this book. See Appendix D for more information on accessing and loading the sample applications.*

Step 1: Starting a New Project

In practice, you would want to create a separate project for your control and a project to test the control. So, to keep this tutorial as real as possible, you'll develop two separate projects. Begin this step-by-step exercise by creating a new project using the following steps:

1. Start Visual Studio .NET if necessary.

2. From the Start Page, select to create a **New Project**.

3. From the New Project dialog box, select **Smart Device Application**.

4. Specify a project name of **RoundButton Demo**.

5. Select a location in which to create the project.

6. Select a project type of **Class Library** and click the **OK** button.

Step 2: Adding References

Since you created your project as a class library, only a small subset of references were added by the wizard. To add the references to your project, perform the following steps:

1. In the Solution Explorer, right-click **References** and click **Add Reference**.

2. Select **System.Drawing** from the Component Name column and then click the **Select** button.

3. Select **System.Windows.Forms** from the Component Name column and then click the **Select** button.

4. Click **OK**.

Step 3: Configuring the Project

To configure the target output folder for your project, perform the following steps:

1. Under the Project menu, select **RoundButton Properties**.

2. Under the Device page of the Text File Property Pages dialog box, set the output file folder to **\Windows\Start Menu\Programs\Apress**.

Step 4: Naming Your Control Class

To change the control's name from Class1.vb to RoundButton.vb, perform the following steps:

1. Click the filename **Class1.vb** in the Solution Explorer.

2. Change the filename in the Properties Box to **RoundButton.vb**.

3. Open the **RoundButton Class** module.

Step 5: Inheriting the Control Class

The RoundButton control is based upon the **Control** class. You accomplish this by adding a single line of code to your **Class** module.

Perform the following steps to add the line of code to inherit the **Control** class:

1. Open the **RoundButton Class** module.

2. Insert **Inherits System.Windows.Forms.Control** in the **Class** module as shown:

```
Public Class RoundButton
    Inherits System.Windows.Forms.Control
End Class
```

Step 6: Creating Class-Level Variables

You need variables to hold the enabled and disabled color of the button. You also need to track the button state as either up or pressed. (You'll see why later.) Add the declarations to the editor so that your code appears as shown:

```
Public Class RoundButton
    Inherits System.Windows.Forms.Control


    Private _buttonDrawnDown As Boolean = False
    Private _btnColor As Color = Color.LightGreen
    Private _btnDisabledColor As Color = Color.DarkGreen
End Class
```

Step 7: Adding the OnPaint Event

You need to draw the control in several locations other than just in the **OnPaint** event. Keeping that in mind, you have a very small and simple event to code. Perform the following steps to add this procedure:

1. Open the **RoundButton Class** module.

2. Add the following code to the **Class** module:

```
Protected Overrides Sub OnPaint( _
        ByVal e As System.Windows.Forms.PaintEventArgs)
    DrawButton(e.Graphics, Me.ForeColor, _btnColor)
    MyBase.OnPaint(e)
End Sub
```

This procedure calls out to your DrawButton routine that we'll get to shortly. In the meantime, notice that you are passing three arguments to the method. The first is a Graphics object that you pull from the **PaintEventArgs** parameter. The second argument is the control's own foreground color. Since you are deriving it from **Control**, you can use the control's existing colors, among other properties, by referencing your base class through the **Me** keyword.

Step 8: Creating Your DrawButton Method

You need to draw the control in several other locations rather than just in the **OnPaint** event. Keeping that in mind, you have another very small and simple event to code. Perform the following steps to add this procedure:

1. Open the **RoundButton Class** module.

2. Add the code in Listing 7-6 to the **Class** module.

Listing 7-6. Custom Drawing Your Own Button

```vbnet
Private Sub DrawButton(ByVal g As Graphics, _
        ByVal fColor As Color, ByVal bColor As Color)
    '    Use the button height as the diameter of the round end
    Dim bRadius As Int32 = Me.ClientRectangle.Height / 2
    '    Create a Brush object and initialize it to Nothing
    Dim sb As Brush = Nothing

    If Me.Enabled Then
        sb = New SolidBrush(bColor)
    Else
        sb = New SolidBrush(_btnDisabledColor)
    End If

    '    Create variables to hold button size for calculations
    Dim aTop As Int32 = Me.ClientRectangle.Top
    Dim aLeft As Int32 = Me.ClientRectangle.Left
    Dim aWidth As Int32 = Me.ClientRectangle.Width
    Dim aHeight As Int32 = Me.ClientRectangle.Height

    '    First, draw the semicircle that is the left end of the button
    g.FillEllipse(sb, aLeft, aTop, 2 * bRadius, 2 * bRadius)
    '    Now, draw the rectangle for the button body
    g.FillRectangle(sb, aLeft + bRadius, aTop, aWidth - (2 * bRadius), aHeight)
    '    Lastly, draw the semicircle that is the right end of the button
    g.FillEllipse(sb, aWidth - (2 * bRadius), aTop, 2 * bRadius, 2 * bRadius)

    '     Now write the text to the button face
    '     Use the font set in the base control property
    Dim fnt As Font = New Font(Me.Font.Name, Me.Font.Size, Me.Font.Style)
    '     Measure the string
    Dim siz As SizeF = g.MeasureString(Me.Text, fnt)
    '     Here we draw the string, centering it in the button's client space
    '     Note that it is centered both horizontally and vertically in the space
    g.DrawString(Me.Text, fnt, New SolidBrush(fColor), _
        (aWidth - siz.Width) / 2, (aHeight - siz.Height) / 2)
    sb.Dispose()
End Sub
```

Step 9: Adding the OnEnabledChanged Event

The basic button is now done and will work. However, you want it to do more than just sit there. If the user changes the state of the button, you need to force it to change its color appropriately. Perform the following steps to add this procedure:

1. Open the **RoundButton Class** module.

2. Add the following code to the **Class** module:

```
Protected Overrides Sub OnEnabledChanged(ByVal e As System.EventArgs)
    Dim g As Graphics = Me.CreateGraphics()
    If Me.Enabled Then
        DrawButton(g, Me.ForeColor, _btnColor)
    Else
        DrawButton(g, Me.ForeColor, _btnDisabledColor)
    End If
    g.Dispose()
    MyBase.OnEnabledChanged(e)
End Sub
```

The **OnEnabledChanged** event is raised when the **Enabled** property of the control is changed. This can occur from code or at design time.

 NOTE *Yes I know you can't do a design time control in Visual Basic .NET. But I want to make this point anyway, because I'll show you in Appendix F how to create this same control in C#. The appendix code will also show you how to build a second DLL, from the same code, that can be used as a design time control that you can add to the Toolbox.*

You don't have a Graphics object passed to you in this method, so you need to create your own. Your form has a **CreateGraphics** method that you use to get a current Graphics object. Remember, you need to dispose of the object when you are done. Just like your mother always told you, "Clean up after yourself!"

Step 10: Handling More Events

Since this is a graphics tutorial, we'll skip the explanation of some of the work in adding multiple events. What is important here is that you see how you need to force a redraw of the button face again after the mouse has touched or released. Again, let me emphasize the fact that you need to create a Graphics object, use its methods to draw, and then dispose of it. It's also important to call the base class's **OnMouseUp** and **OnMouseDown** events to let the base control do its processing. Add the following code to the **RoundButton Class** module:

```
Protected Overrides Sub OnMouseUp(ByVal e As System.Windows.Forms.MouseEventArgs)
    Try
        Dim g As Graphics = Me.CreateGraphics()
        DrawButton(g, Me.ForeColor, _btnColor)
        g.Dispose()
        _buttonDrawnDown = False
        MyBase.OnMouseUp(e)
    Catch
    End Try
End Sub

Protected Overrides Sub OnMouseDown(ByVal e As
System.Windows.Forms.MouseEventArgs)
    Try
        Dim g As Graphics = Me.CreateGraphics()
        DrawButton(g, Color.White, Color.Black)
        g.Dispose()
        _buttonDrawnDown = True
        MyBase.OnMouseDown(e)
    Catch
    End Try
End Sub
```

Step 11: Adding Two Simple Properties

You need two properties to set the button face color to indicate when the button is enabled or disabled. Add the following code to the **RoundButton Class** module:

```
Property ButtonColor() As Color
    Get
        Return _btnColor
    End Get
```

```
        Set(ByVal Value As Color)
            _btnColor = Value
        End Set
End Property
Property ButtonColorDisabled() As Color
        Get
            Return _btnDisabledColor
        End Get
        Set(ByVal Value As Color)
            _btnDisabledColor = Value
        End Set
End Property
```

Step 12: Moving the Stylus Off of the Button

When the stylus touches the button and is then "rolled" off the button face, the button needs to revert to its normal color state. It then needs to be painted back to its depressed state when the stylus again moves over the button. That takes some fancy code that you can add now to the **RoundButton Class** module:

```
Protected Overrides Sub OnMouseMove(ByVal e As System.Windows.Forms.MouseEventArgs)
Try
    If e.Button = MouseButtons.Left Then
        If ((e.X > Me.ClientRectangle.Top And e.X < Me.ClientRectangle.Bottom) _
        And (e.Y > Me.ClientRectangle.Left And e.Y < Me.ClientRectangle.Right))
        Then
            If (_buttonDrawnDown) Then
                '   I'm inside the button face
                Dim g As Graphics = Me.CreateGraphics()
                DrawButton(g, Me.ForeColor, _btnColor)
                g.Dispose()
                _buttonDrawnDown = False
            End If
        Else
                '   Moving outside the button
            If _buttonDrawnDown Then
                Dim g As Graphics = Me.CreateGraphics()
                DrawButton(g, Me.ForeColor, Color.Black)
                g.Dispose()
                _buttonDrawnDown = True
            End If
        End If
```

```
            End If
        '               End If
        MyBase.OnMouseMove(e)
    Catch
    End Try
End Sub
```

Step 13: Testing the Paint Job

Create a new Smart Device Extensions Windows Application (see the tutorial "Step-by-Step Tutorial: Creating an Owner-Drawn Control" in Chapter 5 if you need help). Add the following code to the declaration section of the form:

```
Friend WithEvents btnRound As New RoundButton.RoundButton
```

Then add this code to the **Form_Load** event:

```
btnRound.ButtonColor = Color.Red
btnRound.ButtonColorDisabled = Color.LightGray
btnRound.Top = 10
btnRound.Left = 10
btnRound.Width = 100
btnRound.Height = 20
btnRound.Text = "Touch Me!"
btnRound.Font = New Font("Arial", 8, FontStyle.Bold)
Me.Controls.Add(btnRound)
```

And if you want to see the button actually do something (imagine that!), add this code to the form's class along with a label control named Label1:

```
Private Sub btnRound_Click(ByVal sender As System.Object, _
        ByVal e As System.EventArgs) Handles btnRound.Click
    Label1.Visible = True
End Sub
```

And that, my friend, is the whole story. You have just done a decent amount of graphics work to draw your own custom button. Next, I have two homework assignments for you.

HOMEWORK *Change the code where the text is measured to be centered in the button client space. As the code is currently written, if the text is too big it overlaps the button. Hint: You'll need to check the size and change the font to a different size and then test again.*

 HOMEWORK *Add a new property called **ShowBorder** and implement it. This sounds simple enough. But there's a catch: There's no **DrawArc** method in the .NET Compact Framework, so you can't simply draw a half-circle on the left and right ends.*

Working with Images

The previous section detailed the basics of GDI and did some work with line and shape drawing. This section of the chapter will deal with images such as bitmaps and icons. There are two methods that you can use to draw images. Table 7-2 shows the methods along with their overloads.

Table 7-2. Image Methods and Their Overloads

METHODS	OVERLOADS
DrawIcon	DrawIcon(Icon, Integer, Intger)
DrawImage	Image, x, y×Image, Destination Rectangle, Source Rectangle, Graphics Unit×Image, x, y, Source Rectangle, Graphics Units×Image, Destination Rectangle, Source x, Source y×Source width, Source height, Graphics Unit, Image Attributes

At first glance, it may seem like slim pickings for image drawing, but **DrawImage** overloads add a considerable amount of power to the image graphics. The **DrawIcon** method is about as straightforward as you can get.

```
Dim g As Graphics = Me.CreateGraphics()
g.DrawIcon(ico,  0, 0)
```

You can't change its size or alter it in any fashion. You can load it and display it—simple.

NOTE *In my examples in this chapter, I'll never refer to a graphic by its filename (e.g., MyIcon.ico). When you are working on a device, whether it's an emulator or the real thing, the file paths won't work. While my graphic might be located at C:\Samples\MyIcon.ico on my development machine, that isn't the path of the file on the device. There are just too many things that can go wrong this way. The best way is this: Embed the resource in your executable. In VB 6, that wasn't the easiest thing to do, but .NET has made it very easy. Add the graphic to your project and select it. In the Properties window you should see a property called **Build Action**. Change that to **Embedded Resource** and rebuild. The graphic is now embedded in your application. I'll show in an example later in this chapter how to get the file out of the assembly.*

On the other hand, **DrawImage** is much more flexible. In its simplest form, **DrawImage** is very straightforward:

```
g.DrawImage(bmp, x, y)
```

This method draws the image full size at the provided x/y coordinates. You may be thinking, "Yeah, but what does that bmp variable stand for?" I embed my images in the assembly and get them back out with this code:

```
Dim assm As [Assembly]
Dim str As Stream

assm = [Assembly].GetExecutingAssembly()
str = assm.GetManifestResourceStream("ButtonTest.BookCover.bmp")

Dim bmp As Bitmap = New Bitmap(str)
```

My graphic is called BookCover.bmp, but if you look at the code closely, I am creating the stream from a resource called "ButtonTest.BookCover.bmp". This comes from the fact that when you embed a resource, .NET prepends the project's name onto the string to make it more descriptive. The reason for this is there can be multiple applications in a single assembly. Adding the application's name to the filename ensures a unique ID for every resource found in the assembly. Figure 7-3 shows you the output from this code.

Figure 7-3. An image drawn on a form

Another of the overloads for **DrawImage** allows you to specify a source rectangle and a source unit. The unit is *always* GraphicsUnit.Pixel, as there are no other choices in NETCF. The source rectangle lets you select a subset of the image to display. Figure 7-4 shows the results of the following code, where I only show the top one-half of the book cover.

```
Dim srcRect As Rectangle = New Rectangle(0, 0, _
    bmpBookCover.Width, bmpBookCover.Height/2)
g.DrawImage(bmp, 35, 35, srcRect, GraphicsUnit.Pixel)
```

You can stretch or compress an image by using another overloaded **DrawImage** method. You can specify both a target and a source rectangle in the parameter list, and by making the target rectangle either smaller or larger than the source bitmap, you effectively zoom in and zoom out of an image (see Listing 7-7).

Figure 7-4. Cropping an image using the source region

Listing 7-7. DrawImage with Rectangles

```
Dim srcRect As Rectangle = New Rectangle(0, 0, _
    bmpBookCover.Width, bmpBookCover.Height)
Dim targetRectSmall As Rectangle = New Rectangle(0, 0, _
    bmpBookCover.Width / 2, bmpBookCover.Height / 2)
Dim targetRectLarge As Rectangle = New Rectangle(targetRectSmall.Width, 0, _
    bmpBookCover.Width * 1.5, bmpBookCover.Height * 1.5)

Dim g As Graphics = Me.CreateGraphics()
g.DrawImage(bmpBookCover, targetRectSmall, srcRect, GraphicsUnit.Pixel)
g.DrawImage(bmpBookCover, targetRectLarge, srcRect, GraphicsUnit.Pixel)
g.Dispose()
```

The code in Listing 7-7 produces the output shown in Figure 7-5.

Another overload is very similar to this one, but instead of a source rectangle it takes the x and y position along with the source width and height. What makes this new overload interesting is the last parameter that only exists in this one overload.

```
Overloads Public Sub DrawImage( _
    ByVal image As Image, _
    ByVal destRect As Rectangle, _
    ByVal srcX As Integer, _
```

```
    ByVal srcY As Integer, _
    ByVal srcWidth As Integer, _
    ByVal srcHeight As Integer, _
    ByVal srcUnit As GraphicsUnit, _
    ByVal imageAttr As ImageAttributes _
)
```

Figure 7-5. Stretching and compressing an image

When you read the help information on the ImageAttributes object, you might get a little excited. I mean, look at all of the cool stuff you can do with this class's methods—grayscale adjustment matrices, color adjustment matrices, and gamma correction values. Sounds like *Star Trek* or something, doesn't it? Well, cool your correction matrices jets, because as you read further, only two methods of ImageAttributes are supported in NETCF that deal with the actual image manipulation: **SetColorKey** and **ClearColorKey**.

```
Dim g As System.Drawing.Graphics = Me.CreateGraphics()

Dim ia As Imaging.ImageAttributes = New Imaging.ImageAttributes
ia.SetColorKey(Color.White, Color.White)
Dim bmp As Bitmap = New Bitmap(str)
Dim tarRect As Rectangle = New Rectangle( _
    (Me.ClientRectangle.Width - bmp.Width) / 2, 35, bmp.Width, bmp.Height)
g.DrawImage(bmp, tarRect, 0, 0, bmp.Width, bmp.Height, GraphicsUnit.Pixel, ia)
```

SetColorKey sets the color value that will be treated as transparent in the image. Even though the method signature and help file tell you that you can set a range, you can't. If you try this line of code:

```
ia.SetColorKey(Color.White, Color.Red)
```

you'll get a **System.ArgumentException** when the line executes. If you call **SetColorKey** more than once, only the last color passed is treated as the transparent color. Figure 7-6 shows what the book cover looks like when **Color.White** has been set as transparent and the image is displayed on a light blue form background.

Figure 7-6. Transparent colors in an image

Step-by-Step Tutorial: Displaying a Simple Image

In this tutorial, you'll display a simple icon on a form.

Step 1: Starting a New Project

Begin this step-by-step exercise by creating a new project using the following steps:

1. Start Visual Studio .NET if necessary.

2. From the Start Page, select to create a **New Project**.

3. From the New Project dialog box, select **Smart Device Application**.

4. Specify a project name of **DisplayImageDemo**.

5. Select a location in which to create the project and click the **OK** button.

6. Select a target platform of **Pocket PC** and a project type of **Windows Application** and click the **OK** button.

Step 2: Configuring the Project

To configure the target output folder for your project, perform the following steps:

1. Under the Project menu, select **DisplayImage Properties**.

2. Under the Device page of the Text File Property Pages dialog box, set the output file folder to **\Windows\Start Menu\Programs\Apress**.

Step 3: Adding References

In addition to the standard references added by Visual Studio, you will need to add two more references. To add the references to your project, perform the following steps:

1. In the Solution Explorer, right-click **References** and click **Add Reference**.

2. Select **System.IO** from the Component Name column and then click the **Select** button.

3. Select **System.Reflection** from the Component Name column and then click the **Select** button.

4. Click **OK**.

Step 4: Adding the Image

Obviously, to draw the image, you need to add one to the project. Perform the following steps:

1. In the Solution Explorer, right-click the project name and click **Add | Add Existing Item**.

2. Add an image from your system.

3. Select the image and change its **Build Action** property to **Embedded Resource**.

Step 5: Using a PictureBox

Open Form1 in the designer and drag a PictureBox control from the toolbox to the design surface. Set the properties of the PictureBox as shown in Table 7-3.

Table 7-3. PictureBox Properties

OBJECT	PROPERTY	VALUE
PictureBox1	Location	0, 0
PictureBox1	Size	240, 120
PictureBox1	SizeMode	CenterImage

Add the following code to the form's **OnPaint** event.

```
Dim assm As [Assembly] = [Assembly].GetExecutingAssembly()
Dim str As Stream

str = assm.GetManifestResourceStream("DisplayImageDemo.logo.gif")
Dim imgCorporateLogo As Bitmap = New Bitmap(str)
Me.PictureBox1.Image = imgCorporateLogo
```

The PictureBox works just fine, so why not use it instead of drawing the image? Two reasons come to mind right off. A PictureBox only supports stretching an image, not compressing it. If the image is too large for the picture box, then you have no choice other than to change the graphic to a smaller size. Secondly, you can create a transparent color in your image when you draw it. Using a PictureBox, you don't have that capability. Now let's see how you can draw a simple image on the form.

Step 6: Drawing the Image

Add the following code to the **OnPaint** event:

```
Dim g As Graphics = Me.CreateGraphics()
Dim destRect As Rectangle = New Rectangle(0, 125, imgCorporateLogo.Width / 2, _
    imgCorporateLogo.Height / 2)
Dim srcRect As Rectangle = New Rectangle(0, 0, imgCorporateLogo.Width, _
    imgCorporateLogo.Height)
g.DrawImage(imgCorporateLogo, destRect, srcRect, GraphicsUnit.Pixel)
```

This code draws a smaller version of the logo, compressed to fit on the screen. In Figure 7-7, you can see the top image flows outside of the bounds of the picture box. The lower image on the form is the same one as before, but now it's reduced to fit within a region of the form.

Figure 7-7. Drawing an image or using a PictureBox

Step-by-Step Tutorial: Scrolling an Image

In this tutorial, you'll create a standard Windows form, display an image on the form, and then cause the image to "scroll" around its center point.

 NOTE *I provide a completed version of this application, titled ScrollingImage Demo, under the* **Chapter 7** *folder of the* **Samples** *folder for this book. See Appendix D for more information on accessing and loading the sample applications.*

Step 1: Starting a New Project

Begin this step-by-step exercise by creating a new project using the following steps:

1. Start Visual Studio .NET if necessary.

2. From the Start Page, select to create a **New Project**.

3. From the New Project dialog box, select **Smart Device Application**.

4. Specify a project name of **ScrollingImage Demo**.

5. Select a location in which to create the project and click the **OK** button.

6. Select a target platform of **Pocket PC** and a project type of **Windows Application** and click the **OK** button.

Step 2: Configuring the Project

To configure the target output folder for your project, perform the following steps:

1. Under the Project menu, select **ScrollingImage Properties**.

2. Under the Device page of the Text File Property Pages dialog box, set the output file folder to **\Windows\Start Menu\Programs\Apress**.

Step 3: Adding References

In addition to the standard references added by Visual Studio, you will need to add two more references. To add the references to your project, perform the following steps:

1. In the Solution Explorer, right-click **References** and click **Add Reference**.

2. Select **System.IO** from the Component Name column and then click the **Select** button.

3. Select **System.Reflection** from the Component Name column and then click the **Select** button.

4. Click **OK**.

Step 4: Adding a Start Button

You need to start and stop the scrolling image, so you'll add a button to your form:

1. Show Form1.vb in Design and use the toolbox to add a Button control to the form.

2. Set its properties as shown in Table 7-4.

Table 7-4. Button Properties

OBJECT	PROPERTY	VALUE
Button1	Name	btnToggleScroll
Button1	Location	8, 240
Button1	Size	224, 20
Button1	Text	Start Scrolling

3. Add the following event handler:

```
Private Sub btnToggleScroll_Click(ByVal sender As System.Object, _
        ByVal e As System.EventArgs) Handles btnToggleScroll.Click
    If Me.tmrScroll.Enabled Then
        Me.tmrScroll.Enabled = False
        Me.btnToggleScroll.Text = "Start Scrolling"
    Else
        Me.tmrScroll.Enabled = True
        Me.btnToggleScroll.Text = "Stop Scrolling"
    End If
End Sub
```

Step 5: Creating Form-Level Variables

You want to load the graphic once, so you'll create some variables declared in the form class to use when you draw the image. Add the following code to the form:

```
Private posCurrent As Integer = 0
Private bmpBookCover As Bitmap = Nothing
```

Step 6: Loading the Image

To enhance the speed of your drawing, you want to load the graphic into memory only once. To accomplish that, add the following code to the **Form_Load** event:

```
Dim assm As [Assembly] = [Assembly].GetExecutingAssembly()
Dim str As Stream

str = assm.GetManifestResourceStream("ButtonTest.BookCover.bmp")
bmpBookCover = New Bitmap(str)
```

Step 7: Setting Up a Timer for the Scrolling

Rather than try to get into threading here, revert to your old VB friend, the timer, to regulate the scrolling of your image:

1. Drag a Timer from the Toolbox and drop it onto the form.

2. Set its properties as shown in Table 7-5.

Table 7-5. Timer Properties

OBJECT	PROPERTY	VALUE
Timer1	Name	tmrScroll
Timer1	Interval	50

3. Add the following code for the timer's event handler:

```
Private Sub tmrScroll_Tick(ByVal sender As System.Object,
        ByVal e As System.EventArgs) Handles tmrScroll.Tick
    Me.Invalidate()
End Sub
```

All you do in this example is to invalidate the form's client area. The scrolling is done in the **OnPaint** event.

Step 8: Adding the Scrolling Code

To do the actual scrolling, add code to the **OnPaint** event. The first thing you'll do is to check the status of the timer to see if it's enabled. If it is, then the image will scroll. Listing 7-8 shows the entire code for the **OnPaint** event.

Listing 7-8. Scrolling an Image

```
Protected Overrides Sub OnPaint(ByVal e As System.Windows.Forms.PaintEventArgs)
    If Me.tmrScroll.Enabled Then
        '    Only paint this if the timer is on
        '    Draw the bookcover bitmap from the current position to the end,
        '    and then add the front to the back
        If (posCurrent >= bmpBookCover.Width) Then
            posCurrent = 0
        End If
        Dim rectSrc As Rectangle = New Rectangle(posCurrent, 0, _
            bmpBookCover.Width - posCurrent, bmpBookCover.Height)
        Dim rectSrc2 As Rectangle = New Rectangle(0, 0, _
            posCurrent, bmpBookCover.Height)

        e.Graphics.DrawImage(bmpBookCover, _
            (Me.ClientRectangle.Width - bmpBookCover.Width) / 2, 35, _
            rectSrc, GraphicsUnit.Pixel)
        e.Graphics.DrawImage(bmpBookCover, _
            ((Me.ClientRectangle.Width - bmpBookCover.Width) / 2) _
            + (bmpBookCover.Width - posCurrent), 35, _
            rectSrc2, GraphicsUnit.Pixel)
        posCurrent += 2
    End If
End Sub
```

You added the form-level variable **posCurrent** earlier, and now you see what it's used for. You keep the current x position in the image that's to be drawn on the left side. rectSrc is the right side of the source image that will be drawn on the left side of the display area. rectSrc2 is the left side of the source image that will be drawn on the right side of the display area. You then call **DrawImage** twice, drawing the two pieces to make the image appear to scroll. As the last step, you increment your position pointer by 2 pixels.

HOMEWORK *When you call the **Invalidate** method on the form, you're invalidating the entire form. Write the additional code to invalidate only a portion of the form where the image will be displayed.*

As you play with the code in the previous tutorial, try adjusting the timer interval. You can see the responsiveness of the device's graphics to very small intervals. If you are worried about drawing at short intervals, you can use the code in the preceding example as a test bed for your own work.

Summary

In this chapter, you've seen most, if not all, of the graphics functions and capabilities of NETCF. But there are still many ways to use the graphics beyond the techniques shown. You can create any type of custom controls that you want by doing your own drawing. In fact, I've included another control in the sample code for this chapter that displays a simple calendar that raises events you can use to customize the looks of the displayed calendar.

You can also use the graphics methods to create line charts or bar graphs for displaying data. The ideas are endless; only your time is the limiting factor (I know that's the way it is for me, anyway).

CHAPTER 8

Files and Directories

WHILE THE PROCESS OF DEVELOPING applications for a device and desktop is similar, it is not unusual for a device developer to have far more responsibility for the environment, that is to say the operating system, directory, and file structure, than the desktop developer. Often the only reason that a user has a device is to run your application. In such a situation, your application is often solely responsible for maintaining the underlying directory and file structure.

In this chapter, I'm going to expose you to the **System.IO** namespace of the .NET Compact Framework. This namespace provides device developers with a plethora of file- and directory-related functionality including

- **Querying directories** to obtain a list of the subdirectories and files they hold. This capability provides your application with a method for determining if necessary files exist and are in their appropriate locations.

- **Managing directories** by being able to create, move, and delete directories from within your application, giving you complete control over the directory structure of a device.

- **Setting directory attributes,** providing you with a way to limit access to, protect, and control directories.

- **Localizing your application** through the use of language-specific special folders, including those used for Windows, Start menu shortcuts, and user documents.

- **Determining the directory** where your application resides. You can use this information to access data and configuration files that you have placed in the same directory as your application.

- **Managing the files** that are used by your application. Through the **System.IO** namespace you can create, copy, and delete files.

- **Setting file attributes** as needed for your application to control access.

- **Reading from and writing to text and binary files.**

This chapter is divided into four parts. The first part provides you with an overview of the **System.IO** namespace, introducing you to its key classes and members. The second part focuses on file- and directory-specific functionality that is commonly found in device applications. It is in this section that you will learn how to create, move, and delete directories and files. The third part of this chapter demonstrates how to read and write text and binary files. Finally, in the fourth part you will walk through a step-by-step example that incorporates some of the techniques from this chapter.

System.IO Namespace

Implementing directory- and file-related functionality within your applications requires at least a basic understanding of the **System.IO** namespace. This namespace with its base classes enables you to create, manipulate, and delete directories and files.

Some of the more commonly utilized classes of the **System.IO** namespace are shown in Table 8-1.

Table 8-1. The System.IO Namespace Key Classes

CLASS	DESCRIPTION
BinaryReader	Reads primitive data types as binary values
BinaryWriter	Writes primitive data types as binary values
Directory	Indicates static methods for creating, moving, deleting, and enumerating through directories, subdirectories, and the files they contain
DirectoryInfo	Indicates instance methods for creating, moving, deleting, and enumerating through directories, subdirectories, and the files they contain
File	Represents static methods for creating, copying, moving, deleting, and opening files
FileInfo	Represents instance methods for creating, copying, moving, deleting, and opening files
FileStream	Provides access to a file via a stream of bytes
MemoryStream	Provides access to a memory store via a stream of bytes
Path	Indicates file path information
StreamReader	Reads character-based data from a file

Table 8-1. The System.IO Namespace Key Classes (continued)

CLASS	DESCRIPTION
StreamWriter	Writes character-based data to a file
StringReader	Reads character-based data from a string
StringWriter	Writes character-based data from a string
TextReader	Reads a sequential string of characters
TextWriter	Writes a sequential string of characters

Working with the System.IO Namespace

There are two ways to work with the **System.IO** namespace within your application. First, you can add an Imports statement as shown in Figure 8-1. The advantage to this approach is that it allows you to shorten reference names. For example, instead of having to use the complete naming syntax as follows:

```
System.IO.Directory.GetFiles
```

you could instead use this much easier to type syntax:

```
Directory.GetFiles
```

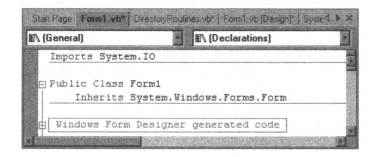

Figure 8-1. Adding a reference to the System.IO namespace

Which leads us to the second approach to working with the **System.IO** namespace—don't add the Imports statement, but simply use the complete naming syntax. Does it require more typing? Certainly, it does. Does it make your code easier to read? I think so. That's why you'll find that throughout this book

I use the full syntax. Plus, if you are getting paid by the number of characters you type, this is definitely the approach to use.

The remainder of this chapter provides details and practical examples of the **System.IO** namespace classes shown in Table 8-1.

NOTE *Throughout the **System.IO** namespace, file paths are used. Under Windows CE and the Pocket PC, paths are driveless. They start with a "\" rather than the C:, D:, etc. For example, the path C:\Program Files on your desktop PC would be \Program Files on your device.*

Managing Directories

While directories, and particularly the management of directories, aren't a large part of the development process of mobile applications, they can play a key part. The need to manage directories can appear in your application in a variety of ways including the following:

- **Handling the creation, modification, and deletion of directories** used with your application. Mobile applications frequently store data locally. Often your application handles directory-related tasks with no involvement from the user.

- **Protecting directories** so that data they hold is not accidentally lost. Through the use of directory and file attributes your application can limit the user from modifying or deleting data outside of your application.

- **Determining the contents of a directory** by checking for new or modified files. The **Directory** and **DirectoryInfo** classes provide collections of sub-directories and files that are contained within a directory.

- **Obtaining the directory names** of special folders, taking into account localization issues. Any application that will have international use needs to incorporate these techniques.

The Directory and DirectoryInfo Classes

The **System.IO** namespace provides two classes that offer directory-specific functionality: **Directory** and **DirectoryInfo**. The key difference between these two classes is that while the **Directory** class provides static methods, the **DirectoryInfo** class offers instance methods instead. I'm going to focus on the

Directory class because I find it more useful. Table 8-2 lists **Directory** class methods that I find particularly helpful in developing Pocket PC applications.

Table 8-2. Methods of the Directory Class

METHOD	DESCRIPTION
CreateDirectory	Creates a directory on the device
Delete	Deletes a directory
Exists	Checks if a directory exists
GetDirectories	Returns the subdirectories contained within a directory
GetFiles	Returns the files contained within a directory
Move	Moves a directory

Let's look at each of these methods in more detail.

Working with Special Folders

Windows CE uses a set of special folders that identify where common information is stored. Special folders point to specific physical folders on a device and serve two purposes. First, they enable an application to identify where key folders are located, such as the **Windows** folder. Second, they take into account localization issues, where folder names need to be altered based upon the language for which a device has been configured.

In Table 8-3, you'll find a list of special folders that are commonly of interest to Pocket PC developers.

Table 8-3. Pocket PC Special Folders

FOLDER	LOCATION	USE
Personal	\My Documents	Stores user data
Programs	\Windows\Start Menu\Programs	Contains applications
Start Menu	\Windows\Start Menu	Contains shortcuts to items that appear in the Start menu
Start Up	\Windows\Startup	Contains applications that will be run when a device is booted
Windows	\Windows	Contains the Windows CE OS files

NOTE   *The folders shown in Table 8-3 are for English-based versions of the Pocket PC OS.*

The **System.IO** namespace, with all of the information it provides, doesn't offer anything on special folders. To access details on special folders, you need to turn to the Windows CE API, specifically the SHGetSpecialFolderPath function.

The SHGetSpecialFolderPath function returns the path to the special folder defined by its **nFolder** argument. The syntax for calling this function is

```
SHGetSpecialFolderPath(HWND hwndOwner,LPTSTR lpszPath,
  int nFolder,BOOL fCreate)
```

The arguments used with the SHGetSpecialFolderPath function are shown in Table 8-4.

Table 8-4. Arguments for the SHGetSpecialFolderPath Function

ARGUMENT	DESCRIPTION
hwndOwner	Specifies the handle to the owner window
lpszPath	Indicates the address of the buffer that will receive the path to the requested special folder
nFolder	Specifies the desired special folder
fCreate	Indicates that the folder should be created if it doesn't already exist

Table 8-5 shows the values, or what are commonly referred to as the CSIDL values, associated with Pocket PC special folders. You would provide a value from this table with the **nFolder** argument.

Table 8-5. CSIDL Numbers for Special Folders

NUMBER	FOLDER
0	Desktop—\My Documents
2	Programs—\Windows\Start Menu\Programs
5	Personal—\My Documents
7	StartUp—\Windows\Startup
11	StartMenu—\Windows\Start Menu
14	Fonts—\Windows\Fonts
16	Favorites—\Windows\Start Menu

Of these CSIDL values, Personal, Programs, Start Menu, and Start Up are the most commonly used.

The **Personal** folder defines the area that is recommended for storing user data. On the Pocket PC this is the **\My Documents** folder. Can you store data elsewhere? Certainly you can.

The **Programs** folder specifies the location where applications are stored. On the Pocket PC, this is the **\Windows\Start Menu\Programs** folder. From a Pocket PC end user's standpoint, applications in this folder are accessed through the **Programs** menu item of the Start menu as shown in Figure 8-2.

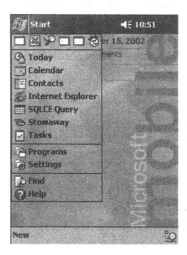

Figure 8-2. The Programs menu item under the Pocket PC Start menu

The Pocket PC **Programs** folder itself is shown in Figure 8-3.

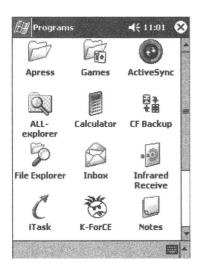

Figure 8-3. The Pocket PC Programs folder

TIP *You can create a folder under the* **Programs** *folder to logically group all of the applications from your company. I used this approach with the* **Apress** *folder shown in Figure 8-3, where I deploy all of the samples used with this book.*

The **StartUp** folder identifies the folder used to store applications that will be run when a Pocket PC is booted. On the Pocket PC this is the **\Windows\Startup** folder. This folder is useful in situations where your applications should always be running.

The **StartMenu** folder points to the folder of items that will appear on the Pocket PC Start menu. On the Pocket PC this is the **\Windows\Start Menu** folder. You can place shortcuts or applications in this folder.

TIP *By adding your application to the Start menu, you make it easy for the end user to access your program.*

NOTE *See Chapter 21 for information on how to add a shortcut for your application to the Start menu during the installation process.*

Figure 8-4 shows the contents of the **Start Menu** folder that corresponds to the Start menu shown in Figure 8-2.

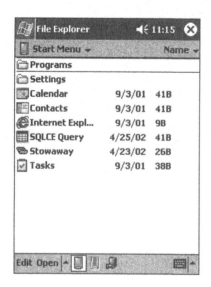

Figure 8-4. The contents of the Start Menu folder

Retrieving Special Folder Information

While calling the SHGetSpecialFolderPath function is laborious from the coding standpoint, it is by no means rocket scientist stuff.

NOTE *To make working with SHGetSpecialFolderPath even easier for you, I've included a module called **GetSpecialFolderPath** under the Chapter 8 section of the **Samples** folder. You simply need to include this module in your applications.*

The first thing that you need to do is define the values that you will use with the **nFolder** argument. Listing 8-1 shows the enumeration declaration of these values.

Listing 8-1. Values Used with the nFolder Argument of SHGetSpecialFolderPath

```
' Pocket PC folder values for use with the SHGetSpecialFolderPath
' function nFolder argument.
Public Enum CSIDL As Integer
    DESKTOP = 0              ' \My Documents
    PROGRAMS = 2            ' \Windows\Start Menu\Programs
    PERSONAL = 5           ' \My Documents
    FAVORITES = 6          ' \Windows\Start Menu
    STARTUP = 7            ' \Windows\StartUp
    STARTMENU = &HB        ' \Windows\Start Menu
    FONTS = &H14           ' \Windows\Fonts
End Enum
```

The second thing that you need to do is to add the SHGetSpecialFolderPath function declaration as shown in Listing 8-2. This declaration needs to be added to the **Declarations** section of a module.

Listing 8-2. Declaring the SHGetSpecialFolderPath Function

```
' Windows API function that returns the paths to common folders.
<System.Runtime.InteropServices.DllImport("coredll.dll")> _
    Private Function SHGetSpecialFolderPath( _
        ByVal hwndOwner As Integer, _
        ByVal lpszPath As String, _
```

```
        ByVal nFolder As CSIDL, _
        ByVal fCreate As Boolean _
        ) As Boolean
    End Function
```

A General Purpose Routine for Calling SHGetSpecialFolderPath

Now, at this point you are ready to call the SHGetSpecialFolderPath function from within your applications. But working with SHGetSpecialFolderPath requires more than just calling the function. There is some work that you need to do before and after making the call. To simplify this part of the process, I've created a general purpose API function wrapper called GetSpecialFolderPath. This function accepts a single argument, **MyCSIDL**, which is the CSIDL of the folder you're retrieving.

 NOTE *Wrappers are functions that encapsulate and isolate complex or detailed code while exposing a simpler interface to the developer. For more information on wrappers see Chapter 17.*

The GetSpecialFolderPath wrapper function is shown in Listing 8-3. Within this function you'll find the call to the SHGetSpecialFolderPath function encased within a Try/Catch statement. This will handle any errors that may occur during the process.

Listing 8-3. The GetSpecialFolderPath Wrapper Function

```
Private Function GetSpecialFolderPath(ByVal MyCSIDL As CSIDL) As String
    Dim strWorkingPath As String = New String(" "c, 260)
    Dim intEndOfPath As Integer

' Retrieve the requested path.
    Try
        SHGetSpecialFolderPath(0, strWorkingPath, MyCSIDL, False)

' Locate the end of the path name.
        intEndOfPath = strWorkingPath.IndexOf(Chr(0))

' Extract just that path name.
        If intEndOfPath > -1 Then
            strWorkingPath = strWorkingPath.Substring(0, intEndOfPath)
        End If
    Catch ex As Exception
        strWorkingPath = ex.Message
    End Try
```

```
' Send the path name back to the calling program.
   Return strWorkingPath


End Function
```

A 260-character string filled with spaces is passed to the SHGetSpecial
FolderPath function. This string is used by SHGetSpecialFolderPath to return the
requested path. The string must be predefined at a length long enough to receive
any path that may be returned. When it is returned, the path will be at the left
end of the 260-character string, followed by a NULL character (ASCII 0). The
GetSpecialFolderPath function simply locates the NULL character, extracts
everything to its left, and returns that substring to the calling program.

The GetSpecialFolderPath function makes retrieving special folder paths
simple. Following are examples of retrieving the **Personal**, **Programs**, **Start
Menu**, and **Startup** special folders.

 NOTE *All of these functions are included in the **GetSpecialFolderPath**
module.*

Retrieving the Personal Special Folder

The GetPersonalFolder function, shown in the following code snippet, returns
the path to the **Personal** special folder by passing the enumerated value of
PERSONAL to the GetSpecialFolderPath function.

```
Public Function GetPersonalFolder() As String
' Return the Personal folder, which on English-based
' devices is \My Documents.
   Return GetSpecialFolderPath(CSIDL.PERSONAL)
End Function
```

Retrieving the Programs Special Folder

The GetProgramFolder function, shown in the following code, returns the path to
the **Programs** special folder by passing the enumerated value of PROGRAMS
to the GetSpecialFolderPath function.

```
Public Function GetProgramsFolder() As String
' Return the Programs folder, which on English-based
' devices is \Windows\Start Menu\Programs.
   Return GetSpecialFolderPath(CSIDL.PROGRAMS)
End Function
```

Retrieving the Start Menu Special Folder

The GetStartMenuFolder function, shown in the following code, returns the path to the **Start Menu** special folder by passing the enumerated value of STARTMENU to the GetSpecialFolderPath function.

```
Public Function GetStartMenuFolder() As String
' Return the Start Menu folder, which on English-based
' devices is \Windows\Start Menu.
    Return GetSpecialFolderPath(CSIDL.STARTMENU)
End Function
```

Retrieving the Startup Special Folder

The GetStartupFolder function, shown in the following code, returns the path to the **Startup** special folder by passing the enumerated value of STARTUP to the GetSpecialFolderPath function.

```
Public Function GetStartupFolder() As String
' Return the Startup folder, which on English-based
' devices is \Windows\Startup.
    Return GetSpecialFolderPath(CSIDL.STARTUP)
End Function
```

Determining If a Directory Exists

The **Directory** class of the **System.IO** namespace contains a method called **Exists** that returns whether or not the specified directory exists. The syntax for this method is

```
Public Shared Function Exists( _
   ByVal path As String _
) As Boolean
```

The **Exists** method returns a **Boolean** value: True if the directory exists, False if it doesn't. Use this line of code to call the **Exists** method from your application:

```
MsgBox(System.IO.Directory.Exists("\Program Files\My Directory"))
```

Creating a Directory

Your application may create a directory on its own or under the direction of the user. On its own, your application may use directories to organize and store data that is gathered by or used with your application. Alternatively, your application may provide functionality that allows your users to control the organization and storage of data, letting them specify the folders that best suit their needs. In either case, at some point your application will need to create directories.

You create directories and subdirectories using the **CreateDirectory** method of the **Directory** class. The syntax for this method is

```
Public Shared Function CreateDirectory( _
   ByVal path As String _
) As DirectoryInfo
```

When calling the **CreateDirectory** method, you must provide the path of the directory to create. An example of this is shown here:

```
System.IO.Directory.CreateDirectory("\Program Files\My Directory")
```

In this example, the directory \Program Files\My Directory will be created.

 NOTE *Paths under Windows CE do not include a drive letter. For example, C:\Windows would be simply \Windows on a device.*

As with all IO-related operations, creating a directory has the potential of generating a runtime error. You need to incorporate error handling into your code to address this potential problem area. An example of this is shown in Listing 8-4.

Listing 8-4. Creating a Directory with Error Handling

```
' Create the directory.
  Try
    System.IO.Directory.CreateDirectory("\Program Files\My Directory")
    Msgbox("The directory was created.")

' An exception occurred.
  Catch ex As Exception
    MsgBox("The following error occurred: " & ex.Message)
  End Try
```

Moving a Directory

Your application can move a directory along with its contents to a new location using the **Move** method of the **Directory** class. The syntax for this method is

```
Public Shared Sub Move( _
    ByVal sourceDirName As String, _
    ByVal destDirName As String _
)
```

The path to the source directory is sourceDirName, and destDirName is the path to the destination directory. An example of using this method is shown here:

```
System.IO.Directory.Move("\Program Files\My Directory", _
    "\Program Files\New Directory")
```

The **Move** method will throw an exception if the source directory doesn't exist or the destination directory already exists. Listing 8-5 shows an example of how you can handle these situations from code. The routine MoveDirectory checks both the source and destination directories before making a call to the **Move** method. The **Move** method itself is contained within a Try/Catch structure, which will handle any other exceptions that may occur.

Listing 8-5. Adding Checks to the Moving of a Directory

```
' Declare the ReturnStatus structure.
Public Structure ReturnStatus
  Dim Success As Boolean
  Dim Message As String
End Structure

Function MoveDirectory(ByVal strSource As String, ByVal strTarget As String) _
  As ReturnStatus
' Moves a directory.
' The strSource argument is the full path to the directory to move.
' The strTarget argument is the full path to the new directory.
  Dim MyReturn As ReturnStatus

' Check to see if source directory exists.
  If Not (System.IO.Directory.Exists(strSource)) Then
    MyReturn.Success = False
    MyReturn.Message = "Source directory does not exist."
    Return MyReturn
    Exit Function
  End If
```

```
' Check to see if target directory exists.
  If System.IO.Directory.Exists(strTarget) Then
    MyReturn.Success = False
    MyReturn.Message = "Target directory already exists."
    Return MyReturn
    Exit Function
  End If

' Move the directory.
  Try
    System.IO.Directory.Move(strSource, strTarget)
    MyReturn.Success = True
    MyReturn.Message = strTarget
    Return MyReturn

' An exception occurred, so let the calling program
' know what happened.
  Catch ex As Exception
    MyReturn.Success = False
    MyReturn.Message = ex.Message
    Return MyReturn
  End Try
End Function
```

Deleting a Directory

You can delete a directory using the **Delete** method of the **Directory** class. This method is overloaded, providing two ways it can be called. The first way, shown in the following code, deletes a single directory:

```
Overloads Public Shared Sub Delete( _
   ByVal path As String _
)
```

Here's an example of calling the **Delete** method using this syntax:

```
System.IO.Directory.Delete("\Program Files\My Directory")
```

The second way of calling this method deletes the directory, as well as any subdirectories and files that it contains. The syntax for this second way of calling the **Delete** method is

```
Overloads Public Shared Sub Delete( _
    ByVal path As String, _
    ByVal recursive As Boolean _
)
```

Set the **recursive** argument to True to include subdirectories and files in the delete process.

Determining the Subdirectories Within a Directory

You can obtain a list of subdirectories contained within a directory using the **GetDirectories** method of the **Directory** class. This method returns an array of strings, with each member in the array holding the name of a single subdirectory.

The **GetDirectories** method is overloaded, providing two ways that it can be called. This first way, shown in the following code, returns all of the subdirectories that are contained within the specified directory. It accepts a single argument, which is the path to the parent directory.

```
Overloads Public Shared Function GetDirectories( _
    ByVal path As String _
) As String()
```

Following is an example of using this first approach. Note that **strDirectories** is declared as an array.

```
Dim strDirectories() as String
strDirectories = _
    System.IO.Directory.GetDirectories("\Program Files\My Directory")
```

 NOTE *If the target directory, in this example \Program Files\My Directory, doesn't contain any subdirectories, an error will be thrown. You should always include error handling around directory and file-related activities.*

The second way to call the **GetDirectories** method returns only those subdirectories that match the search pattern you provide as the second argument. This alternate syntax is shown here:

```
Overloads Public Shared Function GetDirectories( _
    ByVal path As String, _
    ByVal searchPattern As String _
) As String()
```

The code that follows shows a simple example of using this second approach:

```
Dim strDirectories() as String
strDirectories = _
  System.IO.Directory.GetDirectories("\Program Files\My Directory", _
    "tmp*")
```

In this example, only the subdirectories with the prefix of **tmp** will be returned.

As mentioned earlier, the **GetDirectories** method returns an array of strings. Each member of the array contains the name of a subdirectory, including its full path. You can iterate through this array to access each member as shown in Listing 8-6.

Listing 8-6. Iterating Through the Array of Subdirectories

```
Dim strDirectories() As String
Dim strDirectory As String

' Retrieve and sort the list of directories.
  strDirectories = _
    System.IO.Directory.GetDirectories("\Program Files\My Directory")

' Display the directories.
  For Each strDirectory In strDirectories
    Msgbox(strDirectory)
  Next
```

Determining the Files Within a Directory

You can obtain a list of files that are contained within a directory using the **GetFiles** method of the **Directory** class. Similar to the **GetDirectories** method, this method returns an array of strings with each member of the array containing the name of a single file.

The **GetFiles** method is overloaded. It provides two ways that it can be called. The first way as shown here returns all of the files within a directory:

```
Overloads Public Shared Function GetFiles( _
   ByVal path As String _
) As String()
```

The following code demonstrates this first method of calling **GetFiles**:

```
Dim strFiles() As String
strFiles = System.IO.Directory.GetFiles("\Program Files\My Directory")
```

In this example, **GetFiles** will return all of the files contained in \Program Files\My Directory.

 NOTE *If the target directory, in this example \Program Files\My Directory, doesn't contain any files, an error will be generated. You should always include error handling around directory- and file-related activities.*

The second way to call the **GetFiles** method returns only the files that match the search pattern you provide as the second argument. The alternate syntax for this method is

```
Overloads Public Shared Function GetFiles( _
    ByVal path As String, _
    ByVal searchPattern As String _
) As String()
```

The following code demonstrates this second approach to calling the **GetFiles** method:

```
Dim strFiles() As String
strFiles = System.IO.Directory.GetFiles("\Program Files\My Directory", _
    "*.txt")
```

In this example, only files with a .txt extension will be returned.

The **GetFiles** method returns an array of strings, with each member of the array containing a single filename. By iterating through this array, you can access the individual filenames. An example of this is shown in Listing 8-7.

Listing 8-7. Iterating Through the Array of Filenames

```
Dim strFiles() As String
Dim strFile As String

' Retrieve and sort the list of files.
  strFiles = System.IO.Directory.GetFiles(txtSource.Text, "*.*")
```

```
' Display the files.
  For Each strFile In strFiles
    MsgBox(strFile)
  Next
```

Other Directory-Related Functionality

While the **Directory** class offers a wide variety of directory-related capabilities, there are some features and functionality it lacks. Two items of particular interest to Pocket PC developers are working with special folders and obtaining the path to your application. Those items are the topic of this remaining section of managing directories.

Determining the Application's Directory

In developing Pocket PC applications, you often want to know from what directory your application was launched. This information is handy in that it allows you to store configuration files, databases, and other application-related files all together in a single directory.

The **Path** class of the **System.IO** namespace provides a method, **GetDirectoryName**, to use to retrieve your application's directory. An example of retrieving this information is shown here:

```
Dim ApplicationFolder as String
ApplicationFolder = _
     System.IO.Path.GetDirectoryName(Reflection.Assembly. _
     GetExecutingAssembly().GetName().CodeBase.ToString())
```

Conclusion of the Managing Directories Section

As this section shows, the .NET Compact Framework offers developers an incredible amount of control over and information on directories. Understanding how to use the methods provided through the **System.IO** namespace is a key skill in developing well-rounded, comprehensive Pocket PC applications.

This section also exposes you to how the Windows CE API can be used to "fill in the gaps" of functionality not offered through the **System.IO** namespace.

Now let's turn our attention to how the **System.IO** namespace can be used to manage files.

Managing Files

Pocket PC applications frequently involve some sort of file management. Whether that be dealing with text-based configuration files, XML documents, databases, or simple comma-separated files, you will want to know how to copy, move, delete, and work with file attributes. In this section, I'll show you how to leverage the **File** class of the **System.IO** namespace to manage files within the Pocket PC environment.

The File and FileInfo Classes

Similar to the **Directory** and **DirectoryInfo** classes, the **System.IO** namespace contains two classes, **File** and **FileInfo**. These two classes differ in that the **File** class offers static methods while the **FileInfo** class provides instance methods. I prefer the **File** class, finding it more direct and better suited for developing Pocket PC applications. Table 8-6 lists **File** class methods that are commonly used in managing files.

Table 8-6. Methods of the File Class Used to Manage Files

METHOD	DESCRIPTION
Copy	Makes a copy of a file
Delete	Deletes a file
Exists	Checks if a file exists
Move	Moves a file

Let's examine each of these methods in more detail.

Checking If a File Exists

The **File** class of the **System.IO** namespace includes the **Exists** method. As its name would lead you to believe, this method is used to determine whether a file exists. The syntax for the **Exists** method is

```
Public Shared Function Exists( _
   ByVal path As String _
) As Boolean
```

The **Exists** method returns a Boolean value; True if the file exists, False if it doesn't. The following line of code shows an example of calling the **File** class **Exists** method:

```
MsgBox(System.IO.File.Exists("\Program Files\My Directory\working.tmp"))
```

Copying a File

You can easily copy a file from within your application with the **Copy** method. This method is overloaded, providing two ways that it can be called. The first way, as shown in the following code, assumes that the target file doesn't already exist. The syntax for this method is

```
Overloads Public Shared Sub Copy( _
    ByVal sourceFileName As String, _
    ByVal destFileName As String _
)
```

An example of calling the **Copy** method is shown here:

```
System.IO.File.Copy("\Program Files\My Directory\working.tmp", _
    "\Program Files\My Directory\new.tmp")
```

 CAUTION *If you are using this first overloaded method for copying files, you should first verify that the target file doesn't exist. You can perform this check with the **System.IO.File.Exists** method.*

The second way of calling the **Copy** method of the **File** class allows you to specify whether the target file should be overwritten if it already exists. The syntax for this call is

```
Overloads Public Shared Sub Copy( _
    ByVal sourceFileName As String, _
    ByVal destFileName As String, _
    ByVal overwrite As Boolean _
)
```

The third argument to this version of the **Copy** method, **overwrite**, is a Boolean value. Setting this argument to True will cause the overwriting of the target file. An example of calling the overloaded version of this method is shown here:

```
System.IO.File.Copy("\Program Files\My Directory\working.tmp", _
  "\Program Files\My Directory\new.tmp", True)
```

Moving a File

In addition to copying files, you can also move files. The **File** class provides the **Move** method for this. The syntax for this method is

```
Public Shared Sub Move( _
    ByVal sourceFileName As String, _
    ByVal destFileName As String _
)
```

where *sourceFilename* is the path to the source file and *desFileName* is the path to the destination file. An example of calling this method is shown in the following code:

```
System.IO.File.Move("\Program Files\My Directory\working.tmp", _
  "\Program Files\Archive\working.tmp")
```

The point to remember when using this method is that it assumes that the target file doesn't already exist. If in fact it does, an exception will be thrown. Because of that, you need to check for the target file before you perform the move. Listing 8-8 demonstrates a self-contained routine, MoveFile, which provides an example of a proper way to implement the operation of moving files.

Listing 8-8. A Comprehensive Routine for Copying Files

```
' Declare the ReturnStatus structure.
Public Structure ReturnStatus
  Dim Success As Boolean
  Dim Message As String
End Structure

Function MoveFile(ByVal strSource As String, ByVal strTarget As String) _
  As ReturnStatus
' Moves a file.
' The strSource argument is the full path to the file to move.
' The strTarget argument is the full path to the new file.
  Dim MyReturn As ReturnStatus
```

```
' Check to see if source file exists.
  If Not (System.IO.File.Exists(strSource)) Then
    MyReturn.Success = False
    MyReturn.Message = "Source file does not exist."
    Return MyReturn
    Exit Function
  End If


' Check to see if target file exists.
  If System.IO.File.Exists(strTarget) Then
    MyReturn.Success = False
    MyReturn.Message = "Target file already exists."
    Return MyReturn
    Exit Function
  End If


' Move the file.
  Try
    System.IO.File.Move(strSource, strTarget)
    MyReturn.Success = True
    MyReturn.Message = strTarget
    Return MyReturn


' An exception occurred, so let the calling program
' know what happened.
  Catch ex As Exception
    MyReturn.Success = False
    MyReturn.Message = ex.Message
    Return MyReturn
  End Try
End Function
```

 NOTE *The MoveFile routine is included in the **FileRoutines** module, which is included under **Chapter 8** of the **Samples** folder.*

Deleting a File

To delete a file use the **Delete** method of the **File** class. The syntax for this method is

```
Public Shared Sub Delete( _
    ByVal path As String _
)
```

where *path* is the full path to the file to delete. An example of calling this method is shown here:

```
System.IO.File.Delete("\Program Files\My Directory\working.tmp")
```

Obtaining File Attributes

The current attributes for a file can be retrieved from the **Attributes** property of the **FileInfo** class. Notice I said the **FileInfo** class. The .NETCF implementation of the **File** class doesn't provide a method to accomplish this.

The value returned from this property is a combination of the archive, hidden, read-only, and system attribute flags. The following code shows an example of working the **Attributes** property:

```
Dim myFile As System.IO.FileInfo

myFile = New System.IO.FileInfo("\Program Files\My Directory\working.tmp")
MsgBox(myFile.Attributes.ToString)
```

Setting File Attributes

To set the attributes for a file, you use this same **Attributes** property of the **FileInfo** class. An example of setting an attribute is shown in the following code. In this example, first I create an instance of the file working.tmp. Next, I add the read-only attribute to the existing attributes of the file. Finally, I display the adjusted attributes.

```
Dim myFile As System.IO.FileInfo

myFile = New System.IO.FileInfo("\Program Files\My Directory\working.tmp")
myFile.Attributes = myFile.Attributes + IO.FileAttributes.ReadOnly
MsgBox(myFile.Attributes.ToString)
```

Working with Files

Up to this point, this chapter has been concerned with managing directories and files. While management is an important issue, working with files, that is to say, reading from and writing to text and binary files, is another critical skill that you will want to have as a developer of Pocket PC applications.

In this section, I'm going to show you how to do just that, read from and write to both text and binary files. Now, at this point I wouldn't be surprised if you're thinking, "Why in the world would I want to use text files and binary files? I don't use them for desktop applications. They're pretty primitive, aren't they? I have SQL Server CE, what do I need text and binary files for?" Okay, maybe you're not thinking that, but either way remember, in the rough and tumble world of Pocket PC development, often simple is better. Text and binary files are simple. They are simple to create, simple to work with, and most importantly simple to move between a device and an enterprise server. Finally, I've got your attention.

Creating and Opening Files

There are numerous methods provided through the **File** and **FileStream** classes for creating and opening files. In fact, the options are plentiful enough that I could spend a whole chapter on this topic alone. Rather than doing that, I've chosen to demonstrate several of the more commonly used approaches.

The first method uses the **CreateText** method of the **File** class. This method takes a single argument, which is the path to your file, and returns a reference to a StreamWriter. The following code shows an example of this method:

```
Dim sw As System.IO.StreamWriter
sw = System.IO.File.CreateText("\Program Files\My Directory\working.tmp")
```

As you would guess, the **CreateText** method is perfectly suited for situations where you are going to be using a StreamWriter.

A second option allows you to open and automatically create the file. This method is provided through the **StreamWriter** class. Simply specify the path to your file when creating an instance of StreamWriter. The class takes care of the rest. An example of this approach is shown here:

```
Dim sw As System.IO.StreamWriter
sw = New System.IO.StreamWriter("\Program Files\My Directory\working.tmp")
```

Still another commonly used approach makes use of the **FileStream** class. When creating a new instance of this class, you specify the path to your file and whether you want to create and open the file or simply just open an existing file. The following is an example of working with the **FileStream** class:

```
Dim fs As System.IO.FileStream
fs = New _
  System.IO.FileStream("data.tmp", _
  IO.FileMode.OpenOrCreate)
```

Each of these methods has it purpose and appropriate place of use. By no means are these the only ways for creating and opening files through the **System.IO** namespace. My intention here was to provide you with some of the more commonly used approaches.

Understanding Readers and Writers

Before we go any further, we need to have a brief discussion of readers and writers, as they play such a key role in working with files. The .NET Compact Framework offers a set of **Reader** and **Writer** classes for use with text and binary files. There are the **TextReader** and **TextWriter** classes, which are used with files that contain character data. The **StreamReader** and **StreamWriter** classes are used when working with files where particular encoding is needed. The **BinaryReader** and **BinaryWriter** classes allow you to work with primitive types in binary, rather than text format.

Each of these **Reader** classes, **Text**, **Stream**, and **Binary**, offers methods for reading in its respective data types. The corresponding **Writer** classes provide methods for writing out their appropriate data types.

Writing to a File

You write to a file using the **TextWriter**, **StreamWriter**, and **BinaryWriter** classes. If you are going to be writing text-based data to file, you can use either the TextWriter or **StreamWriter** classes. The commonly used methods for these two classes are shown in Table 8-7.

Table 8-7. Methods of the TextWriter and StreamWriter Classes

METHOD	DESCRIPTION
Close	Closes the stream
Flush	Clears the buffer being used by the stream, causing the data to be written to file
Write	Writes data to a stream
WriteLine	Writes text to the stream followed by a line terminator

Listing 8-9 demonstrates using the **StreamWriter** class to write some simple text to file. This example starts by creating an instance of the **StreamWriter** class and opening the file working.tmp. There are two examples of writing to the file. The first writes a static string of text to the file using the **StreamWriter Write** method. The second write uses the **StreamWriter WriteLine** method to add the current date and time. The **WriteLine** method inserts a line terminator as well.

Listing 8-9. Writing to a File Using StreamWriter

```
Dim sw As System.IO.StreamWriter

' Open the file.
  sw = New System.IO.StreamWriter("text.tmp")

' Add some text to the file.
  sw.Write("This content was written at: ")
  sw.WriteLine(DateTime.Now)

' Close the file.
  sw.Close()
```

What if your application isn't writing string data, but instead needs to write numeric data? That's where the **BinaryWriter** class comes in.

If your Pocket PC application needs to write, and subsequently read, specific data types to file, you will want to use the **BinaryWriter** class. Table 8-8 includes commonly used methods of this class.

Table 8-8. Methods of the BinaryWriter Class

METHOD	DESCRIPTION
Close	Closes the stream
Flush	Clears the buffer being used by the stream, causing the data to be written to file
Seek	Sets the position within the stream
Write	Writes binary data to the stream

You add data to a file with the **Write** method of the **BinaryWriter** class. This method is overloaded, providing support for a wide variety of data types. The **Write** method can also be used to write arrays to file.

Listing 8-10 provides an example of using the **BinaryWriter** class to write a couple of values to a file.

Listing 8-10. Writing to a File Using BinaryWriter

```
Dim bolTemp As Boolean = True
Dim bw As System.IO.BinaryWriter
Dim fs As System.IO.FileStream
Dim intTemp As Integer = 13

' Open the file.
 fs = New _
    System.IO.FileStream("data.tmp", _
    IO.FileMode.OpenOrCreate)
 bw = New System.IO.BinaryWriter(fs)

' Write two values to the file.
 bw.Write(bolTemp) ' Write a Boolean
 bw.Write(intTemp) ' Write an integer

' Close the file.
 bw.Close()
```

Reading from a File

The second half of our file discussion addresses reading from files. The **System.IO** namespace provides three classes for this: **TextReader**, **StreamReader**, and **BinaryReader**. As with the **Writer** classes, **TextReader** and **StreamReader** are used with character-based content, and the **BinaryReader** class handles data-specific content.

Commonly used methods of the **TextReader** and **StreamReader** classes are shown in Table 8-9. As you can see, there are several methods for reading content, differing primarily in the amount of data that they return.

Table 8-9. Methods of the TextReader and StreamReader Classes

METHOD	DESCRIPTION
Close	Closes the StreamReader and in effect the file
Peek	Reads the next character from the stream
Read	Reads the next character or characters from the stream
ReadBlock	Reads a block of characters from the stream
ReadLine	Reads a line of characters from the stream
ReadToEnd	Reads from the current position to the end of the stream

The following code fragment provides a simple example of how to read from a file using the **StreamReader** class. In this case, the **ReadToEnd** method is used to read the complete file in at one time, an approach that is typically used with text editors or other note-based applications. If you need more control over the retrieval process, use the **Read**, **ReadBlock**, or **ReadLine** methods.

```
Dim sr As System.IO.StreamReader

sr = System.IO.File.OpenText("text.tmp")
MsgBox(sr.ReadToEnd)
sr.Close()
```

While the **TextReader** and **StreamReader** classes work well with character content, if your application works with numeric data, you will want to use the **BinaryReader** class. With the **BinaryReader** class, you can read data of specific types directly without having to go through any conversion process.

The commonly used methods of the **BinaryReader** class are shown in Table 8-10. Immediately apparent is the large number of **Read** methods, one each for the data types supported by this class.

Table 8-10. Methods of the BinaryReader Class

METHOD	DESCRIPTION
Close	Closes the StreamReader and in effect the file
PeekChar	Reads the next character without advancing a position
Read	Reads from the stream
ReadBoolean	Reads a Boolean value from the stream
ReadByte	Reads a byte from the stream
ReadBytes	Reads a number of bytes from the stream
ReadChar	Reads a character from the stream
ReadChars	Reads a number of characters from the stream
ReadDecimal	Reads a decimal value from the stream
ReadDouble	Reads a double value from the stream
ReadInt16	Reads a signed, 2-byte integer from the stream
ReadInt32	Reads a signed, 4-byte integer from the stream
ReadInt64	Reads a signed, 8-byte integer from the stream
ReadSByte	Reads a signed byte from the stream

Table 8-10. Methods of the BinaryReader Class (continued)

METHOD	DESCRIPTION
ReadSingle	Reads a 4-byte floating point value from the stream
ReadString	Reads a string from the stream
ReadUInt16	Reads an unsigned, 2-byte integer from the stream
ReadUInt32	Reads an unsigned, 4-byte integer from the stream
ReadUInt64	Reads an unsigned, 8-byte integer from the stream

Listing 8-11 provides a simple example of reading numeric data from a file using the **BinaryReader** class. Two values, one Boolean and the other integer, are read from the file.

Listing 8-11. Reading In a Text File All in One Read

```
Dim bolTemp As Boolean
Dim br As System.IO.BinaryReader
Dim fs As System.IO.FileStream
Dim intTemp As Integer

' Open the file.
fs = New _
    System.IO.FileStream("data.tmp", _
    IO.FileMode.Open)
br = New System.IO.BinaryReader(fs)

' Read some numbers from the file.
bolTemp = br.ReadBoolean()
intTemp = br.ReadInt16
MsgBox("Boolean: " & bolTemp.ToString & " - Integer: " & intTemp.ToString)

' Close the file.
br.Close()
```

Working with Network Files

One of the coolest file-related features offered through the **System.IO** namespace is the ability to read and write files directly from a network share. Now, you may be asking, "What's so cool about this? I mean, after all, you're just working with files, right?" Well, files that are centrally stored can be shared between devices and can be processed on the server side. In addition, when working with files on a network share, you use exactly the same programming techniques as you would working with files on a device.

To store files on a network share, simply reference the Universal Naming Convention (UNC) of the computer, share, and filename, in place of the path you would use with device-based files. An example of this is shown in Listing 8-12.

Listing 8-12. Writing to a File Using StreamWriter

```
Dim sw As System.IO.StreamWriter

' Open the file.
  sw = New System.IO.StreamWriter("\\myComputer\myShare\text.tmp")

' Add some text to the file.
  sw.Write("This content was written at: ")
  sw.WriteLine(DateTime.Now)

' Close the file.
  sw.Close()
```

To read from a file stored on a network share, again you would use a UNC, as shown here:

```
Dim sr As System.IO.StreamReader

sr = System.IO.File.OpenText("\myComputer\MyShare\text.tmp")
MsgBox(sr.ReadToEnd)
sr.Close()
```

As you can see from these two examples, working with the **System.IO** namespace's support for network shares is no different from working with local files. Plus, it provides you with another option for handling data, and as a developer of mobile applications, you can never have too many ways to work with data.

 TIP *Just to make your life easier, verify that your Pocket PC device can connect to a network share before attempting to access it from code. Use the Pocket PC File Manager for this. After starting File Manager, simply tap the* **Open** *menu, enter the UNC of your share, and click the* **OK** *button. If everything is configured correctly, you will see the share displayed.*

Step-by-Step Tutorial: Building a Text File Demo

In this step-by-step exercise, you'll create a Pocket PC project that demonstrates reading from and writing to a text file. As part of this exercise, you'll

- Determine the directory where your application is stored.

- Check if a file exists.

- Delete a file.

- Write text to a file.

- Read text from a file.

This simple application provides the basic read and write capabilities that are found at the core of many text editors. In fact, it wouldn't take much to build a Notepad knockoff by combining what you learned here with the basic shell of an editor built in Chapter 6.

 NOTE   *A completed version of this application, titled Text File Demo, is provided under the **Chapter 8** folder of the **Samples** folder for this book. See Appendix D for more information on accessing and loading the sample applications.*

Step 1: Starting a New Project

Begin this step-by-step exercise by creating a new project using the following steps:

1. Start Visual Studio .NET if necessary.

2. From the Start Page, select **New Project**.

3. From the New Project dialog box, select **Smart Device Application**.

4. Specify a project name of **Text File Demo**.

5. Select a location to create the project and click the **OK** button.

Step 2: Configuring the Project

To configure the target output folder for this project, perform the following steps:

1. Under the Project menu, select **Text File Demo Properties**.

2. Under the Device page of the Text File Property Pages dialog box, set the output file folder to **\Windows\Start Menu\Programs\Apress**.

 TIP   *Using **\Windows\Start Menu\Programs** as the output folder will add your application under the **Programs** folder that can be accessed from the Start menu on your Pocket PC device. This is a good way to organize your test applications and make them easy to access.*

 NOTE   *If you are unsure of the purpose of project properties, or how to set them, refer to Chapter 3, which provides a detailed overview of this topic.*

Step 3: Constructing the Interface

The interface for this demo application is simple, consisting of a single TextBox and two Buttons. Figure 8-5 provides an example of how the interface should appear when completed.

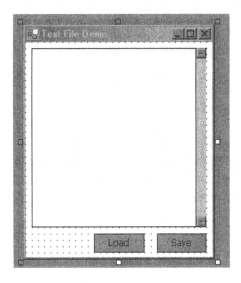

Figure 8-5. The completed interface for the Text File Demo application

Step 4: Setting Properties

Use Table 8-11 to configure the properties for the form and controls.

Table 8-11. Form and Control Properties

OBJECT	PROPERTY	VALUE
Form1	Text	Text File Demo
TextBox	Name	txtContent
TextBox	Multiline	True
TextBox	ScrollBars	Vertical
TextBox	Text	(empty)
Button (left)	Name	btnLoad
Button (left)	Text	Load
Button (right)	Name	btnSave
Button (right)	Text	Save

Resize the TextBox control so that it fills the form as shown in Figure 8-5.

Step 5: Coding the Application

There are three parts to coding this demo—handling each of the buttons and creating a small function that returns the path to your application's directory.

Retrieving the Application's Directory

Start the coding by writing the function that will be used to obtain the application's directory. The following example shows the simple code that is required to implement the function AppPath. You'll use the AppPath function in the **Click** event procedures for both the **Load** and **Save** buttons.

```
Private Function AppPath() As String

' Return the path to this application.
    AppPath = _
```

```
System.IO.Path.GetDirectoryName(Reflection.Assembly. _
GetExecutingAssembly().GetName().CodeBase.ToString())
```

```
End Function
```

> **TIP** *Determining the path to your application is a process that*
> *you will commonly perform within a Pocket PC application. To*
> *make the AppPath function easier to reuse, create the function in*
> *a separate module. Make sure that you define it as Public. To use it*
> *in the future, simply add the module to your project.*

Coding the Load Button

The code behind the **Click** event of the **Load** button is shown in Listing 8-13.
This procedure starts by performing a check to see if the file used in this demonstration already exists. The **Exists** method of the **File** class is used for this. If the
file exists, it is opened and read into the TextBox with a single read. The user is
warned if the file doesn't exist.

Listing 8-13. Coding the Load Button

```
Private Sub btnLoad_Click(ByVal sender As System.Object, _
  ByVal e As System.EventArgs) Handles btnLoad.Click
  Dim sr As System.IO.StreamReader

' Check to see if the file exists. If it does, open and read the file.
  If (System.IO.File.Exists(AppPath() & "\demo.txt")) Then
    sr = System.IO.File.OpenText(AppPath() & "\demo.txt")
    txtContent.Text = sr.ReadToEnd
    sr.Close()

' The file doesn't exist, so tell the user what to do.
  Else
    MsgBox("Demo file does not exist." & _
      " Tap the Save button to create the file", _
      MsgBoxStyle.Information, _
      "File not found")
  End If

End Sub
```

Coding the Save Button

The final bit of code is for the **Click** event of the **Save** button. Listing 8-14 provides the code to place in this event. This is by far the most involved of the four procedures that power this application.

Listing 8-14. Coding the Save Button

```
Private Sub btnSave_Click(ByVal sender As System.Object, _
  ByVal e As System.EventArgs) Handles btnSave.Click
  Dim sw As System.IO.StreamWriter

' Whack the file if it already exists.
  If (System.IO.File.Exists(AppPath() & "\demo.txt")) Then
    MsgBox("Deleting existing version of the demo file.")
    System.IO.File.Delete(AppPath() & "\demo.txt")
  End If

' Open, and create, the file.
  sw = New System.IO.StreamWriter(AppPath() & "\demo.txt")

' Write some text to the file.
  sw.Write("This demo file was created at ")
  sw.WriteLine(DateTime.Now)

' Close the file.
  sw.Close()

End Sub
```

The procedure starts by checking to see if the file exists using the **Exists** method of the **File** class. If the file does exist, it is deleted. This step is accomplished using the **Delete** method of the **File** class. The procedure continues by opening the file. Two **Write** methods are used to add some content to the file. The last step performed is to close the file.

Step 6: Testing Your Application

To test your application, perform the following steps:

1. Select either **Pocket PC Device** or **Pocket PC Emulator** from the Deployment Device combo box.

2. Select **Release** from the Solution Configurations combo box.

3. Click the **Start** button.

Your application will be copied to the target device and run. It should appear as shown in Figure 8-6.

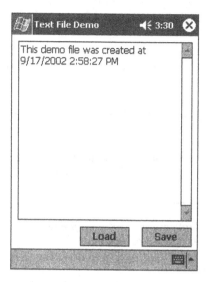

Figure 8-6. The Text File Demo application

Perform the following steps to verify your application is running correctly:

1. Tap the **Save** button to create the demo file.

2. Tap the **Load** button. The contents of the demo file should be loaded into the TextBox.

HOMEWORK *Turn your application into a simple text editor by modifying the **Save** event procedure so that it writes out the contents of the TextBox rather than the current date and time.*

HOMEWORK *Modify your Text File Demo application so that it stores and reads the file from a network share. Refer to the "Working with Network Files" section for details on how this is accomplished.*

Step-by-Step Tutorial: Building a Binary File Demo

In this step-by-step exercise, you'll create a Pocket PC project that demonstrates reading and writing from a binary file. As part of this exercise you'll

- Determine the directory where your application is stored.

- Write to a binary file.

- Read from a binary file.

This application is designed to provide you with all of the basics of working with a binary file.

 NOTE *A completed version of this application, titled Binary File Demo, is provided under the* **Chapter 8** *folder of this book's* **Samples** *folder. See Appendix D for more information on accessing and loading the sample applications.*

Step 1: Starting a New Project

Begin this step-by-step exercise by creating a new project using the following steps:

1. Start Visual Studio .NET if necessary.

2. From the Start Page, select **New Project**.

3. From the New Project dialog box, select **Smart Device Application**.

4. Specify a project name of **Binary File Demo**.

5. Select a location to create the project and click the **OK** button.

Step 2: Configuring the Project

To configure the target output folder for this project, perform the following steps:

1. Under the Project menu, select **Binary File Demo Properties**.

2. Under the Device page of the Text File Property Pages dialog box, set the output file folder to **\Windows\Start Menu\Programs\Apress**.

Step 3: Constructing the Interface

The interface for the Binary File Demo application uses the Noah's Arc approach
to interface design. It includes everything in pairs: two Labels, two TextBoxes, and
two Buttons. Figure 8-7 provides an example of how the interface should appear.

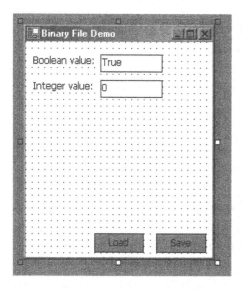

Figure 8-7. The completed interface for the Binary File Demo application

Step 4: Setting Properties

Use Table 8-12 to configure the properties for the form and controls.

Table 8-12. Form and Control Properties

OBJECT	PROPERTY	VALUE
Form1	Text	Binary File Demo
Label (top)	Text	Boolean value:
TextBox (top)	Name	txtBoolean
TextBox (top)	Text	True
Label (bottom)	Text	Integer value:
TextBox (bottom)	Name	txtInteger
TextBox (bottom)	TextAlign	Right

Table 8-12. Form and Control Properties (continued)

OBJECT	PROPERTY	VALUE
TextBox (bottom)	Text	0
Button (left)	Name	btnLoad
Button (left)	Text	Load
Button (right)	Name	btnSave
Button (right)	Text	Save

Step 5: Coding the Application

There are three parts to coding this demo—handling the two buttons and defining a function that returns the path to your application's directory.

Retrieving the Application's Directory

The first piece of code you need is a function that will obtain the application's directory. Here's the code that implements the AppPath function:

```
Private Function AppPath() As String

' Return the path to this application.
    AppPath = _
      System.IO.Path.GetDirectoryName(Reflection.Assembly. _
      GetExecutingAssembly().GetName().CodeBase.ToString())

End Function
```

Coding the Load Button

The code behind the **Click** event of the **Load** button is shown in Listing 8-15. This procedure uses a FileStream to open the data file. It then reads two values, one Boolean and the other integer, before closing the file.

Listing 8-15. Coding the Load Button

```
Private Sub btnLoad_Click(ByVal sender As System.Object, _
    ByVal e As System.EventArgs) Handles btnLoad.Click
    Dim br As System.IO.BinaryReader
    Dim fs As System.IO.FileStream
```

```
' Open the file.
   fs = New _
     System.IO.FileStream(AppPath() & "\demo.dat", _
     IO.FileMode.Open)
   br = New System.IO.BinaryReader(fs)

' Read two values from the file.
   txtBoolean.Text = br.ReadBoolean.ToString
   txtInteger.Text = br.ReadInt16.ToString

' Close the file.
   br.Close()


   End Sub
```

Coding the Save Button

The last bit of coding that is required for this application is for the **Save** button. Listing 8-16 contains the code for the **Click** event of this button. As with the **Load** procedure, a FileStream is used to open the data file. Two values are written to the file after they're converted to the appropriate format.

Listing 8-16. Coding the Save Button

```
Private Sub btnSave_Click(ByVal sender As Object, _
   ByVal e As System.EventArgs) Handles btnSave.Click
   Dim bw As System.IO.BinaryWriter
   Dim fs As System.IO.FileStream

' Open the file.
   fs = New _
     System.IO.FileStream(AppPath() & "\demo.dat", _
     IO.FileMode.OpenOrCreate)
   bw = New System.IO.BinaryWriter(fs)

' Write the two values to the file.
   bw.Write(CBool(txtBoolean.Text))
   bw.Write(CInt(txtInteger.Text))
```

```
' Reset the TextBox controls.
   txtInteger.Text = "True"
   txtBoolean.Text = "0"


' Close the file.
   bw.Close()


   End Sub
```

Step 6: Testing Your Application

To test your application, perform the following steps:

1. Select either **Pocket PC Device** or **Pocket PC Emulator** from the Deployment Device combo box.

2. Select **Release** from the Solution Configurations combo box.

3. Click the **Start** button.

Your application will be copied to the target device and run. It should appear as shown in Figure 8-8. Perform the following steps to verify your application is running correctly:

1. Enter **False** in the first field and an integer number in the second field.

2. Tap the **Save** button to create the demo file.

3. Tap the **Load** button. The contents of the demo file should be loaded into the TextBox.

 HOMEWORK *Modify the Binary File Demo program so that it will accept, store, and retrieve other data types.*

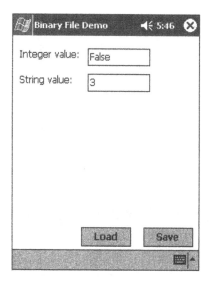

Figure 8-8. The Text File Demo application

Summary

Directories and files—two staples for Pocket PC developers' programming diet. Having a solid understanding of how to manage directories and files is critically important, particularly when your application is in complete control of the device on which it is running.

Managing directories and files is straightforward and simple thanks to the **System.IO** namespace. The **Directory** and **DirectoryInfo** classes can be used to create, move, delete, and query directories. The **File** and **FileInfo** classes allow you to copy, move, delete, and configure files.

Management is only part of what the **System.IO** namespace has to offer. This namespace also is used to read and write text and binary files. Three classes are provided for input: **TextReader**, **StreamReader**, and **BinaryReader**. Three corresponding classes are provided for output: **TextWriter**, **StreamWriter**, and **BinaryWriter**.

I can't stress strongly enough how important text and binary files are as design options for Pocket PC applications. Simple in comparison to a relational database, they are often just what you need. The ease in which they are created, used, and transferred makes them invaluable tools to have in your development skill set.

CHAPTER 9

Introduction
to ADO.NET

WHEN IT COMES TO APPLICATIONS, whether those applications are server, desktop, or device based, they have a common trait—data. Most applications work with data in some fashion, whether that is to gather and store data, to query and view data, or some combination of both storing and viewing. Mobile applications are no different.

In Chapter 8, you were introduced to some of the simpler ways to incorporate data into your mobile applications. While text and binary files will work for many programming needs, when it comes to constructing robust, enterprise applications, you will want something more. That something is ADO.NET.

ADO.NET offers you a wide variety of functionality for you to construct data-enabled applications including the following:

- **Access to both local and remote data** provides you with options on how to incorporate data into your mobile applications.

- **Support for disconnected data** is especially useful with mobile applications. Data can be loaded, updated, and viewed without requiring an active connection to its data source.

- **Integrated support for XML** makes it easy for you to pass data over the Internet and to persist data on the device.

- **Being able to assemble data from a variety of sources** including local or network based, and over the Internet.

- **Robust error handling** that provides a comprehensive way to address problems that may occur when working with data.

The implementation of ADO.NET under the .NET Compact Framework is like everything else under NETCF, a subset of the version provided with the .NET Framework. Even so, it is an incredible improvement over earlier versions of Windows CE programming tools. What makes ADO.NET even more useful to you is that you can leverage your ADO.NET skills between the server, desktop, and device.

In this chapter, I'm going to provide you with an overview of ADO.NET and its key classes. This is just the start of our ADO.NET-related adventure, though. The next five chapters continue this data odyssey, touching on the following topics:

- **Data binding** (Chapter 10) shows how to link the controls that make up your graphical interface to a data source. No longer do you have to code by hand all of your data/form work. Simply set a few properties, and ADO.NET handles the rest.

- **SQL Server CE** (Chapter 11) is the Mini Me version of SQL Server. You will learn what SQL Server CE is, what it includes, how to set it up, and work with it from code.

- **Server-based data** (Chapter 12) is one of the coolest new features offered to mobile developers through the .NET Compact Framework. With ADO.NET, you can now create mobile applications that interact with server-based databases just as you would from a desktop PC. This feature is particularly useful in wireless environments.

- **Device-based data** (Chapter 13) is the hands-on continuation to Chapter 11. You will learn the code side of how to work with SQL Server CE databases.

- **XML** (Chapter 14) is a key component of ADO.NET. It provides mobile developers with a means to transfer data seamlessly to and from a variety of sources. Chapter 14 highlights the XML functionality offered through the **System.Data** and **System.XML** namespaces.

System.Data Namespace

We'll start our discussion of ADO.NET with the namespace through which much of the functionality is provided: **System.Data**. I have listed classes of this namespace commonly used by mobile developers in Table 9-1. You can use these classes to access and work with data that is stored both locally on a device as well as remotely on an enterprise server.

Table 9-1. Key Classes of the System.Data Namespace

CLASS	DESCRIPTION
Constraint	Constraint that is used with DataColumns
ConstraintCollection	Collection of constraints for a DataTable
DataColumn	Column within a DataTable
DataColumnCollection	Collection of DataColumns for a DataTable
DataRow	Row within a DataTable
DataRowCollection	Collection of DataRows for a DataTable
DataSet	Disconnected in-memory storage of data
DataTable	Single table in memory
DataTableCollection	Collection of DataTables for a DataSet
DataView	Class used to manage the data within a DataTable

Working with the System.Data Namespace

As with any namespace, there are two ways to reference the **System.Data** namespace within your application. The first method requires you to add an Imports statement as shown in Figure 9-1. Adding this single statement allows you to shorten reference names. For example, instead of having to use the complete naming syntax as shown here:

```
System.Data.SqlClient.SqlConnection
```

you could instead use the much more easy to type syntax:

```
SqlClient.SqlConnection
```

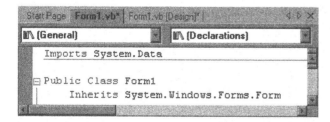

Figure 9-1. Adding a reference to the System.Data namespace

The second approach to working with the System.Data namespace is what I refer to as the longhand method. In place of adding a single reference in the General Declarations section of a module, you instead use complete naming syntax when referring to objects.

Data Providers

The .NET Compact Framework supports two relational data sources: SQL Server and SQL Server CE. This support is delivered through two providers: SqlClient and SqlServerCE, as shown in Table 9-2. Both of these providers are similar in functionality, differing primarily in the source that they work with.

Table 9-2. Data Providers of the .NET Compact Framework

PROVIDER	DESCRIPTION
SqlClient	Provides access to SQL Server databases running on network or desktop servers
SqlServerCe	Provides access to SQL Server CE databases running locally on a device

It is through these providers that your applications access data.

SQL Server Provider

The SQL Server provider is implemented through the **System.Data.SqlClient** namespace. Through this provider, you can access SQL Server from your mobile applications, allowing you to directly query and modify enterprise databases. For all practical purposes, with this provider you can create mobile applications that function identically to desktop applications in the way that they work with data. I list the commonly used classes of this namespace in Table 9-3.

Table 9-3. Key Classes of the System.Data.SqlClient Namespace

CLASS	DESCRIPTION
SqlCommand	Transact-SQL statement or stored procedure that will be executed against the target SQL Server database
SqlConnection	Connection to a SQL Server database
SqlDataAdapter	Class used to fill DataSets and update SQL Server databases
SqlDataReader	Forward-only stream of rows
SqlError	Warning or error returned by the SQL Server provider
SqlErrorCollection	Collection of warnings and errors returned by the SQL Server provider
SqlParameter	Parameter for use with a SqlCommand
SqlParameterCollection	Collection of parameters used with a SqlCommand
SqlTransaction	SQL transaction to be made against a SQL Server database

NOTE *As with all namespaces, you will either need to add an Imports statement to reference the namespace within your application or use the complete name of SqlClient objects when referring to them from within your code, for example, System.Data.SqlClient.SqlCommand.*

SQL Server CE Provider

The SQL Server CE provider is implemented through the **System.Data.SqlServerCe** namespaces. This provider enables you to access SQL Server CE databases that are resident on your device. I have listed the commonly used classes of this namespace in Table 9-4.

Table 9-4. Key Classes of the System.Data.SqlServerCe Namespace

CLASS	DESCRIPTION
SqlCeCommand	Transact-SQL statement that will be executed against the target SQL Server CE database
SqlCeConnection	Connection to a SQL Server CE database
SqlCeDataAdapter	Class used to fill DataSets and update SQL Server CE databases
SqlCeDataReader	Forward-only stream of rows
SqlCeEngine	Properties, methods, and other objects that represent a SQL Server CE database
SqlCeError	Warning or error returned by the SQL Server CE provider
SqlCeErrorCollection	Collection of warnings and errors returned by the SQL Server CE provider
SqlCeParameter	Parameter for use with a SqlCeCommand
SqlCeParameterCollection	Collection of parameters used with a SqlCeCommand
SqlCeRemoteDataAccess	Instance of the SqlCeRemoteDataAccess object
SqlCeReplication	Instance of the SqlCeReplication object
SqlCeTransaction	SQL transaction to be made against a SQL Server CE database

Working with the System.Data.SqlServerCe Namespace

Unlike the System.Data and System.Data.SqlClient namespaces, the System.Data.SqlServerCe namespace is not natively part of the .NET Compact Framework. What this means is that you can't simply add an Imports statement or reference the complete object without first adding a reference to the **System.Data.SqlServerCe** namespace to your project.

To add a reference to the **System.Data.SqlServerCe** namespace to your project, perform the following steps:

1. From the Project menu, select **Add Reference**. The Add Reference dialog box will be displayed as shown in Figure 9-2.

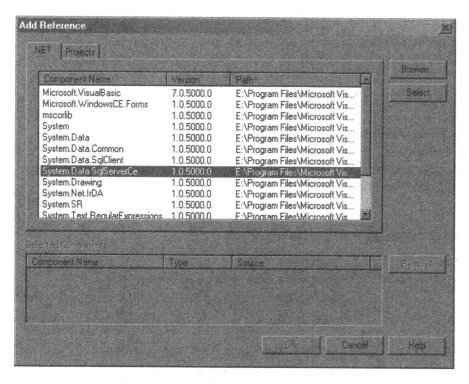

Figure 9-2. The Add Reference dialog box

2. Select **System.Data.SqlServerCe** from the list of components.

3. Click the **Select** button. This will add **System.Data.SqlServerCe** to the Selected Components list.

4. Click the **OK** button to add the reference to your project.

NOTE *After adding this reference, you'll still need to either add an Imports statement for **System.Data.SqlServerCe** or reference objects using their complete name, for example, System.Data. SqlServerCe.SqlCommand.*

The Connection Classes

When it comes to accessing databases, whether that is locally from SQL Server CE or remotely from SQL Server, everything starts with a connection. Both the **System.Data.SqlClient** and **System.Data.SqlServerCe** namespaces include **Connection** classes.

The SqlConnection Class

The **Connection** class for the **System.Data.SqlClient** namespace is **SqlConnection**. You'll use this class to establish a connection to a SQL Server database directly from your device. I list the commonly used methods of the **SqlConnection** class in Table 9-5.

Table 9-5. Methods of the SqlConnection Class

METHOD	DESCRIPTION
BeginTransaction	Starts a database transaction. You will use the SqlTransaction object to commit or roll back a transaction.
Close	Closes the connection to a database.
CreateCommand	Creates and returns a SQLCommand object.
Open	Opens a connection to a database.

I show the commonly used properties of this class in Table 9-6.

Table 9-6. Properties of the SqlConnection Class

PROPERTY	DESCRIPTION
ConnectionString	String that defines how a SQL Server database will be opened
ConnectionTimeout	Amount of time to wait when opening a connection before generating an error
Database	Name of the database to open
DataSource	Instance of SQL Server to which to connect
State	Current state of the connection to the SQL Server database

Opening a Connection to SQL Server

The following code shows an example of opening a connection to a SQL Server database. In this example, the server name is being provided as an IP address, and the database being used is the infamous Northwind.

NOTE *In your applications, you will need to replace the IP address with the address of your server and the database with the name of your database.*

```
Dim cn As System.Data.SqlClient.SqlConnection

' Open the connection.
  cn = New System.Data.SqlClient.SqlConnection( _
    "user id=sa;password=;database=Northwind;server=192.168.1.101")
```

NOTE *For more information on working with the SQL Server connection class, see Chapter 12.*

The SqlCeConnection Class

The **Connection** class for the **System.Data.SqlServerCe** namespace is **SqlCeConnection**. This class is used to connect to a SQL Server CE database that is located on your device. Table 9-7 lists the commonly used methods of the **SqlCeConnection** class and Table 9-8 shows the commonly used properties of this class.

Table 9-7. Methods of the SqlCeConnection Class

METHOD	DESCRIPTION
BeginTransaction	Starts a database transaction. You will use the SqlCeTransaction object to commit or roll back a transaction.
Close	Closes the connection to a database.
CreateCommand	Creates and returns a SQLCeCommand object.
Open	Opens a connection to a database.

Table 9-8. Properties of the SqlCeConnection Class

PROPERTY	DESCRIPTION
ConnectionString	String that defines how a SQL Server CE database will be opened
ConnectionTimeout	Time to wait when opening a connection before generating an error
Database	Name of the database to open
DataSource	Path and filename of the SQL Server CE database
State	Current state of the connection to the SQL Server CE database

Opening a Connection to SQL Server CE

The following code shows an example of opening a connection to a SQL Server CE database. In this example, this is the Northwind database located in the folder **\Windows\Start Menu\Programs\Apress**.

NOTE   *When specifying the data source for a connection, include the complete path to the database.*

```
Dim cn As System.Data.SqlServerCe.SqlCeConnection

' Open the connection.
cn = New _
   System.Data.SqlServerCe.SqlCeConnection( _
      "Data Source=\Windows\Start Menu\Programs\Apress\Northwind.sdf")
```

NOTE   *For more information on working with the SQL Server CE connection class, see Chapter 13.*

The Command Classes

Now that we've discussed connections, we're ready for the next topic: commands. Commands are used to define, query, and modify databases and their contents. As with connections, both the **System.Data.SqlClient** and **System.Data.SqlServerCe** namespaces include **Command** classes.

The SqlCommand Class

The **Command** class for the **System.Data.SqlClient** namespace is **SqlCommand**. This class is used to execute commands against a SQL Server database. I list the commonly used methods of this class in Table 9-9 and the commonly used properties of the **SqlCommand** class in Table 9-10.

Table 9-9. Methods of the SqlCommand Class

METHOD	DESCRIPTION
Cancel	Cancels the execution of a command.
CreateParameter	Creates a parameter object, SqlParameter, for use with a command.
ExecuteNonQuery	Executes a SQL command and returns the number of rows affected. This is commonly used for bulk updates and deletes.
ExecuteReader	Executes a command and returns a SqlDataReader object.
ExecuteScalar	Executes a command and returns the first column in the first row of the query results. Used to obtain summary information from a database.
ExecuteXmlReader	Executes a command and returns an XmlReader object.

One of the cool features of the **SqlCommand** class is the quartet of **Execute** methods that offer you a variety of ways to receive data back from a command.

NOTE   *We'll see other ways that you can receive data back from a database when we look at DataAdapters later in this chapter.*

Table 9-10. Properties of the SqlCommand Class

PROPERTY	DESCRIPTION
CommandText	Command that will be executed. This can be either a SQL statement or the name of a stored procedure.
CommandTimeout	Amount of time to wait when executing a command before generating an error.
CommandType	Property that defines whether CommandText is a SQL command, the name of a table, or the name of a stored procedure.
Connection	Connection to use when executing this command.
Parameters	Collection of parameters to pass when calling a stored procedure.
Transaction	SqlTransaction used when executing this command.

Executing a Command Against SQL Server

I show an example of executing a command against a SQL Server database in Listing 9-1. This example starts by opening a connection to the Northwind database. Next, I define a command with two arguments provided: first, a SQL statement that specifies what the command will do, and second, the connection to the database. Finally, I execute the command. In this example, the command is a SQL Select statement that returns a DataReader object.

Listing 9-1. Executing a Command Against SQL Server

```
Dim cn As System.Data.SqlClient.SqlConnection
Dim cmd As System.Data.SqlClient.SqlCommand
Dim dr As System.Data.SqlClient.SqlDataReader

' Open the connection.
cn = New System.Data.SqlClient.SqlConnection( _
  "user id=sa;password=;database=Northwind;server=192.168.1.101")

' Configure and execute the command.
cmd.CommandText = "SELECT * FROM Customers
cmd.Connection = cn
dr = cmd.ExecuteReader
```

NOTE *For more information on using the **SqlCommand** class, see Chapter 12.*

The SqlCeCommand Class

The **Command** class for the **System.Data.SqlServerCe** namespace is **SqlCeCommand**. This class is used to execute commands against a SQL Server CE database. Table 9-11 shows the commonly used methods of this class.

Table 9-11. Methods of the SqlCECommand Class

METHOD	DESCRIPTION
Cancel	Cancels the execution of a command
CreateParameter	Creates a parameter object, SqlCeParameter, for use with a command
ExecuteNonQuery	Executes a SQL command and returns the number of rows affected
ExecuteReader	Executes a command and returns a SqlCeDataReader
ExecuteScalar	Executes a command and returns the first column in the first row of the query results

NOTE *Unlike the **SqlCommand** class, the **SqlCeCommand** class doesn't support the **ExecuteXMLReader** method.*

In Table 9-12, you'll find commonly used properties of this class.

Table 9-12. Properties of the SqlCeCommand Class

PROPERTY	DESCRIPTION
CommandText	SQL command that will be executed.
CommandTimeout	Amount of time to wait when executing a command before generating an error. NOTE: Timing out a command is of less concern when working with a SQL Server CE database as 1) the data is not usually being shared, and 2) there is no network connection involved.
CommandType	Property that defines whether CommandText is a SQL command or the name of a table. NOTE: The value of StoredProcedure is not supported by this property.
Connection	Connection to use when executing this command.
Parameters	Collection of parameters to pass with this command.
Transaction	SqlCeTransaction to use when executing this command.

Executing a Command Against SQL Server CE

Listing 9-2 shows an example of executing a command against a SQL Server CE database. This example begins by opening a connection to a local copy of the Northwind database. The command then uses this connection to retrieve all of the records from the Customers table into a DataReader.

Listing 9-2. Executing a Command Against SQL Server CE

```
Dim cn As System.Data.SqlServerCe.SqlCeConnection
Dim cmd As System.Data.SqlServerCe.SqlCeCommand
Dim dr As System.Data.SqlServerCe.SqlCeDataReader

' Open the connection.
cn = New _
    System.Data.SqlServerCe.SqlCeConnection( _
    "Data Source=\Windows\Start Menu\Programs\Apress\NorthwindDemo.sdf")

' Configure and execute the command.
cmd.CommandText = "SELECT * FROM Customers"
cmd.Connection = cn
dr = cmd.ExecuteReader
```

NOTE *For more information on using the SqlCeCommand class, see Chapter 13.*

The DataReader Classes

In the previous section, we looked at how the SqlCommand and SqlCeCommand objects return the results of a query in a DataReader object. The obvious question that a developer would ask at this point is, "What is a DataReader object?" A DataReader is a set of records that are read-only and can only be navigated through in a forward motion. I like to think of them as being the one-card solitaire approach to data access.

Because of their characteristics/limitations, DataReaders are ideally suited for producing reports, retrieving and displaying sets of records, filling ListBox and ComboBox controls, and any other activity that *doesn't require you to update the data or move backwards through the data.*

DataReaders are quicker to access than DataSets. They are returned as a raw data stream. This means you really have no good way of telling how many rows (records) there are until you read all the way through the stream.

The **System.Data.SqlClient** and **System.Data.SqlServerCe** namespaces each include **DataReader** classes. I list the most commonly used methods of both of these classes in Table 9-13.

Table 9-13. DataReader Methods

METHOD	DESCRIPTION
Close	Closes the reader. You should always close the reader when you are done.
Read	Moves the reader to the next record.

The SqlDataReader Class

The **DataReader** class for the **System.Data.SqlClient** namespace is **SqlDataReader**. You'll use this class to receive the results of a query made against a SQL Server database.

Listing 9-3 shows how to loop through a SqlDataReader object loading a ListBox with the contents of the CompanyName field from each record.

Listing 9-3. Looping Through a SqlDataReader Object

```
Sub ReadSqlDataReader()
  Dim cn As System.Data.SqlClient.SqlConnection
  Dim cmd As System.Data.SqlClient.SqlCommand
  Dim dr As System.Data.SqlClient.SqlDataReader
Try
' Open the connection.
  cn = New System.Data.SqlClient.SqlConnection( _
    "user id=sa;password=;database=Northwind;server=192.168.1.101")

' Configure and execute the command.
  cmd.CommandText = "SELECT * FROM Customers"
  cmd.Connection = cn
  dr = cmd.ExecuteReader

' Loop through the data.
  While dr.Read()
    ListBox1.Items.Add(dr("CompanyName"))
  End While
Catch
Finally
' Clean up.
  dr.Close()
  cn.Close()
End Try
```

NOTE *The fields in a record can be referred to either by their name, as shown in the preceding example, or by a numeric index that corresponds to the position within a record, with the first field being zero (0).*

SqlCeDataReader

The **DataReader** class for the **System.Data.SqlServerCe** namespace is **SqlCeDataReader**. This class is used to receive the results from a query that is made against a SQL Server CE database.

The example in Listing 9-4 shows how to loop through a SqlDataReader object to load a ListBox with the contents of the CompanyName field from each record.

Listing 9-4. Looping Through a SqlCeDataReader Object

```
    Dim cn As System.Data.SqlServerCe.SqlCeConnection
    Dim cmd As System.Data.SqlServerCe.SqlCeCommand
    Dim dr As System.Data.SqlServerCe.SqlCeDataReader

' Open the connection.
  cn = New _
    System.Data.SqlServerCe.SqlCeConnection( _
    "Data Source=\Windows\Start Menu\Programs\Apress\NorthwindDemo.sdf")

' Configure and execute the command.
    cmd.CommandText = "SELECT * FROM Customers"
    cmd.Connection = cn
    dr = cmd.ExecuteReader

' Loop through the data.
    While dr.Read()
      ListBox1.Items.Add(dr("CompanyName"))
    End While

' Clean up.
  dr.Close()
  cn.Close()
```

NOTE *What you should come away with from these two examples (Listing 9-3 and 9-4) is that the process of working with DataReaders, whether that is the SqlDataReader or the SqlCeDataReader, is identical. This is just another example of the flexibility offered through the .NET Compact Framework.*

The DataAdapter Classes

Just to recap, up to this point we've looked at how to open a connection to either a SQL Server or SQL Server CE database and then use that connection with a command to retrieve data into a DataReader object. Pretty cool, but what if you want to do more than just reading and displaying data? One option would be to use the Command object to update the database directly, using a SQL INSERT, UPDATE, or DELETE statement. Another approach is to use the combination of a DataAdapter with a DataSet. That is the topic of the following sections.

The first part of this combination of classes is the DataAdapter. DataAdapters serve two purposes: They are used to fill a DataSet and to update a database. Simply stated, it is the go-between for a database and a DataSet, an in-memory database, or IMDB.

Both the **System.Data.SqlClient** and **System.Data.SqlServerCe** namespaces contain a **DataAdapter** class. For **System.Data.SqlClient**, that is the **SqlDataAdapter** class. For **System.Data.SqlServerCe**, that is the **SqlCeDataAdapter** class. I show common methods for both of these classes in Table 9-14.

Table 9-14. Methods of the SqlDataAdapter and SqlCeDataAdapter Classes

METHOD	DESCRIPTION
Fill	Loads a DataSet with data retrieved from a database.
FillSchema	Configures a DataSet to match the schema of the database.
Update	Updates the database with the modifications identified within the DataSet. This method uses the SQL commands defined in the InsertCommand, UpdateCommand, and DeleteCommand properties.

Table 9-15 shows commonly used properties of the **SqlDataAdapter** and **SqlCeDataAdapter** classes.

Table 9-15. Properties of the SqlDataAdapter and SqlCeDataAdapter Classes

PROPERTY	DESCRIPTION
DeleteCommand	SQL statement to use when updating a database with deletions made to a DataSet
InsertCommand	SQL statement to use when inserting into a database records that have been added to a DataSet
SelectCommand	SQL statement used to retrieve records from the database to fill a DataSet
UpdateCommand	SQL statement to use when updating a database with updates made to a DataSet

The SqlDataAdapter Class

The example shown in Listing 9-5 demonstrates how to use a DataAdapter to fill a DataSet with data retrieved from a SQL Server database. The top part of this code handles opening a connection and configuring a command. I covered both tasks earlier in this chapter. Now, it is the last couple of lines that we're interested in, where the DataAdapter is created and then used to fill the DataSet.

Listing 9-5. Filling a DataSet from a SQL Server Database

```
Dim cn As System.Data.SqlClient.SqlConnection
Dim cmd As System.Data.SqlClient.SqlCommand
Dim da As System.Data.SqlClient.SqlDataAdapter
Dim ds As System.Data.DataSet

' Open the connection.
cn = New System.Data.SqlClient.SqlConnection( _
    "user id=sa;password=;database=Northwind;server=192.168.1.101")

' Configure the command.
cmd.CommandText = "SELECT * FROM Customers"
cmd.Connection = cn

' Create the DataAdapter and fill the DataSet.
da = New System.Data.SqlClient.SqlDataAdapter(cmd)
da.Fill(ds)
```

The SqlCeDataAdapter Class

In Listing 9-6, you see how to use a DataAdapter to fill a DataSet with data retrieved from a SQL Server CE database. This example begins by connecting to a local SQL Server CE database. It then uses a Command object to create a DataAdapter, which in turn is used to fill a DataSet.

Listing 9-6. Filling a DataSet from a SQL Server CE Database

```
Dim cn As System.Data.SqlServerCe.SqlCeConnection
Dim cmd As System.Data.SqlServerCe.SqlCeCommand
Dim da As System.Data.SqlServerCe.SqlCeDataAdapter
Dim ds As System.Data.DataSet

' Open the connection.
cn = New _
    System.Data.SqlServerCe.SqlCeConnection( _
    "Data Source=\Windows\Start Menu\Programs\Apress\NorthwindDemo.sdf")
```

```
' Configure and execute the command.
cmd.CommandText = "SELECT * FROM Customers"
cmd.Connection = cn
da = New System.Data.SqlServerCe.SqlCeDataAdapter(cmd)
da.Fill(ds)
```

The DataSet Class

DataAdapters are used to put data into a DataSet and pass additions, modifications, and deletions from a DataSet back to a database. But what is a DataSet?

The easiest way to think of a DataSet is as a database in memory. The mistake that developers coming over from ADO commonly make is to try to equate a DataSet to a recordset. While they both contain data, they are in many ways significantly different.

DataSets are *always* disconnected. The structure that comprises a DataSet and the data it contains is not dependent upon any active connection to a database. Yes, DataSets are commonly created from a database, and modifications to a DataSet are typically returned to a database. However, in between those two events, DataSets operate totally independent from the database from which they were created.

DataSets are comprised of one or more DataTables. As the name would lead you to believe, DataTables are equivalent to a table in a database. We'll see more on DataTables later in this chapter. There is a collection of DataTables in each DataSet. This collection can be used to determine what tables a DataSet contains and to iterate through those tables. DataSets also maintain relationships between DataTables.

DataSets provide full support for XML. The schema that defines a DataSet and the data contained within a DataSet can both be persisted to a file as XML. In turn, DataSets can be defined and propagated from XML. Since DataSets are natively XML, they are easily passed via Web services.

DataSet methods that are commonly used in mobile development are shown in Table 9-16.

Table 9-16. DataSet Methods

METHOD	DESCRIPTION
Clear	Clears a DataSet including removing all tables and rows
Clone	Creates an exact copy of a DataSet
HasChanges	Identifies whether a DataSet has changed
ReadXml	Loads XML schema and data into a DataSet
ReadXmlSchema	Loads only XML schema into a DataSet
RejectChanges	Rolls back any changes that have been made to a DataSet
Reset	Resets a DataSet back to its original state
WriteXml	Saves a DataSet as XML schema and data
WriteXmlSchema	Saves the structure of a DataSet as XML schema

Populating a DataSet

Populating, or filling, a DataSet can be accomplished in a variety of ways including the following:

- **Through a DataAdapter's Fill method** as shown in the previous section. This method is used when the data source is either a SQL Server or SQL Server CE database.

- **Directly from an XML file**. You can use this approach to store data locally on a device while the device is disconnected from the data's original source.

- **From a Web service** by calling a method on the service that returns a DataSet.

- **By building the DataSet completely from code.**

Populating a DataSet from a DataAdapter

The **Fill** method of the **DataAdapter** class (either **SqlDataAdapter** or **SqlCeDataAdapter**) can be used to populate a DataSet. Listings 9-5 and 9-6 show examples of using this method to load data from both a SQL Server and SQL Server CE database.

The **Fill** method is overloaded, providing for methods in which it can be called. This method can be used to fill either a DataSet or a DataTable.

Populating a DataSet from an XML File

DataSets can be loaded directly from an XML file without the need of a DataAdapter. The DataSet class includes a **ReadXml** method for this purpose. Following is an example of using this method:

```
Dim ds As System.Data.DataSet

' Populate the DataSet from XML.
  ds.ReadXml("\Windows\Start Menu\Programs\Apress\Northwind.XML")
```

In addition to reading in data, you can also read in the schema for a DataSet from an XML file using the **ReadXmlSchema** method. An example of using this method is shown here:

```
Dim ds As System.Data.DataSet

' Load the schema into DataSet.
  ds.ReadXmlSchma("\Windows\Start Menu\Programs\Apress\NorthwindSchema.XML")
```

Populating a DataSet from a Web Service

Another method to populate a DataSet is by calling a Web service method. The method simply needs to return a DataSet. An example of this is shown in Chapter 16 in the "Passing Data from XML Web Services" section.

Populating a DataSet from Code

If you've got way too much time on your hands or simply like to write lots of code, you might want to consider this method of populating a DataSet. Populating a DataSet from code means that you first create the DataSet, then define its schema, and finally load data into that structure. Listing 9-7 demonstrates defining a simple DataSet schema. In this example, you first create a DataSet and a DataTable. Next, you create three columns for your table: OrderID, Quantity, and CompanyName. You finish by adding a primary key to the table.

Listing 9-7. Defining a DataSet Schema

```
Dim ds As DataSet = New DataSet

' Add the Orders table to the DataSet.
Dim dt As DataTable = ds.Tables.Add("Orders")

' Add three columns to the Orders table.
Dim dc As DataColumn = dt.Columns.Add("OrderID", Type.GetType("System.Int32"))
dt.Columns.Add("Quantity", Type.GetType("System.Int32"))
dt.Columns.Add("CompanyName", Type.GetType("System.String"))

' Define a primary key for the Orders table.
dt.PrimaryKey = New DataColumn() {pkCol}
```

Refreshing a DataSet

Depending upon the design of your application and the source of its data, you may have the need to refresh periodically a DataSet. Remember, DataSets are disconnected from the source. If the source changes, as it may do in a volatile Enterprise environment, you can use the **Fill** method of the **DataAdapter** method to refresh the content of a DataSet.

 TIP *The Timer control works well for scheduling when to refresh a DataSet. Simply set the Timer to the desired time and then call the DataAdapter **Fill** method from within the Timer control's event procedure.*

Clearing a DataSet

At times, you may want to clear completely the contents of a DataSet. This technique is commonly used where you're reusing a single DataSet, maintaining the structure, but loading in different data. The DataSet's **Clear** method is used for this purpose. An example of using this method is shown here:

```
Dim ds As System.Data.DataSet

' Clear the DataSet.
ds.Clear()
```

Saving a DataSet

Just as there are several methods to propagate a DataSet, there are several methods to save a DataSet as well. Typically, the method that you use to save a DataSet will match the method used to load the DataSet. That's to say if you propagated the DataSet from a DataAdapter, you'll usually go through a DataAdapter to save the DataSet. But that's more of a guideline rather than a rule. The requirements of your application may dictate that you load a DataSet through a DataAdapter from an enterprise-based SQL Server database and then save the DataSet locally on the device as XML. There's nothing wrong with that. In fact, that is part of the strength and beauty of the .NET Compact Framework. It gives you many options from which you can construct your mobile solutions.

Saving a DataSet Through a DataAdapter

The **Update** method of the **DataAdapter** class (either the **SqlDataAdapter** or the **SqlCeDataAdapter** class) is used to save modifications within a DataSet to a database. Listing 9-8 shows an example of using the **Update** method with both a SQL Server database.

The DataAdapter **Update** method is overloaded, allowing you to save modifications made to a DataSet, DataTable, or DataRow.

Listing 9-8. Saving a DataSet to a SQL Server Database

```
Dim cn As System.Data.SqlClient.SqlConnection
Dim cmd As System.Data.SqlClient.SqlCommand
Dim da As System.Data.SqlClient.SqlDataAdapter
Dim ds As System.Data.DataSet

' Open the connection.
cn = New System.Data.SqlClient.SqlConnection( _
    "user id=sa;password=;database=Northwind;server=192.168.1.101")

' Configure the command.
cmd.CommandText = "SELECT * FROM Customers"
cmd.Connection = cn

' Create the DataAdapter and fill the DataSet.
da = New System.Data.SqlClient.SqlDataAdapter(cmd)
da.Fill(ds)

' Make some changes to the DataSet here.
```

```
' Save the changes made to the DataSet to the database.
  da.Update(ds)
```

One key point to note is that while this example shows everything happening within a single set of code, it doesn't need to be. You could just as easily fill a DataSet, close the connection to the database, go offline, go wandering about the greater world working with the data, come back online, reconnect to the database, and then finally use the **Update** method of the DataAdapter to store any changes you made.

 NOTE *I chose not to include an example of saving a DataSet back to a SQL Server CE database here because the process is identical to that used with a SQL Server database.*

Saving a DataSet As XML

DataSets can be saved directly to an XML file without the need of a DataAdapter. The **DataSet** class includes a **WriteXml** method for this purpose. An example of using this method is shown here:

```
Dim ds As System.Data.DataSet

' Create and work with the DataSet here...

' Save the DataSet to XML.
  ds.WriteXml("\Windows\Start Menu\Programs\Apress\Northwind.XML")
```

The **WriteXML** method is overloaded, providing two ways that it can be called. The first method is shown in the preceding code where only a path to a filename is provided when calling the method. Calling WriteXML in this fashion will cause the data that a DataSet contains to be written to a file.

The second method for calling the **WriteXML** method makes use of a second argument, **XMLWriteMode**. With this argument, you can control whether to include the schema and changes as part of the output. Table 9-17 shows the values you can use for the **XMLWriteMode** argument.

Table 9-17. Values That Can Be Used with the XMLWriteMode Argument

VALUE	DESCRIPTION
DiffGram	Writes the DataSet as a DiffGram, including both the original and changed values
IgnoreSchema	Writes the data contained within a DataSet, but doesn't include the schema
WriteSchema	Writes both the data and the schema of a DataSet

The following code demonstrates saving both the data and the schema from a DataSet to an XML file:

```
Dim ds As System.Data.DataSet

' Create and work with the DataSet here...

' Save the DataSet to XML.
  ds.WriteXml("\Windows\Start Menu\Programs\Apress\Northwind.XML",
XmlWriteMode.WriteSchema)
```

TIP *Using the **WriteXML** and **ReadXML** methods with a DataSet, you can create an in-memory database without using SQL Server CE. This approach is best suited for prototyping, configuration settings, and applications that use a limited amount of data.*

Saving a DataSet to a Web Service

Another method of saving DataSets is by passing them to a Web service through one of the Service's methods. The method simply needs to be written to accept a DataSet. An example of this is shown in Chapter 16 in the "Passing Data from XML Web Services" section.

The DataTable Class

DataSets are comprised of one or more DataTables. DataTables are like regular tables—they have columns, rows, and constraints. Columns are the fields in your table. You work with columns programmatically through the DataColumn object and the DataTable Columns collection. Rows are the records in your table. You work with rows through the DataRow object and the Rows collection. Constraints enforce the integrity of the data stored in a DataTable. You work with constraints through the Constraint object and the DataTable Constraints collection.

Table 9-18 contains commonly used methods of the DataTable.

Table 9-18. Methods of the DataTable Object

METHOD	DESCRIPTION
AcceptChanges	Commits all changes that have been made to a DataTable since the last time this method was called.
Clear	Empties all data from a DataTable.
GetChanges	Gets all changes that have been made to a DataTable since the last time AcceptChanges was called.
GetErrors	Provides a set of rows containing errors that have occurred while working with a DataTable.
ImportRow	Copies a DataRow into a DataTable.
LoadDataRow	Updates a matching row within a DataTable. If no matching row is found, then the row is added to the table.
NewRow	Adds an initialized row to a DataTable.
RejectChanges	Rolls back any modifications that have been made to a DataTable.
Select	Filters the rows within a DataTable.

Table 9-19 contains a list of commonly used DataTable properties.

Table 9-19. DataTable Properties

PROPERTY	DESCRIPTION
Columns	Collection of the columns within a DataTable
Constraints	Collection of constraints for a DataTable
Rows	Collection of rows within a DataTable
TableName	Name of a DataTable

Populating a DataTable

DataTables are typically populated through the DataAdapter's **Fill** method. They may also be populated from code.

An example of populating a DataTable through a DataAdapter is shown in Listing 9-9. This is a two-step process: First the DataTable is created and then it is added to a DataSet. At the top of this example, a new DataTable object is created. Here, the DataTable is given the name **Customers**, as you're going to use it to store customer data. Near the bottom of this example, you fill the DataTable through the DataAdapter's. Finally, the DataTable is added to your DataSet.

Listing 9-9. Populating a DataTable Through a DataAdapter

```
Dim cn As System.Data.SqlServerCe.SqlCeConnection
Dim cmd As System.Data.SqlServerCe.SqlCeCommand
Dim da As System.Data.SqlServerCe.SqlCeDataAdapter
Dim ds As System.Data.DataSet
Dim dt As New System.Data.DataTable("Customers")

' Open the connection.
cn = New _
    System.Data.SqlServerCe.SqlCeConnection( _
      "Data Source=\Windows\Start Menu\Programs\Apress\Northwind.sdf")

' Configure and execute the command.
cmd.CommandText = "SELECT * FROM Customers"
cmd.Connection = cn
da = New System.Data.SqlServerCe.SqlCeDataAdapter(cmd)
da.Fill(dt)
ds.Tables.Add(dt)
```

 NOTE *Using this process defines both the data and structure of a DataTable.*

Obtaining a List of DataTables in a DataSet

Each DataSet has a collection called **Tables**, which is comprised of all of the DataTables that are contained within the DataSet. You can obtain a list of the DataTables that are part of a DataSet by iterating through this collection as shown in Listing 9-10. In this example, the table names are loaded into a ComboBox control.

Listing 9-10. Obtaining a List of the DataTables in a DataSet

```
Dim ds As System.Data.DataSet
Dim dt As System.Data.DataTable

' Some steps to load the DataSet woud need to be performed first.

' Load a ComboBox with a list of available DataTables.
  For Each dt In ds.Tables
    ComboBox1.Items.Add(dt.TableName.ToString)
  Next
```

Obtaining a List of DataTable Columns

As I mentioned earlier in this section, each DataTable is comprised of a number
of columns that represent the individual fields of data in the table. You can
obtain a list of these columns by iterating through the **Columns** collection of the
DataTable object. I show you an example of this in Listing 9-11. In this example,
I use the column names to define the header column for a ListView control.
A For loop accomplishes this, running from 0, the first member in the collection,
to Count -1, the last member in the collection.

Listing 9-11. Obtaining a List of Columns Within a DataTable

```
Dim dr As DataRow
Dim intCnt As Int16
Dim lvwColumn As ColumnHeader

' Set the view for the ListView control.
  listView1.View = "Details"

' Add the column headers.
  For intCnt = 0 To ds.Tables("Customers").Columns.Count - 1
    lvwColumn = New ColumnHeader
    lvwColumn.Text = _
      ds.Tables("Customers").Columns(intCnt).ColumnName
    lvwDisplay.Columns.Add(lvwColumn)
  Next
```

 NOTE *Members in the Tables collection can be accessed either by
their name, as shown in Listing 9-11, or by their position in the
collection.*

Accessing Data Within a DataTable

Unlike the DataReader, you can move about the DataTable forwards and backwards. You access data within a DataTable through its Rows collection. Each member of the Rows collection corresponds to a record within the table. You can iterate through this collection as shown in Listing 9-12, where a ListView control is used to display the contents of the DataTable.

This example uses a For Each loop along with a DataRow object. A DataRow object contains a collection called **Items**, which in turn contains the individual fields of data within a row.

Listing 9-12. Displaying the Contents of a DataTable

```
Dim dr As DataRow
Dim ds As DataSet
Dim intCnt As Int16
Dim objListItem As ListViewItem

' Perform some statements to load the DataSet.

' Load the data by looping through each of the rows within a table.
For Each dr In ds.Tables("Customers").Rows
    objListItem = New ListViewItem

' Load the first field.
    If dr.IsNull(0) Then
      objListItem.Text = ""
    Else
      objListItem.Text = dr.Item(0)
    End If

' Now the rest of the fields.
    For intCnt = 1 To dr.ItemArray.GetUpperBound(0)
      If (dr.IsNull(intCnt)) Then
        objListItem.SubItems.Add("")
      Else
        Try
          objListItem.SubItems.Add(CStr(dr.Item(intCnt)))
        Catch
          objListItem.SubItems.Add("")
        End Try
      End If
    Next
```

```
' Add the item (record) into the display.
   ListView1.Items.Add(objListItem)
  Next
```

Searching a DataTable

Within a DataTable you can restrict the rows, or records, that you are viewing through the DataTable's **Select** method. The **Select** method is overloaded, supporting the following three ways that it can be called:

- **With only a filter criteria,** which returns rows that match the criteria

- **Matching filter** criteria and sorted in the order specified

- **Matching filter criteria, sorted and of a specific state,** where the state can be rows that were added, modified, deleted and even unchanged

The **Select** method returns an array of DataRows. I give an example of working with the DataTable's **Select** method in Listing 9-13. This example begins by specifying the filter where only rows that have large order amounts are included. We then specify a sort order that will cause the returning rows to be sorted descending by CompanyName.

Listing 9-13. Filtering Rows Using the DataTable Select Method

```
  Dim dt As System.Data.DataTable
  Dim strFilter As String
  Dim strSortOrder As String

' We want to look at only big orders.
  strFilter = "OrderAmount > 1000"

' Sort by the CompanyName column in a descending order.
  strSortOrder = "CompanyName DESC"

' Use the Select method to find all rows matching the filter.
  Dim SelectedRows As DataRow() = _
      dt.Select(strFilter, strSortOrder)
```

TIP *You can use the **Select** method to build a list of rows that have changed in a table, which in turn can be sent back to an enterprise server. This is a simple way to handle data updates, and it minimizes data transfer.*

The DataRow Class

A DataRow object represents an individual row, or record, within a DataTable. You will use the DataRow object to add, modify, delete, and view rows. The commonly used DataRow methods are shown in Table 9-20.

Table 9-20. DataRow Methods

METHOD	DESCRIPTION
AcceptChanges	Commits all changes that have been made to a DataRow since the last time this method was called
BeginEdit	Initiates an edit on a DataRow object while temporarily suspending events that involve validation rules
CancelEdit	Cancels the editing of a DataRow object
Delete	Deletes a DataRow object
EndEdit	Completes an edit on a DataRow object
IsNull	Determines whether a column in the DataRow is null

Item, the commonly used DataRow property, specifies column data. You can think of this as a field within a record.

Adding a Row to a Table

Adding a row to a table is a three-step process. First, you physically create a new row using the **AddRow** method of the DataTable object. Second, you load the row with values. Third, you add the row to the Rows collection of the DataTable. An example of this process is shown in Listing 9-14.

Listing 9-14. Adding a Row to a Table

```
Dim dr As DataRow
Dim dt As DataTable

' Do something to create the DataTable...

' Create the row.
dr = dt.NewRow()
```

```
' Add the data to the row.
  dr("CustomerName") = "Acme Manufacturing"
  dr("Contact") = "John Smith"

' Finally, add the row to the table

  dt.Rows.Add(dr)
```

Modifying a Row

Unlike recordsets, where you always had a current record, to reference a specific row within a DataTable you need to specify an index. In the following example, the first row in the table, row 0, is modified by changing its Contact field.

 NOTE   *We could also refer to the Contact field by its index within the row, rather than by its name.*

```
Dim dt As System.Data.DataTable

dt.Rows(0)("Contact") = "John Smith"
```

Viewing the Contents of a Row

You view the contents of a row within a DataTable by referencing the individual fields of the row. An example of this is shown here:

```
Dim dt As System.Data.DataTable

txtCompany.Text = dt.Rows(0)("CompanyName")
txtContact.Text = dt.Rows(0)("Contact")
```

The DataColumn Class

A DataColumn object represents an individual column, or field, within a table. From the programming standpoint, DataColumns are used primarily for two purposes: to get the name of the column or to configure the column. Obtaining the column name is useful when you are developing an application that will be displaying data from a variety of sources. Configuring a column is used when your application will be modifying the schema of a DataTable.

Table 9-21 provides a list of commonly used properties of the **DataColumn** class.

Table 9-21. DataColumn Properties

PROPERTY	DESCRIPTION
AllowDBNull	Specifies whether a column can contain null values.
AutoIncrement	Defines whether the value of a column will be automatically incremented as new rows are added to the DataTable.
AutoIncrementSeed	Defines a starting value for use with an auto-incrementing column.
AutoIncrementStep	Defines the step, or amount between, each auto incremented number. Use this value to leave space between rows so that you may insert rows between them later.
Caption	Specifies the caption of a column.
ColumnName	Indicates the name of a column.
DataType	Specifies the type of data stored in a column.
DefaultValue	Defines a default value to be used with a column when adding new rows.
Expression	Specifies expression used to calculate the value of a column.
MaxLength	Defines the maximum length of a text column.
ReadOnly	Restricts a column to read only after it is initially added.
Unique	Specifies whether each value in a column must be unique.

Listing the Columns Within a DataTable

Listing 9-11, shown earlier in this chapter, demonstrates how to obtain a list of column names for a table.

Adding a Column to a DataTable

Listing 9-15 demonstrates adding a column to a DataTable. In this example, the column name is CustomerID and it is an Int32 value. The column is further configured, requiring it to contain a value, by setting the **AllowDBNull** property to False.

Listing 9-15. Adding a Column to a DataTable

```
Dim dt As DataTable
Dim newColumn As DataColumn

' Create the column.
newColumn = New DataColumn("CustomerID", System.Type.GetType("System.Int32"))
newColumn.AllowDBNull = False

' Add the column to the DataTable.
dt = New DataTable
dt.Columns.Add(newColumn)
```

The DataView Class

DataViews are similar to standard database views in that they allow you to customize the way you look at the data. In the case of DataViews, this pertains to the data found within a DataTable. You can use DataViews to filter, sort, and edit the data.

DataViews support data binding, which is a common way that they are used with mobile applications. They make it easy to create master/detail forms. Using two DataViews, have one handle the master data and the other the detail data. For example, let's say you are building the classic order/order detail form. In this example, you're using a combo box to hold the order numbers and a ListView to display the order detail. The combo box would be bound to a DataView that contains the list of orders. The ListView would be bound to a DataView that would contain the order details for the currently selected order.

Commonly used methods of the DataView class are shown in Table 9-22.

Table 9-22. DataView Methods

METHOD	DESCRIPTION
AddNew	Adds a row
Delete	Deletes a row
Find	Finds a row using the specified sort key value

Commonly used properties of the DataView class are shown in Table 9-23.

Table 9-23. DataView Properties

PROPERTY	DESCRIPTION
AllowDelete	Defines whether deleting is allowed
AllowEdit	Defines whether editing is allowed
AllowNew	Defines whether adding rows is allowed
Count	Returns the number of rows
Item	Specifies a row within a table
RowFilter	Limits rows that are viewed
RowStateFilter	Sets the filter that is used with the DataView
Sort	Defines the sort column(s) and order
Table	Defines the source DataTable

Creating and Defining a DataView

The example shown in Listing 9-16 demonstrates creating and configuring a DataView. In this example, the DataSet "dv" holds the contents of the Northwind database, including the Orders table. The DataView is configured to limit modifications to adding new rows, to show only the orders for the customer VINET, and to sort the rows in ascending order by the CustomerID field.

Listing 9-16. Setting Up a DataView

```
Dim dv As DataView

' Create and define a DataView.
dv = New DataView

With dv
  .Table = ds.Tables("Orders")
  .AllowDelete = False
  .AllowEdit = False
```

```
    .AllowNew = True
    .RowFilter = "CustomerID = 'VINET'"
    .Sort = "OrderID ASC"
End With


' Bind the DataView to a TextBox control.
  Text1.DataBindings.Add("Text", dv, "OrderID")
```

Step-by-Step Tutorial: Working with ADO.NET

In this step-by-step exercise, you will create an application that demonstrates using ADO.NET to access and display data from three sources: SQL Server, SQL Server CE, and XML. As part of this exercise, you'll

- Retrieve data from a remote SQL Server database.

- Retrieve data from a local SQL Server CE database.

- Save a DataSet as XML.

- Load a DataSet from XML.

- Determine the DataTables that are contained in a DataSet.

- Display the contents of a DataTable.

This application provides examples of working with DataAdapters, DataSets, DataTables, DataRows, and DataColumns.

 NOTE *I provide a completed version of this application, titled ADODOTNET Demo-Complete under the* **Chapter 9** *folder of the* **Samples** *folder. See Appendix D for more information on accessing and loading the sample applications.*

Step 1: Opening the Project

To simplify this tutorial, I've already created the project and the user interface for the ADODOTNET Demo application. This template project is included under the **Chapter 9** folder of the **Samples** folder. To load this project, follow these steps:

1. From the VS .NET IDE Start Page, select to open a project. The Open Project dialog box will be displayed.

2. Use the dialog box to navigate to the **Chapter 9** folder under the **Samples** folder for this book.

3. Select and open the project **ADODOTNET Demo**. The project will be loaded.

Step 2: Examining the User Interface

The user interface of the ADODOTNET Demo application is comprised of four panels, each of which is used with a particular feature of this application. The panels are as follows:

- **pnlCfgSqlServer**—Defines the configuration settings to use when connecting to a SQL Server database. This panel is shown in Figure 9-3.

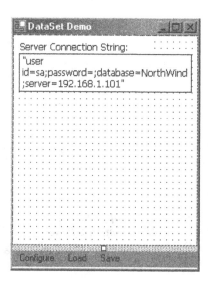

Figure 9-3. The pnlCfgSqlServer panel

- **pnlDisplay**—Displays the data contained within the DataTables. The ComboBox at the top of this panel is loaded with the list of DataTables stored within the DataSet. The ListView at the bottom of the panel displays the data from a selected DataTable. This panel is shown in Figure 9-4.

Figure 9-4. The pnlDisplay panel

- **pnlSelect**—Specifies three items: the SQL statement that will be used when adding a DataTable to a DataSet, the name to give the DataTable, and whether the DataSet should be cleared when adding a DataTable. This panel is shown in Figure 9-5.

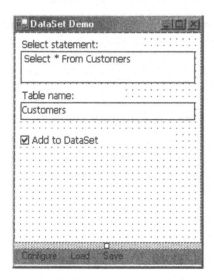

Figure 9-5. The pnlSelect panel

- **pnlXml**—Specifies the filename used when reading and writing a DataSet as XML. This panel is shown in Figure 9-6.

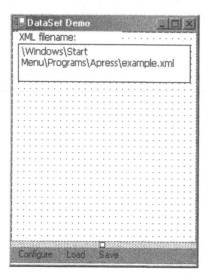

Figure 9-6. The pnlXml panel

Each of these panels is parked just off the right of the viewable form. That is to say, the **Left** property has been set high enough to move the panels out of the user's view. When we want to display the panel, we simply have to set the **Left** property to 0, which moves the panel back within the viewable area of the form.

> **NOTE** *I have already added to the project template the code to display these panels. The routine ShowPanel provides this functionality.*

Step 3: Examining Other Preconfigured Settings

Before you start adding code, there are two other project configurations that we need to examine: project references and module-level declarations.

Project References

Along with designing the user interface for you, I've already added these references to the project:

- System.Data.Common

- System.Data.SqlClient

- System.Data.SqlServerCe

Module-Level Declarations

I've also added this module-level declaration:

```
Dim ds As New System.Data.DataSet
```

This variable is used throughout the application, from loading to displaying and saving.

Included SQL Server CE Database

A SQL Server CE database, NorthwindDemo.sdf, is included with the project. This database will automatically be copied to the same folder as the application.

Step 4: Retrieving Data from SQL Server

Now you're ready to start adding code. You'll begin with the code used to retrieve a DataSet from a SQL Server database. Add the code shown in Listing 9-17 to the **Click** event procedure of the load from SQL Server menu item (**mnuLoadSql Server_Click**).

Listing 9-17. Loading a DataTable from SQL Server

```
Private Sub mnuLoadSqlServer_Click(ByVal sender As System.Object, _
  ByVal e As System.EventArgs) Handles mnuLoadSqlServer.Click

  Dim cn As System.Data.SqlClient.SqlConnection
  Dim cmd As System.Data.SqlClient.SqlCommand
  Dim da As System.Data.SqlClient.SqlDataAdapter

' Establish a connection to the SQL Server database.
  cn = New System.Data.SqlClient.SqlConnection(txtServerConnection.Text)
  cmd = New System.Data.SqlClient.SqlCommand(txtSelect.Text, cn)
  da = New System.Data.SqlClient.SqlDataAdapter(cmd)

' Is this table being added to the DataSet? If not destroy and
' recreate the DataSet.
  If Not chkAddToDataSet.Checked Then
    ds = Nothing
    ds = New System.Data.DataSet
  End If
```

```
' Add the new table.
  Dim dt As System.Data.DataTable = New System.Data.DataTable(txtTableName.Text)
  da.Fill(dt)
  ds.Tables.Add(dt)

' Display the DataSet.
  DisplayData()

End Sub
```

This procedure starts by establishing a connection to the SQL Server database. It uses the values taken from two TextBox controls, txtServerConnection and txtSelect, to connect to and retrieve the requested data. By using these TextBox controls, you can easily change the settings to connect to different servers and databases.

Next, a check is made to see whether the DataSet should be cleared before the new table is added. Since the DataSet (ds) is shared throughout this application, if you don't offer a way to clear it, you will just keep adding tables to the same DataSet, even if the tables don't logically belong together.

With this check completed, the new DataTable is filled from the DataAdapter. Note that when the DataTable object is created, a table name is specified. This name will subsequently be loaded into the ComboBox control on the display page. The DataTable is then added to the DataSet.

Finally, the data is displayed.

Step 5: Retrieving Data from SQL Server CE

To provide support for SQL Server CE databases, add the code shown in Listing 9-18 to the **Click** event procedure of the load from **SQL Server CE** menu item (**mnuLoadSqlCe_Click**).

This procedure is nearly identical to the one you added in the previous step. The key differences are as follows:

- **Provider-specific objects**—To connect to a SQL Server database, you use objects out of the **System.Data.SqlClient** namespace. For SQL Server CE, you use the **System.Data.SqlServerCe** namespace.

- **Single Database**—Unlike the SQL Server example, which will allow you to connect up to any number of servers and databases, the SQL Server CE example is restricted to a single database. Could we make it work with any databases? Certainly, but I've included only one with this project.

Listing 9-18. Loading a DataTable from SQL Server CE

```
Private Sub mnuLoadSqlCe_Click(ByVal sender As System.Object, _
  ByVal e As System.EventArgs) Handles mnuLoadSqlCe.Click

  Dim cmd As System.Data.SqlServerCE.SqlCeCommand
  Dim cn As System.Data.SqlServerCe.SqlCeConnection
  Dim da As System.Data.SqlServerCe.SqlCeDataAdapter

' Establish a connection to the SQL Server CE database.
  cn = New System.Data.SqlServerce.SqlCeConnection("Data Source= " & _
    ApplicationLocation() & "\NorthwindDemo.sdf")
    cmd = New System.Data.SqlServerCE.SqlCeCommand(txtSelect.Text, cn)
    da = New System.Data.SqlServerCE.SqlCeDataAdapter(cmd)

' Is this table being added to the DataSet?
  If Not chkAddToDataSet.Checked Then
    ds.Clear()
  End If

' Add the new table to the DataSet.
  Dim dt As System.Data.DataTable = New System.Data.DataTable(txtTableName.Text)
  da.Fill(dt)
  ds.Tables.Add(dt)

' Display the DataSet.
  DisplayData()

End Sub
```

Step 6: Retrieving Data from an XML File

Compared to the two previous examples, the routine that handles loading
a DataSet from XML is simple. Add the code shown in Listing 9-19 to the **Click**
event for the **Load from XML** menu item (**mnuLoadXML_click**).

In this procedure, the DataSet is loaded using the **ReadXML** method.

Listing 9-19. Loading a DataTable from an XML File

```
Private Sub mnuLoadXML_Click(ByVal sender As System.Object, _
  ByVal e As System.EventArgs) Handles mnuLoadXML.Click
```

```
' Load the DataSet.
  ds.Clear
  ds.ReadXml(txtXML.Text)

' Display the DataSet.
  DisplayData()

  End Sub
```

Step 7: Displaying Data

The routine used to display the contents of a DataSet is the next item to add. The DisplayData routine performs two functions:

- **Loading table names** into the ComboBox that is located on the Display panel. Selecting a table name from the ComboBox will cause the table's data to be displayed.

- **Triggering the display** of the first table.

Add the code shown in Listing 9-20 to your project. This routine begins by emptying the ComboBox of any tables that it might contain. Next, it loops through the DataSet Tables collection, retrieving the names of all of the tables that are contained within the DataSet. Finally, it sets the **SelectedIndex** property of the ComboBox to 0, causing the ComboBox's **SelectedIndexChange** event to fire, which in turn will display the data for the selected table.

Listing 9-20. Loading the ComboBox with the Names of DataTables

```
Sub DisplayData()
  Dim dt As System.Data.DataTable

' Clear the ComboBox control.
  cmbTables.Items.Clear()

' Load the ComboBox with a list of available tables.
  For Each dt In ds.Tables
    cmbTables.Items.Add(dt.TableName.ToString)
  Next

' Finally, trigger the displaying of the first table.
  cmbTables.SelectedIndex = 0

End Sub
```

Displaying a Table

When the user selects a table name from the ComboBox on the Display panel, the contents of that table will be displayed in the ListView control that is part of that same panel (see Figure 9-4).

Add the code shown in Listing 9-21 to the **SelectedIndexChange** event of the ComboBox (**cmbTables_SelectedIndexChanged**).

This event procedure begins by clearing any data from the ListView control. Next, it loops through the Columns collection of the selected table to retrieve and display the names of the columns (fields) in the first row of the ListView control. Finally, a large loop is used to iterate through the Rows collection of the selected table, loading the contents of each data item into the ListView control.

 NOTE *Normally you will want to wrap all of this code within error handling. For simplicity, I elected to not to do this.*

Listing 9-21. Displaying the Data from a DataTable

```
Private Sub cmbTables_SelectedIndexChanged(ByVal sender As Object, _
  ByVal e As System.EventArgs) Handles cmbTables.SelectedIndexChanged

  Dim dr As DataRow
  Dim intCnt As Int16
  Dim lvwColumn As ColumnHeader
  Dim objListItem As ListViewItem

' Clear the ListView control.
  lvwDisplay.Visible = False
  lvwDisplay.Clear()

' Add the column headers.
  For intCnt = 0 To ds.Tables(cmbTables.SelectedIndex).Columns.Count - 1
    lvwColumn = New ColumnHeader
    lvwColumn.Text = _
      ds.Tables(cmbTables.SelectedIndex).Columns(intCnt).ColumnName
    lvwDisplay.Columns.Add(lvwColumn)
  Next

' Get rid of lvwColumn.
  lvwColumn = Nothing
```

```
' Load the data by looping through each of the rows within
' the table.
  For Each dr In ds.Tables(cmbTables.SelectedIndex).Rows
    objListItem = New ListViewItem

' Load the first field.
    If dr.IsNull(0) Then
      objListItem.Text = ""
    Else
      objListItem.Text = dr.Item(0)
    End If

' Now the rest of the fields.
    For intCnt = 1 To dr.ItemArray.GetUpperBound(0)
      If (dr.IsNull(intCnt)) Then
        objListItem.SubItems.Add("")
      Else
        Try
          objListItem.SubItems.Add(CStr(dr.Item(intCnt)))
        Catch
          objListItem.SubItems.Add("""")
        End Try
      End If
    Next

' Add the item (record) into the display.
    lvwDisplay.Items.Add(objListItem)
  Next

' Show the ListBox
  lvwDisplay.Visible = True

' Finally, display the panel that contains the ListView control.
  ShowPanel(pnlDisplay)

End Sub
```

Step 8: Saving Data to an XML File

Saving a DataSet to a file as XML is just as easy as loading an XML file into
a DataSet. Add the code shown in Listing 9-22 to the **Save XML** menu item **Click**
event procedure (**mnuSaveXML_Click**). In this procedure, the **WriteXML**
method of the DataSet object is used to perform the save.

Listing 9-22. Saving a DataSet to an XML File

```
Private Sub mnuSaveXML_Click(ByVal sender As System.Object, _
  ByVal e As System.EventArgs) Handles mnuSaveXML.Click

' Persist the DataSet as XML.
  ds.WriteXml(txtXML.Text)

End Sub
```

Step 9: Testing Your Application

Finally, you're ready to test your application. To test your application, perform the following steps:

1. Select either **Pocket PC Device** or **Pocket PC Emulator** from the Deployment Device combo box.

2. Select **Release** from the Solution Configurations combo box.

3. Click the **Start** button.

Your application will be copied to the target device and run.

Configure Your Settings

The first thing you need to do in testing this application is to configure the settings that will be used when connecting to your SQL Server database. To configure these settings, perform the following steps:

1. Tap on the **Configure** menu. The Configure menu will be displayed.

2. From the Configure menu, tap **SQL Server**. The SQL Server configuration panel will be displayed.

3. Modify the connection setting provided to match your server and database.

Test the SQL Server Component

You're now ready to test your connection to your SQL Server database. To connect to and retrieve a DataSet from your server, perform the following steps:

1. Tap the **Load** menu. The Load menu will be displayed.

2. From the Load menu, tap **from SQL Server**. There will be a brief delay while a connection is made to your server and the DataSet is retrieved. When completed, the Display panel will be shown. An example of this display appears in Figure 9-7.

Figure 9-7. The Display panel loaded with data

Test the SQL Server CE Component

Next, you'll check your connection to the SQL Server CE database. Remember, a sample database was included with the project. To access this database, perform the following steps:

1. Tap the **Load** menu. The Load menu will be displayed.

2. From the Load menu, tap **from SQL Server CE**. As with the SQL Server example earlier, there will be a brief delay while the DataSet is loaded. Upon completion, the Display panel will be shown, this time containing the data from the SQL Server CE database.

Test the XML Save Component

Before you can test the Load XML feature, you first need to save a DataSet to a file as XML. To create this file, perform the following steps:

1. Tap the **Save** menu. The Save menu will be displayed.

2. From the Save menu, tap **as XML**. The DataSet will be written out to file as XML.

Test the XML Load Component

Now you're ready to test loading a DataSet from XML. To test this part of your application, perform the following steps:

1. Tap the **Load** menu. The Load menu will be displayed.

2. From the Load menu, tap **from XML**. There will be a brief pause as the DataSet is first loaded and then displayed.

HOMEWORK   *View the XML content that is generated when saving the DataSet to file. The XML file will be located under the folder \Windows\Start Menu\Programs\Apress. The easiest way to view this file is to copy it to your PC using Mobile Explorer and then open the file in Internet Explorer.*

HOMEWORK   *Try loading several tables into a single DataSet. You can do this from either a SQL Server or SQL Server CE data source. You will need to configure a SQL Select statement for each table. You can do this through the Select statement menu item under the Configure menu. From the display page, see how the different tables are loaded into the ComboBox.*

Summary

Mobile solutions, like desktop solutions, are usually based upon data. The .NET Compact Framework and ADO.NET provide you with a broad selection of data tools, allowing you to create robust, data-enabled mobile applications.

This chapter provided you with an overview to ADO.NET as it is implemented under the NETCF. You learned about the **System.Data** namespace, what it offered, and how to incorporate it within your project and leverage its classes from your applications.

The NETCF version of ADO.NET supports two data providers, SqlClient and SqlServerCe. The SqlClient provider is used to access SQL Server databases. The SqlServerCe provider allows you to access SQL Server CE databases.

There are two key points that you need to hold on to as you finish this chapter. First, how you work with databases, whether they are SQL Server or SQL Server CE databases, is identical, with the exception of connecting to the database itself. Second, ADO.NET is all about XML. You can save and load DataSets as XML just as easy as you can to a database. This is truly powerful stuff and offers tremendous possibilities to mobile application developers.

Finally, remember this is just the start of the data discussions. Chapters 10 through 14 provide far greater detail on the topics of data binding, working with SQL Server CE, working with server and device-based data, and leveraging XML with your mobile applications.

CHAPTER 10

Data Binding

DATA BINDING—MENTIONING THESE TWO WORDS to a group of developers is likely to elicit a wide variety of responses: everything from "Real programmers don't use data binding" to "I wouldn't develop a data application without it." My opinion is that it's another tool at your disposal, and as such, understanding what it is and how it can be effectively utilized is a good thing.

Going back to the early days of Visual Basic, there have always been two ways of displaying data in a form: manual and automatic.

With the manual approach, the developer is responsible for everything. Using this approach, you write code to load fields of data from an underlying data source into individual controls on the form. You write code to know when the user changes the values in the controls. You write code to save the modified values from the controls back to the underlying data source. You write code to navigate about the underlying data source. You write code to handle adding records to and deleting records from the underlying data source. The manual approach is, as I like to say, the perfect alternative if you're being paid for the number of lines of code you write.

The automatic approach is data binding. With data binding, you define a relationship, or a binding, between controls and fields of data in an underlying data source. After that, much of the data-related work either is done completely for you or can be performed with a far simpler and less code-intensive approach. Data binding allows you to quickly build data-enabled applications. It takes away the coding complexities associated with this type of application, freeing you up to focus on creating effective solutions.

Binding to Controls

In this section, we're going to look at the process of binding controls provided through the .NET Compact Framework to underlying data sources. Not to be overly simplistic, but I like to look at this as a two-step task: 1) create the data source, and 2) bind that data source to the appropriate controls. For the most part, I'll focus on these basic tasks with this chapter.

Binding can be more involved than simply binding a control to a data source and forgetting about it, and it often is more complex. Normal data-related tasks, such as validation and navigation, commonly come into play. I'll discuss the basics of both of these topics later in this chapter. As I already mentioned, we'll start with the basics, and nothing is more basic than binding to a simple control.

Binding to Simple Controls

Binding to a single control is simple. In fact, once you have created the underlying data source, it takes only a single line of code.

Listing 10-1 shows an example of binding to two TextBox controls. As you can see, most of the code in this example handles preparing the data source and dealing with any exceptions that may occur. The physical binding process resides within two lines of code, one for each of the TextBox controls.

Listing 10-1. Binding to Simple Controls

```
' Declare the data-related objects.
Dim cn As System.Data.SqlServerCe.SqlCeConnection
Dim cmd As New System.Data.SqlServerCe.SqlCeCommand
Dim da As System.Data.SqlServerCe.SqlCeDataAdapter
Dim dt As System.Data.DataTable = New System.Data.DataTable("Employees")

' Binding to the TextBox controls is performed within this click
' event procedure.
Private Sub cmdBind_Click(ByVal sender As System.Object, _
    ByVal e As System.EventArgs) Handles cmdBind.Click

' Open the connection.
  Try
    cn = New _
    System.Data.SqlServerCe.SqlCeConnection( _
      "Data Source=" & ApplicationLocation() & "\NorthwindDemo.sdf")

' Configure and execute the command.
    cmd.CommandText = "SELECT * FROM Employees"
    cmd.Connection = cn

' Load the DataTable.
    da = New System.Data.SqlServerCe.SqlCeDataAdapter(cmd)
    da.Fill(dt)

' Bind the TextBoxes.
    txtFirstName.DataBindings.Add(New Binding("Text", dt, "FirstName"))
    txtLastName.DataBindings.Add(New Binding("Text", dt, "LastName"))

' Handle any exceptions that may occur.
  Catch sqlex As SqlServerCe.SqlCeException
    MsgBox(sqlex.Message.ToString)
```

```
   Catch ex As Exception
     MsgBox(ex.Message.ToString)
   End Try

End Sub

Private Function ApplicationLocation() As String
' Fetch and return the location where the application was launched.
    ApplicationLocation = _
      System.IO.Path.GetDirectoryName(Reflection.Assembly. _
      GetExecutingAssembly().GetName().CodeBase.ToString())
End Function
```

You define each of the bindings by adding a new binding object to the target control's DataBinding collection. Initially, this collection is empty. Each binding object that you add defines a new binding between a control and an underlying data source. Typically, you'll only add a single binding, your control to a single data field, but you're not limited there. You can bind multiple data fields to a single control. An example of this is shown later in this chapter, in the section "Binding Multiple Fields to a Single Control."

Once you've established this relationship, there is nothing else you need to do. Data will display automatically in the control. Any changes made to the data displayed in a bound control are automatically saved to the underlying data source. And to think, all of this functionality is provided through a single line of code.

NOTE   *The examples in this section are from the Simple Binding project, which is included under **Chapter 10** of the **Samples** folder.*

Binding Multiple Fields to a Single Control

While typically you will use a "one control to one data field" approach when it comes to binding, you are by no means limited to binding a single item to a control. Technically speaking, you can bind as many fields from an underlying data source as there are appropriate properties available on the bound control.

Take for example the following code snippet. In this example, the Checked and Description fields are bound to a single CheckBox control. CheckBox controls work well with dual binding as they provide two visible components: a check box and descriptive text.

```
' Bind the CheckBox.
  CheckBox1.DataBindings.Add(New Binding("Checked", dt, "Selected"))
  CheckBox1.DataBindings.Add(New Binding("Text", dt, "Description"))
```

Binding to a ListBox or ComboBox

The process of binding to either a ListBox or ComboBox is different from that used with a simple control like a TextBox or CheckBox. It involves setting three properties: **DataSource**, **DisplayMember**, and **ValueMember**.

The **DataSource** property specifies the underlying data source. The **DisplayMember** property defines the field from the underlying data source that will appear in the ListBox or ComboBox. The **ValueMember** property defines a value associated with each item displayed.

For example, Listing 10-2 demonstrates binding a ListBox to the Employees table of the NorthwindDemo database. In this example, the **DisplayName** property is set to the LastName field from the data source. This means that when the application runs, the ListBox will be loaded with the last names of all of the employees.

Listing 10-2. Binding to a ListBox

```
' Declare the data-related objects.
Dim cn As System.Data.SqlServerCe.SqlCeConnection
Dim cmd As New System.Data.SqlServerCe.SqlCeCommand
Dim da As System.Data.SqlServerCe.SqlCeDataAdapter
Dim dt As System.Data.DataTable = New System.Data.DataTable("Employees")
Dim loading As Boolean

' Binding to the ListBox control is performed within this Click
' event procedure.
Private Sub btnBind_Click(ByVal sender As System.Object, _
  ByVal e As System.EventArgs) Handles btnBind.Click

' Turn on the loading flag.
  loading = True

' Open the connection.
  Try
    cn = New _
    System.Data.SqlServerCe.SqlCeConnection( _
      "Data Source=" & ApplicationLocation() & "\NorthwindDemo.sdf")

' Configure and execute the command.
    cmd.CommandText = "SELECT * FROM Employees"
    cmd.Connection = cn
```

```
' Load the DataTable.
    da = New System.Data.SqlServerCe.SqlCeDataAdapter(cmd)
    da.Fill(dt)

' Bind the ListBox.
    ListBox1.Visible = False
    ListBox1.DataSource = dt
    ListBox1.DisplayMember = "LastName"
    ListBox1.ValueMember = "FirstName"
    ListBox1.Visible = True

' Handle any exceptions that may occur.
  Catch sqlex As SqlServerCe.SqlCeException
    MsgBox(sqlex.Message.ToString)

  Catch ex As Exception
    MsgBox(ex.Message.ToString)
  End Try

' Turn off the loading flag.
  loading = False

End Sub

Private Function ApplicationLocation() As String

' Fetch and return the location where the application was launched.
  ApplicationLocation = _
    System.IO.Path.GetDirectoryName(Reflection.Assembly. _
    GetExecutingAssembly().GetName().CodeBase.ToString())

End Function
```

In this example, the **ValueMember** property is set to the FirstName field. This means that each of the LastName entries stored within the ListBox will have an associated FirstName.

 NOTE *The **Visible** property of the ListBox is set to False before configuring the DataSource. This hides an abnormality in how the ListBox appears while performing the binding.*

Where the **ValueMember** property typically comes into play is when the user selects an item from the ListBox or ComboBox. Querying the **SelectedValue** property of the control will return the ValueMember value for the selected item.

The following code shows an example of this. Within the **SelectedIndexChanged** event of the ListBox, the **SelectedValue** property is displayed. You may use this technique to implement Master-Detail functionality. An example of this is shown later in this chapter.

NOTE *This example includes the use of a flag called "loading." This flag is set when the ListBox is in the process of being loaded with data, which occurs during the binding process. The flag is used to work around a shortcoming of the ListBox control. Not only does the ListBox control fire its* **SelectedIndexChanged** *when the user selects an item, but also when a new item is added to a list. This "feature" causes programming grief unless you use some technique to tell the difference between events that are caused by loading and those triggered by the user. Hence, the use of the flag.*

```
Private Sub ListBox1_SelectedIndexChanged(ByVal sender As System.Object, _
  ByVal e As System.EventArgs) Handles ListBox1.SelectedIndexChanged
  If (Not loading) Then
    MsgBox(ListBox1.SelectedValue)
  End If
End Sub
```

NOTE *The examples in this section are from the List Binding project, which is included under* **Chapter 10** *of the* **Samples** *folder. For an example of binding to a ComboBox, refer to the Combo Binding project.*

Binding to a DataGrid

The process of binding to a DataGrid is straightforward. Simply load a data source and then assign the data source to the **DataSource** property of the DataGrid.

Listing 10-3 shows an example of this process. As you can see, loading the data source, which in this case is a DataTable, is far more complex than the actual binding part of the process.

Listing 10-3. Binding to a DataGrid

```
' Declare the data-related objects.
Dim cn As System.Data.SqlServerCe.SqlCeConnection
Dim cmd As New System.Data.SqlServerCe.SqlCeCommand
Dim da As System.Data.SqlServerCe.SqlCeDataAdapter
Dim dt As System.Data.DataTable = New System.Data.DataTable("Employees")


' Binding to the DataGrid control is performed within this Click
' event procedure.
Private Sub btnBind_Click(ByVal sender As System.Object, _
   ByVal e As System.EventArgs) Handles btnBind.Click


' Open the connection.
   Try
     cn = New _
     System.Data.SqlServerCe.SqlCeConnection( _
       "Data Source=" & ApplicationLocation() & "\NorthwindDemo.sdf")


' Configure and execute the command.
     cmd.CommandText = "SELECT * FROM Employees"
     cmd.Connection = cn


' Load the DataTable.
     da = New System.Data.SqlServerCe.SqlCeDataAdapter(cmd)
     da.Fill(dt)


' Bind the DataGrid.
     DataGrid1.Visible = False
     DataGrid1.DataSource = dt
     DataGrid1.Visible = True


' Handle any exceptions that may occur.
   Catch sqlex As SqlServerCe.SqlCeException
     MsgBox(sqlex.Message.ToString)

   Catch ex As Exception
     MsgBox(ex.Message.ToString)
   End Try


End Sub
```

```
Private Function ApplicationLocation() As String
' Fetch and return the location where the application was launched.
    ApplicationLocation = _
        System.IO.Path.GetDirectoryName(Reflection.Assembly. _
        GetExecutingAssembly().GetName().CodeBase.ToString())
End Function
```

I will point out one key part of this process. Note that I've sandwiched the setting of the DataGrid's **DataSource** property within two statements: one that hides the control, and another that displays the control. The reason for this is that during the binding process, there is an intermediate point, or stage, where the appearance of the control is, well, not what you would like your users to see. By setting the DataGrid's **Visible** property to False before setting the **DataSource** property, you hide this ugliness from the user.

NOTE   *The examples in this section are from the Grid Binding project, which is included under **Chapter 10** of the **Samples** folder.*

Binding to a PictureBox

The process of binding to a PictureBox is the most complicated of the examples shown in this chapter. This complexity comes as the result of the way SQL Server CE stores images.

Images placed within a SQL Server CE table are stored as a byte stream. This causes a problem when it comes to binding because the **Image** property of the PictureBox control requires an image object, not a byte stream.

You can rectify this formatting difficulty through the implementation of a simple event handler. This handler executes every time the **Format** event of the PictureBox fires. The **Format** event occurs when placing data from the underlying data source into the control. It's within this event that you'll convert the byte stream into an image.

Listing 10-4 demonstrates binding to a PictureBox. As with the other examples in this section, much of the programming work with data binding revolves around establishing the underlying data source.

Listing 10-4. Binding to a PictureBox

```
' Declare the data-related objects.
  Dim cn As System.Data.SqlServerCe.SqlCeConnection
  Dim cmd As New System.Data.SqlServerCe.SqlCeCommand
  Dim da As System.Data.SqlServerCe.SqlCeDataAdapter
  Dim dt As System.Data.DataTable = New System.Data.DataTable("Employees")
```

```vb
Private Sub btnBind_Click(ByVal sender As System.Object, _
  ByVal e As System.EventArgs) Handles btnBind.Click

' Open the connection.
    Try
      cn = New _
      System.Data.SqlServerCe.SqlCeConnection( _
        "Data Source=" & ApplicationLocation() & "\NorthwindDemo.sdf")

' Configure and execute the command.
      cmd.CommandText = "SELECT * FROM Employees"
      cmd.Connection = cn

' Load the DataTable.
      da = New System.Data.SqlServerCe.SqlCeDataAdapter(cmd)
      da.Fill(dt)

' Bind the PictureBox.
      Dim pbBinding As New Binding("Image", dt, "Photo")
      AddHandler pbBinding.Format, AddressOf ConvertImage
      PictureBox1.DataBindings.Add(pbBinding)

' Handle any exceptions that may occur.
    Catch sqlex As SqlServerCe.SqlCeException
      MsgBox(sqlex.Message.ToString)

    Catch ex As Exception
      MsgBox(ex.Message.ToString)
    End Try

  End Sub

  Private Sub ConvertImage(ByVal sender As Object, _
    ByVal cevent As ConvertEventArgs)

' Convert the byte string into an image.
    cevent.Value = New Bitmap(New _
      System.IO.MemoryStream(CType(cevent.Value, Byte())))
    End Sub

  Private Function ApplicationLocation() As String
```

```
' Fetch and return the location where the application was launched.
  ApplicationLocation = _
    System.IO.Path.GetDirectoryName(Reflection.Assembly. _
    GetExecutingAssembly().GetName().CodeBase.ToString())


End Function
```

Implementing the binding of the PictureBox involves these three lines of code:

```
Dim pbBinding As New Binding("Image", dt, "Photo")
AddHandler pbBinding.Format, AddressOf ConvertImage
PictureBox1.DataBindings.Add(pbBinding)
```

The first and third lines here are straightforward. They define a binding object and then add that binding object to the DataBindings collection of the PictureBox. It's the second line, the AddHandler statement, that is the key to binding a PictureBox. This line defines a handler, a routine that runs every time data loads from an underlying data source into the PictureBox.

In this case, that routine is ConvertImage. The ConvertImage routine contains a single line of code, which converts the byte string into an image.

```
cevent.Value = New Bitmap(New _
    System.IO.MemoryStream(CType(cevent.Value, Byte())))
```

That's all there is to binding a PictureBox control to a field in a SQL Server CE table.

 NOTE   *The examples in this section are from the PictureBox Binding project, which is included under **Chapter 10** of the **Samples** folder.*

Moving Between Items

Binding a set of controls on a form is limited without providing the user with some way to move about the underlying data source. What I'm talking about here is giving the user a navigational interface, which enables them to move forward and backward through the data source. This could be a set of buttons, menu items, or toolbar buttons.

Typically, your navigational interface will allow users to move to the first item, the previous item, the next item, and the last item. You control movement about the underlying data source by setting the **Position** property of the BindingContext object. Table 10-1 shows examples of how to move to specific positions.

Table 10-1. Moving Between Items

POSITION	CODE EXAMPLE
First	Me.BindingContext(dt).Position = 0
Previous	Me.BindingContext(dt).Position -= 1
Next	Me.BindingContext(dt).Position +=1
Last	Me.BindingContext(dt).Position = Me.BindingContext(dt).Count – 1

Listing 10-5 provides four event procedures for four buttons: **first**, **last**, **previous**, and **next**. Within each of these respective procedures is a single line of code that repositions the location in the underlying data source. In each of these cases, changing the position causes the values of the bound controls to update.

Listing 10-5. Moving About a Data Source

```
Private Sub btnFirst_Click(ByVal sender As System.Object, _
  ByVal e As System.EventArgs) Handles btnFirst.Click
    Me.BindingContext(dt).Position = 0
End Sub

Private Sub btnLast_Click(ByVal sender As System.Object, _
  ByVal e As System.EventArgs) Handles btnLast.Click
    Me.BindingContext(dt).Position = Me.BindingContext(dt).Count - 1
End Sub

Private Sub btnPrevious_Click(ByVal sender As System.Object, _
  ByVal e As System.EventArgs) Handles btnPrevious.Click
    Me.BindingContext(dt).Position -= 1
End Sub

Private Sub btnNext_Click(ByVal sender As System.Object, _
  ByVal e As System.EventArgs) Handles btnNext.Click
    Me.BindingContext(dt).Position += 1
End Sub
```

Adding an Item

The BindingContext object provides a method, **AddNew**, for adding an item to the underlying data source. You can use this method to implement this type of functionality in your mobile applications.

The **AddNew** method performs two tasks. First, it adds a blank record to the underlying data source. Second, it clears all of the bound fields, preparing them for data entry. Following is an example of calling this method:

```
Private Sub btnAdd_Click(ByVal sender As System.Object, _
  ByVal e As System.EventArgs) Handles btnAdd.Click
    Me.BindingContext(dt).AddNew()
End Sub
```

Deleting an Item

The BindingContext object provides a method, **RemoveAt**, for deleting an item from an underlying data source. You can use this method to implement this type of functionality in your mobile applications.

The **RemoveAt** method accepts a single argument, an integer value, which specifies the item to delete. Commonly, when working with bound data, this will be the current record. Following is an example of this where the current position of the BindingContext object is passed to the **RemoveAt** method. You can determine the current position within the BindingContext object through its **Position** property.

```
Private Sub btnDelete_Click(ByVal sender As System.Object, _
  ByVal e As System.EventArgs) Handles btnDelete.Click
    Me.BindingContext(dt).RemoveAt(Me.BindingContext(dt).Position)
End Sub
```

Canceling an Edit in Progress

While not a function that is frequently used when working with bound controls, there are times when you need to cancel an edit that is in progress. For example, say a user brings up a record, begins to modify the values of fields within that record, and suddenly realizes, "Oops! Wrong record!" At this point, the user wants to quit that activity, restore the current record to its original form, and move on to the appropriate record. There's an easy way to accomplish this: the **CancelCurrentEdit** method.

The following code demonstrates the **CancelCurrentEdit** method of the BindingContext object. Executing the **CancelCurrentEdit** method says to the BindingContext object, "Hey, I've changed my mind. Put everything back the way it was." Simply stated, executing this method throws away any modifications that may have occurred to the bound controls and restores the original values for each control from the underlying data source.

```
Private Sub btnCancel_Click(ByVal sender As System.Object, _
  ByVal e As System.EventArgs) Handles btnCancel.Click
    Me.BindingContext(dt).CancelCurrentEdit()
End Sub
```

 CAUTION   *This is an all-or-nothing approach. Calling the* ***CancelCurrentEdit*** *method throws away the changes made to* all *of the bound controls, not a select control or group of controls.*

Validating Input

Just because you are using bound controls doesn't mean that you have to give up control over validating input. All of the validation techniques that you employ with regular forms will work with bound forms. You can validate as the user types, field-by-field, and as a complete form.

The general rule with bound forms is to perform any validation before moving between records in your underlying data source. This is because moving between records automatically saves the values of the bound controls. At that point, it's too late—you've accepted the bad data.

Listing 10-6 shows a simple example of performing validation before moving about the underlying data source. In this example, four routines handle moving to the first record, the previous record, the next record, and the last record. In these routines, a call to the ValidateInput function, determines whether the values in the form are valid.

Listing 10-6. Validating a Bound Form

```
Private Sub btnFirst_Click(ByVal sender As System.Object, _
  ByVal e As System.EventArgs) Handles btnFirst.Click
    If (ValidateInput) Then
      Me.BindingContext(dt).Position = 0
    End If
End Sub
```

```
Private Sub btnPrevious_Click(ByVal sender As System.Object, _
  ByVal e As System.EventArgs) Handles btnPrevious.Click
    If (ValidateInput) Then
      Me.BindingContext(dt).Position -= 1
    End If
End Sub

Private Sub btnNext_Click(ByVal sender As System.Object, _
  ByVal e As System.EventArgs) Handles btnNext.Click
    If (ValidateInput) Then
      Me.BindingContext(dt).Position += 1
    End If
End Sub

Private Sub btnLast_Click(ByVal sender As System.Object, _
  ByVal e As System.EventArgs) Handles btnLast.Click
    If (ValidateInput) Then

      Me.BindingContext(dt).Position = Me.BindingContext(dt).Count - 1
    End If
End Sub

Function ValidateInput() As Boolean
' Perform some validation here.
  ValidateInput = True
End Function
```

This simple approach to input validation allows you complete control over your data with minimal effort. As I stated earlier in this section, this is by no means the only approach you could use. You can use any of the standard input validation techniques with bound controls including keystroke monitoring and field-by-field validating.

Creating a Master-Detail Form

You can use bound controls to create a variety of application interfaces, including Master-Detail forms. In case you aren't familiar with this terminology, Master-Detail forms present parent-child relationships that exist in a data source. An example of a Master-Detail relationship is customers and orders. Each customer has a number of orders. The customer is the Master. The orders are the Details.

It's easy to create a Master-Detail form using bound controls. Commonly, you will use a ComboBox control for the Master component of the form and a DataGrid for the Detail part of the form. Figure 10-1 shows an example of this type of configuration.

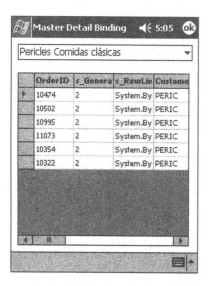

Figure 10-1. A Master-Detail form

Bound controls make creating a Master-Detail form easy. It's a simple two-step process. The first step is to bind the Master component of the form. An example of this process is shown in Listing 10-7. Here, the ComboBox is bound to the CompanyName field of the Customers table. Note that the **ValueMember** property of the ComboBox is set to the CustomerID field. This provides the link between the Master and Detail components of the form.

Listing 10-7. Configuring the Master Component of the Form

```
Private Sub Form1_Load(ByVal sender As System.Object, _
  ByVal e As System.EventArgs) Handles MyBase.Load

' Circumvent the SelectedIndexChanged event while loading the ComboBox.
  loading = True

' Open the connection.
  Try
    cn = New _
      System.Data.SqlServerCe.SqlCeConnection( _
      "Data Source=" & ApplicationLocation() & "\NorthwindDemo.sdf")
```

```
' Configure and execute the command.
    cmd.CommandText = "SELECT * FROM Customers"
    cmd.Connection = cn

' Load the DataSet.
    da = New System.Data.SqlServerCe.SqlCeDataAdapter(cmd)
    da.Fill(customerDT)

' Bind the fields.
    ComboBox1.Visible = False
    ComboBox1.DataSource = customerDT
    ComboBox1.DisplayMember = "CompanyName"
    ComboBox1.ValueMember = "CustomerID"
    ComboBox1.Visible = True

' Handle any exceptions.
  Catch sqlex As SqlServerCe.SqlCeException
    MsgBox(sqlex.Message.ToString)

  Catch ex As Exception
    MsgBox(ex.Message.ToString)
  End Try

  loading = False

' Display orders for the first entry.
  ComboBox1.SelectedIndex = -1
  ComboBox1.SelectedIndex = 0

End Sub
```

The process of binding the ComboBox occurs in the **Form Load** event procedure. As such, it takes place when the application runs. Near the bottom of this procedure, we trigger the second part of the binding process by setting the **SelectedIndex** property of the ComboBox. Setting this property causes the ComboBox's **SelectedIndexChanged** event to fire.

Listing 10-8 shows the code used to bind the Detail component of the form. It's placed within the **SelectedIndexChanged** event of the ComboBox. This event fires every time the user selects a customer from the ComboBox.

Listing 10-8. Configuring the Details Component of the Form

```
Private Sub ComboBox1_SelectedIndexChanged(ByVal sender As System.Object, _
  ByVal e As System.EventArgs) Handles ComboBox1.SelectedIndexChanged

' This flag is set while the control is being loaded.
  If (Not loading) Then
    Try
' Configure and execute the command.
      cmd.CommandText = "SELECT * FROM Orders Where CustomerID='" & _
        ComboBox1.SelectedValue & "'"
      cmd.Connection = cn

    ' Load the DataSet.
      da = New System.Data.SqlServerCe.SqlCeDataAdapter(cmd)
      ordersDT.Clear()
      da.Fill(ordersDT)

    ' Bind the fields.
      DataGrid1.Visible = False
      DataGrid1.DataSource = ordersDT
      DataGrid1.Visible = True

    ' Handle any exceptions.
      Catch sqlex As SqlServerCe.SqlCeException
        MsgBox(sqlex.Message.ToString)

      Catch ex As Exception
        MsgBox(ex.Message.ToString)

    End Try
  End If
End Sub
```

The key to this procedure is the use of the ComboBox's **SelectedValue** property. If you look back to Listing 10-7, the property holds the CustomerID of the
selected customer. We use this value to query the Orders table, retrieving only
the orders for the selected customer. From there, all that remains is to bind the
DataGrid to this resulting DataTable.

That's all there is to it. As you can see, creating a Master-Detail form is easy
using bound controls.

NOTE *The examples in this section are from the Master Detail project, which is included under **Chapter 10** of the **Samples** folder.*

Permanently Saving Data

I need to make one very crucial point regarding data binding and the concept of saving data. If you are new to DataSets, DataTables, and DataAdapters, it's very easy to make the mistake that data modified in a DataSet or DataTable is automatically saved for you. By saved, I mean permanently saved, which is to say written out to a database or to a file as XML.

Let me strongly warn you that this isn't the case with ADO.NET. Data that isn't explicitly saved from DataSets and DataTables before your application exits is permanently lost. This includes data modified through data binding.

Now obviously, if you were to do any prerelease testing at all, you should come to this startling conclusion on your own. Just to save you some heartache and sanity, I wanted to clarify that point here.

CAUTION *Failing to save in-memory data sources before exiting your application will result in the loss of data. Remember, DataSets are disconnected from their source.*

Following is a simple example of saving data before exiting your application. This is just one way to handle permanently saving data from an underlying data source.

```
Dim ds As New System.Data.DataSet("NorthwindDemo")

Private Sub Form1_Closing(ByVal sender As Object, _
   ByVal e As System.ComponentModel.CancelEventArgs) Handles MyBase.Closing
  Save the cached data permanently.
   da.Update(ds)
End Sub
```

NOTE *For more on saving data, see Chapters 9 and 13.*

As I mentioned, saving data as shown in the preceding code example is just one way to approach permanently saving data. While saving data just before an application exits is critical, you should also consider saving your data at other times, such as when data is changed or on a regular timed interval. Doing so limits the liability of losing data through those standard problems that plague mobile developers—loss of power, resetting the device, and user intervention.

You can use the **CurrentChanged** and **PositionChanged** events of the **BindingManagerBase** class to monitor modification to and movement within your underlying data source. Listing 10-9 provides a simple demonstration of adding a delegate for the **PositionChanged** event. Here, a check is made to determine if the underlying data source has been modified. If it has, the DataSet automatically saves the data.

Listing 10-9. Saving Data Within the PositionChanged Event

```
Sub BindControlDemo()
' Create a Binding object for the TextBox control.
  Dim myBinding As New Binding("Text", ds, "Employees.FirstName")
  TextBox1.DataBindings.Add(myBinding)

' Get the BindingManagerBase for the Employees table.
  Dim bmEmployees As BindingManagerBase = Me.BindingContext(ds, "Employees")

' Define a delegate for the PositionChanged event.
  AddHandler bmEmployees.PositionChanged, AddressOf Position_Changed

End Sub

Private Sub Position_Changed(sender As Object, e As EventArgs)
  If (ds.HasChanges) Then
    da.Update(ds)
    ds.AcceptChanges()
  End If
End Sub
```

Working with the BindingContext Object

While I've shown you numerous examples of working with the BindingContext object throughout this chapter, I thought that it might be helpful to summarize its key properties and methods.

Table 10-2 shows commonly used properties of the BindingContext object. You will find that it's practically impossible to develop a binding application without the **Position** property.

Table 10-2. Commonly Used Properties of the BindingContext Object

PROPERTY	DESCRIPTION
Bindings	Collection of bindings being managed.
Count	Number of rows in the underlying list or data source. Useful for navigational purposes.
Position	Current position in the underlying list or data source. Controls the values displayed in the bound controls.

Table 10-3 shows commonly used methods of the BindingContext object. Two of these methods, **AddNew** and **RemoveAt**, appear in all data-bound applications that allow data modifications. The other two methods, **CancelCurrentEdit** and **EndCurrentEdit**, are useful in managing and controlling modifications in progress.

Table 10-3. Commonly Used Methods of the BindingContext Object

METHOD	DESCRIPTION
AddNew	Adds an item to the underlying list or data source.
CancelCurrentEdit	Cancels the edit in progress, discarding any changes to the underlying data. Useful in providing users with a way to cancel an edit they don't want to complete.
EndCurrentEdit	Ends the edit in progress, saving any modifications to the underlying data.
RemoveAt	Removes an item from the underlying list or data source.

Now you're ready to put everything that you've learned on data binding to work. The following section is a detailed, step-by-step tutorial that walks you through the complete process of creating and working with bound controls. If you have any confusion with any part of the binding process, working through this tutorial should put everything in place for you.

Step-by-Step Tutorial: Working with Bound Controls

In this step-by-step exercise, you will create an application that demonstrates working with bound controls. As part of this exercise, you'll

- Connect to a SQL Server CE database.

- Retrieve a DataTable from the database.

- Bind two TextBox controls to the DataTable.

- Navigate about the DataTable.

- Add new records to the DataTable.

- Delete existing records from the DataTable.

- Cancel edits before they are committed.

This application provides all of the fundamentals of creating a bound form. It uses the Employees table from the Northwind database as its source. For simplicity, only the FirstName and LastName fields from this table are included in this example.

 NOTE *I provide a completed version of this application, titled Binding Tutorial–Complete, under* **Chapter 10** *of the* **Samples** *folder for this book. See Appendix D for more information on accessing and loading the sample applications.*

Step 1: Opening the Project

To simplify this tutorial, I've already created the project and the user interface for the Binding Tutorial application. This template project is included under the **Chapter 10** folder of the **Samples** folder. To load this project, follow these steps:

1. From the VS .NET IDE Start Page, select to open a project. The Open Project dialog box will be displayed.

2. Use the dialog box to navigate to the **Chapter 10** folder under the **Samples** folder for this book.

3. Select and open the project **Binding Tutorial**. The project will be loaded.

Step 2: Examining the User Interface

The user interface for the Binding Tutorial application is comprised of two Labels, two TextBoxes, and eight Buttons. Figure 10-2 shows the application's interface.

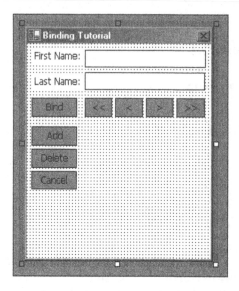

Figure 10-2. The Binding Tutorial application interface

The two TextBox controls will display the data taken from the FirstName and LastName fields of the Employees table.

The eight buttons are comprised of a single **Bind** button, four navigational buttons, and three feature buttons (**Add**, **Delete**, **Cancel**). All of the buttons, with the exception of the **Bind** button, are disabled when the application starts. That's because they are useless until the binding process is complete.

Step 3: Adding the Database

A SQL Server CE database, NorthwindDemo.sdf, needs to be included with your project. It will act as the data source for the binding.

To add the database to your project, perform the following steps:

1. Under the Project menu, select **Add Existing Item**.

2. The Add Existing Item dialog box displays. From this dialog box, navigate to the **Common** folder under the **Samples** folder for this book.

3. From the Files of type ComboBox, select **All Files (*.*)**.

4. Select the file **NorthwindDemo.sdf** and click the **Open** button.

The database appears as part of your project in the Solution Explorer window. To configure the database so that it's copied to your device, perform the following steps:

1. Select the file **NorthwindDemo.sdf** in the Solutions Explorer window.

2. In the Properties window, change the **Build Action** property to **Content**.

When you build your application, the database automatically copies to the same folder as the application.

Step 4: Adding References

You need to add two references to your application. Both are data related, enabling you to work with a SQL Server CE database.

To add these references, perform the following steps:

1. In the Solution Explorer window, right-click the **References** folder. A pop-up menu displays.

2. From the menu, select **Add Reference**.

3. The Add Reference dialog box displays. Select both the **System.Data.Common** and **System.Data.SqlServerCe** components.

4. Click the **OK** button to add the selected components to your project.

Step 5: Declaring Module-Level Objects

This tutorial uses four module-level object variables. These variables hold instances of the Connection, Command, DataAdapter, and DataTable objects.

To define these variables, add the following code to the module level of the form:

```
Dim cn As System.Data.SqlServerCe.SqlCeConnection
Dim cmd As New System.Data.SqlServerCe.SqlCeCommand
Dim da As System.Data.SqlServerCe.SqlCeDataAdapter
Dim dt As System.Data.DataTable = New System.Data.DataTable("Employees")
```

Step 6: Binding the Controls

The first functionality that you'll add to your application handles binding the two TextBox controls to the underlying data source. In this case, that source is the Employees table from the NorthwindDemo database.

To bind the two controls, add the code shown in Listing 10-10 to the **Click** event of the **Bind** button.

Listing 10-10. Binding the Two TextBox Controls

```
Private Sub btnBind_Click(ByVal sender As System.Object, _
  ByVal e As System.EventArgs) Handles btnBind.Click

' Open the connection.
  Try
    cn = New _
      System.Data.SqlServerCe.SqlCeConnection( _
      "Data Source=" & ApplicationLocation() & "\NorthwindDemo.sdf")

' Configure and execute the command.
    cmd.CommandText = "SELECT * FROM Employees"
    cmd.Connection = cn

' Load the DataSet.
    da = New System.Data.SqlServerCe.SqlCeDataAdapter(cmd)
    da.Fill(dt)

' Bind the fields.
    txtFirstName.DataBindings.Add(New Binding("Text", dt, "FirstName"))
    txtLastName.DataBindings.Add(New Binding("Text", dt, "LastName"))

' Handle any exceptions.
  Catch sqlex As SqlServerCe.SqlCeException
    MsgBox(sqlex.Message.ToString)

  Catch ex As Exception
    MsgBox(ex.Message.ToString)
  End Try

' Disable the Bind button.
  btnBind.Enabled = False
```

```
' Enable the other buttons.
  btnFirst.Enabled = True
  btnPrevious.Enabled = True
  btnNext.Enabled = True
  btnLast.Enabled = True

  btnAdd.Enabled = True
  btnDelete.Enabled = True
  btnCancel.Enabled = True

End Sub
```

The code within this **Click** event procedure begins by opening a connection (cn) to the SQL Server CE database NorthwindDemo, which you added to your project back in Step 3.

Next, a command (cmd) retrieves all of the records from the Employees table. A DataAdapter (da) object fills a DataTable (dt) with these records.

Near the middle of this procedure, you bind two TextBox controls to the DataTable. You bind them to the FirstName and LastName fields of the Employees table.

The lower part of the procedure performs exception handling and interface management.

Step 7: Adding the ApplicationLocation Function

To establish a connection to the NorthwindDemo database, your application needs to know the directory where the database resides. Since you configured the database as part of your project, it's copied along with your application to the device and placed in the same directory.

The function ApplicationLocation retrieves the path to where your application resides. Add this function, shown in the following code snippet, to your project:

```
Private Function ApplicationLocation() As String
' Fetch and return the location where the application was launched.
    ApplicationLocation = _
      System.IO.Path.GetDirectoryName(Reflection.Assembly. _
      GetExecutingAssembly().GetName().CodeBase.ToString())
End Function
```

 NOTE   *The ApplicationLocation function appears within the **Click** event procedure of the **Bind** button.*

Step 8: Moving Between Records

Now with the binding in place, you're ready to add code that enables the user to navigate about the DataTable. You will need to add code to each of the four navigational buttons.

Add the code shown in here to the **Click** event of the first record button (<<):

```
Private Sub btnFirst_Click(ByVal sender As System.Object, _
  ByVal e As System.EventArgs) Handles btnFirst.Click
    Me.BindingContext(dt).Position = 0
End Sub
```

Add the following code to the **Click** event of the previous record button (<):

```
Private Sub btnPrevious_Click(ByVal sender As System.Object, _
  ByVal e As System.EventArgs) Handles btnPrevious.Click
    Me.BindingContext(dt).Position -= 1
End Sub
```

Add the following code to the **Click** event of the next record button (>):

```
Private Sub btnNext_Click(ByVal sender As System.Object, _
  ByVal e As System.EventArgs) Handles btnNext.Click
    Me.BindingContext(dt).Position += 1
End Sub
```

Add the code shown here to the **Click** event of the last record button (>>):

```
Private Sub btnLast_Click(ByVal sender As System.Object, _
  ByVal e As System.EventArgs) Handles btnLast.Click
    Me.BindingContext(dt).Position = Me.BindingContext(dt).Count - 1
End Sub
```

At this point, if you were to do nothing else, you would have an application that would allow you to browse about the records that appear in the Employees table. You could also modify the first and last names of employees.

What you wouldn't be able to do is add or delete records. You'll add this functionality in the following steps.

Step 9: Adding a New Record

Adding records to a bound table is simple, requiring only a single line of code. Following is the code that you need to add to the **Click** event of the **Add** button:

```
Private Sub btnAdd_Click(ByVal sender As System.Object, _
  ByVal e As System.EventArgs) Handles btnAdd.Click
    Me.BindingContext(dt).AddNew()
End Sub
```

Step 10: Deleting a Record

Deleting records from a bound table is equally simple. Following is the code that
you need to add to the **Click** event of the **Delete** button:

```
Private Sub btnDelete_Click(ByVal sender As System.Object, _
  ByVal e As System.EventArgs) Handles btnDelete.Click
    Me.BindingContext(dt).RemoveAt(Me.BindingContext(dt).Position)
End Sub
```

Step 11: Canceling an Edit

The final feature to add to your binding demo application handles canceling an
edit that's in progress. Where this functionality comes into play is when users
begin modifying a record and then change their mind. When working with
bound controls, canceling an edit causes the values displayed within the controls to revert to the original values.

Add the code shown here to the **Click** event of the **Cancel** button:

```
Private Sub btnCancel_Click(ByVal sender As System.Object, _
  ByVal e As System.EventArgs) Handles btnCancel.Click
    Me.BindingContext(dt).CancelCurrentEdit()
End Sub
```

Step 12: Testing the Application

Finally, you're ready to test your application. To test your application, perform
the following steps:

1. Select either **Pocket PC Device** or **Pocket PC Emulator** from the
    Deployment Device combo box.

2. Select **Release** from the Solution Configurations combo box.

3. Click the **Start** button.

Your application copies to the target device along with the NorthwindDemo database. Upon completion the application starts.

To test your application, perform the following steps:

1. Tap the **Bind** button. After a brief pause, the bound TextBox controls display the first record.

2. Use the navigational buttons to move about the Employees table.

3. Modify the first or last name of one of the employees. Move to another record and then back to the record you modified. Confirm that the value was saved.

4. Tap the **Add** button. Fill in the fields and move to another record. Move back to your new record to confirm the addition.

5. Move to your new record and tap the **Delete** button. The record is deleted and a new record displayed.

6. To test the **Cancel** button, start to edit either a first or a last name of a record. Tap the **Cancel** button. The original values of the first and last name redisplay.

 HOMEWORK *Add three fields to your form: Address, City, and Region. Verify that the contents of these fields display correctly and can be modified.*

 HOMEWORK *Modify the first button (<<) and last button (>>) so that they are disabled when they aren't functional. That is to say, disable the first button (<<) when on the first record. Disable the last button (>>) when on the last record.*

Summary

Data binding offers an easy way to build applications that display and accept data. The beauty behind binding is that it handles much of the underlying data-related work for you. Binding automatically saves modifications to fields and requires no code on your part. Adding and deleting records is only slightly more complex. Each requires only a single line of code. Likewise, you can cancel edits with a single line of code.

Things would be even easier if you could use the Data Form Wizard to create bound forms that target the .NET Compact Framework. Instead, you must roll your own binding. Even then, you will find that once you have built the basic bound form, creating subsequent forms is quick and easy.

In the next chapter, we'll continue our discussion on data-related items. Chapter 11 provides a detailed overview of SQL Server CE.

Introduction to SQL Server CE

You might be saying to yourself, "SQL Server on Windows CE, no way!" Actually yes, and it's a very good implementation, seeing as how it has to run on a memory- and processor-constrained device. On the device it doesn't run as a service, but is implemented as a normal DLL.

In this chapter, we'll look at what it takes to get SQL Server CE up and running on your device and development work station. The setup work also involves creating a subscription in SQL Server that is required for merge replication. In the following two chapters, I'll cover how you access and maintain data on the server and on the device. I'll start this chapter with an overview of what can be done with this technology and the functionality provided by SQL Server CE. We'll also take a look at a tool that comes with SQL CE called the *Query Analyzer*.

If you ever used SQL Server CE 1.x, you'll be overjoyed to know that you'll be learning about SQL Server CE 2.x. While version 1.x was usable, the setup and maintenance of the database, publications, and subscriptions were not.

In this book, you've already learned about ADO.NET, and we're about to explore SQL Server CE in some detail using that knowledge. What we aren't going to look at is Pocket Access for one very big reason: It isn't supported in the Compact Framework. If you have a Pocket Access database, you have a couple of choices: Throw it away (just kidding), convert it to SQL CE, or use a product by InTheHand (http://www.inthehand.com) called ADOCE .NET Wrapper. This library is designed to efficiently provide access directly to the ADOCE control. This will help you fill the gap as you explore and move over to SQL CE.

What Can You Do with SQL CE?

The potential uses of the Pocket PC, combined with SQL Server CE, are almost limitless! I have seen applications that were used for real estate home sales. A device synchronizes with SQL Server to maintain a list of homes, all the details about the houses, and a picture of each house. Agents can carry their device with them when showing a prospective buyer the area. And if they need directions, they can call up any of the mapping services on the Internet and find the way to a particular home.

The favorite user scenario out of Microsoft is the cookie company that supplies its drivers with ruggedized Pocket PCs to keep track of deliveries and damaged (or eaten) goods. At the beginning and the end of each day, the devices are synchronized with the servers in the main distribution center via SQL Server replication.

NOTE *A ruggedized Pocket PC is one that can take some abuse, unlike the standard Pocket PC devices. A ruggedized device can be dropped from 6 feet or more and not be damaged. It can also be sealed to prevent chemical or electrical contamination. Some models are also able to withstand high temperatures.*

Many areas of the sports business could benefit from data synchronization to and from devices. The amount of data collected and analyzed at sporting events, from hockey to basketball, is amazing. Performing data collection through a Pocket PC and then synchronizing that data with back-end servers is an idea yet to be fully explored.

As you'll see in the next two chapters, this synchronization can be done either on a direct connection to the database, through Web services, or by using synchronization. To understand how to use these capabilities, you first need to know what features SQL CE provides. You might think that, being of reduced size, the SQL CE engine would be crippled or limited at best. The following list shows a few of the features that have been included in SQL Server CE 2.0. Version 1.x was more constrained, but version 2.0 really delivers much of the functionality provided by the server version of SQL.

- Defaults
- Having/group by
- Inner/outer joins
- Multicolumn indexes
- Null support

- One-file database
- Referential integrity
- Subselects (IN)
- Transactions
- Unicode support

SQL CE also provides the basics and then some when it comes to the supported data types. The data types supported are as follows:

- bigint
- binary
- bit
- datetime
- float
- image
- integer

- money
- ntext
- numeric
- real
- smallint
- tinyint
- uniqueidentifier

SQL CE Architecture

In very basic terms, there is an agent on the Pocket PC, SQL Server CE Client Agent, and an agent on the server, SQL Server CE Server Agent, that talk to each other via HTTP requests across either Ethernet, wireless LAN, or wireless WAN. The server client is actually located on a computer that is running Internet Information Server (IIS). Figure 11-1 shows a graphical representation of the layout of the various agents. Authentication for the requests is handled through IIS. The SQL Server database may be located on the same computer as IIS, or it can be on a different computer in a remote location. I'll discuss authentication in more detail later.

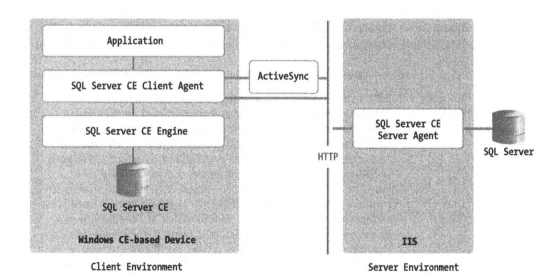

Figure 11-1. Basic architecture

When the SQL Server CE Server Agent receives a request from the client, it connects to the SQL Server and returns any data back to the SQL Server CE Client Agent, again through HTTP requests. These communications can be performed over HTTPS connections for added data security. SQL Server CE can also use the IIS Secure Sockets Layer (SSL) feature to encrypt data that is propagated between the device running SQL Server CE and the computer running SQL Server. To reduce data transfer time, SQL CE compresses the data through the HTTP channel.

If you don't have your device connected to a network, you can also use ActiveSync to connect directly to SQL Server through your desktop's network connection. If you're using Pocket PC 2002, this works without any additional software. However, if you're using any other Windows CE system, then you'll need to use the SQL Server CE Relay application. If you worked with the earlier versions of SQL CE, then you are probably familiar with the relay application. I'm going to assume that by this point most people have bought or upgraded to 2002, so I won't cover the relay in any detail.

The next several pages will discuss installation of the tools in the development environment. To install SQL CE on a device with your application, all you need to do is reference the correct assemblies, and the proper files are copied by default. I'll discuss installing server-side tools, distributors, and publications in the next section. If you don't plan on using data replication, then you don't need to create distributors and publications (hey, the chapter may have gotten a whole lot shorter for you). If you later need to remove the tools, the uninstall feature works well, but you'll need to remove any distributors or publications yourself.

Installing SQL Server CE 2.0

Before you start installing SQL CE, make sure that you have at least Service Pack 1 of SQL Server on whichever machine you plan on installing the server-side tools on.

NOTE *At the time of this writing, Service Pack 3 for SQL Server 2003 has just been released. After you install SP3 on the development computer, you may not be able to run the server-side tool installation. Microsoft's Web site says that if you already have SQL Server CE 2.0 on your computer, you'll be able to install SP3 with no resulting problems with SQL CE. However, if you have no service packs on SQL Server 2003, and you install SP3 and then attempt to install SQL Server CE 2.0, you'll indeed have problems. To install the server tools, you need a service pack for SQL CE. The filename is sqlce20sql2ksp3.exe, and you can read about it and download a copy from the SQL CE Web site at* http://www.microsoft.com/sql/ce. *Be warned that this may indeed change by the time you buy this book and read this note.*

Installing the Development Tools

Once you get started with the installation, you have to make a choice of which tools to install. You already know about the two different agents that go on the server and on the client. When you start the installation, the first dialog box presents a simple choice of what tools you want to install, developer or server. The development tools choice will install the assemblies that are required to build SQL CE applications. The assemblies are also copied to the device during testing and installation to enable the device to work with SQL CE. The server installation creates a virtual directory and copies the SQL Server CE Server Agent files to the directory. I'll cover the server tools installation in detail in the next section.

NOTE *You can download SQL Server CE version 2.0 at* http://www.microsoft.com/sql/ce/downloads/ce20.asp.

Since you're running Visual Studio .NET, you'll already have IIS on your development computer, so you could install both sets of tools. However, to make a point, and to separate the two installations to make the distinction between client and server as obvious as possible, you'll run the installation twice. If you want to run SQL Server CE Server Agent on a computer separate from your development machine, and at some point in the future you will, you need to run the development and server installations separately anyway. Check the **Development Tools** box in the first step; select the drive on which to install the tools in the next step and click **Next**. That's all there really is to installing the development tools.

Installing the Server Tools

The installation of the server tools is very much the same as for the development tools. To install the Server Tools, run the setup program again, only this time, in the first step select **Server Tools** and click **Next**. If you try to run the server tools installation, and you either have no SQL Server service packs on your computer or you have SP3, you'll receive an error message stating that SQL Server CE is compatible with Service Pack 1 or higher (see the note earlier in this chapter that discusses this problem). Once the installation is completed, you'll see the dialog box shown in Figure 11-2.

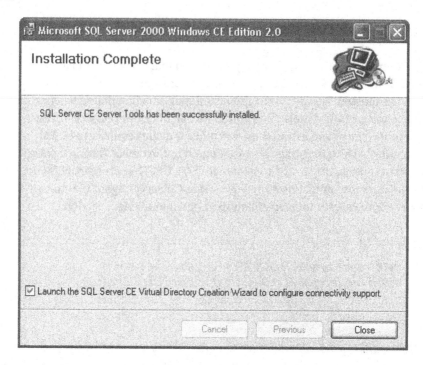

Figure 11-2. Setting up the virtual directory by wizard on installation completion

Notice the check box along the bottom edge of the dialog box. In our earlier discussion about architecture, I mentioned that the computer running IIS was the entry point to SQL Server in communications from the device. This is done through a virtual directory that contains a file called sscesa20.dll. This file is the SQL Server CE Server Agent that I discussed earlier. If you are familiar with SQL Server CE 1.x, you'll appreciate the new Virtual Directory Creation Wizard. In the previous version, the virtual directory and permissions were done by hand and were more difficult than writing the app in the first place (all right, maybe I exaggerate just a little). When you click **Close** in the dialog box shown in Figure 11-2, the Virtual Directory Creation Wizard starts.

This wizard walks you through the steps required to set up the virtual directory and to set permissions, if required, on that directory. The dialog box in Figure 11-3 is used to set the name of the virtual directory and to set the directory to which the virtual folder points. By default the installer puts the files within the SQL CE directory. You can change this path to any folder you like, but you must be sure to copy the correct files into the folder that you chose.

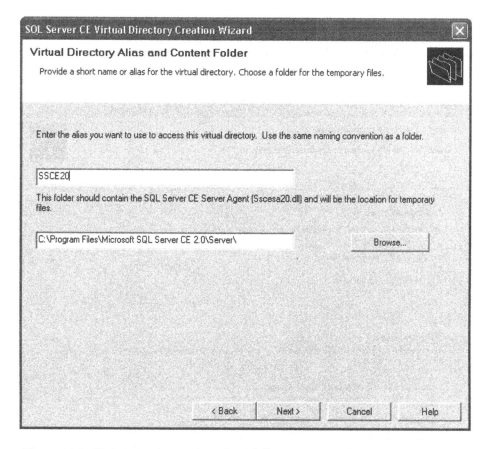

Figure 11-3. Giving a name to your virtual directory

The following files are placed in the default folder by the wizard:

- sscesa20.dll

- sscerp20.dll

- SQL Server CE Connectivity Management.msc

- connwiz20.dll

- connwizr20.dll

The next step, shown in Figure 11-4, is to set the permissions on the directory. The easy way out is to use anonymous authentication, while the more difficult, if not more secure, solution is to use Integrated Windows authentication. In the next series of steps, you'll be using Windows authentication, but we'll look at authentication in more detail in the next section.

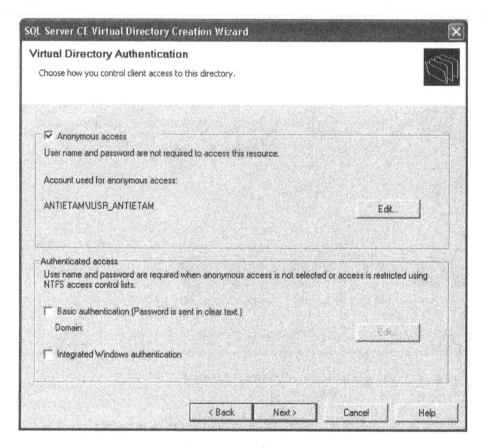

Figure 11-4. Choosing your authentication scheme

Once an authentication scheme has been set, you have the choice to set up the database to handle one or more of your applications to use merge replication as shown in Figure 11-5.

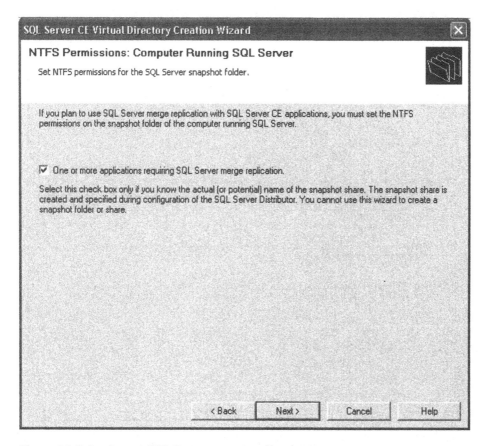

Figure 11-5. Setting up SQL Server merge replication

If you select this check box, then the next step is to specify the directory to be used for the snapshot folder. Figure 11-6 shows the dialog box in which you set the snapshot folder. This folder must be created before you run this wizard step because the wizard doesn't create the folder; it just assigns the appropriate rights for users on the folder. The folder, as explained in the dialog box in Figure 11-5, is created when you set up the publisher/subscription in SQL Server Enterprise Manager.

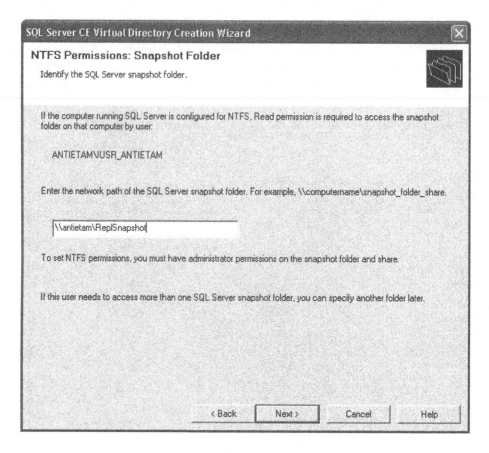

Figure 11-6. Setting your snapshot folder

The final step is a verification of the work that you want done. When you click **Finish** in this final dialog box, the wizard performs the requested directory and permissions work. Once the permissions are set up, you can change them by using either IIS Manager or a utility that comes with SQL CE. You can find the SQL Server CE Connectivity Management console in the virtual directory.

In Figure 11-7, you can see a dialog box similar to the IIS Manager that lets you select either anonymous access or Integrated Windows authentication. When you select Integrated Windows authentication, you'll need to add or modify the permissions for a user on the **NTFS** tab, which is shown in Figure 11-8.

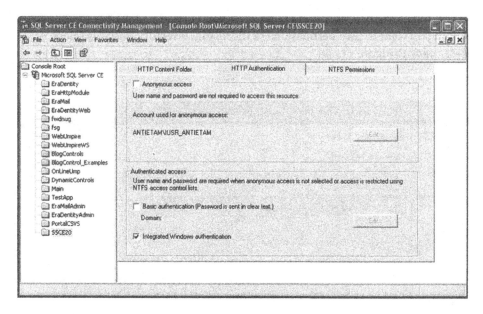

Figure 11-7. Changing authentication after the fact

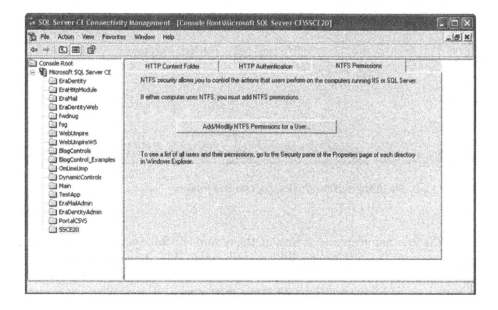

Figure 11-8. Setting the user permissions

In the dialog box shown in Figure 11-9, you enter the name of the users to whom you want to give permissions to the virtual directory that was selected (refer back to Figure 11-7).

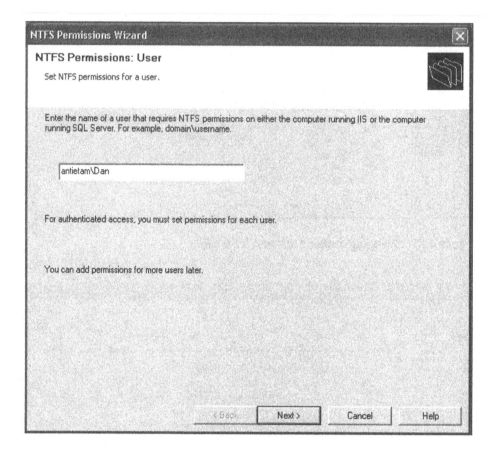

Figure 11-9. Selecting a user who will access the folder

If the user name entered is invalid, the wizard will force you to enter a valid name. Once you have defined a valid user, the dialog box shown in Figure 11-10 will let you set permissions for the user on the directory. Once the user is given permissions, that user can start accessing the database.

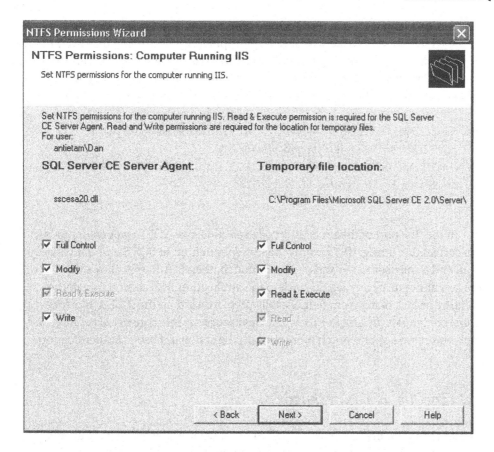

Figure 11-10. Setting the user's permissions

Authentication Choices

Remember the two authentication choices? You can use anonymous access or Integrated Windows authentication to protect the virtual directory that was created by the wizard in the preceding sequence.

 NOTE *Yes, I know there are really three methods. I have skirted around mentioning Basic authentication. I do this for one main reason: Every time it is mentioned in the docs, Microsoft makes a disclaimer similar to this, "Passwords are sent in plain text. This is bad, so don't do it. And if you do, use SSL." Good enough for me, there's enough work to do to implement Integrated Windows authentication.*

Our first look will be at using anonymous access through IIS. You can approach anonymous access two ways: by supplying a user name password for SQL Server validation or by letting IIS route credentials on to SQL Server using the *machinename*\IUSER_*machinename* account. I haven't really covered the code for this yet, so I'll use a very simple example to show you the difference:

```
Dim connString1 As String = "server=192.168.1.101;database=Nwind_SQLCE;"
    connString &= "user id=user;pwd=password;"
Dim connString2 As String = "server=192.168.1.101;database=Nwind_SQLCE;"
    connString &= "Integrated Security=True"
```

In the first part of the preceding code sample I pass SQL Server credentials in the connection string. IIS forwards those credentials on to SQL Server for validation, and if the user name and password match, then SQL Server allows the request and returns any results back to the application. The second part of the code, by its lack of login credentials, tells IIS to forward on the IUSER_*machinename* credentials. In Chapter 13, when we discuss the intimate details of RDA and replication, we'll spend much more time on the setup and use of authentication.

Setting Up a Distributor

As covered in the preceding wizard discussion, when you want to have an application use SQL Server merge replication, you have to specify a snapshot folder (refer back to Figure 11-5). I mentioned that you don't create the folder yourself, but that it is created for you when you create a distributor in SQL Server. If you aren't a SQL Server geek, then you might not know how to set up a subscription (I know I didn't until I started using replication with SQL CE). This section will step you through the process of creating a distributor. You start the wizard by opening the SQL Server Enterprise Manager and navigating the tree to show the database in which you want to create the distributor. Expand the node for the database, right-click the **Replication** node, and choose the menu item **Configure Publishing, Subscribers, and Distribution** as shown in Figure 11-11.

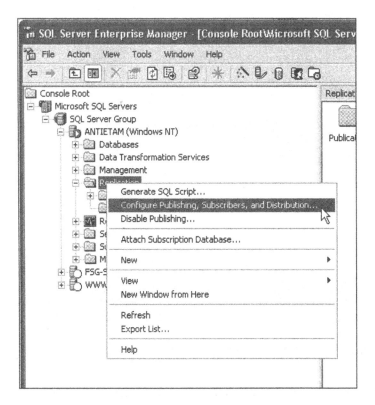

Figure 11-11. Configuring a distributor

The first step of the wizard is the standard welcome screen that gives you a short description of what you are about to get yourself into. So let's take a look at the steps required to do what you need to do.

Once you step further into the process, in most cases you'll accept the default values provided by the wizard. As shown in Figure 11-12, you have to choose which server should act as the distributor. A *distributor* is the server that controls the data flow between your publishers and subscribers. It isn't required to be the same server that hosts the SQL Server containing the database you are publishing. For most standard situations, the distributor is the same as the SQL Server being published, and you therefore use the default value in the wizard.

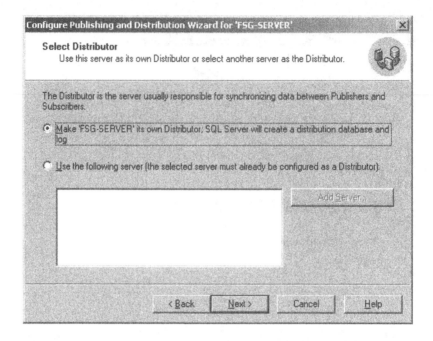

Figure 11-12. Choosing which server to act as the distributor

In order for the data to be synchronized, the SQL Server Agent must be running. The step shown in Figure 11-13 provides an opportunity for you to have the system automatically start up the SQL Server Agent.

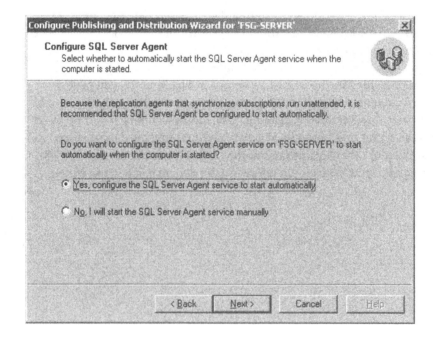

Figure 11-13. Configuring the SQL Server Agent service

Since your replication will fail if this service isn't running, using the default choice of starting when the computer starts is a very smart idea! When using replication, SQL Server requires access to a directory that it calls the *snapshot directory*. This directory stores information about the state of the data that has been published through replication. The snapshot folder needs to be shared and accessible to the database.

Figure 11-14 shows the dialog box for configuring a snapshot folder. In this figure the user is logged in as administrator. That might not be the best idea, as the wizard choices provide a default value that includes the administrator's share (notice the C$ in the path). If you click the **Next** button, you receive an error telling you that this path uses a special share name that might not be available to users who aren't administrators on the computer.

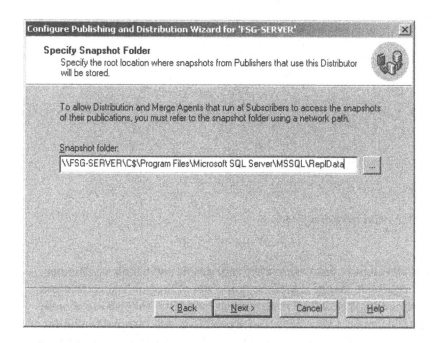

Figure 11-14. Setting the snapshot folder

This error is telling you that if you use the administrator's share you might (actually, you definitely will) have problems later. The reason is that if you authenticate using anonymous access, you'll be logged in as IUSER_*machine-name*, which won't have admin rights to the snapshot directory. You have a better chance of this working if you use Integrated Windows authentication because the login you use might have admin rights. Either way, using an admin-only path for the snapshot folder is risky at best. In Figure 11-15, I have entered a better path, a folder that is defined by a full network path and has been shared. Without the share on the folder, the wizard will fail when trying to locate the folder. The good thing is that the wizard will keep prompting you until you either give up or provide a valid shared folder.

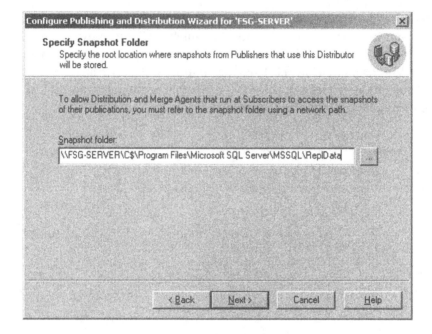

Figure 11-15. A valid snapshot folder

The last two steps of this wizard are pretty simple—you indicate whether you want to review or change any of the properties of the publication that you have just defined and give a final confirmation before the changes are actually made to the SQL Server. I have never had a need to change any parameters at this point in the process. Just in case you're a SQL Server guru, let me qualify that last statement. In the world of publications involving the Pocket PC, SQL Server 2000, and SQL CE, I have never had to use any options beyond what I enter in the normal wizard steps.

Creating a Publication

I promise, cross-my-heart, that this is the last wizard! So far you've created a distributor, but as of yet there are no publications. Think of this process as building a house; you have the foundation, but there is no structure on top of it yet to live in. The distributor is set up, but you still need to create the publication(s) to allow your subscribers to replicate data between the device and the SQL Server. Now, for one more wizard, one more time, one more step 1, here we go!

Let me remind you that this isn't a detailed explanation of publications. The intent here is to give you enough information to drive your database administrator crazy. No, really, it's to give you the basic knowledge and some heads-up notification of what you need to do at a bare minimum to get publications working. For a detailed explanation, you'll want to go to the SQL Server help and look for "Replication Wizard Help" under "Using the SQL Server Tools" in the **Contents** tab.

The first step is typical, introducing you to the process and giving a short explanation of what you are about to do. Figure 11-16 lists all of the databases on the host SQL Server. From this list, you can select a single database for which to create a publication.

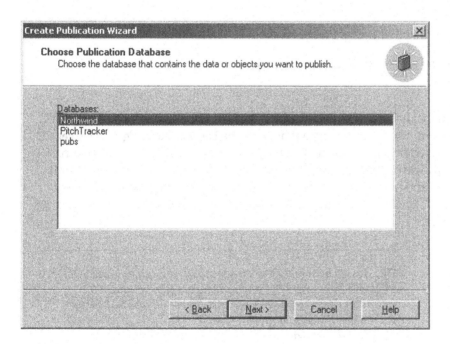

Figure 11-16. Choosing the database to expose to publication

Once you make your selection, you move on to the next step shown in Figure 11-17, where you need to make a choice of which subscription type you want to use. Actually, the choice here is quite easy; for replication of SQL CE database, you *must* choose the **Merge publication** option.

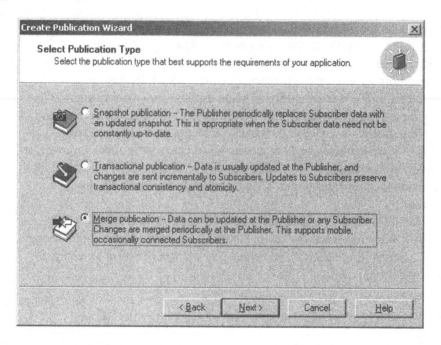

Figure 11-17. Choosing a subscription type

Your next choice is to decide which types of clients will have access to this publication. The obvious choice (I hope) is the **Devices running SQL Server CE** option. In addition, as shown in Figure 11-18, you can also select **Servers running SQL Server 2000** or any of the other choices. Notice that if your server is SQL 2000 and you allow SQL Server 7.0 subscribers, you'll have some limited options. That won't affect your SQL Server CE publications, but it is worth being aware of.

NOTE *Just to be sure that you understand, you can only use SQL replication from SQL CE if your database is SQL Server 2000. Replication doesn't work between SQL Server CE and SQL Server 7.0. I'll make this point again in Chapter 13, when I cover details about Remote Data Access (RDA) and merge replication.*

The publication process needs to know what objects in the database should be exposed. SQL Server calls these *articles*. In the next step, shown in Figure 11-19, you can make a selection for which tables, stored procedures, or views you want to provide to the subscriber.

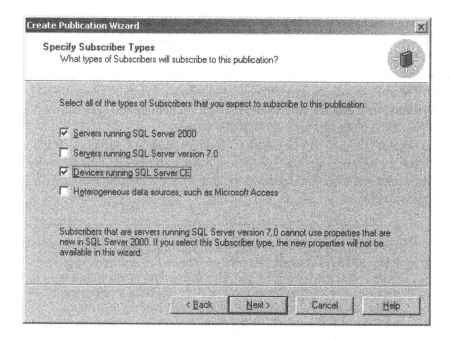

Figure 11-18. Select the correct subscriber type

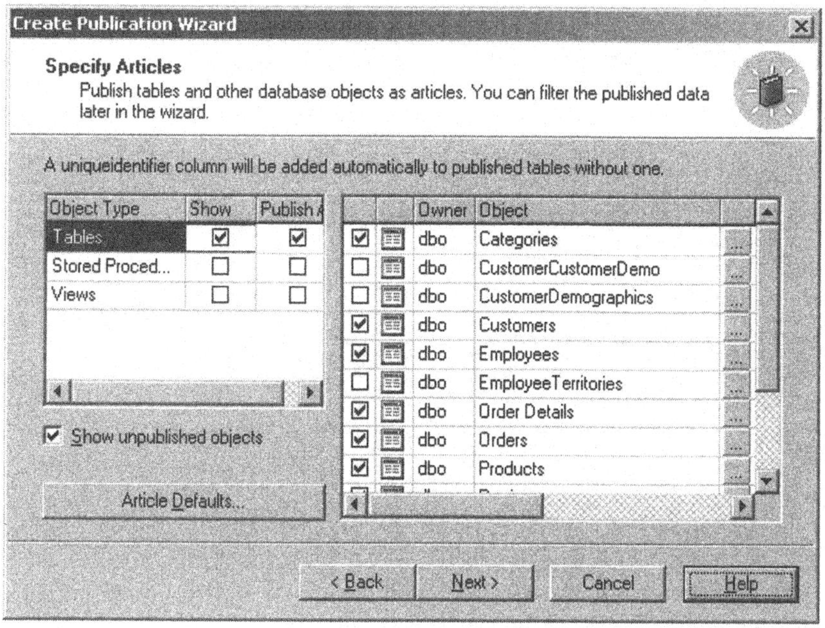

Figure 11-19. Choosing the articles, tables, and stored procedures that you want to publish

Only the articles that you explicitly choose are able to be synchronized through this publication. In this example, I have selected the basic data tables to be shared through this publication. You might only want to publish a very small subset of the tables or views in your database. Through this dialog box, you have full control of what resources are published. Since this isn't a full-blown tutorial on publications, we'll skip the **Article Details** button. Remember, I am simply trying to give you a basic first pass through the wizard.

If you request tables to be published, your tables must have unique IDs in order to track the data and any changes made by the publisher or subscriber. By default the wizard will alter your tables to include a uniqueidentifier column in each published table.

 TIP *If you already have a column on your table that is set up correctly, SQL doesn't add a new column. The correct definition of the entry is that it must be a unique identifier, it can't allow nulls, the default value must be (newid()), and its **Is RowGuid** property must be Yes. The column name doesn't make a difference. If SQL creates a row for you, it is put at the end of the table and is named rowguid.*

The dialog box shown in Figure 11-20 explains your options and what will occur for each option.

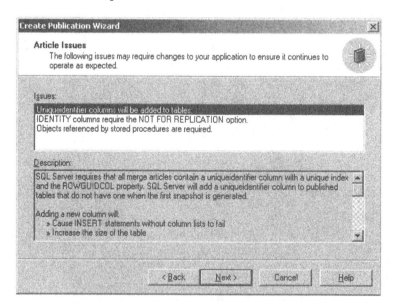

Figure 11-20. Issues with the selected articles

The description text box in the lower portion of the dialog box explains the actions that your selection will cause. If you scroll down through the entire description, you'll see a detailed list of tables that will be altered by this choice.

NOTE *Perhaps you remember from a database class in school, or a session at a conference, or a book that you read that somebody told you to always build your select clauses with explicit filenames. If nobody has, I'll tell you now. Always use explicit field names when building a SELECT statement. The reason some very intelligent person told you this was probably related to performance of the SQL query. Performance studies have shown that qualifying column names in a SELECT statement will greatly increase the performance of the query versus using the *. Okay, now let's say that you didn't follow my suggestion (well, yeah, if this is the first time you heard about it and all of your old code doesn't do it, I'll give you a break—this time), and you did a **SELECT * FROM myTable**. And to make it worse, when you get data out of the data reader you use **indexes (dataReader.Fields(0))**. Now you publish the table, and SQL inserts a new uniqueidentifier column. Although SQL adds the new field at the end of the table, there is still a potential problem: You still face the possibility at a later time of having the rowguid field causing order problems in your SQL statements.*

Now, as shown in Figure 11-21, you have to name your publication. The default name is simply the database name. It is possible to create multiple publications on the same table, so it would be a good idea to create a unique name. Perhaps you can append a string that identifies the intended use of the publication (e.g., Northwind_Sales).

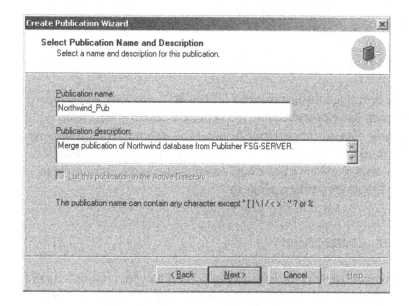

Figure 11-21. Making the publication name have some relationship to its use

As I keep saying, I normally pick the default values presented to me by the wizard and I continue this through the last two steps. The next step gives you the opportunity to really fine-tune your publication by defining filters or performing other customizations. But unless you are very good at the details of publications, let the wizard create the publication without other changes. The final step of the wizard is again the "Are you sure?" question asking you for confirmation before the database changes are made.

NOTE *After the publication is defined, there are still pending changes to the database. Any new uniqueidentifier columns don't get created until the first snapshot of the data is made.*

At this point, if all went well, you have SQL Server configured to support replication from SQL CE. You also should have security set up to allow your users to log in through IIS using either anonymous access, Integrated Windows authentication, or Basic authentication. You'll check in the next section if everything went as expected. On a final note, before we move on, there are two different types of SQL that you just installed: SQL Client for Windows CE and SQL Server CE. The SQL Client for Windows CE is where you have a connection to the database and you talk to it directly using the **System.Data** namespace. I'll cover this extensively in Chapter 12. SQL Server CE is where you talk to a local database on the device. This file on the device has the .sdf extension you'll soon see. Chapter 13 is dedicated to using data on the device and synchronizing it back to SQL Server using merge replication.

Getting Started

Great, you made it through the last sections (or you are a true geek and skipped them) and are ready to write some code. You get Visual Studio open, create a project, add some code to connect to SQL, press F5—and not a thing happens! You're probably thinking, "What happened, I followed all of your $#^@& directions!" Well, as always, there are a few things to watch for, and a trick or two to try to make sure things are working properly.

Testing Your Connection

When you have written some code, how do you know if it's your code or if it's the SQL CE setup that's causing the problem? You need a way to test this, and you can by using Internet Explorer on your device or emulator. To test the SQL installation, you type into the address bar the path to the virtual directory that you created way back at the beginning of this chapter. I show you in Figure 11-22 what my emulator screen looks like when I have a valid connection and everything is set up correctly.

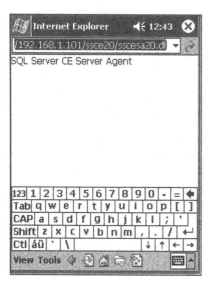

Figure 11-22. If the SQL CE setup is correct, you'll be notified by the Server Agent

If your database is set up correctly, you'll get the same screen. If your connection is bad, or the SQL CE was done incorrectly, you'll get an error. Basically what this means is that if you can't connect through IE, you might as well not even try to get any code to run because it won't. If you do get the error, you'll need to go back and review your virtual directory settings and permissions. In the worst case, you'll need to uninstall and reinstall SQL CE.

Look again at Figure 11-22. I entered the address in the address bar using the IP address of my server. The reason I did this is because the emulator won't resolve domain names. My local server is called Antietam, but from the emulator I must use the IP address of Antietam for the connection to work.

NOTE *You might be asking, "Why didn't you use localhost, you ding dong?" Initially I did use localhost, but it never worked. At first glance it makes perfect sense to use localhost, After all, I am on my development machine, running the emulator, and I want to talk to my local SQL Server. Of course, I would use localhost. NOT! While the emulator is running on the local machine, it is in fact a separate OS that is being hosted by my local machine. While running in the emulator, localhost refers to the emulator, not my development computer.*

When I do this test from my device, I use the following URL: `http://antietam/ssce20/sscesa20.dll`. The same difficulty arises when you are defining your connection string in code. You need to use an IP address when running from a device. If your address is pretty consistent, this isn't really a problem; but if your IP address changes, then any code that worked with the emulator before will fail due to the change.

TIP *I travel a lot and have a different IP every time I change locations. My loop-back adapter connection is yet another IP address. You may experience this same problem for other reasons other than traveling. When I have to handle constantly changing IP addresses, I store the IP address in an external file and load it when I need to build a connection string. I also keep a section of my code commented out that uses the server name. I can easily uncomment it and have my code working properly on the device.*

Hiding Your Data

Many managers are concerned about putting sensitive data on a Pocket PC or other PDA because of the risk of losing the device and along with it all of the data. SQL CE provides two ways of securing your data. You can secure your database with a password that is specified in the connection string of your SqlCeConnection object. When you create the database, you specify the password to be used to protect the database. If someone should gain possession of the database through loss of the device, or some other sneaky means, that person could not open the file programmatically unless he or she had the password. The big "but" here is that he or she could open the database file with a text editor and have access to the text portions of the database. A really determined thief could reap a good deal of information from a text view of the database. Fear not, for there is another option.

You can also encrypt the database so that it isn't viewable with a text viewer. To do this, you add an extra parameter on the line that creates the database. When you specify that you want the database encrypted, you also supply a password to use to access the database in code. The password follows the same rules as in the password-protected option discussed previously. The password may be up to 40 characters long and may contain any combination of numbers, characters, or symbols.

TIP *Don't lose or forget your password. There is no way to retrieve it, and without the password your data will never be heard from again. It will be swimming with the fishes, gone, kaput. Got the idea?*

In Chapter 13, I'll talk in detail about how to create a database programmatically, including how to make the database encrypted or password protected.

Query Analyzer

I won't spend a lot of time on this tool here because the SQL Server CE Books Online does a very good job of explaining the tool and its various options. You can find the explanation in the topic "Using SQL Server CE Query Analyzer" under "Working with SQL Server CE Databases." I do, however, want to bring one thing to your attention that has bitten me in the backside more than once (many times more than once!).

Figure 11-23 shows the Query Analyzer running with a connection to the pscout database. From this point you can run queries, look at data in the tables, and perform just about any database operation that you want. When you are finished, you click the close button in the upper-right corner of the window, and Query Analyzer goes away. But wait! Just because it is gone doesn't mean it has stopped running. In fact, if you remember the default operation of Windows CE, applications aren't terminated, they are just hidden. "Okay, what's the problem?" you ask. The problem is that the Query Analyzer still has a connection to your database, an *exclusive* connection. Do you see the problem yet? If you try to run your application, you'll fail miserably because the database is locked and your commands will throw an exception.

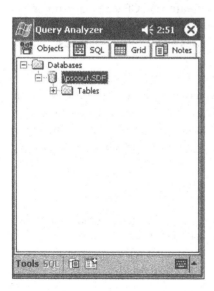

Figure 11-23. The Query Analyzer keeps a connection to your database

NOTE *SQL CE is a* single user *database. That means that only a single user can be connected to the data store at any one time. You can also make your full SQL Server 2000 run in the same single-user mode (I'm sure that there must be a reason why you would want to do this).* Single user *actually may more realistically mean* single application. *It is possible to open two connections to the same data store on different threads in the same application.*

Then you'll open up the Query Analyzer, look at the database, and say to yourself, "Wow, I wonder why that didn't work. My database and tables all look fine." And guess what, you'll click that little close button, try your code again, and it will *fail* again! How many times you do this process depends on how quickly you catch on!

You have two options to fix this. Before you close the analyzer, make sure that you disconnect the database by clicking the toolbar button with the red square in it. Your other choice is to go to the Running Applications dialog box and terminate the process.

Licensing SQL Server CE

The short story about licensing SQL CE is this: SQL CE has no device licensing requirements. What this means is that you can create SQL CE databases on as many devices as you deem appropriate without any special license fees. However, as soon as any portion of your application accesses a SQL Server database, you'll be responsible for a license.

SQL Server 2000 has two modes of licensing: Processor license or client access license (CAL). You can get a license based on the number of processors on the computer running SQL Server. Your other option is a client access license, where each device you have connecting to the server requires a license. By this definition, either RDA or merge replication requires a license because they both "touch" a SQL Server database.

NOTE *You can go to Microsoft's Web site for the details of licensing at* http://www.microsoft.com/sql/howtobuy/production.asp.

Basically, the licensing model for SQL Server CE is analogous to that of MSDE.

Summary

Wow, what a chapter! Since we started some time ago, you've learned how to install SQL CE and create a distributor and publications in SQL Server, and we've looked at several generic topics to SQL Server CE and how to make sure it really works.

In the next two chapters, we'll move back into coding. In Chapter 12, I'll discuss how to write applications for the SQL Client for Windows CE. Then the fun starts in Chapter 13, when we look at what it takes to write SQL CE code to maintain a SQL database on a device. We didn't spend all of the time in this chapter doing setups and installations for nothing, because you'll also see how to use Remote Data Access and merge replication to synchronize your data between your device and SQL Server.

Working with Server-Based Data

IF YOU STAYED WITH ME AND WORKED through the last chapter, you should be ready to get started using SQL CE. Wait, let me correct myself, you should be ready to get started using SQL Server Client for Windows CE. Now, *that's* better. If you thought you would be smart and skip the last chapter, go back, read the chapter, and make sure your SQL is set up and ready. Go ahead, I'll wait.

Okay, now that you're ready, we can start exploring the wonderful world of SQL Server access from a connected device. The code and discussions of this chapter require that you have a live and reliable connection to a SQL database to access the data store. We won't be exploring disconnected data here—that's the focus of the next chapter. A Pocket PC device is mobile and as such won't normally be connected through a hard network connection. The device may, however, be connected through a wireless link to the network. In concept, you could be drinking your latte at Starbucks (http://www.starbucks.com) downtown or at the ballgame, have access to a wireless connection, and be able to send data back and forth to your SQL Server. Ah, working from your box behind home plate, connected to your server data, who would have thought?

The samples in this chapter use the (surprise!) Nwind_SQLCE database. This database was installed on your server during the server-side tools installation that you did in Chapter 11.

My Data, Get My Data

In any situation where you plan on using SQL Server, whether it's from a desktop or from a device, you need to make the connection before you do anything else. In the desktop world, you would drag a table from the Server Explorer and drop it on your form. Unfortunately, the .NET Compact Framework doesn't support the Data Designer functionality. That means that you'll get *real good* at copying and pasting code and connection strings from one project to another. Oh, and while I'm on the subject, remember that the .NET Compact Framework version of the **System.Data.SqlClient** namespace also has no support for transactions that cross servers or for connection pooling. You're limited to transactions that occur only on one server within one database.

TIP *Hopefully, you know about the advantages of connection pooling that .NET provides on the desktop. If you don't, you're about to find out because since NETCF doesn't support pooling, you'll see a significant delay when a connection is made. In programming for the desktop, you'll hear from many sources—and I'm sure that I've said it myself more than once—that you should only keep a connection open for as short of a period as possible and reopen it when you need it. Good advice for a desktop application, but not for a connected device using SQL Server. The best strategy is to create a connection early in the life of the class and keep it open during the entire life of the object. This keeps you from suffering a delay each time a connection is required as you work with your server data. Just be sure to close it when you are finished.*

Instead of looking at this from the perspective of the **SqlClient** namespace, I'm going to discuss how to write an application and cover the various objects as you encounter them. The classes you use in writing connected SQLCE applications require two additional references (that is, above what the VS IDE Wizard puts into a project). You'll need to add references to **System.Data.Common** and to **System.Data.SqlClient**.

NOTE *In Chapter 11, I mentioned another reference, **System.Data.SqlServerCE**. Why am I not discussing it here? Well, that namespace and its classes are used for support of SQL Server on the device in a disconnected state. Those classes support the access of data and support for queries and such of the SQLCE database. I'll get to that in the next chapter.*

To create a connection, you need to create a new instance of SqlConnection and initialize the connection string either through the constructor or using its properties.

```
Dim connString As String
connString = "server=books;database=Nwind_SQLCE;user id=user;pwd=password;"
Dim conNwindCE As SqlConnection = _
    New SqlConnection(connString)
```

NOTE *Hard coding strings usually isn't a very good practice. In this situation, though, it makes the code more readable, and since the connection and other strings are critical to understanding this chapter, I have left them in. The .NET Compact Framework doesn't support using the **Configuration** namespace and so you must handle the strings on your own. This can be done through an external text or XML file. As the alternative to **Configuration** classes, I'll show you in Chapter 20 how to read values from a flat text file. Chapter 14 discusses how you can read values from an XML file.*

If you prefer to use properties, then you'll want to use the **ConnectionString** property of the **SqlConnection** class.

```
Dim conNwindCE As SqlConnection = New SqlConnection
conNwindCE.ConnectionString = "server=books;database=Nwind_SQLCE; " _
    & "user id=user;pwd=password;")
```

One of the benefits of using the property is that I can create one SqlConnection object, open it, close it, and then change the connection string before reopening the connection. This reduces the work on the system to delete the old object and create a new one. There are two basic reasons to use a connection: to fill a DataSet or to make queries on the database.

Querying the Database with the SqlCommand Object

If you want to execute some command on the SQL Server database, this is the class for you. Obviously, the first action you need to do is to create a new instance of the command object. There are four constructors for this class. Each constructor supplies more information than would otherwise be required to be set through a property of the class. A command requires at least a connection object and a command string, and these can easily be passed through the constructor.

```
Dim conNwindCE As SqlConnection = New SqlConnection( _
    "server=192.168.1.101;database=Nwind_SQLCE;user id=user;pwd=password;")
Dim cmdData As SqlCommand = New SqlCommand("SELECT * FROM Customers", _
    conNwindCE)
conNwindCE.Open()
```

When using a SqlConnection object with a command object, be sure that you open the connection before executing the command. The SqlCommand object supports these four methods:

- **ExecuteNonQuery**—Allows you to execute a query that returns no data

- **ExecuteDataReader**—Returns an object from which you can read data

- **ExecuteScalar**—Returns a single value from a query

- **ExecuteXmlReader**—Returns an object from which you can read the data in XML format

The code in Listing 12-1 shows a sequence of calls using the SqlCommand object.

Listing 12-1. Exploring the SqlCommand Object

```
Dim iRet As Integer
Dim conNwindCE As SqlConnection
Dim bRet As Boolean

Try
    Dim connString As String

    '   Create and open a connection.
    connString = "server=antietam;database=Nwind_SQLCE;"
    connString &= "user id=user;pwd=pword;"
    conNwindCE.Open()

    '   Create a command object.
    connString = "SELECT COUNT(*) FROM Customers"
    Dim cmdData As SqlCommand = New SqlCommand(connString, conNwindCE)
    iRet = cmdData.ExecuteScalar()

    '   Reuse the command object for a ExecuteNonQuery call.
    cmdData.CommandText = "DELETE FROM Customers WHERE CustomerID='HILAA'"
    cmdData.ExecuteNonQuery()

    cmdData.CommandText = "SELECT * FROM Customers AS AUTO XML"
    Dim xml As Xml.XmlReader = cmdData.ExecuteXmlReader()

    '   Reuse the command with a DataReader.
    cmdData.CommandText = "SELECT * FROM Customers "
    Dim dr As SqlDataReader = cmdData.ExecuteReader()
    '   Pull data from the reader and do some work.
    dr.Read()
    dr.Close()
Catch ex As Exception
```

```
Finally
    conNwindCE.Close()
End Try
```

NOTE *Alright, you caught me! I made a big deal in Chapter 11 about never using SELECT *, and what do I do in the first code sample? I use SELECT *. I hate to say it, but this is sample code. By this I mean that I have to format it to fit cleanly within the confines of a book page. Due to this restriction, and to keep the listings from becoming too hard to read (and thus hard to comprehend), I use the dreaded * syntax. In my own code I really do qualify the column names. Honestly.*

In the first piece of this code you use the **ExecuteScalar** method to return the count of records in the Customers table using the COUNT(*) TSQL statement. This method returns a single value, even if your SELECT statement returns multiple rows and columns. In this case only the first column of the first row will be returned. Anytime you need a single value back, this is the method to use.

The code in Listing 12-1 also shows the use of **ExecuteNonQuery**. This method is used when you expect no information back about the query or you need a count of rows that were affected by the query. The best examples are UPDATE, DELETE, and INSERT statements.

If you are an XML programmer, then you might like to try the **ExecuteXmlReader** method of the SqlCommand object. I'll spend more time in Chapter 14 discussing XML in NETCF, so for now know that just about everything available on the desktop in XML is also available in NETCF.

NOTE *Notice that I did say "'just about" in the previous sentence <g>. The biggest piece, in my mind, that you'll find missing from the **XML** namespace is XPath. The NETCF team decided that XPath was just a little too heavy to port down to the device. There are ways to work around some of the functionality, and I'll discuss those in Chapter 14.*

Passing Parameters Through a SQL Statement

The **ExecuteNonQuery** portion of Listing 12-1 shows the CustomerID hard coded into the SQL command statement. Obviously, this isn't something to do often in production code, so let me show you a way to code the statement using a variable parameter:

```
cmdData.CommandText = "DELETE FROM Customers WHERE CustomerID=@CustomerID"
Dim parameter As SqlParameter = _
    cmdData.Parameters.Add("@CustomerID", SqlDbType.VarChar, 5)
parameter.Value = strCustomerID
cmdData.ExecuteNonQuery()
```

I've rewritten the code a little in the preceding snippet to use a named parameter in the DELETE statement. Then I add a parameter to the SqlParameterCollection of the command object. Once the **Value** property of the parameter is set, you can execute the **ExecuteNonQuery** method. This style of coding works for all of the various execute methods of the SqlCommand object. The benefit of this technique is that you do not have to build dynamic strings at runtime in order to assemble the correct SQL command string. Another is that the command can be cached and reused by changing the **Value** property, and subsequent calls to the execute method will result in faster execution of the SQL command.

ExecuteDataReader

While this isn't an ADO.NET chapter or book, I think that it is appropriate that we take some time to look at this method in detail before running on to the more famous DataSet and DataAdapter.

NOTE *I'll cover the DataSet and SqlDataAdapter later in this chapter. The coverage here will be limited to how it relates to SQL Server data. For a more extensive discussion on how to implement and use DataSet and SqlDataAdapter, refer back to Chapter 9.*

In the sample shown in Listing 12-1 there is a very simple example of using a SqlDataReader. Now, I don't know about you, but I really *hate* it when I read help information or samples that provide such simple examples that my 2-year old could understand them, but nothing more detailed that would help a real developer make use of the method. In pursuit of a more reasonable, real-world example, we'll step through snippets of code, detailing interesting pieces of the DataReader and conclude the section with a full code listing.

Opening and getting data into a SqlDataReader is easy, if you have the connection string and command object built properly.

```
cmdString = "SELECT COUNT(*), CompanyName, ContactName, rowguid FROM Customers"
cmdData.CommandText = cmdString
Dim dr As SqlDataReader = cmdData.ExecuteReader()
```

Once you've retrieved the data, you can read it, one record at a time, by calling the **Read** method of the class.

```
Dim strValue As String
Dim guidValue As Guid

While dr.Read()
    strValue = dr.Item(0)
    strValue = dr.Item("CompanyName")
    guidValue = dr.Item("rowguid")
    strValue = dr.Item("ContactName")
End While
dr.Close()
```

TIP   *When you create a command string, it is possible to apply your own column names to any table column or aggregate column. In the preceding code, you can only access COUNT(*) as an index since there is no "name" assigned to it. An alternative would be to change the command string to specify a name for the value. The new string would look like "**SELECT COUNT(*) AS Counter, CompanyName, ContactName, rowguid FROM Customers**". With this change, you would then access the value using the code snippet* **strValue = dr.Item("Counter")** *instead of* **dr.Item(0)**.

TIP   *Keep in mind as you work with data returned from a database that some fields may be null. In VB .NET terms, you may have a value returned as Nothing. You'll need to check for Nothing before assigning it to a variable. The check for Nothing would look something like this:* **If dr.Item(4) Is Nothing Then** ...

A DataReader is a *forward only* data-reading object. That is, once you retrieve the data from record 2 and move onto record 3, you *cannot* back up and access that record again without closing the DataReader and calling the **ExecuteReader** method again. This doesn't mean that you must collect data in the row in sequence. In the preceding example, the ContactName field is the third field in the Items collection, but you retrieve it as the last step before reading the next record.

NOTE   *You can force the DataReader into a mode where you must read the row data in a sequential order. See the discussion of the enum value SequentialAccess in the "Overload of DataReader" section a little later.*

NOTE *It is critical that you close the DataReader when you are finished getting the data you need by calling its **Close** method. While the SqlDataReader is open, the connection associated with it is busy and can't be used for any other operation. Not closing the reader will cause your application to consume both memory and connections. Neither is a good thing.*

This might be a good time to mention one of the benefits of using Visual Basic .NET instead of C#. In the preceding code, you use the **Item** property of the DataReader instance to pull the data into a local variable. You aren't required in Visual Basic .NET to perform a cast to the proper variable type. The C# equivalent code looks like the following:

```
while( dr.Read() )
{
    strValue = (string)dr.Item(0);
    strValue = (string)dr.Item("CompanyName");
    guidValue = (Guid)dr.Item("rowguid");
    strValue = (string)dr.Item("ContactName ");
}
```

NOTE *I don't say this to bad-mouth C#. In fact I use C# and Visual Basic .NET pretty much evenly from project to project, so I don't think either one is "better" than the other in every situation. In fact, if I wanted to prove a point, I can think of several situations where I would get more benefits from using C# as opposed to VB .NET. My intent here is to help clarify in your mind the difference so that if you see an example somewhere that uses the C# style of coding you'll understand it.*

The preceding code also shows that you can use either an index to the field or the name of the field. If you don't qualify the column names in the SELECT clause, then you really should use the preceding syntax that defines the item based on the field name, not the index. As you read the documentation, you'll see another set of methods on the DataReader object that are used to get data from the reader into your variables. These are the methods that are of the "Get . . ." syntax. For example, this list includes **GetInt16**, **GetString**, and many others. If you are a Visual Basic .NET developer, two instances may come to mind where these methods are useful. One is when you've saved chunks or blobs of data into the database in a byte array and you need to read it back from the field. The other is if you have a value from the database that isn't a standard .NET variable type. This code is a perfect example:

```
Dim curValue As Data.SqlTypes.SqlMoney
Dim dr As SqlDataReader = cmdData.ExecuteReader()
'   All of the work to open the reader goes here.
'   Pull data from the reader and do some work.
While dr.Read()
    strValue = dr.Item(0)
    curValue = dr.Item(1)
End While
```

When you execute the **dr.Item(1)** line, an **InvalidCastException** is thrown. To correct the line and make it work properly, you use the following syntax:

```
While dr.Read()
    strValue = dr.Item(0)
    curValue = dr.GetSqlMoney(1)
End While
```

Now that you are familiar with the DataReader, let's combine the previous code snippets and look at a larger example in Listing 12-2.

Listing 12-2. A Thorough SqlDataReader Example

```
Dim conNwindCE As SqlConnection
Dim cmdData As SqlCommand

Try
    Dim connString As String

    '   Create and open a connection.
    connString = "server=antietam;database=Nwind_SQLCE;"
    connString &= "user id=user;pwd=pword;"
    conNwindCE.Open()

    '   Reuse the command with a DataReader.
    cmdData.CommandText = "SELECT * FROM Customers "
    Dim dr As SqlDataReader = cmdData.ExecuteReader()
    '   Pull data from the reader and do some work.
    dr.Read()
    dr.Close()

Catch ex As Exception
Finally
    conNwindCE.Close()
End Try
```

Overload of ExecuteReader

There is one overload of the **ExecuteReader** method that provides you with several choices that affect performance, the type of data returned, and the lifetime of the object. The overload takes different parameters, which are described in Table 12-1.

Table 12-1. CommandBehavior Enum

PARAMETER	DESCRIPTION
CloseConnection	The connection used to create the reader is kept open until the DataReader is closed.
Default	This is functionally equivalent to the syntax we have used before, passing no parameter.
KeyInfo	Only the column and primary key information is returned. In SQL Client, the FOR BROWSE clause is appended to the TSQL statement.
SchemaOnly	Returns only the column information.
SequentialAccess	When this parameter is used, the entire row isn't returned at one time. This is done to save memory when your data row contains large amounts of binary data. In this situation, you must retrieve the data from the row in the order that it is defined in the SELECT statement.
SingleResult	Only a single result set is returned.
SingleRow	Only a single row is returned. If multiple result sets are returned, a single row of each set is returned.

Now we all know that in the real world of data access, you have to return data back to a user. Note how you close the connection when you're finished with it in order to not tie up the database. See if you can figure out why the code shown in Listing 12-3 would not do what you want or expect.

Listing 12-3. No Data Is Returned

```
Public Function GetMyData() As SqlDataReader
    Dim conNwindCE As SqlConnection
    Dim cmdData As SqlCommand
    Dim connString As String
```

```
Try
    '   Create and open a connection.
    connString = "server=169.254.223.37;database=Nwind_SQLCE;"
    connString &= "user id=user;pwd=pword;"
    conNwindCE = New SqlConnection(connString)
    conNwindCE.Open()

    '   Create a new command object.
    cmdData = New SqlCommand
    cmdData.CommandText = "SELECT * FROM Customers"
    cmdData.Connection = conNwindCE

    Return cmdData.ExecuteReader()
Catch ex As Exception
    MessageBox.Show(ex.Message)
Finally
    conNwindCE.Close()
End Try
End Function
```

A SqlDataReader keeps a connection open and reads data from the database on *each* invocation of the **Read** method. When the SqlDataReader is returned from this function, the underlying connection is closed, causing your DataReader to also be closed. You'll get an exception when you try to use the returned value. To get this code to work, you need to make two small changes. The first is to change the **ExecuteReader** call to include the **CloseConnection** parameter and the other is to remove the **conNwindCE.Close** method call. Instead of removing the **Close** call, you might want to move it into the Catch block of the exception handler. This is a suggestion that depends heavily on your error handling scheme. Now when the calling routine closes the returned SqlDataReader, the connection is also closed. You can see the complete, updated code in Listing 12-4.

Listing 12-4. Getting Data Back in the SqlDataReader

```
Public Function GetMyData() As SqlDataReader
    Dim conNwindCE As SqlConnection
    Dim cmdData As SqlCommand
    Dim connString As String
```

```
        Try
            '    Create and open a connection.
            connString = "server=169.254.223.37;database=Nwind_SQLCE;"
            connString &= "user id=user;pwd=pword;"
            conNwindCE = New SqlConnection(connString)
            conNwindCE.Open()

            '    Create a new command object.
            cmdData = New SqlCommand
            cmdData.CommandText = "SELECT * FROM Customers"
            cmdData.Connection = conNwindCE

            Return cmdData.ExecuteReader(CommandBehavior.CloseConnection)
        Catch ex As Exception
            MessageBox.Show(ex.Message)
        Finally
        End Try
    End Function
```

In an earlier code snippet of the previous section, I mentioned that it doesn't make a difference if you read from the fields of a row in sequential order. You may have thought I was daft when I said that, and under one circumstance that statement isn't true. If you specify SequentialAccess in the call to **ExecuteReader**, then the following code will raise an **InvalidOperationException**:

```
cmdData.Connection = conNwindCE
Dim dr As SqlDataReader = cmdData.ExecuteReader(CommandBehavior.SequentialAccess)
'    Pull data from the reader and do some work.
While dr.Read()
    curValue = dr.GetSqlMoney(1)
    strValue = dr.Item(0)
End While
dr.Close()
```

You must read the values in order, and you can't go back to read a value a second time. The SequentialAccess enum is used to read large byte arrays out of the database without having to hold the entire field in memory at a single time. One other enum value that begs for a description is the SingleResult value.

You may not be aware of the fact that the **CommandText** of the SqlCommand object can include more than one T-SQL statement. Listing 12-5 shows an example of how you can return a series of result sets using a SqlDataReader.

Listing 12-5. Retrieving Multiple Result Sets

```
Public Sub GetResultSets()
    Dim conNwindCE As SqlConnection
    Dim cmdData As SqlCommand
    Dim connString As String
    Dim dr As SqlDataReader

    Try
        '   Create and open a connection.
        connString = "server=169.254.223.37;database=Nwind_SQLCE;"
        connString &= "user id=user;pwd=pword;"
        conNwindCE = New SqlConnection(connString)
        conNwindCE.Open()

        '   Create a new command object.
        cmdData = New SqlCommand
        cmdData.CommandText = _
            "SELECT * FROM Customers;SELECT * FROM CustOrderHist"
        cmdData.Connection = conNwindCE

        dr = cmdData.ExecuteReader()
        While dr.Read

        End While

        If dr.NextResult() Then
            While dr.Read

            End While
        End If
    Catch ex As Exception
        MessageBox.Show(ex.Message)
    Finally
        dr.Close()
        conNwindCE.Close()
    End Try
End Sub
```

A close look at the **CommandText** value in Listing 12-5 shows that you make two SELECT calls separated by a semicolon. Each of these statements represents a *result set*. After the call to **ExecuteReader**, you have access to the first result set and can read it as you would normally read data returned in a SqlDataReader. When the current result set is exhausted, access to the next set is obtained by calling **dr.NextResult**(). The **NextResult** method returns a **Boolean** value that indicates whether or not another result exists. Defensive programming will tell you that you need to check the return value of **NextResult**.

 NOTE *Combining two or more SQL statements in the same command text does* not *mean that the statements are handled as a transaction. If the first SELECT statement fails, then the second might still execute. The behavior here depends on the severity level of the failure. You might also be tempted to combine multiple UPDATE commands in the command text. If you do, you must understand that if one fails there is no transaction boundary to roll back or force other changes to occur. It is possible to use the* **BeginTransaction** *method of the SqlConnection object to control transactions from the client side. It is better to handle transactions on the server rather than have client-side code performing transactions. This is especially true in the .NET Compact Framework. Transactions aren't distributed, and if the back-end database scheme ever changes, creating distributed data, your client applications will fail. It is always better to handle transactions on SQL Server. (See the "Doing Transactions" section later in this chapter for a full description of how to use the* **BeginTransaction** *method).*

If you don't want multiple result sets returned, you can specify the SingleResult enum in the call to **ExecuteReader**, and you'll restrict the returned data to a single result set. You might be wondering why I don't just take the second SELECT statement out of the **CommandText** value. I could edit the select string, and in this situation that would probably be a better option. But what if I was calling a stored procedure that returned multiple result sets? In that situation, I can't simply change the select statements.

Clearing the Air About Stored Procedures

You may have read in various articles and papers—at least I know I have—that you can't use stored procedures from SQL CE. For that to be a true statement, you need to remember that SQL CE can be either SQL Client for Windows CE or SQL Server CE. When writing SQL Client code, as demonstrated in this chapter, you can indeed use stored procedures because you're actually accessing a back-end SQL Server engine that, of course, has stored procedures. When writing an application that uses *device* data and the local SQL Server CE, stored procedures are, however, not supported.

You can see an example in Listing 12-6 of code that combines SQL Client and a SqlDataReader.

Listing 12-6. Using Stored Procedures

```
Dim conNwindCE As SqlConnection
Dim cmdData As SqlCommand
Dim curValue As Data.SqlTypes.SqlMoney

Try
    Dim connString As String

        '   Create and open a connection.
    connString = "server=169.254.223.37;database=Nwind_SQLCE;"
    connString &= "user id=user;pwd=pword;"
    conNwindCE = New SqlConnection(connString)
    conNwindCE.Open()

        '   Reuse the command with a DataReader.
    cmdData = New SqlCommand
    cmdData.CommandType = CommandType.StoredProcedure
    cmdData.CommandText = "Ten Most Expensive Products"

    cmdData.Connection = conNwindCE
    Dim dr As SqlDataReader = cmdData.ExecuteReader()
        '   Pull data from the reader and do some work.
    While dr.Read()
        strValue = dr.Item(0)
        curValue = dr.GetSqlMoney(1)
    End While
    dr.Close()
Catch ex As Exception
Finally
    conNwindCE.Close()
End Try
```

If the called stored procedure returns multiple result sets, you can access each in the same manner shown in the previous section. Listing 12-6 shows a very simple call that requires no parameters to the stored procedure. You can see in Listing 12-7 the extra code required to pass parameters to the stored procedure.

Listing 12-7. Using Stored Procedures with Parameters

```
Dim conNwindCE As SqlConnection
Dim cmdData As SqlCommand

Try
    Dim connString As String
    Dim paramCustomerID As SqlParameter

    '    Create and open a connection.
    connString = "server=192.168.1.101;database=Nwind_SQLCE;"
    connString &= "user id=sa;pwd=antietam;"
    conNwindCE = New SqlConnection(connString)
    conNwindCE.Open()

    '    Create a new SqlCommand object.
    cmdData = New SqlCommand
    cmdData.CommandType = CommandType.StoredProcedure
    cmdData.CommandText = "CustOrderHist"

    cmdData.Parameters.Add("@CustomerID", "ALFKI")
    cmdData.Connection = conNwindCE
    Dim dr As SqlDataReader = cmdData.ExecuteReader()

    '    Pull data from the reader and do some work.
    While dr.Read()
        Dim retValue = dr.Item(0)
    End While
    dr.Close()
Catch ex As Exception
Finally
    conNwindCE.Close()
End Try
```

There are any number of methods of assigning parameters to a stored procedure. Another method is to declare a SqlParameter variable, assign its properties, and add that to the SqlCommand object parameter collection.

```
paramCustomerID = New SqlParameter("@CustomerID", SqlDbType.NVarChar)
paramCustomerID.Value = "ALFKI"
cmdData.Parameters.Add
```

For more information on writing stored procedures and how to call them using ADO.NET, take look at these books:

- *ADO.NET and ADO Examples and Best Practices for VB Programmers, Second Edition* by Bill Vaughn (Apress. ISBN: 1-893115-68-2)

- *Database Programming with Visual Basic .NET, Second Edition* by Carsten Thomsen (Apress. ISBN: 1-59059-032-5)

- *The Handbook for Reluctant Database Administrators* by Josef Finsel (Apress. ISBN: 1-893115-90-9)

When you read these books, be sure to check the discussions about using output parameters from stored procedures. If you use return values only in a stored procedure, you are limited to returning a single value. For better performance and the ability to get multiple values back, consider output parameters. The following code snippet shows how you would write the call to return a value through a parameter:

```
paramCustomerID = New SqlParameter("@CustID", SqlDbType.Int)
paramCustomerID.Direction = ParameterDirection.Output
cmdData.Parameters.Add("@CustID")
cmdDataParameters.ExecuteNonQuery()
Dim custID As Integer = paramCustomerID.Value;
```

DataSets and DataAdapters

Early on I mentioned that there were two basic methods of using a SqlConnection to get data out of a database. We've discussed the SqlCommand, and now we'll look at using the connection object to get data into a DataSet. A DataSet is, in very general terms, an in-memory database. It can contain multiple tables that can be from any number of different databases. Relationships can be defined that tie the tables together inside the DataSet. You can then bind this database to a grid or other object and display your data. You can also change the view of the data by defining sort and filter criteria on the tables of the DataSet. But before you can do anything with the DataSet, you must fill it with data, and that is what you are about to learn how to do.

In Listing 12-8, you can see how you initialize the DataAdapter through its constructor using the same connect string used in previous examples. Once the DataAdapter is initialized, you fill the DataSet.

Listing 12-8. Filling a DataSet

```
Public Function GetMyDataSet() As DataSet
    Dim conNwindCE As SqlConnection
    Dim adapterData As SqlDataAdapter
    Dim cmdData As SqlCommand
    Dim connString As String

    Try
        '    Create and open a connection.
        connString = "server=169.254.223.37;database=Nwind_SQLCE;"
        connString &= "user id=user;pwd=pword;"
        conNwindCE = New SqlConnection(connString)

        '    Create a new command object.
        adapterData = New SqlDataAdapter("SELECT * FROM Customers", connString)

        Dim ds As DataSet = New DataSet
        adapterData.Fill(ds)
        Return ds
    Catch ex As Exception
        MessageBox.Show(ex.Message)
    Finally
    End Try
```

NOTE   *When you fill a DataSet using the SqlDataAdapter, you'll always be returned a valid DataSet. But what if your query returns nothing? Like I said, you still get back a valid DataSet that contains a valid DataTable. So how do you know that it is blank? Well, as I found out early in my ADO.NET days, you don't do it by checking for Nothing because you always get back a valid DataSet. You check for no results by looking at the **Count** property of the DataRowCollection object of the DataTable.*

Bear in mind that a DataSet has no knowledge of where its data came from and holds no connection open. Notice in Listing 12-8 that I don't explicitly open or close the connection. The *DataAdapter* handles the connection for me. When you pass a DataSet back to a calling method, that method is free to browse the data, create child DataSets from the original, filter the data, or change the data in the DataSet. This is all done with no connection to and no effect on the data back on the server(s).

Probably the most common use of a DataSet is to bind it to a control that has a **DataSource** property.

```
Try
    Dim ds As DataSet = GetMyDataSet()
    Me.DataGrid1.DataSource = ds.Tables(0)
Catch ex As Exception
    Dim str As String = ex.Message
End Try
```

The results of running the preceding code and the code in Listing 12-8 is shown in Figure 12-1.

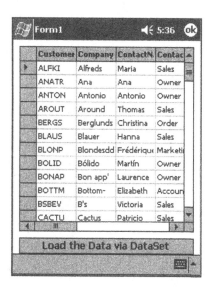

Figure 12-1. Binding a DataSet to a DataGrid

You can access the data stored in the DataSet in various ways. For the sake of completeness, let's walk through one example here. You can get a more detailed look at DataSets in Chapter 9. This example, as shown in Listing 12-9, uses the same code in Listing 12-8 to set up the connections and to fill the DataSet and then walks through the Rows collection of the first table in the DataSet and retrieves data from the row.

Listing 12-9. Reading Data from a DataSet

```
Dim conNwindCE As SqlConnection
Dim adapterData As SqlDataAdapter
Dim cmdData As SqlCommand
Dim connString As String
```

```
Try
    '    Create and open a connection.
    connString = "server=192.168.1.101;database=Nwind_SQLCE;"
    connString &= "user id=sa;pwd=antietam;"
    conNwindCE = New SqlConnection(connString)

    '    Create a new command object.
    adapterData = New SqlDataAdapter("SELECT * FROM Customers", connString)

    Dim ds As DataSet = New DataSet
    adapterData.Fill(ds)

    Dim strCustomerID As String
    Dim strCustomerName As String
    Dim strContactName As String

    For Each dr As DataRow In ds.Tables(0).Rows
        strCustomerID = dr.Item(0)
        strCustomerName = dr.Item(1)
        strContactName = dr.Item("ContactName")
    Next
    Return ds
Catch ex As Exception
    MessageBox.Show(ex.Message)
Finally
End Try
```

The code inside the For Each block should look very similar to the code used to get data from the DataReader object in the earlier section.

 HOMEWORK   *Create a new project, and in that project create a DataSet based on four tables: Customers, Orders, Order Details, and Products. Create an interface to show all four tables independently and an additional form to show the related data in a DataGrid.*

Doing Transactions

Earlier in the chapter I made a quick reference to transactions. Basically, you can do them using the SQL Server Client for Windows CE, but only within a single database and on a single server. In other words, distributed transactions covering multiple databases or multiple servers aren't supported in the .NET Compact

Framework SQL implementation. This leaves you with the ability to wrap transactions on a single server and to be sure that all SQL statements are successfully completed and that your data is intact. Listing 12-10 shows how you implement a transaction in SQL Server.

Listing 12-10. How to Code a Transaction

```
Dim conNwindCE As SqlConnection
Dim cmdData As SqlCommand
Dim connString As String
Dim transNwindCE As SqlTransaction

Try
    '    Create and open a connection.
    connString = "server=169.254.223.37;database=Nwind_SQLCE;"
    connString &= "user id=user;pwd=pword;"
    conNwindCE = New SqlConnection(connString)
    conNwindCE.Open()


    '    This is different; I created the command from the connection
    '    instead of using the New statement, keeping you on your toes!
    Dim cmdNwindCE As SqlCommand = conNwindCE.CreateCommand()


    '    Create a transaction.
    transNwindCE = conNwindCE.BeginTransaction("ShowTransaction")
    cmdNwindCE.Connection = conNwindCE
    cmdNwindCE.Transaction = transNwindCE


    cmdNwindCE.CommandText = "INSERT INTO <more stuff>"
    cmdNwindCE.ExecuteNonQuery()
    cmdNwindCE.CommandText = "INSERT INTO <different stuff>"
    cmdNwindCE.ExecuteNonQuery()
    '   If the statements succeed, commit the transaction.
    transNwindCE.Commit()
Catch ex As SqlException
    '    Something went wrong; by calling Rollback,
    '    the database is restored to its previous condition.
    transNwindCE.Rollback("ShowTransaction")
    MessageBox.Show("An exception of type " & _
        ex.GetType().ToString() & _
        " has occurred")
Finally
    conNwindCE.Close()
End Try
```

The only complexity in implementing transactions is the overload of the **BeginTransaction** method. There are a series of enumeration flags called IsolationLevel enums. These values are passed as parameters to **BeginTransaction** and determine how data is maintained during the life of a transaction. This enumeration has the **FlagsAttribute**, which allows you to combine the various flags as needed. Table 12-2 lists the flags and provides a short description of each.

Table 12-2. IsolationLevel Enumeration Values

FLAG	DESCRIPTION
Chaos	Pending changes from highly isolated transactions can't be overwritten.
ReadCommitted	Dirty reads are avoided by holding shared locks while the data is being read. Data can be changed before the end of the transaction. This may cause unrepeatable reads.
ReadUncommitted	Dirty reads are permitted. No exclusive locks are honored and no shared locks are issued.
RepeatableRead	Locks are placed on all data in the query. This prevents other users from updating the data and thus prevents nonrepeatable reads.
Serializable	A range lock is placed on the DataSet, thus preventing other users from updating rows in the locked portion of the DataSet.

In addition to handling transactions in the code on your device, you can also utilize transaction in the stored procedures. In fact, while you can't do distributed transactions from NETCF code, you can use the transactions on the server to handle distributed transactions. The better practice is to handle transactions on the server. Microsoft has put a lot of work into SQL Server to do the advanced database work, like transactions. Take advantage of that work.

 HOMEWORK *Open up your SQL Server test database (please, not one in production!) and create a new stored procedure that does some updates, using TSQL transaction syntax. Then create a project that calls the stored procedure.*

TIP *If you want to do some advanced reading on transactions, I have a recommendation. A book written back in 1987,* Concurrency Control and Recovery in Database Systems *by Philip A. Bernstein, Vassos Hadzilacos, and Nathan Goodman, is now available for free download, subject to the notice that appears on the book's copyright page. The book is being made available electronically because the hardcover version, published by Addison-Wesley Longman, is out of print. While 1987 may seem like a long time ago, the material in this book is still very much applicable to the work you do today. You can download the book from* `http://research.microsoft.com/~philbe/`.

SQL Error Handling

In the previous sections, I think I've done a pretty good job of skirting the error handling code in the Catch block, don't you? Well, it's time to correct that right now. If you've run any code in .NET using SQL Server, you might have noticed that by default, the **Message** string of the Exception object is pretty useless if you use the same code you might use on the desktop.

```
Try
    '     Code goes here.
Catch ex As Exception
    MessageBox.Show(ex.Message)
Finally
End Try
```

I changed the code in Listing 12-9 to have an invalid table name (**SELECT * FROM Customer**). The error was trapped with the preceding code snippet and the results shown in Figure 12-2.

In other areas of NETCF and the desktop framework, the **Message** property of the Exception object gives a more than adequate description of the error. The problem here is that you are trapping a specific SqlException with a generic Exception object. With the base **Exception** class, you have very little information to go on from within your code. The interesting part here is if you look in the debugger and explore the **ex** variable you'll see something like what is shown in Figure 12-3. I've pulled the **ex** variable into the Watch window to make it a little more clear what we're looking at.

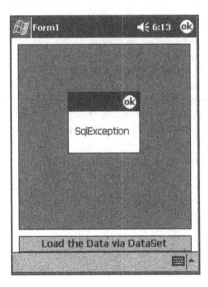

Figure 12-2. An error message, yes, but not a helpful one

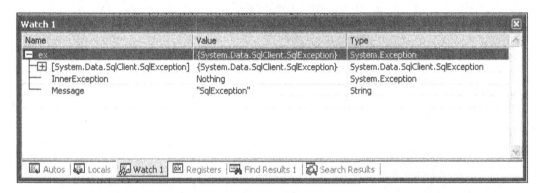

Figure 12-3. A SqlCeException in the Exception object

You can see the System.Data.SqlClient.SqlException object in the Watch window, but you don't have access to it through code. You access this information by changing the code in the Catch block, as shown in Listing 12-11.

Listing 12-11. Handling SqlClient Errors

```
Try
        Code goes here.
    Catch ex As SqlException
        MessageBox.Show(ex.Message)
    Catch ex As Exception
        MessageBox.Show(ex.Message)
    End Try
```

This code works as expected. The debugger view of the SqlException can be seen in Figure 12-4. MessageBox.Show displays the message associated with the last exception defined by the Exception object. Yes, I said the last exception. If you've worked with databases for very long, including MS Access and SQL Server, you'll know that multiple errors can be reported. In MS Access, this often shows itself by several message boxes popping up for a single "error." In .NET SQL Client, multiple exceptions are returned in the **Errors** property of the SqlException object. Listing 12-12 shows a very basic implementation of how to view all of the exceptions that may be present in the Errors collection.

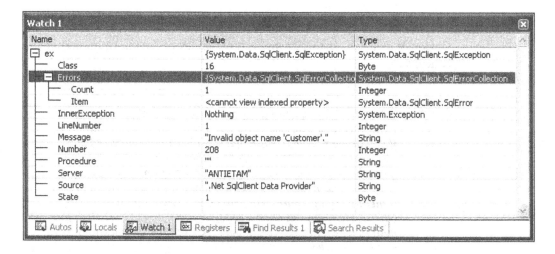

Figure 12-4. *Detailed information about the SQL error*

NOTE   *You only get this detailed help message if you have installed ssceerror20en.dll with your application. The .NET Compact Framework has removed error strings from the standard libraries to reduce the footprint on the device. You'll certainly want this library on your device while writing the code and in the beta stages of product testing. Whether you want to ship your finished product with the extra DLL is up to you.*

Listing 12-12. Handling Multiple SQL Client Errors

```
Try
    '     Code goes here.
    Catch ex As SqlException
        Dim errCollection As SqlErrorCollection = ex.Errors
        For Each err As SqlError In errCollection
            MessageBox.Show(err.Message)
        Next
    Catch ex As Exception
        MessageBox.Show(ex.Message)
    End Try
```

Obviously, you can customize any sort of display of the information that you can conceive.

NOTE *In SQL help, and other sources too, you might see exception handlers that create event logs and write the error information to them for later review. This might seem like a broken record but, again, not in NETCF. The .NET Compact Framework doesn't implement the classes required to write to or read from event logs. And I suppose that makes sense. Always remember, just because you see something in the samples in help doesn't mean that it will work in NETCF. Microsoft has done a good job specifying in the help information which methods work in NETCF, but the samples are still all desktop samples.*

In the next chapter, we'll review much of this exception discussion again when we discuss the SqlCeException object.

Summary

As technology grows, you'll see more and more devices connected through a wireless connection to your network, no matter where you might be located. If you are developing applications that run on connected devices, then you can use the SQL Server Client for Windows CE to access, view, and manipulate your server-side data. Using SQL Client from your device gives you the flexibility to use either ad-hoc SQL statements or to use stored procedures on the SQL Server.

Your choice of using either DataSets or DataReaders is entirely up to you. They each have benefits, depending on what you plan to do with the data. If you need data in a stream to just parse or review, then the SqlDataReader may be the choice for you. If you want to be able to hold onto the data (maybe even cache it in a local state as XML), review it, make changes, and then submit those changes back to the server, you'll need the abilities of the DataSet. While I can show you how to fill either one with data, I can't tell you what the best choice is for you.

In this chapter, we've discussed how to handle data that is stored on the remote SQL Server. We haven't discussed having a SQL CE database on your device. When using the SQL Server Client for Windows CE, you never keep data local on the device. In the next chapter, where I talk about disconnected data, I'll cover a new namespace: **System.Data.SqlServerCe**. This collection of classes will provide you the foundation to write code to store your data locally and to share and synchronize that data with your remote SQL Server.

All of the code presented in this chapter can be found under the **Chapter 12** folder of the **Samples** folder for this book. See Appendix D for more information on accessing and loading the sample applications.

CHAPTER 13

Working with Device-Based Data

I MAY BE A LITTLE PREJUDICED ABOUT THIS, but I think that handling device-based data is where the real power of SQL CE comes into play. After all, a Pocket PC, and yes I realize that the .NET Compact Framework is for more than Pocket PC development, is made to be mobile. It is supposed to be disconnected from the network so that you can walk around your warehouse, yard, house, or whatever and be able to make notes about the inventory on the shelves or the condition of your garden. When you and I used the eMbedded Visual Tools to write applications, having our data disconnected from the server was the default. We had, for the most part, Pocket Access and that was it. When we dropped the device into a cradle, the data was synchronized back to a database on our desktop and the world was fine.

But with the advent of the .NET Compact Framework, we are looking at a move to SQL Server as the de facto database on the device. To get up and running quickly, you need some background information about SQL CE (not the SQL Client that was discussed in the last chapter) before you start the real work of learning how to implement Remote Data Access (RDA) and merge replication.

When you commit to using SQL CE, you are forsaking all other databases. There is currently no provider that lets you pass data from a SQL CE database to an MS Access or Oracle database. This is not to say that you couldn't write your own, just that nothing is available commercially yet to let you communicate between different databases.

As you work deeper into this chapter, you'll see how to create tables in your client code. In Chapter 11 we discussed the allowable data types and functions that can be used by SQL CE. You may want to go back and review those lists to refresh your memory before you get started with the sample code in this chapter.

Covering the Database Basics

The first example will concern itself with creating and using a database that is not, and never will be, connected to an instance of SQL Server. SQL CE is a very good database that allows you to use the fundamentals of ADO.NET, such as data binding, while still using a local database. A SQL CE database can't be created on the desktop, so it must be created on the device. You can use the SQL CE

Query application to create the database and build the tables, but I find that tedious and frustrating at best. If a user inadvertently deletes the database, you can't just pick up the device and rebuild that database. So the best choice, in my mind anyway, is to create the database and its tables in code. The code in Listing 13-1 shows how you use a new namespace and its classes to create a new database and tables.

Listing 13-1. Creating a Database

```
Imports System.Data.SqlServerCe
Public Class DataInterfaceDisconnected
    Private m_localDatabaseName As String = "\My Documents\Chapter13.sdf"
    Private m_localDataSource As String = "Data Source=" & m_localDatabaseName

    Private Function CreateDatabase(bEncrypt As Boolean, bPassword As String)
        Dim boolCreateNewDatabase As Boolean = True

        '   Does the database already exist?
        If System.IO.File.Exists(m_localDatabaseName) Then
            '   Ask if we should delete it, delete for simplicity now.
            boolCreateNewDatabase = False
        End If

        If boolCreateNewDatabase Then
            Dim eng As SqlCeEngine = New SqlCeEngine(m_ localDataSource)
            eng.CreateDatabase()

            '   Get a connection to the database.
            Dim localConnection As SqlCeConnection
            localConnection = New SqlCeConnection(m_ localDataSource)
            localConnection.Open()

            '   Create the tables.
            Dim buildTables As StringBuilder = New StringBuilder()

            buildTables.Append("CREATE TABLE Books (")
            buildTables.Append( _
                "BookID uniqueidentifier DEFAULT (newid()) not null")
            buildTables.Append(", Title nvarchar(100) not null")
            buildTables.Append( _
                ", AuthorID int REFERENCES Authors(AuthorID) not null")
            buildTables.Append(", ISBN nvarchar(25) not null")
            buildTables.Append(", PubDate nvarchar(50) not null")
            buildTables.Append(", Pages int not null")
            buildTables.Append(", Price nvarchar(10) not null")
```

```
        buildTables.Append(", Cover nvarchar(100)  null")
        buildTables.Append(")")

        Dim cmdCreateTable As SqlCeCommand
        cmdCreateTable = New SqlCeCommand( _
            buildTables.ToString(), localConnection)
        cmdCreateTable.CommandType = CommandType.Text
        cmdCreateTable.ExecuteNonQuery()
      End If
    End Sub
End Class
```

NOTE *In my own code, I don't hard code either connection or database path strings. I do it here to make the values used clear to you. I would recommend that you don't hard code strings. Why would you not want to store strings in the code? Well, as I mentioned before, if the IP address of IIS changes, you need to get the new string into the code. Or you may want to internationalize your application and* My Documents *may not be* My Documents *in Germany or some other non-English language country. If you insert a CompactFlash (CF) card into the device, you might want to change the database location to the card. These types of settings can be read from an external file or files. If you have experience on the desktop, you might think that you would use **System.Configuration**. However, the **Configuration** namespace is not supported in NETCF. You will have to find other ways to get load strings from an external file. For alternatives, I'll show you in Chapter 20 how to read values from a flat text file, while Chapter 14 discusses how you can read values from an XML file.*

TIP *You could use more than one text or XML file for various strings required by your application. This would let you download files to change only a specific string without affecting other string values used in other parts of the application. Database connection strings have no relation to application strings for UI or other data storage, so why do they have to be grouped in the same file?*

If you recall from Chapter 12, you didn't use any namespaces that were different from the regular desktop ADO.NET namespace. The examples for that chapter were talking to SQL Server more or less directly. Now you will be working disconnected in SQL CE, and that requires you to specify a new namespace,

System.Data.SqlServerCe. You will need to add a reference to the SqlServerCe.dll in order to use this namespace. Figure 13-1 shows the Add Reference dialog box with this reference highlighted.

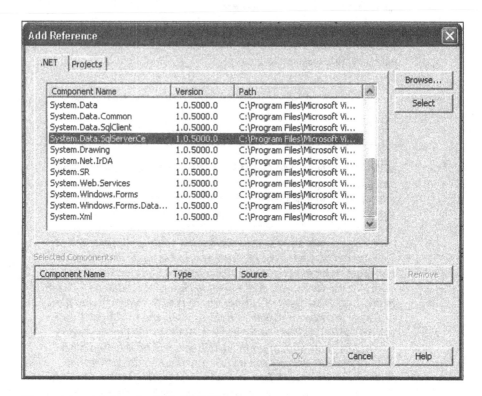

Figure 13-1. Adding the SQL CE DLL

I make it a habit to always use a string constant for my database name, defined as private in the scope of the class. This lets me change the database name in a single location and have it recognized throughout the class.

TIP *Another habit I have is to put all of my database code into one of two classes. In Listing 13-1 you see a class named* **DataInterfaceDisconnected**. *This class is used for all code where I only work with SQL CE to maintain a local database that will never see SQL Server. I also have a class named* **DataInterface** *that contains the code required for Remote Data Access and merge replication (you will see this class in a later section). The* **DataInterface** *class also has code that talks to a local SQL CE database, but it knows that at some time data will be moved between the device and SQL Server. The object of this is to keep all of the code related to databases in a single location. I don't have connection strings and database name strings spread across forms, classes, and whatever. I have written my classes in such a way that I only need to copy the classes to a new project, change a couple of strings, and I have full database functionality in the new applications.*

In this example, I demonstrate creating the database in the **My Documents** folder on the device. You can put the file anywhere on your device that you see fit.

TIP *Hi, me again. One thing you should consider, especially when using SQL CE, is to add a CompactFlash card (or some similar item) to your device. No matter how reliable (or not) your device is, if something drastic happens, you are in jeopardy of losing your data when the device fails. Placing the data on a CompactFlash card accomplishes two things: It provides a safety net in case your device dies and more RAM for applications. While SQL CE databases may not be very large, it doesn't take much to run down your available memory on the device with storage along with running applications and their memory requirements. You can also install your application from a CompactFlash card (see Chapter 21). For my applications, I use a 64MB CompactFlash card and I access the database using this string:* **\Storage Card\MyDatabase.sdf**.

NOTE *All CF cards are not equal. If you plan on using one for your database (or other storage), you need to investigate some of the different products available. One card's performance over another may be insignificant or may be as much as 100 times slower. If you are performing a query on a database that is stored on a CF card, and it seems to be taking an unusually long time, the problem might be the card and not your application or device. Move the database to the device to see if the execution time changes. If the difference is significant, you might want to look at a different CF card.*

In Listing 13-1, the code to actually create the database consists of two lines:

```
Dim eng As SqlCeEngine = New SqlCeEngine(m_localDatabaseName)
eng.CreateDatabase()
```

The rest of the code is dedicated to adding tables to your newly created database. The code to add the table should look familiar to the code presented in Chapter 12. This snippet shows how you set up a connection to your local SQL CE database:

```
'   Get a connection to the database.
Dim localConnection As SqlCeConnection
localConnection = New SqlCeConnection(m_localDatabaseName)
localConnection.Open()
```

Instead of using a SqlConnection as you did in Chapter 12 or in ADO.NET on the desktop, you create a SqlCeConnection. All of the standard full framework classes are duplicated on the .NET Compact Framework and the objects have the additional "Ce" in the class name. Table 13-1 lists the SQL Server Ce classes that NETCF supports. We'll discuss each of these classes in detail, and you'll get a chance to work some sample code for each as you progress through this chapter.

Table 13-1. A Short Introduction to the SQL Server CE Database Classes

CLASS	DESCRIPTION
SqlCeEngine	Collects information relevant to a warning or error returned by the data source. This class can't be inherited.
SqlCeConnection	Represents an open connection to the database.
SqlCeCommand	Represents a SQL statement that will be run against the database.
SqlCeDataAdapter	Represents a set of data commands and a database connection that are used to fill the DataSet and update the data source.
SqlCeDataReader	Provides a way of reading a forward-only stream of data rows from a data source.
SqlCeParameter	Represents a parameter to a SqlCeCommand and, optionally, its mapping to a DataSet.
SqlCeCommandBuilder	Automatically generates single-table SQL statements that will allow data from a DataSet to be reconciled with the SQL Server CE database.
SqlCeError	Collects information relevant to a warning or error returned by the data source.
SqlCeException	The exception that is thrown when the underlying provider returns a warning or error from a SQL Server CE data source.

Once the connection is made and opened, you have to build the SQL command in a string that will create the table. This string is then used as a parameter, along with your connection object, to construct the SqlCeCommand object.

```
Dim cmdCreateTable As SqlCeCommand
cmdCreateTable = New SqlCeCommand(buildTables, localConnection)
cmdCreateTable.CommandType = CommandType.Text
cmdCreateTable.ExecuteNonQuery()
```

Obviously, you can create additional SQL command strings to build more tables and add them to the database. There are a few options we need to look at before you can move on to adding and retrieving data from your newly created database.

Protecting the Database

Recall from Chapter 11 that I mentioned that you could password protect or encrypt a SQL CE database. This is done when the database is created. You password protect the database by adding an additional parameter to the connect string. The following code shows the connect string needed to password protect your database:

```
Dim dataSource = "DataSource=\Protected.sdf;Password='passw0rd'; "
```

Similarly, if you want to encrypt the database you use the following line of code:

```
dataSource = "DataSource=\Encrypted.sdf;Password='passw0rd';Encrypt
Database=True"
```

The connection string is the same for both password-protected and encrypted databases. Returning to the code in Listing 13-1, the following snippet shows how you would create the connection object if the database was protected:

```
'   Get a connection to the database.
Dim localConnection As SqlCeConnection
Dim localConnectString As String

localConnectString = "DataSource=" & m_localDatabaseName & "Password=passw0rd"
localConnection = New SqlCeConnection(localConnectString)
localConnection.Open()
```

NOTE *I made a very similar note in a previous chapter but this warrants a reminder. Do not forget the password. If you don't have the password, then your data is as good as gone!*

TIP *Pay close attention in the next few sections. You might be planning to connect your data to SQL Server through RDA or replication and think that none of this really applies to you, but you would be wrong! Once the database is created, the remainder of the code you'll see is the same as you'll be using with a local SQL CE database that will connect to a server. If your data is replicated on the server, your application will no doubt still add information collected from the device to be added to the server-side data store. So, don't think you are above the next few sections; they will be useful later.*

Once you password protect your database, the Query Analyzer will prompt you for the password each time you try to view the database. Figure 13-2 shows the dialog box that pops up when you open a password-protected SQL CE database.

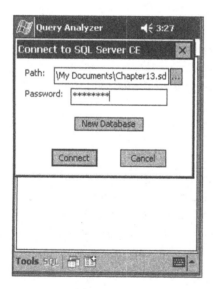

Figure 13-2. Query Analyzer with protected database

Manipulating Data in the Database

Your database has been created and the tables added. Now you are ready to work with the data in the tables. The first order of business, before you can edit data, is to add new data to your tables. The code in Listing 13-2 is pretty similar to what you've seen already and should look much like the desktop ADO.NET code with which you might be familiar.

Listing 13-2. Adding Data to Tables

```
Dim localConnection As SqlCeConnection
localConnection = New SqlCeConnection(m_localDataSource)

Dim insertData As String
insertData = "INSERT INTO Authors (Name) VALUES('Fergus')"

Dim cmdCreateTable As SqlCeCommand

localConnection.Open()
cmdCreateTable = New SqlCeCommand(insertData, localConnection)
cmdCreateTable.CommandType = CommandType.Text
cmdCreateTable.ExecuteNonQuery()
localConnection.Close()
```

This code is similar to that where you created the table in your fresh database because both code snippets use the **ExecuteNonQuery** method of the **SqlCeCommand** class. In fact, this code can be used for any SQL statement that doesn't require a return value. This leads me to this: In the **DataInterface** classes that I show you how to create in this chapter, you can add a function that takes as its parameter a SQL command string and performs all of the required connection work behind the scenes. This method is shown in Listing 13-3.

Listing 13-3. Using a Subroutine to Provide Common Functionality

```
Public Sub RunNonQuery(ByVal sqlCommandText As String)
    Dim localConnection As SqlCeConnection
    localConnection = New SqlCeConnection(m_localDataSource)

    Dim cmdCreateTable As SqlCeCommand

    localConnection.Open()
    cmdCreateTable = New SqlCeCommand(sqlCommandText, localConnection)
    cmdCreateTable.CommandType = CommandType.Text
    cmdCreateTable.ExecuteNonQuery()
    localConnection.Close()
```

```
        cmdCreateTable.Dispose()
        localConnection.Dispose()
End Sub
```

The variations for this code are endless. For example, the SqlCeConnection object could be created in the class constructor and only opened and closed in any methods that use it. If the connection is created in the class's constructor, you have a little more to worry about. For instance, how do you dispose of the connection when you are finished with the class? The simple answer is that you implement the IDisposable interface from the framework. You can see the full implementation in the accompanying source code for this chapter.

NOTE *In the code within this chapter, I show connections being created, opened, closed, and disposed of to illustrate the entire sequence of code required to make this functionality work. However, in the DeviceData solution I include with the code for this chapter (under **Chapter 13** in the **Samples** folder), I take liberties to create better designed code that at first glance may not be as obvious to you when reviewing the code for the first time.*

Creating the connection object early in the life of the class and holding it does not consume the SQL connection. The connection is tied up only while the connection is actually opened. Notice that you also dispose of both the connection and command object before you leave the function. This is somewhat analogous to the Visual Basic 6 practice of setting variables to Nothing as you are leaving scope.

NOTE *I don't mean to imply that calling **Dispose** and setting variables to Nothing are exactly the same. What I am looking at more is the practice of cleaning up after yourself when leaving scope. I have made it a practice since VB4 to always set my local variables to Nothing when leaving scope. In .NET, with its nondeterministic garbage collection, memory is not released as soon as you call **Dispose**. This is more of an indication to the garbage collector that you are finished and it can collect and release any resources associated with the object. If a .NET object has a **Dispose** method, I would suggest that you call that method before leaving scope to help the garbage collector do a better job of cleaning up.*

Calling **Dispose** ensures a timely cleanup of the resources that are related to the objects. Once data is inserted into your tables, it would be useful to get access to the data so that you can do something with it. As in Chapter 12, you can use a DataReader or a DataSet.

The DataReader in SQL CE is used as shown in Listing 13-4. This code should also look familiar to the previous code because the sequence of steps is the same: Create a connection, create a command, open the connection, and execute the command.

Listing 13-4. Using the DataReader to Recall Data

```
Public Function GetData() As SqlCeDataReader
    Try
        Dim localConnection As SqlCeConnection
        localConnection = New SqlCeConnection(m_localDataSource)

        '   Get the data.
        Dim dr As SqlCeDataReader
        Dim cmdGetData As SqlCeCommand

        localConnection.Open()
        cmdGetData = New SqlCeCommand("SELECT * FROM Books", localConnection)
        cmdGetData.CommandType = CommandType.Text
        dr = cmdGetData.ExecuteReader(CommandBehavior.CloseConnection)

        Return dr
    Catch ex As SqlCeException
        MessageBox.Show(ex.Message)
    End Try
End Function
```

To pull data back as a DataSet is just as simple. Listing 13-5 does highlight one change to the roll we have been on. Notice that the DataSet object is not CeDataSet or SqlCeDataSet like all of the other classes have been. In fact, ADO.NET doesn't distinguish DataSet to be of SQL, OleDb, or Oracle as it does with other classes such as connections and commands. The same holds true for the .NET Compact Framework. A DataSet is a stand-alone data structure that has no direct relationship with the source of the data, so it does not carry the extra name baggage that you might expect.

Listing 13-5. Using a DataSet to Recall Data

```
Public Function GetDataSet() As DataSet
    Try
        Dim localConnection As SqlCeConnection
        localConnection = New SqlCeConnection(m_localDataSource)
```

```
'   Get the data.
    Dim da As SqlCeDataAdapter = New SqlCeDataAdapter
    Dim ds As DataSet = New DataSet
    da.SelectCommand = New SqlCeCommand("SELECT * FROM Books",
localConnection)
    da.Fill(ds)

    Return ds
Catch ex As SqlCeException
    MessageBox.Show(ex.Message)
End Try
End Function
```

All of the code we have discussed so far has been applied to a SQL CE database (which carries the SDF extension) that resides only on a device with no connection to the greater world at large. But there is a bigger world out there! There are mountains to climb, rivers to swim, and database servers to connect to. With that in mind, let's take it to another level.

Remote Data Access

Also known as RDA, this type of data access provides a simple way for a Microsoft Windows CE–based application to access data from a remote SQL Server database table and store that data in a local SQL Server CE database table. In RDA speak, you get data from the server by doing a *pull*. The data is stored on the device in a SQL CE database with the .sdf extension, the same as you created in the previous sections.

Once the data is on the local device, a user can read, update, or delete the data in the tables. After the data has been changed, you put it back on the server by doing a *push*. The work you do on the device database is accomplished in the same manner that you added data in the previous sections.

Using RDA, you can additionally execute SQL statements against the remote SQL Server database. You can add or delete records directly in the remote database, or you can call stored procedures on the remote server.

RDA is best suited for disconnected devices, as opposed to a connected SQL Client for Windows CE. The data packages being sent over the wire are compressed to optimize performance. To get a better feel for how RDA works, I'll walk you through the steps that occur whenever communication from the device to the remote server is performed. Figure 13-3 shows how the communication flows between the device database and the server database.

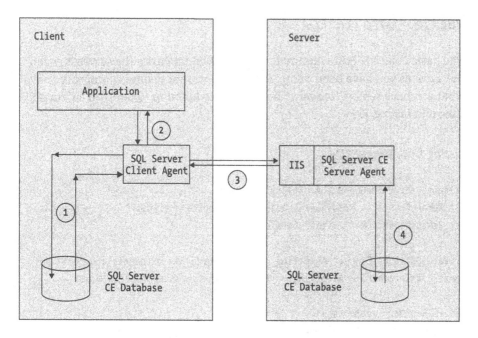

Figure 13-3. RDA architecture

When your application performs a data pull (retrieves data from the server), the SQL Server CE Client Agent forwards the request to the SQL Server CE Server Agent, through IIS, using HTTP. The Server Agent then connects with SQL Server and invokes the client's SQL request. The data is then passed back to the Client Agent and moved into the client database. It is possible to track any changes made to the device database, and I'll demonstrate how when I cover the code to perform a pull.

When you perform a push, the Client Agent collects any changed or added records from the device database and passes them, using HTTP, through IIS and to the Server Agent. The Server Agent performs the inserts or updates on the remote SQL Server and reports any errors back to the device.

RDA uses optimistic concurrency control for the data that is pulled and pushed between the device and the server. In plain English this means that when changes are moved from the device database to the server database, any changes made between the pull and push may be overwritten. If the insert, update, or delete operations do result in a conflict, RDA manages the resulting error by passing the error information back to the device in an error table. SQL Server CE only supports row-level record tracking. When a push is performed, some records may succeed while others may fail. The exact functionality is determined by the specifics of the pull method. We'll discuss this in detail in the following sections.

As the developer, you are responsible for the handling of the conflicts that occur and are reported back to you in the error table.

Pulling Data in RDA

The basic code structure required to do a pull of data from the server is much the same as you have been doing. RDA does introduce some complexity above what you have seen previously. The most basic function to perform a data pull is shown in Listing 13-6.

Listing 13-6. Simple RDA

```
Private _strRemoteConnect As String
_strRemoteConnect = "provider=sqloledb;data source=antietam;"
_strRemoteConnect &= "Initial Catalog=Books;"

Private _strLocalConnect As String = "Data Source=\My Documents\Chapter13.sdf "
Const _strInternetURL As String = "http://antietam/ssce20/sscesa20.dll"

Public Sub DownloadBooks()
    DropLocalTable("localBooks")

    Try
        Dim rda As SqlCeRemoteDataAccess= New SqlCeRemoteDataAccess()
        rda.InternetLogin = String.Empty
        rda.InternetPassword = String.Empty
        rda.InternetUrl = _strInternetURL
        rda.LocalConnectionString = _strLocalConnect
        rda.Pull("localBooks", _
            "SELECT * FROM Books", _
            _strRemoteConnect, _
            System.Data.SqlServerCe.RdaTrackOption.TrackingOnWithIndexes)
    Catch ex As SqlCeException
        MessageBox.Show(ex.Message)
    End Try
End Sub
```

Without a doubt this code will require some explanation. The first few lines are connection string definitions. There is a remote connection string to the remote server, and a local connection string to the device database. A third constant string is the URL to the virtual directory that you created when you installed the server tools (way back in Chapter 11). These strings are all kept as class-level variables as they are used throughout the methods of the **DataInterface** class.

TIP *It can be very confusing as you write more RDA and replication code as to which connection string you are referencing from place to place. One way to help keep things straight is to name the various objects using the local and remote designation in the variable name. I often use the prefix "local" when I am talking about a local database or connection string. In contrast, I use the prefix "remote" to name a connection or object that resides on or references a remote object. For example _localConnectionString would point to the local SQL CE database while _remoteConnectionString points to the remote SQL Server database. I also like to name my local tables the same name as the remote database tables, adding the "local" prefix to the name to distinguish them. This distinction helps me keep things straight in my head, and in the code. You'll appreciate how complicated it can get in the next few sections.*

I mentioned earlier that I keep all of my database code, or at least as much as possible, in separate classes. The class called **DataInterface** contains all of the code to handle RDA and replication and the supporting functions needed to query and maintain the database. Once all of the string constants are initialized, you can pull the data from the remote database.

Before you can pull data down to the device database, you need to remove the old table. The pull tries to create a new table to hold the incoming data and raises an exception if the table already exists.

NOTE *If the database does not exist before the **Pull** method is called, you must create it before you make a call to the **Pull** method. In other words, SQL will create tables for you but not the database. Being required to create the database before calling RDA methods, you have control over whether the database is password protected and/or encrypted. More about protecting the database later in this chapter.*

This is a very important point and may be a deal breaker if you are looking at using RDA. If the table that you want to pull contains hundreds or even thousands of records, you will have to pull all the rows each time. If you are connected through a poor-quality connection, you can see the problems that may arise. In this case, you might want to look at replication as the alternative, because replication only moves the records back and forth that have changed or been added since the last synchronization.

Next you have to instantiate and initialize the SqlCeRemoteDataAccess object. Listing 13-6 uses the overloaded constructor that requires no parameters, initializing the data through the class properties.

```
Dim rda As SqlCeRemoteDataAccess= New SqlCeRemoteDataAccess()
rda.InternetLogin = String.Empty
rda.InternetPassword = String.Empty
rda.InternetUrl = _strInternetURL
rda.LocalConnectionString = _strLocalConnect
```

Because in this first example you use anonymous access through IIS, the **InternetLogin** and **InternetPassword** properties are set to String.Empty. We'll look at using other authentication in a later section. With the SqlCeRemoteDataAccess object configured correctly, it's time to pull your data down to your device database.

```
rda.Pull("localBooks", _
    "SELECT * FROM Books", _
    _strRemoteConnect, _
    System.Data.SqlServerCe.RdaTrackOption.TrackingOnWithIndexes)
```

There are three overloads for the **Pull** method; all three require a minimum of three parameters. The first parameter is the name of the local table where the data will be stored. The second is the SQL command text to be passed to the SQL Server CE Client for submission to the remote database, and the third required parameter is the connect string to the remote SQL Server. The fourth parameter, used in the preceding code, tells SQL CE what tracking is in effect for the pulled data. The RdaTrackOption enum values and descriptions are shown in Table 13-2.

Table 13-2. RdaTrackOption Enum Values

ENUM MEMBER	DESCRIPTION
TrackingOff	SQL Server CE does not track changes to the pulled table. No primary key constraints are created.
TrackingOffWithIndexes	SQL Server CE does not track changes to the pulled table. If indexes or primary key constraints existed on the remote SQL Server table, they are created on the device data table.
TrackingOn	SQL Server CE tracks all changes to the pulled table. Primary key constraints related to the requested data are created on the local table.
TrackingOnWithIndexes	SQL Server CE tracks all changes to the pulled table. Primary key constraints and indexes that existed on the remote SQL Server table are created on the device data table.

If you plan to push updated data back to the remote SQL Server database, then you must use either the TrackingOn or TrackingOnWithIndexes values of RdaTrackOption. There are several constraints that you need to be aware of. The SELECT statement used to pull the data must return an updatable DataSet; if not, an exception will be thrown. The SELECT statement may reference a view or stored procedure, but again, the returned DataSet must be updatable. Among other things, an updatable DataSet can only contain data rows from a single table, and that table must have a primary key defined. One last potential gotcha: Any indexes on the remote SQL Server table are only created on the device database table if the column or columns that make up the index are included in the SELECT statement.

The last overload of the **Pull** method takes a fifth parameter that gives the name of the error table to create in the device database should an error occur when the data is pushed back to the server. This parameter can only be provided if tracking is turned on.

Pushing Data Back to the Server

Your application is moving right along. You have a database, and you have pulled data from the server down to the device. Your users, bless their little hearts, have made changes to the data, and now they want to copy that data back up to the server. With all of the constants already worked out and explained, the push code is pretty straightforward, as you can see in Listing13-7.

Listing 13-7. Pushing Data Back to the Server

```
Try
    With _rda
        .InternetLogin = String.Empty
        .InternetPassword = String.Empty
        .InternetUrl = _strInternetURL
        .LocalConnectionString = _strLocalConnect
        .Push("localBooks", _
            _strRemoteConnect, _
            System.Data.SqlServerCe.RdaBatchOption.BatchingOn)
    End With
Catch ex As SqlCeException
    Dim q As String = ex.Message
End Try
```

The setup for the call to **Push** is the same as that for **Pull**. The first parameter of **Push** is the local table to be pushed back to the remote server, and the second parameter is the connect string to the server. The third parameter is an RdaBatchOption enum that specifies how SQL Server should handle any conflicts and errors. The RdaBatchOption enum values are explained in Table 13-3. If no value is specified, the default is to turn batching off.

Table 13-3. RdaBatchOption Enum

ENUM MEMBER	DESCRIPTION
BatchingOff	SQL Server CE does not batch the rows submitted to the remote server. Each row to be inserted, deleted, or updated is handled as an independent transaction. The transaction is not dependent on any other transaction. Errors are reported back to the error table specified in the Pull method.
BatchingOn	SQL Server CE sends all changes as a single transaction. If any one fails, they are all rolled back. SQL Server attempts to apply each change even when one fails. Each change that failed is reported back in the error table specified in the Pull method call.

Authenticating with IIS

Like just about every other example I've ever seen, you have RDA working using anonymous authentication. But you, my friend, are going to take it a step further and protect your IIS virtual directory with Basic authentication. You might think that all you have to do is change two lines of code and all should be fine. That is partially correct, all you really have to do in code is to make two small changes, but the problem is in setting up IIS to handle authentication using something other than anonymous access. So, let's do the easy part first.

```
_rda.InternetLogin = "webUser"
_rda.InternetPassword = "passw0rd"
```

The part that is a little more difficult is getting the server end, IIS and SQL Server, set up properly. To do that, I am going to take you through a short tutorial that will hopefully save you some time.

Step-by-Step Tutorial: Beyond Anonymous

There are two pieces that you need to be certain you have set up properly: IIS authentication mode and the user login in SQL Server.

Step 1: Create a Login Account

When you use either Basic authentication or Integrated Windows authentication, an account must exist on the computer that is hosting IIS for the user whose credentials are being used.

Step 2: Set Directory Security

Remember that virtual directory you created long, long ago? You need to go back to that folder and look at its Properties dialog box. Select the **Security** tab and add the user that will be logging in through IIS to the list. Figure 13-4 shows the dialog box with my login, Dan (ANTIETAM\Dan), highlighted.

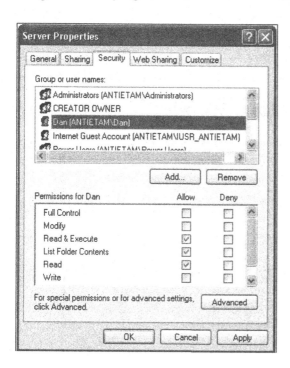

Figure 13-4. Security for your virtual directory

 NOTE *Rather than adding each user to the directory, you can also create a new group and add that group to the list of groups or user names that have access to the directory. I have created a group called "Web Users" that has access through IIS to my SQL Server. You still need an account on the server doing the IIS hosting; you just don't need to add it to the security for the directory.*

Step 3: Set Security in IIS

1. Open Internet Information Services and right-click the virtual directory you set up in SQL CE.

2. Select **Properties** from the menu.

3. Select the **Directory Security** tab.

4. Click the **Edit** button for authentication control (see Figure 13-5).

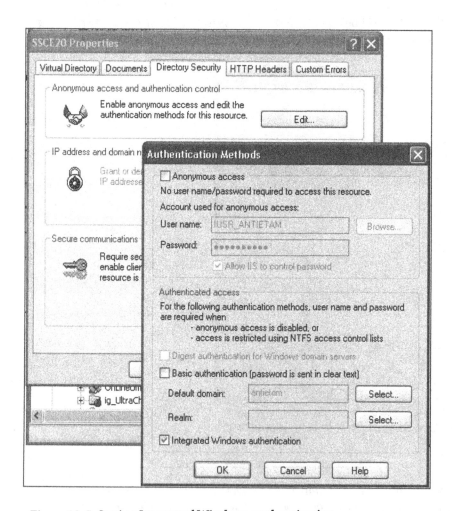

Figure 13-5. Setting Integrated Windows authentication

5. Select the **Integrated Windows Authentication** check box. Alternatively, you can select **Basic authentication** (see Figure 13-6). When you select the latter option, another dialog box pops up, warning you about a potential problem with this authentication (see Figure 13-7). The problem is that Basic authentication sends the user name and password as clear text. As the dialog box says, a malicious hacker could intercept the information and get access to the logon information for the account. Dismiss the dialog box by clicking the **OK** button.

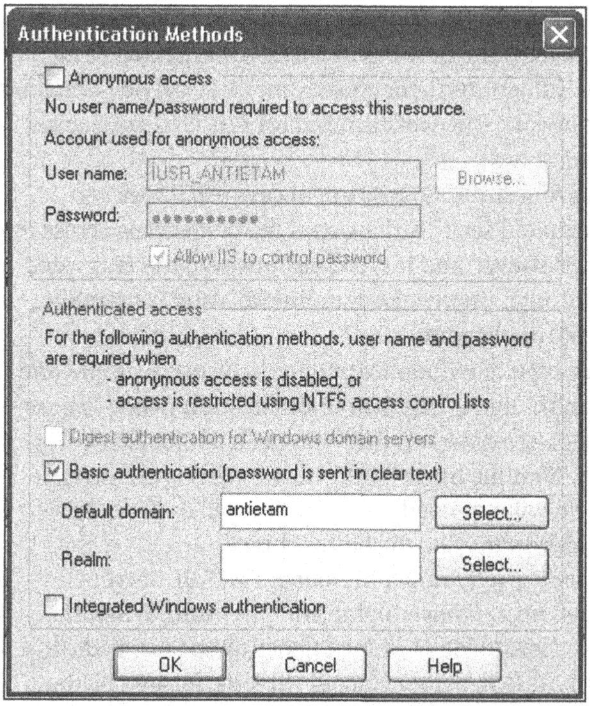

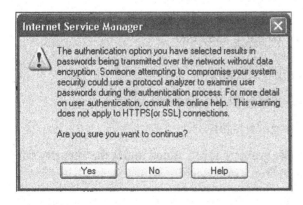

Figure 13-6. Setting Basic authentication

Figure 13-7. Be careful with Basic authentication

NOTE *The Default domain field shown in Figure 13-6 tells IIS to search that domain first if no domain is provided in the login string from the client. While this is what is supposed to happen, it doesn't seem to do anything when used from the Pocket PC. Maybe it's just me, but be careful, because it might not just be me.*

About this time you should be asking yourself what's the difference between Integrated Windows authentication and Basic authentication. There is one difference that really matters, and that is the fact that Basic authentication sends the user name and password across the network in a Base-64 encoded string. Other than this encoding, the values aren't encrypted and can easily be obtained by anyone "sniffing" on the network. The work around for this is to use Secure Sockets Layer (SSL) encryption.

That sounds pretty serious doesn't it? So why not always use Integrated Windows authentication? Integrated security does send the credentials across the network as encrypted tokens. However, and this is a big however, the encrypted information can't be passed through proxy servers or firewalls and is therefore really only useful for an intranet application.

The decision about which type of authentication to use is not a simple one to make. A good rule of thumb though is this: If your application needs to pass credentials through a firewall or proxy server, then you need to consider using SSL and Basic authentication. If on the other hand you are writing an intranet application or are sure that you will not need to cross a firewall or proxy server, Integrated Windows authentication may be the better choice.

Either way, the process works pretty much the same. The SQL Server CE Client supplies a valid Windows account user name and password. When IIS receives the credentials, it attempts to log in. If the login attempt succeeds, the connection is made to the remote SQL Server, and all work performed by the SQL Server CE Server Agent is done under the identity of the specified Windows account. If the login attempt fails, the request is rejected. Basic authentication requires that each client have a valid Windows account.

Step 4: Set Security in SQL Server

1. Open SQL Server Enterprise Manager.

2. Open the **Security** node under the database of interest.

3. Select **Logins** and create a new login.

4. Add the same user or user group that you added under the **Security** tab of the virtual directory in Step 2 previously.

5. Open the Properties dialog box for the newly added user or group (see Figure 13-8).

6. Select the **Grant access** radio button.

7. Select the **Data Access** tab (see Figure 13-9).

8. Select the **db_datareader** and **db_datawriter** check boxes so that they are checked, and close the dialog box.

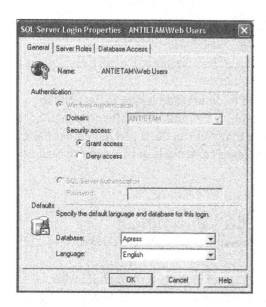

Figure 13-8. Setting the default database

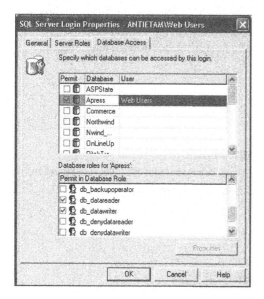

Figure 13-9. Setting access rights to the database

That's the setup that you need to do on the IIS/SQL Server box.

> **TIP** *If you wanted to force a user to log in as a member of a group instead of an individual, you might try to change the security access shown in Figure 13-9 to **Deny Access**. Unfortunately, the security access setting overrides the group permissions, and the user can no longer log into SQL Server. You can either delete the user from SQL Server logins or remove the database from the users list of databases to which he or she has access.*

I mentioned earlier that all you had to do was add values to the code for **InternetPassword** and **InternetLogin** properties of the SqlCeRemoteDataAccess object. While that is true, there is more that you can do. If you remember back in Listing 13-6, you supply SQL Server login credentials in your remote connection string.

```
Private _strRemoteConnect As String
_strRemoteConnect = "provider=sqloledb;data source=antietam; "
_strRemoteConnect &= "Initial Catalog=Books;User ID=sa;Password=right"
```

If you do not change these values, you are logging in through IIS with a Windows account and then using SQL Server authentication to access SQL Server. Makes sense, right? That is a perfectly acceptable approach. You can also change the connect string and use the same Windows account to log in to SQL Server that you used to gain access through IIS. In Listing 13-8 I show code that will pull data from the remote server table Authors and place it into the device database table localAuthors. The major difference between this code and the earlier listing is that you are now using Basic authentication instead of anonymous access.

Listing 13-8. Using Integrated Security

```
Public Sub DownloadBooks()
    Dim strSQL As String = "SELECT * FROM Authors"
    Dim _strRemoteConnect As String = "provider=sqloledb;data source=antietam; "
    _strRemoteConnect &= "Initial Catalog=apress;Integrated Security=SSPI;"

    DropLocalTable("localAuthors")

    Try
        Forms.Cursor.Current =Forms.Cursors.WaitCursor
        With _rda
            .InternetLogin = "Antietam\Dan"
            .InternetPassword = "<password>"
```

```
            .InternetUrl = "http://antietam/ssce20/sscesa20.dll"
            .LocalConnectionString = "Data Source=\Chapter13.SDF"
            .Pull("localAuthors ", _
                strSQL, _
                _strRemoteConnect, _
                System.Data.SqlServerCe.RdaTrackOption.TrackingOnWithIndexes, _
                "pushErrors")
        End With
    Catch ex As SqlCeException
        Dim q As String = ex.Message
    Finally
        Forms.Cursor.Current =Forms.Cursors.Default
    End Try
End Sub
```

 NOTE *From the code side, there is no difference between Integrated Windows authentication and Basic authentication. The account credentials are passed in the same manner, and the connection strings, both local and remote, are the same.*

Another difference is the change to the remote connection string. Instead of using a SQL Server user name and password, you are using integrated security. When we use integrated security instead of user name/password values, the login that was used at IIS is the same one used at SQL Server.

The code in Listing 13-8 uses the Dan account on the Antietam computer to authenticate against IIS and SQL Server. With the proper setup on the IIS and SQL Servers, you should now be able to easily use advanced authentication instead of Anonymous access.

Working with SQL CE

Once you have data on the device, I suppose you also need a way to work with that data. Most of the code you write for this purpose is basic ADO.NET-style code. There will be a few differences due to the nature of the .NET Compact Framework. Back in Listing 13-6 I introduced a method to drop a local table and said that we would get to it later. Well, it's later, so let's take a look at the code in Listing 13-9.

Listing 13-9. Dropping a Table in SQL CE

```
Private Sub DropLocalTable(ByVal tableName As String)
    Dim cn As System.Data.SqlServerCe.SqlCeConnection = Nothing
    Dim cmd As System.Data.SqlServerCe.SqlCeCommand

    Try
        '    Drop the existing local table.
        cn = New SqlCeConnection("Data Source=\ Chapter13.SDF")
        cn.Open()

        cmd = New SqlCeCommand("DROP TABLE " & tableName, cn)
        cmd.ExecuteNonQuery()

    Catch ex As SqlCeException
        '    Eat the error.
        Dim p As String = ex.Message
    Finally
        If Not cn Is Nothing Then
            cn.Close()
        End If
    End Try
End Sub
```

NOTE *You will see in many samples a local connect string that has much more in it than the data source. An example would be a connect string like this: "Provider=Microsoft.SQLSERVER.OLEDB. CE.2.0;Data Source=\ssce.sdf". You don't need the extra information, and in fact I have found that connections often don't work with anything more than the data source.*

The steps are familiar: Create a SqlCeConnection object using the correct connect string. Then create a SqlCeCommand object that uses the connection object and the SQL select string that you want executed. Open the connection, run the query, close the connection, and you're done. Of course, there are a few details. In Listing 13-9, I also have an exception handler that will close the connection whether there is an exception thrown or not. This code drops the existing table. If the table does not exist and an exception is thrown, it is caught and not sent on to the caller. In the code in Listing 13-10, I show you how to use the **ExecuteReader** method of the SqlCeCommand object instead of the **ExecuteNonQuery** method of Listing 13-9.

Listing 13-10. Creating a SqlCeDataReader

```
Public Function GetCustomerTable() As SqlCeDataReader
    Dim cn As System.Data.SqlServerCe.SqlCeConnection
    Dim cmd As System.Data.SqlServerCe.SqlCeCommand
    Dim dr As System.Data.SqlServerCe.SqlCeDataReader

    Try
        cn = New SqlCeConnection("Data Source=\ Chapter13.SDF")
        cn.Open()

        cmd = New SqlCeCommand("SELECT * FROM localAuthors", cn)
        return cmd.ExecuteReader(System.Data.CommandBehavior.CloseConnection)
    Catch ex As SqlCeException
        MessageBox.Show(ex.Message)
    Finally
        '    The connection is closed when the DataReader is closed
        '    if( cn != null )
        '        cn.Close();
        '    Normally I would not have these lines commented out but I left them
        '    in to emphasize the point that I do NOT want to close the connection
    End Try
End Function
```

To retrieve data from the device table, you can use a SqlCeDataReader. As you learned in Chapter 12, overloads of the **ExecuteReader** method allow you some flexibility of how to handle the connection. In Listing 13-10 you delay the close of the connection until the DataReader object is destroyed.

The code examples in the previous two listings and a basic knowledge of ADO.NET (as provided in Chapter 9) should give you enough information and background to be able to write code to do just about any data manipulation you need on your device-side data.

Running T-SQL on a Remote SQL Server

In addition to pushing and pulling data to and from a remote SQL Server, you can also execute Transact-SQL (T-SQL) commands on the data on the remote server. This is accomplished by using the **SubmitSql** method of the SqlCeRemoteDataAccess object as shown in Listing 13-11.

Listing 13-11. Submitting Commands to the Server

```
Private _strRemoteConnect As String = "provider=sqloledb;data source=antietam; "
strRemoteConnect &= "Initial Catalog=apress;IntegratedSecurity=SSPI";

Public Sub ExecuteTsqlCommand(ByVal sqlCommandText As String)
    Try
        Forms.Cursor.Current = Forms.Cursors.WaitCursor

        _rda.InternetLogin = "Antietam\Dan"
        _rda.InternetPassword = "<password>"
        _rda.InternetUrl = "http://antietam/ssce20/sscesa20.dll"
        _rda.LocalConnectionString = "Data Source=\Chapter13.sdf"
        _rda.SubmitSql(sqlCommandText, _strRemoteConnect)
    Catch ex As SqlCeException
        Dim q As String = ex.Message
    Finally
        Forms.Cursor.Current = Forms.Cursors.Default
    End Try
End Sub
```

The setup to make the **SubmitSql** call is identical to that for either a push or pull of data. Also, as in all of the previous code, you can use SQL Server authentication or either of the Windows authentication methods, Basic or Integrated Windows.

You now know everything needed to set up and run Remote Data Access from your .NET Compact Framework application. We have also looked at how to manipulate the data on the device using local SQL CE commands. After the previous discussion, you might not think that RDA is the easy way to get data back and forth from the server. But as you are about to see, there is still more to do to use merge replication.

Merge Replication

Replication in SQL Server CE is based on Microsoft SQL Server 2000 merge replication. While RDA let you do simple push and pulls of the data, you were responsible for maintaining data integrity when conflicts or errors arose. Merge replication allows data to be updated autonomously on the portable device and the server when the device is connected. The data on the device can then later be merged back to the remote SQL Server when the device is again connected.

In Chapter 11, you set up a distributor and a publication. When you defined the publication, you specified which fields of a table were to be exposed to subscribers. Through the publication, you can define and maintain what data is to be published to various sites. Publications also support row filtering so that only certain rows of a table are exposed to subscribers.

For instance, say you run a very large snack food company that has hundreds of trucks delivering hundreds of different products to customers around the world. Why would a driver in Fort Worth, Texas, care about the inventory for Mom's Grocery in Iowa? The driver probably wouldn't, and that is where row filtering comes in. Each device, normally associated with a driver, will have some identifier so that only the data rows of interest to that driver are synchronized with his or her device.

The architecture of replication is very similar to that of RDA. Figure 13-10 shows the components and flow between them for replication.

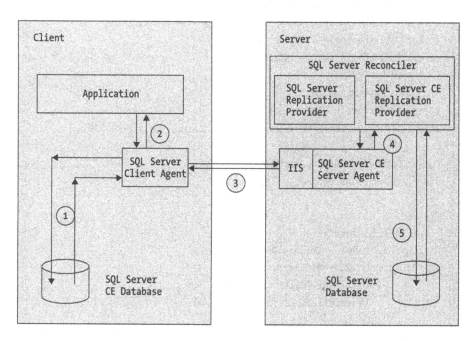

Figure 13-10. Replication architecture

The client side is the same as RDA, the changes are on the server side, where there is an additional agent that handles the replication. The SQL Server Reconciler hosts two different providers, one working on behalf of the device and one on behalf of SQL Server. Replication does have an ability to handle conflicts, and a discussion between the two providers is what will resolve the conflict. Enough of this talk. We'll discuss more specifics, and when to use replication versus remote data access, in a later section. It's time now to look at some code (see Listing 13-12).

Listing 13-12. SQL CE Replication

```
Public Sub Replication()
    Dim cerepl As SqlCeReplication = New SqlCeReplication
    cerepl.InternetLogin = "Antietam\Dan"
    cerepl.InternetPassword = "<password>"
    cerepl.InternetUrl = "http://antietam/ssce20/sscesa20.dll"

    '    Set the publisher.
    cerepl.Publication = "Apress_Pub"
    cerepl.PublisherDatabase = "Apress"
    cerepl.Publisher = "Antietam"
    cerepl.PublisherSecurityMode = SecurityType.NTAuthentication
    cerepl.PublisherLogin = String.Empty
    cerepl.PublisherPassword = String.Empty

    '    Set the subscriber.
    cerepl.Subscriber = "Apress_Sub"
    cerepl.SubscriberConnectionString = "data source=\Chapter13.SDF"

    Cursor.Current = Cursors.WaitCursor
    Dim flagChanges As Boolean = False

    Try
        cerepl.Synchronize()
        Cursor.Current = Cursors.Default
        If cerepl.PublisherChanges > 0 _
                Or cerepl.PublisherConflicts > 0 _
                Or cerepl.SubscriberChanges Then
            flagChanges = True
        End If
    Catch ex As SqlCeException
        Dim q As String = ex.Message
    Finally
        Cursor.Current = Cursors.Default
    End Try
End Sub
```

The object of our desire (sorry, I couldn't resist) in replication is the **SqlCeReplication** class. The majority of the code in Listing 13-12 is involved with the initialization of the SqlCeReplication object. The **InternetLogin**, **InternetPassword**, and **InternetUrl** properties are the same as when you work with the **SqlCeRemoteDataAccess** class. Replication involves a publisher and a subscriber. The publisher you set up when you installed the server tools of SQL

CE. Figure 13-11 shows the Apress database in SQL Server Enterprise Manager. I created a publisher called Apress_Pub that I assign to the SqlCeReplication objects' **Publication** property.

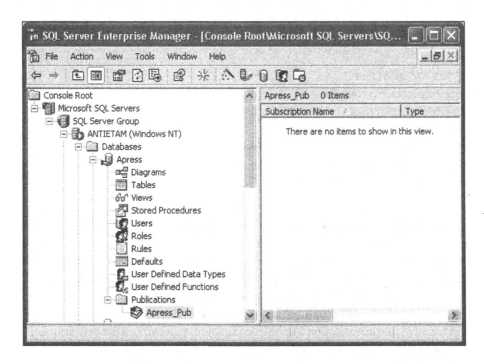

Figure 13-11. Publications on Antietam database

TIP *As you might have noticed by now, I am big on careful naming of objects. By default, the wizards try to name the publication the same name as the publisher. I find that to be very confusing. I like to append "_Pub" to the end of the name of publisher to make it as obvious as possible. Obviously, this only works with a single publication on a database. Later you will see that I append "_Sub" to the publisher name to denote my subscriber. You'll have to be more creative to name multiple publications and subscribers on the same publisher.*

PublisherDatabase is the name of the database from which the data is published, in this case Antietam, while **Publisher** is the server that is hosting the publisher. The next properties of the replication object are those involved with the security and login to the remote SQL Server. In Listing 13-12 you specify **NTAuthentication** as the security mode for this replication. **NTAuthentication**

takes the credentials that were used to authenticate with IIS and passes them on to SQL Server as the authentication credentials. Since you use **NTAuthentication**, you do not supply values for the **PublisherLogin** and **PublisherPassword** properties. The alternative is to use **DBAuthentication** as the publisher security mode, in which case you must supply a login and password as shown in the following code snippet:

```
'    Set the publisher.
cerepl.Publication = "Apress_Pub"
cerepl.PublisherDatabase = "Apress"
cerepl.Publisher = "Antietam"
cerepl.PublisherSecurityMode = SecurityType.DBAuthentication
cerepl.PublisherLogin = "webUser"
cerepl.PublisherPassword = "passw0rd"
```

After the publisher information has been completed, you need to initialize the information for the subscriber. In this example, you use Apress_Sub as the name of the subscriber. The device database is the subscriber, and this name uniquely defines this particular database. Other devices would have different subscription names. The **SubscriberConnectionString** is the same connection string you have been using to point to your local database.

After all of this initialization has been completed, you can call the **Synchronize** methods of SqlCeReplication to actually synchronize the data between the remote server and your local database. In Listing 13-12 I use three properties of the **SqlCeReplication** class to see if any changes were made to the database.

```
If cerepl.PublisherChanges > 0 _
        Or cerepl.PublisherConflicts > 0 _
        Or cerepl.SubscriberChanges Then
    flagChanges = True
End If
```

The number of conflicts or changes is provided through the three properties shown in the preceding code snippet. Those values can then be used to report back the results of the synchronization to the user.

```
MessageBox.Show("Synchronization Complete:" & vbCrLf & _
    "Publisher changes = " + cerepl.PublisherChanges.ToString() & vbCrLf & _
    "Publisher conflicts = " + cerepl.PublisherConflicts.ToString() & vbCrLf & _
    "Subscriber changes = " + cerepl.SubscriberChanges.ToString(), _
    "Apress", _
    MessageBoxButtons.OK, _
    MessageBoxIcon.Asterisk, _
    MessageBoxDefaultButton.Button1)
```

It's amazing really that the code for RDA and replication is rather simple and straightforward. You can cut and paste most everything except the various connect strings and credentials. That is why you create two classes that contain all of the code for connected and disconnected data handling. You can see the full code for both classes in the sample code under **Chapter 13** in the **Samples** folder.

Row Filtering

Now that you have seen how you use the publications from the database, it's time to look a little more at how to filter data based on the user doing the synchronization. There are two ways that you can do what SQL Server calls *row filtering*. The least scalable option would be to create a different publication for each user who needs to synchronize data. In the publication, you can specify a WHERE clause based on the filtering criteria. You might want to filter based on delivery area, and your WHERE clause for each publication could specify a different delivery code. If you have a large number of users, the administration of this design would be a nightmare. And if business picks up and you add 30 new drivers, you will have to create 30 new publications.

The second option is called *dynamic filtering*. Dynamic filters allow you to create a single publication and filter the returned data based on the connection properties from the replication object. To implement this method, you need to add a column to the published tables that identifies each customer to a driver. You can use the **InternetLogin** property of the replication as the value of this field. Then using a common SQL function such as SUSER_SNAME(), you can create a WHERE clause in the publication that looks like the following:

```
WHERE DriverID = SUSER_SNAME()
```

Now when you synchronize, you'll only get back the rows that have your login ID as the value in the DriverID column of the table.

This method, dynamic filters, is easily supported and easier to maintain than the multiple publication method. If you have a large number of new drivers, all that is required is a change to the customer records' DriverID value to filter the data being sent out to the drivers.

NOTE *When using dynamic filtering with SQL Server CE, you must set the optimize synchronization option when you create the publication or run the stored procedure **sp_runmergepublication**.*

TIP *I could spend another chapter discussing replication and filtering. Instead, let me point you in the direction of more information: You can go to SQL Server CE Books Online. You can get more detailed information about setting up publications in the SQL Server Online Help. The point is, if it's not in the CE Help, be sure to look in the Server Help.*

RDA or Replication, That Is the Question

So here you are, ready to run out and save the world from unsynchronized data. But which outfit should your superhero wear? Does your superhero use Remote Data Access or merge replication? They both have benefits. (Is that the easy way out or what!) With RDA the client is the controlling factor in what data gets transferred from the server, whereas with replication, the publication, and thus the server, controls the data being distributed. A change on the database may create a lot of work to be done on the code side to accommodate the changes.

For scalability, replication may be the best choice. For a central location, the server, you decide what data is delivered by changing the publication. As your business grows, you can add new users and change the data being distributed without changing a single client, all of whom may be spread around the country.

If your data on the device is basically static, and you only download it for informational purposes, then RDA may be the better way to handle your data. Using RDA may also be a better choice if you create new data on the device and add it to the server tables without attempting to update existing data. Replication requires a little more overhead and resources, which you may not need if you have a small operation, uploading data where the chance of conflicts with the data on the server is small.

The choice between RDA and replication comes down to scalability and data conflicts. Scalability is hard to pin down because what I think is scalable may not be to you. So let's look at something a little more concrete—data conflict and resolution.

Conflict and Resolution

When synchronization occurs, the Merge Agent on the publisher detects conflicts and then determines which data is accepted. Conflicts usually occur between updates made from different subscribers.

SQL Server CE only supports row-level tracking. This was done to save storage space on the device because row-level tracking involves less overhead for tracking changes.

NOTE *Publications on SQL Server allow column-level tracking in addition to row-level tracking. But since SQL CE does not support column-level tracking, any changes made on any column in a row will be flagged as a conflict.*

After a conflict is detected by the Merge Agent, it launches the conflict resolver specified when the publication was created. Other than the default resolver, you can implement your own custom resolver to deal with specific conflicts in your data. SQL Server CE subscriber conflicts are always detected, resolved, and logged at the publisher.

Summary

Devices, by their nature, are meant to be disconnected. When you are working with data that you need to move between a remote database and your device, you need to choose how to get that data from one database to the other. The options we looked at in this chapter are Remote Data Access and merge replication.

Remote Data Access is easier to implement in code and on the server. But RDA has limitations that may affect its performance in a large enterprise application. Resolving conflicts in RDA is more of a manual process. You can have conflicts reported back to you in an error table and then you are responsible, in code, for resolving the conflicts.

Replication is a more complicated system to set up. It requires you to create and maintain one or more publications on the database server. Those publications can be as simple as the wizard defaults that we discussed in Chapter 11 or they can become quite complex when you implement custom resolvers and dynamic filtering. While the code is slightly more involved, it is nothing when compared to the work in setting up the server. However, once publications have been set up, scalability in the enterprise is much easier to accomplish. Adding users and changing filters is easily done in a central location, reducing the need for software updates on the client devices.

Which is better is your choice, not mine. Hopefully after reading this chapter and reviewing the code samples and consulting help, you will be able to make an educated decision about which road to pursue.

Working with XML

THE PROMISE OF XML HAS BEEN, among other things, the ability to store data in just about any format you need; but, as you may have suspected, you have a somewhat limited range of choices for data storage in the .NET Compact Framework. Your choices? SQL Server CE, custom data files, text files, or XML files. We spent the last three chapters discussing SQL Server CE, and that might be your best option based on the business model that you're working under. However, there are situations in which you might not want to use SQL Server CE, even in its disconnected mode. In that case, you're pretty much reduced to using either your own data file format or XML files to store your data.

Not that XML is a bad option to pursue. In fact, in many situations you might want to use XML files in conjunction with other data storage mechanisms. If you've spent any time on the desktop working with .NET, you'll no doubt be familiar with the **Configuration** namespace and its set of classes.

This chapter isn't even going to try to provide you with an exhaustive coverage of XML and all of its industry-specific derivatives. What I'll cover here is the basic structure of an XML file and how to read and write to that file. We'll also look at how you can use the tools in the IDE to assist you in building XML files for the device. To accomplish this goal, I'll step you through the code required to implement the supported classes of the **System.Xml** namespace on the Pocket PC and then look at the desktop tools that can help you build your XML files easier than the tedious method of creating them by hand.

Basic XML

While I won't spend pages and pages explaining XML (there are more than enough books on the market that do that for you), I do think that it's important to have a few basics of XML up front to be sure we have some consistent level of understanding. As a longtime VB6 developer, I never did much, if anything, with XML. And, to be honest, once I started programming in .NET, the **Xml** namespace is the one I probably had the hardest time getting my head around. In the normal life of daily programming, the hidden secrets of XML have no real effect on your work. If you're writing Web services, you don't need to know XML, as that is all taken care of for you behind the scenes. But since you *will* be reading, writing, and parsing XML documents from your NETCF application, it'll be important to know a few terms and the basic structure of an XML document.

An XML document has a structured format that makes it extensible and flexible. Listing 14-1 shows a very basic XML document.

Listing 14-1. A Standard, Simple XML Document

```
<?xml version="1.0" encoding="utf-8" ?>
<Baseball>
    <Leagues>
        <League>
            <Name>American</Name>
            <LeagueID>10</LeagueID>
        </League>
        <League>
            <Name>National</Name>
            <LeagueID>11</LeagueID>
        </League>
    </Leagues>
    <Teams>
        <Team>
            <Name>Texas Rangers</Name>
            <TeamID>1</TeamID>
            <Wins>4</Wins>
            <Losses>5</Losses>
        </Team>
        <Team>
            <Name>Anaheim Angels</Name>
            <TeamID>2</TeamID>
            <Wins>7</Wins>
            <Losses>2</Losses>
        </Team>
        <Team>
            <Name>Oakland Athletics</Name>
            <TeamID>3</TeamID>
            <Wins>5</Wins>
            <Losses>4</Losses>
        </Team>
        <Team>
            <Name>Seattle Mariners</Name>
            <TeamID>4</TeamID>
            <Wins>5</Wins>
            <Losses>4</Losses>
        </Team>
    </Teams>
</Baseball>
```

The first line of the document is an XML declaration, and while there is currently only a single version of XML, this line always shows a version number of 1.0. The *encoding* value tells the parser what language will be found in the document. The next line defines the first *element* of the document, which is often called the *root element*. Inside the Baseball element are the child elements. In this example, there is a collection of League elements and a collection of Team elements. Notice that this listing is constructed using nothing but elements. Another way to build an XML file is by using *attributes*. Listing 14-2 shows how to build the same information into a document using elements and attributes.

Listing 14-2. A Standard, Simple XML Document, Using Attributes

```
<?xml version="1.0" encoding="utf-8"?>
<Baseball>
    <Leagues>
        <League Name="American" LeagueID="10" />
        <League Name="National" LeagueID="11" />
        <League Name="Texas" LeagueID="12" />
    </Leagues>
</Baseball>
```

The League element still exists as in the previous example, but in this code the element is combined with two attributes, Name and LeagueID. This is as basic as you can make the XML document structure. And, for now, this is good enough to get you started reading and writing XML documents. Listings 14-1 and 14-2 will be the basis for learning how to read a file based on the **Xml** namespace.

> **NOTE** *It's okay to mix blocks of element-only XML in the same document as blocks of element/attribute XML. In fact, this is common practice. So when it comes to XML, you can have your cake and eat it, too.*

Unlike HTML, XML tags *must* be properly structured to avoid ambiguity of the markup in the document. In HTML it isn't always necessary to close off tags (<P> comes to mind as the biggest offender in HTML). An XML parser won't take an educated guess like an HTML parser does; if the structure is bad, the XML parser raises an error. You can get help to verify the structure of your XML documents through the use of document type definitions (DTDs) or an XML schema. I'll cover these two topics later.

NOTE *Maybe I would have been better off to not even mention DTD here. But if I didn't, you might say, "Hey, what about DTD?" So I'll give you a few seconds to think about what I am about to tell you. The NETCF **Xml** namespace doesn't support document type definitions. The desktop framework has a class in the **Xml** namespace called **XmlValidatingReader** that can validate your XML document against the embedded DTD. This method isn't supported in NETCF, and in fact, if you place DTD in your XML document, you'll get an exception from XmlTextReader. What this means is that you'll need to handle your XML validation using XML schemas. This is actually a good option as the DataSet and XmlTextReader are implemented to make it easy to use and create schemas.*

TIP *XML names are case sensitive! If you edit some string in an XML document, be sure you keep the case of all letters the same. If you inadvertently change them, your code will no longer work. And, of course, you'll find this out just before you're supposed to leave for a skiing trip and a big release is due in 2 days.*

So, if both elements and attributes can be used, how do you know when to use which? Each has benefits and each has shortcomings. Much of the decision will be based on personal preference, but let me point out a couple of items to help you make your choice. In general, representing data with elements will take up more space than when using attributes. If you have a very large document being transmitted over a phone connection from your device, this could be a real concern.

If you need to store data that contains markup characters (&, >, etc.), then you can use a CDATA section. CDATA constructs can only be used in an element.

```
<comment>Combined the Rangers [![ CDATA[&]]>
Angels have fewer wins than the Yankees</comment>
```

The preceding listing shows how you would represent the text "Rangers & Angels" inside of an element. This would not be possible if you were using attributes. You would have to use those nasty &lt, &gt, &amp sequences to represent the <, >, & characters in your attributes. CDATA makes it a little less tedious.

Attributes are very good for adding descriptive information to an element. In Listing 14-2, the LeagueID attribute describes the League element. This is more intuitive than adding another element as a child to League to define its ID. In most cases, either works fine, and if you search on the Internet long enough, you'll be able to find arguments supporting both approaches. Speaking of searching the Internet, the following sites will give you a sampling of what you can find:

- http://www.codehound.com

- http://www.javaworld.com/javaworld/jw-04-1999/jw-04-xml.html

The first site, CodeHound, has a page that exclusively searches XML sites, making the results a little more targeted than your everyday search engine.

Using the XmlTextReader

We have two code listings that need to be read to retrieve data, one that is element based and the other that is attribute based. Before getting into the specifics, though, you need to know how to do something as simple as open an XML file and read it. You can see in Listing 14-3 the code required to open and read a file.

Listing 14-3. Reading a File with XmlTextReader

```
Dim dr As XmlTextReader
Dim fs As FileStream = New FileStream(AppPath()  & "XMLFile1.xml",
FileMode.Open)
Dim sb As StringBuilder = New StringBuilder
dr = New XmlTextReader(fs)
While dr.Read()
    sb.Append(String.Format("{0} {1} {2}" & vbCrLf, dr.NodeType, dr.Name,
    dr.Value.ToString()))
End While
TextBox1.Text = sb.ToString()
dr.Close()
fs.Close()
```

The code in Listing 14-3 opens an XML file (the file shown in Listing 14-1) using a FileStream object and, using XmlTextReader, walks through the file, adding each element to a string that is displayed in the text box. The output of this code can be seen in Figure 14-1. You can see in the output that the Name element is bracketed by Element/EndElement tags. There are also node types displayed as WhiteSpace and followed by a line feed (and thus a blank line).

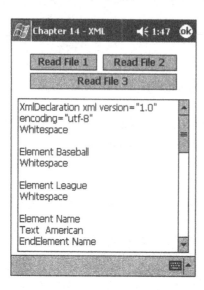

Figure 14-1. Looking at a file of XML elements

NOTE *Like DataReader, which was discussed in Chapter 9 and in Chapters 11 through 13, XmlTextReader is very fast and is a forward-only data pipe. XmlTextReader reads a single node from the file at a time, without validating the markup against the schema.*

If you want to display the file without the white spaces, you can do so by adding the following line to the code in Listing 14-3:

```
dr.WhitespaceHandling = WhitespaceHandling.Significant
```

In XML, there are such things as significant white space and insignificant white space. The preceding line tells XmlTextReader to show only the significant white space that is encountered in the document. Normally, however, you aren't looking to display an XML file and are more interested in reading the data stored in the file. In particular, you want to get data from the elements of the document in Listing 14-1.

NOTE *I mentioned back in Chapter 7 about the problems caused by trying to reference image paths in a program. The same sort of problem comes up again as you try to open and save files in these XML demos. If you use a hard-coded path, then the files aren't copied for you when the application is deployed by the debugger. I would use the old Visual Basic method **App.Path** if it existed in .NET, but it doesn't. What's a developer to do except to dive into the .NET Framework and find an alternative?*

```
Private Function AppPath() As String
        ' Fetch the location where the application was launched.
        AppPath = _
          System.IO.Path.GetDirectoryName(Reflection.Assembly. _
          GetExecutingAssembly().GetName().CodeBase.ToString())
      End Function
```

 NOTE *This code uses reflection to retrieve information about the currently running application. If you need a function to replace the beloved **App.Path**, this code will do it for you. And for nostalgic reasons, it even has a name that will make you think, for a minute, that you are back in VB 6.*

Reading Data from Elements

As you saw in the previous code segment, it's easy to walk through the file and look at nodes and values. Luckily, though, XmlTextReader makes it even easier to pull data from an element in the document. Let's say you want to obtain a list of all of the leagues in the file and their associated IDs. The grunt way is to perform a read operation until you find the node in which you're interested and then perform another read operation and look at the value of the element. In Listing 14-4, you can see another way to get the data from the element, using the **ReadElementString** method of XmlTextReader.

Listing 14-4. Using the ReadElementString Method of XmlTextReader

```
Dim dr As XmlTextReader
Dim fs As FileStream = New FileStream("\xmlfile1.xml", FileMode.Open)
Dim sb As StringBuilder = New StringBuilder
```

```
dr = New XmlTextReader(fs)
dr.WhitespaceHandling = WhitespaceHandling.Significant
While dr.Read()
    If dr.NodeType = XmlNodeType.Element And dr.Name = "League" Then
        '     Now we are in the element of interest.
        '     Read the next two elements and get their data.
        dr.Read()
        sb.Append(String.Format("Name: {0}  ", dr.ReadElementString()))
        sb.Append(String.Format("ID: {0}" & vbCrLf, dr.ReadElementString()))
    End If
End While
TextBox1.Text = sb.ToString()
dr.Close()
fs.Close()
```

This code finds all of the League elements and builds a string based on the values of the Name and ID elements contained in the League element. Notice that the **ReadElementString** method advances the reader to the next element. Remember back in Listing 14-3 that repeatedly calling **Read** returns node types of Element and EndElement. Using **ReadElementString** skips those node types and positions the reader at the next element. If you try to put a **Read** method call between the two calls to **ReadElementString**, you'll raise an exception because you aren't on an element and therefore unable to perform a read.

> **NOTE** *If you know anything about XML, right now you might be asking yourself why I am not using an XPath method such as **SelectSingleNode** to locate and read the value from the League elements. One big reason comes to mind: XPath and its associated methods aren't supported on the .NET Compact Framework.*

Writing Data to Elements

Great, now you can read an XML file, but if you are going to use this file as some sort of data store, you'll need to be able to make changes to the values and write them back to the file. First you need to know the basics of how to write using the **XmlTextWriter** class, and the code in Listing 14-5 shows these basics.

Listing 14-5. Writing XML Through XmlTextWriter

```
Private Sub WriteNewXmlFile()
    Dim dw As XmlTextWriter
    Dim fsOut As FileStream = New FileStream(AppPath() _
        & "XmlTestFile.xml", FileMode.Create)

    dw = New XmlTextWriter(fsOut, System.Text.Encoding.UTF8)
    dw.Formatting = Formatting.Indented
    dw.Indentation = 4

    dw.WriteStartElement("Baseball")
    dw.WriteStartElement("Teams")
    dw.WriteStartElement("Team")
    dw.WriteElementString("Name", "Texas Rangers")
    dw.WriteElementString("Manager", "Buck Showalter")
    dw.WriteElementString("Stadium", "Ballpark in Arlington")
    dw.WriteEndElement()
    dw.WriteStartElement("Team")
    dw.WriteStartElement("Name")
    dw.WriteString("Anaheim Angels")
    dw.WriteEndElement()
    dw.WriteStartElement("Manager")
    dw.WriteString("Mike Scioscia")
    dw.WriteEndElement()
    dw.WriteStartElement("Stadium")
    dw.WriteString("Edison Field")
    dw.WriteEndElement()        '    Close the Stadium element.
    dw.WriteEndElement()        '    Close the Team element.
    dw.WriteEndElement()        '    Close the Teams element.
    dw.WriteEndElement()        '    Close the BaseBall element.
    dw.Close()
    fsOut.Close()
End Sub
```

As shown in the code, there are two ways that you can write an element out to the file. The first, and preferred by those who are keyboard impaired, is the simple **WriteElementString** method that is used in the portion of the listing that writes the information about the Texas Rangers. This one line takes care of the beginning element, the text, and the ending element. The other option is to specifically call the **WriteStartElement** and **WriteEndElement** methods, sandwiched around the **WriteString** method. This technique was used in the listing to write the Angels information to the file.

NOTE *Sometimes I may sound like a broken record, but I want to remind you that when you are finished using a FileStream, XmlTextWriter, or an XmlTextReader object, you need to call the **Close** method. I keep saying this because it's important to remember and critical to the performance and reliability of your .NET applications. To prove a point, if you remove the **Close** method calls in Listing 14-5 and try to open the file to dump its contents to a text box, you get a **System.IO.IOException**.*

XmlTextWriter exposes 27 **Write** methods for various data types and different pieces of an XML document. The various methods are explained thoroughly in the .NET documentation and in numerous books, so I won't delve into them any further here. One point I do want to make is about opening either a reader or writer. In these examples, I have initially created a FileStream object and used that in the constructor for the XmlTextReader or XmlTextWriter objects. I could just as well have used code similar to the following:

```
Dim dw As XmlTextWriter
dw = New XmlTextWriter("\XmlTestFile.xml", System.Text.Encoding.UTF8)
```

One of the advantages of using a stream object is that you have more control over how the file is opened. The FileMode enum parameter in the FileStream constructor lets you specify if the file is opened as a read-only or write-only file. It also lets you tell the stream to create, append, or delete an old file before operating on the file. The XmlTextWriter constructor has one mode, truncate and overwrite. If that is all you need, then the code is simpler to write without using the FileStream object.

Using Attributes in the XML Document

You may also have seen XML documents formatted like the one shown in Listing 14-6, using *attributes* in addition to the elements you have already discovered.

Listing 14-6. An XML Document Using Attributes

```
<?xml version="1.0" encoding="utf-8"?>
<Baseball>
    <Leagues>
        <League Name="American" LeagueID="10" />
        <League Name="National" LeagueID="11" />
        <League Name="Texas" LeagueID="12" />
    </Leagues>
```

```
    <Teams>
        <Team Name="Texas Rangers" TeamID="1" Wins="7" Loses="9" />
        <Team Name="Anaheim Angels" TeamID="2" Wins="8" Loses="8" />
        <Team Name="Oakland Athletics" TeamID="3" Wins="8" Loses="8" />
        <Team Name="Seattle Mariners" TeamID="4" Wins="9" Loses="7" />
    </Teams>
</Baseball>
```

Reading Attributes in the Document

In the previous sections, elements hold all of the information in the document. The work to read and write an XML document using attributes is a little different than what you saw in the last section. The code in Listing 14-7 is a simple routine to walk through an XML document and print out the elements and their attributes.

Listing 14-7. Listing a Document's Elements and Attributes

```
Private Sub ReadXmlAttributes(ByVal fileName As String)
    Dim dr As XmlTextReader
    Dim strPath As String = AppPath() & fileName

    dr = New XmlTextReader(strPath)
    dr.WhitespaceHandling = WhitespaceHandling.None
    TextBox1.Text = String.Empty

    While dr.Read()
        If dr.NodeType = XmlNodeType.Element Then
            TextBox1.Text &= dr.Name.ToString() & "Name: " & _
                vbTab & dr.GetAttribute("Name") & vbCrLf
        , End If
    End While
    dr.Close()
End Sub
```

One nice thing about XmlTextReader is that if you try to access an attribute on an element where none exists, you don't get an exception raised. If you want to check to see if the element has an attribute, you can adjust your code to use the **HasAttributes** property of XmlTextReader.

```
While dr.Read()
    If dr.NodeType = XmlNodeType.Element And dr.HasAttributes Then
        TextBox1.Text &= "(" & dr.Name.ToString() & ") Name: " & _
            vbTab & dr.GetAttribute("Name") & vbCrLf
    End If
End While
```

This code will remove the elements with no attributes (Baseball and Teams) that are shown in the XML file of Figure 14-2. The output of the code is shown in Figure 14-3.

Figure 14-2. The baseball XML file, containing elements with and without attributes

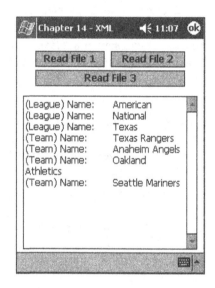

Figure 14-3. Outputting a file, removing elements with no attributes

As in the examples using elements, there is one major problem with accessing the data in this manner. You've hard-coded attribute names in the element, which can be a problem if the format of the document changes. When using elements only, you have the same problem: how to adjust your code at runtime to handle new information or format changes in the document.

The **XmlTextReader** class has two methods that allow you to look at all attributes that are associated with a particular element. Listing 14-8 shows how to use the **MoveToFirstAttribute** and **MoveToNextAttribute** methods to display all of the attributes in an element and Figure 14-4 shows the output of the code.

Listing 14-8. Looking at All of the Attributes Dynamically

```
Private Sub ReadXmlAttributesDynamic(ByVal fileName As String)
    Dim dr As XmlTextReader
    Dim strPath As String = AppPath() & fileName

    dr = New XmlTextReader(strPath)
    dr.WhitespaceHandling = WhitespaceHandling.None
    TextBox1.Text = String.Empty

    While dr.Read()
        If dr.NodeType = XmlNodeType.Element And dr.HasAttributes Then
            TextBox1.Text &= "(" & dr.Name.ToString() & ")" & vbCrLf
            '    Walk and look at all elements.
            dr.MoveToFirstAttribute()
            TextBox1.Text &= vbTab & "{" & dr.Name & "}" & _
                vbTab & dr.Value & vbCrLf
            While dr.MoveToNextAttribute
                TextBox1.Text &= vbTab & "{" & dr.Name & "}" & _
                    vbTab & dr.Value & vbCrLf
            End While
            dr.MoveToElement()
        End If
    End While
    dr.Close()
End Sub
```

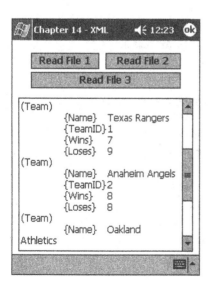

Figure 14-4. Reading the attributes in an element dynamically

The **MoveToElement** method sets the "pointer" back to the element that owns the attributes. In the current example, this is really not required. However, if you want to do more work with the element itself using other methods of the reader, then this call would be required to get the reader to point back to the correct location in the stream.

Writing Attributes to the Document

Your next step is to see how to create an XML document using attributes. You'll be creating the counterpart to the document that was created back in Listing 14-5. As you can see in Listing 14-9, you have to open a stream for the new file, write the beginning elements for Baseball and Teams, and include a **WriteStartElement** method for each team you are adding.

Listing 14-9. Creating a Document Using Attributes

```
Private Sub WriteNewXmlFileWithAttributes()
    Dim dw As XmlTextWriter
    Dim fsOut As FileStream = New FileStream( _
        AppPath() & "\XmlOutAttrib.xml", FileMode.Create)

    dw = New XmlTextWriter(fsOut, System.Text.Encoding.UTF8)
    dw.WriteStartElement("Baseball")
    dw.WriteStartElement("Teams")
    dw.WriteStartElement("Team")
    dw.WriteAttributeString("Name", "Texas Rangers")
    dw.WriteAttributeString("Manager", "Buck Showalter")
    dw.WriteAttributeString("Stadium", "Ballpark in Arlington")
    dw.WriteEndElement()    '    Close the Team element.
    dw.WriteStartElement("Team")
    dw.WriteAttributeString("Name", "Anaheim Angels")
    dw.WriteAttributeString("Manager", "Mike Scioscia")
    dw.WriteAttributeString("Stadium", "Edison Field")
    dw.WriteEndElement()    '    Close the Team element.
    dw.WriteStartElement("Team")
    dw.WriteAttributeString("Name", "Oakland Athletics")
    dw.WriteAttributeString("Manager", "Ken Macha")
    dw.WriteAttributeString("Stadium", "Network Associates Coliseum")
    dw.WriteEndElement()    '    Close the Team element.
    dw.WriteStartElement("Team")
```

```
        dw.WriteAttributeString("Name", "Seattle Mariners")
        dw.WriteAttributeString("Manager", "Bob Melvin")
        dw.WriteAttributeString("Stadium", "SAFECO Field")
        dw.WriteEndElement()    '    Close the Team element.
        dw.WriteEndElement()    '    Close the Teams element.
        dw.WriteEndElement()    '    Close the BaseBall element.
        dw.Close()
        fsOut.Close()
End Sub
```

The difference from the previous examples is that instead of creating a new element and writing data to that element, you call the **WriteAttributeString** method to add attributes to the current element. After all attributes are written, the element is closed with a call to **WriteEndElement** and the next element is created until all elements and their attributes are written to your file. And since I am trying to set a good example for you, note that I also closed both the DataReader and the file string. The file created from this code is displayed in the browser, as shown in Figure 14-5.

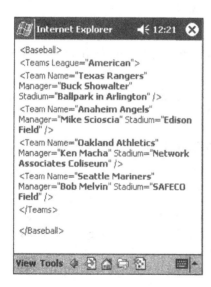

Figure 14-5. The baseball XML file, with attributes

Using **WriteAttributeString** works well when you have a simple attribute to put into the element. The **XmlTextWriter** class has a variety of methods to write data to the document. Table 14-1 shows a subset of those methods.

Table 14-1. XmlTextWriter Methods to Write Data to the XML Document

METHOD	DESCRIPTION
WriteAttributes	Writes out all of the attributes in current scope of an XmlTextReader. This is often used when copying portions of one document to another.
WriteBase64	Writes the given byte array to the stream encoded as Base64.
WriteBinHex	Writes the given byte array to the stream as binhex.
WriteCData	Writes the given string inside a CDATA block (<![CDATA[ ]]>).
WriteChars	Writes the specified number of characters from the given char array.
WriteComment	Writes the given string inside a comment marker (<!-- -->).
WriteElementString	Writes the element with the given string.
WriteEndAttribute	Writes the closing tag for the open attribute.
WriteEndDocument	Writes the closing of any open element or attribute.
WriteEndElement	Writes the closing element.
WriteNode	Writes the current node in XmlTextReader to the XmlTextWriter stream, moving the reader to the start of the next sibling.
WriteRaw	Writes the given markup directly into the document.
WriteStartAttribute	Writes the start of an attribute.
WriteStartDocument	Writes the XML declaration found at the top of the document.
WriteStartElement	Writes the given start tag.
WriteString	Writes out the given text. Several conversions are made when the text is written. The &, <, > characters are replaced with &, <, and >. Single quotes are replaced with ' and double quotes are replaced with ".

NOTE *I have kept away from an explanation of advanced XML data, like CDATA and entities, for a reason. I did so to make the code in this chapter simpler and easier to follow. The purpose of the previous sections is to get you familiar enough with writing and reading simple XML documents so that you can create your own configuration files. If you need to know the intimate details of complex XML, you can find a plethora of other books dedicated to this subject. Often when I read an XML book (or a chapter in some other book), it's like giving a calculus book to my third grader. After the title, I'm lost! In this book, I'm just trying to show the basics, nothing more. If you have the basics down and feel comfortable with them, you can move on as you see fit.*

Step-by-Step Tutorial: Creating a Configuration Reader

I gave you several good lectures in Chapters 11 through 13 about not keeping connection strings and such in your code. Now it's time to put my money where my mouth is. This tutorial will walk you through setting up an application that will open a configuration file and read the requested value.

Step 1: Starting a New Project

Begin this step-by-step exercise by creating a new project using the following steps:

1. Start Visual Studio .NET if necessary.

2. From the Start Page, select **New Project**.

3. From the New Project dialog box, select **Smart Device Application**.

4. Specify a project name of **XmlConfigReader Demo**.

5. Select a location to create the project.

6. Select the project type **Windows Application** and click the **OK** button.

Step 2: Adding an XML File

You need an XML file to read your configuration data from, and you can add it to your project from the Solution Explorer. To do so, perform the following steps:

1. In the Solution Explorer, right-click the project name and click the **Add |
   Add New Item** menu selection.

2. Select **XML File** from the Add New Item dialog box, name the file
   app.config in the Name text box, and click the **Open** button.

3. Replace the file contents (without the line breaks) with the following
   information:

```
<Application>
  <Settings>
    <Setting Name="ConnectString" Value="provider=sqloledb;
        data source=antietam;Initial Catalog=apress;" />
    <Setting Name="URLString"
        Value="http://fsg-server/ssce20/sscesa20.dll" />
    <Setting Name="DataSource"
        Value="DataSource=\Storage Card\Chapter13.sdf" />
  </Settings>
</Application>
```

4. You want Visual Studio to copy this file to your application directory for
   you. Select the **app.config** file in the Solution Explorer, click the **Build
   Action** property in the Properties window, and select **Content** from the
   drop-down list. By default, this value is set to None.

5. Save and close the file.

Step 3: Adding Controls to the Form

You need an interface to get input and display the output. Add two TextBox
controls and a Button control to the form and set the properties as shown in
Tables 14-2 through 14-4.

Table 14-2. TextBox1 Properties

OBJECT	PROPERTY	VALUE
TextBox1	Location	8, 24
TextBox1	Size	216, 22
TextBox1	Text	ConnectionString
TextBox1	Name	txtInput

Table 14-3. TextBox2 Properties

OBJECT	PROPERTY	VALUE
TextBox2	Location	8, 112
TextBox2	Size	216, 22
TextBox2	Text	<empty>
TextBox2	MultiLine	True
TextBox2	Name	txtOutput

Table 14-4. Button Properties

OBJECT	PROPERTY	VALUE
Button1	Location	8, 56
Button1	Size	216, 20
Button1	Text	Go Get It
Button1	Name	btnGoGetIt

Step 4: Creating a ConfigReader Class

With the idea of making this into a real class that all of your future applications can use, you're going to create a new class that can be expanded and moved to its own project later. To create the class, perform the following steps:

1. If not already in the code window, move there by pressing the F7 key.

2. Add a new class definition to the Form1.vb file by including the following code:

```
Public Class ConfigReader
    Public Sub New()
    End Sub
End Class
```

3. The configuration file that you created back in Step 3 will follow the same rules for configuration files on the desktop framework. For now that means it will be located in the same directory as your application. Add the following code to the **ConfigReader** class:

```
Private Function AppPath() As String
    ' Fetch the location where the application was launched.
    AppPath = _
        System.IO.Path.GetDirectoryName(Reflection.Assembly. _
        GetExecutingAssembly().GetName().CodeBase.ToString())
End Function
```

4. You need a method that will take a parameter specifying the setting name that returns a string to represent the value. Add the following code to the **ConfigReader** class:

```
Public Function GetConfig(ByVal fieldName As String) As String
    Dim dr As XmlTextReader
    Dim strPath As String = AppPath() & "\app.config"

    Try
        dr = New XmlTextReader(strPath)
        dr.WhitespaceHandling = WhitespaceHandling.None

        While dr.Read()
            If dr.NodeType = XmlNodeType.Element _
            And dr.HasAttributes Then
                If dr.Name.ToString() = "Setting" Then
                    '   Walk and look at all elements.
                    dr.MoveToFirstAttribute()
                    If dr.Name = "Name" Then
                        If dr.Value = fieldName Then
                            'Get the next attribute.
```

```
                                While dr.MoveToNextAttribute()
                                    If dr.Name = "Value" Then
                                        Return dr.Value
                                    End If
                                End While
                            End If
                        End If
                    End If
                End If
            End While
            '    If we get here, nothing was found.
            Return String.Empty
        Finally
            dr.Close()
        End Try
    End Function
```

5. Create an event handler for the **btnGoGetIt** button by returning to the
    designer and double-clicking the button. To call your new **GetConfig**
    method, add the following code to the event handler:

```
Dim cfr As ConfigReader = New ConfigReader

cfr = New ConfigReader
txtOutput.Text = cfr.GetConfig(txtInput.Text)
```

Your new class now calls into your app.config file and pulls the value associated with the requested name in the Setting element.

HOMEWORK   *The tutorial code might return the wrong value (or no
value) if more than one element in the file has a **Setting** property.
In your sample app.config file, a Setting element only occurs inside
the Settings element. Add the code to make sure that you only look
for the Name/Value pairs inside a Settings element.*

HOMEWORK   *What good is a configuration class that can't write new
data back to the file? Add to the tutorial code and provide a method
to write new elements or update current values in your configuration file.*

DOM Navigation of Your Documents

An alternative to XmlTextReader and XmlTextWriter is the Document Object Model (DOM) interface. The DOM interface loads the entire document into memory at one time, so, unlike the forward-only stream-based classes, you can explore and freely move around in the document.

NOTE   *This last statement should raise a big red flag. What is one of the key concerns in applications running on memory-constrained (that was a hint) devices? Memory, of course! If your XML document is very large, then you might not want to use the DOM to read and analyze the data. When would you use the DOM? One instance would be if you need access to a large portion of the documents data. If you need only a small portion of the data, then you might be better off using one of the streaming methods to read or write the file. If you have several documents to parse through at the same time, you might be better off using the **XmlTextReader** class instead of the DOM. If you have several documents open with DOM, then you are using a lot of memory, and that might not be a good thing. In general, remember that the DOM classes require greater resources than the stream-based classes. Recall that XmlTextReader only brings a single node into memory at a time, whereas the DOM loads the entire document and requires no memory for the schema.*

Reading Elements with the DOM

Listing 14-10 shows you how to read all of the teams from the document created in Listing 14-9. The output of Listing 14-10 is shown in Figure 14-6.

Listing 14-10. Reading a File Using the DOM

```
Private Sub ReadingWithDOM()
    Dim xd As XmlDocument = New XmlDocument

    xd.Load(AppPath() & "\XmlOutAttrib.xml")
    Dim teams As XmlNodeList

    TextBox1.Text = String.Empty
    teams = xd.GetElementsByTagName("Team")
```

```
    For Each xm As XmlNode In teams
        For Each att As XmlAttribute In xm.Attributes
            TextBox1.Text &= att.Name & ":  " & att.Value() & vbCrLf
        Next
        TextBox1.Text &= vbCrLf
    Next
End Sub
```

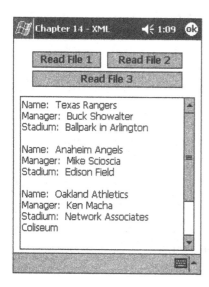

Figure 14-6. A view from the DOM

After the document is loaded, the **GetElementsByTagName** method is called. This method returns an XmlNodeList object that contains a list of all descendent elements that match the name specified in the method argument. You can then walk through each element in the list, accessing the attributes through an XmlAttribute object.

> **NOTE** *As you review the documentation in Visual Studio, you'll notice that most of the methods for the DOM are supported in the .NET Compact Framework. But you'll also notice a consistent pattern to what isn't available, and that is anything to do with **SelectNodes** or any methods that require XPath expressions. I am sure that I've mentioned this before, but here I go again: The .NET Compact Framework doesn't support XPath. This means if you want to get a list of nodes that is more specific than that returned by **GetElementsByTagName**, you won't be able to use **SelectNodes** to do it.*

The .NET Compact Framework doesn't support the **GetElementsByID** method found in the full framework. Again, you are forced to do a little more work to both structure your XML in a consistent format and to get the data out of the file.

Writing Elements with the DOM

Now that you can read data out of your XML file, let's see if you can write something back into the file. Listing 14-11 shows how you use the DOM interface to add a new Team element to your XML file.

Listing 14-11. Writing to a Document with the DOM

```
Dim xd As XmlDocument = New XmlDocument
xd.Load(AppPath() & "\XmlOutAttrib.xml")

Dim xe As XmlElement = xd.CreateElement("Team")
xe.SetAttribute("Name", "New York Yankees")
xe.SetAttribute("Manager", "Joe Torre")
xe.SetAttribute("Stadium", "Yankee Stadium")
Dim teams As XmlNodeList = xd.GetElementsByTagName("Teams")

teams.Item(0).AppendChild(xe)
xd.Save("\XmlTest10.xml")
```

This code shows that you open the XML document just as you do when you want to read from the document. In fact, you can open the document and use the same object to write or read without closing or changing the state of the object. Notice the call to **GetElementsByTagName** in the listing. If you tried to add the new Team element to the document, it would throw an **InvalidOperationException** at runtime. You need to take care that you add the new element to the correct node in the document.

 HOMEWORK   *Using the DOM interface, create a class that reads and writes from an application configuration file. The class should have at least two methods, **GetSetting** and **SaveSetting**. You can use some ideas from the previous homework assignment in which you create the code to write to a configuration file using the **XmlTextWriter** class.*

As you can see, reading data from and writing data to an XML file can be tedious work. But what other way do you have to manipulate data besides XML?

Other than SQL Server, there aren't many choices. One option you do have is to store your data in an XML file but manipulate it through a DataSet, which we'll look at next.

Working with XML Data Using a DataSet

The first step to using a DataSet to massage your XML data is to load the XML document into the DataSet. This is done using the **ReadXml** method as shown in Listing 14-12.

Listing 14-12. Massaging XML Data Using a DataSet

```
Private Sub ManipulateXmlDataDataSet()
    Dim ds As DataSet = New DataSet

    ds.ReadXml(AppPath() & "\XmlTest10.xml")
    Dim tab As DataTable = ds.Tables(0)
    For Each dr As DataRow In tab.Rows
        Dim str() As Object = dr.ItemArray()
    Next
    Dim ddr As DataRow = tab.NewRow()
    ddr(0) = "1"
    ddr(1) = "National"
    tab.Rows.Add(ddr)


    tab = ds.Tables(1)
    For Each dr As DataRow In tab.Rows
        Dim str() As Object = dr.ItemArray()
    Next
    ddr = tab.NewRow
    ddr(0) = "Atlanta Braves"
    ddr(1) = "Bobby Cox"
    ddr(2) = "Turner Field"
    ddr(3) = 1
    tab.Rows.Add(ddr)

  Dim xw As XmlWriter = New XmlTextWriter( _
        AppPath() & "\XmlTest11.xml", System.Text.Encoding.UTF8)
    ds.WriteXml(xw, Data.XmlWriteMode.WriteSchema)
    ds.WriteXmlSchema(AppPath() & "\XmlTest10.xsd")
End Sub
```

I could probably have chosen an easier example to start with, but what the heck, it'll be fun. The XML document used for this example is the same as before with only a simple modification. Notice in Figure 14-7 that the Teams element now has an attribute specifying the league to which the teams belong. At present, only the single Teams element is shown.

Figure 14-7. A new attribute added to the Teams element for the sample XML file

When the DataSet loads the document, it has to create a table (or tables in this case) to hold the data. For your test file, two tables are created. The first table has a single row that has two fields whose values are American and the number 0. The second table has 5 rows (one for each team in the file). The fields are the team name, the manager, the name of the stadium, and an integer number. The integer is the key that relates this table to the first table. If you do some snooping around in the Watch windows while running the program, you can see in the DataSet object that the Relations object contains an item. Exploring this item, you can see that the DataSet has created keys on both tables and set up a relationship between those two keys. The Teams element has become the ParentTable, while the Team elements are defined as the ChildTable.

To verify this programmatically, the code in Listing 14-12 adds a new row to the first table using a new number for the index. You then get a reference to the Teams table and add a new row to it. After adding the new data, the file is saved to memory. To write the data back to an XML file, you use the **WriteXml** method. The .NET Compact Framework doesn't support several of the desktop overloads for this method, and in fact you are reduced to two choices. One is shown earlier where you pass an XmlTextWriter object to the **WriteXml** method along with an enum value that tells the framework whether the schema should be written out or ignored, or whether the data should be written as a DiffGram. The other overload supported by NETCF is shown next. Using this method, you specify a filename directly without having to create an XmlTextWriter. However, this does limit you to writing only the XML data to the file.

```
ds.WriteXml("\XmlTest11.xml")
```

Listing 14-12 also shows how you can write the schema for your data out to an XSD file by calling the **WriteSchema** method on the DataSet object. Figure 14-8 shows that the code indeed added a new Teams element along with the corresponding Team element for the Atlanta Braves.

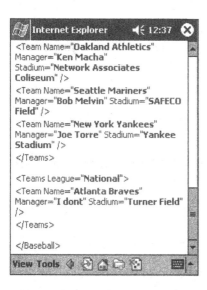

Figure 14-8. New data in a DataSet written to XML

Looking at Data Schemas

When working in NETCF, you're a little limited in your use of schema files. NETCF doesn't support enough of the Schema object to be useful, and you can't specify the XSD file as a parameter to any calls. The best opportunity to use schemas is when loading and saving data from a DataSet. Listing 14-13 shows you the simple code to load the data, along with the schema, from an XML document into a DataSet.

Listing 14-13. Using a Schema with a DataSet

```
Dim ds As DataSet = New DataSet
Dim xmlPath As String = AppPath() & "\XmlTest11.xml"

' Create new FileStream to read the schema with.
Dim fsReadXml As New System.IO.FileStream(xmlPath, System.IO.FileMode.Open)
' Create an XmlTextReader.
Dim xmlReader As New System.Xml.XmlTextReader(fsReadXml)
' Load the data from the XML document.
ds.ReadXml(xmlReader)
' Close the XmlTextReader.
xmlReader.Close()
```

The **ReadXml** method of the DataSet has a couple more overloads not shown in Listing 14-13. Of particular interest is the method that lets you specify how you wish to handle the schema associated with the data.

```
' Load the data from the XML document.
ds.ReadXml(xmlReader, XmlReadMode.IgnoreSchema)
```

The second parameter of the **ReadXml** method tells the DataSet how to handle any schema. The valid enums are explained in Table 14-5.

Table 14-5. Handling the Schema in a DataSet

ENUM	DESCRIPTION
Auto	Is set to ReadSchema if a schema already exists; is set to InferSchema if no schema is found in the DataSet and none is found in the document.
DiffGram	Reads a DiffGram, applying changes as appropriate.
Fragment	Reads XML documents, such as those generated by executing FOR XML queries, against an instance of SQL Server.
IgnoreSchema	Ignores any schema found in the document and reads data into the schema existing in the DataSet. Any data that doesn't match the existing schema is discarded.
InferSchema	Ignores any schema found in the document and infers the schema from the data found in the DataSet.
ReadSchema	Reads any schema from the document, if found, and loads the data.

NOTE *Now, with all of that said, let me tell you this. (You might want to have a seat first!) In reality, despite the fact that this all seems to work, everything compiles, and no exceptions are thrown, the truth is that the .NET Compact Framework doesn't do any XML schema validation. If I create a schema, change the data in a document to be in violation of the just created schema, and reload the document, I get no exception thrown. In a future release, XML schema validation may be implemented, but for now it isn't. You can use the schema information when, or if, you transfer the document back to a server application. The full framework can use the schema information to validate the information in the document.*

Using XML Serialization

Here's a chapter covering XML, and I haven't talked about serialization. I haven't because, from a developer's point of view, NETCF doesn't support serialization. The framework itself does indeed use serialization of objects to move data through XML Web services. But this functionality isn't exposed to a user of NETCF. The following code won't compile because XmlSerializer doesn't exist in the .NET Compact Framework:

```
Dim serializer As New XmlSerializer(GetType(PurchaseOrder))
Dim writer As New StreamWriter(filename)
Dim po As New PurchaseOrder
```

But to muddy the waters a little, it's possible to add serialization attributes to the elements of your classes and structures to advise the serializer on how to serialize the object into the outgoing stream:

```
Public Class Address
    <XmlAttribute()> _
    Public Name As String
    Public Street1 As String
    Public Street2 As String

    ' Setting the IsNullable property to false instructs
    ' XmlSerializer that the XML attribute will not appear if
    ' the City field is set to a null reference.
    <XmlElementAttribute(IsNullable:=False)> _
    Public City As String
    Public State As String
    Public Zip As String
End Class
```

So remember, you can decorate your class variables but you can't call the serializer yourself.

Summary

This chapter provided you with an overview of how to read and write XML documents. You learned about XmlTextReader, XmlTextWriter, and the DOM interface exposed through an XML document.

There were several homework assignments in the chapter. I hope you did them or will do them before you check out my solutions. I have provided code for the homework along with an example that puts all of the snippets of the chapter into a program that shows you how it fits together. You can find the solutions under the **Chapter 14** folder of the **Samples** folder. Be sure to check Appendix D for information on accessing the sample applications. But I would assume that by the time you've gotten to Chapter 14, you've already looked at Appendix D!

Some of the power and pizzazz of XML documents lose their luster when applied to the .NET Compact Framework. In the small footprint of NETCF, they become another way to hold data and configuration strings. While you can still use XML for more than simple data storage, if you do, you'll have more work than you are used to on the desktop. Whether you choose to use an XmlReader, XmlWriter, the DOM interface, or a DataSet to manipulate your XML data is entirely up to you. The DOM is easier to manipulate (my opinion, of course) but the stream classes consume fewer resources. The DataSet is nice, and if your data is very complex, then it might be a better choice than either streams or DOM.

I hope that you understand that there are entire 300-plus page books that do nothing but talk about XML. Admittedly, a lot of those books talk about XPath and other objects that are unsupported on the .NET Compact Framework. What I've done here is to give you a start to understanding XML and hopefully to show you a few ways to use XML files on your device.

CHAPTER 15

Mobile Networking

IF YOU'RE A DESKTOP DEVELOPER switching over to mobile development, chances are that network programming is something that you seldom do, if not at all. The reason for this is that most desktop applications simply don't require this type of functionality. As a mobile developer, understanding and embracing the concepts of network programming is paramount to your success. Enhancing your skill set to include various network programming techniques is essential, because often the success of a mobile application hinges on a single item—moving data to and from a server.

Now before I go any further, I need to define some parameters. Network programming, whether it's on a device, a desktop PC, or a server, is a broad and involved topic. Whole books are dedicated to the topic of network programming. Comprehensive discussions of networking and programming over networks can be overwhelming to the novice. Given the limitations I have to work with here, that is this single chapter, I've chosen to focus on the networking concepts and implementations that I have found to be the most useful in developing mobile solutions. We'll be looking at three topics:

- Working with the HTTP protocol to communicate to Web servers

- How to use TCP programming with your mobile applications

- Leveraging infrared data association (IrDA) from within your applications

You'll find that this trinity of networking methodologies provides you with a good sampler plate of ways of passing data both to and from a server, as well as between devices. When combined with the database skills you learned in Chapters 9 through 13, the XML techniques from Chapter 14, and the Web Service capabilities shown in Chapter 16, you should have everything you need to link your mobile solutions to your existing enterprise systems.

We'll start our discussion of networking with HTTP, the protocol of the World Wide Web.

Working with the HTTP Protocol

Many developers mistakenly assume that HTTP, the protocol of the World Wide Web, has little benefit or use in the world of mobile development. While HTTP isn't an integral piece to every mobile application, it does offer developers another alternative for moving data back and forth between a device and a server. And having just one more way to move data is always a good thing when it comes to creating mobile solutions.

HTTP most commonly is used between a browser application, such as Pocket IE, and a Web server, such as Microsoft's Internet Information Server (IIS). However, use of this protocol isn't limited to a browser/server relationship. Your mobile applications can make use of the HTTP protocol to talk to Web servers, just as if they were browsers. Since your application looks like a browser to the server, your application can request content from the server, and submit data to the server, just as you could from a browser.

In this section, I'll show you examples of how to do both. As you'll see, the .NET Compact Framework makes working with the HTTP protocol quick and simple.

A Word About Connectivity

Before you get started, I'm going to say something that may seem to be right out of Homer Simpson's mouth, but it needs to be said. For your NETCF mobile application to be able to access an Internet resource, the device itself must be able to reach that resource. In the case of an application that is going to be leveraging the HTTP protocol to communicate to Web servers, this means the device needs to be able to reach that Web server.

Now, there are a variety of ways that a device can access a Web server. Starting with ActiveSync version 3.5 and later, any device that has established an ActiveSync connection to a desktop PC can access a Web server through that PC, assuming that the PC has Internet access. That means you can slap your Pocket PC down in the cradle, fire off ActiveSync, and surf the Internet with Pocket IE, if you like.

Devices that have Ethernet capabilities, whether that is through a wireless or tethered Ethernet card, can access Internet-based Web servers directly, although somewhat problematically. The issue here is with the connection settings. If you have an ActiveSync connection to a PC over Ethernet, you can access resources on the Internet, just as you could through a USB or serial connection. If your device doesn't have an ActiveSync connection, as would typically be the case when your application is being run in the field, you must configure the device setting so that the network card connects to **The Internet** rather than **Work**. An example of this is shown in Figure 15-1.

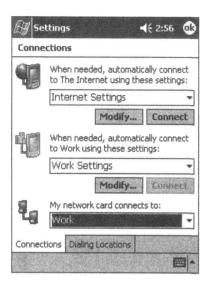

Figure 15-1. The Pocket PC Connection Settings dialog box

For testing purposes with Ethernet-enabled devices, again, as long as you have an ActiveSync connection established between your device and your development PC, your application can access the Internet through the PC. This feature keeps you from having to go through a bad configuration shuffle of toggling your network card setting between **Work** and **The Internet** to test your application.

Working with URIs

It's important that you understand the role of URIs, or Uniform Resource Identifiers, within the .NET Compact Framework. URIs define two key parts in network communications: the protocol that will be used and the target. The protocol may be HTTP, as you'll see in this section, FTP, or any of a variety of other Internet protocols. The target is the server that your mobile application will be communicating with.

The server can be defined by either a TCP address, for example 192.168.1.100, or by a DNS name, such as www.apress.com. Obviously, to be able to use a DNS name, your device's communication settings must include the address of a DNS server.

The URI used to specify the target contains these components:

- **Scheme identifier**—Defines the protocol, such as HTTP

- **Server identifier**—Specifies the TCP address or DSN name

- **Path identifier**—Indicates the requested content

- **Query string (optional)**—Specifies parameters being passed to the server

For example, the URI `http://www.apress.com/testpage.aspx?id=10112` can be broken down into these parts:

- **Scheme identifier**—http

- **Server identifier**—www.apress.com

- **Path identifier**—/testpage.aspx

- **Query string**—?id=10112

Should You Use the WebRequest and HTTPWebRequest Class?

The .NET Compact Framework offers two sets of classes that can be used to request content, or as it's more commonly referred to, a resource, from a Web server—**WebRequest** and **HTTPWebRequest**. The **WebRequest** class is more general purpose in nature and can be used to make requests not only to a Web server using the HTTP protocol, but also to other servers using other common Internet protocols, such as FTP.

In comparison, the **HTTPWebRequest** class is used only to make HTTP requests. As a single-purpose class, it offers several HTTP-specific features in the form of methods and properties, such as exposing common HTTP header values, and is generally more robust and well rounded in the HTTP-related functionality it provides.

In most applications, the **WebRequest** class provides you with everything that you need in the way of HTTP functionality. I like how this class allows you to use similar programming techniques with a variety of Internet protocols. The samples shown in this section demonstrate how to use the **WebRequest** class.

As you might expect, there are corresponding **WebResponse** and **HTTPWebResponse** classes, which are used in conjunction with the **WebRequest** and **HTTPWebRequest** classes. These response classes are used to retrieve the content that your mobile applications requested.

Working with the NetworkStream Class

To send and receive content to and from the Internet, your application will use Stream objects and the **System.Net** classes. Whether that content is a Web page, XML, a directory listing from an FTP server, or something else, your application will use **Stream.Write** and **Stream.Read** to send and receive that content.

Steams allow you to communicate with a variety of protocols. One of their key benefits is that they allow your application to process data as it arrives, rather than waiting for the entire set of data to be received.

In this section, you'll see an example of how the **NetworkStream** class is used to send and receive data via the HTTP protocol.

Retrieving a Web Page

The first use of the HTTP protocol we'll examine is to have your mobile application retrieve a Web page. Now you may be wondering why you would want to retrieve a Web page from a mobile application. There are a variety of reasons you may want to do this including

- To incorporate content available on the Internet into your application. For example, you may want to display a weather forecast, sports scores, news highlights, or even maps based upon a GPS reading taken from the device.

- To integrate your mobile application into existing third-party Web-based applications. Many vendors now provide HTTP interfaces to their applications. You can create mobile extensions of these systems using the techniques presented in this section.

- To extend your own enterprise systems to a mobile platform. Products such as SQL Server and Exchange can be accessed from Web-based clients, including your mobile applications written in the .NET Compact Framework.

- To create mobile applications that are firewall friendly. Most corporations that make use of firewalls commonly make port 80, the port typically used with the HTTP protocol, accessible. Your mobile solutions can therefore leverage this configuration without any additional work by your security support groups.

This is just a few of the many reasons of why the HTTP protocol is both so appealing and useful to the mobile developer.

Retrieving a Web page from your application using the **WebRequest** class is simple. The process is as follows:

1. Use the **Create** method of the WebRequest object to initiate a new WebRequest. As part of this request, you'll provide a URI that specifies the page you are interested in.

2. Use the **GetResponse** method of the WebRequest object to send a request for the desired page. The method returns an instance of a WebResponse object, which in turn will be used to retrieve the content from the Web server.

3. Use the **GetResponseStream** of the WebResponse object to retrieve the data stream from the Web server.

4. Use the StreamReader object to convert the data stream to text.

5. Parse and work with the text content as required.

Listing 15-1 shows a complete example of this process. What's important to note here is that if you strip away the dimension statements at the top of this listing and the exception handling statements later, the actual process of retrieving, converting, and displaying the content takes only five lines of code.

 NOTE   *This code is taken from the HTTPDemo project, which can be found under the **Chapter 15** folder of the **Samples** folder for this book. See Appendix D for more information on accessing and loading the sample applications.*

Listing 15-1. Retrieving a Page from a Web Server

```vbnet
Imports System.Net
Imports System.IO

Private Sub btnFetchHttp_Click(ByVal sender As System.Object, _
  ByVal e As System.EventArgs) Handles btnFetchHttp.Click
  Dim Reader As StreamReader
  Dim Response As WebResponse
  Dim ResponseStream As Stream
  Dim Request As WebRequest

' Toggle on the wait cursor.
  Cursor.Current = Cursors.WaitCursor
  txtSource.Text = "[waiting]"
```

```
    Try

' Retrieve the requested page.
        Request = WebRequest.Create(txtUrl.Text)
        Request.Timeout = 60000
        Response = Request.GetResponse
        ResponseStream = Response.GetResponseStream

' Convert the response to text.
        Reader = New StreamReader(ResponseStream)
        txtSource.Text = Reader.ReadToEnd
' The request failed, so figure out why.
' Was it an invalid URI (URL)?
    Catch uriex As UriFormatException
        txtSource.Text = "The page you requested is in an invalid format."

' Was there a problem with either the Web response or request objects?
    Catch webex As WebException
        txtSource.Text = "An exception occurred relating to the use of " & _
            "a web response or request object. The specific exception was:" & _
            vbCrLf & webex.Message

' Did some type of general exception occur?
    Catch ex As Exception
        txtSource.Text = "A general exception occurred while attempting to " & _
            "retrieve the requested page." & _
            vbCrLf & ex.Message()

' Clean up before exiting.
    Finally
        Cursor.Current = Cursors.Default
        Response.Close()

    End Try

End Sub
```

NOTE *Listing 15-1 demonstrates a synchronous request. An example of an asynchronous request is shown later in this chapter.*

TIP *When making a request to a Web server, set the **Timeout** property of the Request object to control the amount of time your application will wait for a response. In Listing 15-1, I set the time-out to 60 seconds (60,000 milliseconds).*

Exception Handling with Web Requests

Most of the lower part of Listing 15-1 is comprised of code used to handle any exceptions that might occur. While Appendix E addresses exception handling in greater detail, I wanted to draw your attention to the exception handling code used with Listing 15-1, as it demonstrates three key components that you should incorporate into your HTTP-based applications.

At the top of the exception handling code is a Catch statement that handles invalid URIs. UriFormatExceptions are generated when the URI that you provide is formatted incorrectly.

```
' Was it an invalid URI (URL)?
  Catch uriex As UriFormatException
    txtSource.Text = "The page you requested is in an invalid format."
```

TIP *Always include a check for the UriFormatException when you are allowing the user to enter in a URI or URL.*

Next is a Catch statement that handles exceptions generated by either the WebRequest or WebResponse objects. Depending upon the complexity and needs of your application, you may want to wrap uses of the WebRequest and WebResponse objects within their own Try, Catch, Finally statements.

```
' Was there a problem with either the Web response or request objects?
  Catch webex As WebException
    txtSource.Text = "An exception occurred relating to the use of " & _
      "a web response or request object. The specific exception was:" & _
      vbCrLf & webex.Message
```

Finally, you complete the exception handling code with a general purpose Catch statement, which handles any unforeseen problems that are encountered.

Sending Data to a Web Server

While requesting static Web pages is a useful technique in the development of mobile solutions, the real power that your applications can leverage from the HTTP protocol involves sending data to a Web server. There are two key reasons that you would want to send data to a Web server: to define the content of a page being returned to your application and to transfer data from a device for storage on an enterprise server.

Defining the content of a page you request allows you to create an environment where you can query an enterprise server via the HTTP protocol for particular information. For example, say you are creating a mobile application that will be used by salespersons working out on the road. The application is designed such that it makes queries through a Web server to retrieve information on pending customer orders from a back-end enterprise database. A salesperson, through the mobile application, can specify the customers that he or she will be visiting so that only the orders for those customers are retrieved. The Web server in response can then deliver back order details as either HTML or XML, depending upon your application needs.

The second reason for using the HTTP protocol to send data to a Web server involves passing data from the device for storage on an enterprise server. The process of getting data from a device to a server is always one of the key items in any mobile solution. With the HTTP protocol and Web servers, you have just one more way of transferring this data. Continuing with the salesperson example, you could easily create a mobile application in which the salesperson would enter orders on the device, which in turn would be transferred from the device through a Web server to an enterprise database, by using the HTTP protocol.

If this all seems too good to be true, wait until you see how easy it is to implement.

The Client Side

To send data to a Web server from your mobile application using the HTTP protocol, you simply need to add a query string to the URI that you pass to the server as part of your request. For example:

```
http://192.168.1.100/PostingData/Echo.aspx?barcode=0123456789&qty=20
```

In this example, the ASP.NET Web page echo.aspx is being requested. The query string included with this request includes two data items, **barcode**, with a value of 0123456789, and **qty**, with a value of 20.

That's all there is to it. Simply extend the URI to include the data that you're passing. This data could be taken from fields on a form, read in from a file, or retrieved from an underlying data source such as a Pocket Access or SQL Server CE database.

The Server Side

On the server side of things, the process is equally simple. With ASP.NET, you can extract the data values from QueryString with a few lines of code. Listing 15-2 shows an example of the process used to retrieve and display both the **barcode** and **qty** data items that were passed to the echo.aspx page in Listing I5-1.

Listing 15-2. Server-Side Code That Retrieves the Values Passed

```
Private Sub Page_Load(ByVal sender As System.Object, ByVal e As _
    System.EventArgs) Handles MyBase.Load
' Echo the values received.
    Response.Write("<B>Barcode: </B>")
    Response.Write(Request.QueryString.Item("barcode"))
    Response.Write("<BR>")
    Response.Write(" <B>Quantity: </B>")
    Response.Write(Request.QueryString.Item("qty"))
End Sub
```

Using the QueryString collection of the Request object, you reference the individual data items by name. While Listing 15-2 shows these values are echoing back to the requesting application, you could just as easy store these values away in an enterprise database.

NOTE *This example demonstrates an HTTP GET request. The .NET Compact Framework also supports HTTP POST requests through the **WebRequest** and **HTTPWebRequest** classes.*

NOTE *For more on programming with ASP.NET, see* Programming the Web with Visual Basic .NET *by Constance Petersen, Lynn Torkelson, and Zac Torkelson (Apress, 2002).*

Asynchronous HTTP Requests

In the examples shown up to this point, the Web requests have all been made synchronously. In a synchronous request, the client application waits for a response from the server before continuing. Depending upon your application needs, this pause may or may not be acceptable.

For example, let's say you were developing a barcode scanning application that scans packages in a warehouse and then sends those scans on to a Web server via the HTTP protocol. The user is just scanning one package after another, as fast as he or she is able to. If the application has to wait 3, 4, 5, or more seconds for the server to respond, it may impact how the job is performed.

In this type of situation, you have two options: You could either move the sending of the data to a background thread, or you could make the request to the server asynchronously. The beauty behind asynchronous requests is that they don't wait for a server response. They simply make the request and return control to the application. The trick to using this approach is that your application must provide some additional code to handle the server's response at a later time.

Making an asynchronous request is more complicated than the synchronous method. You need to keep track of the request state and provide a callback routine that will receive and process the server's response when it occurs. To illustrate how this is done, I'll start by showing you how to store the state of a request.

Listing 15-3 contains a description of the **RequestState** class used to preserve the state of the asynchronous Web request. Its WebRequest and Stream instances are used to hold the current resource request, the stream that is received in response, and a StringBuilder, which contains the response. All of this is defined within the **New** procedure of the class.

Listing 15-3. Class Used to Store the State of the Request

```
Imports System.IO
Imports System.Net
Imports System.Text

' This class stores the state of the request.
Public Class RequestState
   Private Shared BUFFER_SIZE As Integer = 1024
   Public requestData As StringBuilder
   Public bufferRead() As Byte
   Public request As WebRequest
   Public response As WebResponse
   Public responseStream As Stream
```

```
        Public Sub New()
          bufferRead = New Byte(BUFFER_SIZE) {}
          requestData = New StringBuilder("")
          request = Nothing
          responseStream = Nothing
        End Sub
    End Class
```

The process of initiating an asynchronous Web request is similar to that used for a synchronous request. Listing 15-4 demonstrates this process using a format similar to the example shown in Listing 15-1.

Listing 15-4. Initiating the Request

```
Private Sub btnAsyncFetchHttp_Click(ByVal sender As System.Object, _
    ByVal e As System.EventArgs) Handles btnAsyncFetchHttp.Click
    Dim AsyncResult As IAsyncResult
    Dim Request As WebRequest
    Dim rs As RequestState

' Toggle on the wait cursor.
    Cursor.Current = Cursors.WaitCursor
    txtSource.Text = "[waiting]"

    Try

' Request the page asynchrounously.
        Request = WebRequest.Create(txtUrl.Text)
        rs = New RequestState
        rs.request = Request
        AsyncResult = CType(Request.BeginGetResponse(AddressOf ResponseCallback, _
            rs), IAsyncResult)

' The request failed, so figure out why.
' Was there a problem with either the Web response or request objects?
    Catch webex As WebException
        txtSource.Text = "An exception occurred relating to the use of " & _
            "a web response or request object. The specific exception was:" & _
            vbCrLf & webex.Message
```

```
' Did some type of general exception occur?
  Catch ex As Exception
    txtSource.Text = "A general exception occurred while attempting to " & _
      "retrieve the requested page." & _
      vbCrLf & ex.Message()

  Finally
' Toggle off the wait cursor.
    Cursor.Current = Cursors.Default

  End Try

End Sub
```

In the middle of Listing 15-4 is the code used to initiate the asynchronous request. This part of the code starts by creating an instance of the **RequestState** class, described in Listing 15-3. A call to the **BeginGetResponse** method of the Request object initiates the asynchronous response. You pass to this method the address of the callback routine ResponseCallback. This routine will be fired when the server responds.

Listing 15-5 shows the ResponseCallback routine. In this routine, the **EndGetResponse** method of the WebRequest object is called to complete the asynchronous request from the Web server. An instance of the response stream is created, from which you begin to read the response asynchronously, by providing a second callback routine—ReadCallback.

Listing 15-5. Processing the Asynchronous Response

```
Sub ResponseCallback(ByVal AsyncResult As IAsyncResult)
  Dim AsyncResultRead As IAsyncResult
  Dim rs As RequestState
  Dim Request As WebRequest
  Dim Response As Stream

  Try

' Configure the state of the request to be asynchronous.
    rs = CType(AsyncResult.AsyncState, RequestState)
    Request = rs.request

' Terminate the asynchronous response.
    rs.response = Request.EndGetResponse(AsyncResult)
```

```
' Retrieve the response.
    Response = rs.response.GetResponseStream
    rs.responseStream = Response

' Initiate reading the response.
    AsyncResultRead = Response.BeginRead(rs.bufferRead, 0, BUFFER_SIZE, _
        AddressOf ReadCallBack, rs)

' The request failed, so figure out why.
' Was there a problem with either the Web response or request objects?
  Catch webex As WebException
      txtSource.Text = "An exception occurred relating to the use of " & _
          "a web response or request object. The specific exception was:" & _
          vbCrLf & webex.Message

' Did some type of general exception occur?
  Catch ex As Exception
      txtSource.Text = "A general exception occurred while attempting to " & _
          "retrieve the requested page." & _
          vbCrLf & ex.Message()
  End Try

End Sub
```

The reading of the response stream is handled by the ReadCallback routine. This routine reads the data that is waiting and then starts another asynchronous read, repeating this process until all of the response has been received. Listing 15-6 shows an example of this technique.

Listing 15-6. Reading the Response

```
Sub ReadCallBack(ByVal AsyncResult As IAsyncResult)
    Dim AsyncResultRead As IAsyncResult
    Dim rs As RequestState
    Dim Response As Stream
    Dim ReadCount As Integer

    Try
      rs = CType(AsyncResult.AsyncState, RequestState)
      Response = rs.responseStream
      ReadCount = Response.EndRead(AsyncResult)
```

```
' Is there anything waiting to read?
    If (ReadCount > 0) Then
        rs.requestData.Append(Encoding.ASCII.GetString(rs.bufferRead, 0, _
            ReadCount))
        AsyncResultRead = Response.BeginRead(rs.bufferRead, 0, BUFFER_SIZE, _
            AddressOf ReadCallBack, rs)

' You are done, so display the source for the requested page.
    Else
        If rs.requestData.Length > 1 Then
            Dim sringContent As String
            sringContent = rs.requestData.ToString()
            txtSource.Text = sringContent
        End If
        Response.Close()

    End If

' The request failed, so figure out why.
' Was there a problem with either the Web response or request objects?
    Catch webex As WebException
        txtSource.Text = "An exception occurred relating to the use of " & _
            "a web response or request object. The specific exception was:" & _
            vbCrLf & webex.Message

' Did some type of general exception occur?
    Catch ex As Exception
        txtSource.Text = "A general exception occurred while attempting to " & _
            "retrieve the requested page." & _
            vbCrLf & ex.Message()
    End Try

End Sub
```

While at first glance this asynchronous approach may seem to be far more complicated than the synchronous method, in actuality, once you strip out the extra declarations and error handling, you'll see that in fact only 10 to 12 more lines of actual code are required.

I would recommend that you be familiar with both approaches, as each method has its use in the development of mobile solutions.

NOTE *The code presented as part of this discussion on asynchronous requests is taken from the HTTPDemo project, which can be found under the **Chapter 15** folder of the **Samples** folder for this book. See Appendix D for more information on accessing and loading the sample applications.*

HTTP Requests with SSL

There is just one more HTTP-related subject that you need to learn about: making HTTP requests with SSL. SSL, or Secure Socket Layer, enables you to transfer data securely over the HTTP protocol. Normally, data is passed between a Web client, which in this case would be your application, and a Web server as clear text. While in many cases this may not be an issue, there will be instances when you'll want to protect the data you are passing.

The good news is that both the WebRequest and WebResponse objects support and use SSL natively. There is absolutely nothing you need to do on the client end other than specify a URI starting with HTTPS, rather than HTTP.

Now that you have a pretty good understanding of what the WebRequest and WebResponse objects can do for your application development, let's look at a lower, more flexible form of Internet communication—programming with the TCP objects.

Working with the TCP Objects

While the WebRequest and WebResponse objects allow you to easily communicate using Internet standard protocols, there may be times when you need to create custom interfaces between your client and device applications. That's where the TCP objects, provided as part of the .NET Compact Framework, come in.

The TCP objects are built upon the **Socket** class, which allows you to send and receive data over a network as streams. That network could be something as large as the Internet or a much more controlled environment, such as a network within a building; or you can even use something as simple as communication between a device and a PC via the docking cradle. The beauty of the TCP objects is that regardless of which approach you use to communicate—the Internet, a local network, a phone connection, or the docking cradle—the method in which you communicate is exactly the same.

Rather than spend pages discussing the theory behind TCP communications and exploring the **Socket** class, I'm instead going to show you how to build a basic TCP client-server application. Along the way, you'll learn the key concepts behind working with TCP. You'll learn how to package, send, and receive data. The techniques that you learn here can be applied to a wide variety of situations. We'll start with the server side of things.

Developing a TCP Server

A TCP server is simply an application that monitors a port waiting for someone to request a connection. In building a TCP server component, you'll use the **TcpListener** class. The basics of creating a TCP server using the **TcpListener** class are as follows:

1. Open a port for listening.

2. Start listening.

3. Check if there are any pending requests from a client.

4. Accept a client request.

5. Receive a data packet from the client.

6. Process the data packet.

7. Build a response packet.

8. Return the packet to the client.

TCP servers can be designed to operate in a one-to-one mode, in which there is a single client connection, or in a many-to-one mode, in which multiple clients can access the server at the same time. The sample that is presented as part of this discussion is a many-to-one example, because that is both the more complicated and more frequently used approach.

NOTE *The code presented as part of this discussion is taken from the TCP Server project, which can be found under the **Chapter 15** folder of the **Samples** folder for this book. See Appendix D for more information on accessing and loading the sample applications.*

The TCP Server project, along with the matching TCP Demo project, which implements the client, demonstrates a simple barcode scanning application that stores scans locally on the device, and then subsequently forwards the scans to the server via TCP.

The Basic Server

As I mentioned earlier in this section, the TCP objects are build upon the **Sockets** class, which is defined within the **System.Net.Sockets** namespace. Including a reference to this namespace, as shown in the following code line, simplifies the coding process and the typing required to work with the TCP objects:

```
Imports System.Net.Sockets
```

To enable your TCP server to handle multiple clients, you need to provide some infrastructure to manage the connections. Your server uses a small number of variables to accomplish this.

The variable **ActiveThreads** stores the number of clients that are currently connected. Tracking this number allows you to limit the number of connections based upon your server capabilities.

```
Dim ActiveThreads As Integer          ' Threads currently active
```

Used in conjunction with the **ActiveThreads** variable is the variable **MaxConnections**, which specifies the maximum number of client connections allowed at one time.

```
Dim MaxConnections As Integer = 100   ' Maximum # of connections
```

The **StopListener** variable terminates the TCP server application, and correctly cleans up all of the threads that are being used to handle the client connections.

```
Private StopListener As Boolean       ' Flag to control server
```

All of these variables are defined at the module-level of a form, so that they will be available throughout the application. You also need to create an instance of the **TCPListener** class, which is the cornerstone of this application.

```
Dim Listener As TcpListener
```

Step 1: Opening a Port for Listening

The first step of implementing the server component is to open the port to which you'll be listening. In actuality, there are two key configurations when it comes to TCP communications.

The first configuration is the port number. The port is the channel on which the server is listening. Valid port numbers are 1 to 65,536. The lower 1024 port numbers are reserved for common Internet protocols, such as HTTP and FTP. For example, Web servers, which use the HTTP protocol, monitor port 80; FTP servers monitor ports 20 and 21.

The second configuration is the IP address. Servers can monitor one or more IP addresses. For a simple server that contains a single networking card, the IP address the server would monitor would be the IP address assigned to the server. In cases where the server has multiple cards, you can either specify one of the server's IP addresses or configure things so that the server monitors all of its addresses.

Listing 15-7 shows an example of creating an instance of the TCPListener object that listens to all IP addresses on a port that is specified from the contents of the **Port** text box. This text box is part of the simplistic interface shown in Figure 15-2. In this example, the port number is predefined with the value of 1234.

Listing 15-7. Opening a Port and Starting to Listen

```
Public Sub New()
    MyBase.New()

'This call is required by the Windows Form Designer.
    InitializeComponent()

'Add any initialization after the InitializeComponent() call.

' Open a port for listening.
    Listener = New TcpListener(System.Net.IPAddress.Any, txtPort.Text)
    Listener.Start()

    timMain.Enabled = True

End Sub
```

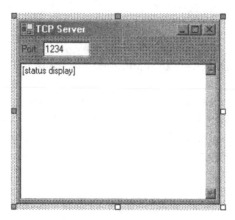

Figure 15-2. The interface to the TCP server application

NOTE *In your application, the port number can be any number between 1 and 65,536, just as long as both the client and server applications are using the same number. For a list of standard ports, see* http://www.iana.org/assignments/port-numbers. *A list is also available in your C:\WINNT\system32\drivers\etc directory in the "services" file.*

Step 2: Starting to Listen to the Port

The second step that the server needs to perform is to start listening to the port. This task is accomplished by issuing the **Listen** method of the TcpListener object. Listing 15-7 shows this occurring right after configuring the object's IP address and port number.

Step 3: Checking If There Are Any Pending Requests

The TCP server checks for pending client requests by polling the TcpListener object via its **Pending** method. This method returns a response of true when a client is attempting to connect to the server and returns a false value when there are no pending requests.

To implement this polling process, the TCP server application uses a Timer control that is configured to fire every 1/10th of a second. The **Tick** event procedure for the Timer control is examined in the following discussion.

This routine starts by first checking to see if a request is pending. If there isn't a request pending, the routine simply exits.

```
Private Sub timMain_Tick(ByVal sender As System.Object, _
  ByVal e As System.EventArgs) Handles timMain.Tick

    Dim CurrentThreadStart As ThreadStart
    Dim CurrentThread As Thread
    Dim ThreadCount As Integer

' Is there a client waiting to connect? If not, exit this routine.
  If Not Listener.Pending() Then
    Exit Sub
  End If
```

If a connection is pending, then you first disable the timer, forcing any other pending or new requests to wait until after you process this first request.

```
' If you get to here there is a client waiting. Temporarily disable
' the timer so that you don't try to process any additional connections
' until this one is complete.
  timMain.Enabled = False
```

Next, you check to make sure that the maximum number of acceptable connections has not been exceeded.

```
' Have you reached the maximum number of connections you'll accept? If
' so, turn the timer back on and leave the requesting client
' waiting.
  If ActiveThreads > MaxConnections Then
    timMain.Enabled = True
    Exit Sub
  End If
```

Step 4: Accepting Client Requests

If you get to this point of the Timer **Tick** event procedure, then you're going to accept the client's request. The server is designed to handle each request in its own thread. To implement this, you first create a new thread and then start the thread. You should note as part of creating the thread you specify that the thread should run the procedure **ProcessRequest**, which will handle processing the communication with this client.

```
' If you get to here then you are going to accept the client. Define a new
' thread to use with this connection.
```

```
    CurrentThreadStart = New ThreadStart(AddressOf ProcessRequest)
    CurrentThread = New Thread(CurrentThreadStart)

' Start the thread.
    CurrentThread.Start()
```

All that is left is to increment the counter used to track the number of active clients. Before exiting, you start the Timer again so that it can process the next request.

```
' Have all of the other threads wait while you increment the counter.
    SyncLock CurrentThread
        ActiveThreads += 1
    End SyncLock

' You're done, so restart the timer.
    timMain.Enabled = True

End Sub
```

Step 5: Receiving Data from the Client

Within the TCP server application, data from an individual client is received by the **ProcessRequest** routine. In this routine, you start by using the **AcceptSocket** method of the TcpListener object to accept the client's connection.

```
Protected Sub ProcessRequest()
    Dim Buffer(100) As Byte
    Dim Bytes As Integer
    Dim CurrentThread As Thread
    Dim CurSocket As Socket
    Dim InboundPacket As String
    Dim OutboundPacket As String
    Dim Temp As String

' Get the current running thread.
    CurrentThread = System.Threading.Thread.CurrentThread()

' Accept the pending socket request.
    CurSocket = Listener.AcceptSocket

' Listen on this socket until you are told to stop.
    While Not StopListener
```

To determine if any client data is waiting, you check the **Available** property of the instance of the TcpListener object. If data is waiting, you use the **Receive** method of the TcpListener object to retrieve it into a byte array. After converting the byte array to a string, it's ready for processing.

```
' Is there anything waiting to be read? If so, read it.
    If CurSocket.Available > 0 Then
      Bytes = CurSocket.Receive(Buffer, Buffer.Length, 0)
      SyncLock CurrentThread
      InboundPacket = System.Text.Encoding.Default.GetString(Buffer)
      End SyncLock
      Exit While
    End If


' Relinquish control to the system so that the other threads may run.
    Application.DoEvents()


' Check to see if the connection is still active.
    If Not CurSocket.Connected Then
      StopListener = True
    End If
  End While
```

Step 6: Processing the Data Packet

The packet you receive from the client is processed by the ProcessPacket function. I'll discuss this packet in greater detail later in this section. For now, you simply need to know that this function returns a string that will in turn be sent back to the client.

```
' Process the packet that was received.
  OutboundPacket = ProcessPacket(InboundPacket)

' Update the display to show both the message received and sent.
  txtDisplay.Text += vbCrLf & InboundPacket
  txtDisplay.Text += vbCrLf & OutboundPacket
```

Step 7: Building a Response Packet

The response that is returned by the ProcessPacket function must first be converted from a string into a byte array before it can be sent to the client.

```
' Format the return message.
  Buffer = System.Text.Encoding.Default.GetBytes(OutboundPacket.ToCharArray)
```

Step 8: Returning the Packet to the Client

After this, the **Send** method of the TcpListener object is used to send the server's response.

```
' Send the messsage to the client.
  CurSocket.Send(Buffer, Buffer.Length, 0)
  CurSocket.Close()
  SyncLock CurrentThread
  ActiveThreads -= 1
  End SyncLock

End Sub
```

Processing the Request and Building a Response

At the heart of any TCP client-server application you'll find routines that process requests and create responses. In the case of the TCP server application, both of these tasks are handled within a single function—ProcessPacket.

While there are any number of ways to package data for sending between a TCP client and server, one common approach is to build a package that is comprised of a header component and a data component. Within the header component you'll typically find a packet identifier, which defines the type of packet, a timestamp, and other identifying information. The data component is just that, the data being sent. Usually you'll separate the individual pieces or fields of data that comprise both the header and the data components using some type of delimiter, such as a comma or a pipe (|) character. I prefer the pipe character because it's far less likely to appear within the data itself, whereas a comma is fairly common.

Listing 15-8 shows the ProcessPacket function. This function expects the client's packet as an argument and sends back the packet to return to the client.

Listing 15-8. The ProcessPacket Function

```
Function ProcessPacket(ByVal InboundPacket As String) As String
  Dim OutboundPacket As String
  Dim Params As String() = Nothing
  Dim ResultString As String

' Parse the packet.
  Params = InboundPacket.Split("|")

' Determine what type of packet you received.
  Select Case Params(0)

    Case "DAT" ' Data message

' Build the message header.
      OutboundPacket = "DRP|"

' Add the dual-device info.
      OutboundPacket += "SUCCESS|"
      OutboundPacket += Now.ToString & "|"

    Case Else ' Unknown message type
      Return "unknown"

  End Select

' Return the packet.
  Return OutboundPacket

End Function
```

The function begins by parsing the inbound packet up into its respective pieces using the Split function. The Split function divides a string into a set of fields based upon the delimiter you specify. It returns an array in which these individual items are stored.

As I stated, the first field is commonly used to define the packet type. By checking this field, you can create a routine that will handle a variety of packets. In the example shown in Listing 15-8, only a single packet type, "DAT", or data, is provided. You could easily expand this routine to include packets for logging on (LOG), requesting updates to configurations (CFG), checking to see if any messages are waiting for the client (MSG), or any other pertinent communications.

In the case of this example, the response packet is nothing more than the packet header of "DRP", which signifies data received, along with a "SUCCESS" field and a timestamp.

The server as described here handles any number of clients and, with some minimal modifications, any variety of data packet types. Now that you have an understanding of how the server side works, let's turn to the client side of TCP communications.

Developing a TCP Client

In comparison to the server component, creating a TCP client requires minimal effort. The client needs only to perform the following tasks:

1. Establish a connection to the server.

2. Build the data packet.

3. Send the packet to the server.

4. Wait for a response from the server.

5. Read the response.

6. Convert the response to a string.

 NOTE *The code presented as part of this discussion is taken from the TCP Demo project, which can be found under the **Chapter 15** folder of the **Samples** folder for this book. See Appendix D for more information on accessing and loading the sample applications.*

Step 1: Establishing a Connection to the Server

The first step that the client needs to perform is to establish a connection to the server. This is accomplished through the **Connect** method of the TcpClient object.

You need to provide two key pieces of information when calling this method: the IP address and port number that the server is monitoring.

```
' Connect to the server.
  Client = New TcpClient
  Try
    Client.Connect(txtIP.Text, txtPort.Text)
```

```
Catch ex As Exception
  MsgBox("Connection failed: " & ex.Message)
  Exit Sub
End Try
```

In this sample code, the exception code handles any errors that might occur. If the connection succeeds, then you continue on with the next step—building the data packet.

Step 2: Building the Data Packet

Once you've established a connection to the server, you're ready to build the packet you'll be sending. When I'm talking about building a packet, I don't mean concatenating the data together, adding a packet identifier, including a date stamp, and such. Although those tasks do need to be performed, what I'm referring to is converting the data packet from a string to a byte array.

The actual conversion process is straightforward using the **System.Text** namespace. Simply pass your string to the **GetBytes** method, which returns to you a byte array.

```
' Build the message.
  Dim myMessage As String = "This is a test..."
  Dim OutBuffer() As Byte
  OutBuffer = System.Text.Encoding.Default.GetBytes(myMessage.ToCharArray)
```

With the packet in its right form, you're ready to send it off to the server.

Step 3: Sending the Packet to the Server

Sending the packet to the server is accomplished by calling the **Write** method of the NetworkStream object provided through the **GetStream** method of the TcpClient object. You pass to the byte buffer you created in step 2 to the **Write** method.

```
' Send the message.
  Client.GetStream().Write(OutBuffer, 0, OutBuffer.Length)
```

At this point, the client must wait for the server's response. As was shown with the WebRequest example earlier in this chapter, TCP communications can be performed either synchronously or asynchronously. This example demonstrates the synchronous method, which is more commonly used.

Step 4: Waiting for a Response from the Server

In a synchronous implementation, the client must wait for the server's response. Typically, this is accomplished by implementing a simple loop that monitors the NetworkStream object provided through the TcpClient for data. The **DataAvailable** property of the NetworkStream object is set to true as data arrives.

```
' Wait for a response.
  While Not Client.GetStream.DataAvailable()
    Application.DoEvents()
  End While
```

Once you've determined that there's data present, you need to retrieve that data.

Step 5: Reading the Response

You retrieve data from the NetworkStream object provided through the TcpClient using the **Read** method. You need to pass to this method a byte array that is large enough to handle the packets you're using. In this example, that buffer is set to 1000 bytes.

```
' Read the server's response.
  Dim InBuffer(1000) As Byte
  Dim ReturnMessage As String

  ReturnMessage = ""
  While Client.GetStream.DataAvailable()
    Client.GetStream().Read(InBuffer, 0, InBuffer.Length)
    ReturnMessage &= System.Text.Encoding.Default.GetString(InBuffer, _
      0, InBuffer.Length)
  End While
```

Having retrieved the response, the only step left is to convert the byte array to a string.

Step 6: Converting the Response to a String

The final step is to convert the byte array back into a string, making it easier to work with and parse into its respective pieces, as was demonstrated with the server discussion earlier in this section.

In this example, the string **ReturnMessage** is used to hold the converted string. You convert the byte array to a string using the **GetString** method provided through the **System.Text** namespace.

```
' Read the server's response.
  Dim InBuffer(1000) As Byte
  Dim ReturnMessage As String

  ReturnMessage = ""
  While Client.GetStream.DataAvailable()
    Client.GetStream().Read(InBuffer, 0, InBuffer.Length)
    ReturnMessage &= System.Text.Encoding.Default.GetString(InBuffer, _
      0, InBuffer.Length)
  End While
```

Once the complete string has been retrieved, you're ready to process that string, just as you did on the server. And with that you've completed the whole communication process from initiation, to the client sending a message, to the server receiving that message, processing that message, building a response, and sending it back to the client, where it's received and processed by the client.

As you can see, although it requires a bit more coding than the WebRequest/WebResponse approach, TCP offers an incredible amount of flexibility and functionality with a minimal amount of additional code.

Asynchronous TCP Communication

Before we wrap up our discussion of TCP communications, I want to point out the basics of how you would go about implementing an asynchronous TCP interface. There are three key items that you'll need to change in your client application: where you connect to the server, when you send data, and when you receive data from the server.

Asynchronous TCP Connection

In the examples shown earlier in this section, the client connected to the server using the **Connect** method. With an asynchronous connection, the client will use the **BeginConnect** and **EndConnect** methods in place of the **Connect** method.

The **BeginConnect** method initiates a connection request. When calling this method, you'll provide a routine that will be called when the server responds to your connection request.

After handling the server's connection response, you'll need to call the **EndConnect** method to finalize the connection request.

Asynchronous TCP Sends and Receives

To send data synchronously to the server, you've previously used the **Write** method. To send data asynchronously, you'll use two methods, **BeginWrite** and **EndWrite**. To receive data synchronously, you've previously used the **Read** method. To receive data asynchronously, you'll use **BeginRead** and **EndRead**.

When calling both the **BeginRead** and **BeginWrite** methods, you'll need to provide a routine that will be called when the requested operation is performed. Within the routine you provide you'll need to call either the **EndRead** or **EndWrite** method, depending upon the operation you're performing to complete the process.

Step-by-Step Tutorial: Working with TCP

In this step-by-step exercise, you'll create an application that demonstrates passing data via TCP. As part of this exercise, you'll

- Create a server that will listen for client connections.

- Create a client that will connect to a server.

- Send data from a client.

- Receive data from a client on the server.

- Send data from the server.

- Receive data from a server on the client.

This application provides all of the fundamentals of working with TCP.

 NOTE *I include a completed version of both the client and server applications, titled TCPDemo - Complete and TCP Server - Complete, under the **Chapter 15** folder of the **Samples** folder for this book. See Appendix D for more information on accessing and loading the sample applications.*

Step 1: Opening the Server Project

To simplify this tutorial, I've already created the server project and the user interface for the TCP server application. This template project is included under the **Chapter 15** folder in the **Samples** folder. To load this project, follow these steps:

1. From the VS .NET IDE Start Page, select to open a project. The Open Project dialog box will be displayed.

2. Use this dialog box to navigate to the **Chapter 15** folder under the **Samples** folder for this book.

3. Select and open the project **TCP Server**. The project will be loaded.

Step 2: Examining the Server's User Interface

The user interface for the TCP server application is comprised of several controls: a Label and two TextBox controls. Figure 15-3 shows the application's interface.

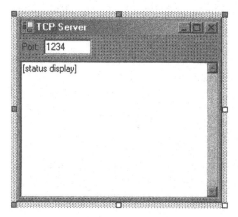

Figure 15-3. The interface to the TCP server application

The TCP server application is a Windows application. It's designed to run on a desktop PC and communicate to a device either via the docking cradle or through a wireless Ethernet connection.

Step 3: Defining General Purpose Settings

Before you jump into the server component, you'll first need to define some settings and configurations. First add the following Imports statements above the form's class construct:

```
Imports System.Net.Sockets
Imports System.Threading
```

Next, add the following declarations at the module level of the form:

```
Dim ActiveThreads As Integer              ' Number of threads currently active
Dim Listener As TcpListener
Dim MaxConnections As Integer = 100       ' Maximum # of connections to support
Private StopListener As Boolean           ' Flag that controls listening process
```

Step 4: Initiating the Listening Process

The implementation of the server's listening process is handled in the **New** procedure, which is located within the Windows Form Designer region of code. Add the following lines of code to this procedure:

```
' Open a port for listening
  Listener = New TcpListener(System.Net.IPAddress.Any, txtPort.Text)
  Listener.Start()

  timMain.Enabled = True
```

The server will listen to all IP addresses that are present on the test PC, monitoring the port as defined by the **Text** property of the TextBox txtPort.

Step 5: Adding the Code to Accept Client Connections

The server uses the Timer control's **Tick** event procedure to check for pending client connections. Add the code shown in Listing 15-9 to this procedure.

Listing 15-9. Watching for TCP Client Connections

```
Private Sub timMain_Tick(ByVal sender As System.Object, _
   ByVal e As System.EventArgs) Handles timMain.Tick
   Dim CurrentThreadStart As ThreadStart
   Dim CurrentThread As Thread
   Dim ThreadCount As Integer
```

```
' Is there a client waiting to connect? If not, exit this routine.
  If Not Listener.Pending() Then
    Exit Sub
  End If


' If you get to here, there is a client waiting. Temporarily disable
' the timer so that you don't try to process any additional connections
' until this one is complete.
  timMain.Enabled = False


' Have you reached the maximum number of connections you'll accept? If
' so, turn the timer back on and leave the requesting client
' waiting.
  If ActiveThreads > MaxConnections Then
    timMain.Enabled = True
    Exit Sub
  End If


' If you get to here, then you are going to accept the client. Define a new
' thread to use with this connection.
  CurrentThreadStart = New ThreadStart(AddressOf ProcessRequest)
  CurrentThread = New Thread(CurrentThreadStart)


' Start the thread.
  CurrentThread.Start()


' Have all of the other threads wait while you increment the counter.
  SyncLock CurrentThread
    ActiveThreads += 1
  End SyncLock


' You're done, so restart the timer.
  timMain.Enabled = True


End Sub
```

This procedure starts by checking to see if a client connection is pending. If there isn't one, then the routine simply exits.

If a connection request is waiting, the server first checks to see if the maximum connection limit has been reached. If not, the connection is accepted and assigned to a new thread for processing. Note that the thread will run a routine called ProcessRequest, which handles communicating with each client.

Step 6: Processing a Client's Request

Within the ProcessRequest routine you'll find the code used to process the communications with each client. Add the code shown in Listing 15-10 to the form code of the server.

Listing 15-10. Processing a Client's Request

```
Protect  Protected Sub ProcessRequest()
  Dim Buffer(100) As Byte
  Dim Bytes As Integer
  Dim CurrentThread As Thread
  Dim CurSocket As Socket
  Dim InboundPacket As String
  Dim OutboundPacket As String
  Dim Temp As String

' Get the current running thread.
  CurrentThread = System.Threading.Thread.CurrentThread()

' Accept the pending socket request.
  CurSocket = Listener.AcceptSocket

' Listen on this socket until you are told to stop.
  While Not StopListener

' Is there anything waiting to be read? If so, read it.
    If CurSocket.Available > 0 Then
      Bytes = CurSocket.Receive(Buffer, Buffer.Length, 0)
      SyncLock CurrentThread
      InboundPacket = System.Text.Encoding.Default.GetString(Buffer)
      End SyncLock
      Exit While
    End If

' Relinquish control to the system so that the other threads may run.
    Application.DoEvents()

' Check to see if the connection is still active.
    If Not CurSocket.Connected Then
      StopListener = True
    End If
  End While
```

```
' Process the packet that was received.
  OutboundPacket = ProcessPacket(InboundPacket)

' Update the display to show both the message received and sent.
  txtDisplay.Text += vbCrLf & InboundPacket
  txtDisplay.Text += vbCrLf & OutboundPacket

' Format the return message.
  Buffer = System.Text.Encoding.Default.GetBytes(OutboundPacket.ToCharArray)

' Send the messsage to the client.
  CurSocket.Send(Buffer, Buffer.Length, 0)
  CurSocket.Close()
  SyncLock CurrentThread
  ActiveThreads -= 1
  End SyncLock

End Sub
```

This procedure starts by retrieving the active thread. It then accepts the pending connection request of that thread, before entering a loop where the server stays until it has retrieved all of the data that the client passed.

Upon completion of the data retrieval, the server sends the data to the ProcessPacket function, where the data is parsed into its various pieces. The ProcessPacket function returns a packet that will be sent on to the client. Both the packet received from the client and the packet being returned to the client will be displayed on the server's interface.

Finally, the return packet is sent to the client, and the server closes the connection before exiting.

Step 7: Processing the Packet

The ProcessPacket function is responsible two tasks: parsing the input packet and building the output packet. Add the code shown in Listing 15-11 to perform these functions.

Listing 15-11. Processing a Packet

```
Function ProcessPacket(ByVal InboundPacket As String) As String
  Dim OutboundPacket As String
  Dim Params As String() = Nothing
  Dim ResultString As String
```

```
' Parse the packet.
  Params = InboundPacket.Split("|")

' Determine what type of packet you received.
  Select Case Params(0)

     Case "DAT" ' Data message

' Build the message header.
        OutboundPacket = "DRP|"

' Add the dual-device info.
        OutboundPacket += "SUCCESS|"
        OutboundPacket += Now.ToString & "|"

     Case Else ' Unknown message type
        Return "unknown"

  End Select

' Return the packet.
  Return OutboundPacket

End Function
```

The ProcessPacket function begins by splitting the inbound packet up into its respective parts. In this demonstration, the first field of the inbound packet is used to define the packet type. There is only a single packet type sent from the client, "DAT", for data.

The ProcessPacket function will build a response that includes a packet header of "DRP".

That completes the server side of things. Next we'll turn our attention to the client component.

Step 8: Opening the Client Project

To simplify this tutorial, I've already created the client project and the user interface for the TCPDemo (client) application. This template project is included under the **Chapter 15** folder in the **Samples** folder. To load this project, follow these steps:

1. From the VS .NET IDE Start Page, select to open a project. The Open Project dialog box will be displayed.

2. Use this dialog box to navigate to the **Chapter 15** folder under the **Samples** folder for this book.

3. Select and open the project **TCPDemo**. The project will be loaded.

Step 9: Examining the Client's User Interface

The user interface for the TCPDemo application is comprised of two Label controls, three TextBox controls, and two Button controls. Figure 15-4 shows the application's interface.

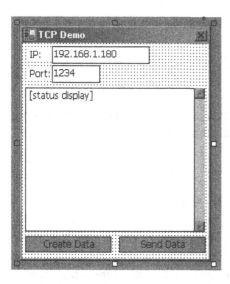

Figure 15-4. The interface to the TCPDemo application

The TCPDemo application is a Pocket PC application.

Step 10: Defining General-Purpose Settings

Before you jump into the client component, you'll first need to define some settings and configurations. First add the following Imports statement above the form's class construct:

```
Imports System.Net.Sockets
```

Next, add the following declarations at the module level of the form:

```
' Example scan record structure.
  Structure ScanRecord
     Dim Barcode As String
     Dim TimeStamp As DateTime
     Dim Qty As Integer
  End Structure

' Queue of scans on the device.
  Dim Scans As New Collection
```

These declarations define first a structure, ScanRecord, and an array, Scans, that will be used to store your dummy scans that are passed as part of this TCP demonstration.

Step 11: Generating the Dummy Scans

The scans used with this demonstration are generated by clicking the **Create Data** button on the client application interface. To implement this functionality, add the code shown in Listing 15-12 to the **Click** event procedure of the **Create Data** button.

Listing 15-12. Code Used to Create Dummy Scans

```
Private Sub btnCreate_Click(ByVal sender As System.Object, _
   ByVal e As System.EventArgs) Handles btnCreate.Click
   Dim Scan As ScanRecord

   Cursor.Current = Cursors.WaitCursor
```

```
' Create the data.
' First record.
  Scan.Barcode = "11111"
  Scan.TimeStamp = Now
  Scan.Qty = 11
  Scans.Add(Scan)
  txtDisplay.Text += vbCrLf & "scanned item 11111"

' Pause for effect.
  System.Threading.Thread.CurrentThread().Sleep(500)

' Second record.
  Scan.Barcode = "22222"
  Scan.TimeStamp = Now
  Scan.Qty = 22
  Scans.Add(Scan)
  txtDisplay.Text += vbCrLf & "scanned item 22222"

' Pause for effect.
  System.Threading.Thread.CurrentThread().Sleep(500)

' Third record.
  Scan.Barcode = "33333"
  Scan.TimeStamp = Now
  Scan.Qty = 33
  Scans.Add(Scan)
  txtDisplay.Text += vbCrLf & "scanned item 33333"

' Toggle the buttons.
  btnCreate.Enabled = False
  btnSend.Enabled = True

  Cursor.Current = Cursors.Default

End Sub
```

The code within this procedure is straightforward. It begins by creating three scans, after which it disables the **Create Data** button and enables the **Send Data** button.

Step 12: Sending Data to the Server

The code that is responsible for sending data to the server is contained within
the **Click** event procedure of the **Send Data** button. Listing 15-13 shows the code
that you need to add to this event.

Listing 15-13. Sending Data to the Server

```
Private Sub btnSend_Click(ByVal sender As System.Object, _
   ByVal e As System.EventArgs) Handles btnSend.Click
   Dim Counter As Integer
   Dim InboundPacket As String
   Dim OutboundPacket As String
   Dim Scan As ScanRecord

' Loop through the data sending it to the server.
   For Each Scan In Scans
      OutboundPacket = "DAT|"
      OutboundPacket += Scan.Barcode & "|"
      OutboundPacket += Scan.TimeStamp & "|"
      OutboundPacket += Scan.Qty & "|"

' Send the message.
      InboundPacket = SendMessage(OutboundPacket)

' Display the return message.
      txtDisplay.Text += vbCrLf & InboundPacket

   Next

' Clear out the collection after the data has been sent.
   For Counter = Scans.Count - 1 To 0 Step -1
     Scans.Remove(1)
   Next

' Toggle the buttons.
   btnSend.Enabled = False
   btnCreate.Enabled = True

End Sub
```

At the heart of this routine is a loop that is used to run through the Scans collection. Within this loop each scan is first packaged up and then sent to the server

for processing. The SendMessage function is called to send each packet to the server. The server's response to each packet is displayed on the client's interface.

Near the bottom of the event procedure the scan collection is emptied and then the two buttons are toggled, preparing the interface for the next test.

Step 13: Sending a Message

The SendMessage routine handles packaging a message, sending that message to the server, and receiving a response back from the server. Encapsulating all of these operations into a single function makes it easy to quickly build TCP-based applications.

To include the SendMessage function in the client application, add the code shown in Listing 15-14.

Listing 15-14. Sending a Message to the Server

```
Function SendMessage(ByVal myMessage As String) As String
  Dim Client As TcpClient
  Dim InBuffer(1000) As Byte
  Dim OutBuffer() As Byte
  Dim ReturnMessage As String

' Connect to the server.
  Client = New TcpClient
  Try
    Client.Connect(txtIP.Text, txtPort.Text)
  Catch ex As Exception
    MsgBox("Connection failed: " & ex.Message)
    Return "[no signal]"
  End Try

' Build the message.
  OutBuffer = System.Text.Encoding.Default.GetBytes(myMessage.ToCharArray)

' Send the message.
  Client.GetStream().Write(OutBuffer, 0, OutBuffer.Length)

' Wait for a response.
  While Not Client.GetStream.DataAvailable()
    Application.DoEvents()
  End While
```

```
' Read the server's response.
  ReturnMessage = ""
  While Client.GetStream.DataAvailable()
    Client.GetStream().Read(InBuffer, 0, InBuffer.Length)
    ReturnMessage &= System.Text.Encoding.Default.GetString(InBuffer, 0, _
      Buffer.Length)
  End While

' Close the connection.
  Client.Close()

' Send back the response.
  Return ReturnMessage

End Function
```

This function begins by establishing a connection to the server. Next, it packages the client's message up into a packet and sends that packet to the server. The function then waits for the server's response, which in turn is converted from a byte array to a string and returned to the client.

Step 14: Testing the Applications

Since this TCP demonstration is comprised of two applications, you'll need to perform some additional steps to test each program. To start the server application, do the following:

1. Select **Release** from the Solution Configurations combo box.

2. Click the **Start** button.

The server application will start running on your development PC. To start the client application, perform the following steps:

1. Select either **Pocket PC Device** or **Pocket PC Emulator** from the Deployment Device combo box.

2. Select **Release** from the Solution Configurations combo box.

3. Click the **Start** button.

With both applications running, perform the following steps to verify the TCP communication:

1. Click the **Create Data** button on the client. You should see a listing of the individual scan records being created.

2. Click the **Send Data** button on the client. On the server, you should see a listing of the records being received. On the client, you should see the server's response to each message.

HOMEWORK *Modify the client and server, adding a second packet type, a logon packet.*

Working with the IrDA Objects

The final form of communication that I want to present in this chapter involves the infrared port found on all Pocket PC devices. *Infrared communication*, or *IR communication* as it's commonly referred to, is best suited for situations where you need to transfer data between two devices.

What type of data can you transfer between devices using IR? Just about anything, including configuration settings, individual items such as a contact or an appointment, and even complete databases.

There are some limitations to take into account when considering using IR communications as part of your applications. IR is a line-of-sight communication, which means the IR port of the sender and the receiver must be in line and unobstructed with each other. Also, the IR hardware used in most Pocket PC devices is far more limited in range and spread than your common household remote control.

Generally speaking, IR communication is best suited for situations where you can butt two devices up next to each other. If these limitations are acceptable in your application setting, you'll be amazed at how easy it is to implement IR-based communications.

IrDA communications is much like TCP communications in that there's a server and a client. The server initiates a listening process and then waits for a client to connect. Once a client connects, the server looks for and reads any data that was sent by the client.

On the client side of an IrDA communication model, the client first establishes a connection and then sends the data to the IrDA server.

In this section, I'll walk you through the complete process, starting with the server component.

Adding a Reference to the IrDA Namespace

In order to incorporate IrDA communication functionality into your mobile applications that leverage the .NET Compact Framework, you'll need to add a reference to the **System.Net.IrDA** namespace.

Developing an IrDA Server

An IrDA server application is similar to a TCP server in that it listens for a client to connect to. It's different from the TCP server in that the server computer is in fact another Pocket PC device.

The actual number of steps in the process of listening for and responding to a client is more limited under IrDA than what I showed for TCP. To create an IrDA server, you need to

1. Listen for a client.

2. Accept the client's connection.

3. Read the stream of data passed from the client.

4. Process the client's data.

5. Close the connection.

We'll examine each of these steps in greater detail in the following section.

 NOTE   *The code presented as part of this discussion is taken from the IrDADemo project, which can be found under the **Chapter 15** folder of the **Samples** folder for this book. See Appendix D for more information on accessing and loading the sample applications.*

Step 1: Listening for a Client

IrDA server applications are built using the **IrDAListener** class. The first step in creating a server involves creating an instance of the **IrDAListener** class and then using the **Start** method provided through this class to begin listening for the client.

You must provide each instance of the IrDAListener object you create with a service name for use with the object. The service name, much like the TCP IP address and port number, will in turn be used by the IrDA client to connect to the server. In the following example, the server name is "IRDA_DEMO":

```
Dim ServiceName As String = "IRDA_DEMO"
Dim listener As IrDAListener = New IrDAListener(ServiceName)

' Wait for client connection.
  listener.Start()
```

Once your server has started listening, you're ready to wait for a client's connection.

Step 2: Accepting the Client's Connection

After an IrDA server application initiates the listening process, it next executes the **AcceptIrDAClient** method, which causes the server application to pause while it waits for a client to connect. The server is effectively paused, waiting for the client.

```
' Accept client connection.
    client = listener.AcceptIrDAClient()
```

Once the connection is made, the **AcceptIrDAClient** method will return an IrDAClient object, through which the server will be able to retrieve the data sent by the client.

Step 3: Reading the Data Passed from the Client

With the connection in hand, the IrDA server is ready to read the data sent from the client. Just as is the case with TCP communication, data passed using IrDA is passed as streams. To retrieve that data, the server application uses the **Read** method of the Stream object. This method returns the data in a byte array as shown in the following code:

```
Dim BytesRead As Integer = 0
Dim Buffer(BufferLength) As Byte
Dim stream As System.IO.Stream = Nothing

stream = client.GetStream()
BytesRead = stream.Read(Buffer, 0, BufferLength)
```

At this point the server has the data sent by the client.

Step 4: Processing the Client's Data

The IrDA server can either convert the buffer to a string, as shown with the TCP example, or work with it in its byte form. The following code shows an example of the latter, where the byte form is used directly. Here you are checking the value of the first byte and configuring a setting on the server application based upon that value.

```
' Read and process the data that the client sent.
  BytesRead = stream.Read(Buffer, 0, BufferLength)
  Select Case Buffer(1)
    Case 0
      Me.BackColor = System.Drawing.Color.Red
    Case 1
      Me.BackColor = System.Drawing.Color.Blue
    Case 2
      Me.BackColor = System.Drawing.Color.Green
    Case 3
      Me.BackColor = System.Drawing.Color.Yellow
    Case 4
      Me.BackColor = System.Drawing.Color.Black
    Case 5
      Me.BackColor = System.Drawing.Color.White
  End Select
```

Step 5: Closing the Connection

The final part of the server process is to close the connection to the client. This involves three steps—closing the stream, closing the connection, and terminating the listening process.

```
' Clean-up before exiting.
  If (Not stream Is Nothing) Then
    stream.Close()
  End If

  If (Not client Is Nothing) Then
    client.Close()
  End If

  listener.Stop()
```

Now that you've seen the server side of IrDA communications, let's turn our attention to the client side.

Developing an IrDA Client

Like the IrDA server, the IrDA client is similar to its TCP counterpart. To create an IrDA client, you need to

1. Connect to the server.

2. Send the data.

3. Close the connection.

We'll examine each of these steps in greater detail in the following section.

 NOTE *The code presented as part of this discussion is taken from the IrDADemo project, which can be found under the **Chapter 15** folder of the **Samples** folder for this book. See Appendix D for more information on accessing and loading the sample applications.*

Step 1: Connecting to the Server

The first step that the client needs to perform is to connect to the server. This process is initiated by creating a new instance of IrDAClient and passing to that instance the service name of the server. In the following example, the service name is "IRDA_DEMO", which matches the name used with the server example, as shown previously in this section.

```
Dim ServiceName As String = "IRDA_DEMO"
client = New IrDAClient(ServiceName)
```

The client application will pause at this point while it waits to establish the connection. You'll need to add error checking to this process to handle situations where this process fails.

NOTE *Typically, the client will know the service name being used by the IrDA server application. In situations where the client doesn't know the name of the server or in environments where there are multiple IrDA servers, you can use the **DiscoverDevices** method of the IrDAClient object. This method returns a list of servers that are presently listening for clients.*

Step 2: Sending the Data

With the connection established to the server, the client is ready to send its data. As was shown with the server, the client uses streams to pass the data. The **GetStream** method of the IrDAClient object returns a stream that you can use to communicate with the server.

```
Dim Buffer(BufferLength) As Byte

stream = client.GetStream()
stream.Write(Buffer, 0, BufferLength)
```

The **Write** method of the stream object sends a byte array from the client to the server.

Step 3: Closing the Connection

When the client completes the process of sending its data, it should close both the stream and the connection to the IrDA server.

```
If (Not stream Is Nothing) Then
  stream.Close()
End If
client.Close()
```

There you have it, the complete process of using IrDA and the IR port on your Pocket PC devices to send data between devices.

Step-by-Step Tutorial: Working with IrDA

In this step-by-step exercise, you'll create an application that demonstrates passing data via the IrDA protocol. As part of this exercise, you'll

- Create a server that will listen for client connections.

- Create a client that will connect to a server.

- Send data from a client.

- Receive data from a client.

This application provides all of the fundamentals of working with IrDA.

 NOTE *I provide a completed version of this application, titled IrDADemo - Complete, under the **Chapter 15** folder of the **Samples** folder for this book. See Appendix D for more information on accessing and loading the sample applications.*

Step 1: Opening the Project

To simplify this tutorial, I've already created the project and the user interface for the IrDADemo application. This template project is included under the **Chapter 15** folder in the **Samples** folder. To load this project, follow these steps:

1. From the VS .NET IDE Start Page, select to open a project. The Open Project dialog box will be displayed.

2. Use this dialog box to navigate to the **Chapter 15** folder under the **Samples** folder for this book.

3. Select and open the project **IrDADemo**. The project will be loaded.

Step 2: Examining the User Interface

The user interface for the IrDADemo application is comprised of several controls: a ListBox and two Buttons. Figure 15-5 shows the application's interface.

The IrDADemo application is both a client and a server. To test it, you'll need to run it on two devices, one acting as the server, the other as the client. The application demonstrates sending a color setting (taken from the ListBox) from the client to the server, where it's applied to the server's form.

Figure 15-5. The interface to the IrDADemo application

Step 3: Defining General-Purpose Settings

Before you jump into the client and server components, you'll first need to define some settings and configurations. First add the following Imports statements above the form's class construct:

```
Imports System.Net
Imports System.Net.Sockets
Imports System.Text
```

Next, add the following declarations at the module level of the form. BufferLength is used to define the length of the byte array the client passes to the server. NumberOfRetries specifies the number of attempts that the client should make while trying to connect to the server. ServiceName is the name that both the client and server will use to establish the connection between them.

```
Private BufferLength As Integer = 2
Private NumberOfRetries As Integer = 5
Private ServiceName As String = "IRDA_DEMO"
```

Step 4: Creating the Server

The IrDA server component of this demonstration application is implemented in the **Click** event procedure of the **Listen** button. Add the code shown in Listing 15-15 to this procedure.

Listing 15-15. Implementing the IrDA Server

```
Private Sub btnListen_Click(ByVal sender As System.Object, _
  ByVal e As System.EventArgs) Handles btnListen.Click
  Dim BytesRead As Integer = 0
  Dim Buffer(BufferLength) As Byte
  Dim listener As IrDAListener = New IrDAListener(ServiceName)
  Dim client As IrDAClient = Nothing
  Dim stream As System.IO.Stream = Nothing

  Try

' Wait for client connection.
    listener.Start()

' Accept client connection.
    client = listener.AcceptIrDAClient()  ' Blocking call
    stream = client.GetStream()

' Read and process the data that the client sent.
    BytesRead = stream.Read(Buffer, 0, BufferLength)
    Select Case Buffer(1)
      Case 0
        Me.BackColor = System.Drawing.Color.Red
      Case 1
        Me.BackColor = System.Drawing.Color.Blue
      Case 2
        Me.BackColor = System.Drawing.Color.Green
      Case 3
        Me.BackColor = System.Drawing.Color.Yellow
      Case 4
        Me.BackColor = System.Drawing.Color.Black
      Case 5
        Me.BackColor = System.Drawing.Color.White
    End Select

' Handle any exceptions that might occur.
  Catch ex As Exception
    MsgBox(ex.Message)

  Finally
```

```
' Clean-up before exiting.
  If (Not stream Is Nothing) Then
    stream.Close()
  End If

  If (Not client Is Nothing) Then
    client.Close()
  End If

  listener.Stop()
End Try

End Sub
```

This procedure starts by listening for a client. It's listening using the service name of "IRDA_DEMO". It then accepts the connection from the client. From this connection the server is able to retrieve a stream object, which in turn is used to retrieve the data that was sent by the client.

The bottom part of the **Click** event procedure contains code that extracts the color sent from the client, which in turn is used to configure the **BackColor** property of the form. Finally, the stream and the connection are closed, completing the process.

Step 5: Creating the Client

Like the server, the client is implemented within the **Click** event procedure of a button. In the case of the client, that button is the **Send** button. Add the code shown in Listing 15-16 to the **Click** event procedure of that button.

Listing 15-16. Implementing the IrDA Client

```
Private Sub btnSend_Click(ByVal sender As System.Object, _
  ByVal e As System.EventArgs) Handles btnSend.Click
  Dim Buffer(BufferLength) As Byte
  Dim client As IrDAClient = Nothing
  Dim CurrentTries As Integer = 0
  Dim stream As System.IO.Stream = Nothing

' Send the selected color.
  Buffer(1) = lstColor.SelectedIndex
```

```
' Loop while trying to send the data.
  Do
    Try
      client = New IrDAClient(ServiceName)
    Catch se As SocketException
      MsgBox(se.Message)
      Exit Sub
    Catch ex As Exception
      MsgBox(ex.Message)
      Exit Sub
    End Try
    CurrentTries = CurrentTries + 1
  Loop while client is Nothing and CurrentTries < NumberOfRetries

' A timeout occurred while attempting to connect to server.
  If (client Is Nothing) Then
    MsgBox("Timeout trying to send.")
    Exit Sub
  End If

' You have a connection, so send the data.
  Try
    stream = client.GetStream()
    stream.Write(Buffer, 0, BufferLength)
    MsgBox("Data sent.")
  Catch ex As Exception
    MsgBox(ex.Message)
  Finally
    If (Not stream Is Nothing) Then
      stream.Close()
    End If
    client.Close()
  End Try

End Sub
```

This procedure starts by storing the color selection into the byte array. Next, the client attempts to connect to the server, using the service name of "IRDA_DEMO". This code is wrapped within a Try-Catch construct to handle any errors that may occur. Particularly, it's designed to handle situations where the server could not be found.

Once a connection is established, a Stream object is used to send the data to the server. The stream's **Send** method is used for this purpose. Upon completion of the send process, the client closes first the stream and then the connection.

Step 6: Testing the Application

Since the IrDADemo application is both client and server, you'll need to run it on two devices so that it can be tested. To start it on a single device, perform the following steps:

1. Select either **Pocket PC Device** or **Pocket PC Emulator** from the Deployment Device combo box.

2. Select **Release** from the Solution Configurations combo box.

3. Click the **Start** button.

The application copies to the target device and starts. After starting the application on the second device, perform the following steps to verify the IrDA communication:

1. Line up the IR ports on both devices.

2. On the device acting as the server, tap the **Listen** button.

3. On the device acting as the client, select a color and then tap the **Send** button.

4. After a brief pause, you should see the color of the server's form change to the color you selected on the client.

 HOMEWORK *Modify the interface to include a TextBox control. Change both the server and client components to pass the text from the TextBox via IrDA.*

Summary

Networking, while often ignored by the desktop developer, is frequently the cornerstone of mobile development. In this chapter, we looked at three different methods of networking—HTTP, TCP, and IrDA. Each method brings a certain set of capabilities and liabilities. Each is suited for a particular purpose. Knowing how to work with each of these methods will give you more options when it comes to developing mobile solutions, and, well, mobile development is all about options.

The HTTP protocol is best suited for use with existing Web servers. With this protocol, you can send data to and from servers. In many cases, you can seamlessly incorporate your mobile applications into existing Web applications.

TCP is by far the most flexible and powerful of the options demonstrated in this chapter. With TCP, you can create custom client and server components that can communicate over the Internet, a wireless network, a phone line, and through the docking cradle.

IrDA, while certainly the most limited method of communicating of the three, has its place. When all you need to do is pass a bit of simple data from one Pocket PC device to another, IrDA offers a simple method without requiring any additional hardware.

CHAPTER 16

XML Web Services

IF THERE'S ONE FEATURE OR capability of .NET that has received the most public attention, it most certainly must be XML Web services. XML Web services offer developers a straightforward and simple way to extend the functionality of their enterprise across the Internet. Obviously, XML Web services are immensely attractive to mobile developers because they provide access to the enterprise from a device.

The .NET Compact Framework allows mobile developers to easily access XML Web services just as they would from a desktop application written against the .NET Framework. While the .NET Compact Framework does have some limitations when it comes to XML Web services (which will be detailed later in this chapter), for the most part, the most commonly used and helpful functionality of XML Web services is provided for use in your mobile applications.

XML Web services are not difficult to use. While much of the publicly available publications on XML Web services tend to be heavy in theory and light in practical examples, I'm going to take the opposite approach in this chapter. We'll instead concentrate on the details of implementing and incorporating XML Web services into your .NET Compact Framework applications. Along the way, you will learn

- Basics of XML Web services

- The NETCF limitations regarding XML Web services

- How to create an XML Web service

- How to access an XML Web service from your mobile application

- Techniques for passing various types of data from an XML Web service including structures, objects, and DataSets

XML Web services can be leveraged by your mobile applications for numerous reasons. They can be used to obtain information on the fly, such as retrieving a detailed map based upon your current GPS position. XML Web services can be used to query an enterprise database, regardless of the vendor of that database. For example, you could use XML Web services to deliver order status to salespeople while they are on the road. XML Web services can pass DataSets, allowing the client to work with data in a detached method. This data can be altered and subsequently returned to the XML Web service for processing. They can be used to update your application's software, providing you an easy way to deliver updates to the field. This is just a few of the multitude of uses for XML Web services.

We'll start our discussion of XML Web services with a brief overview of what they are, how you find out about them, and how they are incorporated into your application.

 NOTE *To be able to work through the samples demonstrated in this chapter, you will need a server running Microsoft's Internet Information Server (IIS) and the .NET Framework. For testing purposes, this system could be your development PC.*

Understanding XML Web Services

Of all of the discussions, white papers, articles, and books I've seen on XML Web services, none of them have described this technology as simply as I feel it should be. XML Web services are nothing more than subroutines and functions that you publicly expose for access over the Internet or intranet. These publicly exposed subroutines and functions appear as methods to the application consuming the XML Web service.

Pretty much anything that you can do in a normal subroutine or function, you can do within an XML Web service method. You can implement business rules; access enterprise data sources; interface to messaging systems, such as Microsoft Exchange or SMTP servers; and even call other XML Web services.

There are two key features to XML Web services. First, XML Web service methods are a black box to the client application. That is to say, the client application has no idea of what is being performed within an XML Web service method. This allows you to hide sensitive details within the confines of a method, and at the same time take the complexity out of the mobile developer's hands. Second, XML Web services can be updated at any time. You can change the logic within a method without having to alter all of the client applications that leverage the XML Web service. For example, you could switch a method that calls an Oracle database to one that calls a SQL Server database without having any impact on the client application.

As you would guess by their name, XML Web services pass data as XML. They communicate via the HTTP (and HTTPS) protocols, which means they are firewall friendly. While the examples shown in this chapter are based upon Microsoft products only, XML Web services are by no means limited to Microsoft platforms. From your .NET Compact Framework applications, you can call XML Web services that run under a variety of operating systems.

While I mentioned that I was going to limit the discussion of the theory behind XML Web services, there are some key concepts that you need to understand before we move on to the practical steps in implementing and using Web services. Three items in particular, finding a list of XML Web services, obtaining a description of an XML Web service, and determining what an XML Web service offers, are critical to working with XML Web services. We'll look at each of these topics in the following section.

Finding XML Web Services

XML Web services are literally spread throughout the Internet. To state the obvious, to be able to leverage these XML Web services from within your mobile applications, you must know 1) that they exist, and 2) where they exist. That's where UDDI, or Universal Description, Discovery, and Integration, comes in. Think of UDDI as the yellow pages for XML Web services.

UDDI is an industry standard for registering XML Web services. Through UDDI you can search for XML Web services that may meet your application's needs. UDDI Web sites host information on a variety of XML Web services, making it easy for you to locate and obtain details on publicly available XML Web services.

NOTE *You can obtain more information on UDDI at either the UDDI Web site (*http://www.uddi.org*) or the Microsoft UDDI Web site (*http://uddi.microsoft.com*).*

Visual Studio .NET 2003 allows you to both search and publish to a UDDI registry. To use the VS .NET 2003 IDE to connect to a UDDI server, search for and examine XML Web services by perform the following:

1. On the Visual Studio .NET 2003 Start Page, click the **Online Resources** tab.

2. From the **Online Resources** tab, select **XML Web Services**. The XML Web service interface will be displayed as shown in Figure 16-1.

3. Select an item from the Category combo box.

4. In the Search for text box, enter a keyword associated with the XML Web service you want to locate.

5. Click the **Go** button.

Figure 16-1. The interface for finding and publishing XML Web services

Matching XML Web services will be displayed as shown in Figure 16-2. To add references to an XML Web service to your project, simply click the associated **Add as web reference to your project** link.

Figure 16-2. The resulting list of XML Web services returned from the search

Obtaining a Description of an XML Web Service

Now that you have a way to locate XML Web services, the next step is determining what an XML Web service has to offer. This determination is handled through a process that is commonly referred to as *discovery*.

The discovery process provides the location of the files that describe an XML Web service. These locations are contained within a *DISCO file*. The term *DISCO* comes from the abbreviation of DISCOvery. DISCO files have the extension .disco. Visual Studio .NET–generated DISCO files have the extension .vsdisco. Listing 16-1 shows the DISCO file for the Demo XML Web service presented throughout this chapter.

Listing 16-1. The Contents of the Demo Service's DISCO File

```
<?xml version="1.0" encoding="utf-8"?>
<discovery xmlns:xsd="http://www.w3.org/2001/XMLSchema"
xmlns:xsi="http://www.w3.org/2001/XMLSchema-instance"
xmlns="http://schemas.xmlsoap.org/disco/">
  <contractRef ref=http://192.168.1.180/WebServiceDemo/Demo.asmx?wsdl
   docRef=http://localhost/WebServiceDemo/Demo.asmx
   xmlns="http://schemas.xmlsoap.org/disco/scl/" />
  <soap address=http://192.168.1.180/WebServiceDemo/Demo.asmx
   xmlns:q1="http://tempuri.org/WebServiceDemo/Demo" binding="q1:DemoSoap"
   xmlns="http://schemas.xmlsoap.org/disco/soap/" />
</discovery>
```

Take a moment to examine this file. Note the following:

- Opening and closing <discovery> tags

- The reference to the WSDL file, which defines what an XML Web service offers

- The reference to the .asmx file, which you will use when adding a Web reference to your project

NOTE *In Listing 16-1, 192.168.1.180 is the TCP/IP address of the machine where the XML Web service resides.*

Now that you know how to find XML Web services and obtain information about them, let's look at how you go about determining what an XML Web service has to offer. That description is provided through the Web Services Description Language (WSDL) document, which you learn about in the DISCO file. WSDL documents are the topic of the following section.

Determining What an XML Web Service Offers

XML Web services are, by definition, public functions and subroutines exposed as methods. Developers who want to call these methods must know the programmatic interface that is provided by the XML Web service—that is to say, what methods and properties an XML Web service exposes, the arguments for the methods, what the methods return, and what data types are used.

Web services are described through the Web Services Description Language, or WSDL. Visual Studio .NET 2003 uses WSDL files to build proxy objects for you automatically, allowing you to easily incorporate and work with XML Web services within your NETCF applications.

The WSDL for an XML Web service is stored in a file with a .wsdl extension. As you might expect, this file is in XML format. Listing 16-2 shows the WSDL file for the demonstration XML Web service presented throughout this chapter.

Listing 16-2. The Contents of the Demo Service's WSDL File

```
<?xml version="1.0" encoding="utf-8"?>
<definitions xmlns:http=http://schemas.xmlsoap.org/wsdl/http/
 xmlns:soap="http://schemas.xmlsoap.org/wsdl/soap/"
 xmlns:s="http://www.w3.org/2001/XMLSchema"
 xmlns:s0="http://tempuri.org/WebServiceDemo/Demo"
 xmlns:soapenc="http://schemas.xmlsoap.org/soap/encoding/"
 xmlns:tm="http://microsoft.com/wsdl/mime/textMatching/"
 xmlns:mime="http://schemas.xmlsoap.org/wsdl/mime/"
 targetNamespace="http://tempuri.org/WebServiceDemo/Demo"
 xmlns="http://schemas.xmlsoap.org/wsdl/">
  <types>
    <s:schema elementFormDefault="qualified"
  targetNamespace="http://tempuri.org/WebServiceDemo/Demo">
      <s:import namespace="http://www.w3.org/2001/XMLSchema" />
      <s:element name="CalcPay">
        <s:complexType>
          <s:sequence>
            <s:element minOccurs="1" maxOccurs="1" name="Hours"
              type="s:float" />
            <s:element minOccurs="1" maxOccurs="1" name="Rate" type="s:float" />
          </s:sequence>
```

```
      </s:complexType>
  </s:element>
  <s:element name="CalcPayResponse">
    <s:complexType>
      <s:sequence>
        <s:element minOccurs="1" maxOccurs="1" name="CalcPayResult"
          type="s:float" />
      </s:sequence>
    </s:complexType>
  </s:element>
  <s:element name="StructureDemo">
    <s:complexType>
      <s:sequence>
        <s:element minOccurs="0" maxOccurs="1" name="ListingNumber"
          type="s:string" />
      </s:sequence>
    </s:complexType>
  </s:element>
  <s:element name="StructureDemoResponse">
    <s:complexType>
      <s:sequence>
        <s:element minOccurs="1" maxOccurs="1" name="StructureDemoResult"
          type="s0:ListingSpecs" />
      </s:sequence>
    </s:complexType>
  </s:element>
  <s:complexType name="ListingSpecs">
    <s:sequence>
      <s:element minOccurs="0" maxOccurs="1" name="ListingNumber"
        type="s:string" />
      <s:element minOccurs="0" maxOccurs="1" name="Address"
        type="s:string" />
      <s:element minOccurs="1" maxOccurs="1" name="Rooms" type="s:int" />
      <s:element minOccurs="1" maxOccurs="1" name="Bedrooms"
        type="s:float" />
      <s:element minOccurs="1" maxOccurs="1" name="Baths" type="s:float" />
      <s:element minOccurs="1" maxOccurs="1" name="Size" type="s:int" />
      <s:element minOccurs="0" maxOccurs="1" name="Price" type="s:string" />
    </s:sequence>
  </s:complexType>
  <s:element name="ClassDemo">
    <s:complexType>
      <s:sequence>
        <s:element minOccurs="0" maxOccurs="1" name="ListingNumber"
          type="s:string" />
```

639

```
              </s:sequence>
            </s:complexType>
          </s:element>
          <s:element name="ClassDemoResponse">
            <s:complexType>
              <s:sequence>
                <s:element minOccurs="0" maxOccurs="1" name="ClassDemoResult"
                  type="s0:DemoClass" />
              </s:sequence>
            </s:complexType>
          </s:element>
          <s:complexType name="DemoClass">
            <s:sequence>
              <s:element minOccurs="0" maxOccurs="1" name="ListingNumber"
                type="s:string" />
              <s:element minOccurs="0" maxOccurs="1" name="Address"
                type="s:string" />
              <s:element minOccurs="1" maxOccurs="1" name="Rooms" type="s:int" />
              <s:element minOccurs="1" maxOccurs="1" name="Bedrooms"
                type="s:float" />
              <s:element minOccurs="1" maxOccurs="1" name="Baths" type="s:float" />
              <s:element minOccurs="1" maxOccurs="1" name="Size" type="s:int" />
              <s:element minOccurs="0" maxOccurs="1" name="Price" type="s:string" />
            </s:sequence>
          </s:complexType>
          <s:element name="DsDemo">
            <s:complexType />
          </s:element>
          <s:element name="DsDemoResponse">
            <s:complexType>
              <s:sequence>
                <s:element minOccurs="0" maxOccurs="1" name="DsDemoResult">
                  <s:complexType>
                    <s:sequence>
                      <s:element ref="s:schema" />
                      <s:any />
                    </s:sequence>
                  </s:complexType>
                </s:element>
              </s:sequence>
            </s:complexType>
          </s:element>
        </s:schema>
      </types>
```

```
<message name="CalcPaySoapIn">
  <part name="parameters" element="s0:CalcPay" />
</message>
<message name="CalcPaySoapOut">
  <part name="parameters" element="s0:CalcPayResponse" />
</message>
<message name="StructureDemoSoapIn">
  <part name="parameters" element="s0:StructureDemo" />
</message>
<message name="StructureDemoSoapOut">
  <part name="parameters" element="s0:StructureDemoResponse" />
</message>
<message name="ClassDemoSoapIn">
  <part name="parameters" element="s0:ClassDemo" />
</message>
<message name="ClassDemoSoapOut">
  <part name="parameters" element="s0:ClassDemoResponse" />
</message>
<message name="DsDemoSoapIn">
  <part name="parameters" element="s0:DsDemo" />
</message>
<message name="DsDemoSoapOut">
  <part name="parameters" element="s0:DsDemoResponse" />
</message>
<portType name="DemoSoap">
  <operation name="CalcPay">
    <input message="s0:CalcPaySoapIn" />
    <output message="s0:CalcPaySoapOut" />
  </operation>
  <operation name="StructureDemo">
    <input message="s0:StructureDemoSoapIn" />
    <output message="s0:StructureDemoSoapOut" />
  </operation>
  <operation name="ClassDemo">
    <input message="s0:ClassDemoSoapIn" />
    <output message="s0:ClassDemoSoapOut" />
  </operation>
  <operation name="DsDemo">
    <input message="s0:DsDemoSoapIn" />
    <output message="s0:DsDemoSoapOut" />
  </operation>
</portType>
```

```
<binding name="DemoSoap" type="s0:DemoSoap">
  <soap:binding transport=http://schemas.xmlsoap.org/soap/http
style="document" />
  <operation name="CalcPay">
    <soap:operation
soapAction="http://tempuri.org/WebServiceDemo/Demo/CalcPay" style="document" />
    <input>
      <soap:body use="literal" />
    </input>
    <output>
      <soap:body use="literal" />
    </output>
  </operation>
  <operation name="StructureDemo">
    <soap:operation
soapAction="http://tempuri.org/WebServiceDemo/Demo/StructureDemo"
style="document" />
    <input>
      <soap:body use="literal" />
    </input>
    <output>
      <soap:body use="literal" />
    </output>
  </operation>
  <operation name="ClassDemo">
    <soap:operation
soapAction="http://tempuri.org/WebServiceDemo/Demo/ClassDemo"
style="document" />
    <input>
      <soap:body use="literal" />
    </input>
    <output>
      <soap:body use="literal" />
    </output>
  </operation>
  <operation name="DsDemo">
    <soap:operation soapAction="http://tempuri.org/WebServiceDemo/Demo/DsDemo"
      style="document" />
    <input>
      <soap:body use="literal" />
    </input>
    <output>
      <soap:body use="literal" />
    </output>
  </operation>
```

```
    </binding>
    <service name="Demo">
      <port name="DemoSoap" binding="s0:DemoSoap">
        <soap:address location="http://localhost/WebServiceDemo/Demo.asmx" />
      </port>
    </service>
</definitions>
```

The thing to note here is the length of this WSDL document. It's several pages long, all to define the interface for a simple XML Web service that exposes four—that's right, four—methods. Now, thankfully, you don't have to create these documents by hand. Visual Studio .NET 2003 generates them for you.

TIP *As you work through the remainder of this chapter and examine the sample XML Web service that's presented, I would suggest you turn back from time to time to this WSDL code and examine how each property and method is described.*

Figure 16-3 shows this same WSDL code within Internet Explorer. Here you can more clearly see the definition of the **CalcPay** method, with its two arguments, **Hours** and **Rate**. Both arguments are of the data type **Single**.

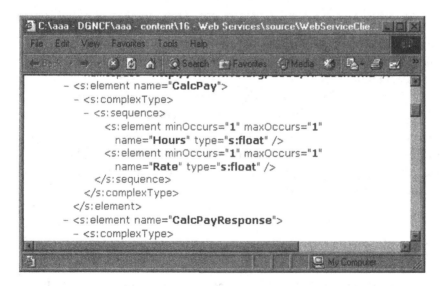

Figure 16-3. The WSDL code for the demo XML Web service

TIP *You can use Internet Explorer or another XML viewing utility to simplify viewing WSDL files.*

Now that you have a basic understanding of how you go about locating an XML Web service, discovering what that XML Web service has to offer, and determining the methods and properties exposed by the XML Web service, let's look at what Web service functionality is absent from the .NET Compact Framework.

Web Service Limitations with NETCF

The implementation of Web services under the .NET Compact Framework is a limited version of the Web service capabilities offered through the .NET Framework. The functionality that is most notably absent is

- The inability to host Web services. The .NET Compact Framework limits you to creating client applications that access Web services.

- Support for typed DataSets. While your mobile application can still access and retrieve DataSets from a Web service, the DataSets can't be typed. We'll see more on the topic of retrieving DataSets later in this chapter.

- Only basic and digest authentication are supported for use in securing the access of Web services from mobile applications. NTLM, the most secure method of HTTP authentication, is not supported under the .NET Compact Framework.

- No support for binary serialization and deserialization.

Now that you have a basic understanding of the concepts behind XML Web services, let's turn our attention to the process of creating both an XML Web service and the client to consume that service.

Creating an XML Web Service

The best way to learn about XML Web services is to create and consume XML Web services. In the remainder of this chapter, I'm going to walk you through the process of creating both an XML Web service and the NETCF client application that will consume that service. The approach I'm using will give you an understanding of

- How to create an XML Web service

- The process of adding methods to an XML Web service

- The various forms of data that can be returned from an XML Web service, including structures, objects, and DataSets

- How to call an XML Web service asynchronously, allowing your application to perform other activities while waiting for a response from the Web service

I'll start this discussion by showing you how to create a simple XML Web service.

Creating the XML Web Service Project

For the most part, this book has presented techniques and guidance on creating mobile applications. And while I could certainly just show you how to consume Web services, oftentimes your mobile solution will require you to create the XML Web service as well. That's why in this section we are going to slip over to the desktop or server side to examine the process used to create XML Web services.

NOTE *To re-create the examples on creating Web services, you'll need a machine running Microsoft's Internet Information Server. IIS can be running on your development PC, a server within your enterprise, or at an ISP.*

To start an XML Web service project, perform the following steps:

1. From the Start Page, click the **New Project** button. The New Project dialog box will be displayed as shown in Figure 16-4.

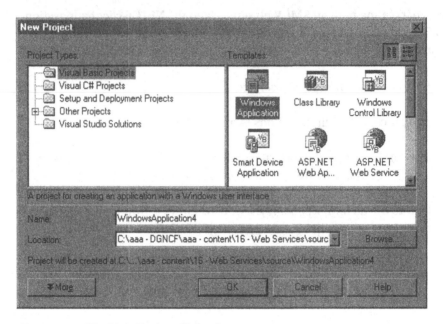

Figure 16-4. The New Project dialog box

2. In this dialog box, select the **Visual Basic Projects** folder and then the
    ASP.NET Web Service project template.

3. Note that when you select the ASP.NET Web Service project template
    that the Name field is disabled and the Location field is switched to
    `http://localhost/` followed by the name of your Web service. This loca-
    tion defines where your Web service will be created. The term *localhost*
    refers to your machine. You'll need to change this location to the IP
    address of the machine on which you'll run the Web service, whether
    that be your own development machine or another server. Figure 16-5
    shows the dialog box after I've modified the location to the IP address of
    my machine.

4. The last item you need to configure for your new project is the name of
    the Web service itself. For the purpose of the examples shown through-
    out the remainder of this chapter, that name is WebServiceDemo.
    Figure 16-6 shows the New Project dialog box as it appears with the con-
    figuration complete.

5. Click the **OK** button to create the XML Web service project.

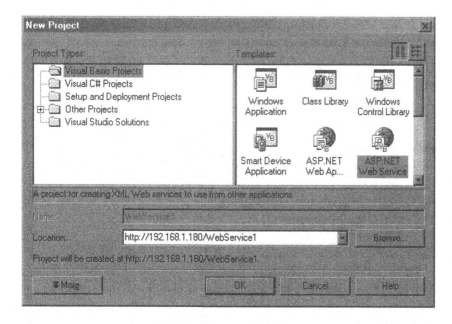

Figure 16-5. Configuring the IP address of the server

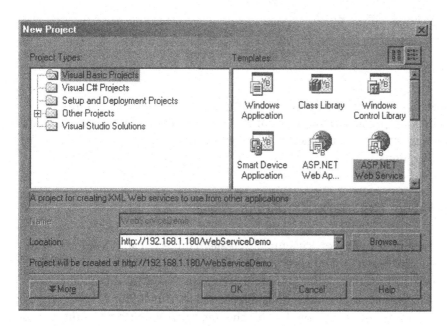

Figure 16-6. Configuring the name of the XML Web service

The ASP.NET Web Service template creates a shell of an XML Web service for you. Listing 16-3 shows the starter code that is provided for you.

Listing 16-3. Starter Code Provided with the ASP.NET Web Service Template

```
Imports System.Web.Services

<System.Web.Services.WebService(Namespace :=
 "http://tempuri.org/WebServiceDemo/Service1")> _
Public Class Service1
    Inherits System.Web.Services.WebService
[Web Services Designer Generated Code]
    ' WEB SERVICE EXAMPLE
    ' The HelloWorld() example service returns the string Hello World.
    ' To build, uncomment the following lines then save and build the project.
    ' To test this Web service, ensure that the .asmx file is the start page
    ' and press F5.
    '
    '<WebMethod()> _
    'Public Function HelloWorld() As String
    '    Return "Hello World"
    'End Function

End Class
```

Note that in the lower part of this listing there is a section of commented-out code that contains a simple example of how you implement a method. You'll be working with this method shortly, but before that, you need to make a couple of modifications.

Modifying the Default Class Name

When the ASP.NET Web Service template creates a project, it adds a default class module called **Service1**. This class module describes the service your XML Web service will be providing. While you could certainly go with this default name, as with most cases of automatic naming, there is usually something far more appropriate. For the example presented in this chapter, you're going to name this service Demo. You will need to perform the following steps to implement this change:

1. Rename the class file from Service1.asmx to **Demo.asmx**.

2. Rename the Service1 class to **Demo**. You will need to do this from the code window.

You're now ready to add a method to your new service.

Adding Methods

As I've already stated, methods are nothing more than subroutines and functions. It shouldn't surprise you then that to add a method to a Web service, you simply add a subroutine or function to the class module that defines the service.

There is one small difference between how you implement a method for a Web service and the creation of a standard subroutine or function—the addition of the <WebMethod()> attribute.

Listing 16-4 shows an example of the syntax for adding a WebMethod attribute. The difference between a normal subroutine or function and a Web service method is nothing more than the attribute tag <WebMethod()>.

Listing 16-4. Adding a WebMethod Attribute

```
<WebMethod()> _
Public Function CalcPay(ByVal Hours As Single, ByVal Rate As Single) As Single

' Calculate the employee's pay.
  Return Hours * Rate

End Function
```

Adding a Method to Your Web Service

At this point, your Web service has no methods. You're going to correct that by removing the comments in front of the **HelloWorld** method. To accomplish this, perform the following steps:

1. Open up the **Demo** class module if necessary.

2. Locate the block of commented code that defines the **HelloWorld** method.

3. Remove the comment characters from the front of each line of this method, starting with the Web service attribute line (<WebMethod()>) and continuing on through the End Function statement of the **HelloWorld** function.

That's it. Your newly created Web service now contains a single method called **HelloWorld**. Listing 16-5 shows the new method as it should appear.

Listing 16-5. The HelloWorld Method

```
' WEB SERVICE EXAMPLE
' The HelloWorld() example service returns the string Hello World.
' To build, uncomment the following lines then save and build the project.
' To test this Web service, ensure that the .asmx file is the start page
' and press F5.
'
<WebMethod()> _
Public Function HelloWorld() As String
   Return "Hello World"
End Function
```

This method does nothing more than return the string **"Hello World"**, which isn't anything in itself to get excited about, but it does demonstrate the basic functionality of XML Web services.

Testing Your Web Service

Now you're ready to test your Web service. One of the cool features of developing an XML Web service within Visual Studio .NET 2003 is the ability to test a Web service without having to create a client application.

To test your XML Web service, click the **Start** button on the Visual Studio .NET toolbar. Your Web service will first be built and then displayed within a browser window as shown in Figure 16-7.

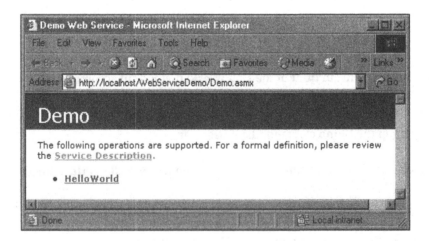

Figure 16-7. Testing your Web service from within Visual Studio .NET

I want to highlight a few key points shown in Figure 16-7. First, note the contents of the address bar—http://localhost/WebServiceDemo/Demo.asmx. Both the name of your XML Web service project, WebServiceDemo, and the name of the service class, **Demo**, are part of the address.

Second, notice the link to the service description. Remember from earlier in this chapter, service descriptions are stored in WSDL documents. Clicking the Service Description link will display the contents of the WSDL document as shown in Figure 16-8. Note that in Figure 16-8 I've scrolled to the section of this document that defines both the **HelloWorld** method and the response returned from this method.

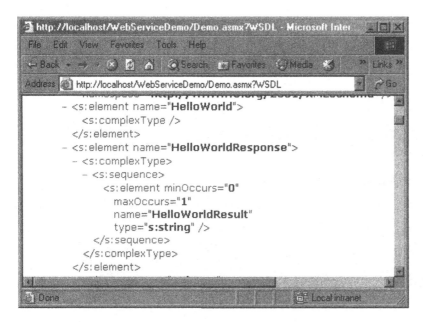

Figure 16-8. Viewing the WSDL document for your Web service

The third point that I want you to see in Figure 16-7 is the link to the **HelloWorld** method. Clicking this link takes you to a browser page where you can test your Web method. This feature is a tremendous capability as it allows you to test your Web methods without having to create a client application. Clicking the HelloWorld link causes the test page shown in Figure 16-9 to be displayed.

Clicking the **Invoke** button on this test page calls your Web method and returns the result in the form of XML. The resulting XML is displayed in a new browser window as shown in Figure 16-10.

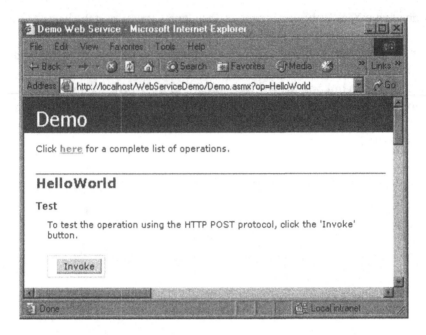

Figure 16-9. Testing the HelloWorld method

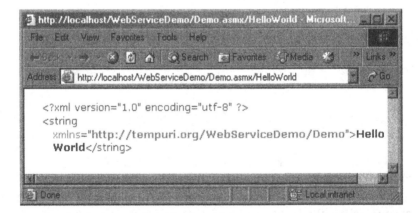

Figure 16-10. The result returned from calling the HelloWorld method

NOTE *The XML Web service project demonstrated throughout this chapter, WebServiceDemo, can be found under the **Chapter 16** folder in the **Samples** folder for this book. See Appendix D for details on loading and working with the sample applications.*

Now that you have the basic process of creating an XML Web service, let's turn our attention to creating a .NET Compact Framework application that consumes the Web service.

Creating a Web Service Client

As the previous section demonstrated, creating an XML Web service is, at its basic levels, pretty straightforward and easy. Now, let's look at what it takes to consume, or use, your new Web service from within a client application.

Adding Web service functionality to your mobile application requires three steps:

1. Adding a Web reference for the XML Web service.

2. Creating an instance of the Web service class.

3. Consuming (calling) the Web service methods.

Details of each of these steps are presented in the following sections.

Adding a Web Reference

Before you can call an XML Web service from within your mobile application, you must first add a Web reference to the service. Doing so will cause Visual Studio .NET 2003 to automatically create the proxy object, which is needed to communicate to the selected XML Web service.

To add a Web reference to an XML Web service to your mobile application, perform the following steps:

1. Open your mobile application within the Visual Studio .NET 2003 IDE.

2. Under the Project menu, select **Add Web Reference**.

3. The Add Web Reference dialog box will be displayed. In the URL field of this dialog box, enter the URL of XML Web service as shown in Figure 16-11.

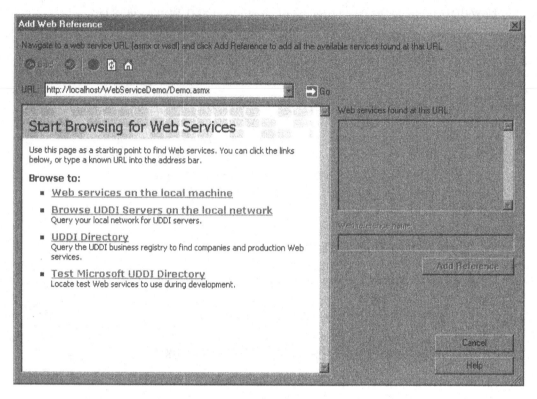

Figure 16-11. The Add Web Reference dialog box as it first appears

---

TIP *If you are developing the XML Web service yourself, an easy way to get the URL of the service is to copy it from your browser's address bar and paste it into the URL field when testing the service.*

---

4. Click the **Go** button. Information on the selected XML Web service will be retrieved and displayed in the body of the dialog box.

NOTE *The body of the Add Web Reference dialog box works just as if you were accessing the selected service via a browser.*

---

5. In the Web reference name field, enter the name to assign to this reference within your project.

NOTE *In the examples shown throughout this chapter, the Web reference name has been set to Chapter16.*

6. Click the **Add Reference** button.

Web references that are added to your project appear in a folder within the **Web References** folder of the Solution Explorer window. You can configure the properties of your Web reference by selecting the reference itself, or the files that are part of a reference in the Solution Explorer window.

TIP *If you are developing both the Web service and the client at the same time, you will need to update the Web reference in the client as you make changes to the Web service. To do this, simply right-click the Web reference in the Solution Explorer window and then select **Update Web Reference** from the context-sensitive menu.*

Now that you have a reference to the XML Web service added to your project, you're ready to turn your attention to the code required to create an instance of an XML Web service class and to consume its methods.

Creating an Instance of the Web Service Class

Like any object created from a class, before you can work with a class provided by the Web service, you must first create an instance of that class.

In the following example, ws is the name of the object with which you'll be working, Chapter16 is the name of the Web reference, and **Demo** is the name of the class, or what is more commonly referred to as the service, with which you will be working.

```
Dim ws As New Chapter16.Demo
```

Where you place the declaration of the Web service variable depends upon the needs of your application. All of the normal variable scope-related issues apply here as they would with any VB .NET variable.

NOTE *If you are following along with the two projects demonstrated throughout this chapter, WebServiceDemo and WebServiceClient, you'll note that Demo is the name given to the class module within the Web service project.*

With the addition of this single line of code, you're ready to begin working with the methods and properties provided through the Web service.

Consuming Web Service Methods

Finally, you're ready to work with the methods provided by the Web service. The following example demonstrates calling the **HelloWorld** method of the Demo Web service.

```
Dim ws As New Chapter16.Demo
MessageBox.Show(ws.HelloWorld())
```

 NOTE *The client project demonstrated throughout this chapter, WebServiceClient, can be found under the Chapter 16 folder in the Samples folder for this book. See Appendix D for details on loading and working with the sample applications.*

As you can see, creating and working with Web services is much about classes. All of the techniques of adding properties and methods to a class apply to Web services as well. From the client side of things, the process of creating an instance of and working with a class defined by a Web service is no different than that used with any other class.

Now that you have a basic understanding of the process of creating and consuming a Web service from both the server and client side, let's turn our attention to how you go about passing various forms of data between the two.

Passing Data from XML Web Services

First the basics: You use the same techniques to pass data to and from an XML Web service method as you would with any other method that you implement through a class module. And while there are some limitations imposed by the implementation of Web services under the .NET Compact Framework, as referenced earlier in this chapter, you will find that you have a broad assortment of alternatives for passing data between a Web service and a client application.

In this section, I'm going to show you how to pass data as arrays, structures, objects, and DataSets. These methods for passing data, along with the more common data types (**integer**, **string**, etc.) provide you with a fairly solid set of options with which to construct your mobile applications. We'll start our discussion with arrays.

Passing Arrays from XML Web Services

In situations where you need to pass blocks of structured data between a Web service and a client application, you may want to consider arrays. When combined with structures, which are discussed later in this section, arrays offer you a clean and manageable way to pass large amounts of data.

For example, say you're creating a mobile real estate listing application. The client application queries a Web service to obtain home listings. Within the Web service method, each listing is added to an array, which is subsequently returned to the client. Each listing is as an item in an array. Within the client application, you simply need to iterate through the array to access and display details about each listing.

From the Web server side, adding a method that returns an array is straightforward. Listing 16-6 shows a simple demonstration of this process.

Listing 16-6. Returning an Array from a Web Method

```
<WebMethod()> _
Public Function RetrieveArray() As String()
  Dim Working(3) As String

' Load the array.
  Working(0) = "first item"
  Working(1) = "second item"
  Working(2) = "third item"
  Working(3) = "fourth item"

' Load the array.
  Return Working

End Function
```

The size of the array can vary depending upon the amount of data that needs to be returned. While the return argument of the Web method is defined as an array, the size of the array isn't specified. This enables you to vary the size of the array returned, depending upon your application needs.

On the client side, calling a Web method that returns an array is shown in Listing 16-7.

Listing 16-7. Calling a Web Method That Returns an Array

```
Private Sub btnRetrieveArray_Click(ByVal sender As System.Object,
  ByVal e As System.EventArgs) Handles btnRetrieveArray.Click
  Dim ws As New Chapter16.Demo
  Dim myArray as String()

' Call the RetrieveArray Web service method.
  Cursor.Current = Cursors.WaitCursor
  myArray = ws.ReturnArray ()
  Cursor.Current = Cursors.Default

' Display the first item.
  MessageBox.Show(myArray(0))

End Sub
```

As you can see, incorporating arrays is pretty straightforward. I think they are ideally suited for situations where you need to pass blocks of data and don't want to use DataSets.

As I mentioned earlier in this section, arrays are particularly useful when combined with structures, which we'll be discussing next.

Passing Structures from XML Web Services

Structures provide you with a way to incorporate complex data types into your Web methods. For example, let's say you are building that mobile real estate application. The client application makes a call to the Web service to retrieve the listing of a house. That listing is comprised of the typical listing details including price, size, number of bedrooms, number of baths, and size of the lot. This is a perfect situation in which to use structures.

To create a Web method that returns a structure, you need to do two things: 1) define the structure that will be passed, and 2) create the method that returns this structure.

Listing 16-8 shows the first part of this process, defining the structure. As you can see, this is just a plain vanilla structure definition.

Listing 16-8. Defining a Structure for Use with a Web Method

```
Public Structure ListingSpecs
   Public ListingNumber As String
   Public Address As String
   Public Rooms As Integer
   Public Bedrooms As Single
   Public Baths As Single
   Public Size As Integer
   Public Price As String
End Structure
```

The key point to note from this listing is the fact that the structure is declared as public. It needs to be this way so that the client application will be able to see it. Since the Web method is going to return this structure, you have to provide the client with a description of the structure. Again, this is no different from what you would do with a class module through which you want to expose a structure definition.

With the structure defined, you're ready to create the Web method that will make use of the structure. Listing 16-9 provides an example that makes use of the ListingSpecs structure just described.

Listing 16-9. Creating a Web Method That Returns a Structure

```
<WebMethod()> _
Public Function StructureDemo(ByVal ListingNumber As String)
   As ListingSpecs
   Dim mySpec As ListingSpecs

' Grab the specs for the requested listing.
   Select Case ListingNumber
      Case "11111"
         mySpec.ListingNumber = "11111"
         mySpec.Address = "111 Main Street"
         mySpec.Rooms = 10
         mySpec.Bedrooms = 3
         mySpec.Baths = 2.5
         mySpec.Size = 2400
         mySpec.Price = "$240,000"
      Case "22222"
         mySpec.ListingNumber = "22222"
         mySpec.Address = "222 East Maple Street"
```

```
        mySpec.Rooms = 8
        mySpec.Bedrooms = 2
        mySpec.Baths = 1.5
        mySpec.Size = 1800
        mySpec.Price = "$190,000"
    Case "33333"
        mySpec.ListingNumber = "33333"
        mySpec.Address = "333 Front Street"
        mySpec.Rooms = 9
        mySpec.Bedrooms = 3
        mySpec.Baths = 2
        mySpec.Size = 2050
        mySpec.Price = "$225,000"
    End Select


    ' Return the selected listing.
    Return mySpec

End Function
```

There are four points that I want to focus on in this example. First, the **StructureDemo** Web method accepts a single argument, which contains the listing number of the house for which the client application is requesting details.

Second, the Web method will return a ListingSpec structure, as defined by the function description.

Third, this method has been simplified for clarity. Where I use a simple Select Case statement to return one of three available listings, in actuality you would most probably be retrieving a listing from a database. What I wanted to demonstrate here was the loading of the structure.

Fourth, at the bottom of Listing 16-9, you can see where the structure is returned to the client application.

You could easily combine the example on passing arrays with this structure example to create a Web method that passes an array of structures. For example, let's say the client application allows the user to specify a set of criteria for a house, such as a price limit, location, and minimum size. It then calls a Web method to retrieve all of the listings that match the specified criteria. One way to accomplish this would be to create an array of the ListingSpecs structure and fill that array with details on each of the matching homes.

With the Web service part in place, we're ready to look at the client side. There are three key points to the client implementation shown in Listing 16-10. First is the creation of the instance of the Web service. Second is the declaration of the variable **Listing**, which is of the type **Chapter16.ListingSpecs**. This is how the public structure that you defined in the Web service appears to the client. Third, you call the Web method, which returns a structure containing the requested information.

Listing 16-10. Calling the StructureDemo Web Method

```
Private Sub cmbStructureListings_SelectedIndexChanged(ByVal sender As _
   System.Object, ByVal e As System.EventArgs) Handles _
   cmbStructureListings.SelectedIndexChanged

   Dim ws As New Chapter16.Demo
   Dim Listing As Chapter16.ListingSpecs

' Call the Structure Demo Web Service method.
   Cursor.Current = Cursors.WaitCursor
   Listing = ws.StructureDemo(cmbStructureListings.Text)
   Cursor.Current = Cursors.Default

' Display the listing.
   DisplayStructureListing(txtStructureListing, Listing)

End Sub
```

At the bottom of Listing 16-10 is a call to the DisplayStructureListing routine. Listing 16-11 shows the details of this routine. The only thing that I want to point out here is that that all of the individual data types are exposed through the ListingSpecs structure defined in the Web service.

Listing 16-11. The DisplayStructureListing Routine

```
Sub DisplayStructureListing(ByVal myTextBox As TextBox, _
   ByVal Listing As Chapter16.ListingSpecs)
   Dim temp As String

' Format the listing.
   temp = "Price: " & Listing.Price & vbCrLf
   temp += "Address: " & Listing.Address & vbCrLf
   temp += "Square Feet: " & Listing.Size & vbCrLf
   temp += "Baths: " & Listing.Baths & vbCrLf
   temp += "Bedrooms: " & Listing.Bedrooms & vbCrLf
   temp += "Rooms: " & Listing.Rooms & vbCrLf

' Display the listing.
   myTextBox.Text = temp

End Sub
```

An example of the output produced by the DisplayStructureListing routine is shown in Figure 16-12. The details of a listing are displayed within a single text box.

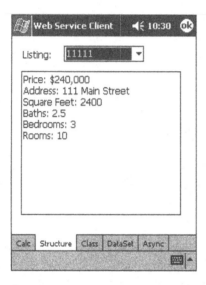

Figure 16-12. The results returned from the StructureDemo Web method

---

NOTE *The example demonstrated in this section is part of the demo applications included with this chapter. The Web method and structure definition can be found in the WebServiceDemo project. The client's call to this Web method is demonstrated on the* **Structure** *tab of the client application. This client application can be found in the WebServiceClient project. Both of these projects are provided with the sample applications for this book. See Appendix D for further details on working with the sample applications.*

Having looked at arrays and structures, we'll next look at a third way to pass data from a Web service—through objects.

Passing Objects from XML Web Services

When I talk about passing data as an object, what I mean is creating a class that includes properties for each of the individual data items you require. This approach is very similar to structures and can be used interchangeably.

To create a Web method that returns an object, you need to do two things: 1) define the class that will be passed, and 2) create the method that returns an instance of the class—the object.

Listing 16-12 shows the first part of this process, defining the class. This is a simple class comprised of nothing more than a set of properties.

Listing 16-12. Defining the Class That Will Be Used with the Web Method

```
Public Class DemoClass
   Public ListingNumber As String
   Public Address As String
   Public Rooms As Integer
   Public Bedrooms As Single
   Public Baths As Single
   Public Size As Integer
   Public Price As String
End Class
```

The key point to note from this listing is the fact that the class is declared as public, just as it was with the structure definition, so that the client application will be able to see it. Since the Web method is going to return an instance of this class, we have to provide the client with a description of the class so that the client application can create its own instance in which to receive the Web method returned.

With the class defined, you're ready to create the Web method that will make use of the class. Listing 16-13 provides an example that makes use of the **DemoClass** class just described.

Listing 16-13. Creating a Web Method That Returns an Object

```
<WebMethod()> _
Public Function ClassDemo(ByVal ListingNumber As String) As DemoClass
   Dim myDemo As New DemoClass

' Grab the specs for the requested listing.
   Select Case ListingNumber
     Case "11111"
       myDemo.ListingNumber = "11111"
       myDemo.Address = "111 Main Street"
       myDemo.Rooms = 10
       myDemo.Bedrooms = 3
       myDemo.Baths = 2.5
       myDemo.Size = 2400
       myDemo.Price = "$240,000"
```

```
      Case "22222"
        myDemo.ListingNumber = "22222"
        myDemo.Address = "222 East Maple Street"
        myDemo.Rooms = 8
        myDemo.Bedrooms = 2
        myDemo.Baths = 1.5
        myDemo.Size = 1800
        myDemo.Price = "$190,000"
      Case "33333"
        myDemo.ListingNumber = "33333"
        myDemo.Address = "333 Front Street"
        myDemo.Rooms = 9
        myDemo.Bedrooms = 3
        myDemo.Baths = 2
        myDemo.Size = 2050
        myDemo.Price = "$225,000"
    End Select

  ' Return the selected listing.
    Return myDemo

End Function
```

As with this structure example, there are four points that I want to focus on in this example. First, the **ClassDemo** Web method accepts a single argument that contains the listing number of the house for which the client application is requesting details.

Second, the Web method will return a DemoClass object, as defined by the function description. This object is an instance of the **DemoClass** class described earlier in this section.

Third, like the structure example, this method has been simplified for clarity. A simple Select Case statement returns one of three available listings.

Fourth, at the bottom of Listing 16-13 you can see where the object is returned to the client application.

Just as I suggested with the structure demo, you could easily combine the example on passing arrays with this object example to create a Web method that passes an array of objects.

With the Web service method written, we're ready to turn our attention to the client side. There are three key points to the client implementation shown in Listing 16-14. First, you start by creating an instance of the Web service. Second is the declaration of the variable **Listing**, which is of the type **Chapter16.DemoClass**. This is how the public class that you defined in the Web service appears to the client. Third, you call the Web method, which returns an object containing the requested information.

Listing 16-14. Calling the ClassDemo Web Method

```
Private Sub cmbClassListings_SelectedIndexChanged(ByVal sender As _
  System.Object, ByVal e As System.EventArgs) Handles _
  cmbClassListings.SelectedIndexChanged
  Dim ws As New Chapter16.Demo
  Dim Listing As Chapter16.DemoClass

' Call the Class Demo Web Service method.
  Cursor.Current = Cursors.WaitCursor
  Listing = ws.ClassDemo(cmbClassListings.Text)
  Cursor.Current = Cursors.Default

' Display the listing.
  DisplayClassListing(txtClassListing, Listing)

End Sub
```

At the bottom of Listing 16-14 is a call to DisplayClassListing. This routine is similar enough to the DisplayStructureListing routine that I will forgo discussing it in detail.

 NOTE   *The example demonstrated in this section is part of the demo applications included with this chapter. The Web method and class definition can be found in the WebServiceDemo project. The client's call to this Web method is demonstrated on the **Class** tab of the client application. This client application can be found in the WebServiceClient project. Both of these projects are provided with the sample applications for this book. See Appendix D for further details on working with the sample applications.*

Now that you've seen several examples of manually building the data blocks you return from a Web service, let's look at another approach in which you pass DataSets to and from a Web service.

Passing DataSets from XML Web Services

The last form of data passing that I want to discuss involves DataSets. Using this approach, your Web methods can return a DataSet to the client application. From there, the client can work with that DataSet just as it would any other untyped DataSet.

The beauty behind this approach is that it offers a clean, easy-to-implement way of providing access to enterprise-based data from your mobile application, all of which is delivered in the confines of the familiar DataSet. The source of the enterprise data can be anything that you can access from a normal desktop VB .NET application, including all of the sources that support OLEDB or ODBC. This includes Oracle, SQL Server, and Microsoft Access, just to name a few.

Now, passing DataSets to a NETCF application from an XML Web service is not without limitations. As I mentioned at the beginning of this chapter, the .NET Compact Framework lacks support for receiving typed DataSets from an XML Web service. The size of the DataSet as it's returned as XML is another consideration. Small amounts of data can turn into large amounts of XML. Even with these shortcomings, I still feel that the combination of DataSets and XML Web services is an enticing option for your mobile applications.

An example of returning a DataSet from a Web method is shown in Listing 16-15. There are three key points to this example. First, the function definition specifies that the Web method will return a DataSet. Second, the ADO .NET code is required to connect to a data source, retrieve some data, and load that data into the DataSet. Third, the Web method returns the DataSet.

Listing 16-15. The Web Method That Returns a DataSet

```
<WebMethod()> _
Public Function DsDemo() As DataSet
  Dim strSQL As String
  Dim cn As SqlClient.SqlConnection
  Dim da As SqlClient.SqlDataAdapter
  Dim ds As DataSet

' Retrieve the Employees table.
  strSQL = "SELECT * FROM Employees"
  cn = New SqlClient.SqlConnection("Server=localhost;UID=sa;Database=Northwind")
  da = New SqlClient.SqlDataAdapter(strSQL, cn)

' Add the table to a dataset.
  ds = New DataSet
  da.Fill(ds, "Employees")

' Return the dataset.
  Return ds

End Function
```

In this example, the data being returned is the Employees table taken from the SQL Server database Northwind running on the same machine as the XML Web service. It would require minimal work to extend the functionality of this Web method to access data from another source or data stored on another machine. You could even go further by adding a set of arguments to this Web method where you could specify the connection settings and the data to be retrieved, either in the form of a SQL statement, the name of a table, or a stored procedure.

On the client side, the process of calling this Web method is simple. Listing 16-16 demonstrates the client routine that calls the **DsDemo** Web method. The client routine then uses the DataSet returned to bind a DataTable to a DataGrid control. With less than a dozen lines of code, your client application can retrieve and display a whole table from an enterprise database. Now, that's my type of coding.

Listing 16-16. Calling the DsDemo Web Method

```
Private Sub btnGrabData_Click(ByVal sender As System.Object, _
  ByVal e As System.EventArgs) Handles btnGrabData.Click
  Dim ws As New Chapter16.Demo
  Dim ds As DataSet

' Retrieve the data.
  Cursor.Current = Cursors.WaitCursor
  ds = ws.DsDemo

' We need a DataTable for the binding process.
  Dim dt As DataTable = ds.Tables(0)

' Bind the DataGrid.
  DataGrid1.Visible = False
  DataGrid1.DataSource = dt
  DataGrid1.Visible = True
  Cursor.Current = Cursors.Default

End Sub
```

An example of the **DataSet** tab interface after making a call to the **DsDemo** Web method is shown in Figure 16-13.

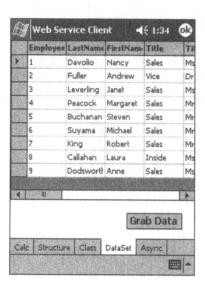

Figure 16-13. Displaying the DataSet returned by the DsDemo Web method

NOTE *The example demonstrated in this section is part of the demo applications included with this chapter. The **DsDemo** Web method can be found in the WebServiceDemo project. The client's call to this Web method is demonstrated on the **DataSet** tab of the client application. This client application can be found in the WebServiceClient project. Both of these projects are provided with the sample applications for this book. See Appendix D for further details on working with the sample applications.*

Returning Updates to XML Web Services

The obvious question when learning how to retrieve DataSets from an XML Web service is, "How do I return updates to the Web service?" The process is simple. You need to add another Web method to your XML Web service that accepts an updated DataSet from the client. The Web method then uses that DataSet to update the original data source.

Listing 16-17 demonstrates the code required to implement this update Web method in the Web service. While there are only two lines of code in this function, they each merit discussion. The first line uses the **Update** method of the DataAdapter to update the data source. The second line is a bit more involved. The function needs to return the updated DataSet, which now notes that the updates have been made to the data source, to the client application so that the client doesn't still think that there are changes that need to be saved.

Listing 16-17. Adding an Update Method to the Web Service

```
<WebMethod()> _
Public Function DsUpdate(ds As DataSet) As DataSet

' Update the data source.
  da.Update(ds)

' Return the updated dataset.
  Return ds

End Function
```

Listing 16-18 shows the client side of working with this Web method. Sending updates to the Web service requires a single line of code.

Listing 16-18. Saving DataSet Updates from the Client Application

```
Private Sub btnSaveData_Click(ByVal sender As System.Object, _
  ByVal e As System.EventArgs) Handles btnSaveData.Click
  Dim ws As New Chapter16.Demo
  Dim ds As DataSet

' Save the data.
  Cursor.Current = Cursors.WaitCursor
  ds = ws.DsUpdate(ds)
  Cursor.Current = Cursors.Default

End Sub
```

NOTE *For more on DataSets, DataAdapters, and working with data in your mobile applications, see Chapters 9, 10, and 12.*

Now that you know how to pass data back and forth from a Web service, we have just a single topic left to discuss—making asynchronous calls to an XML Web service.

Asynchronous Calls to Web Services

Up to this point in our discussion of XML Web services, all of the samples have demonstrated synchronous calls to a Web service. With synchronous calls, the client application makes a call to the Web service and waits until the service responds.

In many cases, this is exactly what you'll want to do. Going back to the mobile real estate listing application example, when users specify a set of criteria for homes they are interested in and then tap the "retrieve" button, there is really nothing else to do. They want to look at listings, and you need to go get them. Everybody is just taking a little tech siesta while you wait for the Web service to return the requested data.

But what if a user doesn't want to wait for a response? Consider this slightly altered example of the mobile real estate listing application: Instead of users having to wait for a new list of homes to be returned, they can go off and do other things, such as viewing the current list of homes that have already been delivered to their device.

That's where asynchronous calls to XML Web services come into play. Asynchronous calls don't require your application to wait. There are two approaches to implementing asynchronous calls: polling and callbacks. *Polling* involves performing some type of looping operation while continually checking to see if the call has completed. *Callbacks*, while slightly more complicated to implement, offer a more elegant approach and allow you to make multiple calls to a Web service in succession while waiting for responses.

Both approaches are completely implemented on the client side. No modifications need to be made to the Web service at all to support asynchronous calls.

 NOTE *The reason that you don't need to make any modifications to your Web service is that Visual Studio .NET 2003 automatically creates two additional methods for each method you define, a **Begin** and an **End** method, for use with asynchronous calls. For example, if you defined a **DsDemo** method, VS .NET would include two additional methods, **BeginDsDemo** and **EndDsDemo**.*

Asynchronous Calls Using Polling

Implementing asynchronous calls with polling is easy. It involves three steps. First, you call the **Begin** method of a Web service. Next, you loop, checking the status of the request. Finally, after determining that the request has completed, you retrieve the server's response.

Listing 16-19 shows an altered version of calling the DataSet Web method asynchronously using polling.

Listing 16-19. Calling the DsDemo Web Method Asynchronously

```
Private Sub btnGrabData_Click(ByVal sender As System.Object, _
   ByVal e As System.EventArgs) Handles btnGrabData.Click
   Dim ws As New Chapter16.Demo
   Dim ds As DataSet
   Dim myResult as IAsyncResult

' Retrieve the data.
   myResult = ws.BeginDsDemo(Nothing, Nothing)

' Wait for the response.
   While (myResult.IsComplete = False)
    ' Peform a delay - allow the user to do other things.
   Wend

' Retrieve the response.
   ds = ws.EndDsDemo(myResult)

' We need a DataTable for the binding process.
   Dim dt As DataTable = ds.Tables(0)

' Bind the DataGrid.
   DataGrid1.Visible = False
   DataGrid1.DataSource = dt
   DataGrid1.Visible = True

End Sub
```

The first thing to note is that the call to the **DsDemo** method has been replaced with a call to the **BeginDsDemo** method. This initiates the asynchronous call to the Web service. This call returns an IAsyncResult object, which will continue to query to determine when the Web service responds.

After making the call to **BeginDsDemo**, you jump into a loop in which you check the status of the return. When the **IsComplete** property of the IAsyncResult object becomes true, you exit the loop.

The final step involves retrieving the response from the IAsyncResult object. This is accomplished by calling the matching asynchronous **End** method, **EndDsDemo**, passing the IAsyncResult object you received when this request was initiated. That's all there is to it.

While polling is useful, I prefer callbacks because they are more flexible. We'll look at making an asynchronous call using callbacks next.

Asynchronous Calls with Callbacks

Making asynchronous calls using callbacks involves creating and providing a routine that will be called when the Web service request completes. Although this approach may seem a bit confusing the first time that you use it, in actuality it's no more difficult or time consuming to implement than the polling approach. I prefer callbacks over polling for their flexibility, performance, and elegance of code.

Calling a Web service asynchronously using callbacks is similar to doing so using polling. Listing 16-20 shows an altered version of the DataSet Web method call using an asynchronous callback approach.

Listing 16-20. Calling the DsDemo Web Method Asynchronously with a Callback

```
Private Sub btnGrabData_Click(ByVal sender As System.Object, _
  ByVal e As System.EventArgs) Handles btnGrabData.Click
  Dim cb As New AsyncCallback(AddressOf DisplayCallBack)
  Dim ws As New Chapter16.Demo
  Dim ds As DataSet

' Retrieve the data.
  ws.BeginDsDemo(cb, Nothing)

End Sub
```

Like the polling example, you're still going to be calling the **BeginDsDemo** method. Note though that the first argument has been altered to specify the callback routine, which is a subroutine that will be executed when the Web service responds. This routine, DisplayCallBack, accepts an argument of type **IAsyncResult**, which you previously examined in the polling example. Also note that the object variable, **cb**, was declared as the type **AsyncCallback**.

Listing 16-21 shows the DisplayCallBack routine. Within this routine, you retrieve the response from the Web service before binding the DataSet to the DataGrid control.

Listing 16-21. The Callback Routine

```
Sub DisplayCallBack(ByVal ar As IAsyncResult)

' Retrieve the response.
  ds = ws.EndDsDemo(ar)

' We need a DataTable for the binding process.
  Dim dt As DataTable = ds.Tables(0)
```

```
' Bind the DataGrid.
  DataGrid1.Visible = False
  DataGrid1.DataSource = dt
  DataGrid1.Visible = True

End Sub
```

As I stated, while the use of callbacks might initially seem a bit confusing, they are in fact marginally more complicated in nature than straight synchronous calls.

Aborting an Asynchronous Call

One issue that you may encounter when using asynchronous calls is the need to terminate a call to a Web service that's pending. This can be accomplished through the use of the **Abort** method of the IAsyncResult object. Listing 16-22 shows an example of this technique.

Listing 16-22. Terminating a Method Called Asynchronously

```
Private Sub btnGrabData_Click(ByVal sender As System.Object, _
  ByVal e As System.EventArgs) Handles btnGrabData.Click
  Dim ws As New Chapter16.Demo
  Dim ds As DataSet
  Dim myResult as IAsyncResult

' Retrieve the data.
  myResult = ws.BeginDsDemo(Nothing, Nothing)

' Wait for the response.
  While (myResult.IsComplete = False)
  ' Peform a delay - allow the user to do other things.

  ' If we have waited too long, terminate the request.
    myResult.Abort()
    Exit Sub
  Wend

' Retrieve the response.
  ds = ws.EndDsDemo(myResult)
```

```
' We need a DataTable for the binding process.
  Dim dt As DataTable = ds.Tables(0)

' Bind the DataGrid.
  DataGrid1.Visible = False
  DataGrid1.DataSource = dt
  DataGrid1.Visible = True


End Sub
```

Now that you have an understanding of the key Web service concepts and techniques, let's put them to use in the following tutorial.

Step-by-Step Tutorial: Building a Web Service Client

In this step-by-step exercise, you'll create an application that demonstrates accessing two different Web services that are available on the Internet. The first service provides a 9-day weather forecast for a specified zip code. The second Web service provides stock quote details for companies based upon the stock symbols you provide.

As part of this exercise, you'll do the following:

- View each Web service in a browser.

- View the XML content returned from the services.

- Add references for the two services to a mobile application.

- Call each service.

- Display the information returned from each service.

This application provides you with all of the fundamentals of working with Web services.

 NOTE *I provide a completed version of this application, titled Web Service Sampler - Complete, under the **Chapter 16** folder of the **Samples** folder for this book. See Appendix D for more information on accessing and loading the sample applications.*

NOTE *To be able to work through this sample demonstration, you'll need a server running Microsoft's Internet Information Server and the .NET Framework. For testing purposes, this system could be your development PC.*

Step 1: Opening the Project

To simplify this tutorial, I've already created the project and the user interface for the Web Service Sampler application. This template project is included under the **Chapter 16** folder of the **Samples** folder. To load this project, follow these steps:

1. From the VS .NET IDE Start Page, select to open a project. The Open Project dialog box will be displayed.

2. Use the dialog box to navigate to the **Chapter 16** folder under the **Samples** folder for this book.

3. Select and open the project **Web Service Sampler**. The project will be loaded.

Step 2: Examining the User Interface

The user interface for the Web Service Sampler application is built using a tab interface. This interface is comprised of two tabs, one for weather and the other for stocks. Each tab is comprised of the identical set of controls: a Label, a TextBox, a Button, and a ListView. Figure 16-14 shows the application's interface.

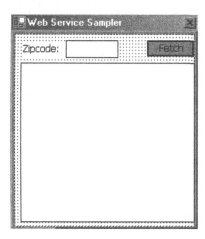

Figure 16-14. The Web Service Sampler application interface

The text box is where the user enters a zip code on the **Weather** tab, or stock symbols on the **Stock** tab. The ListView on each tab displays the information returned from the Web service.

Step 3: Viewing the Weather Service in a Browser

Before you attempt to integrate any XML Web service into your application, I recommend that you always first view that Web service from within a browser. That's where you're going to start with the Weather service that you'll be incorporating into your sampler application.

To view the Weather Web service in a browser, perform the following steps:

1. Open your browser.

2. On the address line, enter the following:

   http://www.ejse.com/WeatherService/Service.asmx

3. This document provides an interface to the Web service as shown in Figure 16-15. Select the **GetExtendedWeatherInfo** method.

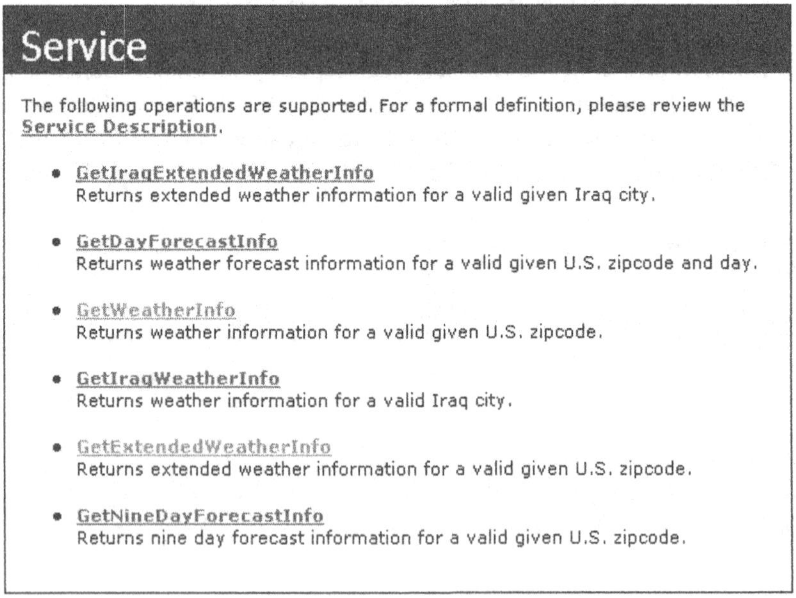

Figure 16-15. The methods offered by the Weather Web service

4.   The browser interface to this method will display as shown in Figure 16-16. Enter the zip code of your location and click the **Invoke** button.

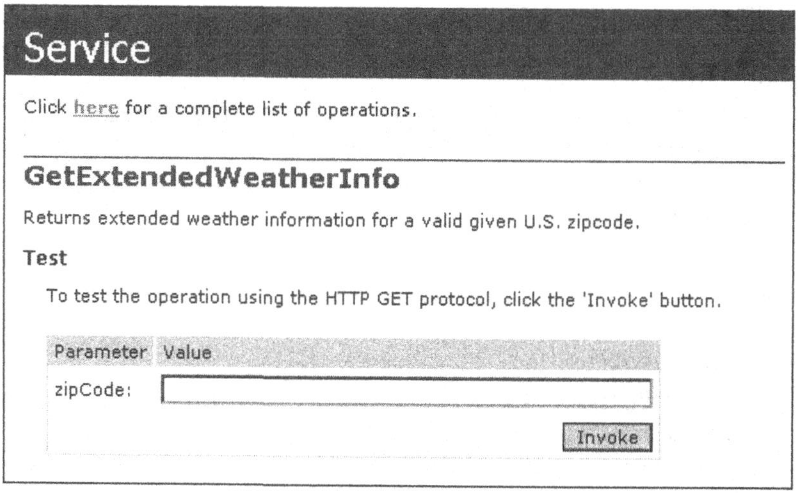

Figure 16-16. Testing the GetExtendedWeatherInfo method

Step 4: Viewing the XML Returned from the Weather Service

After a brief pause, the response from the Web service will display. Listing 16-23 shows the XML returned for the 10010 zip code. Note that this Web method returns today's current weather within the <Info> tag, followed by a series of tags, one for each of the next 9 days. It's the 9 days that you're interested in. You'll see how to leverage these daily forecasts from within your application later in this example.

Listing 16-23. The 9-Day Forecast Returned as XML

```
<?xml version="1.0" encoding="utf-8" ?>
- <ExtendedWeatherInfo xmlns:xsd=http://www.w3.org/2001/XMLSchema
  xmlns:xsi="http://www.w3.org/2001/XMLSchema-instance"
  xmlns="http://ejse.com/WeatherService/">
- <Info>
  <Location>New York, NY</Location>
  <IconIndex>26</IconIndex>
  <Temperature>39°F</Temperature>
  <FeelsLike>30°F</FeelsLike>
```

```
<Forecast>Cloudy</Forecast>
<Visibility>Unlimited</Visibility>
<Pressure>30.52 inches and rising</Pressure>
<DewPoint>37°F</DewPoint>
<UVIndex>1 Minimal</UVIndex>
<Humidity>93%</Humidity>
<Wind>From the East Northeast at 16 gusting to 22 mph</Wind>
<ReportedAt>Central Park, NY</ReportedAt>
<LastUpdated>Friday, April 18, 2003, at 10:51 AM Eastern Daylight
   Time.</LastUpdated>
</Info>
- <Day1>
<Day>Sat</Day>
<Date>Apr 19</Date>
<IconIndex>30</IconIndex>
<Forecast>Partly Cloudy</Forecast>
<High>59°</High>
<Low>44°</Low>
<PrecipChance />
</Day1>
- <Day2>
<Day>Sun</Day>
<Date>Apr 20</Date>
<IconIndex>30</IconIndex>
<Forecast>Partly Cloudy</Forecast>
<High>64°</High>
<Low>43°</Low>
<PrecipChance />
</Day2>
- <Day3>
<Day>Mon</Day>
<Date>Apr 21</Date>
<IconIndex>26</IconIndex>
<Forecast>Cloudy</Forecast>
<High>61°</High>
<Low>54°</Low>
<PrecipChance />
</Day3>
- <Day4>
<Day>Tue</Day>
<Date>Apr 22</Date>
<IconIndex>30</IconIndex>
<Forecast>AM Clouds / PM Sun</Forecast>
<High>66°</High>
<Low>47°</Low>
```

```
  <PrecipChance />
  </Day4>
- <Day5>
  <Day>Wed</Day>
  <Date>Apr 23</Date>
  <IconIndex>30</IconIndex>
  <Forecast>Partly Cloudy</Forecast>
  <High>61°</High>
  <Low>43°</Low>
  <PrecipChance />
  </Day5>
- <Day6>
  <Day>Thu</Day>
  <Date>Apr 24</Date>
  <IconIndex>34</IconIndex>
  <Forecast>Mostly Sunny</Forecast>
  <High>63°</High>
  <Low>42°</Low>
  <PrecipChance />
  </Day6>
- <Day7>
  <Day>Fri</Day>
  <Date>Apr 25</Date>
  <IconIndex>30</IconIndex>
  <Forecast>Partly Cloudy</Forecast>
  <High>58°</High>
  <Low>43°</Low>
  <PrecipChance />
  </Day7>
- <Day8>
  <Day>Sat</Day>
  <Date>Apr 26</Date>
  <IconIndex>30</IconIndex>
  <Forecast>Partly Cloudy</Forecast>
  <High>59°</High>
  <Low>45°</Low>
  <PrecipChance />
  </Day8>
- <Day9>
  <Day>Sun</Day>
  <Date>Apr 27</Date>
  <IconIndex>30</IconIndex>
  <Forecast>Partly Cloudy</Forecast>
```

```
<High>60°</High>
<Low>46°</Low>
<PrecipChance />
</Day9>
</ExtendedWeatherInfo>
```

Step 5: Adding the Web Reference for the Weather Service

Now that you have an understanding of this service, you're ready to begin incorporating it into the sampler application. The first step is to add a Web reference to the Weather service. To accomplish this, perform the following steps:

1. Under the Project menu, select **Add Web Reference**.

2. The Add Web Reference dialog box will display. In the URL field of this dialog box, enter the following:

   ```
   http://www.ejse.com/WeatherService/Service.asmx
   ```

3. Click the **Go** button. Information on the service will be retrieved and displayed within the body of the dialog box.

4. Click the **Add Reference** button to add the Web reference to your application.

5. In the Solution Explorer window, verify that the Web reference for the Weather service is added. Note that there is both a DISCO and WSDL file added for the service.

Step 6: Calling the Weather Service

Next, you need to add code to call the Weather service. There are two pieces of code that you need to add. Listing 16-24 shows the code that you need to add to the **Click** event procedure of the **Fetch** button.

Listing 16-24. Calling the Weather Service

```
Private Sub btnFetchWeather_Click(ByVal sender As System.Object, _
  ByVal e As System.EventArgs) Handles btnFetchWeather.Click
  Dim ws As New com.ejse.www.Service
  Dim forecast As com.ejse.www.ExtendedWeatherInfo
  Dim aDaysForecast As com.ejse.www.DayForecastInfo
```

```
' Retrieve the forecast.
  Cursor.Current = Cursors.WaitCursor
  forecast = ws.GetExtendedWeatherInfo(txtZipcode.Text)
  Cursor.Current = Cursors.Default

' Clear any existing forecast.
  lvwWeather.Items.Clear()

' Display the forecast for the first day.
  aDaysForecast = forecast.Day1
  AddDaysForecast(aDaysForecast)

' Display the forecast for the second day.
  aDaysForecast = forecast.Day2
  AddDaysForecast(aDaysForecast)

' Display the forecast for the third day.
  aDaysForecast = forecast.Day3
  AddDaysForecast(aDaysForecast)

' Display the forecast for the fourth day.
  aDaysForecast = forecast.Day4
  AddDaysForecast(aDaysForecast)

' Display the forecast for the fifth day.
  aDaysForecast = forecast.Day5
  AddDaysForecast(aDaysForecast)

' Display the forecast for the sixth day.
  aDaysForecast = forecast.Day6
  AddDaysForecast(aDaysForecast)

' Display the forecast for the seventh day.
  aDaysForecast = forecast.Day7
  AddDaysForecast(aDaysForecast)

' Display the forecast for the eighth day.
  aDaysForecast = forecast.Day8
  AddDaysForecast(aDaysForecast)

' Display the forecast for the ninth day.
  aDaysForecast = forecast.Day9
  AddDaysForecast(aDaysForecast)

End Sub
```

At the top of this event procedure you will find the declarations for the Web service and the object variable that will hold the response from the Web service. The Weather service returns an ExtendedWeatherInfo object, which in turn is comprised of a series of DayForecastInfo objects, one for each of the 9 days.

After making a call to the Weather service, you extract and process forecasts for each of the days, one at a time.

Next, you'll need to add the AddDaysForecast routine, shown in Listing 16-25, to the sample application. This routine handles loading individual forecasts into the ListView control. The routine accepts a single argument of type **DayForecastInfo**, which is the forecast of a single day.

Listing 16-25. Displaying the Forecast for a Single Day

```
Sub AddDaysForecast(ByVal aDaysForecast As com.ejse.www.DayForecastInfo)
  Dim lvItem As ListViewItem

' Add the forecast for the specified day to the ListView.
  lvItem = New ListViewItem
  With lvItem
    .Text = aDaysForecast.Date
    .SubItems.Add(aDaysForecast.High)
    .SubItems.Add(aDaysForecast.Low)
    .SubItems.Add(aDaysForecast.Forecast)
  End With
  lvwWeather.Items.Add(lvItem)

End Sub
```

Now that you have the weather report functioning, we can turn our attention to the stock report part of this demonstration.

Step 7: Viewing the Stock Service in a Browser

Just as you did with the Weather service, you're going to start your work with the Stock service by first viewing the service from within a browser. To view the Stock Web service in a browser, perform the following steps:

1. Open your browser.

2. On the address line, enter the following:

   http://www.swanandmokashi.com/HomePage/WebServices/StockQuotes.asmx

3. This document provides an interface to the Web service as shown in Figure 16-17. Select the **GetStockQuotes** method.

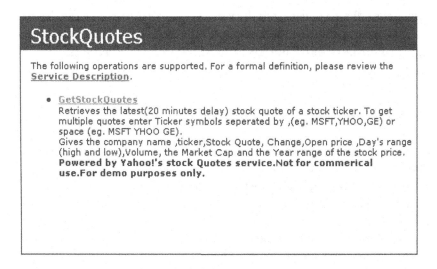

Figure 16-17. The methods offered by the Stock Web service

4. The browser interface to this method will display as shown in Figure 16-18. Enter the symbols for stocks, separating each symbol with a comma. Click the **Invoke** button to retrieve the quotes.

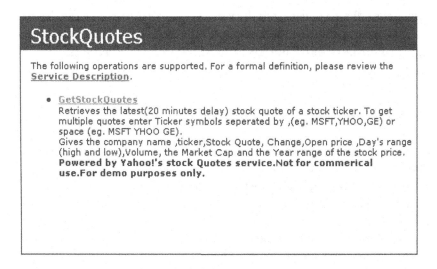

Figure 16-18. Testing the GetStockQuotes method

Step 8: Viewing the XML Returned from the Stock Service

After a brief pause, the response from the Web service will display. Listing 16-26 shows the XML returned for the stock symbols MSFT and COKE. You'll see how to leverage the individual quote objects from within your application later in this example.

Listing 16-26. The Stock Quotes Returned as XML

```xml
<?xml version="1.0" encoding="utf-8" ?>
- <ArrayOfQuote xmlns:xsd=http://www.w3.org/2001/XMLSchema
 xmlns:xsi="http://www.w3.org/2001/XMLSchema-instance"
 xmlns="http://swanandmokashi.com/">
- <Quote>
  <CompanyName>MICROSOFT CP</CompanyName>
  <StockTicker>MSFT</StockTicker>
  <StockQuote>25.50</StockQuote>
  <LastUpdated>4:01pm</LastUpdated>
  <Change>0.00</Change>
  <OpenPrice>24.77</OpenPrice>
  <DayHighPrice>25.54</DayHighPrice>
  <DayLowPrice>24.74</DayLowPrice>
  <Volume>58516864</Volume>
  <MarketCap>273.4B</MarketCap>
  <YearRange>20.705 - 29.48</YearRange>
  </Quote>
- <Quote>
  <CompanyName>COCA COLA BOTT</CompanyName>
  <StockTicker>COKE</StockTicker>
  <StockQuote>50.30</StockQuote>
  <LastUpdated>4:00pm</LastUpdated>
  <Change>0.00</Change>
  <OpenPrice>50.41</OpenPrice>
  <DayHighPrice>50.41</DayHighPrice>
  <DayLowPrice>49.50</DayLowPrice>
  <Volume>14706</Volume>
  <MarketCap>454.9M</MarketCap>
  <YearRange>41.30 - 70.45</YearRange>
  </Quote>
  </ArrayOfQuote>
```

Step 9: Adding the Web Reference for the Stock Service

Now that you have an understanding of this service, you're ready to begin incorporating it into the sampler application. The first step is to add a Web reference to the Stock service. To accomplish this, perform the following steps:

1. Under the Project menu, select **Add Web Reference**.

2. The Add Web Reference dialog box will display. In the URL field of this dialog box, enter the following:

   ```
   http://www.swanandmokashi.com/HomePage/WebServices/StockQuotes.asmx
   ```

3. Click the **Go** button. Information on the service will be retrieved and displayed within the body of the dialog box.

4. Click the **Add Reference** button to add the Web reference to your application.

5. In the Solution Explorer window, verify that the Web reference for the Stock service is added. Note that there is both a DISCO and WSDL file added for the service.

Step 10: Calling the Stock Service

Next, you need to add code to call the Stock service. Listing 16-27 shows the code that you need to add to the **Click** event procedure of the **Fetch** button.

Listing 16-27. Calling the Stock Service

```
Private Sub btnFetchStock_Click(ByVal sender As System.Object, _
  ByVal e As System.EventArgs) Handles btnFetchStock.Click
  Dim ws As New com.swanandmokashi.www.StockQuotes
  Dim quotes() As com.swanandmokashi.www.Quote
  Dim quote As com.swanandmokashi.www.Quote
  Dim lvItem As ListViewItem

' Retrieve the stock information.
  Cursor.Current = Cursors.WaitCursor
  quotes = ws.GetStockQuotes(txtSymbol.Text)
  Cursor.Current = Cursors.Default
```

```
' Clear any existing stocks.
  lvwStock.Items.Clear()

' Display the stock details
  For Each quote In quotes
    lvItem = New ListViewItem
    With lvItem
      .Text = quote.StockTicker
      .SubItems.Add(quote.StockQuote)
      .SubItems.Add(quote.Change)
      .SubItems.Add(quote.Volume)
    End With
    lvwStock.Items.Add(lvItem)
  Next

End Sub
```

At the top of this event procedure you will find the declarations for the Web service and the object variable that will hold the response from the Web service. The Stock service returns an array of objects of type **Quote**. Each Quote object contains details on a particular stock.

After receiving the array of quotes back from the Web service, you loop through the array, adding each quote to the display.

That completes the development work. You're now ready to test the Web Service Sampler application.

Step 11: Testing the Application

To test your application, perform the following steps:

1. Select either **Pocket PC Device** or **Pocket PC Emulator** from the Deployment Device combo box.

2. Select **Release** from the Solution Configurations combo box.

3. Click the **Start** button.

Your application copies to the target device. Upon completion the application starts.

To test your application, perform the following steps:

1. On the **Weather** tab, enter your zip code into the input field and tap the **Fetch** button. After a brief pause, the ListView is loaded with a 9-day forecast for your location.

2. Switch to the **Stock** tab. Enter a set of stock symbols into the input field and tap the **Fetch** button. After a brief pause, the ListView is loaded with the stock details.

NOTE *To enter multiple symbols, separate each symbol with a comma.*

HOMEWORK *Add another XML Web service to this application. What that service is, you can decide. Search the UDDI listings for something that you believe would be useful, interesting, or just cool to play with. Add a tab page to the application for querying and displaying information returned from the Web service.*

Summary

Hopefully, you come away from this chapter with what I feel are the three key points about XML Web services: They are not as complicated as they appear to be, they are easy to create and use, and they offer a tremendous amount of opportunity and functionality to mobile applications.

The first point is that XML Web services are nowhere near as complicated as they are made out to be in some publications. From the simplest standpoint, they are nothing more than public functions and subroutines that are accessible over the Internet. While all of the Web service/SOAP/HTTP discussions are interesting and have their place, to the developer attempting to craft a mobile solution, Web services are in fact Internet-based functions and subroutines that are easily incorporated into your applications.

The second point is that Visual Studio .NET 2003 makes it easy to create both XML Web services and the client applications to consume those services. You saw just how easy it was to create a Web service using the VS .NET project template. Adding Web service methods requires nothing more than a basic understanding of functions and subroutines.

The third point is that consuming and working with XML Web services is simple once you have a basic understanding of the process. All you need to do is add a Web reference to the service, create an instance of that service in code, and then you're ready to call the methods offered by the service.

XML Web services offer developers an easy and powerful way to access and leverage enterprise data from within their mobile applications. Whether your applications incorporate wireless networking, dial-up technologies, or just the docking cradle, you should examine and consider what XML Web services offer you in the way of connectivity.

CHAPTER 17

Working with Unmanaged Code

WHEN YOU WRITE CODE in .NET, whether in NETCF or the desktop framework, you're creating *managed* code. In NETCF, managed code is created by using either C# or Visual Basic .NET as your programming language. Managed code runs under the watchful eye of the .NET runtime and is guaranteed, by the runtime, to be safe. For one thing, being "safe" means that the code you write can't and won't write outside your application space. The intermediate language (IL) code generated by the managed compilers is verified at runtime to be sure that the code runs safely. On the desktop, a feature called Code Access Security (CAS) makes certain that the application will only run if it has the proper execution rights on the machine running the code. While NETCF doesn't support CAS, the runtime still does verification of the code at runtime.

On the other hand, you have *unmanaged* code, which is usually written in C++ and isn't under the watchful eye of the .NET runtime. Windows dynamic link libraries (DLLs) are a good example of unmanaged code, as are the ADOCE libraries used in the eMbedded Visual Tools to program against Microsoft Access. These APIs don't use managed code and don't have built-in type libraries like .NET assemblies do. They also use different data types than managed code does. The .NET assemblies call the standard Windows API for you. This "jump" to the Windows API is hidden by the classes provided by the framework.

While .NET in general and the .NET Compact Framework in particular supply an interface to much of the Windows API through managed code, there will be times when you need to access functionality outside of the framework. When those times come, and they will, you'll need to know how to access unmanaged code. The ability to interoperate with the Windows APIs from the .NET platform is done using Platform Invoke, or P/Invoke. *Platform Invoke* is a service that enables managed code to call unmanaged, publicly exported functions implemented in DLLs.

In addition to using the Windows API or other existing libraries, you might have reason to write your own unmanaged libraries. One example would be if you require an application to talk to hardware that has no .NET interface. In this case, you'll need to write your own unmanaged library and call it from your .NET Compact Framework. If you write your own libraries, then you have to step over to the eMbedded Visual Tools and write it in C++ 3.0. At the time of writing, eMbedded Visual C++ 4.0 doesn't have an SDK for the Pocket PC. Another example, which will be covered in detail later in this chapter, is when you just can't write managed code in Visual Basic .NET to call a system API. Certain constructs that can't be handled in Visual Basic can be done by writing an unmanaged DLL and calling it from your managed application.

The first step in making a P/Invoke call is to create a function declaration in much the same way you would in Visual Basic 6 using the Declare statement. In .NET, the enhanced version of Declare is DllImport.

Examining DllImport

If you have programmed in Visual Basic 6, then you should be familiar with the Declare statement used to call a function found in an external DLL. To refresh your memory, take a look at the following code:

```
Declare Auto Function MsgBox  Lib "user32" _
    Alias MessageBox32 (ByVal hWnd As Integer, ByVal text As String, _
    ByVal Caption As String, ByVal Typ As Interger ) As Integer
```

In a Declare statement, you specify the function you want to call in the external DLL and build its parameter list along with any return value. If you're comfortable with Declare statements, you can continue to use them in .NET. However, if you want to move more completely into .NET, then you'll want to use the .NET version of Declare, which is called DllImport.

```
<DllImport("Coredll.dll")>
Public Function GetSystemMetrics(nIndex As Integer) As Integer
End Function
```

The preceding code shows an example of using DllImport. What you're actually doing with DllImport is applying the **DllImportsAttribute** class to a prototype of the function to be called.

 NOTE *To learn more about writing and applying attributes to your .NET code, read the forthcoming title by Jason Bock and Tom Barnaby,* Applied .NET Attributes *(Apress, 2003).*

Notice that you actually build a function body, or sub body, just as if you were creating a regular method. You then apply the attribute, and NETCF knows that you're setting up to call a method in an external module.

NOTE *If you have read or worked in .NET for any length of time, you have surely heard somebody throw out the term P/Invoke. Like me, you may have been impressed the first few times you heard it. And then you used it on your coworkers to show how "smart" you were when it came to .NET. To bring it all down a notch or two, P/Invoke is nothing more than DllImport. Now you can go to lunch and use DllImport in a sentence and amaze your friends or spouse.*

Like any good .NET class, **DllImportAttribute** has a series of fields, and these are shown in Table 17-1. You'll explore some of these later as you work through the code in this chapter.

Table 17-1. DllImportAttribute Fields

METHOD	DESCRIPTION
EntryPoint	Specifies the name, or ordinal number, that is to be called in the library. Supported on CE.
SetLastError	When set to True, it enables the caller to use the Marshal.GetLastWin32Error method. Supported on CE.
CallingConvention	Specifies the calling convention used when passing parameters. Supported on CE.
CharSet	Controls how string values are marshaled. Supported on CE.
BestFitMapping	Specifies whether best-fit mapping behavior when converting Unicode characters to ANSI characters is enabled.
ExactSpelling	Allows the runtime to search for similar names based on the specified CallingConvention.
ThrowOnUnmappableChar	Specifies if an exception is thrown if an unmappable Unicode character is encountered.

Reasons to Use Unmanaged Code

Now that you know about DllImport, you might wonder why you would want to call into unmanaged code. There are several reasons why you would need to use the information presented in this chapter. The explanation in the previous section gives away reason one, and that is to access functionality that exists in the system but isn't exposed through .NET. Following are a few more reasons:

- To call into a system dll

- To call Win32 dlls (MSMQ as an example)

- To write your own unmanaged code (ActiveSync provider)

- To use native callbacks

- To enable interprocess communication

- To allow direct OEM Adaptation Layer (OAL) access

- To allow raw speed (lots of math)

Applied Examples

Rather than prattle on endlessly talking about doing the P/Invoke thing, I'll just show you how to write some code. In the remainder of this chapter, you're going to learn to solve some problems involving calls to unmanaged code. I could talk about this and that for 10 or 15 pages, and you might get something out of my diatribe that would help you write code to access unmanaged code. However, the best way for you to learn about P/Invoke is to write code, so that is how I'm going to proceed for the remainder of the chapter. The following sections will each be dedicated to a specific example that will explain and create an application that can do a specific task in the unmanaged code world. The code presented in each section will independent of all other sections, making it easy for you to comprehend and digest.

NOTE *In the **Chapter 17** folder of the **Samples** folder, you'll find a single solution. This solution contains classes for each of the sections that you're about to cover, in addition to several forms that are used to test the unmanaged code classes. The sample solution also contains classes that won't be covered in this chapter, but that you might find interesting. See Appendix D for more information on accessing and loading the sample applications.*

Using the Soft Input Panel

Rather than jump in with a complex and convoluted example, let's start with something a little easier. A frequent question that I get asked and is often raised in the various newsgroups is how to show and hide the Soft Input Panel (SIP).

This is a good starting example because it's straightforward. In Listing 17-1, you can see a portion of the **SipOperation** class that relates to the show and hide operations.

Listing 17-1. P/Invoke to Hide and Show the SIP

```
Public Enum SIPStatus As Integer
    SipOff = &H0
    SipOn = &H1
    SipDocked = &H2
    SipLocked = &H4
End Enum

<DllImport("coredll.dll")> _
Private Shared Function SipShowIM(ByVal i As SIPStatus) As Boolean
End Function

Public Shared Sub Show()
    SipShowIM(SIPStatus. SipOn)
End Sub

Public Shared Sub Hide()
    SipShowIM(SIPStatus. SipOff)
End Sub
```

 NOTE *If you've already opened the project and looked at the code, you can see there's a lot more to this class than just handling SIP visibility. I'll cover the more advanced methods of this class later in the chapter.*

Why does this example use the **Shared** keyword? When you use this identifier on a class method, you're telling the runtime that although there may be two or more instances of this class, there will only be a single instance of this method. When a method doesn't use class-level variables, then using **Shared** is one way to reduce the memory footprint of the class. Also, when you call a **Shared** method, you do *not* need to create an instance of the class first. You make the call by qualifying the method with either the class or structure name. You can also qualify the method name with a specific instance of the class or structure, remembering that it's the same method being called from all instances of the class or structure. So, use the **Shared** keyword when you want to expose methods that don't require access to instance data. For a good example, look at the **Shared** methods of the **String** class. There are many methods exposed that work on **String** but don't have a relationship to the underlying string class data.

> **NOTE** *It's also possible to use the **Shared** keyword on the class constructor. If you use **Shared New**, then that constructor will only execute when the first instance of the class is instantiated. You might use this constructor to initialize **Shared** variables that are defined in the class or other work that needs to be done on a class basis and not an instance basis.*

From the earlier discussion about DllImport, you should understand right away that you are calling the method named **SipShowIM**, which is found in the coredll.dll library. This method also takes a single parameter and returns a value. In the C++ world, the definition for **SipShowIM** looks like the following:

```
BOOL WINAPI SipShowIM(DWORD);
```

Note in this declaration that the argument is passed as the enum type, which is declared as a **System.UInt32**. The conversion from the variable types in C++ prototypes to variable types in Visual Basic .NET is the single biggest challenge to any P/Invoke call made to the system API or to your own custom DLLs. In this case, a C++ **DWORD** is an unsigned 32-bit variable that maps to the .NET variable type of **System.UInt32**. When specifying a type for an enum, you only have the choices of **Byte**, **Short**, **Integer**, and **Long**. You have to know that in .NET, a VB **Integer** is the same as an **Int32**. The return types are a little less convoluted because a .NET **Boolean** variable maps directly to the C++ **BOOL** variable type.

> **NOTE** *Technically, a **DWORD** is unsigned. It's also permissible in some situations to use **Int32** as the managed version of **DWORD**. The difference is that if the **DWORD** is being used as a bit mask, then the most significant bit (MSB) may be important. To be safe, it's better to always use **UInt32** as the variable type in managed code. Another opportunity for confusion is BOOL. BOOL is actually defined as a 32-bit value. Technically it's incorrect to return a simple **System.Boolean** value instead of an **Int32**. However, it's more convenient to get a True or False back rather than an **Int32** that needs to be converted to a **Boolean**. The question is, Is this workable or technically correct? Only you have the answer.*

Once the DllImport statement is set up correctly, making the call to the API is as simple as calling any function whose source resides in your application.

```
SipShowIM(SIPStatus.SipOn)
```

In this example, the class method is defined as a sub and the **BOOL** returned from the API call is discarded.

As you do more work with P/Invoke, you'll find that you're constantly referring back to the original declaration, in C++, of many of your methods to see what the prototype for a particular variable was. This is especially true as you're working on a new P/Invoke call and things aren't going so well. A trick I use is to keep the C++ prototype in my VB .NET source code for reference later.

```
'     BOOL WINAPI SipShowIM(DWORD)
<DllImport("coredll.dll")> _
Private Shared Function SipShowIM(ByVal i As Int32) As Boolean
End Function
```

Having this information close at hand makes debugging the methods easier and serves as a good reference the next time you need to create a new DllImport.

When you're copying sample code from the help files or from code in another project, use caution, especially if the sample might be from Visual Basic 6 code. The following declaration, although it looks good, will cause your P/Invoke call to crash:

```
Private Shared Function MoveWindow(ByVal hwnd As IntPtr, _
    ByVal x As Long,  ByVal y As Long, ByVal nWidth As Long, _
    ByVal nHeight As Long, ByVal bRepaint As Boolean) _
    As Int32
End Function
```

The problem is rather subtle. In this code, the parameters for x, y, nHeight, and nWidth are specified as **Long** values. In .NET, a **Long** is 64 bits, but the API call only expects 32-bit values to be passed. This means that instead of getting 22 bytes pushed onto the stack, your application will be pushing 38 bytes on the stack, causing the underlying system library to "get a little confused" and crash your application. Be careful, be very careful.

TIP *Now, before you think that I know all of these API methods by heart, I'll fill you in on a little secret: the eMbedded Visual Tools 3.0—2002 Edition. Download your copy today from* http://www.microsoft.com/downloads/details.aspx?FamilyId=F 663BF48-31EE-4CBE-AAC5-0AFFD5FB27DD&displaylang=en. *The eMbedded Visual Tools have the include files that contain all of the information that you need to call into the system APIs. If installed in the default location, you can find the files in the* **C:\Windows CE Tools\wce300\Pocket PC 2002\include** *folder. In addition to these files, the eMbedded Visual Tools IDE comes with several very useful tools that aren't included in Visual Studio .NET: the Remote File Viewer, Remote Spy++, and Remote Registry Editor, to name a few.*

Getting Power Information from the Device

If one piece of hardware will cause you problems more regularly than any other, it'll most likely be the battery on your device. In order for your application to handle any scenario that your device can throw at it, it will be important to be able to know how much life is left in the batteries on the device. This example will get into a little more of the details of DllImport while also showing how to retrieve information about the battery and power status on a device. In this section, we'll look at the newer of two functions related to battery information on the device. The older version is GetSystemPowerStatus, while the one I'll cover is GetSystemPowerStatusEx.

Setting Up for the Call

Before you can think about calling an API, you need to get all of the declarations correct. The DllImport statement shown a little later in Listing 17-2 has the required library in which the method's entry point is found. Additionally, this statement also defines the SetLastError field. When this field is set, the runtime marshaler calls the **GetLastError** system API method and caches the return value for the managed code to retrieve through a call to the managed method **GetLastWin32Error**.

NOTE *This is one of the reasons that you would use the DllImport attribute instead of a Declare statement. If you use the Declare statement, then you're forced to use the **GetLastError** P/Invoke call, which can be inaccurate. From the time that your call fails and you call back through the marshaler to get the error code with **GetLastError**, the value in the OS may have been over- written by another failed API call. When you use DllImport with the SetLastError field set to True, then you can be assured that your error value is never overwritten. The default value of **SetLastError** is False for C# and True for Visual Basic. So why this discussion and why include it in DllImport at all? One word— clarity. It's important to make your code as clear as possible for others and for yourself. Instead of relying on the default scope of variables, declare them as Private or Public. Instead of "knowing" that the default is SetLastError:=True, explicitly specify it. One more word—multiapplication. The PPC is becoming more than a simple device running a single application at a time. With mul- tiple applications running on the device, the possibility of getting invalid error codes back from **GetLastError** increases.*

TIP *If you're going to use .NET, then use it and leave the old VB 6 syntax behind. Many people continue to use VB 6 code constructs that, while still supported in .NET, have .NET counterparts. DllImport and Declare are one example, Try/Catch and On Error are another. There are advantages to the .NET counterparts that make the move to full .NET worthwhile. If you use Try/Catch instead of On Error, you can significantly decrease the size of your IL code. If you use DllImport, you have more flexibility on how you can call unmanaged code and get data back from the unmanaged side.*

If you decide to make **SetLastError** equal to False, then you would need to use the **GetLastError** P/Invoke call. The declaration for that method is included in Listing 17-2.

Listing 17-2. Declarations for Retrieving Battery Information

```
' BOOL WINAPI GetSystemPowerStatusEx(
' PSYSTEM_POWER_STATUS_EX pStatus, BOOL fUpdate );
<DllImport("coredll" , SetLastError:=True)> _
Public Shared Function GetSystemPowerStatusEx( _
    ByRef pStatus As tagSystemPowerStatusEx2, _
    ByVal fUpdate As Boolean) As Boolean
End Function
```

```vb
'DWORD WINAPI GetSystemPowerStatusEx2(
'PSYSTEM_POWER_STATUS_EX2 pSystemPowerStatusEx2,
'ByVal dwLen As Int32,BOOL fUpdate)
<DllImport("coredll", SetLastError:=True)> _
Public Shared Function GetSystemPowerStatusEx2( _
    ByRef sps As SystemPowerStatusEx2, _
    ByVal dwLen As Int32, _
    ByVal fUpdate As Boolean) As Boolean
End Function

<DllImport("Coredll.dll")> _
Public Shared Function GetLastError() As Int32
End Function

<StructLayout(LayoutKind.Sequential)> _
Public Structure SystemPowerStatusEx
    Public ACLineStatus As Byte
    Public BatteryFlag As Byte
    Public BatteryLifePercent As Byte
    Public Reserved1 As Byte
    Public BatteryLifeTime As Int32
    Public BatteryFullLifeTime As Int32
    Public Reserved2 As Byte
    Public BackupBatteryFlag As Byte
    Public BackupBatteryLifePercent As Byte
    Public Reserved3 As Byte
    Public BackupBatteryLifeTime As Int32
    Public BackupBatteryFullLifeTime As Int32
End Structure

<StructLayout(LayoutKind.Sequential)> _
Public Structure SystemPowerStatusEx2
    Public ACLineStatus As Byte
    Public BatteryFlag As Byte
    Public BatteryLifePercent As Byte
    Public Reserved1 As Byte
    Public BatteryLifeTime As Int32
    Public BatteryFullLifeTime As Int32
    Public Reserved2 As Byte
    Public BackupBatteryFlag As Byte
    Public BackupBatteryLifePercent As Byte
    Public Reserved3 As Byte
    Public BackupBatteryLifeTime As Int32
    Public BackupBatteryFullLifeTime As Int32
```

```
      The Ex2 version has these additional fields.
    Public BatteryVoltage As Int32
    Public BatteryCurrent As Int32
    Public BatteryAverageCurrent As Int32
    Public BatteryAverageInterval As Int32
    Public BatteryAHourConsumed As Int32
    Public BatteryTemperaure As Int32
    Public BackupBatteryVoltage As Int32
    Public BatteryChemistry As Byte
End Structure


Private _PowerStatus As SystemPowerStatusEx2
```

> **NOTE** *But why use something that is unreliable? Using **GetLastError** is opening yourself up to a bug that may be hard to find. Always use the **Marshal.GetLastWin32Error** call.*

One of the parameters to the **GetSystemPowerStatus** method is a structure through which the values are returned. In this case, the structure is nothing more than a series of **Byte** and **Int32** variables, which is an easy structure to pass through the NETCF runtime marshaler. It's advisable, though not always required, to specify the layout of the structure being passed through the marshaler. In Listing 17-2, you can see that the StructLayout attribute has been applied to the structure.

The LayoutKind value, a field of the StructLayout attribute, can be either of three values, Auto, Sequential, or Explicit. When set to Auto, the .NET default, you're letting the runtime engine decide what the best layout is for your structure when marshaling it to unmanaged code. In the example in Listing 17-2, sequential layout means that the elements of the structure are laid out in memory just as they appear in the structure definition. The third option, Explicit, is designed to allow explicit layout of the elements in a structure. When you use StructLayout.Explicit, you then use another attribute called FieldOffset to set the exact alignment of all the members of the structure.

```
<StructLayout(LayoutKind.Explicit)> _
Public Structure Rect
    <FieldOffset(0)> Public left As Int32
    <FieldOffset(4)> Public top As Int32
    <FieldOffset(8)> Public right As Int32
    <FieldOffset(12)> Public bottom As Int32
End Structure
```

Oddly enough, while NETCF supports Explicit, it doesn't support FieldOffset. So that leaves you with two options instead of three. This makes passing structures that contain bit-level definitions like the DCB impossible without a wrapper class to massage a byte array to the desired information.

NOTE *In addition to the lack of the FieldOffset attribute, I've run into another discrepancy between the full framework and NETCF. When working on the desktop framework, there are two additional members of the StructLayout attribute, Pack and CharSet, that have been left out of NETCF. The Pack member lets you define the packing of your structure when you define StructLayout as Sequential. The default packing for managed code is 8, whereas the default for unmanaged code is 4. For most system API calls, the default will be fine, as it is in the example in Listing 17-2. However, caution should be used when writing any custom libraries to make sure that you use the standard API packing of 4.*

Learning the business of calling unmanaged code is a matter of persistence and of learning what you can and can't do. For example, if you note the C++ prototype of **GetSystemPowerStatusEx2**, you'll note that the return value is defined as a **DWORD**. However, the DllImport declares the return value as Boolean and the call works just fine. This trick works because the runtime marshals the 4-byte value **DWORD** back and converts it to a Boolean as specified by the DllImport statement. This process just discards the upper 2 bytes of the **DWORD**. If you're depending on a value to be returned in the upper bytes of the value, don't use this conversion. With this method, the return value is the size of the SystemPowerStatusEx2 structure. Any value that isn't zero is converted to True by the runtime marshaler.

NOTE *Be warned, this is a hack. The proper way is to define the variables as **UInt32** and convert them in your code to the desired end type. Letting the marshaler make conversions is probably not the best idea, even though it's easier.*

The second value defined in the parameter list is the size of the SystemPowerStatusEx2 structure, and the third parameter is whether to use cached values or to get fresh data from the device driver.

Making the Call

Once you have the P/Invoke methods and the related structures defined, you can then make the call into unmanaged code. Listing 17-3 shows the code required to make the unmanaged call and to populate the SystemPowerStatusEx2 structure. This structure contains every detail about the state of the device power system. While this structure contains as many as 20 pieces of data, only a few are of interest to most programmers.

Listing 17-3. Calling the System for Battery Information

```vb
Public Sub Refresh()
    Dim bRet As Boolean = False
    Try
        Dim sizeOf As Int32 = Marshal.SizeOf(_PowerStatus)
        bRet = GetSystemPowerStatusEx2(_PowerStatus, sizeOf, True)
    Catch ex As Exception
    End Try


    If Not bRet Then
        Try
            Dim sps As SystemPowerStatusEx = New SystemPowerStatusEx
            If GetSystemPowerStatusEx(sps, True) Then
                '    Store in our class-level SystemPowerStatusEx2 structure.
                _PowerStatus.ACLineStatus = sps.ACLineStatus
                _PowerStatus.BatteryFlag = sps.BatteryFlag
                _PowerStatus.BatteryLifePercent = sps.BatteryLifePercent
                _PowerStatus.BatteryLifeTime = sps.BatteryLifeTime
                _PowerStatus.BatteryFullLifeTime = sps.BatteryFullLifeTime
                _PowerStatus.BackupBatteryFlag = sps.BackupBatteryFlag
                _PowerStatus.BackupBatteryLifePercent = _
                    sps.BackupBatteryLifePercent
                _PowerStatus.BackupBatteryLifeTime = sps.BackupBatteryLifeTime
                _PowerStatus.BackupBatteryFullLifeTime = _
                    sps.BackupBatteryFullLifeTime
            End If
        Catch ex As Exception
        End Try
    End If
End Sub
```

NOTE *In order for the data coming back from the P/Invoke call to be accurate and complete, it's the responsibility of the device manufacturers to write proper drivers that populate this data. If the call succeeds, but you still have problems with the data, check with the device manufacturer. And speaking of device manufacturers, the documentation states that the **GetSystemPowerStatusEx2** call isn't supported on the emulator. Whether a particular method works or not is determined by the OEM that made the device. The emulator manufacturer in this case didn't implement the **GetSystemPowerStatusEx2** call. If a particular device doesn't implement **GetSystemPowerStatusEx2**, NETCF isn't going to raise an exception. Be ready to verify that the returned values make sense. Don't blindly accept that they are valid.*

As with many other system API methods, a value of zero is returned if the function fails. The **GetSystemPowerStatusEx2** method returns the size of the data structure, which you ignore and cast to a Boolean value when it's successful. If you need to know the size of some object, as you do for the second parameter to the **GetSystemPowerStatusEx2** method, you can use the **SizeOf** method in the **Marshal** class. This method returns the size of the object in unmanaged code. The value returned from **Marshal.SizeOf** is passed into your P/Invoke call. You also ask the system to get fresh data by passing True as the third parameter. Upon successful completion of the call, the class scope variable **_PowerStatus** contains the information you need. For the **GetSystemPowerStatusEx** method, the values from its data structure are copied into the SystemPowerStatusEx2 structure variable.

In the **BatteryInformation** class in the **Chapter 17** folder under the **Samples** folder, each piece of information in the class-level SystemPowerStatusEx2 structure is exposed as a property. A full explanation of the fields in the returned structure is shown in Table 17-2.

Table 17-2. SystemPowerStatus Member Descriptions

MEMBER	DESCRIPTION
ACLineStatus	A value representing either online, offline, on backup power, or unknown.
BackupBatteryFlag	A value representing either low, high, critical, charging, no battery, or unknown.
BackupBatteryFullLifeTime	The number of seconds of backup battery life if battery was at full charge, or BATTERY_LIFE_UNKNOWN.
BackupBatteryLifePercent	The percentage of full backup battery charge remaining. Valid values range from 0 to 100, or BATTERY_PERCENTAGE_UNKNOWN.

Table 17-2. SystemPowerStatus Member Descriptions (continued)

MEMBER	DESCRIPTION
BackupBatteryLifeTime	The number of seconds of backup battery life remaining, or BATTERY_LIFE_UNKNOWN.
BackupBatteryVoltage	The number of millivolts (mV) of backup battery voltage. Valid values can range from 0 to 65535.
BatteryAHourConsumed	The average number of milliamp hours (mAh) of long-term cumulative average discharge. Valid values range from 0 to –32768. This value is reset when the batteries are charged or changed.
BatteryAverageCurrent	The average number of milliamps of short-term device current drain. Valid values range from 0 to 32767 for charge and 0 to –32768 for discharge.
BatteryAverageInterval	The number of milliseconds (mS) that is the time constant interval used in reporting BatteryAverageCurrent.
BatteryChemistry	A value representing either alkaline, nickel cadmium, nickel metal hydride, lithium ion, lithium polymer, or unknown.
BatteryCurrent	The number of milliamps (mA) of instantaneous current drain. Valid values range from 0 to 32767 for charge and 0 to –32768 for discharge.
BatteryFlag	A value representing either low, high, critical, charging, no battery, or unknown.
BatteryFullLifeTime	The number of seconds of battery life if battery was at full charge, or BATTERY_LIFE_UNKNOWN.
BatteryLifePercent	The percentage of the full battery charge remaining. Valid values can range from 0 to 100, or BATTERY_PERCENTAGE_UNKNOWN (–1).
BatteryLifeTime	The number of seconds of battery life remaining, or BATTERY_LIFE_UNKNOWN (–1).
BatteryTemperature	The battery temperature reported in 0.1 degrees Celsius increments. Valid values range from –3276.8 to 3276.7.
BatteryVoltage	The number of millivolts (mV) of battery voltage. Valid values range from 0 to 65535.
Reserved1	Will be set to zero.
Reserved2	Will be set to zero.
Reserved3	Will be set to zero.

Listing 17-4 shows an example of the properties that are exposed. The **ACLineStatus** values have corresponding string representations and the **LineStatus** property returns those values. If you really want the numeric value, there is a corresponding **LineStatusN** method that returns the raw numeric value.

Listing 17-4. Getting Data Back from Your Class

```
Public ReadOnly Property LineStatus() As String
    Get
        If _PowerStatus.ACLineStatus = 0 Then
            Return "OffLine"
        ElseIf _PowerStatus.ACLineStatus = 1 Then
            Return "OnLine"
        Else
            Return "Unknown"
        End If
    End Get
End Property


Public ReadOnly Property LineStatusN() As Byte
    Get
        Return _PowerStatus.ACLineStatus
    End Get
End Property


Public ReadOnly Property BatteryFlagN() As Byte
    Get
        Return _ PowerStatus..BatteryFlag
    End Get
End Property
```

Working with the Windows Registry

First, there are some legal formalities that need to be covered.

This section implies no benefit or detriment to the reading and writing of data into or out of the registry. Any damage done to the device cannot be blamed on the author's inclusion of information of how to access the registry. Known side effects of using the registry consist of system problems, nausea, hair loss, and partial blindness in the left eye.

You need to decide whether it's good or bad to use the registry. Years ago Microsoft used to promote INI files. Then somewhere around Windows 3.1 the storage medium of choice became the Windows Registry. "Store everything in there, we do," said Microsoft. And now, XML has arrived, and because configuration files are now XML based, you no longer have a need to access the registry. COM is dead (cough! cough!), so stay out of the registry. However, good or bad, you may decide that you do need to write something into the registry. At the very least, you may need to get a value from the registry that contains some critical bit of system information. To do this, you need access to the system APIs that relate to registry access. These API calls are bad enough in the Visual Basic 6 world. If you have mastered registry calls in VB 6, then this will be a piece of cake. This section will show you how to use P/Invoke calls to create, write, and read registry keys.

Setting Up for the Call

When you're working with API methods that pass strings as parameters, you need to double-check the API method name. The system often provides a method that works with wide characters (Unicode) and single-byte characters. This is the reason that there is a new field in the DllImport attribute as shown in Listing 17-5.

Listing 17-5. Declarations for Registry API Calls

```
' WINADVAPI LONG APIENTRY RegQueryValueExW(
'     IN HKEY hKey, IN LPCWSTR lpValueName,
'     IN LPDWORD lpReserved, OUT LPDWORD lpType, IN OUT LPBYTE lpData,
'     IN OUT LPDWORD lpcbData);
<DllImport("Coredll.dll", EntryPoint:="RegQueryValueExW")> _
Private Shared Function RegQueryValueEx( ByVal hKey As Int32, _
ByVal lpValueName As String, ByVal lpReserved As Int32, _
ByRef lpType As Int32, ByVal lpData As String, _
ByRef lpcbData As Int32 ) As Int32
End Function


<DllImport("Coredll.dll", EntryPoint:="RegQueryValueExW")> _
Private Shared Function RegQueryValueLong( ByVal hkey As Int32, _
    ByVal lpValueName As String, ByVal lpReserved As Int32, _
    ByRef lpType As Int32, ByRef lpData As Int32, _
    ByRef lpcbData As Int32 ) As Int32
End Function
```

```
<DllImport("Coredll.dll", EntryPoint:="RegQueryValueExW")> _
Private Shared Function RegQueryValueString( ByVal hkey As Int32, _
    ByVal lpValueName As String, ByVal lpReserved As Int32, _
    ByRef lpType As Int32, ByVal lpData As StringBuilder, _
    ByRef lpcbData As Int32 ) As Int32
End Function
```

NOTE *You can find all of the definitions for all of the registry methods and constants in the winreg.h header file. This file can be found in C:\Windows CE Tools\wce300\Pocket PC 2002\include, assuming you installed it in the default location.*

When you call into an unmanaged library, you're required to specify an entry point in that library where execution is to start. The examples in Listings 17-1 and 17-2 didn't specify the EntryPoint field because the name specified in the Function declaration was the same name as the entry point. The difference here is that the declaration uses names other than the entry point's name: the generic names RegQueryValueEx, RegQueryValueString, and RegQueryValueLong. The header file winreg.h defines two functions, or entry points, RegQueryValueExA and RegQueryValueExW. The function terminating with an *A* is for ASCII characters, whereas the function ending with *W* is for wide, or Unicode, characters. Remembering that NETCF manages all strings as Unicode, it should be obvious that you want to use the wide character function, whose entry point is RegQueryValueExW.

NOTE *What's that you say, all Unicode? Absolutely! NETCF uses UTF-16 or UTF-8 to represent characters (UTF being Unicode Transformation Format). In case you don't know, Unicode is a format that lets you store the simple English letter characters as well as the more complex characters of such languages as Chinese and Arabic. Using Unicode, you can store up to 65,000 different characters. Having NETCF and the Pocket PC use Unicode as the base storage option allows you to globalize your application with only a little extra work. For more information on Unicode, you can visit* http://www.unicode.org.

The code in Listing 17-5 declares three functions that call into the same entry point in coredll.dll with the fifth parameter, the one that returns the requested value, different in each. RegQueryValueString and RegQueryValueLong are self-explanatory in that the former expects a string value back while the latter expects an **Int32** value. By changing the output parameter to either **StringBuilder** or

Int32, you force the marshaler to make a conversion for you from the type specified as LPBYTE in the system declaration.

You can use other techniques to return a string value back through a method parameter, but this example uses a **StringBuilder** variable. The last and as of yet undiscussed method declared in Listing 17-5 is used to get information back from the registry about the type of data being retrieved.

Making the Call

There are three publicly exposed methods to query a value in a registry key. One is to return an unknown value; the other two are directly tied to the two previously discussed methods for returning a string or a 32-bit integer. You make the call to **QueryValue** as shown in the following code snippet:

```
Dim oRet As Object = reg.QueryValue( _
    Registry.tagRegistryRootKeys.HkeyCurrentUser, _
    "SOFTWARE\Microsoft\Internet Explorer\Main", _
    "DaysToKeep")
```

This method requires parameters to specify the root key, the key of interest, and the element of the requested key whose data you want to see. The method returns an object that you can then query in order to discover the type of data returned. Listing 17-6 shows the sequence of calls required in accessing registry keys. You first need to open the requested key and use the returned handle to make the call to RegQueryValueEx. After this is completed, you're also required to close the previously opened key.

Listing 17-6. Getting Data Back from Your Class

```
Public Function QueryValue(ByVal lSection As Int32, ByVal sKeyName As String, _
        ByVal sValueName As String) As Object
    Dim lRet As Int32
    Dim hkey As Int32
    Dim vValue As Object

    Try
        If RegOpenKeyEx(lSection, sKeyName, 0, KeyAllAccess, hkey) = 0 Then
            lRet = QueryValueEx(hkey, sValueName, vValue)
        End If
    Catch ex As Exception
        Throw ex
```

```
        Finally
            RegCloseKey(hkey)
        End Try
        Return CType(vValue, Object)
    End Function
```

The actual P/Invoke calls are shown in Listing 17-7. In this code, you use the
RegQueryValueEx method to call to unmanaged code and get the type of data
being stored in the specified registry key. You do this by passing zero as the fifth
parameter instead of a valid data structure to accept the returned data. The system sees the zero, and instead of returning data, returns information about the
key in the **lType** and **lenData** variables. **lType** tells you whether the data stored in
the key is string or numeric and **lenData** is the length of the data stored in the
key. If the data is of type **String** then **lenData** is the length of the string.

Listing 17-7. Making the P/Invoke Calls to the Registry

```
Private Function QueryValueEx(ByVal lhKey As Int32, _
        ByVal szValueName As String, ByRef vValue As Object) As Int32
    Dim lenData As Int32
    Dim intRet As Int32
    Dim lType As Int32
    Dim lValue As Int32
    Dim sValue As StringBuilder

    intRet = RegQueryValueEx(lhKey, szValueName, 0, lType, 0, lenData)

    Select Case lType
        Case RegistryDataType.String
            sValue = New StringBuilder(lenData)
            intRet = RegQueryValueString(lhKey, szValueName, 0, lType, _
                sValue, lenData)
            If intRet = tagReturnValues.NoError Then
                vValue = sValue.ToString
            Else
                vValue = String.Empty
            End If
        Case RegistryDataType.Number
            intRet = RegQueryValueLong(lhKey, szValueName, 0, lType, _
                lValue, lenData)
            If intRet = tagReturnValues.NoError Then
                vValue = lValue
            End If
```

```
        Case Else
            intRet = -1
    End Select
    Return intRet
End Function
```

Once you know the type of data that needs to be returned, you call the appropriate method, **RegQueryValueString** or **RegQueryValueLong**, check if the call was successful, and pass the data back through the vValue function parameter. The registry function definitions are some of the trickiest to get right when you have to convert from the C++ definition to a DllImport statement.

And sometimes the error messages that you receive from the OS aren't the most helpful. The error shown in Figure 17-1 would seem to imply that the registry call I made isn't supported by the system. But what that error really means is that somewhere in the definition of the function a parameter is defined incorrectly. If you get such an error, you might have a return value set as Boolean instead of a string or a parameter set as ByVal instead of ByRef.

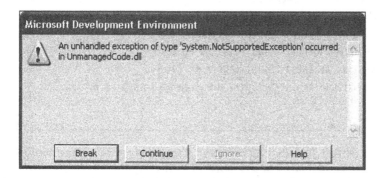

Figure 17-1. While something might be wrong, it's not what this message says it is

The point being, don't give up just because the system seems to say that the method isn't supported.

Using Cryptography on the Device

Security of data is critical, perhaps more so on a device than on a desktop machine, because it can easily be lost or stolen. Connection strings or passwords stored in plain text in a configuration file are of particular concern. The full framework has a very good **Cryptography** class that can be used to perform any number of different encryptions on strings or files. But alas, the **Cryptography** class isn't supported in NETCF. What is a developer to do? Fear not, ye faint of heart, because this section will step you through how to call into the unmanaged world of the system cryptography methods.

Setting Up for the Call

The definitions for the methods in coredll.dll aren't that difficult once you see that the big scary names in the C++ definitions translate into simple .NET types. For instance, Listing 17-8 shows the definition for the **CryptEncrypt** method found in coredll.dll. The first two parameters, HCRYPTKEY and HCRYPTHASH, are defined in C++ as unsigned long pointers.

Listing 17-8. Required Declarations to Use Cryptography API

```
'WINADVAPI BOOL WINAPI
'CryptEncrypt(HCRYPTKEY hKey, HCRYPTHASH hHash,
'     BOOL Final, DWORD dwFlags, BYTE *pbData,
'     DWORD *pdwDataLen, DWORD dwBufLen);
<DllImport("coredll.dll", EntryPoint:="CryptEncrypt", SetLastError:=True)> _
    Public Shared Function CryptEncrypt(ByVal hKey As IntPtr, _
    ByVal hHash As IntPtr, ByVal Final As Boolean, _
    ByVal dwFlags As Int32, ByVal pbData As Byte(), _
    ByRef pdwDataLen As Int32, ByVal dwBufLen As Int32) As Boolean
End Function
```

NOTE *You can find all of the definitions for all of the cryptography methods and constants in the wincrypt.h header file. This file can be found in* **C:\Windows CE Tools\wce300\Pocket PC 2002\include**, *assuming you installed it in the default location.*

Visual Basic has no representation of an unsigned long pointer and no realization of pointers in general. However, in NETCF you use the **IntPtr** variable type to represent pointers. The remainder of the method parameters are straightforward variable types that you have seen before.

This is a good time to look at when a variable should be declared as ByVal or ByRef in the Visual Basic function declaration. The C++ definitions in Listing 17-5 include the compiler directives **IN** and **OUT** for each parameter, so it was very obvious what the role of the variable was to be. The C++ definition in Listing 17-8 isn't as helpful so it's useful to look at how you can decide. If you're an old C++ or C developer, you already know, but many Visual Basic 6 developers may not.

In general, and there may be an exception out there somewhere, all parameters that are defined as pointers, DWORD *pdwDataLen being an example, should be declared ByRef, while all other parameters can be declared ByVal. The idea here is that the DWORD pointer is "pointing" to some location in memory that the API method will write its data into. Mixing ByRef and ByVal definitions is probably the most frequent problem found in API method definitions.

Now with that said, let's look at an exception. The C++ definition shows the parameter where the data is returned, pbData, as being BYTE *, but the Visual Basic .NET definition defines the variable as ByVal. The difference here is that when an array is passed as a parameter, it is passed by default as a "pointer" to the array of data that is in your application process space. If the parameter was defined as ByRef, the call won't succeed because in that case you're actually passing a pointer to a pointer, not what is expected by the API.

One last close encounter before moving on to making the call. The following code shows a snippet from the C++ header file:

```
// Algorithm classes
#define ALG_CLASS_ANY          (0)
#define ALG_CLASS_SIGNATURE    (1 << 13)
#define ALG_CLASS_MSG_ENCRYPT  (2 << 13)
#define ALG_CLASS_DATA_ENCRYPT (3 << 13)
#define ALG_CLASS_HASH         (4 << 13)
#define ALG_CLASS_KEY_EXCHANGE (5 << 13)
```

Unless you have done some computer science classes or had a C/C++ background, these definitions would be Greek to you. The << signs represent the shift operator in C++. A shift moves, or shifts, the bits of the number to the left 1 bit. The Visual Basic equation to calculate the value of 5 << 13 is shown in the following code line:

```
5 * Math.Pow(2, 13) = 40990
```

In other words, the pseudo code would look like this:

```
NumberToShift * Math.Pow(2, PlacesToShift)
```

The **ALG_CLASS_KEY_EXCHANGE** constant is defined as 5 << 13, which, using the preceding equation, evaluates to 40,990. The Visual Basic equivalent of the preceding defines is shown in the following code:

```
'// Algorithm classes
Private Const ALG_CLASS_ANY As Int32 = 0
Private Const ALG_CLASS_SIGNATURE As Int32 = 8192
Private Const ALG_CLASS_MSG_ENCRYPT As Int32 = 16384
Private Const ALG_CLASS_DATA_ENCRYPT As Int32 = 24576
Private Const ALG_CLASS_HASH As Int32 = 32768
Private Const ALG_CLASS_KEY_EXCHANGE As Int32 = 40990
```

The source file in the samples folder that contains the full list of definitions and declarations (and of course all of the code) is Cryptography.vb. This file contains most of the constants that are defined in the C++ header file. All of them aren't used in the class code, but they can be used as references for your future work in writing your own P/Invoke method calls.

Making the Call

In order to encrypt a string, and this pertains to the full framework as well, you need to supply some value to use as a key. This can usually be any string value that is unique for each company's implementation of the encryption algorithms. This key is what makes the encrypted text private. In this example, a unique key, or password, is defined in the class scope:

```
Private Const _password As String = "77709C1B61834c68AFAE8BB93323EAC7"
```

If you are observant, you may have noticed that this key is nothing more than a registry-formatted GUID with the hyphens (-) removed. Your keys may be as creative or as simple as you like. The example **CryptoAPI** class exposes two methods for encrypting a string and two methods for decrypting a string.

```
Public Function EncryptString(ByVal strData As String, ByVal password As String) _
        As String
    Return EncryptStringEx(strData, password)
End Function
Public Function EncryptString(ByVal strData As String) As String
    Return EncryptStringEx(strData, _password)
End Function
```

One method uses the class's encrypt key value, whereas the other lets the developer pass a string representing a different encryption key. If you pass the string into the **EncryptString** method, be sure to remember the value of the string so you can pass it to the **DecryptString** method later. The code to encrypt a string looks like the following:

```
txtEncrypt.Text = ctp.EncryptString(Me.txtEncrypt.Text)
```

The class's implementation of this method takes the input string and passes it to the internal **EncryptStringEx** method along with the encrypt key defined in the class.

```
Public Function EncryptString(ByVal strData As String) As String
    Return EncryptStringEx(strData, _password)
End Function
```

 NOTE *Before you get too far into the code, let's take a second to touch on an important topic. When you encrypt a string, its length will increase. In this chapter's sample code, the value of **Encrypt This!** after encryption is **dYYFfWn5Ngsq+CxsQ6Yuhw==**. That is an increase of almost 100 percent in string size. The change is dependent on your source string and your password. The point is, if you're encrypting x number of characters, don't expect x number of characters back.*

Now comes the fun. While the definitions for the cryptography API calls aren't that difficult, the same can't be said about the code that must make a series of calls to unmanaged code to actually do the encrypting. There is a very definite series of calls that *must* be made in order for the encryption to work. Along the way, you must supply what seems like an infinite number of constants, Trues, Falses, and other variables. The code to perform the encryption and to make the calls to unmanaged code is shown in Listing 17-9.

Listing 17-9. Calling the System Crypto Methods

```
Private Function EncryptStringEx(ByVal strData As String, _
        ByVal password As String) As String
    Dim hProv As IntPtr
    Dim phKey As IntPtr

    Dim retVal As Boolean = CryptAcquireContext(hProv, Nothing, _
        Nothing, PROV_RSA_FULL, 0)
    Dim hHash As IntPtr = IntPtr.Zero
    retVal = CryptCreateHash(hProv, CALG_MD2, IntPtr.Zero, 0, hHash)
    If Not retVal Then
        Dim retError As Integer = Marshal.GetLastWin32Error()
        Return String.Empty
    End If

    Dim byteValue As Byte() = System.Text.Encoding.ASCII.GetBytes(password)
    Dim byteValueLen As Int32 = byteValue.Length
    retVal = CryptHashData(hHash, byteValue, byteValueLen, 0)
```

```vb
        If Not retVal Then
            Dim retError As Integer = Marshal.GetLastWin32Error()
            Return String.Empty
        End If


        retVal = CryptDeriveKey(hProv, CALG_DES, hHash, _
                CRYPT_EXPORTABLE, phKey)
        If Not retVal Then
            Dim retError As Integer = Marshal.GetLastWin32Error()
            Return String.Empty
        End If


        byteValue = System.Text.Encoding.ASCII.GetBytes(strData)
        Dim bLen As Integer = byteValue.Length
        Dim requiredLen As Int32 = byteValue.Length
        Dim encryptedLen As Int32 = byteValue.Length


        '   Get the size of the buffer for the encrypted string.
        retVal = CryptEncrypt(phKey, IntPtr.Zero, True, 0, Nothing, _
            requiredLen, encryptedLen)
        If Not retVal Then
            Dim retError As Integer = Marshal.GetLastWin32Error()
            Return String.Empty
        End If


        ' Resize the array to hold extra data after encryption.
        ReDim Preserve byteValue(requiredLen)
        encryptedLen = byteValue.Length
        retVal = CryptEncrypt(phKey, IntPtr.Zero, True, 0, byteValue, bLen, _
            encryptedLen)
        If Not retVal Then
            Dim retError As Integer = Marshal.GetLastWin32Error()
            Return String.Empty
        End If
        CryptDestroyHash(hHash)
        CryptDestroyKey(phKey)
        CryptReleaseContext(hProv, 0)


        Return System.Convert.ToBase64String(byteValue, 0, bLen)
    End Function
```

Several preliminary steps must be done before you can make that single call to **CryptEncrypt**. The first order of business is to acquire a context that is used in the remainder of the function. This implementation uses both the default container and default service provider provided by the system. This is done by passing Nothing as the second and third parameters. The requested provider type is PROV_RSA_FULL. The PROV_RSA_FULL provider type supports digital signatures and data encryption. It's considered a general-purpose cryptographic service provider (CSP).

The next step is to get a handle to a CSP hash object, the CryptCreateHash function. This handle is used in the subsequent call to CryptHashData. After the hash and the context handles have been obtained, the password is prepared for use by the crypto API. In most stream operations in .NET, a byte array is required instead of a string. To convert a string to a byte array, use the **System.Text.Encoding.ASCII.GetBytes** method as shown in Listing 17-9.

When the password has been converted to a byte array, it's then hashed by calling the CryptHashData function. This function uses the hash object handle that was created in the call to CryptCreateHash.

The next step is to create a cryptographic session key that derives from your base data. The **CryptDeriveKey** method uses the context handle and the hash handle, which now contains information about the hashed password, to generate a key that guarantees that you can, using the same base data, generate an identical key when you need to decrypt the string at a later time. If you want to generate random keys to encrypt a string, you could use the CryptGenKey function. If you did this, you would need a way to store the key to be used at decrypt time.

It's now time to make the call to **CryptEncrypt**. Actually, you call this method twice in the implementation. The first call is strictly to get the size of the buffer required to hold the encrypted string value. It's possible to just create a large buffer, pass that buffer to **CryptEncrypt**, and then look at the string coming out and trim it to length. This class takes the extra step to get the size and fill the buffer on the second call. Either way works, which you decide to choose boils down to personal preference. After the second call to **CryptEncrypt**, your encrypted byte array is in the **byteValue** variable.

Being the good .NET programmer that you are, you also clean up after yourself by closing the key, the hash handle, and the context handle. However, at this point, your data isn't a string but a byte array. To convert it to a string, use the **System.Convert.ToBase64String** method.

Decrypting the string follows much the same path. One difficulty to overcome is how to convert the encrypted string into an array of bytes.

```
Dim byteValue As Byte() = System.Convert.FromBase64String(strData)
```

The preceding line of code does a superb job of changing the Base64-encoded encrypted string into a byte array.

NOTE *In writing and testing the encryption code, I came to the realization that just because the header file defines nine different algorithm identifiers, you can't use them all. In the code in Listing 17-9, I used CALG_MD2 for the CryptCreateHash function call and CALG_DES for the CryptDeriveKey function call. In trying various combinations of the other identifiers, I was unable to find another combination that performed as expected. That isn't to say that others won't work, just that I didn't keep trying to fix something that I had working.*

TIP *Look at the source code for this section. There is also a function exposed by the class that hashes a string. A hash is a one-way operation, and there is no way to get the original string back. Just the kind of thing you want to use when storing passwords into a database.*

HOMEWORK *Add to the **CryptoAPI** class the ability to store the password used to encrypt the string in the encrypted string.*

Writing Your Own DLLs

No matter how hard you try, there will be times when you just can't make managed code do what you want it to do. The scope of this book is Visual Basic .NET. You have undoubtedly heard the explanation that VB .NET is as powerful as C#. That is indeed true most of the time, and one of the times when it's not is in calling unmanaged APIs. When using C#, you can take advantage of the **unsafe** and **fixed** keywords. The unsafe statement basically tells the .NET runtime that you'll be doing direct memory management, which means that you'll be using pointers. When you use unsafe code blocks, you're "turning off" the runtime's code verification. In other words, when using **unsafe** the runtime doesn't check to be sure that the code is accessing only the memory owned by the process.

The fixed statement goes hand in hand with the unsafe statement. When the runtime runs the garbage collector, it's highly probable that your variables will move as memory is freed and released from managed memory. If you were using pointers, it's very likely that the runtime would relocate the variables and cause your application to crash. The fixed statement pins the variable to a specific address, keeping the garbage collector from moving the variable.

Thankfully, or not, there is no equivalent to **unsafe** or **fixed** in Visual Basic .NET. If you really have to do something like this, you could write a component in C# and use it from your Visual Basic .NET application, or you could take another tactic and write the code in C++ and call it through P/Invoke. Another reason to create an external DLL that you access from NETCF is when you need to call an API that requires a structure that has more complex embedded objects inside them.

It's easy to call API methods that take the simple variable types, but you can't pass a structure that has a member that is a string type. Also, if a structure contains something more complex, such as a RECT object (the Win32 rectangle object), you can't easily pass it through a P/Invoke call. In the following tutorial, you'll create an eMbedded Visual C++ DLL that hides the complexity of the SHSipInfo API.

The SHSipInfo call can do several things, one of which is to tell you if the SIP is visible or hidden.

Step-by-Step Tutorial: Creating an Unmanaged DLL

In this tutorial, you'll create a dynamic link library that you can call from your managed Visual Basic application. You'll be adding the ability to check if the SIP is visible and also to find out which SIP panel is currently active. This sample also assumes that you have eMbedded Visual Tools 3.0 installed on your system. If you don't have it installed, I encourage you to do so. There are several useful tools in the package that aren't provided in Visual Studio .NET.

 NOTE   *I provide a completed version of this application, titled SipInfo, under the **Chapter 17** folder of the **Samples** folder for this book. See Appendix D for more information on accessing and loading the sample applications.*

Step 1: Starting a New Project

In practice, you would want to create a separate project for your control and a project to test the control. So, to keep this tutorial as real as possible, you'll develop two separate projects. Begin this step-by-step exercise by creating a new project using the following steps:

1.   Start eMbedded Visual C++.

2.   From the File menu, select **New**.

3.   From the **New** dialog box, select **WCE Dynamic-Link Library**.

4. Adjust the location text box to change where the project is to be placed.

5. Enter a project name of **SipInfo**.

6. Select the CPUs that you want to support.

7. Click **OK**.

8. In Step 1 of 1, select **A DLL that exports some symbols**.

9. Click **Finish**.

Step 2: Adding Link Libraries

To add the link libraries to the project that are required by your yet-to-be-added new code, perform the following steps:

1. From the **Project** menu, select **Settings**.

2. Select **All Configurations** in the **Settings for:** drop-down box in the Project Settings dialog box.

3. Select the **Link** tab.

4. Add **aygshell.lib** and **ole32.lib** to the **Object/libraries modules:** text field. Separate the two values by a space from each other and any other items in the text box.

5. Click **OK**.

Step 3: Adding a Function to Export

The purpose of your library is to implement calls to the **SHSipInfo** method found in the aygshell system library. To add the required code, perform the following steps:

1. Select the **Files** tab in the workspace tool window on the left of the workspace.

2. Open the SipInfo.cpp file by double-clicking the filename under **Source Files**.

3. Add the code in Listing 17-10 to the code file after the **DllMain** method.

Listing 17-10. Making a Call to SHSipInfo for Visible State

```
extern "C" __declspec(dllexport) bool WINAPI IsSipVisible(void)
{
    int ret;
    RECT rcDesktop;
    RECT rcSip;
    DWORD fdwFlags = 0;

    rcDesktop.bottom = 0;
    rcDesktop.left = 0;
    rcDesktop.right = 0;
    rcDesktop.top = 0;

    rcSip.bottom = 0;
    rcSip.left = 0;
    rcSip.right = 0;
    rcSip.top = 0;

    SIPINFO sipInfo;
    sipInfo.cbSize = sizeof(sipInfo);
    sipInfo.fdwFlags = fdwFlags;
    sipInfo.rcVisibleDesktop = rcDesktop;
    sipInfo.rcSipRect = rcSip;
    sipInfo.dwImDataSize = 0;
    sipInfo.pvImData = 0;
    ret = SHSipInfo(SPI_GETSIPINFO, 0, &sipInfo, 0);
    return (0 != (sipInfo.fdwFlags & SIPF_ON));
}
```

Most important to getting the correct format of a library so that its functions can be accessed from managed Visual Basic .NET is to ensure the method signature is correct. If you get that wrong, there is no way that your call will ever succeed. In order for your method to be exposed to the outside world, it must be exported. This is done by prefixing the function name with __declspec(dllexport). When working with DllImport, you'll need to be concerned about the calling convention (this will be covered in more detail when we discuss how to call the library you're currently creating). This choice is simple since WINAPI is the only convention supported by NETCF. The WINAPI portion of the declaration specifies the correct calling convention.

By default, C++ "mangles" the function name. This means that the name is "decorated" to allow method overloading. This default behavior needs to be turned off so that the name you enter in the function declaration is the name that you call from NETCF. This is accomplished by specifying **extern "C"** in the function declaration.

The rest of the line is the actual definition of the function call. In this example, the function takes no parameters (void) and returns a bool value. This is the basis of all methods that you wish to export from your libraries.

The code inside the function defines to RECT structures and fills them with default data. A SIPINFO structure is then defined and its default values are set. Once the variables are all defined and populated, SHSipInfo is called. The first parameter of SHSipInfo is specified as SPI_GETSIPINFO, which tells the method that data is to be returned about the status of the SIP. Other values will set the status of the SIP or get and set which SIP is currently active. More code will be added later that will get the active SIP. The last line of your function returns True if the SIPF_ON flag was set in the flag's element of the SIPINFO structure.

Step 4: Adding the include Directives

In C++, you need to add include files in the project. These files are where the compiler and linker get the information they need to resolve function signatures, constants, and other definitions. To add the required includes, add the following code to SipInfo.cpp:

```
#include "stdafx.h"
#include "SipInfo.h"
#include "aygshell.h"
#include "Objbase.h"
```

Step 5: Adding Code to Query the Current SIP

Since you have made a library, it would be a shame to waste it on a single exported function. SHSipInfo can provide more information than whether the SIP is visible or not. Of particular interest is which input method is currently active. The Pocket PC comes with three standard input methods (IMs): Block Recognizer, Letter Recognizer, and Keyboard. Each IM is identified by a unique GUID. If you were to build your own or buy a third-party IM, they would also have unique identifiers. SHSipInfo can be used to get the GUID (CLSID) of the active IM. To add the required code, perform the following steps:

1. Open the SipInfo.cpp file if it isn't already open.

2. Add the code in Listing 17-11 to the code file after the **IsSipVisible** method that you added earlier.

Listing 17-11. Getting the Current Input Method Identifier

```
extern "C" __declspec(dllexport) char* WINAPI
    GetCurrentInputMethod(void)
{
    int ret;
    RECT rcDesktop;
    RECT rcSip;
    DWORD fdwFlags = 0;

    rcDesktop.bottom = 0;
    rcDesktop.left = 0;
    rcDesktop.right = 0;
    rcDesktop.top = 0;

    rcSip.bottom = 0;
    rcSip.left = 0;
    rcSip.right = 0;
    rcSip.top = 0;

    CLSID sid;
    SIPINFO sipInfo;
    sipInfo.cbSize = sizeof(sipInfo);
    sipInfo.fdwFlags = fdwFlags;
    sipInfo.rcVisibleDesktop = rcDesktop;
    sipInfo.rcSipRect =  rcSip;
    sipInfo.dwImDataSize = 0;
    sipInfo.pvImData = 0;

    ret = SHSipInfo(SPI_GETCURRENTIM, 0, &sid, 0);

    OLECHAR* str = OLESTR("aaaaaaaaaaaaaaaaaaaaaaaaaaaaaaaaaaaaaaaa");
    StringFromCLSID(sid, &str);
    return (char*)str;
}
```

This function starts out just like the IsSipVisible function does. The ending is a little different however. The GUID (CLSID) is returned in the **sid** variable of the SHSipInfo call. Then a buffer the correct size is allocated and the CLSID copied into the string buffer. The return value of this function is a pointer to a string. There may be other ways to return the string value, but this method works, to prove a point that you may find useful in the future.

Step 6: Setting the Build Type

When you tell eMbedded Visual C++ to build the project, it needs to know which platform you are targeting, the emulator or a device. The emulator is represented by x86, whereas a device is represented by ARM. To set the target correctly, perform the following steps:

1. Be certain that the **WCE Configuration** toolbar is visible.

2. Click the **Select Active Configuration** drop-down box.

3. For emulation debugging, choose the **Win32 (WCE x86) Debug** item.

4. For device debugging, choose the **Win32 (WCE ARM) Debug** item.

You may have more choices than ARM and x86 based on what other SDKs are installed on your system.

Step 7: Building and Deploying the Library

To build the library, you can either press F7 or select **Build SipInfo** from the Build menu. The location where the file is copied is defined on the **Debug** tab of the Project Settings dialog box for the project. By default, and you should probably leave it this way, the DLL is copied to the Windows directory. When you build the library, the IDE automatically downloads a copy of the library to the directory on the target, emulator, or device.

If you're really interested to see if the file was placed in the proper directory, don't try to use the device's File Explore feature because it doesn't show you DLL files. To do this you need to start the Remote File Viewer tool, which can be found under the Tools menu in the eMbedded Visual C++ IDE. If you navigate to the \Windows directory, you should see SIPinfo.dll. If you don't, check the build output in the IDE to make certain that everything went fine.

Calling Your Unmanaged Library

The earlier examples were used to explain how to build function definitions, and add DllImportAttributes to those declarations, found in the system libraries. Now it's time to write the code to access the SipInfo library. The discussion in the first section of this chapter barely touched the methods that are available in the **SipOperation** class. This next section will use the SipInfo unmanaged library to detail the rest of the **SipOperation** class (Listing 17-12).

The SipInfo library has two additional methods not covered in the tutorial. The two new methods are variations on the **GetCurrentInputMethod** discussed in the tutorial. The function declarations for the four methods exposed by the SipInfo library are shown in Listing 17-12. To bring the C++ declarations together with the Visual Basic declarations, the C++ prototypes are included in the listing. The **IsSipVisible** method is an easy call, taking no parameters and returning a Boolean value.

Listing 17-12. Function Declarations for the SipInfo Unmanaged Library

```
'extern "C" __declspec(dllexport) bool WINAPI IsSipVisible(void)
<DllImport("SipInfo.dll", EntryPoint:="IsSipVisible")> _
Private Shared Function IsSipVisible() As Boolean
End Function


' char* WINAPI GetCurrentInputMethod(void)
<DllImport("SipInfo.dll", EntryPoint:="GetCurrentInputMethod")> _
Private Shared Function GetCurrentInputMethod() As IntPtr
End Function


'int WINAPI GetCurrentInputMethodID(void)
<DllImport("SipInfo.dll", EntryPoint:="GetCurrentInputMethodID")> _
Private Shared Function GetCurrentInputMethodID() As Int32
End Function


'int GetCurrentInputMethodEx(OUT LPSTR pInputMethodId, IN OUT LPDWORD lpcbData)
<DllImport("SipInfo.dll", EntryPoint:="GetCurrentInputMethodEx")> _
Private Shared Function GetCurrentInputMethodEx(ByVal lpData As String, _
    ByRef lpcbData As Int32) As Int32
End Function
```

The **GetCurrentInputMethod** is a little different as you can see from both the declaration and the way it's called as shown in the following code:

```
Dim uig As IntPtr
Dim str As String
uig = GetCurrentInputMethod()
str = Marshal.PtrToStringUni(uig)
```

This method actually returns the pointer to a string, which, once it's back in managed code, needs to be marshaled back to a string. The string returned is the GUID that serves as an identifier for the active IM. This method would be used in a situation where you're employing a custom input method. When you're only using the standard IMs, the better method to call would be **GetCurrentInputMethodID**. The GetCurrentInputMethodID function returns 1 for the keyboard, 2 for the numeric keyboard, 3 for the block recognizer, and 4 for the letter recognizer. These are the standard input methods on the Pocket PC. If you have defined and are using a custom IM, then the method returns a 5. If an error is encountered, a –1 is returned.

A common implementation used by system APIs is to return a string through the parameter list, along with a variable that specifies the size of the string buffer. The fourth function, GetCurrentInputMethodEx, provides an example of how you can create your own function to do the same type of call.

Even if you're not a C++ programmer, you should be able to do some of the simple calls required in the C++ unmanaged code. In the help for the eMbedded Visual Tools, many of the API calls give C++ examples. To write an unmanaged library, you just have to create the shell, which you now have an example of, and copy the code from help into your new files. And if you get stuck, you can always find some C++ bigot who would be glad to show you how inferior VB is and write the C++ code for you.

HOMEWORK   *Add another function to the SipInfo library that sets the IM to one of the three standard IMs supplied on the Pocket PC. When the library builds correctly, write the managed code to call the method.*

Staying in the Managed World

Perhaps you want to call out to one of those nasty Windows API calls but you don't know anything about C++ and you don't want to ask one of "those" programmers for help. Don't give up just yet, because you do have a managed option; but be warned that this technique isn't for those with a weak stomach. Were you one of those VB 6 cowboys who loved to allocate memory using the Windows API? Did you ever call out to the strcpy function to copy strings to get a little better performance than VB was able to give? If you were, then you're going to love this next example. If you weren't, then hold on because here we go.

In the previous discussions, you've learned that marshaling on NETCF is a little constrained. When it comes to calling to unmanaged code, strings embedded in a class or structure are the biggest shortfall. NETCF doesn't automatically marshal strings embedded in a class or structure, so you have to do it manually. In C#, you do that using the **unsafe** and **fixed** keywords, which don't exist in Visual Basic .NET. But instead of writing a library to hide the call for you, it's possible to allocate and "pin" memory using managed Visual Basic .NET code.

A good example of embedded strings in a class is the Notification API. The main problem with using the Notification API from managed code is the fact that there are two embedded strings in the CE_NOTIFICATION_TRIGGER structure. The code in Listing 17-13 shows the method declaration along with the problem structure.

Listing 17-13. Setting Up for the Notification API Call

```
<DllImport("coredll.dll", SetLastError:=True)> _
Private Shared Function CeSetUserNotificationEx(ByVal h As IntPtr, _
    ByRef nt As CE_NOTIFICATION_TRIGGER, _
    ByVal un As IntPtr) As IntPtr
End Function

Private Structure CE_NOTIFICATION_TRIGGER
    Public dwSize As UInt32
    Public dwType As UInt32
    Public dwEvent As UInt32
    Public lpszApplication As IntPtr
    Public lpszArguments As IntPtr
    Public startTime As SYSTEMTIME
    Public endTime As SYSTEMTIME
End Structure
```

The two strings **lpszApplication** and **lpszArguments** are declared in the structure as **IntPtr** variables. Getting these strings initialized in managed code without the use of **unsafe** and **fixed** is the trick. Listing 17-14 shows the method where the call to the API is made.

Listing 17-14. Calling the Notification API.

```
Private Shared Function CeSetUserNotification( _
    ByVal notificationType As CNT_TYPE, _
    ByVal notificationEvent As NOTIFICATION_EVENT, _
    ByVal application As String, _
    ByVal arguments As String, _
    ByVal startTime As SYSTEMTIME, _
    ' ByVal endTime As SYSTEMTIME) As IntPtr

    Dim nt As CE_NOTIFICATION_TRIGGER = New CE_NOTIFICATION_TRIGGER
    With nt
        dwEvent = Convert.ToUInt32(notificationEvent)
        dwType = Convert.ToUInt32(notificationType)
```

```
            ' Get size of unmanaged object(nt).
            dwSize = Convert.ToUInt32(Marshal.SizeOf(nt))
            startTime = startTime
            endTime = endTime
            lpszApplication = StringToHLocal(application)
        End With
    Dim hNotify As IntPtr
    Try
        ' Put the command line arguments on the heap (if there are any).
        nt.lpszArguments = StringToHLocal(arguments)

        ' For time-based notifies, parm 0 and 2 do not matter.
        hNotify = CeSetUserNotificationEx(IntPtr.Zero, nt, IntPtr.Zero)

        If IntPtr.op_Equality(hNotify, IntPtr.Zero) Then
            Dim Exception As String = String.Format("{0} event failed; _
                getLasterror={1}", notificationEvent.ToString(), _
                Marshal.GetLastWin32Error())
            Throw New Exception(Exception)
        End If
    Finally
        LocalFree(nt.lpszArguments)
        LocalFree(nt.lpszApplication)
    End Try
    Return hNotify
End Function
```

This method instantiates and initializes the notification trigger structure and passes the structure to the desired Windows API. What should look foreign to you are the calls to **StringToHLocal**. This method, shown in Listing 17-15, allocates memory on the local heap. Once the API is called, the return value is compared to IntPtr.Zero to see if the notification call worked as expected. The memory that was allocated by **StringToHLocal** is freed in the Finally block.

Listing 17-15. Allocating Memory on the Local Heap

```
Private Shared Function StringToHLocal(ByVal s As String) As IntPtr
    ' Make sure that there is something to allocate.
    If s Is Nothing Or s.Trim.Length = 0 Then
        Return IntPtr.Zero
    End If
```

```
'      The Length method returns ASCII length, we want UNICODE Length.
    Dim len As Integer = 2 * (1 + s.Length)
    '      Allocate on heap & return handle to it for marshaling.
    Dim hLocal As IntPtr = AllocHLocal(len)
    If IntPtr.op_Equality(hLocal, IntPtr.Zero) Then
        '      I hate when that happens.
        Throw New OutOfMemoryException
    Else
        '      Copy array out of managed code.
        Marshal.Copy(s.ToCharArray(), 0, hLocal, s.Length)
        Return hLocal
    End If
End Function


Private Shared Function AllocHLocal(ByVal bytes As Integer) As IntPtr
    Return (LocalAlloc(LPTR, Convert.ToUInt32(bytes)))
End Function
```

 NOTE *This is a very good example of when to place code into a Finally block. It's bad practice to allocate system resources (file handles, memory, etc.) and then not let them go when finished. To be certain that the memory allocated on the heap is freed, no matter what happens in the method, the calls to LocalFree are placed in the Finally block.*

What happens in the **StringToHLocal** method is the real "magic" that makes all of this work. First a buffer in which the string will be stored is allocated. The string is then copied into the buffer using the **Marshal.Copy** method. The "pointer" to this memory is passed back to be assigned into the notification array. Now in the call to CeSetUserNotificationEx the strings are being handled as memory pointers, which the NETCF marshaler can handle just fine. While this technique works fine, it might be just as foreign to a VB 6 developer as making a new DLL to handle the calls on your behalf. Even though it's closer to the system than most VB developers prefer to be, it's still an excellent way of working around the limitations of NETCF marshaling.

MessageWindow

There will be times when your application will need to listen to an unmanaged application. For instance, you might have a hardware device driver that collects data and posts a message for some application to handle. NETCF has no window handles to use for this purpose. There is, however, a class in the System.WindowsCE.Forms assembly, **MessageWindow**, that provides the ability for your NETCF application to intercept messages. The first step in using **MessageWindow** is to derive a new class as shown in Listing 17-16.

Listing 17-16. Deriving a Class from MessageWindow

```
Imports Microsoft.WindowsCE.Forms

Public Class MessageHandler
    Inherits Microsoft.WindowsCE.Forms.MessageWindow
    Private _ParentForm As Form

    Public Sub New(ByVal frm As Form)
       _ParentForm = frm
    End Sub

    Private Sub New()
    End Sub

    Protected Overrides Sub WndProc(ByRef msg As Message)
        Select Case msg.Msg
            Case &H401
                DirectCast (_ParentForm, frmMessages).MessageInBox( _
                    msg.LParam.ToInt32)
        End Select

        MyBase.WndProc(msg)
    End Sub
End Class
```

TIP   *I am sure that you use **Convert** and **CType** for conversions all of the time, right? There is a less-well-known method called **DirectCast**, which is used in Listing 17-13. **DirectCast** is very similar to **CType** with one exception: **DirectCast** can be faster. **DirectCast** requires the runtime type of an object variable to be the same as the specified type. When this is true, **DirectCast** executes faster than **CType**. **CType** is compiled inline, and for that reason, if the types don't match up correctly, it's faster to use than **DirectCast**.*

In addition to supplying the **WndProc** method, we'll discuss the Case statement code shortly. This class also exposes a **New** method that requires the caller to pass an instance of a form to the constructor. The default constructor with no parameters is made private to force the caller to pass in the form instance. With this reference to a form, you can now call into any public method exposed by the form.

 TIP *Let me save you some debugging time, if I may. In Listing 17-13 the method signature for* **WndProc** *is correct. However, it's very easy to get this signature wrong and cause your application not to work. Let's suppose that some author and developer, whose name shall remain anonymous, wrote the signature as follows:*

```
Public Overloads Sub WndProc(ByRef msg As Message)
```

The preceding signature looks fine and the compiler certainly says nothing bad about it, so it must work, right? Wrong. By using Overloads instead of Overrides, the event chain is short-circuited and the method never gets called.

Using the example of a device sending a message to the hosting application, the next step is to create a class that generates some data. Listing 17-17 shows a very basic class that generates a Windows message inside a separate thread.

Listing 17-17. Generating Data to Display Using a New Class

```
Public Class DataGenerator
    Private _th As Thread = Nothing
    Private Shared i As Int32 = 0
    Private messageWindowHwnd As IntPtr
    Private _useEvent As Boolean = False

    Public Delegate Sub DataUpdate(ByVal count As Int32)
    Public Event DataChanged As DataUpdate

    Public Sub New(ByVal rate As Int32, ByVal hWnd As IntPtr, _
        ByVal bUseEvent As Boolean)
        Dim ts As ThreadStart = New ThreadStart(AddressOf CollectData)
        _th = New Thread(ts)
        messageWindowHwnd = hWnd
        _useEvent = bUseEvent
    End Sub
```

```
        Public Sub Start()
            _th.Start()
        End Sub

        Public Sub [Stop] ()
            _th = Nothing
        End Sub

        Public Sub CollectData()
            While i < 100
                SyncLock i.GetType
                    i += 1
                    Dim q As IntPtr = New IntPtr(i)
                    If _useEvent Then
                        RaiseEvent DataChanged(i)
                    Else
                        Dim msg As Message = Message.Create(Me.messageWindowHwnd, _
                            &H401, IntPtr.Zero, q)
                        MessageWindow.PostMessage(msg)
                    End If
                End SyncLock
            End While
        End Sub
End Class
```

TIP *Look back up the code listing a little and find the **Public Sub Stop()** method. Did you notice the square brackets around the word "Stop"? You might be familiar with this from the ADO days of VB 6 in which you would use the square brackets to "wrap" a variable in a SQL statement. Normally this was to embed spaces in the variable or parameter name. In .NET, you can use the square brackets to tell the compiler that you want to use the word even though it's a reserved word in .NET. So if you want to use a command or statement, in your own class or namespace scope, that is already used by .NET, you can enclose it in square brackets.*

NOTE *While this isn't a .NET tutorial book, it's useful to explain a few things once in a while, just in case you aren't familiar with certain .NET concepts. In Listing 17-14, I enclose some code inside a SyncLock block statement. SyncLock is used to synchronize access to a particular block of code. In this situation, you don't want the thread, or another thread, to try to enter the code block while you're attempting to send a message to the calling app. The lock is placed on a **Shared** variable so that it's the same variable for any and all instances of the class. If you've ever heard of the term deadlocking, this is how you can do it. If execution of the code inside the SyncLock block never leaves the block, every thread that tries to call this method will sit and wait indefinitely. While threading is useful, and fun, it can cause very hard-to-solve problems. Use threading only after much consideration and design.*

There are two important notes to be made about this code. One of the parameters that you pass in is a Windows handle that is provided by the **MessageWindow** class. You'll see how this call is made shortly. The second important point is the construction and posting of the outgoing message. The WindowsCE.Form assembly provides a **Message** class that is used to create the message and a method on the **MessageWindow** class that provides a way to send or post a message.

NOTE *You would normally want to use the **PostMessage** method when passing a message to another window. **SendMessage** is a synchronous call that will cause your code to stop execution and wait for the window on the other end to receive the message and to process it. **PostMessage**, on the other hand, just puts the message into the message queue of the other application and keeps on running.*

When the message is created, the handle of the class derived from MessageWindow is passed as the target of the message. In this example the code uses a hard-coded message number of &H401. You'll be better off using the RegisterWindowsMessage API to create a message number that is guaranteed to be unique by the system. The wParam is set to IntPtr.Zero because you aren't using it in this example, and the lparam is set to an **IntPtr** that was created with the value of your incrementing variable.

The code in Listing 17-17 also has an option to notify the user by raising an event. In the declaration section of the class, there is a **Delegate** method defined that accepts a single **Int32** parameter, matching the data that is also passed through the message.

Now, to pull it all together, your client creates the class derived from **MessageWindow** and an instance of the data generator.

```
Private WithEvents _dataGenerator As Apress.DataGenerator
Private _messageWindow As MessageHandler

Private Sub btnStart_Click(ByVal sender As System.Object, _
        ByVal e As System.EventArgs) Handles btnStart.Click
    _messageWindow = New MessageHandler(Me)
    _dataGenerator = New Apress.DataGenerator(10, _messageWindow.Hwnd, True)
    _dataGenerator.Start()
End Sub
```

The data generator class posts the message to your MessageHandler, which in turn calls the form's **MessageInBox** method (refer back to Listing 17-16). The main purpose of the **MessageInBox** method, shown in the following code snippet, is to update a label on the form's surface.

```
Public Sub MessageInBox(ByVal count As Int32)
    Me.lblDataDisplay.Text = count.ToString()
    Me.lblDataDisplay.Refresh()
End Sub
```

The alternative method discussed is to raise an event to the form. The code to handle the event is shown here:

```
Private Sub testfunc(ByVal count As Int32) Handles _dataGenerator.DataChanged
    If Not CalledOnFormThread() Then
        _count = count
        Me.Invoke(New EventHandler(AddressOf UpdateWithInvoke))
    Else
        Me.lblDataDisplay.Text = count.ToString()
    End If
End Sub
```

Notice the call to the method **CalledOnFormThread**. This method checks to see if the caller is the forms thread. If you attempt to update a UI on a thread other than the forms UI thread, you'll have a 76 percent chance of definitely raising an exception. Why 76 percent? I don't know, I just made that number up. But the point is that you *should* get an exception. However, it's possible to get by with writing from the wrong thread.

NOTE *Before you think I'm nuts (maybe it's too late for that), let me explain. In an application I was creating, as long as I only wrote to the form from the wrong thread, everything worked fine. But when I then wrote to a control on the form from the correct thread, my application crashed. If I wrote to the form first with the correct thread, any attempt to write with the wrong thread caused an exception. Go figure.*

To force the call to occur from your UI thread, the **Invoke** method of the form is called. This method forces the call to be made, using the specified delegate, on the thread that owns the control's underlying window handle. In this case, the control is the Label and the underlying window is frmMessage.

Again, we bump into one of those places where the full framework has a little better solution. NETCF only supports the **Invoke** method that takes a single parameter, the delegate to call. The full framework supports a second overload that takes an object so that data can be passed to the delegate. To work around this, the code sets a class-level variable that is then used in the **Delegate** method.

CalledOnFormThread checks the current thread context against the thread that was in context when the form was being created.

```
Private myFormThread As System.Threading.Thread = _
    System.Threading.Thread.CurrentThread

Private Function CalledOnFormThread() As Boolean
    If Me.myFormThread.Equals(System.Threading.Thread.CurrentThread) Then
        ' The call was made on the form's thread.
        Return True
    End If

    ' The call was made on a thread other than the form's thread.
    Return False
End Function
```

Once you have this all together, the application will run and display numbers in the label scrolling from 0 to 100. Using this same basic layout, you can receive Windows messages from any type of client.

Summary

It's possible to write an entire application without ever needing to call unmanaged code. It's also very likely that at some time, maybe sooner than you think, you'll need to access a Windows API or another unmanaged code library. The examples discussed in this chapter cover a good number of the data types that you'll need if the opportunity to use P/Invoke presents itself. If you ever pushed the limits in Visual Basic 6, using DllImport and calling through the interoperability layer isn't really any harder.

And if you need more help, additional resources are available. The sample code for this chapter has more classes that weren't covered. There will also be new classes posted to the Web sites where you find the sample code. Several good articles appear on Microsoft Web sites that talk about using unmanaged code. The three articles at the following URLs are the ones that you might find most useful:

- http://msdn.microsoft.com/library/default.asp?url=/library/en-us/
  dnnetcomp/html/netcfintrointerp.asp

- http://msdn.microsoft.com/library/default.asp?url=/library/en-us/
  dnnetcomp/html/netcfadvinterop.asp

- http://smartdevices.microsoftdev.com/Learn/Articles/621.aspx

One resource that deserves some special attention is Open NETCF (http://www.opennetcf.org). OpenNETCF.org is maintained by the members of the OpenNETCF Advisory Board. This group is an independent source for .NET Compact Framework development working under the spirit of the open source movement. Of particular interest to this chapter is the open source project that they call the WinAPI Library. This assembly is written in C# and provides managed wrappers for a growing list of functions in the Windows API. You can download binaries or source if you want to take a look at how the C# world lives.

So, all of this might look confusing. But don't be afraid to experiment. And if you get stuck, there are people and places willing to help you.

CHAPTER 18

Working with POOM

INCLUDED AS PART OF THE software bundled with every Pocket PC is a set of applications that are referred to jointly as *Pocket Outlook*. Individually, these are the Calendar, Contacts, Inbox, Notes, and Tasks applications.

Although functionally these applications operate in a stand-alone fashion, they are designed for use in conjunction with their larger, better-known desktop equivalent, Microsoft Outlook. Between these two platforms of PIM applications resides ActiveSync, which natively handles synchronizing data between Microsoft Outlook and the Pocket Outlook applications.

From the development point of view, Pocket Outlook offers two opportunities. First, it provides a repository of specific data, that being contacts, appointments, and tasks. Second, it comes with automatic synchronization, allowing you to be worry free of how this data moves between a device and its associated PC.

The Pocket Outlook Object Model

Applications access Pocket Outlook data through the Pocket Outlook Object Model, or as it's more commonly referred to, POOM. This COM-based library provides an object hierarchy that simplifies the process of creating, modifying, and displaying appointments, tasks, and contacts.

The problem is that, unlike applications written in eMbedded Visual C++ or eMbedded Visual Basic, those that target the .NET Compact Framework don't natively have access to COM libraries, which means, among other things, you can't directly leverage POOM.

As with all NETCF-to-COM situations, the workaround is to create a non-COM dynamic link library, or DLL. This DLL acts as a go-between for your NETCF application and the COM object. The DLL is written using eMbedded Visual C++, which as I've already mentioned can directly access COM objects, including POOM. The DLL exposes a standard NETCF-friendly interface that in turn can be PInvoked from your application.

Now, as you may have already guessed, this isn't a trivial process. It requires a detailed understanding of eMbedded Visual C++, the Pocket Outlook Object Model, and creating DLLs and PInvoking DLLs from a NETCF application. Given the right amount of time and effort, you probably could struggle through this on your own. Luckily, there are two sources of aid that can significantly shorten this process: the POOM sample on the GotDotNet Web site and the Pocket Outlook .NET component offered by InTheHand.

GotDotNet's POOM Sample

The POOM sample offered on the GotDotNet Web site demonstrates creating a DLL written in eMbedded Visual C++. You learn how to call this DLL from a NETCF application. While somewhat limited in functionality, offering access to contacts only, it does show the key points and concepts behind leveraging POOM from a .NET Compact Framework application.

One downside of this sample is that it's written completely in eMbedded Visual C++, and converting the NETCF component to Visual Basic .NET isn't a trivial task.

This sample is available for download at http://www.gotdotnet.com/team/netcf/ Samples.aspx.

InTheHand's Pocket Outlook .NET

The second option available to NETCF developers is the Pocket Outlook .NET component from InTheHand, a software development shop that specializes in NETCF. Pocket Outlook .NET is a set of .NET classes that allow full read/write access to the Appointments, Contacts, and Tasks features of Pocket Outlook.

Unlike the GotDotNet sample application, Pocket Outlook .NET is a library DLL that you can add to your .NET Compact Framework projects to provide a robust object hierarchy. This greatly simplifies incorporating POOM into your applications.

The Pocket Outlook .NET library supports data binding, so you can quickly build PIM-enabled applications using standard NETCF components such as the DataGrid and ComboBox.

From my point of view, Pocket Outlook .NET is the way to go when you need to work with Pocket Outlook data. It's easy to use, offers the right set of features, and is priced right for even the smallest of development shops. This is a cool product. In fact, all of the examples and tutorials in the remainder of this chapter utilize Pocket Outlook .NET.

For more information on this product, see http://www.inthehand.com.

Accessing POOM from NETCF

As I've already mentioned, there are two ways to access POOM from the .NET Compact Framework. The first involves creating your own native-code DLL.

Detailing this approach is outside of the scope of this chapter because of its complexity.

The second approach makes use of the Pocket Outlook .NET component from InTheHand. All of the examples and tutorials that follow make use of this component. You'll need to download and install this component to follow along or utilize any of the techniques demonstrated in the remainder of this chapter.

Working with the Pocket Outlook .NET Component

Once you've downloaded and installed the Pocket Outlook .NET component, there are a few steps that you need to perform to make use of this component within your .NET Compact Framework applications:

1. Add a reference to the Pocket Outlook .NET component.

2. Import the **PocketOutlook** namespace.

3. Define the OutlookApplication object.

These steps are detailed in the following sections.

Adding a Reference to the Pocket Outlook .NET Component

The first step that you need to perform is to add a reference to the Pocket Outlook .NET component. To accomplish this, perform the following steps:

1. With your project open, in the Solutions Explorer window right-click the **References** folder.

2. From the pop-up menu, select **Add Reference**.

3. The Add Reference dialog box will display. From the list at the top of this dialog box, select **InTheHand.PocketOutlook**.

4. Click the **Select** button. The InTheHand.PocketOutlook component will be added to the Selected Components window at the bottom of the dialog box as shown in Figure 18-1.

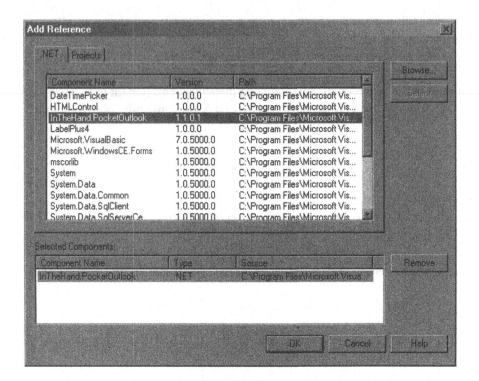

Figure 18-1. Adding the reference to the Pocket Outlook component

5. Click the **OK** button, adding the reference to your project.

Importing the PocketOutlook Namespace

The second step that you need to perform is to add an Imports statement at the top of your form module. To accomplish this, perform the following steps:

1. Open the code window for your form.

2. Navigate to the top of that code window.

3. Add the following line of code to the module:

```
Imports InTheHand.PocketOutlook
```

Defining the OutlookApplication Object

The third step that you need to perform is to declare a variable for the
OutlookApplication object. This object is the interface to the Pocket Outlook
Object Model. You must always include it in your application.

Following is an example of declaring a variable for this object. Typically, this
declaration will occur at the module or project level of your application, so that
the OutlookApplication is available across a broad scope.

```
[at the module level]
Dim poApplication As New OutlookApplication
```

NOTE *When this line of code executes, your application automatically logs in to the Pocket Outlook data source. Unlike working with POOM directly, where you need to log in before performing any task, the InTheHand Pocket Outlook .NET component performs this step for you.*

Obtaining Help on the Pocket Outlook .NET Component

The installation package for the Pocket Outlook .NET component includes a help
file titled Object Model Documentation. The installation process creates a shortcut to this document. To access this documentation, perform the following steps:

1. Click the **Start** menu.

2. From the Start menu, select **Programs.**

3. From Programs, select **InTheHand**.

4. From InTheHand, select **Pocket Outlook .NET Wrapper**.

5. From Pocket Outlook .NET Wrapper, select the shortcut to **Object Model Documentation**.

This help system provides an overview of the object hierarchy provided
through the Pocket Outlook .NET component. It's not intended as a how-to guide,
but rather as a reference. If you're looking for how-to material, then the rest of
this chapter is for you, starting with how to work with Pocket Outlook tasks.

An Important Consideration for Developers Using POOM

When developing an application that uses POOM to modify and query data within Pocket Outlook, you must always keep in mind that the data you are working with is also accessible directly by the user from the native applications themselves—Contacts, Appointments, and Tasks. What that means is the data you are incorporating into your application may be altered outside of your application in a way that may adversely affect your programming scheme.

Working with Tasks

The Pocket Outlook .NET component provides the ability to work with three facets of the Pocket Outlook data: tasks, contacts, and appointments. I'll start the discussion of this component with tasks.

From the developer's point of view, tasks can be used for a variety of purposes. For example, they could be used within a maintenance application to record follow-up work to be completed. In a delivery system, tasks could be used to note items for the next delivery. A CRM application could record steps to perform for a particular customer.

At the core of the task functionality provided through the Pocket Outlook .NET component from InTheHand is the **Tasks** property and the Task object. We'll look at each of these items in greater detail next.

The Tasks Property

The **Tasks** property of the OutlookApplication object provides access to a collection of the tasks that reside on a device. In actuality, the **Tasks** property furnishes an interface to the **Tasks** folder, provided through POOM. This property links through to an Items collection that contains all of the tasks.

We'll see several examples later in this section in which the **Tasks** property along with its Items collection is used to retrieve tasks.

The Task Object

You work with individual tasks through the Task object. Commonly used properties of this object are shown in Table 18-1. Frequently used methods of the Task object are shown in Table 18-2.

Table 18-1. Commonly Used Properties of the Task Object

PROPERTY	DESCRIPTION
Body	Defines the text of the notes accompanying a task
Categories	Indicates the categories for which a task is assigned
Complete	Indicates whether the task is complete
DateCompleted	Specifies the date that a task was completed
DueDate	Specifies the date that a task is due
Importance	Dictates the importance of a task
IsRecurring	Indicates whether a task is a single instance or recurs
Oid	Defines the unique identifier for a task
ReminderSet	Indicates whether to remind the user of the task
StartDate	Specifies the date that a task starts
Subject	Indicates the subject for a task

Table 18-2. Commonly Used Methods of the Task Object

METHOD	DESCRIPTION
Copy	Creates a copy of an existing task
Delete	Deletes a task
Display	Displays a task using the native Task interface
Save	Saves modifications to a task

While these tables might serve you well for reference, a set of practical examples follows that demonstrates commonly performed task-related operations.

Retrieving All Tasks

One of the most common functions involving tasks is the retrieving of a task(s). You can retrieve tasks in several ways:

- As a collection of all tasks

- As a subset of all tasks

- As a single task

We'll start by looking at how to retrieve all tasks, as it's a frequently used approach and the easiest method for retrieving tasks. Listing 18-1 provides a simple example of retrieving all of the tasks that are resident on a device.

Listing 18-1. Retrieving All of the Tasks

```
Imports InTheHand.PocketOutlook

[at the module level]
Dim poApplication As New OutlookApplication
Dim myTasks As OutlookItemCollection

Private Sub btnLoad_Click(ByVal sender As System.Object, _
  ByVal e As System.EventArgs) Handles btnLoad.Click

' Retrieve all of the tasks.
  myTasks = poApplication.Tasks.Items

End Sub
```

The key parts to this example are

- The Imports statement, which must be located at the top of a module.

- The declaration statement for the OutlookApplication object.

- The declaration of the OutlookItemCollection object, which can hold a collection of any Outlook items. In our case, it will hold a collection of tasks.

- Loading the collection of tasks from the OutlookApplication object, poApplication, into the OutlookItemCollection, myTasks.

At this point, the collection myTasks contains a set of task objects, one for each task that is resident on your test device. You can loop through this collection to propagate a ListBox or ComboBox, view specific task information, or reference a specific task within the collection.

Retrieving Select Tasks

There are times when you only want to retrieve specific tasks—either a single task, or perhaps a subset of tasks. Happily, it's easy to do using the **Restrict** method of the Items collection. Listing 18-2 demonstrates retrieving a subset of tasks. This example retrieves only those tasks with the category "demo".

Listing 18-2. Retrieving Select Tasks

```
Imports InTheHand.PocketOutlook

[at the module level]
Dim poApplication As New OutlookApplication
Dim myTasks As OutlookItemCollection

Private Sub btnSelect_Click(ByVal sender As System.Object, _
  ByVal e As System.EventArgs) Handles btnSelect.Click

  Dim strCategory As String
  Dim strQuery As String

' Retrieve the selected tasks.
  strCategory = "demo"
  strQuery = "[Categories] = " & ControlChars.Quote & strCategory & _
    ControlChars.Quote
  myTasks = poApplication.Tasks.Items.Restrict(strQuery)

End Sub
```

Much of the preparatory work is identical to that required to retrieve all of the tasks. You still need to add the Imports statement, declare the OutlookApplication object variable, and declare the OutlookItemCollection object variable.

The code used to select only the tasks you're interested in is located near the bottom of Listing 18-2. There you build a query string, which is nothing more than the WHERE part of a SQL SELECT statement. This query string is subsequently used with the **Restrict** method to retrieve only those tasks in which you're interested.

NOTE *You can restrict tasks based upon any property provided through the Task object.*

Displaying a Task

One of the cool features provided through POOM is the ability to display Pocket
Outlook data in its native application interface—that's to say, just like it would
appear to users had they gone into the Tasks application and selected to view
a particular task.

POOM includes a method, **Display**, which is provided through the Pocket
Outlook .NET component. Listing 18-3 demonstrates working with this method.

Listing 18-3. Displaying a Task

```
Imports InTheHand.PocketOutlook

[at the module level]
Dim poApplication As New OutlookApplication
Dim myTasks As OutlookItemCollection

Private Sub btnDisplay_Click(ByVal sender As System.Object, _
  ByVal e As System.EventArgs) Handles btnDisplay.Click

  Dim myTask As Task

' Retrieve all of the tasks.
  myTasks = poApplication.Tasks.Items

' Display the first task.
  myTask = myTasks.Item(0)
  myTask.Display()

End Sub
```

As with the two previous examples, you start by adding the Imports statement
and declaring the variables for OutlookApplication and OutlookItemCollection.

At the bottom of Listing 18-3 you'll see that all of the tasks are first retrieved.
From this collection of tasks, you extract a single task, the first, into a Task object
variable. This object provides the **Display** method, which in turn is called to display the selected task.

Adding a Task

Adding a new task is a three-step process. First, you need to create a new task. Second, you need to configure the task. Third, you need to save the task. Listing 18-4 demonstrates adding a task.

Listing 18-4. Adding a Task

```
Imports InTheHand.PocketOutlook

[at the module level]
Dim poApplication As New OutlookApplication

Private Sub btnAdd_Click(ByVal sender As System.Object, _
    ByVal e As System.EventArgs) Handles btnAdd.Click

    Dim myTask As Task

' Create a new task.
    myTask = poApplication.CreateTask

' Configure the task.
    With myTask
        .Body = "This is a sample task."
        .Categories = "demo"
        .DueDate = Today.Date
        .Importance = Importance.High
        .ReminderOptions = ReminderOptions.Dialog
        .ReminderSet = True
        .StartDate = Today.Date
        .Subject = "sample task"

' Finally, save the task.
        .Save()
    End With

End Sub
```

As with all of the previous examples, you start by adding the Imports statement and declaring the variables for OutlookApplication and OutlookItemCollection.

At the bottom of Listing 18-4 you'll see the three steps that I described. First, the **CreateTask** method of the OutlookApplication object is used to create your new task. Second, properties of the new task are loaded. Third, the Task object's **Save** method is called to save the task.

Modifying a Task

Modifying a task is similar to adding a task, only instead of creating a new task, you load a Task object with an existing task. Listing 18-5 shows how to modify a task.

Listing 18-5. Modifying a Task

```
Imports InTheHand.PocketOutlook

[at the module level]
Dim poApplication As New OutlookApplication
Dim myContacts As OutlookItemCollection

Private Sub btnModify_Click(ByVal sender As System.Object, _
  ByVal e As System.EventArgs) Handles btnModify.Click

  Dim myTask As Task

' Retrieve all of the tasks.
  myContacts = poApplication.Tasks.Items

' Modify the first task.
  myTask = myTasks.Item(0)
  With myTask
    .Body = "This is updated content."
    .Save()
  End With

End Sub
```

Once again, you start by adding the Imports statement, declaring the variables for OutlookApplication and OutlookItemCollection. At the bottom of Listing 18-5 you'll see where the task is first retrieved (along with all other tasks) and then loaded into the Task object. At this point, you can modify any of the Task object's properties. Finish the modification process by calling the Task object's **Save** method.

Now that you've seen the basics of working with tasks, let's pull it all together in a comprehensive example.

Step-by-Step Tutorial: Working with Tasks

In this step-by-step exercise, you will create an application that demonstrates working with tasks within Pocket Outlook. As part of this exercise, you'll

- Connect to Pocket Outlook.

- Retrieve a list of all tasks.

- Retrieve a list of tasks based upon their **Category** property.

- Display a task.

- Add a task.

This application provides all of the fundamentals of working with tasks within Pocket Outlook.

NOTE *To complete this tutorial, you will need the PocketOutlook component from InTheHand, available at* http://www.inthehand.com.

NOTE *I provide a completed version of this application, titled Tasks - Complete, under the **Chapter 18** folder of the **Samples** folder for this book. See Appendix D for more information on accessing and loading the sample applications.*

Step 1: Opening the Project

To simplify this tutorial, I've already created the project and the user interface for the Tasks Tutorial application. This template project is included under the **Chapter 18** folder of the **Samples** folder. To load this project, follow these steps:

1. From the VS .NET IDE Start Page, select to open a project. The Open Project dialog box will be displayed.

2. Use this dialog box to navigate to the **Chapter 18** folder under the **Samples** folder for this book.

3. Select and open the project **Tasks**. The project will be loaded onto your computer.

Step 2: Examining the User Interface

The user interface for the Tasks Tutorial application comprises several controls: a ListBox, four Buttons, and a TextBox. Figure 18-2 shows the application's interface.

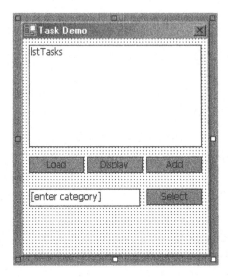

Figure 18-2. The Tasks application interface

The ListBox will display available tasks.
The four buttons for the Tasks Tutorial application function as follows:

- The **Load** button triggers loading a list of all tasks into the ListBox.

- The **Display** button triggers displaying the selected task.

- The **Add** button adds a new task with predefined values.

- The **Select** button retrieves a list of tasks for a select category.

The TextBox allows the user to specify the name of a category.

Step 3: Adding a Reference to the PocketOutlook Component

You need to add a single reference to your application to enable you to work with the Pocket Outlook Object Model from a .NET Compact Framework application.

To add this reference, perform the following steps:

1. In the Solution Explorer window, right-click the **References** folder.
    A pop-up menu displays.

2. From the menu, select **Add Reference**.

3. The Add Reference dialog box displays. Select the
    InTheHand.PocketOutlook component.

4. Click the **OK** button to add the selected component to your project.

Step 4: Adding the Imports Statement

The first line of code you'll be adding imports the **PocketOutlook** namespace.
This allows you to reference and work with the PocketOutlook elements within
your code without having to fully qualify each element.

To import the **PocketOutlook** namespace, perform the following steps:

1. Open the code window for the form.

2. At the top of the module, above the line that declares the **Form** class,
    add the following line of code:

```
Imports InTheHand.PocketOutlook
```

Step 5: Declaring Module-Level Objects

This tutorial uses two module-level object variables. These variables hold instances
of the PocketOutlook OutlookApplication and OutlookItemCollection objects.

To define these variables, add the following code to the module level of
the form:

```
Dim poApplication As New OutlookApplication
Dim myTasks As OutlookItemCollection
```

Step 6: Loading a List of All Tasks

The first functionality that you'll add to the application is to display a list of all
tasks. Obtaining this list is simple. Loading the list into your ListBox requires
nothing more than a For loop for running through the collection.

The first part of this step obtains a list of tasks. While you could simply reference the Tasks collection of the OutlookApplication object, you are instead going to retrieve a copy of the Tasks collection into a collection of its own. Having a collection of tasks that matches those tasks displayed in your ListBox makes it easier to display the details of an individual task. You'll see more on this later in the tutorial.

The code required to retrieve the Tasks collection is shown in Listing 18-6. Add this code to the **Click** event procedure of the **Load** button. In this procedure, you create a copy of the Tasks collection through the OutlookApplication.Contacts.Items collection.

Listing 18-6. Retrieving a List of All Tasks

```
Private Sub btnLoad_Click(ByVal sender As System.Object, _
  ByVal e As System.EventArgs) Handles btnLoad.Click

' Store the collection of tasks for future use.
  myTasks = poApplication.Tasks.Items

' Load the list of tasks.
  LoadTasks()

End Sub
```

Displaying the list of tasks is triggered at the bottom of the procedure shown in Listing 18-6. The **LoadTasks** procedure is a general-purpose procedure that displays the contents of the myTasks collection in a ListBox.

To define the **LoadTasks** procedure, add the code shown in Listing 18-7 to your form module. The heart of this procedure is the For loop located near its bottom. This loop iterates through all of the tasks stored within the myTasks collection, adding the **Subject** property of each task to the ListBox. Remember, myTasks is a collection of tasks. Each item in this collection is a Task object, with all of its properties and methods.

Listing 18-7. The LoadContacts Procedure

```
Sub LoadTasks()
  Dim intCount As Integer
  Dim myTask As Task

' First, make sure that the list box is empty.
  lstTasks.Items.Clear()
```

```
' Next, load the tasks into the list box.
  For intCount = 0 To myTasks.Count - 1
    myTask = myTasks.Item(intCount)
    lstTasks.Items.Add(myTask.Subject)
  Next

End Sub
```

Step 7: Displaying a Task

The process of displaying a task is easy because of the functionality provided through the Pocket Outlook Object Model. Calling the **Display** method of the Task object results in the task being displayed using the default task interface.

To display a task, add the code shown in Listing 18-8 to the **Click** event procedure of the **Display** button.

Listing 18-8. Displaying a Task

```
Private Sub btnDisplay_Click(ByVal sender As System.Object, _
  ByVal e As System.EventArgs) Handles btnDisplay.Click

  Dim myTask As Task

' Display the selected task.
  If (lstTasks.SelectedIndex <> -1) Then
    myTask = myTasks.Item(lstTasks.SelectedIndex)
    myTask.Display()
  End If

End Sub
```

Earlier in this tutorial, I mentioned the use of a collection to hold a list of Task objects. This is where that approach pays off. Since the collection myTasks matches the tasks displayed in the ListBox in a one-to-one relationship, it's easy to display a single task. All that you need to do is to create an instance of the task and then call the **Display** method of that task.

Step 8: Adding a Task

Adding a task is a three-step process. First, you need to create the task. Second, you configure the properties of the task. Third, you save the task.

In this tutorial, the task that is added is predefined, which is to say that the user has no input in the matter. Insert the code shown in Listing 18-9 into the **Click** event of the **Add** button.

Listing 18-9. Adding a Task

```
Private Sub btnAdd_Click(ByVal sender As System.Object, _
    ByVal e As System.EventArgs) Handles btnAdd.Click

    Dim myTask As Task

' Create a new task.
    myTask = poApplication.CreateTask

' Configure the task.
    With myTask
        .Body = "This is a sample task."
        .Categories = "demo"
        .DueDate = Today.Date
        .Importance = Importance.High
        .ReminderOptions = ReminderOptions.Dialog
        .ReminderSet = True
        .StartDate = Today.Date
        .Subject = "sample task"

' Finally, save the task.
        .Save()
    End With

' Let the user know that the task was added.
    MessageBox.Show("task added...")

End Sub
```

Step 9: Loading a List of Select Tasks

The last feature that you're going to add to this application is the ability to select a subset of the tasks list—in this case, all of the tasks from a specific category.

Add the code shown in Listing 18-10 to the **Click** event of the **Select** button. At the heart of this procedure are two steps—the building of the selection string and then the use of this string with the **Restrict** method. The result is the creation of a collection of tasks that match the desired criteria.

Listing 18-10. Selecting a Subset of the Tasks

```
Private Sub btnSelect_Click(ByVal sender As System.Object, _
  ByVal e As System.EventArgs) Handles btnSelect.Click

  Dim strQuery As String

' Retrieve the selected tasks.
  strQuery = "[Categories] = " & ControlChars.Quote & txtCategory.Text & _
    ControlChars.Quote
  myTasks = poApplication.Tasks.Items.Restrict(strQuery)

' Load the list of tasks.
  LoadTasks()

End Sub
```

Step 10: Testing the Application

Finally, you're ready to test your application. To begin, you need to copy the application to your target device by performing the following steps:

1. Select either **Pocket PC Device** or **Pocket PC Emulator** from the Deployment Device combo box.

2. Select **Release** from the Solution Configurations combo box.

3. Click the **Start** button.

Your application copies to the target device along with the PocketOutlook component. Upon completion, the application starts.

To verify the functionality of your application, perform the following steps:

1. Tap the **Load** button. After a brief pause, the ListBox is loaded with all of the tasks that are resident on your device.

2. Select a task from the ListBox. Tap the **Display** button. The selected task displays in the default Tasks interface. Close the selected task.

3. Tap the **Add** button. A message box displays confirming the addition of the task. To verify this addition, tap the **Load** button. The task named "sample task" should appear in the ListBox.

4. Enter a category into the TextBox (you can always use the "demo" category, which was added in the previous step). Tap the **Select** button. All of the tasks that are within this category are loaded into the ListBox.

> **NOTE** *The availability of tasks for a specific category is dependent upon the tasks resident on your test device.*

> **HOMEWORK** *Add a button to this application that will modify an existing task. The task to modify is the one selected within the ListBox.*

Next, we'll turn our attention to accessing, creating, and modifying contacts through the Pocket Outlook Object Model.

Working with Contacts

The second of the trifecta of Pocket Outlook data sources is contacts. Contacts offer developers a variety of application opportunities. They provide an easy way to incorporate contact data into a mobile application without all of the overhead of having to roll your own contact code.

As with tasks, contacts provide a **Categories** property, which is useful in identifying contacts that apply specifically to your application. Contacts are accessed through the **Contacts** property and the Contact object of the Pocket Outlook .NET component. Each of these items is covered in the following section.

The Contacts Property

The **Contacts** property of the OutlookApplication object provides access to a collection of contacts that are resident on a device. This property provides an interface to the **Contacts** folder within POOM, within which resides the contacts.

Several of the examples presented in this section demonstrate the use of the **Contacts** property along with its Items collection in working with contacts.

The Contact Object

All work with contacts themselves is handled through the Contact object. Commonly used properties of this object are shown in Table 18-3. Frequently used methods of the Contact object are shown in Table 18-4.

Table 18-3. Commonly Used Properties of the Contact Object

PROPERTY	DESCRIPTION
Body	The notes accompanying a contact
BusinessAddressCity	The city portion of the contact's address
BusinessAddressState	The state portion of the contact's address
BusinessAddressStreet	The street portion of the contact's address
BusinessFaxNumber	The fax number for the contact
BusinessTelephoneNumber	The business number for the contact
Categories	The categories for which the contact is assigned
CompanyName	The name of the contact's company
EmailAddress1	The e-mail address for the contact
FileAs	How the contact is filed (typically last name first)
MobileTelephoneNumber	The contact's cell phone number

NOTE *This is only a small subset of the properties provided by the Contact object. The properties detailed in Table 18-3 are the ones that I've found to be the most useful within a normal mobile business application. Your applications may benefit from the use of the remaining properties and as such, you should familiarize yourself with the complete property list through the Pocket Outlook .NET documentation.*

Table 18-4. Frequently Used Methods of the Contact Object

METHOD	DESCRIPTION
Copy	Creates a copy of an existing contact
Delete	Deletes a contact
Display	Displays a contact using the native Contact interface
Save	Saves modifications to a contact

While you will find both of these tables are useful for reference, the following sections, along with the examples, provide a quick-start approach to incorporating contact data into your applications.

Retrieving All Contacts

While it's unusual that your application will want to retrieve a list of all contacts (that is, unless you're creating a Contacts application knockoff), I'm still going to start this section by showing you how this is accomplished. As with tasks, you can retrieve contacts in several ways:

- As a collection of all contacts

- As a subset of all contacts

- As a single contact

Listing 18-11 demonstrates how to retrieve all contacts. Please note that, depending upon the number of contacts you have resident on a device, this could result in a sizeable collection.

Listing 18-11. Retrieving All of the Contacts

```
Imports InTheHand.PocketOutlook

[at the module level]
Dim poApplication As New OutlookApplication
Dim myContacts As OutlookItemCollection

Private Sub btnLoad_Click(ByVal sender As System.Object, _
  ByVal e As System.EventArgs) Handles btnLoad.Click

' Retrieve all of the contacts.
  myContacts = poApplication.Contacts.Items

End Sub
```

The key parts of this example are as follows:

- The Imports statement, which must be located at the top of a module.

- The declaration statement for the OutlookApplication object.

- The declaration of the OutlookItemCollection object, which holds a collection of any Outlook items. In this example, it's a collection of contacts.

- Loading the collection of contacts from the OutlookApplication object, poApplication, into the OutlookItemCollection, myContacts.

At this point, the collection myContacts contains a set of contact objects, one for each contact that resides on the test device. As with any collection, you can loop through the collection to access individual contacts and view specific contact information.

Retrieving a Range of Contacts

With contacts, it is more common that you will need to retrieve a subset of all contacts, rather than retrieve all contacts. This subset might be comprised of only those contacts that begin with the letter *A,* or even as restrictive as a single contact.

Retrieving a subset of contacts is easily accomplished with the use of the **Restrict** method of the Items collection. Listing 18-12 demonstrates the use of this method. In this example, only contacts that begin with the letter *A* are returned.

Listing 18-12. Retrieving a Range of Contacts

```
Imports InTheHand.PocketOutlook

[at the module level]
Dim poApplication As New OutlookApplication
Dim myContacts As OutlookItemCollection

Private Sub btnSelect_Click(ByVal sender As System.Object, _
  ByVal e As System.EventArgs) Handles btnSelect.Click

  Dim strA As String = "A"
  Dim strB As String = "B"
  Dim strQuery As String

' Retrieve contacts that begin with the letter A.
  strQuery = "[FileAs] >= " & ControlChars.Quote & strA & _
    ControlChars.Quote
  strQuery = strQuery & " AND [FileAs] < " & strB & _
    cmbPrefix.Items(cmbPrefix.SelectedIndex + 1) & ControlChars.Quote

  myContacts = poApplication.Contacts.Items.Restrict(strQuery)

End Sub
```

Much of the preparatory work is identical to that required to retrieve all contacts. You still need the Imports statement and to declare both the OutlookApplication and OutlookItemCollection objects.

The interesting code appears at the bottom of Listing 18-12. Here you build a query string, which restricts the contacts returned to only those that begin with the letter *A*. Applying this string to the **Restrict** method provides just the contacts that you're interested in.

 NOTE *You can restrict contacts using any of the properties provided through the Contact object. While typically this will be the FileAs property, you are by no means limited to it alone.*

Displaying a Contact

As you have already seen with tasks, POOM provides the ability to easily access and leverage the native application interface of a data type through your application. What users see is a contact, displayed in the typical contact interface.

This functionality is provided through the **Display** method of the Contact object. Listing 18-13 shows an example of this technique.

Listing 18-13. Displaying a Contact

```
Imports InTheHand.PocketOutlook

[at the module level]
Dim poApplication As New OutlookApplication
Dim myContacts As OutlookItemCollection

Private Sub btnDisplay_Click(ByVal sender As System.Object, _
  ByVal e As System.EventArgs) Handles btnDisplay.Click

  Dim myContact As Contact

' Retrieve all of the contacts.
  myContacts = poApplication.Contacts.Items

' Display the first contact.
  myContact = myContacts.Item(0)
  myContact.Display()

End Sub
```

As with the two previous contact examples, you need to add the Imports statement and declaration of the variables for both OutlookApplication and OutlookItemCollection to your module.

At the bottom of Listing 18-13 you'll see that all of the contacts are first retrieved. You could use a subset of the contacts or even a single contact as the starting point. I've chosen to demonstrate all contacts here because it's the easiest to understand.

From this collection of contacts, you extract a single contact, the first, into a Contact object of its own. It's through this Contact object that you gain access to the **Display** method, which in turn is called to display the selected contact.

Adding a Contact

Adding a contact is a three-step process. First, you need to create a new contact. Second, you need to configure the contact. Third, you need to save the contact. Listing 18-14 demonstrates adding a contact.

Listing 18-14. Adding a Contact

```
Imports InTheHand.PocketOutlook

[at the module level]
Dim poApplication As New OutlookApplication

Private Sub btnAdd_Click(ByVal sender As System.Object, _
  ByVal e As System.EventArgs) Handles btnAdd.Click

  Dim myContact As Contact

' Create a new contact.
  myContact = poApplication.CreateContact

' Configure the contact.
  With myContact
    .Birthday = CDate("01/01/1960")
    .Body = "This is a sample contact."
    .BusinessTelephoneNumber = "888-555-0001"
    .Categories = "demo"
    .CompanyName = "Acme"
    .Email1Address = "joe.acme@acme.com"
    .FileAs = "Acme, Joe"
    .FirstName = "Joe"
    .LastName = "Acme"
    .Title = "President"
```

```
' Finally, save the contact.
   .Save()
  End With

End Sub
```

As with all of the previous contact examples, you need to start by adding the Imports statement and declaring the variables for OutlookApplication and OutlookItemCollection.

At the bottom of Listing 18-14 you'll see the three steps I described. First, the **CreateContact** method of the OutlookApplication object is called to create your new contact. Second, you configure the properties of the new contact. Third, the Contact object's **Save** method is called to save the contact.

Modifying a Contact

Modifying a contact is similar to adding a contact, only instead of creating a new contact you load a Contact object from an existing contact. Listing 18-15 demonstrates this process.

Listing 18-15. Modifying an Existing Contact

```
Imports InTheHand.PocketOutlook

[at the module level]
Dim poApplication As New OutlookApplication
Dim myContacts As OutlookItemCollection

Private Sub btnModify_Click(ByVal sender As System.Object, _
  ByVal e As System.EventArgs) Handles btnModify.Click

  Dim myContact As Contact

' Retrieve all of the contacts.
  myContacts = poApplication.Contacts.Items

' Modify the first contact.
  myContact = myContacts.Item(0)
  With myContact
    .BusinessTelephoneNumber = "888-555-0001"
    .Save()
  End With

End Sub
```

As with all of the previous contact examples, you start by adding an Imports statement and declaring the variables for OutlookApplication and OutlookItemCollection. At the bottom of Listing 18-15, you'll find where the contact is first retrieved. In this example, all of the contacts are retrieved, but only the first contact is loaded into the Contact object. From this point, you are free to modify any of the Contact object's properties. You finish the modification process by calling the Contact object's **Save** method.

Now that you've seen the basics of working with contacts, let's put all of these techniques together into a comprehensive example.

Step-by-Step Tutorial: Working with Contacts

In this step-by-step exercise, you'll create an application that demonstrates working with contacts within Pocket Outlook. As part of this exercise, you'll

- Connect to Pocket Outlook.

- Retrieve a list of all contacts.

- Retrieve a list of contacts based upon the first letter of their name.

- Display a contact.

- Add a contact.

This application provides all of the fundamentals of working with contacts within Pocket Outlook.

> **NOTE** *To complete this tutorial you'll need the PocketOutlook component from InTheHand at* http://www.inthehand.com.

> **NOTE** *I provide a completed version of this application, titled Contacts - Complete, under the **Chapter 18** folder of the **Samples** folder for this book. See Appendix D for more information on accessing and loading the sample applications.*

Step 1: Opening the Project

To simplify this tutorial, I've already created the project and the user interface for the Contacts Tutorial application. This template project is included under the **Chapter 18** folder in the **Samples** folder. To load this project, follow these steps:

1. From the VS .NET IDE Start Page, select to open a project. The Open Project dialog box will be displayed.

2. Use this dialog box to navigate to the **Chapter 18** folder under the **Samples** folder for this book.

3. Select and open the project **Contacts**. The project will be loaded onto your computer.

Step 2: Examining the User Interface

The user interface for the Contacts Tutorial application is comprised of several controls: a ListBox, four Buttons, and a ComboBox. Figure 18-3 shows the application's interface.

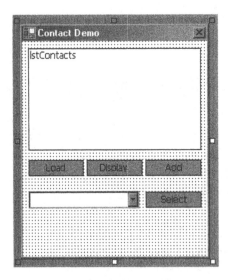

Figure 18-3. The Contacts application interface

The ListBox will display available contacts.

The four buttons for the Contacts Tutorial application function as follows:

- The **Load** button triggers loading a list of all contacts into the ListBox.

- The **Display** button triggers displaying the selected contact.

- The **Add** button adds a new contact with predefined values.

- The **Select** button retrieves a list of contacts that begin with a specific letter.

The ComboBox provides a list from which the user may select an alphabetical subset of the contacts. The ComboBox has been preloaded with all of the letters of the alphabet.

Step 3: Adding a Reference to PocketOutlook

You need to add a single reference to your application to enable you to work with the Pocket Outlook Object Model from a .NET Compact Framework application.
To add this reference, perform the following steps:

1. In the Solution Explorer window, right-click the **References** folder. A pop-up menu displays.

2. From the menu, select **Add Reference**.

3. The Add Reference dialog box displays. Select the **InTheHand. PocketOutlook** component.

4. Click the **OK** button to add the selected component to your project.

Step 4: Adding the Imports Statement

The first line of code you'll be adding imports the **PocketOutlook** namespace. This allows you to reference and work with the PocketOutlook elements within your code without having to fully qualify each element.
To import the **PocketOutlook** namespace, perform the following steps:

1. Open the code window for the form.

2. At the top of the module, above the line that declares the **Form** class, add the following line of code:

```
Imports InTheHand.PocketOutlook
```

Step 5: Declaring Module-Level Objects

This tutorial uses two module-level object variables. These variables hold instances of the PocketOutlook OutlookApplication and OutlookItemCollection objects.

To define these variables, add the following code to the module level of the form:

```
Dim poApplication As New OutlookApplication
Dim myContacts As OutlookItemCollection
```

Step 6: Loading a List of All Contacts

The first functionality that you'll add to the application is to display a list of all contacts. Obtaining this list is simple. Loading the list into your ListBox requires nothing more than a For loop for running through the collection.

The first part of this step obtains a list of contacts. While you could simply reference the Contacts collection of the OutlookApplication object, you are instead going to retrieve a copy of the Contacts collection into a collection of its own. Having a collection of contacts that matches those contacts displayed in your ListBox makes it easier to display the details of an individual contact. You'll see more on this later in the tutorial.

The code required to retrieve the Contacts collection is shown in Listing 18-16. Add this code to the **Click** event procedure of the **Load** button. In this procedure, you create a copy of the Contacts collection through the OutlookApplication. Contacts.Items collection.

Listing 18-16. Retrieving a List of All Contacts

```
Private Sub btnLoad_Click(ByVal sender As System.Object, _
  ByVal e As System.EventArgs) Handles btnLoad.Click

' Store the collection of contacts for future use.
  myContacts = poApplication.Contacts.Items

' Load the list of contacts.
  LoadContacts()

End Sub
```

Displaying the list of contacts is triggered at the bottom of the procedure shown in Listing 18-16. The **LoadContacts** procedure is a general-purpose procedure that displays the contents of the myContacts collection in a ListBox.

To define the **LoadContacts** procedure, add the code shown in Listing 18-17 to your form module. The heart of this procedure is the For loop located near its bottom. This loop iterates through all of the contacts stored within the myContacts collection, adding the **FileAs** property of each contact to the ListBox. Remember, myContacts is a collection of contacts. Each item in this collection is a Contact object, with all of its properties and methods.

Listing 18-17. The LoadContacts Procedure

```
Sub LoadContacts()
  Dim intCount As Integer
  Dim myContact As Contact

' First, make sure that the list box is empty.
  lstContacts.Items.Clear()

' Next, load the contacts into the list box.
  For intCount = 0 To myContacts.Count - 1
    myContact = myContacts.Item(intCount)
    lstContacts.Items.Add(myContact.FileAs)
  Next

End Sub
```

Step 7: Displaying a Contact

The process of displaying a contact is easy because of the functionality provided through the Pocket Outlook Object Model. Calling the **Display** method of the Contact object results in the contact being displayed using the default contact interface.

To display a contact, add the code shown in Listing 18-18 to the **Click** event procedure of the **Display** button.

Listing 18-18. Displaying a Contact

```
Private Sub btnDisplay_Click(ByVal sender As System.Object, _
  ByVal e As System.EventArgs) Handles btnDisplay.Click

  Dim myContact As Contact

' Display the selected contact.
```

```
      If (lstContacts.SelectedIndex <> -1) Then
         myContact = myContacts.Item(lstContacts.SelectedIndex)
         myContact.Display()
      End If

End Sub
```

Earlier in this tutorial, I mentioned using a collection to hold a list of Contact objects. This is where that approach pays off. Since your collection myContacts matches the contacts displayed in the ListBox in a one-to-one relationship, it's easy to display a single contact. All that you need to do is to create an instance of the contact and then call the **Display** method of that contact.

Step 8: Adding a Contact

Adding a contact is a three-step process. First, you need to create the contact. Second, you configure the properties of the contact. Third, you save the contact.

In this tutorial, the contact that is added is predefined, which is to say that the user has no input in the matter. Insert the code shown in Listing 18-19 into the **Click** event of the **Add** button.

Listing 18-19. Adding a Contact

```
Private Sub btnAdd_Click(ByVal sender As System.Object, _
   ByVal e As System.EventArgs) Handles btnAdd.Click

   Dim myContact As Contact

' Create a new contact.
   myContact = poApplication.CreateContact

' Configure the contact.
   With myContact
      .Birthday = CDate("01/01/1960")
      .Body = "This is a sample contact."
      .BusinessTelephoneNumber = "888-555-0001"
      .Categories = "demo"
      .CompanyName = "Acme"
      .Email1Address = "joe.acme@acme.com"
      .FileAs = "Acme, Joe"
```

```
    .FirstName = "Joe"
    .LastName = "Acme"
    .Title = "President"

' Finally, save the contact.
    .Save()
  End With


' Let the user know that the contact was added.
  MessageBox.Show("contact added...")


End Sub
```

Step 9: Loading a List of Select Contacts

The last feature that you're going to add to this application is the ability to select a subset of the contacts list. In this case, you're going to select all of the contacts that begin with a specific letter—for example, only those contacts that begin with the letter *A*.

Add the code shown in Listing 18-20 to the **Click** event of the **Select** button. At the heart of this procedure are two steps—the building of the selection string and then the use of this string with the **Restrict** method. The result is the creation of a collection of contacts that match the desired criteria.

Listing 18-20. Selecting a Subset of the Contacts

```
Private Sub btnSelect_Click(ByVal sender As System.Object, _
  ByVal e As System.EventArgs) Handles btnSelect.Click

  Dim strQuery As String

' Retrieve the selected contacts.
  strQuery = "[FileAs] >= " & ControlChars.Quote & cmbPrefix.Text & _
    ControlChars.Quote

' Use a range for anything other than contacts beginning with the letter "Z".
  If (cmbPrefix.Text < "Z") Then
    strQuery = strQuery & " AND [FileAs] < " & ControlChars.Quote & _
      cmbPrefix.Items(cmbPrefix.SelectedIndex + 1) & ControlChars.Quote
  End If
```

```
  myContacts = poApplication.Contacts.Items.Restrict(strQuery)

' Load the list of contacts.
  LoadContacts()

End Sub
```

Step 10: Testing the Application

Finally, you're ready to test your application. To begin, you need to copy the application to your target device by performing the following steps:

1. Select either **Pocket PC Device** or **Pocket PC Emulator** from the Deployment Device combo box.

2. Select **Release** from the Solution Configurations combo box.

3. Click the **Start** button.

Your application copies to the target device along with the PocketOutlook component. Upon completion the application starts.

To verify the functionality of your application, perform the following steps:

1. Tap the **Load** button. After a brief pause, the ListBox is loaded with all of the contacts that are resident on your device.

2. Select a contact from the ListBox. Tap the **Display** button. The selected contact displays in the default Contacts interface. Close the selected contact.

3. Tap the **Add** button. A message box displays, confirming the addition of the contact. To verify this addition, tap the **Load** button. The contact for "Acme, Joe" should appear in the ListBox.

4. Select a letter from the ComboBox. Tap the **Select** button. All of the contacts that begin with the selected letter are loaded into the ListBox.

NOTE *The availability of contacts that begin with a specific letter is dependent upon the contacts resident on your test device.*

HOMEWORK *Add a button to this application that will modify an existing contact. The contact to modify is the one selected within the ListBox.*

Next, we'll turn our attention to accessing, creating, and modifying appointments through the Pocket Outlook Object Model.

Working with Appointments

The last piece of Pocket Outlook data we have to examine is appointments. As with tasks and contacts, the Pocket Outlook .NET component makes working with appointments an easy task.

From the development standpoint, appointments offer a powerful way to integrate mobile applications with back-end scheduling systems. From your application, through Pocket Outlook, ActiveSync, Outlook, and finally an enterprise server, you have a seamless path for the delivery of appointment-related data. This functionality can be used to schedule maintenance, meetings, followups, or any task that is date and time specific.

Appointment functionality is exposed to the .NET Compact Framework through the Pocket Outlook .NET component from InTheHand. This component's **Appointments** property and Appointment object are the subjects to this section.

The Appointments Property

The **Appointments** property of the OutlookApplication object provides access to the collection of appointments resident on a device. In actuality, the **Appointments** property provides an interface to the **Appointments** folder. The underlying Pocket Outlook Object Model supplies access to this folder. This property links through to an Items collection that contains the actual appointments. This section includes several examples of the **Appointments** property along with its Items collection.

The Appointment Object

Individual appointments are created and modified through the Appointment object. Commonly used properties and methods for this object are shown in Tables 18-5 and 18-6 respectively.

Table 18-5. Commonly Used Properties of the Appointment Object

PROPERTY	DESCRIPTION
AllDayEvent	Specifies whether this is an all-day event
Body	Defines the notes accompanying an appointment
Categories	Specifies the categories for which this appointment is assigned
Duration	Indicates the length of the appointment
End	Specifies when the appointment ends
Location	Indicates where the appointment takes place
ReminderSet	Specifies whether a reminder is configured for an appointment
Start	Indicates when the appointment starts
Subject	Indicates the subject of an appointment

Table 18-6. Commonly Used Methods of the Appointment Object

METHOD	DESCRIPTION
Cancel	Sends a cancellation of a meeting request
Copy	Creates a copy of an existing appointment
Delete	Deletes an appointment
Display	Displays an appointment using the native Appointment interface
Save	Saves modifications made to an appointment
Send	Sends a meeting request to the recipient list for an appointment

While these tables serve well for reference purposes, a set of practical demonstrations follow that provide detailed examples of commonly performed appointment-related operations.

Retrieving All Appointments

Whether or not you retrieve all appointments is going to be dependent upon your applications. Typically, you won't, instead opting for a range of dates under which the appointments fall. As with tasks and contacts, there are several ways that you can retrieve appointments:

- As a collection of all appointments

- As a subset of all appointments

- As an individual appointment

We'll start by looking at how to retrieve all appointments. It's the simplest method, and while not the most commonly used approach, it's still utilized within mobile applications. Listing 18-21 demonstrates this process.

Listing 18-21. Retrieving All of the Appointments

```
Imports InTheHand.PocketOutlook

[at the module level]
Dim poApplication As New OutlookApplication
Dim myAppointments As OutlookItemCollection

Private Sub btnLoad_Click(ByVal sender As System.Object, _
  ByVal e As System.EventArgs) Handles btnLoad.Click

' Retrieve all of the appointments.
  myAppointments = poApplication.Appointments.Items

End Sub
```

The keys to this example are as follows:

- The Imports statement, which must be located at the top of a module.

- The declaration statement for the OutlookApplication object.

- The declaration of the OutlookItemCollection object, which can hold a collection of any Outlook items. In this case, it will hold a collection of appointments.

- Loading the collection of appointments from the OutlookApplication object, poApplication, into the OutlookItemCollection, myAppointments.

At this stage, the collection myAppointments contains a set of appointment objects, one for each appointment that resides on the device. You can loop through this collection to view information on specific appointments.

Retrieving Appointments for a Given Date

While you may at times retrieve a list of all appointments, more commonly your application will want only those appointments that fall within a certain range of dates.

Listing 18-22 demonstrates retrieving a subset of appointments. First, appointments for today are grabbed. Next, appointments for tomorrow are retrieved. Finally, how to select appointments for the next week is shown.

Listing 18-22. Retrieving Appointments for Specific Dates

```
Imports InTheHand.PocketOutlook

[at the module level]
Dim poApplication As New OutlookApplication
Dim myAppointmens As OutlookItemCollection

Private Sub btnSelect_Click(ByVal sender As System.Object, _
  ByVal e As System.EventArgs) Handles btnSelect.Click

  Dim strQuery As String
  Dim tmpDate As Date

' Retrieve appointments for today.
  strQuery = "[Start] = " & _
    ControlChars.Quote & Date.Today.ToShortDateString & _
    ControlChars.Quote
  myAppointments = poApplication.Calendar.Items.Restrict(strQuery)

' Retrieve appointments for tomorrow.
  tmpDate = Date.Today.AddDays(1)
  strQuery = "[Start] = " & _
    ControlChars.Quote & tmpDate.Date.ToShortDateString & ControlChars.Quote
  myAppointments = poApplication.Calendar.Items.Restrict(strQuery)

' Retrieve appointments for this next week.
  tmpDate = Date.Today.AddDays(7)
  strQuery = "[Start] >= " & _
    ControlChars.Quote & Date.Today.ToShortDateString & ControlChars.Quote
  strQuery = strQuery & " AND [Start] < " & ControlChars.Quote & _
    tmpDate.Date.ToShortDateString & ControlChars.Quote
  myAppointments = poApplication.Calendar.Items.Restrict(strQuery)

End Sub
```

The preparatory work for this example is identical to that required by the previous example. You have to include the Imports statement and the declaration of both the variables for OutlookApplication and OutlookItemCollection.

Each of the sections of code that select appointments for today, tomorrow, and the next week make use of the **Restrict** method to retrieve the appropriate data. As you can see, the key to these Restrict statements is some creative date manipulations.

 NOTE *While this example focuses on restricting appointments by their start date, you can in fact restrict appointments based upon the values of any of their properties.*

Displaying an Appointment

As you've already seen with tasks and contacts, POOM provides you with the ability to access the native application interface of its data types through your application. What users will see is an appointment, displayed in the Pocket PC appointment interface.

This functionality is provided by the **Display** method of the Appointment object. Listing 18-23 shows an example of this technique.

Listing 18-23. Displaying an Appointment

```
Imports InTheHand.PocketOutlook

[at the module level]
Dim poApplication As New OutlookApplication
Dim myAppointments As OutlookItemCollection

Private Sub btnDisplay_Click(ByVal sender As System.Object, _
  ByVal e As System.EventArgs) Handles btnDisplay.Click

  Dim myAppointment As Appointment

' Retrieve all of the appointments.
  myAppointments = poApplication.Appointments.Items

' Display the first appointment.
  myAppointment = myAppointments.Item(0)
  myAppointment.Display()

End Sub
```

As with both of the examples involving retrieving appointments, you need to add to your application declarations for the Imports statement and the variables for both OutlookApplication and OutlookItemCollection.

At the bottom of Listing 18-23 you'll see the code used to display an appointment. First, a collection of all appointments is retrieved. Next, a single appointment is selected, in this case the first appointment, and this appointment is used to create an Appointment object. It's through this Appointment object that you gain access to the **Display** method, which causes the appointment to be displayed.

Adding an Appointment

Adding an appointment is a three-step process. First, you need to create a new appointment. Second, you need to configure the appointment. Third, you need to save the appointment. Listing 18-24 demonstrates this process.

Listing 18-24. Adding an Appointment

```
Imports InTheHand.PocketOutlook

[at the module level]
Dim poApplication As New OutlookApplication

Private Sub btnAdd_Click(ByVal sender As System.Object, _
  ByVal e As System.EventArgs) Handles btnAdd.Click

  Dim myAppointment As Appointment

' Create a new appointment.
  myAppointment = poApplication.CreateAppointment

' Configure the appointment.
  With myAppointment
    .Body = "This is a sample appointment."
    .Categories = "demo"
    .End = DateAdd(DateInterval.Hour, 1, Now)
    .Location = "New York"
    .Start = Now
    .Subject = "demo appointment"

' Finally, save the appointment.
    .Save()
  End With

End Sub
```

As with the previous appointment examples, you start by adding the Imports statement and declaring the variables for OutlookApplication and OutlookItemCollection.

At the bottom of Listing 18-24 is the code that performs the three steps required to add an appointment. First, a call is made to the **CreateAppointment** method of the OutlookApplication object. Second, the properties of the new appointment are configured. Finally, the Appointment object's **Save** method is called to save the appointment.

Modifying an Appointment

The process of modifying an appointment is similar to adding an appointment, only instead of creating a new appointment, you load an existing appointment into an Appointment object. Listing 18-25 demonstrates this process.

Listing 18-25. Modifying an Existing Appointment

```
Imports InTheHand.PocketOutlook

[at the module level]
Dim poApplication As New OutlookApplication
Dim myAppointments As OutlookItemCollection

Private Sub btnModify_Click(ByVal sender As System.Object, _
  ByVal e As System.EventArgs) Handles btnModify.Click

  Dim myAppointment As Appointment

' Retrieve all of the appointment.
  myAppointments = poApplication.Appointments.Items

' Modify the first appointment.
  myAppointment = myAppointments.Item(0)
  With myAppointment
    .Body = "This is updated content."
    .Save()
  End With

End Sub
```

As with all of the previous appointment examples, you start by adding an Imports statement and declaring the variables for OutlookApplication and OutlookItemCollection. At the bottom of Listing 18-25, you'll find where the appointment is first retrieved. In this example, all of the appointments are retrieved, but only the first appointment is loaded into the Appointment object. From this point, you're free to modify any of the Appointment object's properties. You finish the modification process by calling the Appointment object's **Save** method.

Now that you've seen the basics of working with appointments, let's put all of these techniques together into a comprehensive example.

Step-by-Step Tutorial: Working with Appointments

In this step-by-step exercise, you'll create an application that demonstrates working with appointments within Pocket Outlook. As part of this exercise, you'll

- Connect to Pocket Outlook.

- Retrieve a list of all appointments.

- Retrieve a list of appointments for today, tomorrow, and the next week.

- Display an appointment.

- Add an appointment.

This application provides all of the fundamentals of working with appointments within Pocket Outlook.

 NOTE *To complete this tutorial, you'll need the PocketOutlook component from InTheHand, available at* http://www.inthehand.com.

 NOTE *I provide a completed version of this application, titled Appointments - Complete, under the **Chapter 18** folder of the **Samples** folder for this book. See Appendix D for more information on accessing and loading the sample applications.*

Step 1: Opening the Project

To simplify this tutorial, I've already created the project and the user interface for the Appointments Tutorial application. This template project is included under the **Chapter 18** folder in the **Samples** folder. To load this project, follow these steps:

1. From the VS .NET IDE Start Page, select to open a project. The Open Project dialog box will be displayed.

2. Use this dialog box to navigate to the **Chapter 18** folder under the **Samples** folder for this book.

3. Select and open the project **Appointments**. The project will be loaded onto your computer.

Step 2: Examining the User Interface

The user interface for the Appointments Tutorial application is comprised of several controls: a ListBox, four Buttons, and a ComboBox. Figure 18-4 shows the application's interface.

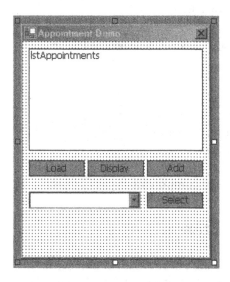

Figure 18-4. The Appointments application interface

The ListBox will display available appointments.

The four buttons for the Appointments Tutorial application function as follows:

- The **Load** button triggers loading a list of all appointments into the ListBox.

- The **Display** button triggers displaying the selected appointment.

- The **Add** button adds a new appointment with predefined values.

- The **Select** button retrieves a list of appointments for today, tomorrow, or the next week.

The ComboBox provides three time-range options from which to choose: today, tomorrow, and next week. These values have been preloaded.

Step 3: Adding a Reference to PocketOutlook

You need to add a single reference to your application to enable you to work with the Pocket Outlook Object Model from a .NET Compact Framework application.
To add this reference, perform the following steps:

1. In the Solution Explorer window, right-click the **References** folder. A pop-up menu displays.

2. From the menu, select **Add Reference**.

3. The Add Reference dialog box displays. Select the **InTheHand.PocketOutlook** component.

4. Click the **OK** button to add the selected component to your project.

Step 4: Adding the Imports Statement

The first line of code you'll be adding imports the **PocketOutlook** namespace. This allows you to reference and work with the PocketOutlook elements within your code without having to fully qualify each element.
To import the **PocketOutlook** namespace, perform the following steps:

1. Open the code window for the form.

2. At the top of the module, above the line that declares the **Form** class, add the following line of code:

```
Imports InTheHand.PocketOutlook
```

Step 5: Declaring Module-Level Objects

This tutorial uses two module-level object variables. These variables hold instances of the PocketOutlook OutlookApplication and OutlookItemCollection objects.

To define these variables, add the following code to the module level of the form:

```
Dim poApplication As New OutlookApplication
Dim myAppointments As OutlookItemCollection
```

Step 6: Loading a List of All Appointments

The first functionality that you'll add to the application is to display a list of all appointments. Obtaining this list is simple. Loading the list into your ListBox requires nothing more than a For loop for running through the collection.

The first part of this step obtains a list of appointments. While you could simply reference the Appointments collection of the OutlookApplication object, you are instead going to retrieve a copy of the Appointments collection into a collection of its own. Having a collection of appointments that matches those appointments displayed in your ListBox makes it easier to display the details of an individual appointment. You'll see more on this later in the tutorial.

The code required to retrieve the Appointments collection is shown in Listing 18-26. Add this code to the **Click** event procedure of the **Load** button. In this procedure, you create a copy of the Appointments collection through the OutlookApplication.Appointments.Items collection.

Listing 18-26. Retrieving a List of All Appointments

```
Private Sub btnLoad_Click(ByVal sender As System.Object, _
    ByVal e As System.EventArgs) Handles btnLoad.Click

' Store the collection of appointments for future use.
    myAppointments = poApplication.Calendar.Items

' Load the list of appointments.
    LoadAppointments()

End Sub
```

Displaying the list of appointments is triggered at the bottom of the procedure shown in Listing 18-26. The **LoadAppointments** procedure is a general-purpose procedure that displays the contents of the myAppointments collection in a ListBox.

To define the **LoadAppointments** procedure, add the code shown in Listing 18-27 to your form module. The heart of this procedure is the For loop located near its bottom. This loop iterates through all of the appointments stored within the myAppointments collection, adding the **Subject** property of each appointment to the ListBox. Remember, myAppointments is a collection of appointments. Each item in this collection is an Appointment object, with all of its properties and methods.

Listing 18-27. The LoadAppointments Procedure

```
Sub LoadAppointments()
   Dim intCount As Integer
   Dim myAppointment As Appointment

' First, make sure that the list box is empty.
   lstAppointments.Items.Clear()

' Next, load the appointments into the list box.
   For intCount = 0 To myAppointments.Count - 1
     myAppointment = myAppointments.Item(intCount)
     lstAppointments.Items.Add(myAppointment.Subject)
   Next

End Sub
```

Step 7: Displaying an Appointment

The process of displaying an appointment is easy because of the functionality provided through the Pocket Outlook Object Model. Calling the **Display** method of the Appointment object results in the appointment being displayed using the default appointment interface.

To display an appointment, add the code shown in Listing 18-28 to the **Click** event procedure of the **Display** button.

Listing 18-28. Displaying an Appointment

```
Private Sub btnDisplay_Click(ByVal sender As System.Object, _
   ByVal e As System.EventArgs) Handles btnDisplay.Click

   Dim myAppointment As Appointment
```

```
' Display the selected appointment.
  If (lstAppointments.SelectedIndex <> -1) Then
    myAppointment = myAppointments.Item(lstAppointments.SelectedIndex)
    myAppointment.Display()
  End If

End Sub
```

Earlier in this tutorial, I mentioned using a collection to hold a list of Appointment objects. This is where that approach pays off. Since your collection myAppointments matches the appointments displayed in the ListBox in a one-to-one relationship, it's easy to display a single appointment. All that you need to do is to create an instance of the appointment and then call the **Display** method of that appointment.

Step 8: Adding an Appointment

Adding an appointment is a three-step process. First, you need to create the appointment. Second, you configure the properties of the appointment. Third, you save the appointment.

In this tutorial, the appointment that is added is predefined, which is to say that the user has no input in the matter. Insert the code shown in Listing 18-29 into the **Click** event of the **Add** button.

Listing 18-29. Adding an Appointment

```
Private Sub btnAdd_Click(ByVal sender As System.Object, _
  ByVal e As System.EventArgs) Handles btnAdd.Click

    Dim myAppointment As Appointment

' Create a new appointment.
  myAppointment = poApplication.CreateAppointment

' Configure the appointment.
  With myAppointment
     .Body = "This is a sample appointment."
     .Categories = "demo"
     .End = DateAdd(DateInterval.Hour, 1, Now)
     .Location = "New York"
     .Start = Now
     .Subject = "demo appointment"
```

```
' Finally, save the appointment.
  .Save()
End With


' Let the user know that the appointment was added.
  MessageBox.Show("appointment added...")


End Sub
```

The key point to bring away from this sample is the configuration of two properties, **Start** and **End**. In the case of this sample, you set the start of the appointment to the present time. The end of the appointment is set to 1 hour from now. Obviously, this is an impractical example. Why would anyone want to set an appointment to start right now? Still, you get the idea. The **Start** and **End** properties are pivotal items when it comes to appointments, and the date-related functionality provided through the .NET Compact Framework makes working with dates easy.

Step 9: Loading a List of Select Appointments

The last feature that you're going to add to this application is the ability to select appointments for either today, tomorrow, or the next week.

Add the code shown in Listing 18-30 to the **Click** event of the **Select** button. At the heart of this procedure are two steps—the building of the selection string and then the use of this string with the **Restrict** method. The result is the creation of a collection of appointments that match the desired criteria.

Listing 18-30. Selecting a Subset of the Appointments

```
Private Sub btnSelect_Click(ByVal sender As System.Object, _
  ByVal e As System.EventArgs) Handles btnSelect.Click

  Dim strQuery As String
  Dim tmpDate As Date

' Retrieve the selected appointments.
  Select Case cmbDates.Text
    Case "today"
      strQuery = "[Start] = " & ControlChars.Quote & _
        Date.Today.ToShortDateString & ControlChars.Quote
```

```
    Case "tomorrow"
      tmpDate = Date.Today.AddDays(1)
      strQuery = "[Start] = " & ControlChars.Quote & _
        tmpDate.Date.ToShortDateString & ControlChars.Quote
    Case "next week"
      tmpDate = Date.Today.AddDays(7)
      strQuery = "[Start] >= " & ControlChars.Quote & _
        Date.Today.ToShortDateString & ControlChars.Quote
      strQuery = strQuery & " AND [Start] < " & ControlChars.Quote & _
        tmpDate.Date.ToShortDateString & ControlChars.Quote
  End Select

  myAppointments = poApplication.Calendar.Items.Restrict(strQuery)

' Load the list of appointments.
  LoadAppointments()

End Sub
```

Selecting appointments for today is the easiest. You simply need to set the criteria to the present date. Selecting appointments for tomorrow is only slightly more complicated. Some simple date math is used to add one day to the present date before performing the selection. Selecting the appointments for the next week is by far the most complicated of the three, and even then it's not rocket science. Here a compound select statement along with some date math is used to specify a range of dates for the selection.

Step 10: Testing the Application

Finally, you're ready to test your application. To begin, you need to copy the application to your target device by performing the following steps:

1. Select either **Pocket PC Device** or **Pocket PC Emulator** from the Deployment Device combo box.

2. Select **Release** from the Solution Configurations combo box.

3. Click the **Start** button.

Your application copies to the target device along with the PocketOutlook component. Upon completion the application starts.

To verify the functionality of your application, perform the following steps:

1. Tap the **Load** button. After a brief pause, the ListBox is loaded with all of the appointments that are resident on your device.

2. Select an appointment from the ListBox. Tap the **Display** button. The selected appointment displays in the default Appointment interface. Close the selected appointment.

3. Tap the **Add** button. A message box displays confirming the addition of the appointment. To verify this addition, tap the **Load** button. The appointment named "This is a sample appointment." should appear in the ListBox.

4. Select a date range option from the ComboBox. Tap the **Select** button. All of the appointments for that range are loaded into the ListBox.

NOTE *The availability of appointments that fall within a specific timeframe is dependent upon the appointments resident on your test device.*

HOMEWORK *Add a button to this application that will modify an existing appointment. The appointment to modify is the one selected within the ListBox.*

Summary

The Pocket Outlook Object Model is the gateway to Outlook-specific data. POOM is not only a fun word to say, but also a powerful resource for developers. POOM allows you to integrate seamlessly your mobile applications into the standard core applications found on every Pocket PC.

The Pocket Outlook .NET component from InTheHand makes working with POOM easy from within your NETCF applications. It offers a solid set of tools to deal with the most useful of Pocket Outlook data: tasks, contacts, and appointments. Rather than having to write your own native-language DLL, and spending months of development time, you can be up and working with Pocket Outlook data in a few hours.

Building Help Systems

HELP SYSTEMS ARE FEATURES that you expect every "well-rounded" application to include. In the case of a Pocket PC application, they're even more important. This is simply because users of Pocket PC applications are typically, well, mobile. Expecting your users to carry around a user's guide is impractical. That means the only information users will have to aid their understanding of your application is the help system you provide.

Although the purposes behind Pocket PC and other Windows-based help systems may be the same—to offer users guidance and direction—the manner in which they're implemented varies greatly. Windows-based help systems offer a robust environment comprised of multimedia objects, complex search capabilities, pop-up definitions, and graphical hot spots. Pocket PC help systems are simplistic in comparison, providing a minimalist environment that's based solely upon simple HTML linking techniques.

That doesn't mean that the limitations of the Pocket PC Help environment make it impossible to create effective help systems. With some careful planning, a simple development tool, and a basic understanding of HTML, you can easily and quickly produce highly useful help systems for your applications. Building help systems for the Pocket PC is simple, requiring nothing more than a basic understanding of HTML and Microsoft Notepad. If you prefer a tool that's a bit more robust than Notepad, you can use Microsoft FrontPage, Microsoft Visual Studio .NET, or any other HTML editor that you're comfortable with.

In this chapter, I'll walk you through the development of Pocket PC help systems. We'll start with an overview of the Pocket PC help system itself to make sure you know the basics. Then, we'll create and test some help files. Finally, you'll see how to call help files from your Pocket PC applications.

 NOTE *I've limited the scope of the discussion within this chapter to Pocket PCs, but the topics covered here apply to any devices that are supported by the initial release of the .NET Compact Framework.*

A Pocket PC Help System

The Pocket PC help system is for all practical purposes a specialized HTML browser. Like other browsers, its basic form of navigation is through hyperlinks.

To select a topic, Pocket PC users simply have to tap on the appropriate link with their stylus.

The Pocket PC help system consists of several key components. First is the **Help** menu item, which is located under the Start menu as shown in Figure 19-1. This item provides easy access to all of the help topics that are presently on the user's device.

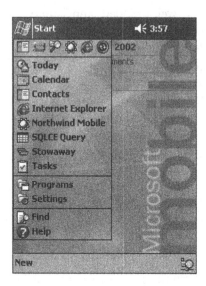

Figure 19-1. The Help item at the bottom of the Start menu

Second is the Help Contents, shown in Figure 19-2, which is displayed when the user taps the **Help** item from the Start menu. This list of help topics is generated dynamically from the list of shortcut files located in the **\Windows\Help** folder.

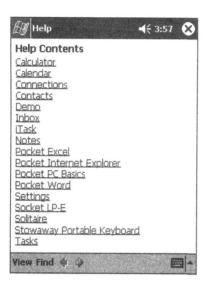

Figure 19-2. The Pocket PC Help Contents screen

The menubar of the Pocket PC help system, shown at the bottom of
Figure 19-2, provides easy access to commonly used functionality. Table 19-1
lists the capabilities of each of the items that comprise this menubar, going from
left to right.

Table 19-1. Help System Menubar Functions

ITEM	FUNCTION
View menu	Enables the user to navigate to either the Help Contents or a list of all help topics that reside on the Pocket PC
Find menu	Provides access to the help system Find screen
Back arrow	Moves to the previous topic or screen
Forward arrow	Moves to the next topic or screen

There are two key functions behind the Pocket PC help system: finding
a particular topic and viewing topics. I will discuss each of these in more detail
in the following sections.

Finding a Help Topic

The help system's Find feature provides a link to the Pocket PC Find utility. This lets users search the help files on their device for particular keywords. An example of the Find interface is shown in Figure 19-3. In this example, I searched for any documents that contain the word *development;* three instances were found—in the Overview, Getting Started, and Contacting Us sections.

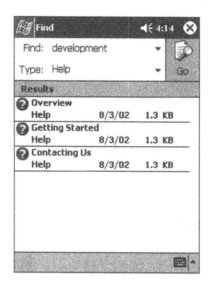

Figure 19-3. The Pocket PC help system find feature

Viewing a Help Topic

Selecting a topic from Help Contents or from the Find utility will result in the topic being displayed in the Pocket PC Help utility. Figure 19-4 shows an example of this.

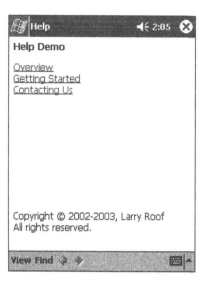

Figure 19-4. The Help Demo system

The beauty behind Pocket PC Help is that it's easy to use, and as we'll see later in this chapter, easy to construct. As you will see in the following section, HTML can be used to create simple yet elegant help systems.

Constructing Help Systems

Now that you have a basic understanding of the functionality and use of the Pocket PC help system, we are ready to begin our discussion on constructing help systems.

As I mentioned earlier in this chapter, Pocket PC help systems are quick and easy to construct. Often they can be designed, coded, and tested within the course of a single day. From the developer's standpoint, all that's required is a basic understanding of HTML.

The Help System Architecture

Pocket PC help systems are typically comprised of only two files: the help file itself and a shortcut file that points to the help file.

The help file contains all of the help content that is being offered for the application. This file can be anything from very simplistic to involved, depending upon your needs.

The shortcut file for a help file must reside in the **\Windows\Help** folder. The sole purpose of this file is to point to your application's help file. Figure 19-5 shows the **\Windows\Help** folder loaded with the common Pocket PC help file shortcuts.

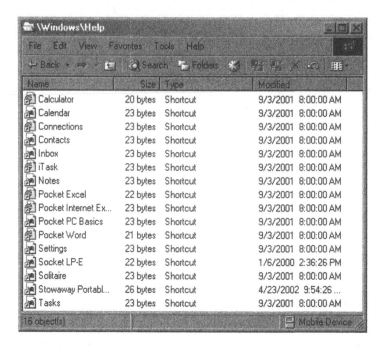

Figure 19-5. The shortcut files within \Windows\Help

Help System Tools

To build help systems for the Pocket PC, you will need the following tools:

- **A tool that you will use to build your help files**—This can be anything from Microsoft Notepad, to your favorite HTML editor, to Microsoft Visual Studio .NET. I prefer Notepad as it lends itself well to the process of repetitive modifications and testing where I construct, view, and refine a Pocket PC help file.

- **File Explorer and Mobile Explorer**—These two utilities are used to copy files quickly and easily to your device for testing. You need to get the file to the device so that you can see how your help system looks within the Pocket PC help system.

- **A Pocket PC device**—While you could certainly test in the emulator, I prefer the device for two reasons. First, in the end the help system is going to be used on a device, so why not test it on one? Second, I think the testing and refinement process is quicker using a device rather than the emulator.

- **The Pocket PC help system for displaying your work**—Since your help files are standard HTML documents, if you tap on them in Pocket Explorer, they will be displayed in Pocket Internet Explorer. This won't give you the results you are looking for. Your help file will be displayed as one continuous page. The Pocket PC help system looks for specific tags that dictate how your help is displayed.

Help Development Process

Developing a help system is all about having a process, one which streamlines creating, deploying, and testing help content. The approach I uses is as follows:

1. Start with determining everything that your help system needs to cover. Microsoft Word in outline mode works well for this. Don't make the mistake of just starting to write content without a plan. You'll end up with spaghetti help.

2. With your outline in hand, it's time to prepare your development environment. Open up Microsoft Notepad, File Explorer, and Mobile Explorer. Notepad is used to construct the help text. The two Explorers are used to copy revisions to your device for testing. Set File Explorer to the source directory, that's to say the directory on your PC where you'll be saving your work. Set Mobile Explorer to the target directory, the folder on your device where you'll be copying the files. Now you're ready to simply drag-and-drop your help file between the two Explorers.

3. Start by creating the shortcut file for your help. You'll need this to be able to correctly launch your help system for testing. Using Notepad, create the shortcut file that will point to your help file. This file needs to be placed in the **\Windows\Help** folder on your device.

4. Now it's time to create the actual help file. For this you will use Microsoft Notepad. I like to build the outline first, inserting all of the appropriate links necessary to move between topics.

5. Copy your help file to your device.

6. Test your help system. Access **Help** under the Start menu. If you created and placed your shortcut correctly, it will appear along with the other help topics.

7. Tap on a help topic to view your work. Leave the Pocket PC help system open. Move back to the help system contents between testing revisions of your help.

After implementing the outline of your help system, you are ready to add the content. Use the preceding process to complete your help file.

The Shortcut File

To be able to test your help file, you will need a shortcut file that points to your help file. This file must reside in the **\Windows\Help** folder on your device.

The Pocket PC help system builds its Help Contents screen using the names of the shortcut files located in this directory. Because of this, you should give some thought to the filename you use for this file. For example, the help file for the Pocket PC Calculator program is named calc.htm. The shortcut file that points to this help file is named Calculator.lnk. When the Pocket PC help system displays its Help Contents page, it's the name of the shortcut file, Calculator, that appears as part of the list.

The shortcut file is a simple ASCII text file that contains a single line. The format for this line is as follows:

- At the left of the line is a number followed by the pound (#) sign. The number indicates the number of characters in the path to your help file.

- To the right of the pound (#) sign is the complete path to your help file. Typically, this file would reside in the **Windows** folder, but it can be placed anywhere.

The contents of the Calculator shortcut file are shown here:

```
17#\windows\calc.htm
```

At the left is the number 17, signifying that there are 17 characters in the path to the Calculator help system. Following that is the mandatory pound (#) sign. To the right of the pound (#) sign is the path to the help file.

During the installation of your application, you will need to install this shortcut file in the **\Windows\Help** folder on the target device. Your help file will need to be placed in the folder that is referenced in the shortcut file.

The Help File

As I stated earlier in this chapter, a help file is nothing more than an HTML document. A help file can be viewed using Pocket Internet Explorer just like any other HTML document.

The PegHelp Tag

What turns your HTML document into a help document is a special HTML tag combined with the Pocket PC help system.

The special HTML tag is <!-- PegHelp --!>. You will insert this tag into your help file to separate and define each topic area.

NOTE *The syntax of the <!-- PegHelp --!> tag is specific. It must contain the space before and after "PegHelp".*

The <!-- PegHelp --!> tag is placed *at the end* of each topic. The Pocket PC help system searches for these tags when it processes your help system. It uses these tags for navigation and display.

TIP *You may find it useful to insert HTML comments into your help file to identify the individual topics. Microsoft uses the comment tag <!-- **Topic Break** --!>, which I think works well.*

The Main_Contents Attribute

When the Pocket PC help system processes your help file, it looks for an HTML anchor tag (<A>) that has the name attribute **Main_Contents**. For all practical purposes, this is the launch point for your help file. Listing 19-1 shows an example of this, an excerpt from the Calculator help file where the main contents for that help is defined.

Listing 19-1. The Main Contents Definition for the Calculator Help File

```
<!-- PegHelp -->

<p><a name="Main_Contents"></a><b>Calculator Help</b>
<!-- CS topic for calc app-->

<ul></ul><p><b>How to</b><br>

<a href="calc.htm#basic">Use the Basic Calculator</a><br>
<a href="calc.htm#currency">Use the Currency Calculator</a><br>
<a href="calc.htm#shortcuts">Use Hardware Buttons</a>

<P> <!-- PegHelp --><hr><!-- *****Topic Break**** -->
```

Note the anchor tag <a name="Main_Contents"> located near the top of Listing 19-1. Immediately below that are three additional anchor tags that define the three entries in the main contents for the Calculator help. Figure 19-6 shows the resulting screen as it's displayed by the Pocket PC help system.

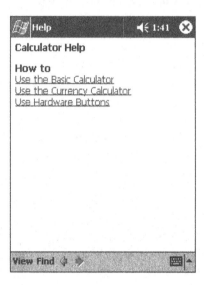

Figure 19-6. The Calculator help main contents screen

Adding Images

Add images to a help file with the <IMG> tag. Images within a help file are limited to the bitmap format. This can be either the standard format (.BMP) or the limited-version format (.2BP) that has been carried forward from Windows CE version 1.

An example of adding an image to a help file is shown in the following HTML text. In this case, the image stored in the file SaveButton.bmp is inserted.

```
<IMG SRC="SaveButton.bmp">
```

NOTE *What I don't like about adding images to a help file is that every image must reside in a separate file on the device. This means that all of these little bitmap files are cluttering up a folder, commonly the **Windows** folder. I find that with some creative text you don't need any images. Web designers have been doing this for years by changing the font, size, and color of the text.*

Supported HTML Tags

The Pocket PC help system will correctly interpret and display all of the HTML
tags supported by Pocket Internet Explorer. Generally, this is a far greater selection than you would ever find use for in a help file. In Table 19-2, I have identified
several HTML tags that are useful in the construction of help files.

Table 19-2. HTML Tags Frequently Found in Help Files

TAG	DESCRIPTION
<!-- -->	Indicates an embedded comment. Useful in documenting your help file.
<!-- PegHelp -->	Identifies the end of a topic.
<A>	Specifies an anchor, which is used to create links to topics.
<B>	Highlights selected text by making it bold.
<BODY>	Specifies the beginning of the body section of the file.
 	Inserts a line break in your help content.
<FONT>	Defines a particular font to use. This should be used sparingly and with the understanding of which fonts work well on a device.
<H#>	Specifies the size of heading to use.
<HEAD>	Defines the area containing information about an HTML document.
<I>	Displays selected text in italics.
<IMG>	Displays images within you help file.
<KEYWORD>	Defines keywords used by the Pocket PC help system Find feature.
<LI>	Defines an item in a list.
<OL>	Defines a numeric item in a list.
<P>	Starts a new paragraph. Useful in formatting bodies of content.
<TABLE>	Defines the start of a table.
<TD>	Defines a cell in a table.
<TH>	Defines a heading for a table.
<TR>	Defines a row in a table.
<UL>	Adds an unordered list.

Tips for Building Successful Help Files

The keys to building a successful help file are keeping it clean and simple. Stated another way, you need to say what needs to be said, and nothing more, in a straightforward, easy-to-navigate fashion.

Some rules of thumb to follow are

- **Keep topics to a single page**—The less the user has to scroll, the better your help system will be. My preference is multiple single pages over long scrolling pages. They are easier to understand and navigate.

- **Keep graphics to a minimum**—Images are a mainstay of desktop help systems. On a device, they eat up precious screen space and litter folders with bitmap files.

- **Be consistent**—Minimize the fonts that you use.

- **Keep the topic hierarchy to a minimum**—I've found that a hierarchy of three levels works well, two is even better. A flowcharting tool, such as Microsoft's Visio program, is helpful for this.

- **Use a font that is easy to read**—Making the font really small so that you can fit everything in doesn't help in the end. I rarely use anything other than the default font.

Now that you've a general understanding of what a help file is and how it's constructed, we'll turn our attention to a detailed tutorial that brings all of the pieces together.

Step-By-Step Tutorial: Building a Help File

In this tutorial, I will walk you through the step-by-step process of building a help file. In this tutorial, you will learn

- How to create a shortcut file

- Where to place the shortcut file

- How to construct the shell of a help file

- How to create a table of contents for your help file

- How to add topics to a help file

- How to add find capabilities to a help file

- How to test your help file on a device

As part of this tutorial, you'll be creating an application called Help Demo. Before you get too excited, I should let you know that the sole purpose behind this application is to show how to link an application to a help file. The application itself has no real usefulness.

Overview of the Help Demo System

The Help Demo system application that you'll be building in this tutorial is, well, a help demo system. It offers all of the key elements of a Pocket PC help file in a simplistic example. The Help Demo system contains a main contents section with three topics: Overview, Getting Started, and Contacting Us. Each of these topics has their own areas within the help file. The main contents page of Help Demo is shown in Figure 19-7.

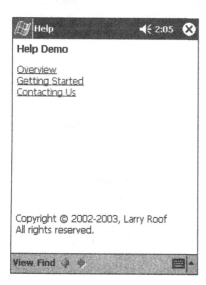

Figure 19-7. The main contents page of Help Demo

Step 1: Creating a Shortcut File

The first step in creating Help Demo is to define the shortcut file that will provide the link between the Pocket PC help system and the Help Demo file. To create this file, perform the following steps:

1. Open Microsoft Notepad.

2. Enter **17#"\Windows\Demo.htm"** into Notepad.

3. Save the file using the name **Demo.lnk**.

4. Leave Notepad open, as you will be using it in subsequent steps.

NOTE   *A complete version of the Demo shortcut file is included in the **Chapter 19** folder of the sample applications.*

The single line that you added to the shortcut file defines the location, \Windows, and the filename, Demo.htm, of your help system. The 17# is stating that there are 17 characters in the path.

Step 2: Placing the Shortcut File

Next, you will copy your newly created shortcut file to your device. This is all setup work in preparation to testing your help system later.

1. Open File Explorer and navigate to the folder where you saved the shortcut file.

2. Open Mobile Explorer and navigate to the **\Windows\Help** folder.

3. Drag the **Demo** shortcut file from File Explorer to Mobile Explorer.

Perform the following steps to verify that your shortcut has been added to the Pocket PC help system:

1. On your device, tap the **Start** menu.

2. From the Start menu, select **Help**.

The Pocket PC help system will be displayed. Verify that Demo has been added to the Help Contents.

Step 3: Constructing the Help File Shell

With the shortcut file is in place, you're ready to begin construction of the Demo help file. To construct the shell for this file, perform the following steps:

1. Start a new file in Notepad.

2. Enter the HTML text shown in Listing 19-2.

3. Save the file as **Demo.htm**.

Listing 19-2. The Demo Help File Shell

```
<HTML>
<HEAD>
<TITLE> Demo Help System</TITLE>
</HEAD>
<BODY BGCOLOR="#FFFFFF" TEXT="#000000">
</BODY>
</HTML>
```

> **NOTE** *A complete version of the Demo help file is included in the **Chapter 19** folder of the sample applications.*

At this point, all you're creating is an HTML shell for your help file. We'll add the table of contents, topics, and find keywords in the following sections.

Step 4: Adding the Table of Contents

The table of contents is the first page displayed for the help file. To add a table of contents to the Demo help file, perform the following:

1. Add the HTML text shown in Listing 19-3 to the Demo file. This text should be added right after the <BODY> tag.

2. Save the file.

Listing 19-3. HTML Defining the Table of Contents

```
<!-- PegHelp -->

<P><A NAME="Main_Contents"></A><B>Help Demo</B>
<BR>
<BR>
<A HREF="Demo.htm#Overview">Overview</A><BR>
<A HREF="Demo.htm#Getting_Started">Getting Started</A><BR>
<A HREF="Demo.htm#Contacting_Us">Contacting Us</A><BR
<BR><BR><BR><BR>
<BR><BR><BR><BR>
<BR><BR><BR><BR>
<BR>
Copywrite (c) 2002-2003, Larry Roof<BR>
All rights reserved.

<P> <!-- PegHelp --><hr><!-- *****Topic Break**** -->
```

There are several items to note in the preceding code. First is the addition of the anchor tag (<A>) that contains the name attribute Main_Contents.

NOTE *The name Main_Contents must be used. The Pocket PC Help engine keys off this word combination.*

Below the Main_Contents anchor tag are three anchor tags that define links to the three topics. Each references a jump to a location within the Help Demo document by referencing Demo.htm#anchor name.

Finally, note the series of line break tags (<BR>) followed by the copyright notice. I included this as an example of fitting content into a single page that doesn't require scrolling on the user's part.

Step 5: Adding Topics

Adding topics to a help file requires two steps. First, you must insert an HTML anchor tag to provide a link to the topic. That is what you did in step 4. Second, you must add the HTML content for the topic itself.

To add the contents for each topic to Help Demo, follow these steps:

1. Insert the HTML content from Listing 19-4 into the Demo help file immediately after the code you entered in the step 4 section.

2. Save the file.

Listing 19-4. The Contents for Topics Within the Demo Help File

```
<A NAME="Overview"></A>
<B>Overview</B><BR><BR>
This is the Overview section.

<P> <!-- PegHelp --><hr><!-- *****Topic Break**** -->
<A NAME="Getting_Started"></A>
<B>Getting Started</B><BR><BR>
This is the Getting Started section.

<P> <!-- PegHelp --><hr><!-- *****Topic Break**** -->
<A NAME="Contacting_Us"></A>
<B>Contacting Us</B><BR><BR>
This is the Contacting Us section.

<P> <!-- PegHelp --><hr>
```

NOTE   *In the preceding code, the name attributes for the three anchor tags, Overview, Getting_Started, and Contacting_Us, match the names used with the three links defined in the step 4 section.*

Step 6: Adding Find Capabilities

The last piece that you need to add to your help file defines the find keywords. Specify find keywords with the HTML keyword tag (<KEYWORD>). The **VALUE** attribute of this tag defines particular keywords. The **HREF** attribute provides the link to the point in your help file where the keyword links.

To add find capabilities to the Demo help file, do the following:

1. Insert the HTML content from Listing 19-5 into the Demo help file immediately after the </TITLE> tag.

2. Save the file.

Listing 19-5. Defining Find Keywords

```
<KEYWORD VALUE="Help Demo" TITLE="Demo Help" HREF="Demo.htm#Main_Contents">
<KEYWORD VALUE="help;development;overview" TITLE="Overview"
 HREF="Demo.htm#Overview">
<KEYWORD VALUE="help;development;learning" TITLE="Getting Started"
 HREF="Demo.htm#Getting_Started">
<KEYWORD VALUE="help;development;contacting" TITLE="Contacting Us"
 HREF="Demo.htm#Contacting_Us">
</HEAD>
```

This series of tags defines several keywords that will be associated with the Demo help file: **help**, **development**, **overview**, **learning**, and **contacting**.

Step 7: Testing the Demo Help File

The last step of this tutorial tests the Demo help file. To perform the test:

1. In Mobile Explorer, navigate to \Windows. This is the location to which the shortcut file points.

2. Drag the Demo help file from File Explorer, on your PC, to Mobile Explorer, on your device.

3. From the Pocket PC help system contents page, select **Demo**.

4. The Help Demo contents will be displayed. Click each of the links to verify their functionality. Tap the back button to move between the Help Demo contents and each topic.

 NOTE *In real life, I would recommend testing each point along the way. It will minimize the errors you encounter and simplify debugging your help files.*

Implementing Help Files

Building the shortcut and content files is only half of the process of adding help to your application. With just these two files, the user will only be able to access help for your application by selecting **Help** under the Start menu. Typically, you will want to provide a link to your help file from within your application itself. That is the topic of this section.

Adding Help to Your Application

Adding help functionality to your application involves three steps. First, the interface of your application needs to be modified to incorporate a method in which the user can access your help. Typically, this is accomplished through menu items. Second, you must include declarations for calling the CreateProcess function from the Windows CE API. Third, you must call the CreateProcess function when the user taps on a menu item.

The CreateProcess function is used to launch the Pocket PC help system, which is contained in the executable **PegHelp.exe**.

NOTE   *For more information on calling functions from the Windows CE API, see Chapter 17.*

The Help Demo Application

The Help Demo application is a simple NETCF program that demonstrates integrating help files into an application. An example of this application is shown in Figure 19-8.

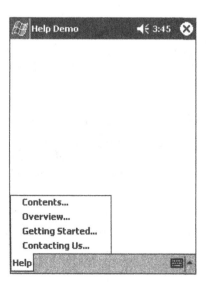

Figure 19-8. The Help Demo application

NOTE   *A complete version of the Demo shortcut file is included in the **Chapter 19** folder of the sample applications.*

This application is painfully simple. Its interface is comprised of a single, four-item Help menu. From this menu, the user can access the main contents of the help system, or go directly to any of three sections: Overview, Getting Started, or Contacting Us.

NOTE   *For more information on building menus, see Chapter 6.*

Adding Declarations

To be able to call the CreateProcess function, you must add two items to the declaration section of your application: a class defining **ProcessInfo** and the **DLLImport** for CreateProcess.

ProcessInfo is used with the last argument when calling the CreateProcess function. Its declaration is shown in Listing 19-6.

Listing 19-6. Declaration of the ProcessInfo Class

```
Public Class ProcessInfo
   Public hProcess As IntPtr
   Public hThread As IntPtr
   Public ProcessID As IntPtr
   Public ThreadID As IntPtr
End Class
```

Listing 19-7 shows the declaration for the **DLLImport** for CreateProcess. The two arguments that are of interest to you are **imageName** and **cmdLine**. The **imageName** argument defines the executable to launch—in this case, PegHelp.exe, or the Pocket PC help system. The **cmdLine** argument is used to pass the name of the file to load into the Pocket PC help system.

Listing 19-7. Declaration of the CreateProcess Function

```
<System.Runtime.InteropServices.DllImport("coredll.dll")> _
  Protected Shared Function CreateProcess( _
    ByVal imageName As String, _
    ByVal cmdLine As String, _
    ByVal lpProcessAttributes As IntPtr, _
    ByVal lpThreadAttributes As IntPtr, _
    ByVal boolInheritHandles As Int32, _
    ByVal dwCreationFlags As Int32, _
    ByVal lpEnvironment As IntPtr, _
    ByVal lpCurrentDir As IntPtr, _
    ByVal si() As Byte, _
    ByVal pi As ProcessInfo) As Int32
  End Function
```

Calling Help Files

With the declarations in place, you can implement the functionality behind
each of the four menu items: **Contents**, **Overview**, **Getting Started**, and
Contacting Us.

Listing 19-8 shows the menu **Click** event for the **Contents** menu item.
Within this code is a call to CreateProcess that passes the file **demo.htm** to be
displayed by the Pocket PC help system.

Listing 19-8. The Click Event Procedure for the Contents Menu Item

```
Private Sub mnuHelpContents_Click(ByVal sender As System.Object, ByVal e As _
  System.EventArgs) Handles mnuHelpContents.Click
  Dim si(128) As Byte
  Dim pi As New ProcessInfo()

' Launch help at the contents section.
  CreateProcess("peghelp.exe", "demo.htm", IntPtr.Zero, _
    IntPtr.Zero, 0, 0, IntPtr.Zero, IntPtr.Zero, si, pi)
End Sub
```

The menu **Click** event procedure for the **Overview** menu item is shown in
Listing 19-9. To access the specific section of the Demo help file, you simply
need to alter the second argument to the CreateProcess call, passing the value
demo.htm#Overview.

Listing 19-9. The Click Event Procedure for the Overview Menu Item

```
Private Sub mnuHelpOverview_Click(ByVal sender As System.Object, ByVal e As _
  System.EventArgs) Handles mnuHelpOverview.Click
  Dim si(128) As Byte
  Dim pi As New ProcessInfo()

' Launch help for the Overview topic.
  CreateProcess("peghelp.exe", "demo.htm#Overview", _
    IntPtr.Zero, IntPtr.Zero, 0, 0, IntPtr.Zero, _
    IntPtr.Zero, si, pi)
End Sub
```

The menu Click event procedure for the **Getting Started** menu item is shown in Listing 19-10. It's identical to the **Click** event procedure for the **Overview** menu item with the exception of the second argument, which has been set to demo.htm#Getting_Started.

Listing 19-10. The Click Event Procedure for the Getting Started Menu Item

```
Private Sub mnuHelpGetting_Click(ByVal sender As System.Object, ByVal e As _
  System.EventArgs) Handles mnuHelpGetting.Click
  Dim si(128) As Byte
  Dim pi As New ProcessInfo()

' Launch help for the Getting Started topic.
  CreateProcess("peghelp.exe", "demo.htm#Getting_Started", _
    IntPtr.Zero, IntPtr.Zero, 0, 0, IntPtr.Zero, _
    IntPtr.Zero, si, pi)
End Sub
```

The menu **Click** event procedure for the **Contacting Us** menu item is shown in Listing 19-11. Like the previous two procedures, the only change required to access the appropriate help is to alter the second argument to the CreateProcess call, changing it to demo.htm#Contacting_Us.

Listing 19-11. The Click Event Procedure for the Contacting Us Menu Item

```
Private Sub mnuHelpContacting_Click(ByVal sender As System.Object, ByVal e As _
  System.EventArgs) Handles mnuHelpContacting.Click
  Dim si(128) As Byte
  Dim pi As New ProcessInfo()
```

```
  Launch help for the Contacting Us topic.
  CreateProcess("peghelp.exe", "demo.htm#Contacting_Us", _
    IntPtr.Zero, IntPtr.Zero, 0, 0, IntPtr.Zero, _
    IntPtr.Zero, si, pi)
End Sub
```

As you see, adding help links to your application is simple. The CreateProcess function allows you to link either to the contents section of your help system or to a specific topic.

The only drawback with linking to a particular topic directly is that the user doesn't have an easy way to return to the contents. Figure 19-9 shows an example of this. Note how the back button is disabled.

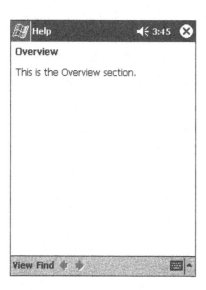

Figure 19-9. The Overview section as it appears when called directly

Delivering Help Files

The final part of the help file process involves installing your help files on the user's system. Remember, there are two help files, the content file and the shortcut file, that you will need to include in your setups, plus any bitmaps you may have included in your content. The content file can be installed anywhere. The shortcut file must be placed in the **\Windows\Help** folder.

Summary

No application is complete without a help system. A help system can significantly improve the effectiveness and usefulness of your application.

In this chapter, you learned the basics about the Pocket PC help system. It is a simple system compared to the help environment offered under other Windows operating systems.

You learned that creating a help system requires nothing more than a basic understanding of HTML and a simple editing tool, like Microsoft Notepad. Shortcut files that are used to point to help files are defined with a single line of text. Help files themselves are constructed using standard HTML tags.

The most complicated part of adding help to your Pocket PC applications is the process of calling your help file from within your application. This step requires you to reach outside of the .NET Compact Framework, to the Windows CE API. While this can be challenging, by reading Chapter 17 and referencing the examples included with this chapter, you should have minimal problems.

In the next chapter, we'll continue our discussion on preparing an application for delivery. Chapter 20 covers user settings: what they are and how you can easily incorporate them into your applications.

Application Settings

WHEN YOU'VE FINISHED AN application and finally get it into the customers' hands, you often want the ability to store application-specific information when the program runs. You might want to store a serial number or a hashed version of one. Other times, you might want to store a user's name and company to display later on a splash screen. The full .NET Framework supports a **System.Configuration** class that handles the grunt work to store and retrieve application settings (in an XML format). Unfortunately, the .NET Compact Framework doesn't support this namespace, so if you want to handle configuration settings, you have to do it yourself.

After reading and working the examples in Chapter 17, you might think that you'll just work with the good old standby, **GetPrivateProfileString**, and its brothers and sisters. Being the good, anti-registry, Visual Basic 6.0 developer that you are, that's how you've probably always done it. One problem: These methods aren't supported by the underlying OS, so don't plan on using them in NETCF.

Instead, this chapter will show you how to develop a class that supports three methods of storing user settings by using managed code. Each of these methods will use portions of NETCF that have been covered in previous chapters. In particular, this chapter will use XML (Chapter 14), text files (Chapter 8), and the registry (Chapter 17) to write user settings to storage for recovery later. Each of the mentioned chapters gave examples of how to use or access the specific technology. The difference in this chapter is that we're going to take those earlier portions of this book and use them in a more directed manner—saving and restoring application settings.

Developing the Foundation

The **UserSettings** class is designed to provide a consistent public face for each of the three methods. To do that, the classes are all derived from an interface class. The interface defines six methods that each derived class must implement.

Basing Classes on Interfaces

This book isn't written as a VB .NET tutorial. The assumption has been made that you have some experience with the desktop version of Visual Basic .NET and will know how to write standard code. Interfaces are new to many VB developers, and as such, you might not have explored them yet on the desktop. Rather than try to spend time explaining them here, I've included a couple of references to other Apress books that will provide you with the knowledge you need to grasp the entirety of this chapter:

- *Programming VB .NET: A Guide for Experienced Programmers,* by Gary Cornell and Jonathan Morrison (Apress, 2001. ISBN: 1-893115-99-2)

- *Visual Basic .NET and the .NET Platform: An Advanced Guide,* by Andrew Troelsen (Apress, 2001. ISBN: 1-893115-26-7)

The methods are modeled loosely from the **GetPrivateProfile** methods exposed by the Windows API. You can read or write a string or a number (defined in Windows as a DWORD), get a listing of all the sections holding the application's data, or delete an entry from an existing section. The interface definition is shown in Listing 20-1.

Listing 20-1. The Base Interface Class

```
Public Interface UserSettings
    Function ReadSettingInt(ByVal section As String, ByVal entry As String, _
        ByVal defaultVal As Int32) As Int32
    Function ReadSettingString(ByVal section As String, ByVal entry As String, _
        ByVal defaultVal As String) As String
    Function WriteSettingString(ByVal section As String, ByVal entry As String, _
        ByVal dataValue As String) As Boolean
    Function WriteSettingInt(ByVal section As String, ByVal entry As String, _
        ByVal dataValue As Int32) As Boolean
    Function GetSectionNames() As String()
    Sub DeleteKey(ByVal SectionName As String, ByVal entry As String)
End Interface
```

Once the interface is defined, it's implemented by each class that needs to present users with a similar set of functionality. Each class implements the interface. The following code shows the syntax for a class implementing your new UserSettings interface:

```
Public Class IniSettings
    Implements UserSettings
End Class
```

The next topic has been covered previously in this book, but it always helps to mention important code snippets and ideas more than once for reinforcement. It's not a simple task to get the path or name of your application at runtime. To handle that functionality, this project has a class called **SettingSupport** with a series of methods that provide the information for both the running application and the calling application as shown in Listing 20-2.

Listing 20-2. Getting Application Information

```
Public Class SettingSupport
    Public Shared Function CallingAppPath() As String
        CallingAppPath = _
            System.IO.Path.GetDirectoryName(Reflection.Assembly. _
            GetCallingAssembly().GetName().CodeBase.ToString())
    End Function
    Public Shared Function CallingAppName() As String
        CallingAppName = _
            Reflection.Assembly.GetCallingAssembly().GetName().Name
    End Function
    Public Shared Function AppPath() As String
        ' Return the path to this application.
        AppPath = _
        System.IO.Path.GetDirectoryName(Reflection.Assembly. _
            GetExecutingAssembly().GetName().CodeBase.ToString())
    End Function
    Public Shared Function AppName() As String
        AppName = _
            Reflection.Assembly.GetExecutingAssembly().GetName().Name
    End Function
End Class
```

The **CallingAppPath** and **CallingAppName** methods get the information not for yourself, but for the calling application. You'll need this functionality when you have one assembly started or loaded by a parent, or calling, assembly. The child assembly may reside in the GAC or some other location on the device. If you're writing settings, you'll want to store information in the location of the calling assembly, not the called assembly.

NOTE *As always, the code for this chapter can be found in the* **Chapter 20** *folder of the* **Samples** *folder for this book. See Appendix D for information on accessing and loading the sample applications. This solution is made up of two projects, a test windows application and a class library project that holds the class that we'll be looking at in detail in the rest of this chapter.*

Working with Settings in an INI File

Although the INI file might seem like the easiest option to start this discussion with, it isn't. This example is strictly grunt text-file parsing, nothing more and nothing less. Grunt text parsing can often get more complex than other algorithms that you might write. And this gives the file I/O methods a good workout.

The UserSettings interface doesn't specify a constructor, because constructors can't be defined in an interface, so each class can implement construction in any way it sees fit. All three of the classes to be covered implement identical constructors.

```
Private Sub New()
End Sub

Private _AppName As String
Private _fileName As String

Public Sub New(ByVal strAppName As String)
    _AppName = strAppName
    _fileName = SettingSupport.AppPath() & "\" & strAppName & ".ini"
End Sub
```

The preceding code shows the constructors for the **IniSettings** class. The **New** method that takes no parameters and has a Private scope so that, in order to create one of these classes, you *must* pass the strAppName parameter. The classes were implemented this way, instead of using the **SettingSupport.AppName** method discussed earlier, to provide a more flexible naming of the configuration files. In this implementation, the location is always going to be in the same directory as the application. That could easily be changed if you want to make the modifications to the classes. Once constructed, you can call any of the methods provided by the class.

Before you can read a value from the INI file, you have to write a value to the file. The first method to be covered therefore is **WriteSettingString**.

NOTE *The **WriteSettingInt** method won't be covered in this chapter because it features almost exactly the same code as **WriteSettingString**. The Int32 parameter is converted to a string and that string is written to the file using **WriteSettingString**. In fact, **WritePrivateProfileInt** doesn't exist in the Win32 API. It was added to this project because when writing to the registry, strings and numbers are handled differently. In order to make all of the class methods interchangeable, the **WriteSettingInt** method was added to the interface, and hence to all three classes.*

Earlier you saw a code snippet that showed how a class implements an interface, and now you'll see how that class implements each method defined in the interface. A class must have a method matching the signature of each method in the interface. To tell the compiler that a method is the one that implements a particular method of the interface, you decorate the method name with the **Implements** keyword.

```
Public Function WriteSettingString(ByVal section As String, _
    ByVal entry As String, _
    ByVal defaultVal As String) As Boolean _
    Implements UserSettings.WriteSettingString
```

Note the last portion of the preceding code. This method is responsible for implementing the **WriteSettingString** method of the UserSettings interface. If you so desired, you could change the name of the method as it's implemented in your derived class to something other than the name that is specified by the interface. As long as the method has a matching parameter list and return value, it can implement an interface method.

The code in Listing 20-3 shows how to get the file opened, or created, and ready for writing. This implementation sets several variables that will be used for position counting and setting the state of the search. It then goes on to build, in INI file format, the name of the section, enclosed by square brackets ([and]), and the name of the key followed by an equal (=) sign. To check if the file exists, **WriteSettingString** uses the **Exists** method of the **System.IO.File** class. If the file exists, it's opened and both a **StreamReader** and **StreamWriter** variable are declared. The reader is initialized by calling the **Open** method of the **File** class while the writer is initialized by creating a new instance of the writer.

Listing 20-3. Getting Ready to Access the INI File

```
Public Function WriteSettingString(ByVal section As String, _
        ByVal key As String, _
        ByVal defaultVal As String) As Boolean _
        Implements UserSettings.WriteSettingString
    Dim posSection As Int32
    Dim iPos As Int32 = 0
    Dim bEntryFound As Boolean = False

    Dim strSection As String = "[" & section & "]"
    Dim strKey As String = key & "="

    Dim strInput As String = String.Empty

    If (System.IO.File.Exists(_fileName)) Then
        '    If it does exist, open it, read in the entire file.
        Dim sr As System.IO.StreamReader
        Dim sw As System.IO.StreamWriter
        sr = System.IO.File.OpenText(_fileName)
        sw = New StreamWriter(_fileName& ".txt")
```

TIP *I originally added a .tmp extension to the temporary write file instead of a .txt extension. That works fine until you want to open the file on the device. There is no association for .tmp, so touching the file won't open the file for viewing. There is, however, an association for .txt, so if you name your files with that extension, all you need to do to view the file is touch it in the explorer. Also, INI extensions don't have associations. I'm lazy; I want to do as little additional work as possible, so if I can do something, like viewing a file, in a simple manner, then I'll do it. If at all possible, name your files, at least during debugging, using file extensions that open for easy viewing.*

This is only one of several techniques that you can use to read and write to files. If you're an old VB 6 developer, then this method most resembles the way you would have done it in the past. This implementation opens one file to read in the existing file and then writes the new values into the temporary file. Once everything works as expected, the original file is deleted, or renamed, and the temporary file renamed to the original filename.

For the purpose of refreshing old brain cells, an example INI file is shown in Listing 20-4. It's also important to get some naming conventions straightened out. The [Info] string is referred to in this chapter as a section marker. Each section is preceded by a marker and continues until a new marker is found. The data entries inside a section are key-value pairs.

Listing 20-4. Sample INI File Entries

```
[Info]
Name=INTL
Version=1.00.000
DiskSpace=8000    ;DiskSpace requirement in KB

[Startup]
CmdLine=
Product=Standard SDK for Windows CE .NET
PackageName=STANDARD_SDK.msi
MsiVersion=1.00.5104.0
EnableLangDlg=Y

[0x0409]
TITLE=Choose Setup Language
DESCRIPTION=Select the language for this installation from the choices below.
OK=OK
Cancel=Cancel
```

Listing 20-5 contains the remainder of the code used to read each line of the file and to save it back out to the temporary file. There are several items to note in the code. The **ReadLine** method will return Nothing when it has reached the end of the file. With .NET built to raise exceptions for almost everything, this would seem to be a good place to raise an end-of-file exception. But this method doesn't, so be sure to write your code to check for Nothing and exit the loop.

Listing 20-5. Reading and Searching

```
    Try
        While True
            strInput = sr.ReadLine()
            If strInput Is Nothing Then
                Exit While
            End If
            If strInput.StartsWith(strSection) Then
                '
                '    Write the section marker out to the temp file.
                sw.WriteLine(strInput)
                '
                '    Read in one line at a time, looking for an entry match.
                '    or for the next section
                Dim intInput As Int32
```

```vbnet
                    While True
                        strInput = sr.ReadLine()
                        If strInput Is Nothing Then
                            Exit While
                        End If
                        If strInput.StartsWith("[") And Not bEntryFound Then

                            '
                            '    Didn't find the key.
                            '    Write our new data to the temp file.
                            sw.WriteLine(strKey & defaultVal)
                            '    Write the section header to file.
                            sw.WriteLine(strInput)
                            Exit While
                        ElseIf strInput.IndexOf(strKey) = -1 Then
                            '    Not the key I wanted
                            sw.WriteLine(strInput)
                        Else
                            '    FOUND IT!!'    Write the new value to the file.
                            sw.WriteLine(strKey & defaultVal)
                            bEntryFound = True
                        End If
                    End While
                Else
                    '    Anything other than a section marker
                    '    needs to be saved to our temp file.
                    sw.WriteLine(strInput)
                End If
            End While
            '    Successful read of the entire file.
            '    Be sure to close the file first.
            sr.Close()
            sw.Close()
            '    Copy the new file over the old file.
            System.IO.File.Copy(_fileName & ".txt", _fileName, True)
        Catch ex As Exception
            MsgBox(ex.Message)
        Finally
            sw.Close()
            sr.Close()
        End Try
    Else
        Dim sw As System.IO.StreamWriter
        sw = New StreamWriter(_fileName)
        sw.WriteLine(strSection)
```

```
        sw.WriteLine(strKey & defaultVal)
        sw.Close()
    End If
End Function
```

A significant number of methods are included in the **String** class, too many to know them all until you spend a significant amount of time working with them. One method in particular is **StartsWith**. In old Visual Basic 6 code, you would have had to specify the comparison to start at zero and continue for a specified number of characters. In .NET, you make a call like the following code snippet:

```
If strInput.StartsWith("[Startup]") Then
End If
```

You may recall from your days of Windows and VB 6 that the entries in an INI are case insensitive. The code just presented is case sensitive because the string comparisons are case dependent. To be clear, "Startup" won't match "StartUp".

 HOMEWORK   *Alter the IniSettings code to be case insensitive. There are a couple of ways that this can be done. Hints: the **ToLower** and **ToUpper** methods, and the **CompareInfo** class.*

If the file doesn't exist in the application directory then the last code block creates the file by creating a new StreamWriter using the filename in the constructor. The section header is written to the file as is the new key and value pair. The **ReadSettingString** method is very similar to the write method in that you read in one line at a time, check the content of the line, and act accordingly. The principles are the same as they are with many of the .NET class method calls. You can see the read implementation in this chapter's source code.

 HOMEWORK   *Fix the code in Listing 20-5 to respect white spaces between sections in the file. If the entry to write doesn't exist, have it written into the file on the line immediately after the last item of the section. Remember, the current implementation will write the new entry after the spaces, immediately before the next section marker.*

HOMEWORK   *Add the **DeleteSection** and the **GetSectionNames** methods to the interface and implement them in each of the three classes.*

NOTE   *Solutions to the homework assignments can be found in the code folder for this chapter.*

Working with Settings in an XML File

This section would be much shorter if NETCF supported XPath functions, but it doesn't. You could take this code up to a project on the desktop, but I really suggest that you learn and use XPath instead when writing code for the full framework. Before you can understand how to parse the file, you need to know what the file looks like. A sample configuration file, in XML format, is shown in Listing 20-6.

Listing 20-6. An Application XML Config File

```
<configuration>
  <Section Name="Info">
    <Key Name="Name" Value="INTL" />
    <Key Name="Version" Value="1.00.000" />
    <Key Name="DiskSpace" Value="8000" Comment=";DiskSpace requirement in KB"/>
  </Section>
  <Section Name="Startup">
    <Key Name="CmdLine" Value="" />
    <Key Name="Product" Value="Standard SDK for Windows CE .NET" />
    <Key Name="PackageName" Value="STANDARD_SDK.msi" />
    <Key Name="MsiVersion" Value="1.00.5104.0" />
    <Key Name="EnableLangDlg" Value="Y" />
  </Section>
  <Section Name="0x0409">
    <Key Name="TITLE" Value="Choose Setup Language" />
    <Key Name="DESCRIPTION" Value="Select the language for this installation" />
    <Key Name="OK" Value="OK" />
    <Key Name="Cancel" Value="Cancel" />
  </Section>
</configuration>
```

Hopefully you can see that the XML configuration file in Listing 20-6 is structured to imitate the data in the INI file shown in Listing 20-4. Each section of the INI file has a matching Section element with a Name attribute. Each key-value pair of the INI file has an XML element, Key, with Name and Value attributes containing the data that was stored in the INI file. Keeping the data structure of your configuration file in mind, it's time to start processing the file.

Reading from an XML Settings File

After the last section, you should expect the first step to be building a filename that is in the correct directory with the correct file extension. The file is read using an XmlTextReader. While XML in general may be new to you, handling XML documents using an XmlTextReader is very much like parsing text. The flow of the code in Listing 20-7 is straightforward. This listing shows a series of **Read** method calls followed by a check to see if the data returned matches the information requested. The **Read** method of an XmlTextReader returns True if a node was read and False if there was no node to read.

Listing 20-7. Reading a Value from an XML Config File

```
Private Function ReadSettingValue(ByVal section As String, _
     ByVal entry As String, ByVal defaultVal As String) As String
  Dim dr As XmlTextReader
  Dim strPath As String = SettingSupport.CallingAppPath() _
     & "\" & "TestFrame" & ".config"
  Dim strRetValue As String = defaultVal

  Try
     dr = New XmlTextReader(strPath)
     dr.WhitespaceHandling = WhitespaceHandling.None

     While dr.Read()
         '    Look for the <configuration> section.
         '    This lets us add several pieces in the config file.
         If dr.Name = "configuration" Then
             '     We are in the correct space, now for the requested section.
             While dr.Read
                 If dr.NodeType = XmlNodeType.Element AndAlso _
                     dr.Name = "Section" AndAlso dr.HasAttributes Then
                     '    See if the attribute is the section we are looking for.
                     dr.MoveToFirstAttribute()
```

```
                    If dr.Name = "Name" And dr.Value = section Then
                       '    We found the section,
                       '    now look for the correct entry (key) item.
                      While dr.Read
                          If dr.NodeType = XmlNodeType.Element AndAlso _
                              dr.HasAttributes AndAlso _
                              dr.Name.ToString() = "Key" Then
                              ' Walk and look at all elements.
                              dr.MoveToFirstAttribute()
                              If dr.Name = "Name" AndAlso _
                                    dr.Value = entry Then
                                 ' Get the next attribute.
                                 dr.MoveToNextAttribute()
                                 If dr.Name = "Value" Then
                                      Return dr.Value
                                 End If
                              End If
                          End If
                      End While
                    End If
                End If
            End While
        End If
    End While
    '    If we get here, nothing was found.
    Return defaultVal
  Finally
      dr.Close()
  End Try
End Function
```

Once a node has been read, you can query its properties to find out what kind of node it is and if it contains the correct data. Maybe this is a little simplistic, but each line in the example config file is an element node.

 NOTE   *This is only true because this example features a very simple XML file. If you were to have a more complex file, then all lines would not be an element. This is discussed in more detail in Chapter 14.*

The code looks first for the configuration element, and once it's found the code reads from a file until it finds the correct section. If the correct section is found, the code then reads node by node until it finds the requested name-value key. If no match is found, the default value passed through the parameter list is returned to the caller. When an element is found that matches, the Key element for example, it then becomes necessary to read the attributes of that element. As a safety precaution, it's important to make sure that attributes do exist in the element before blindly trying to read them. To be sure that attributes exist, you can use the **HasAttributes** method of the XmlTextReader to check for their presence.

Writing to an XML Settings File

One thing the .NET Framework and the .NET Compact Framework have going for them is the ability to attack a problem from several different directions. In Listing 20-7, the XML file is parsed using a reader. In this section, the solution to the problem is addressed by the use of the **XmlDocument** class. When using the reader, you derive every bit of information from the reader object itself. Each read returns a new element. All of the parsing of the file is done using elements. When an element is found that matches the application criteria, the attributes of the element are checked and the appropriate actions are taken.

The big difference in this section is that the file will be parsed by loading the entire file into memory and then examining the nodes of the document.

 NOTE *We had a discussion back in Chapter 14 about the advantages or disadvantages of loading the entire XML document into memory at one time using the **XmlDocument** class. Normally a configuration file isn't thousands of records long (or at least let's hope not), so loading a file of perhaps 100 nodes should not cause a big memory problem.*

It turns out that using the **XmlDocument** class greatly simplifies parsing the XML file. Using an XmlTextReader is fine to read the file, but how about having to write back a single changed element of the file? That requires opening an XmlTextWriter, reading the file, writing pieces of it back to file as needed, making the changes, etc. Using the XmlTextWriter for this purpose would not make you a happy camper.

The easy solution to making changes to an XML document, in the absence of XPath, is to use the **XmlDocument** class. As the code in Listing 20-8 shows, the first step is to create a new XmlDocument instance and to load the file. If the file doesn't exist, an XmlException is thrown. In this situation, a new file is created and the proper nodes are written to the file.

Listing 20-8. Writing to the XML Settings File Using the XmlDocument Class

```
Public Function WriteSettingValue(ByVal section As String, _
        ByVal key As String, ByVal dataValue As String) As Boolean
    Dim xd As XmlDocument = New XmlDocument
    '   Does the file exist?
    Try
        xd.Load(m_sXMLFileName)

        Dim xe As XmlElement = xd.DocumentElement

        '   Check the name to see if the node is <configuration
        If xe.Name = "configuration" Then
            '   Each child node is a 'section' marker.
            For Each xce As XmlElement In xe.ChildNodes
                '   Make certain of the structure of the file
                If xce.Name = "Section" Then
                    '   Check the attribute of the section.
                    If xce.Attributes(0).Name = "Name" And _
                            xce.Attributes(0).Value = section Then
                        '   AppendChild removes the element if it exists.
                        Dim xe2 As XmlElement = xd.CreateElement("Key")
                        xe2.SetAttribute("Name", key)
                        xe2.SetAttribute("Value", dataValue)
                        xce.AppendChild(xe2)
                    End If
                End If
            Next
        End If
        '   Write the document back to disk.
        xd.Save(m_sXMLFileName)
    Catch ex As XmlException
        '   File does not exist
        Dim newDoc As XmlDocument = New XmlDocument
        Dim xe As XmlElement
        xe = newDoc.CreateElement("configuration")
        Dim sectionElement As XmlElement = newDoc.CreateElement("Section")
        sectionElement.SetAttribute("Name", section)

        Dim keyElement As XmlElement = newDoc.CreateElement("Key")
        keyElement.SetAttribute("Name", section)
        keyElement.SetAttribute("Value", dataValue)
        sectionElement.AppendChild(keyElement)
```

```
          newDoc.AppendChild(sectionElement)
          newDoc.Save(m_sXMLFileName)      Finally
      End Try
  End Function
```

The solution as presented here makes a rather significant shortcut. The assumption is that there is nothing in the XML file other than the <configuration> element. If configuration isn't the first element in the file, then the routine won't work. The first element will have a value of Settings, for example, and the first If condition will fail and the routine exit without doing any file parsing.

HOMEWORK *Fix the code in Listing 20-8 to allow for the configuration file to have multiple elements.*

Once the file is loaded, you need to get the root node through the **DocumentElement** property. Once the root element is obtained, the method walks through the child nodes looking for a match to the section name. This method does check to be sure that the inner nodes are named properly and if one isn't it skips that node.

The For Each statement walks the nodes which are the section names shown in Listing 20-6: Info, Startup, and 0x0409. When the correct section is located, no more parsing is needed. The new element is created, its attributes set to the desired values, and the **AddChild** method is called. If the element already exists, then it's deleted first and then added back. If it doesn't exist, then it's added. The beauty of this is that the amount of node walking is reduced significantly. There is no need to see if the name-value pair already existed or not. It isn't important to the write routine if the element has been replaced or added.

After the element has been updated, there is no use in continuing to walk the nodes of the document, so an Exit For statement sends execution out of the loop and right to the **Save** method of the XmlDocument. No close exists for an XmlDocument object, and neither does a **Dispose** method. If you stop to think for a minute, you'll notice no file or other resources are being held open. The XmlDocument is an in-memory copy of the document. The file was opened, read, and closed. It seems a little odd to call the **Save** method of the XmlDocument object while still working with the data. But it works, and the file is saved on top of the original file.

If you use the **XmlTextReader** class, an XML file is easier to parse than a flat text file. The node elements that are created by each read from the reader represent a very convenient way of accessing a file's data. In comparison to the INI file, where any line could possibly contain just about anything, XML parsing is a breeze. If you know a little about XML formats and use the **XmlDocument** class, then parsing the file is even easier.

Working with Settings in the Registry

There is no hidden reason for saving the registry for the end; it just worked out that way. But after the pain of string and node parsing in the previous sections, this section will be a piece of cake. The class created in this section will also implement the UserSettings interface and supply all of the methods required by the interface, just like the previous classes did.

Since this class uses the UserSettings interface, it has to support the same idea of filenames, sections, and name-value pairs. To implement this structure, the **RegistrySettings** class stores its data in the registry as shown in Figure 20-1.

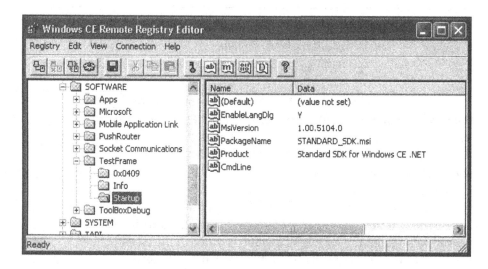

Figure 20-1. Application data stored in the Registry

The value passed into the constructor, the filename, is used as a key name placed under the already existing SOFTWARE registry key. Each section is represented by another registry key placed under the filename key. Lastly, each name-value pair is stored as a string or DWORD inside the registry key.

When you install a new software package on your desktop, it will often ask whether the application should be available to you or to any user of the computer. What happens is that the registry settings are stored in either the local machine key or in the current user key. Along those same lines, the **RegistrySettings** class lets you save the settings at a machine or user level. By default, settings are stored in the local machine root. To get the settings stored in the user's root, you use an overloaded constructor and pass True to make it "private."

As shown in Listing 20-9, the default constructor is set to Private. The two public constructors require an application name, just as the constructors in the previous two classes do.

Listing 20-9. Constructing a RegistrySettings Class

```
Private _AppName As String
Private _RootKey As RegistryAPI.RegistryRootKeys
Private _BaseSubKey As String

Private Sub New()
End Sub

Public Sub New(ByVal strAppName As String)
    _AppName = strAppName
    _BaseSubKey = "Software\" & strAppName & "\"
    _RootKey = RegistryAPI.RegistryRootKeys.HkeyLocalMachine
End Sub
Public Sub New(ByVal strAppname As String, ByVal bPrivate As Boolean)
    _AppName = strAppname
    _BaseSubKey = "Software\" & strAppname & "\"
    If bPrivate Then
        _RootKey = RegistryAPI.RegistryRootKeys.HkeyCurrentUser
    Else
        _RootKey = RegistryAPI.RegistryRootKeys.HkeyLocalMachine
    End If
End Sub
```

If you would prefer a different location for your keys to be created, you can change the value assigned to the _BaseSubKey variable in the constructors. After the _RootKey variable has been assigned, the rest of the calls go quite smoothly. The code in Listing 20-10 shows everything required to read and write to the registry through your **RegistrySettings** class.

Listing 20-10. Reading, Writing, and the Registry

```
Public Function ReadSettingString(ByVal section As String, _
        ByVal entry As String, _
        ByVal defaultVal As String) As String _
        Implements UserSettings.ReadSettingString
    Dim ra As RegistryAPI = New RegistryAPI
    Dim retEntry As String
    If ra.QueryValue(_RootKey, _BaseSubKey & section, entry, retEntry) Then
        Return retEntry
    Else
        Return defaultVal
    End If
End Function
```

```
Public Function WriteSettingString(ByVal section As String, _
        ByVal entry As String, _
        ByVal dataValue As String) As Boolean _
        Implements UserSettings.WriteSettingString
    Dim ra As RegistryAPI = New RegistryAPI

    Return ra.SetValue(_RootKey, _BaseSubKey & section, entry, dataValue)
End Function
```

The code is simple because all of the registry complexity is hidden in the **RegistryAPI** class. In Chapter 17, you built a class that provided access to the system registry. This class is based on the work you did earlier. The class included in this project has had a few enhancements to clarify the interface.

Summary

The big question still exists: How, or where, do you store your application data? This chapter has helped you solve the coding portion, after you've decided which technique to use. This chapter also presented a little more in-depth usage of file IO, registry access, and XML file handling. These examples are by no means the only way to accomplish the storage of user settings.

The **XmlSettings** class could have used an XmlDocument object to read the file, and then the parsing could have been done using the DOM. If you're an XML developer, you might prefer that technique. If you're new to XML, then the approach taken in this chapter looks a little more like the Visual Basic 6 style of code and will be easier to digest.

The **IniSettings** class could also been have implemented by doing a **ReadToEnd** method call to pull the entire file in at once and then parse the string in memory, replacing segments of the text and writing it back to the file when finished. The **Chapter 20** folder under the **Samples** folder contains the code discussed in the chapter. Additionally, the sample code also has another version of each class that implements the alternative methods that were just mentioned.

After reading this chapter, reviewing the code, and doing the homework assignments, you should have a good foundation for the next time you need to store a piece of data for your application. File IO is one of the basics of programming, and unless you stick to SQL Server CE or some other database, you'll want to master the processes that ensure your application can read and write data.

CHAPTER 21

Creating Setups for Your Applications

SETUPS CAN BE LOOKED at as the last step in the development process or the first step in the delivery process. Either way, they play a pivotal role in the success of an application. A good setup can set the stage for a successful application, providing the user with a positive first impression of your application. A bad setup can overshadow even the best applications, causing the user to lose confidence and your application to fail.

Setups can range from easy to complex. At the bare minimum, they handle the installation of an application. As they become more involved, setups can add items to the Pocket PC registry, and create directories and shortcuts. Regardless of their complexity, all setups should make it easy for the end user to uninstall an application and all of its associate files.

In this chapter, I'll lead you through the development of a setup for your NETCF applications. We'll start with an overview of the setup process. You'll learn what's involved and how it's performed. Next, you'll learn how to create a basic setup using the Visual Studio .NET development environment. From there, I'll show you how to create a custom setup that provides you with more control over the setup process. Finally, you'll learn how to create a supporting desktop setup that will handle launching your application setup from a PC.

Setup Fundamentals

Creating setups for a NETCF application is similar to the approach used for other Windows applications. Application setups are delivered using Cabinet files, which are more commonly referred to as Cab files, after their .cab file extension. Cab files serve two purposes: 1) they compress and store files so that they may be easy distributed, and 2) they make sure that all of the files and settings required by an application are correctly handled.

Applications built with SDE require the .NET Compact Framework to be resident on the target device. In addition, if the application makes use of SQL Server CE, you'll need to install the SQLCE components as well.

Your setup routine will need to take all of this into consideration. Potentially, it could need to include multiple Cab files, one for your application, the second for the .NET Compact Framework and the SQL Server CE Cabs.

Installing NET Compact Framework

Smart Device Extensions for Visual Studio .NET includes a set of processor-specific Cab files that handle the installation of the .NET Compact Framework. These Cab files are located on your development PC under the default path of

```
C:\Program Files\Microsoft Visual Studio.NET\CompactFrameworkSDK\vx.xxxx\Windows CE
```

where *x.xxxx* is the version number of the .NET Compact Framework you have installed on your system. As shown in Figure 21-1, you'll need to select the appropriate version of netcf.cjk.ppc3.*xxx*.cab (where *xxx* is the processor type) for your device from either the wce300 or wce400 directories (depending upon the version of the target device's operating system) and then the processor type of your device (ARM, MIPS, SH3, etc.).

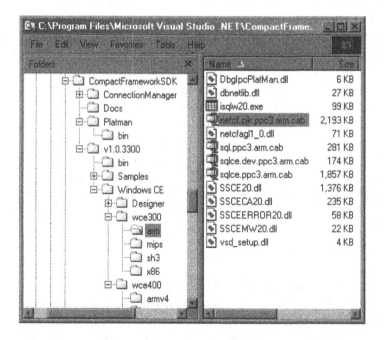

Figure 21-1. The Cab file used to install NETCF on an iPaq Pocket PC

NOTE *If the .NET Compact Framework is already installed on a Pocket PC, it doesn't need to be reinstalled unless your application is built using a newer version of the NETCF.*

Installing SQL Server CE

Smart Device Extensions also includes a set of processor-specific Cab files that handle installing SQL Server CE. These Cab files are located on your development PC under the path

```
C:\Program Files\Microsoft Visual Studio NET\CompactFrameworkSDK\vx.xxxx\Windows CE
```

where *x.xxxx* is the version number of the .NET Compact Framework you have installed. As shown in Figure 21-2, you'll need to select the appropriate version of sql.ppc3.*xxx*.cab, sqlce.dev.ppc3.*xxx*.cab, and sqlce.ppc3.*xxx*.cab (where *xxx* is the processor type) for your device from either the wce300 or wce400 directories (depending upon the version of the target device's operating system) and then the processor type of your device (ARM, MIPS, SH3, etc.).

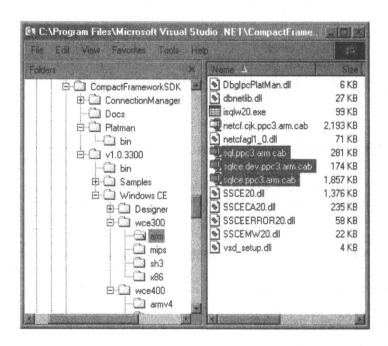

Figure 21-2. The Cab files used to install SQL Server CE on a iPaq Pocket PC

 NOTE *If the SQL Server CE components are already installed on a Pocket PC, they don't need to be reinstalled unless your application is built using a newer version of SQLCE.*

Installing Your Application

As with the .NET Compact Framework and SQL Server CE, your application will be deployed and installed as a Cab file. Later in this chapter, you'll learn how to create a Cab file for your application.

Selecting the Origin of Installation

The NET Compact Framework, SQL Server CE, and your application can be installed from a variety of sources such as the following:

- Directly on the device

- A CF card

- A PC through an ActiveSync connection

- The network

Regardless of the method you choose, each of the components, NETCF, SQL Server CE, and your application, are still being delivered as Cab files. The following sections discuss each of these four methods of installation.

Installing Your Application Manually on the Device

The easiest method to install a Cab file is to manually run the Cabs on the target device. Since this approach is based upon a set of manual steps, it's best suited for situations where technical support staff is involved, such as initial device setups and troubleshooting.

Follow these steps to perform a manual installation on a device:

1. Copy the Cab file to the device.

2. On the device, launch File Explorer.

3. Using File Explorer, navigate to the directory where you copied the Cab file.

4. Tap on the Cab file in File Explorer to launch the installation.

NOTE *Upon completion of the installation, the Cab file will be deleted from the device.*

Installing Your Application from a CF Card

CompactFlash cards, or CF cards, provide a good option for deploying applications and supporting framework. They include two key installation features. First, they offer an easy method for delivery of an application. Simply load the required Cab files onto a CF card and insert the card into the target device. Second, you can leverage the AutoRun capabilities offered through Windows CE, where you can automatically launch and run your setups when the CF card is installed in a device.

To create a CF-based installation, you need to follow these steps:

1. Create an AutoRun.exe file that will launch the Cab file to install your application.

2. Copy the AutoRun.exe file to the appropriate directory on the CF card.

3. Copy your Cab file to the CF card.

Creating AutoRun.exe

Creating an AutoRun application can be anything from simple and straightforward, to complex and involved, depending upon your installation needs. At its simplest, AutoRun only needs to launch your application's Cab file. The coding of AutoRun becomes more complex as you add functionality to check if your application is already installed, to check if either the .NET Compact Framework or SQL Server CE are present, to remove earlier versions of your application or supporting components, or to do any other tasks that you may need to perform to prepare a device for your application.

NOTE   *While AutoRun.exe can be built using SDE, this will only work in situations where you are sure that the target device already has the .NET Compact Framework installed. It's that old "what came first, the chicken or the egg" thing. If you are unsure about NETCF being resident on the device, you'll need to create AutoRun using eMbedded Visual C++. An example of creating an AutoRun application can be found in Pocket PC SDK.*

TIP   *Your AutoRun application will be launched when the CF card is installed or removed. To aid you in handling this, a command line argument of **install** is passed to your application when the card is inserted. No value is passed to your application when the card is removed.*

Copying AutoRun.exe to the CF Card

For the AutoRun functionality to work, your AutoRun application needs to be copied to a CPU-specific directory on the CF card. The directory name must match a predefined list of processor type values shown in Table 21-1.

Table 21-1. Windows CE Processor Values

PROCESSOR NAME	VALUE
ARM720	1824
Hitachi SH3	10003
Hitachi SH4	10005
MIPS R4XXX	4000
StrongARM SA11XX	2577

Figure 21-3 shows the contents of a CF card that includes directories for SH3, SH4, MIPS, and StrongArm devices.

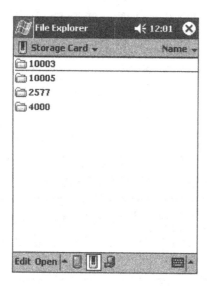

Figure 21-3. Storage card with directories for four separate processor types

Copying Cab Files to the CF Card

The final step to creating a CF card setup is to copy the Cab files to the card. In the example shown in Figure 21-3, you would need to copy the appropriate processor-specific Cab files for each of the four processor types, SH3, SH4, MIPS, and StrongArm, to their respective directories.

 TIP *Normally, Cab files are deleted after they are run. By marking them as read-only, you can circumvent this functionality, enabling you to reuse the same CF card for multiple installs.*

Installing Your Application from the Desktop

The process becomes slightly more complex if your application setup will be performed from a desktop PC, through a docking cradle to a device. In this situation, you'll need two setups, one for the desktop PC and one for the device. The device setup is the Cab file. The desktop setup is an executable that performs two functions. First, it copies your Cab files onto the desktop PC. Second, it starts Application Manager (CeAppMgr.exe). Application Manager then takes over to copy your Cab file to the device and subsequently launches the installation.

Application Manager handles adding and removing applications from devices as well as deleting application files from the PC that initiated the installation. You use an INI file to provide installation instructions to Application Manager.

The Application Manager INI File

The format for the Application Manager INI file is shown in Listing 21-1. This INI file is comprised of two sections, CEAppManager and component_name. The CEAppManager section defines general information about the file. The component_name section provides the details for your application's installation.

Listing 21-1. Format of the Application Manager INI File

```
[CEAppManager]
Version = 1.0
Component = component_name
```

```
[component_name]
Description = descriptive_name
{Uninstall = uninstall_name}
{IconFile = icon_filename}
{IconIndex = icon_index}
{DeviceFile = device_filename}
CabFiles = first cab {, second cab}
```

Table 21-2 provides a brief description of the sections and items that are found in an Application Manager INI file.

Table 21-2. Items in an Application Manager INI File

ITEM	DESCRIPTION
component_name	Identifies the name of the section for the application.
descriptive_name	Indicates the string that will appear in the Description field of the Application Manager when the user chooses the application.
uninstall_name	Identifies the application's uninstall registry key name. This must match the name found for the key HKLM\Software\Microsoft\Windows\CurrentVersion\Uninstall.
icon_filename	Identifies the desktop icon file.
icon_index	Specifies the numeric index into *icon_filename*.
device_filename	Indicates the filename that will be displayed along with the icon specified by *icon_filename*.
cab_filename	Specifies the filename of the Cab file(s) to be installed.

Launching Application Manager

Application Manager is launched by running CeAppMgr.exe, passing your INI file as a command line argument. This executable is installed along with Microsoft ActiveSync. You can start CeAppMgr.exe either manually or, as it is more commonly done, through a secondary desktop setup routine.

TIP *If you are experiencing problems with Application Manager, you can configure your system to provide a series of simple debugging messages as your INI file is processed. This is accomplished by adding the registry entry ReportErrors under **HKLM\Software\ Microsoft\Windows CE Services\AppMgr**. ReportErrors is a **DWORD** type with a value of 1 as shown in Figure 21-4.*

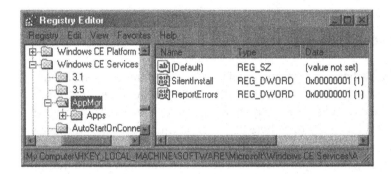

Figure 21-4. Adding a debugging setting to the registry

Creating a Desktop Setup

Desktop setups can be created with any application that allows you to copy your Cab files to a PC and then launch Application Manager. Two companies, InstallShield Software (http://www.installshield.com) and Wise Solutions (http://www.wise.com), provide commercial-grade installation development packages that provide this functionality. The downside of these products is that they're a tad pricey.

On the cheaper side of things, Spb Software House (http://www.softspb.com) offers a free setup product called EZSetup. While this application isn't as robust as the products from InstallShield and Wise, it functions quite well for most setups.

 NOTE *If you are going to write your own desktop setup, you'll need to find where Application Manager is located on the installation PC. The full name and path of Application Manager is stored in the registry value of HKLM\software\Microsoft\Windows\ CurrentVersion\App Paths\CEAppMgr.exe.*

Installing Your Application from the Network

Installs can be launched from a network as well. The easiest way to implement this is with Pocket Internet Explorer. Simply access a network-based Web page that contains a link to your application's Cab file. If needed, you can use Microsoft's Mobile Internet Toolkit to aid in the construction of this Web page. This approach works well in environments where the devices are connected via wireless networking.

Building Cab Files

Now that you have a basic understanding of Cab files, how they are used, and what needs to be installed with your application, let's turn our attention to the process of building Cab files. I'll start by showing you how to create a basic Cab file using Visual Studio .NET. From there I'll walk you through a detailed overview on creating more advanced setups that can be used to create shortcuts, make entries in the registry, handle processor-specific issues, and copy files to multiple directories.

Building Basic Cab Files

The easiest way to create a Cab file for your application is to let Visual Studio .NET do all of the work for you. One of the features with Smart Device Extensions is an additional menu item within the Visual Studio .NET interface that can be used to create simple Cab files.

To build a simple Cab file for an application, follow these steps:

1. Open the project for your application within Visual Studio .NET.

2. Select **Release** from the Solutions Configuration drop-down combo box, as shown in Figure 21-5.

Figure 21-5. Setting the solutions configuration

3. From the Build menu, select **Build Cab File**, as shown in Figure 21-6.

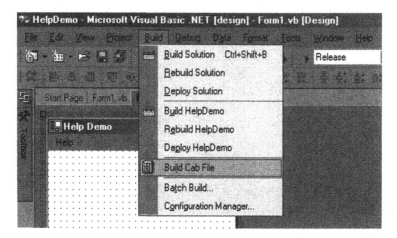

Figure 21-6. The Build Cab File menu item

4. Several command windows will be briefly displayed as your application is being built. When these windows are cleared, your Cab file is complete.

 NOTE *No message or acknowledgment is displayed to inform you that the Cab file has been generated. After the last of the command windows close, you'll simply be returned to the Visual Studio .NET interface.*

Basic Cab File Output

Output from this basic Cab building process is stored in a directory located under the directory where your application resides. You'll find the individual Cab files under the subdirectory \bin\release. An example of this hierarchy is shown in Figure 21-7.

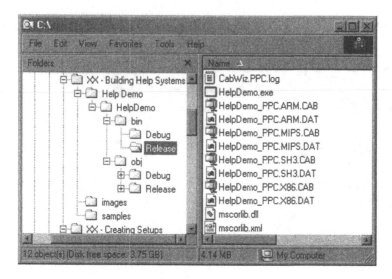

Figure 21-7. The location of Cab files generated through VS .NET

In the example shown in Figure 21-7, there were several Cabs generated, one for each of the target platform processor types. In this figure, you can see the four Cabs, one each for the StrongArm, MIPS, SH3, and X86 processor types. This is because the deployment device was a Pocket PC, and these four processor types are supported for that device.

At this point, you could copy the appropriate Cab file to your target device, open up File Explorer on the device, tap on your Cab file, and your application would be installed.

 CAUTION *Remember, for your application to be able to run, you'll need to install the .NET Compact Framework and, if required, SQL Server CE. Refer to the appropriate sections earlier in this chapter for additional instructions on installing these two products.*

As I mentioned at the start of this section, this is the easy method for installing applications. What you give up for this ease is flexibility and configurability.

If you are unsure where your project and its files are located on your development PC, you can use the following steps to determine their location:

1. Open your project in Visual Studio .NET.

2. In the Solutions Explorer window, right-click your project. A context-sensitive menu will be displayed.

3. From that menu select **Properties**. The Property Pages dialog box will be displayed.

4. From that dialog box open the **Common Properties** folder and select **General**.

5. Under the Information section of that page will be an entry for **Project Folder**. This is where your project is located. It's under this location that you'll find the output generated through the Cab build process.

Building Advanced Cab Files

The Cab file generated from within the Visual Studio .NET interface offers nothing more than the basic functionality of installing your application. If you need anything else, such as creating shortcuts or defining registry entries, you'll have to create a custom installation file. That is the topic of this section.

Cab file generation is controlled through definitions and settings provided in an INF file. INF files have the same format as INI files, that is to say they are divided into sections and directives. An example of the INF file format is shown in Listing 21-2.

Listing 21-2. A Section of an Example INF File

```
[Version]
Signature="$Windows NT$"
Provider="My Company"
CESignature="$Windows CE$"

[CEStrings]
AppName="HelpDemo"
InstallDir=%CE1%\%AppName%

[CEDevice]
VersionMin=3.00
VersionMax=3.99
```

The settings in an INF file are used to define the following:

- The name of the company that developed the application

- The versions of Windows CE on which the application will run

- Processor-specific settings

- Location of files that will be included in the Cab

- The target destinations for the files included in the Cab

- Registry entries

- Shortcuts for your application

INF files are used with the Cab Wizard application, Cabwiz.exe. This command line utility uses settings taken from your INF file to generate the individual processor-specific Cab files used to deploy your application.

Creating an INF File

The first step in creating custom installations is to create an INF file. As mentioned earlier in this chapter, INF files are similar to INI files. They're simple ASCII text files that can be edited with Microsoft Notepad. INF files are comprised of sections, each defining specific configurations for your Cab files.

INF Sections

INF files are divided up into the sections shown in Table 21-3. Some of these sections are required, others are optional.

Table 21-3. The Sections of an INF File

SECTION	DESCRIPTION
Version	Defines the company that created the application
CEStrings	Defines strings (variables) used to specify the name of your application and the default location where your application will be installed
Strings	Defines general purpose strings for use with the installation
CEDevice	Defines the device platforms that are supported by your application
DefaultInstall	Defines the default configurations for your application
CopyFiles	Defines the files that will be copied to the device
AddReg	Defines the registry entries that will be added for your application
CEShortcuts	Defines the shortcuts that will be created for use with your application
SourceDisksNames	Defines where source files used to create your Cab files are located
SourceDisksFiles	Defines the source files that will be included in your Cab files
DestinationDirs	Defines the directories on the device where your application will be installed

A detailed description of each of these sections follows.

The Version Section

While this section has three directives, as shown in Table 21-4, only the **Provider** directive is of any real interest, as the other two must always be set to predefined values. The **Provider** directive defines the name of the individual or company that created the application.

Table 21-4. Version Section Directives

DIRECTIVE	DESCRIPTION
Signature	The name of the operating system under which the Cab file was built.
Provider	The name of the individual or company that created the application.
CESignature	The name of the operating system on which the Cab being built will run. Use "$Windows CE$".

> **NOTE** *This section is mandatory and must be included in your INF file.*

The following is a sample Version section where the provider has been defined:

```
[Version]
Signature="$Windows NT$"
Provider="Larry Roof"
CESignature="$Windows CE$"
```

The CEStrings Section

This section defines two strings that are used elsewhere throughout an INF file: **AppName** and **InstallDir**, which are described in Table 21-5. Strings are nothing more than variables. When referenced within an INF file, their value is substituted in place of the name of the string.

Table 21-5. CEStrings Section Directives

DIRECTIVE	DESCRIPTION
AppName	The name of your application
InstallDir	The default installation directory for your application

NOTE *This section is mandatory and must be included in your INF file.*

A sample CEStrings section is shown in the following code:

```
[CEStrings]
AppName="Help Demo"
InstallDir=%CE1%\%AppName%
```

The Strings Section

While the CEStrings section defines two specific strings, **AppName** and **InstallDir**, the Strings section is used to define other strings for use within an INF file. There are no predefined strings in this section.

NOTE *This section is optional. Include this section only if you need to define your own strings.*

The following code shows a simple Strings section where a single string, **MyRegPath**, is defined. You could use the string **MyRegPath** elsewhere within your INF file to refer to Software\My Company\My Application through the format %MyRegPath%.

```
[Strings]
MyRegPath = Software\My Company\My Application
```

The CEDevice Section

The CEDevice section defines the platforms on which your application will run. Target platforms can be further restricted to particular processor types, and minimum and maximum versions of an operating system. Table 21-6 lists the directives that are supported under the CEDevice section.

Table 21-6. CEDevice Section Directives

DIRECTIVE	DESCRIPTION
ProcessorType	The processor types supported by your application
UnsupportedPlatforms	Platforms that aren't supported by your application
VersionMin	The minimum version of Windows CE under which your application will run
VersionMax	The maximum version of Windows CE under which your application will run

 NOTE *This section is optional. Include this section only if you need to restrict use of your application by platform, processor type, or operating system version.*

The following code shows an example of limiting your application for use with versions of Windows CE between 3.0 and 3.99:

```
[CEDevice]
VersionMin = 3.00
VersionMax = 3.99
```

While this first example is fairly straightforward, the CEDevice section can be confusing because of its syntax and flexibility. Not only does it allow you to define nonspecific settings, that is to say settings that apply to all devices, it also allows you to define settings for specific devices.

Listing 21-3 offers a small example of the flexibility provided by this section. Here two sections, CEDevice and CEDevice.SH3, are defined.

Listing 21-3. A More Involved CEDevice Section

```
[CEDevice]
VersionMin = 3.00
VersionMax = 4.99

[CEDevice.SH3]
ProcessorType = 10003
UnsupportedPlatforms = "HPC", "HPC Pro"
VersionMin = 3.00
VersionMax = 3.99
```

The CEDevice section defines settings that will be applied to all target devices. In this case, your application will run under versions of Windows CE between 3.0 and 4.99.

The CEDevice.SH3 section further restricts settings for SH3 processors, providing support only for versions of Windows CE between 3.0 and 3.99. It also excludes any HPC or HPC Pro devices, effectively limiting use to Pocket PCs.

NOTE *Specific directives, like those shown for the SH3 processor, take precedence over nonspecific directives listed under the CEDevice section.*

NOTE *For a list of processor types, refer to Table 21-1, which appears earlier in this chapter.*

The DefaultInstall Section

The DefaultInstall section is used to provide a variety of information on the installation process including the following:

- What files to install

- Where files should be installed

- What shortcuts to create

- What registry entries to create

- The name of a custom setup DLL, if used

- A list of self-registering DLLs

Table 21-7 provides a list of the directives supported under the DefaultInstall section.

Table 21-7. DefaultInstall Section Directives

DIRECTIVE	DESCRIPTION
CopyFiles	Defines one or more sections that list the files to install with your application. Each section listed is separated by a comma.
AddReg	Defines one or more sections that list the registry entries to be set. Each section listed is separated by a comma.
CEShortcuts	Defines one or more sections that list the shortcuts for use with your application. Each section listed is separated by a comma.
CESetupDLL	Indicates the name of the custom setup DLL that will be run when the Cab file is installed.
CESelfRegistering	Specifies the filenames of the self-registering DLLs that will be installed. Each filename is separated by a comma.

NOTE   *This section is mandatory and must be included in your INF file. Within this section two directives, **CopyFiles** and **AddReg**, are mandatory; the other three directives, **CEShortcuts**, **CESetupDLL**, and **CESelfRegistering**, are optional.*

Listing 21-4 shows an example DefaultInstall section. Within this section three subsequent sections, CommonFiles, SharedFiles, and RegistrySettings, are defined. The CommonFiles and SharedFiles sections each list a single file to be copied, HelpDemo.exe and PocketAccess.dll, respectively. The RegistrySettings section lists a single registry entry, RetryAttempts, that will be created under the HKEY_LOCAL_MACHINE root, using the path defined by the string **MyRegPath**.

Listing 21-4. An Example DefaultInstall Section

```
[DefaultInstall]
CopyFiles=CommonFiles,SharedFiles
AddReg=RegistrySettings

[CommonFiles]
HelpDemo.exe,,,0

[SharedFiles]
PocketAccessInterface.dll,,,0

[RegistrySettings]
HKLM,%MyRegPath%,RetryAttempts,0x00010001,5
```

The CopyFiles Section Syntax

Entries under a CopyFiles section follow this syntax:

```
destination file, source file,, flags
```

NOTE *The third argument in the copy file syntax is empty. Leave this argument blank.*

Table 21-8 describes the individual arguments that are used when defining items under the CopyFile section.

Table 21-8. Copy File Syntax

ITEM	DESCRIPTION
Destination File	Specifies the name of the file as it will appear on the device.
Source File	Indicates the name of the source file; same as the destination file if not provided.
Flags	Specifies actions to be performed while copying the file. Refer to Table 21-9 for supported flag values.

Table 21-9 lists the flag values for use for the third argument with items defined under the CopyFiles section.

Table 21-9. Supported Flag Values

VALUE	DESCRIPTION
0x00000001	Warns users if they try to skip copying this file after encountering an error
0x00000002	Prohibits the user from skipping the copying of this file
0x00000010	Doesn't overwrite an existing file
0x00000400	Copies a file only if a previous version of the file already exists
0x20000000	Doesn't copy file if existing file is newer
0x40000000	Ignores date on target file
0x80000000	Creates a reference for shared DLL

Listing 21-5 shows an example where two files are copied—the application and a shared library. For the application, HelpDemo.exe, the flag value of 0x20000000 is used so that the file is copied to the device only if it has a more recent timestamp than the existing copy of this file. For the shared file, PocketAccessInterface.dll, you specify that a reference be created.

Listing 21-5. An Example CopyFiles Section

```
[DefaultInstall]
CopyFiles=CommonFiles

[CommonFiles]
HelpDemo.exe,,,0x20000000

[SharedFiles]
PocketAccessInterface.dll,,,0x80000000
```

The AddReg Section Syntax

Entries under the AddReg section follow this syntax:

```
registry root name, subkey, value name, flags, value
```

Table 21-10 describes the individual arguments that are used with entries in the AddReg section.

Table 21-10. Registry Entry Syntax

ITEM	DESCRIPTION
registry root name	Indicates the root under which this entry will be made. Refer to Table 21-9 for details.
subkey	Indicates the subkey under which this entry will be made.
value name	Specifies the name under which this entry will be made. If this item is omitted, the default registry value will be used.
flags	Specifies information about this key. Refer to Table 21-10 for details.
value	Indicates the value for this entry.

Table 21-11 provides a list of the registry root values. These values define the registry root under which an entry will be made.

Table 21-11. Registry Root Values

VALUE	DESCRIPTION
HKCR	HKEY_CLASSES_ROOT
HKCU	HKEY_CURRENT_USER
HKLM	HKEY_LOCAL_MACHINE

Table 21-12 provides a list of registry flag values that are used to define the data type for a registry entry.

Table 21-12. Registry Flag Values

VALUE	DESCRIPTION
0x00000000	Specifies REG_SZ data type
0x00000001	Specifies REG_BINARY data type
0x00000002	Indicates not to overwrite existing registry entries
0x00010000	Specifies REG_MULTI_SZ data type
0x00010001	Specifies REG_DWORD data type

The following code snippet shows an example of creating a registry entry for RetryAttempts. The flag value of 0x00010001 signifies that the data type for this entry will be DWORD. The value is set to 5.

```
[DefaultInstall]
AddReg=RegistrySettings

[RegistrySettings]
HKLM,%MyRegPath%,RetryAttempts,0x00010001,5
```

The CEShortcuts Section Syntax

Entries under the CEShortcuts section follow this syntax:

```
shortcut_ name, shortcut_type_flag, target_file/path, standard_destination_path
```

Table 21-13 describes the individual arguments that are used with entries in the CEShortcuts section.

Table 21-13. Shortcut Syntax

ITEM	DESCRIPTION
shortcut_filename	The shortcut name
shortcut_type_flag	Numeric value (0 for shortcut to a file, any other value for shortcut to a folder)
target_file/path	The destination file or folder.
standard_destination_path	Either a %CEx% or %InstallDir% path

In the example shown in the following code snippet, a shortcut for Help Demo is created. The shortcut is for a file, as signified by the second argument value of 0. It will point to the file HelpDemo.exe.

```
[DefaultInstall]
CEShortcuts=Shortcuts

[Shortcuts]
Help Demo,0,HelpDemo.exe
```

The SourceDisksNames Section

The SourceDisksNames section specifies the location, the directory or directories, where your source files reside on your development PC. Each directory is associated with an ID. This ID is in turn used in the SourceDisksFiles section to define the path for the files that comprise your application.

The SourceDisksNames section supports platform-specific settings, which enable you to define separate locations for the source files required by the various platforms your application supports. Table 21-14 lists the directives that can be used under this section.

Table 21-14. SourceDisksNames Section Directives

DIRECTIVE	DESCRIPTION
disk_id	This value is associated with a directory. It will be subsequently used in the SourceDisksFiles section.
comment	A literal string that describes a location.
path	The path to the source directory.

NOTE   *This section is mandatory and must be included in your INF file.*

The following lines of code show an example of a SourceDisksNames section. In this example, three paths are defined. The first path, with the disk ID of 1, specifies general files that will be installed on all systems regardless of their processor type. This typically would be used for media files, help files, and configuration files. The second and third paths, with the disk ID of 2, specify directories that contain processor-specific files.

```
[SourceDisksNames]
1=,"Help Demo - General",,"C:\Help Demo"
[SourceDisksNames.ARM]
2=,"Help Demo - ARM",,"C:\Help Demo\ARM"
[SourceDisksNames.SH3]
2=,"Help Demo - SH3",,"C:\Help Demo\SH3"
```

The SourceDisksFiles Section

The SourceDisksFiles section specifies the files that are required by your application. Each entry in this section defines a file and the path where that file resides. Paths for files are specified using disk IDs defined in the SourceDisksNames section.

This section supports platform-specific settings that enable you to define separate locations for the source files required with various platforms. Table 21-15 lists the directives that can be used under this section.

Table 21-15. SourceDisksFiles Section Directives

DIRECTIVE	DESCRIPTION
filename	Name of file including extension. Long filenames must be included in quotes.
disk_id	Directory ID number as defined in the SourceDisksNames section.

NOTE   *This section is mandatory and must be included in your INF file.*

The following code snippet demonstrates including both general files, along with platform-specific files. The general file, HelpDemo.htm, will be copied from the path defined by disk ID 1. The processor-specific file, HelpDemo.exe, will be copied from the path defined by disk ID 2.

```
[SourceDisksFiles]
HelpDemo.htm=1
[SourceDisksFiles.ARM]
HelpDemo.exe=2
[SourceDisksFiles.SH3]
HelpDemo.exe=2
```

NOTE   *Both disk IDs need to be defined in the SourceDisksNames section before they can be used here.*

The DestinationDirs Section

The DestinationDirs section defines where files will be copied to on the target device. Table 21-16 lists the directives that can be used under this section.

Table 21-16. DestinationDirs Section Directives

DIRECTIVE	DESCRIPTION
file_list_section	The section names referenced by CopyFiles definitions under the DefaultInstall section
subdir	The directory on the device where all of the files from a particular section will be copied

NOTE   *This section is mandatory and must be included in your INF file.*

The following code demonstrates defining destination locations for the files defined under the CommonFiles and SharedFiles sections. Both of these sections must be declared by the CopyFiles entry in the DefaultInstall section before they can be used here.

```
[DestinationDirs]
CommonFiles = 0,%CE1%\Help Demo
SharedFiles = 0,%CE2%
```

The entries in the DestinationDirs section make use of macro strings. Macro strings act as variables for specific directories on a target device. These predefined strings are used to handle localization issues. In the preceding example, the macro string **%CE1%** is used. Under English-based Pocket PC devices, this string points to the Program Files directory. When this macro substitution is performed within the INF file, the common files will be copied to Program Files\Help Demo. The section macro string, **%CE2%**, refers to the Windows directory under English-based versions of the Pocket PC.

Macro Strings

Macro strings are for all practical purposes nothing more than variables that you can use within your INF files. They can be substituted in any place that you would use directory paths. Macro strings are predefined for you. They handle localization issues and will contain the appropriate value based upon the language on which the target device is configured. Don't assume all your users will have English versions of the PPC O/S installed. It's an assumption that will certainly come back to haunt you.

The value of macro strings will vary depending upon the version and language of the Windows CE operating system under which your application is running. Table 21-17 lists the English language equivalents for macro strings on Pocket PC 2002 and Pocket PC 2000 devices.

Table 21-17. English Language Macro Strings

STRING	POCKET PC 2002	POCKET PC 2000
%CE1%	\Program Files	\Program Files
%CE2%	\Windows	\Windows
%CE4%	\Windows\Startup	\Windows\Startup
%CE5%	\My Documents	\My Documents
%CE6%	Not applicable	\Program Files\Accessories
%CE7%	Not applicable	\Program Files\Communication
%CE8%	\Program Files\Games	\Program Files\Games
%CE11%	\Windows\Start Menu\Programs	\Windows\Start Menu\Programs
%CE12%	Not applicable	\Windows\Start Menu\Programs\Accessories
%CE13%	Not applicable	\Windows\Start Menu\Programs\Communications
%CE14%	\Windows\Start Menu\Programs\ Games	\Windows\Start Menu\Programs\Games
%CE15%	\Windows\Fonts	\Windows\Fonts
%CE17%	\Windows\Start Menu	\Windows\Start Menu

Platform-Specific Settings

Several INF file sections support platform-specific settings, enabling you to further define configurations as needed for various target platforms. The INF file sections that support this feature are

- CEDevice

- DefaultInstall

- SourceDisksNames

- SourceDisksFiles

To specify settings for a particular platform, you include the name of the platform as part of the section name. The example shown in Listing 21-6 demonstrates four platform-specific sections, one each for ARM, SH3, MIPS, and X86 (the emulator).

Listing 21-6. Example of Platform-Specific Settings

```
[DefaultInstall]
CopyFiles=CommonFiles

[DefaultInstall.ARM]
CopyFiles=ARMFiles

[DefaultInstall.SH3]
CopyFiles=SH3Files

[DefaultInstall.MIPS]
CopyFiles=MIPSFiles

[DefaultInstall.X86]
CopyFiles=X86Files
```

NOTE *Platform-specific settings are used in conjunction with general settings as shown in Listing 21-6, where there is a general section for DefaultInstall along with more specific sections for each of the four processor types.*

Building Your Cab Files

After creating your INF file, you're ready to generate your Cab files. I say files because you typically would generate a set of Cab files, one for each of the target processors. Cab files are creating using the Cab Wizard command line utility. The filename for this utility is Cabwiz.exe. You'll find the Cabwiz utility under

```
\Program Files\Microsoft Visual Studio .NET\CompactFrameworkSDK\vx.x.xxxx\bin
```

where *x.xxxx* is the version of NETCF installed on your development machine.

 NOTE *For the Cab Wizard executable to operate correctly, Cabwiz.exe must be located in the same directory as Makecab.exe and Cabwiz.ddf.*

The command line syntax for the Cab Wizard utility is

```
Cabwiz.exe "inf_file" [/dest dest_directory] [/err error_file] [/cpu
  platform_label [platform_label]]
```

Table 21-18 details each of the arguments to the Cab Wizard command line.

Table 21-18. Syntax of the Cab Wizard Utility

ARGUMENT	DESCRIPTION
inf_file	Specifies the full path and filename to your INF file.
/dest	Indicates the directory where the Cab files will be created. If no directory is specified, the Cab files will be created in the same directory as the INF file.
/err	Specifies the filename where all build warnings and errors will be written. If an error file isn't provided, then all warnings and errors will be displayed as message boxes.
/cpu	Creates a separate Cab file for each platform label that you specify. Each label you specify must match platform-specific sections you have defined in your INF file; this must be the last argument on the command line.

Following is a demonstration of the Cab Wizard syntax:

```
cabwiz.exe "c:\help demo\HelpDemo.inf" /dest "c:\help demo\cabs" /err
  "HelpDemoBuild.err" /cpu arm sh3
```

In this example, the INF file is c:\help demo\HelpDemo.inf. The destination where the Cabs will be placed is c:\help demo\cabs. Any warnings or errors generated by the Cab Wizard will be placed in HelpDemoBuild.err. Two Cabs will be produced: one for ARM processors and another for SH3 processors.

NOTE *Cabwiz.exe must be called using its full path in order for it to correctly run.*

Step-by-Step Tutorial: Examining a Basic Cab Build

Earlier in this chapter you were shown how to create a basic setup from within the Visual Studio .NET IDE. When you run a build from within Visual Studio .NET, two files, an INF and batch file, are automatically generated behind the scenes. These files provide a good starting point for understanding how INF files work and how the Cab Wizard is used to produce Cabs.

In this tutorial, I am going to walk you through both of these files starting with the INF file.

Step 1: Viewing the Automatically Generated INF File

The INF file that is generated when you select **Build Cab File** from the Build menu of the Visual Studio .NET IDE is created in the directory \obj\release under your project directory, as shown in Figure 21-8.

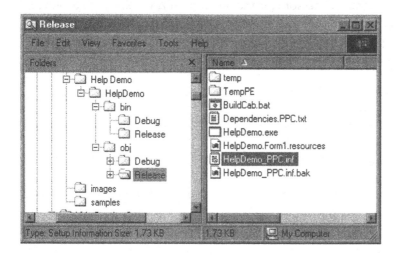

Figure 21-8. The INF file generated through the build process

Analyzing this INF file serves two purposes. First, it provides a good introduction to the layout of INF files. Second, it provides you with a good starting point for construction of your own INF files. To aid you in this learning process, I'll walk you through the contents of an INF file generated through Visual Studio .NET.

The first section of the auto-generated INF file is the Version section. All of these directives will be the same regardless of the project being built.

```
[Version]
Signature="$Windows NT$"
Provider="My Company"
CESignature="$Windows CE$"
```

In the CEStrings section, the **AppName** string is set to the name of your project. The **InstallDir** string is set to a subdirectory of your project name appended to **%CE1%** (\Program Files for English language devices).

```
[CEStrings]
AppName="HelpDemo"
InstallDir=%CE1%\%AppName%
```

In the CEDevice section, the **VersionMin** and **VersionMax** directives are used to limit your application to Windows CE versions 3.00 to 3.99.

```
[CEDevice]
VersionMin=3.00
VersionMax=3.99
```

There are five DefaultInstall sections, one general purpose section, DefaultInstall, and four processor-specific sections for ARM, SH3, MIPS, and X86 processors. Each of these sections contains a **CopyFiles** directive, which defines a subsequent section in the INF file. The processor-specific sections also have a **CESetupDLL** directive that defines vsd_setup.dll.

```
[DefaultInstall]
CopyFiles=Files.Common

[DefaultInstall.ARM]
CopyFiles=Files.ARM
CESetupDLL=vsd_setup.dll

[DefaultInstall.SH3]
CopyFiles=Files.SH3
CESetupDLL=vsd_setup.dll
```

```
[DefaultInstall.MIPS]
CopyFiles=Files.MIPS
CESetupDLL=vsd_setup.dll

[DefaultInstall.X86]
CopyFiles=Files.X86
CESetupDLL=vsd_setup.dll
```

The SourceDisksNames section defines the location of the project directory.

```
[SourceDisksNames]
1=,"Common1",,"C:\HelpDemo\obj\Release\"
```

The four processor-specific SourceDisksNames sections define the location for the ARM, SH3, MIPS, and X86-specific directories.

```
[SourceDisksNames.ARM]
2=,"ARM_Setup",,"C:\Program Files\Microsoft Visual Studio
.NET\CompactFrameworkSDK\v1.0.3300\Windows CE\wce300\ARM\"

[SourceDisksNames.SH3]
3=,"SH3_Setup",,"C:\Program Files\Microsoft Visual Studio
 .NET\CompactFrameworkSDK\v1.0.3300\Windows CE\wce300\SH3\"

[SourceDisksNames.MIPS]
4=,"MIPS_Setup",,"C:\Program Files\Microsoft Visual Studio
.NET\CompactFrameworkSDK\v1.0.3300\Windows CE\wce300\MIPS\"

[SourceDisksNames.X86]
5=,"X86_Setup",,"C:\Program Files\Microsoft Visual Studio
.NET\CompactFrameworkSDK\v1.0.3300\Windows CE\wce300\X86\"
```

The SourceDisksFiles section defines the single executable to include in the Cab.

```
[SourceDisksFiles]
HelpDemo.exe=1
```

The four processor-specific SourceDisksFiles sections define the setup DLL, vsd_setup.dll.

```
[SourceDisksFiles.ARM]
vsd_setup.dll=2

[SourceDisksFiles.SH3]
vsd_setup.dll=3

[SourceDisksFiles.MIPS]
vsd_setup.dll=4

[SourceDisksFiles.X86]
vsd_setup.dll=5
```

The DestinationDirs section defines where to install both the general and processor-specific files on the target device. All of the files will be installed into the directory defined by the string **%InstallDir%**, which is defined as **%CE1%\%AppName%**, where **%CE1%** is \Program Files (again on English language devices) and **%AppName%** is HelpDemo, resulting in the installation directory of \Program Files\HelpDemo.

```
[DestinationDirs]
Files.Common=0,%InstallDir%
Files.ARM=0,%InstallDir%
Files.SH3=0,%InstallDir%
Files.MIPS=0,%InstallDir%
Files.X86=0,%InstallDir%
```

Finally, a set of sections define the CopyFiles directives for both general and processor-specific files.

```
[Files.Common]
HelpDemo.exe,,,0

[Files.ARM]
vsd_setup.dll,,,0

[Files.SH3]
vsd_setup.dll,,,0

[Files.MIPS]
vsd_setup.dll,,,0

[Files.X86]
vsd_setup.dll,,,0
```

Step 2: Viewing the Automatically Generated Batch File

At the same time that Visual Studio .NET generates the INF file, it also creates a batch file, which is used to build your Cab file. This batch file, BuildCab.bat, is created in the same directory as the INF file.

The BuildCab.bat file contains a single statement to run Cabwiz.exe. The statement starts with a full path reference to Cabwiz.exe. Next is the name of the INF file, HelpDemo_PPC.inf, that was generated by Visual Studio .NET. Following the INF file is the **/dest** argument, which specifies the location where the Cab files will be created. The **/err** argument is next, indicating where errors will be written. Finally, the **/cpu** argument specifies the generation of four Cabs, one each for ARM, SH3, MIPS, and X86 processors.

```
"C:\Program Files\Microsoft Visual Studio
 .NET\CompactFrameworkSDK\v1.0.3300\Windows CE\..\bin\..\bin\cabwiz.exe"
"C:\HelpDemo\obj\Release\HelpDemo_PPC.inf" /dest "C:\HelpDemo\bin\Release" /err
CabWiz.PPC.log /cpu ARM SH3 MIPS X86
```

The Easy Way to Building Custom Cabs

The files mention in this tutorial, the INF and batch files that are automatically generated by Visual Studio .NET, provide you with a good starting point for creating your own custom setups. All that you need to do is modify the files to suit your needs and then rerun the batch file to produce your own custom Cab files.

Step-by-Step Tutorial: Building a Custom Installation

This next tutorial walks you through the complete process of building a custom Cab installation from scratch. It includes instructions on creating an INF file, generating Cab files, building an INI file to use with Application Manager, constructing a desktop setup, and finally running the complete setup.

The application that will be used for this demonstration is the Help Demo application that I show you how to create in Chapter 19.

Step 1: Building the INF File

The first step in the process is to construct the INF file that will be used to generate the Cab files. The Cab files will in turn be used to perform the installation on the target device.

The Help Demo application used for this sample is simple. It's comprised of a single executable, HelpDemo.exe, and a single help file, Demo.htm.

In this setup, the executable will be copied to the directory \Program Files\Help Demo. The help file will be copied to the \Windows directory. A shortcut for the Help Demo executable will be added to the Start menu.

Creating the File

INF files can be created with Microsoft Notepad. After starting a new file, save the file with the extension .inf.

Adding the Version Section

The first section to add to the INF file is the Version section shown in the following code. In this example, I've set the provider directive to my name.

```
[Version]
Signature="$Windows NT$"
Provider="Larry Roof"
CESignature="$Windows CE$"
```

Adding the CEStrings Section

Add the following code to the CEString section of your INF file. The **AppName** string is set to **Help Demo**, the name of the example application. The **InstallDir** string is defined as **%CE1%\%AppName%**. The string **CE1** translates to \Program Files under English language devices. The two strings combined together result in a path of \Program Files\Help Demo.

```
[CEStrings]
AppName="Help Demo"
InstallDir=%CE1%\%AppName%
```

Adding a CEDevice Section

Add the following code to the CEDevice section of your INF file. These settings limit the versions of Windows CE under which the Help Demo application will run to versions 3.00 to 3.99.

```
[CEDevice]
VersionMin = 3.00
VersionMax = 3.99
```

Adding a DefaultInstall Section

The DefaultInstall section is the most complicated of this example INF file. Add the code shown in Listing 21-7 to your INF file.

Listing 21-7. The DefaultInstall Section

```
[DefaultInstall]
CopyFiles=AppFiles,WindowsFiles
CEShortcuts=Shortcuts

[AppFiles]
HelpDemo.exe,,,0x20000000

[WindowsFiles]
Demo.htm,,,0x20000000

[Shortcuts]
Help Demo,0,HelpDemo.exe
```

In this code, the **CopyFiles** directive is used to define two sections, AppFiles and WindowsFiles, which will list the files used by the Help Demo application. The files listed under AppFiles will end up in the application directory on the device. The files under WindowsFiles will be copied to the Windows directory.

The **CEShortcuts** directive defines the Shortcuts section where the shortcut HelpDemo.exe will be defined.

Under the AppFiles section is the file HelpDemo.exe. The WindowsFiles section contains the file Demo.htm. Both of these files are configured so that they won't overwrite newer versions. This is accomplished by setting the flags argument to 0x20000000.

In the Shortcuts section, a single shortcut is defined for the Help Demo executable.

Adding a SourceDisksNames Section

The following code defines the SourceDisksName section for your INF file. The directory where HelpDemo.exe and Demo.htm reside, C:\Help Demo, is specified in this section.

```
[SourceDisksNames]
1=,"Help Demo - General",,"C:\Help Demo"
```

Adding a SourceDisksFiles Section

The following code defines the SourceDisksFiles section for your INF file. Here you specify two files, HelpDemo.exe and Demo.htm, for copying to the target device. The location of both of these files is 1, which was defined under the SourceDisksNames section as C:\Help Demo.

```
[SourceDisksFiles]
HelpDemo.htm=1
Demo.htm=1
```

Adding a DestinationDirs Section

You need to add the code that follows to your INF file to define the DestinationDirs section. This section specifies where the application files defined under the CopyFiles section will be copied. Remember, the CopyFiles section is part of the DefaultInstall section. The files defined under the AppFiles section will be copied to \Program Files\Help Demo. Those files defined under the WindowsFiles section will be copied to \Windows.

```
[DestinationDirs]
AppFiles = 0,%CE1%\Help Demo
WindowsFiles = 0,%CE2%
```

Step 2: Generating the Cab Files

With the INF file complete, you are now ready to generate the Cab files for your application. Three Cab files will be created, one each for the ARM, SH3, and MIPS processors.

To build your Cab file, execute the command line shown here:

```
"C:\Program Files\Microsoft Visual Studio
.NET\CompactFrameworkSDK\v1.0.3300\Windows CE\..\bin\..\bin\cabwiz.exe"
"C:\Help Demo\Help Demo.inf"
/dest "C:\Help Demo\cabs\"
/err CabWizardErros.log
/cpu ARM SH3 MIPS
```

NOTE *In the preceding example I have broken the command line into separate lines to make it easier to read. In actuality this should be a single command line.*

Executing this line will produce three Cab files, one for each processor type. You could stop here and simply copy the appropriate Cab file to the target device and launch the installation manually. For this example, though, you are going to take this a step further and create a desktop setup program.

Step 3: Creating the Application Manager INI File

The next part of this tutorial covers creating an INI file that will provide Application Manager with information on your application. Using Microsoft Notepad, create the file Demo.ini. In this file, place the contents shown here:

```
[CEAppManager]
Version = 1.0
Component = HelpDemo

[HelpDemo]
Description = Help Demo
CabFiles = HelpDemo.cab
```

This INI file is divided into two sections. The first section is the required CEAppManager section. It contains the Version and the Component keys. The Component key references the section HelpDemo, which provides details on the application.

The HelpDemo section contains two keys, Description and CabFiles. Description provides simple text that will be displayed to the user. CabFiles lists the Cab file that was produced under step 2 earlier in this tutorial.

NOTE *This setup assumes that the .NET Compact Framework already exists on the target device. If that wasn't the case, you would need to add the NETCF Cab file to this INI file.*

Step 4: Monitoring Application Manager

When you install your application from the desktop using Application Manager, ActiveSync, which is handling the installation, stores messages generated from the installation in the file wcesetup.log. This file is created in a temporary directory.

If the installation is successful, the log file is copied to the directory in which ActiveSync is installed. If the installation fails, the file is copied to the directory specified by the TMP environment variable. This file can be very useful when debugging a setup routine.

Step 5: Building a Desktop Setup

The final step in this tutorial is the building of a desktop setup. This setup will be run on a PC and will facilitate the installation of your application on a device that is connected to that PC.

As mentioned earlier in this chapter, you can use a variety of third-party installation utilities that can be employed to create desktop setups. All that a utility of this type needs to do is copy files to the users' PCs and then launch Application Manager, passing your INI file.

For this part of the example, you're going to use EzSetup, a free setup utility from Spb Software House (http://www.softsb.com). I've chosen EzSetup for use here as it is simple to use, provides the basic functionality that is needed in most applications, and, well, is free.

EzSetup uses a command line interface to generate setups. The command line syntax for EzSetup is

```
ezsetup -l language -i inifilename -r readme.txt -e eula.txt -o output.exe
```

Table 21-19 provides descriptions for each argument in the EzSetup command line.

Table 21-19. Syntax Used by EzSetup

ARGUMENT	DESCRIPTION
-l	Specifies the language of the installation program. Valid values are English, German, and French.
-i	Specifies the INI file that will be fed to Application Manager. The Cab files specified in this INI file must reside in the same directory.
-r	Specifies a text file that contains a readme message for the user. This message will be displayed on the first page of the installation dialog box.
-e	Specifies a text file that contains your end-user licensing agreement. This message will be displayed on the second page of the installation dialog box. The user won't be able to continue without accepting the agreement.
-o	Specifies the name of the setup executable that will be generated.

Creating a Readme File

Using Microsoft Notepad, create a simple readme file. Name this file **readme.txt.**

Creating a EULA File

Using Microsoft Notepad, create a simple eula file. Name this file **eula.txt.**

Generating the Setup

Both the readme file (readme.txt for this example) and end-user licensing agreement file (eula.txt) are then used to produce the setting using the command line shown here:

```
ezsetup -l english -i demo.ini -r readme.txt -e eula.txt -o DemoSetup.exe
```

 CAUTION   *EzSetup requires a space on both sides of any equal signs (=) in your INI file, even though Application Manager doesn't.*

If you have done everything correctly up to this point, EzSetup will produce the setup application DemoSetup.exe.

Step 6: Running the Setup

Finally, you are ready to test your setup. Launch DemoSetup.exe. After it starts, the readme file instructions you defined in readme.txt will be displayed. An example of this is shown in Figure 21-9.

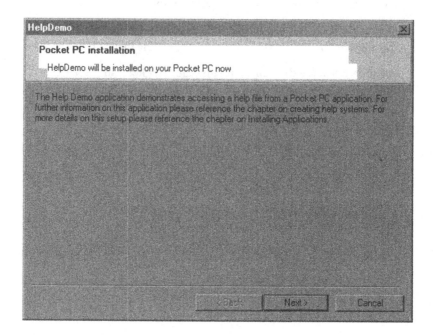

Figure 21-9. The readme page of the EzSetup installation

Clicking the **Next** button displays your licensing agreement. Figure 21-10 demonstrates this part of the installation process.

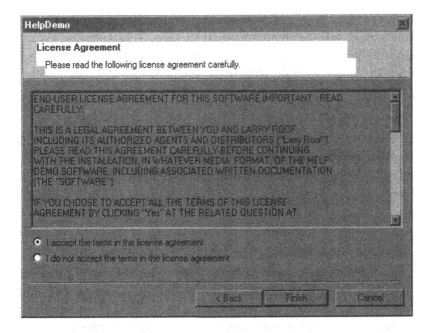

Figure 21-10. The license agreement page from the EzSetup installation

Accepting the agreement and clicking **Finish** will initiate the installation. Here, Application Manager is called to handle the device installation as shown in Figure 21-11.

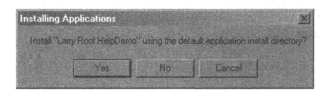

Figure 21-11. Application Manager handling the installation

A Note on Testing Setups

Many developers make the mistake of testing their installation routines on their development PC and development device. This is a sure recipe for disaster. While it's fine to perform initial testing on your development systems, final testing should be performed on what I refer to as "vanilla" systems. A vanilla system is just that, a plain PC or device that don't have any development tools or components installed. It should be a simple PC, ActiveSync, and a device configuration.

Testing with this configuration ensures that your installation will perform correctly regardless of the existing environment on the target PC and device. Using this approach will correctly test for situations where the .NET Compact Framework and SQL Server CE components are required by your application but don't exist on the target device.

 TIP *If you don't have a second device to use to test your installations, you can reset your existing device back to its factory settings when testing. This will remove any existing components from your device. You may want to back up your device before performing the reset so that you can easily return it to its original state.*

Summary

Setups are the last thing you do in developing an application and the first thing that the user experiences in using your application. A good setup can "set the table" for your application, giving the user a feeling of confidence and putting everything in its place for your application to run correctly. A bad setup can frustrate the user, hinder the performance of your application, and even cause the best written applications to fail.

Setups for the Pocket PC are more complicated, as they frequently contain two components, desktop and device. While the build functionality offered through the Visual Studio .NET interface is simple to use, you'll find that it will frequently not meet your needs. As this chapter demonstrates, custom installations are easy to build once you develop an understanding of the process and the format of the configuration files.

CHAPTER 22

Producing Reports

WHEN MICROSOFT INTRODUCED Pocket PCs, the concept of mobile computing took a tremendous leap forward. Suddenly, Windows developers had a powerful portable environment within which they could extend enterprise solutions. The Pocket PC's hardware prowess combined with the common Windows look-and-feel of the interface was appealing to both developers and users alike.

Developing applications for Pocket PCs forces desktop developers to revisit, reconsider, and adjust their programming practices. Not least among these adjustments is the limited support offered through the Pocket PC operating system and the Pocket PC development tools for reporting and printing.

In this chapter, I'll walk you through some techniques and third-party products you may use to implement reporting and printing in your mobile applications. I'll show you

- The basics of generating reports through the NETCF

- How to create HTML-based reports and display those reports

- PrinterCE.NetCF, a third-party component that enables your applications to send output to both network and portable printers

- HP's Mobile Printing Toolkit for .NET, which makes it simple to send reports to printers via your device's IR port and Bluetooth, and over the network

- Report CE, a report formatting and generation utility for the Pocket PC

The .NET Compact Framework offers nothing in the form of reporting tools. There is no compact equivalent to Crystal Reports, nor any printing functionality provided.

In addressing these shortcomings, developers have two options: 1) code around the limitation, or 2) purchase a third-party solution. In this chapter, we'll look at both approaches. First, using the roll-your-own code approach, you'll see how you can combine HTML and the NETCF to produce reports that users will view on their Pocket PC device. Next, we'll look at a printer component from Field Software that allows you to create and send print content to both mobile and network-based printers. Hewlett-Packard also offers a printing product. I'll show you the basics of working with that product as well. Finally, we'll look at a report generation tool, Report CE, that can be leveraged from your Pocket PC applications. While it's not Crystal Reports, it certainly goes a long way in making up for NETCF's absence of reporting capabilities.

Producing HTML Reports

If you have ever worked with ASP or ASP.NET, you'll be right at home with this form of Pocket PC reporting. Simply stated, it uses HTML to format reports. This HTML content can in turn be displayed either in Pocket IE or within your application through a third-party HTML viewer control.

This approach to reporting is simple. It's a three-step process:

1. Retrieve the data that will appear in your report from the data source.

2. Format the report by combining your data with HTML tags.

3. Display the HTML content to the user.

The HTML report approach is best suited for situations in which you want to provide a rich, device-based report. Note that I'm not talking about printing here—this is an on-device approach. That's just one of the limitations of HTML reports. The other has to do with the viewing limitation imposed by the Pocket PC itself. Developing HTML content that displays well on its small screen is at best a challenge. The key to this whole approach is creating HTML content that's easy to view on a screen that's 240×320 pixels.

The following section walks you through the complete process of HTML reporting, from retrieving the data, to producing the HTML content, and finally to displaying the content. In this example, you'll be displaying the report using Pocket IE. As I mentioned earlier, this is one of two ways to display HTML content. The second way is with IntelliProg's HTMLViewer control. There is a sample showing this optional method immediately following the discussion of the HTML Reporting sample.

Examining the HTML Reporting Sample

Figure 22-1 shows the sample report produced by the HTML Reporting sample application as it appears within Pocket IE.

Figure 22-1. The HTML-based report as it's displayed within Pocket IE

NOTE   *You'll find the HTML Reporting sample application under the **Chapter 22** folder in the **Samples** folder for this book. See Appendix D for more information on accessing and loading the sample applications.*

The key to the HTML Reporting sample application is the **Click** event procedure for the **Display Report** button. Listing 22-1 displays the contents of this procedure. This procedure is nothing more than a series of subroutine and function calls:

- **RetrieveData**—Gathers the data

- **ProductReport**—Formats the report

- **SaveReport**—Saves the report to a file

- **DisplayReport**—Displays the report in Pocket IE

Note that the calls to this quartet of routines are inserted between two simple configurations that control the cursor. By toggling the wait cursor on and off, you provide the user with a visual indicator that the report generation is in progress.

Listing 22-1. The Contents of the Display Report Button Click Event

```vb
Private Sub btnDisplayReport_Click(ByVal sender As System.Object, _
  ByVal e As System.EventArgs) Handles btnDisplayReport.Click

  Dim ReportFile As String = "\Windows\Start Menu\Programs\Apress\report.html"
  Dim ReportHtml As String

' Let the user know that there is a process in progress.
  Cursor.Current = Cursors.WaitCursor

' Retrieve the data.
  RetrieveData()

' Generate the report.
  ReportHtml = ProduceReport()

' Save the report.
  SaveReport(ReportHtml, ReportFile)

' Display the report.
  DisplayReport(ReportFile)

' We are done so reset the cursor.
  Cursor.Current = Cursors.Default

End Sub
```

Gathering the Data

The HTML Reporting sample application gets its data from a SQL Server CE database. In this case, a SQLServerCE DataReader is loaded with the contents of the Customers table from the NorthwindDemo database. Listing 22-2 shows the code used to accomplish this task.

Listing 22-2. Retrieving Customer Data from the Database

```vb
Sub RetrieveData()

' Open the connection.
  cn = New _
    System.Data.SqlServerCe.SqlCeConnection( _
    "Data Source=\Windows\Start Menu\Programs\Apress\NorthwindDemo.sdf")
  cn.Open()
```

```
' Configure and execute the command.
  cmd.CommandText = "SELECT * FROM Customers"
  cmd.Connection = cn
  dr = cmd.ExecuteReader

End Sub
```

The process used to retrieve the data is straightforward. A SqlCeCommand selects all of the records from the Customers table. The DataReader in turn is loaded with these records.

NOTE *For more on retrieving data from a SQL Server CE database, see Chapters 11 and 13.*

Formatting the Report

The data that's held within the DataReader is in turn used to produce the HTML content of your report. As I mentioned earlier in this chapter, the HTML reporting option is very similar to ASP or ASP.NET development in the fact that you're using HTML tags combined with your data to create an HTML document.

Listing 22-3 demonstrates this process. The ProduceReport routine shown in this listing has three sections. The first section produces the document header, that is to say, the opening HTML tags. This includes tags for the document itself, the body, a header, a table, and the table's header row.

Listing 22-3. Generating the HTML Content

```
Function ProduceReport() As String
  Dim HTML As String

' Build the report header.
  HTML = "<HTML>"
  HTML += "<BODY>"
  HTML += "<H1><FONT COLOR=Blue>Customer List</FONT></H1>"
  HTML += "<TABLE>"
  HTML += "<TR>"
  HTML += "<TD><B>COMPANY</B></TD>"
  HTML += "<TD><B>CONTACT</B></TD>"
  HTML += "<TD><B>PHONE</B></TD>"
```

```
' Loop through the data.
  While dr.Read()
    HTML += "<TR>"
    HTML += "<TD><FONT SIZE=-2>" & dr("CompanyName") & "</TD>"
    HTML += "<TD><FONT SIZE=-2>" & dr("ContactName") & "</TD>"
    HTML += "<TD><FONT SIZE=-2>" & dr("Phone") & "</TD>"
    HTML += "</TR>"
  End While

' Add the report footer.
  HTML += "</TABLE>"
  HTML += "</BODY>"
  HTML += "</HTML>"

' Return the report.
  Return HTML

End Function
```

In the middle of Listing 22-3 you'll find the code that combines the customer's data taken from the DataReader with some simple HTML formatting. By looping through the DataReader, you can generate the body of your report with a few lines of code.

Finally, at the bottom of the listing, an HTML footer is added to the report. At this point, the report is complete. Your next step involves saving the report to file before it's displayed within Pocket IE.

Saving the Report

Before the report can be displayed within Pocket IE, you need to save it to a file. Listing 22-4 demonstrates how this is accomplished. Using a System.IO.StreamWriter object, you open the report file, write out your HTML content, and then close the report file.

Listing 22-4. Storing the Report in a File

```
Sub SaveReport(ByVal ReportHtml As String, ByVal ReportFile As String)
  Dim sw As System.IO.StreamWriter

' Open the file.
  sw = New System.IO.StreamWriter(ReportFile)
```

```
' Write the report.
  sw.Write(ReportHtml)

' Close the file.
  sw.Close()

End Sub
```

NOTE *For more on writing to files, see Chapter 8.*

Displaying the Report

Finally, you're ready to display the report to the user. This is accomplished by launching Pocket IE programmatically from within the sample application, passing your report file as a command line argument. Listing 22-5 shows the code used to implement this functionality.

Listing 22-5. Launching Pocket IE and Displaying the Report

```
Sub DisplayReport(ByVal ReportFile As String)
   Dim pi As ProcessInfo
   Dim si() As Byte
   Dim intResult As Int32

' Launch Pocket IE to display the report.
   intResult = LaunchApplication("\Windows\iexplore.exe", ReportFile, Nothing, _
     Nothing, 0, 0, Nothing, Nothing, si, pi)

End Sub
```

TIP *Pocket IE, like other versions of Microsoft's browsers, does not refresh a document unless forced to. What that means in the case of this example is that if you use a single filename to output your reports, then the user will have to tap the refresh button on Pocket IE to see the report after each generation. A simple workaround to this problem is to create each report in a temporary file that has a unique name.*

Don't be misled by the simplicity of the DisplayReport routine. What enables this routine to be so simple is the **CreateProcess** module that's part of the HTML Reporting project. Within this module, you'll find the declaration for the Windows CE API function CreateProcess and the wrapper routine LaunchApplication, which simplifies calling CreateProcess.

The CreateProcess API function is one development tool that you'll want to be familiar with. It allows you to launch another executable from within your application. In this case, it's Pocket IE. You can use this same function to launch executables from within your mobile applications.

> **NOTE** *The **CreateProcess** module offers a simple example of lever-aging the Pocket PC API. For more on this subject, see Chapter 17.*

As I mentioned at the start of this chapter, there are two ways to deliver HTML-based reports: through Pocket IE and with an HTML viewing control. Let's take a look at the control approach.

The HTMLViewer Alternative Approach

While the Pocket IE offers one alternative for displaying HTML content, its downside is that the display is separate from the application. While typically this isn't a major concern, you do have to deal with the issue of the user switching between Pocket IE and your application, refreshing the content within Pocket IE, and terminating Pocket IE (if so desired within the functionality of your mobile solution).

There is a second method to display HTML content. This approach requires the third-party HTMLViewer control from IntelliProg. You can obtain a trial version of this control at IntelliProg's Web site (http://www.intelliprog.com).

The IntelliProg HTMLViewer control allows you to display HTML content within your mobile application. The advantage of this approach over the Pocket IE method demonstrated in the previous example is that you have full control over the display.

> **NOTE** *You'll find the HTML Reporting with HTMLViewer sample application under the **Chapter 22** folder in the **Samples** folder for this book. See Appendix D for more information on accessing and loading the sample applications.*

Figure 22-2 shows the sample report produced by this application as it appears to the user.

Figure 22-2. The HTML-based report as it's displayed by the HTMLViewer control

NOTE *You'll need to obtain a copy of IntelliProg's HTMLViewer control to run this sample application.*

As with the previous HTML example, the key to the HTMLViewer version is within the **Click** event procedure for the **Display Report** button. Listing 22-6 shows the contents of this procedure. This procedure is nothing more than a set of subroutine and function calls:

- **RetrieveData**—Gathers the data

- **ProductReport**—Formats the report

- **DisplayReport**—Displays the report in an HTMLViewer control

As with the previous example, the calls to the routines are inserted between two cursor configurations, which again are intended to provide the user with a visual indicator that the report generation is in progress.

Listing 22-6. The Contents of the Display Report Button Click Event

```
Private Sub btnDisplayReport_Click(ByVal sender As System.Object, _
  ByVal e As System.EventArgs) Handles btnDisplayReport.Click
  Dim ReportHtml As String
```

```
' Let the user know that there is a process in progress.
  Cursor.Current = Cursors.WaitCursor

' Retrieve the data.
  RetrieveData()

' Generate the report.
  ReportHtml = ProduceReport()

' Display the report.
  DisplayReport(ReportHtml)

' We are done so reset the cursor.
  Cursor.Current = Cursors.Default

End Sub
```

Notice that the SaveReport function is absent from this version of the HTML Reporting program. You don't need this step because you can place the HTML report directly into the HTMLViewer control. We'll look at that process next.

Displaying the Report

The code behind both the HTML report and HTML report with HTMLViewer samples is identical with the exception of the DisplayReport routine. Listing 22-7 shows how simple it is to display HTML content within IntelliProg's HTMLViewer control.

Listing 22-7. Displaying the Report in an HTMLViewer Control

```
Sub DisplayReport(ByVal ReportHtml As String)
' Display the report by loading it into the HTML control.
  htmlViewer.SetText(ReportHtml)
End Sub
```

To display an HTML report, use the **SetText** method of the HTMLViewer control, passing the report that was formatted earlier.

Configuring the Report View

Another feature of IntelliProg's HTMLViewer control is the ability to toggle between fit-to-screen mode and normal mode. This allows you to offer your users two ways to view reports. The sample program demonstrates this feature through the check box, shown in the lower-left corner of Figure 22-2. Listing 22-8 shows the minimal code required to implement this functionality.

Listing 22-8. Controlling the Report View

```
Private Sub chkFitToWindow_CheckStateChanged(ByVal sender As System.Object, _
  ByVal e As System.EventArgs) Handles chkFitToWindow.CheckStateChanged

' Toggle the HTML viewer mode.
  htmlViewer.FitToWindow = chkFitToWindow.Checked
End Sub
```

You use the **FitToWindow** property of the HTMLViewer control to specify how content is displayed. In this application, I simply pass along the **Checked** property of the CheckBox control.

Summary of Producing HTML Reports

As this section demonstrates, producing HTML reports is simple and straightforward. If you have any background in ASP or ASP.NET, you'll have no trouble embracing this method of reporting.

With HTML-based reporting, you have two methods of displaying the output: either through Pocket IE or within your application using an HTMLViewer control.

The primary downside of this reporting approach is that it doesn't allow you to produce a printed version of your reports. If your mobile applications absolutely need printed output, read on.

Producing Printed Reports

If your application needs to print a report rather than just view the report on the device, you have three good options. The first option is to use the PrinterCE.NetCF component from Field Software Products. This component enables applications written to NETCF to print to a wide variety of mobile and network printing devices. Field Software offers a trial version of its PrinterCE.NetCF component at its Web site, http://www.fieldsoftware.com. The second option is to use the Report CE product from Syware. Think of Report CE as a Crystal Reports for the Pocket PC. You can learn more about Report CE at Syware's Web site, http://www.syware.com. The third printing option is HP's Mobile Printing Toolkit for .NET, which offers developers the ability to print files via the IR port, Bluetooth, and through the network. Note I said "files," meaning your application will need to first save its report to a file. More information on HP's toolkit can be found at http://www.hp.com.

Some developers may argue that there's a fourth approach, one in which you write code to handle communicating to a specific printer. I'm not fond of this old-school approach to printing for these reasons:

- It is incredibly labor intensive.

- It is printer specific, often limiting your application to a single printer or family of printers.

- It requires a solid understanding of how a specific type of printer communicates and the format of the print language it supports.

It's because of these limitations that we'll focus the discussion of printing options to the first three alternatives: the PrinterCE.NetCF component, Report CE, and the Mobile Printing Toolkit for .NET.

Producing Printed Reports with PrinterCE.NetCF

The first printing option that we'll examine is the PrinterCE.NetCF component from Field Software. This component offers developers tremendous printing flexibility, but requires a fair bit of coding and formatting to produce the desired results. It provides a wide variety of functionality:

- It includes support for both VB .NET and C# .NET under NETCF.

- It's easy to use. You don't have to worry about device contexts, bit-blits, or other complexities.

- You have complete control over the appearance of text including the font, size, style, color, rotation, and page position (or you can have PrinterCE.NetCF automatically position multiple rows of text for you).

- Both auto-word wrap and page feed options are available.

- It provides a wide variety of drawing objects including lines, ellipses, rectangles, and rounded rectangles. You can select size, location, line width, color, and fill.

- It supports printing of images including bitmaps, JPG, and GIF. You can control the size, aspect ratio, and rotation of the printed image.

- Full color printing is available.

- It lets you print using infrared, Bluetooth, serial, and network connections.

- Custom printer support is included for a variety of commercial and industrial printers.

- Fast text-only printing to any ASCII printer is available.

A trial version of the PrinterCE.NetCF component is available online at http://www.fieldsoftware.com/PrinterCE_NetCF.htm.

To help you get started with the PrinterCE.NetCF component, I've created a sample application called PrinterCE .NET Demo.

NOTE   *You'll find this project under the **Chapter 22** folder in the **Samples** folder for this book. See Appendix D for more information on accessing and loading the sample applications.*

NOTE   *To use this sample, you'll need to obtain a trial version of the PrinterCE.NetCF component from the Field Software Web site.*

Examining the PrinterCE .NET Demo

The purpose behind this demo isn't as much to show you how to create a robust report as it is to show the process behind working with the PrinterCE.NetCF component. You incorporate the PrinterCE.NetCF component into your Pocket PC applications as follows:

1. Add a reference to the PrinterCE.NetCF component to your project.

2. Add the **FieldSoftware.PrinterCE.NetCF** Imports statement to your form's code module.

3. Dimension a variable as a PrinterCE type.

4. Create a new instance of the PrinterCE object.

5. Configure the instance of the PrinterCE object.

6. Use the various **Draw** methods of the PrinterCE object to produce output.

7. Use the **EndDoc** method to complete your printing output.

Step 1: Adding a Reference to the PrinterCE.NetCF Component

To work with the PrinterCE.NetCF component, you need to add a reference to the component to your Pocket PC project. To add this reference, perform the following steps:

1. In the Solution Explorer window, right-click the **References** folder. A pop-up menu displays.

2. From the menu, select **Add Reference**.

3. The Add Reference dialog box displays. Select the **PrinterCE.NetCF** component.

4. Click the **OK** button to add the selected component to your project.

Step 2: Importing FieldSoftware.PrinterCE.NetCF

To simplify the process of working with the PrinterCE.NetCF component, you should add an Imports statement to the top of your form module. The syntax of this statement is as follows:

```
Imports FieldSoftware.PrinterCE_NetCF
```

Step 3: Dimensioning the PrinterCE Variable

All of your printing work will be carried out through a PrinterCE object. To accomplish this, you must first dimension a variable as this type.

```
Dim prce As PrinterCE
```

Step 4: Creating an Instance of the PrinterCE Object

Next, you're ready to use this variable to create a new instance of the PrinterCE object. When creating the object, you can specify 1) an exception level, at which printing terminates, and 2) your developer license key.

```
prce = New PrinterCE(PrinterCE.EXCEPTION_LEVEL.ABORT_JOB, "YourLicense")
```

Step 5: Configuring the PrinterCE Object

You're almost ready to begin output of your report. Before proceeding onto that, this is a good time to configure the settings for the PrinterCE object. In the example that follows, I've specified that the user will be prompted to select the desired printer:

```
prce.SelectPrinter(True)
```

> **NOTE** *PrinterCE allows you either to specify a printer or to request the user to select a printer. This flexibility allows you to single-source a type of printer for some applications while enabling your application to support a wide variety of printers in other instances.*

In your application, you may want to specify the margins, size of the paper, orientation, and scale, among other options. You'll see a demonstration of these types of configurations in the next PrinterCE.NetCF example.

Step 6: Producing Your Report

You're now ready to begin producing output. PrinterCE provides a number of **Draw** methods that you can use to produce your report. Following is a simple example of outputting plain text:

```
prce.DrawText("The PrinterCE .NET Demo")
```

> **NOTE** *More on the PrinterCE's **Draw** methods can be found later in this section.*

Step 7: Sending Your Report

Finally, the report is ready to send. To complete the process and submit the print job, you call the **EndDoc** method of the PrinterCE object.

```
prce.EndDoc()
```

Bringing It All Together

Listing 22-9 shows how the preceding examples fit together. Here, the simple phrase "The PrinterCE .NET Demo" is sent to a printer.

Listing 22-9. A Simple Example of the PrinterCE.NetCF Component

```
Private Sub Button1_Click(ByVal sender As System.Object, _
   ByVal e As System.EventArgs) Handles Button1.Click
   Dim prce As PrinterCE

   Try
' Create an instance of the PrinterCE component.
      prce = New PrinterCE(PrinterCE.EXCEPTION_LEVEL.ABORT_JOB, "YourLicense")

' Prompt the user for the target printer.
      prce.SelectPrinter(True)

' Print out a simple message.
      prce.DrawText("The PrinterCE .NET Demo")

' Complete the print document, which in turn submits the print job.
      prce.EndDoc()

' Handle any errors that occur.
   Catch exc As PrinterCEException
      MessageBox.Show("PrinterCE Exception", "Exception")

' Clean up.
   Finally
      prce.ShutDown()
   End Try

End Sub
```

Working with the PrinterCE Object

Now that you have a general understanding of the process of working with the
PrinterCE.NetCF component, let's look at another sample application that
demonstrates more of the functionality offered by this product.

The Northwind Mobile Application

The Northwind Mobile application allows the user to view customer orders and print invoices.

NOTE *You'll find this project under the* **Chapter 22** *folder in the* **Samples** *folder for this book. See Appendix D for more information on accessing and loading samples.*

Figure 22-3 provides an example of how a customer's order appears to the user. Figure 22-4 shows a sample invoice produced by the application.

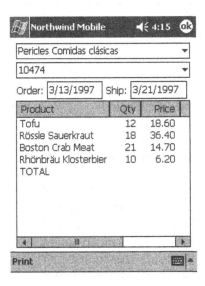

Figure 22-3. Examining an order with the Northwind Mobile application

Account Number	Order Number	Payment Due By	
06-036171-408	R52581782D-AB	4/15/2003	**$1,249.10**

Pericles Comidas clásicas
1217 5th Avenue
New York, NY 10010

To avoid Late Payment charge, full payment must be received by 4/15/2003

THANK YOU FOR YOUR PROMPT PAYMENT

PLEASE RETURN THIS STUB WITH PAYMENT   TO ENSURE PROPER CREDIT, PLEASE WRITE YOUR ACCOUNT NUMBER ON YOU CHECK

Product	Quantity	Unit Price	Item Total
Tofu	12	18.60	$223.20
Rössle Sauerkraut	18	36.40	$655.20
Boston Crab Meat	21	14.70	$308.70
Rhönbräu Klosterbier	10	6.20	$62.00

Figure 22-4. A sample invoice produced by the Northwind Mobile application

Examining the Northwind Mobile Application

A detailed discussion of this application is outside of the scope of this chapter, as much of the application deals with displaying order information. I'm going to focus on the module that produces the invoice. The code for this module, shown throughout this section, is called when the user taps the **Print** menu option.

What you should immediately notice is that this is a lengthy routine. As I already mentioned, for what PrinterCE.NetCF offers in the way of printing functionality and flexibility it exacts as cost lengthy code. You are required to send commands to create every piece of your report, from the text you write, to the lines you add, for boxes, shading, and images you apply. It's certainly a coding process that isn't for the faint of heart.

Looking through this code, you'll see at the top of the module the exact same setup code found in the previous example, where you create an instance of the PrinterCE object and then configure that instance. Note that here the configuration is more involved as you define margins, page orientation, and other items.

Next is the code used to generate the invoice. You'll find examples of a variety of the capabilities offered through the PrinterCE.NetCF component, including the quartet of **Draw** methods: **DrawText**, **DrawLine**, **DrawRect**, and **DrawRoundedRect**. As Figure 22-4 demonstrates earlier, these four methods can be combined to create some truly powerful results.

NOTE *I've broken up the module code with comment paragraphs throughout to further define the code.*

```
Private Sub PrintInvoice()
   Dim curItemTotal As Single
   Dim curTotalAmount As Single
   Dim intCounter As Integer
   Dim prce As PrinterCE

' Create an instance of the printer object.
   prce = New PrinterCE(PrinterCE.EXCEPTION_LEVEL.ABORT_JOB, "YourLicense")

' Prompt the user to select printing attributes.
   prce.SelectPrinter(True)

' Set up the layout and margins.
   With prce
      .PrOrientation = PrinterCE_Base.ORIENTATION.PORTRAIT ' Portrait mode
      .ScaleMode = PrinterCE_Base.MEASUREMENT_UNITS.INCHES ' Work in inches
      .PrLeftMargin = 0.5
      .PrTopMargin = 0.7
      .PrRightMargin = 0.5
      .PrBottomMargin = 0.7
      .DrawWidth = 0.02

' Begin to draw the invoice starting with the top rectangle.
      .DrawRect(0, 0, 5.7, 0.5)
```

You can leverage rectangles, lines, and shading to spice up your reports, giving them a preprinted appearance. This is very different from single-font, no-graphic reporting that's frequently associated with mobile printing.

```
' Add a shaded rectangle.
      .FillColor = System.Drawing.Color.LightGray
      .FillStyle = PrinterCE.FILL_STYLE.SOLID
      .DrawRect(0, 0, 5.7, 0.25)
      .DrawLine(2, 0, 2, 0.5)
      .DrawLine(3.8, 0, 3.8, 0.5)
```

```
' Add the top headers.
    .FontSize = 12
    .FontBold = True
    .ForeColor = System.Drawing.Color.Black
    .JustifyHoriz = PrinterCE_Base.JUSTIFY_HORIZ.CENTER
    .JustifyVert = PrinterCE_Base.JUSTIFY_VERT.CENTER

    .DrawText("Account Number", 1, 0.125)
    .DrawText("Order Number", 2.9, 0.125)
    .DrawText("Payment Due By", 4.75, 0.125)
```

You can use shading to enhance the appearance of your printed output. Following is the code used to create the total amount box found in the upper-left corner of the invoice:

```
' Add the total amount box. This is accomplished by drawing a
' black box with a smaller white box over the top of it.
    .FillColor = System.Drawing.Color.DarkGray
    .DrawRect(5.7, 0, 7.5, 0.7)
    .ForeColor = System.Drawing.Color.White
    .FontSize = 9
    .FontBoldVal = 1000        ' Set to maximum value.
    .DrawText("PLEASE PAY THIS AMOUNT", 6.6, 0.1)
    .FillColor = System.Drawing.Color.White
    .DrawRoundedRect(5.8, 0.2, 7.4, 0.6, 0.15, 0.15)

' Set the drawing color back to black after finishing the white box.
    .ForeColor = System.Drawing.Color.Black

' Add late payment box.
    .FontSize = 12
    .FontBold = False
    .DrawRect(5, 1.9, 7.5, 2.6)
    .DrawText("To avoid Late Payment charge,", 6.25, 2.05)
    .DrawText("full payment must be received by", 6.25, 2.25)

' Add invoice footer.
    .JustifyHoriz = PrinterCE_Base.JUSTIFY_HORIZ.LEFT
    .FontSize = 8
    .DrawText("PLEASE RETURN THIS STUB WITH PAYMENT", 0, 2.8)
    .JustifyHoriz = PrinterCE_Base.JUSTIFY_HORIZ.RIGHT
    .DrawText("TO ENSURE PROPER CREDIT, PLEASE WRITE YOUR " & _
        "ACCOUNT NUMBER ON YOU CHECK.", 7.5, 2.8)
    .FontSize = 14
    .FontBold = True
```

```
        .FontItalic = True
        .JustifyHoriz = PrinterCE_Base.JUSTIFY_HORIZ.CENTER
        .DrawText("THANK YOU FOR YOUR PROMPT PAYMENT", 2.5, 2.5)


' Add the item header bar.
        .FillColor = System.Drawing.Color.LightGray
        .FillStyle = PrinterCE.FILL_STYLE.SOLID
        .DrawRect(0, 3.1, 7.5, 3.35)
        .DrawLine(2, 3.1, 2, 3.35)
        .DrawLine(3.8, 3.1, 3.8, 3.35)
        .DrawLine(5.7, 3.1, 5.7, 3.35)
```

You have complete control of the size and type of font that you use with your
reports. You can alter and combine fonts to produce any desired appearance.

```
' Add the item header titles.
        .FontSize = 12
        .FontBold = True
        .FontItalic = False
        .ForeColor = System.Drawing.Color.Black
        .JustifyHoriz = PrinterCE_Base.JUSTIFY_HORIZ.CENTER
        .JustifyVert = PrinterCE_Base.JUSTIFY_VERT.CENTER

        .DrawText("Product", 1, 3.225)
        .DrawText("Quantity", 2.9, 3.225)
        .DrawText("Unit Price", 4.75, 3.225)
        .DrawText("Item Total", 6.75, 3.225)


' Fill in data component of the invoice. Some of the content
' is hard coded, but could just as easily be retrieved from a
' database.
        .FontBold = False
        .FontItalic = False
        .FillStyle = PrinterCE.FILL_STYLE.TRANSPARENT


' Print the account number and order number.
        .DrawText("06-036171-408", 1, 0.375)
        .DrawText("R52581782D-AB", 2.9, 0.375)


' Add the due dates.
        .DrawText(DateAdd(DateInterval.Day, 30, Date.Today), 4.75, 0.375)
        .FontSize = 12
        .DrawText(DateAdd(DateInterval.Day, 30, Date.Today), 6.25, 2.45)
```

Here, in the middle of the invoice generation routine, you find the code used to extract line items from the user interface and insert them into the output. You could just as well be retrieving these values from a DataReader object as shown in the HTML examples.

```
' Add the line items.
    .FontSize = 14
    For intCounter = 0 To lvwOrder.Items.Count - 2
        .JustifyHoriz = PrinterCE_Base.JUSTIFY_HORIZ.LEFT
        .DrawText(lvwOrder.Items(intCounter).Text, 0, _
            3.5 + (intCounter * 0.25))
        .JustifyHoriz = PrinterCE_Base.JUSTIFY_HORIZ.RIGHT
        .DrawText(lvwOrder.Items(intCounter).SubItems(1).Text, _
            2.9, 3.5 + (intCounter * 0.25))
        .DrawText(lvwOrder.Items(intCounter).SubItems(2).Text, _
            5.0, 3.5 + (intCounter * 0.25))

' Calculate and print the total of this line item.
        curItemTotal = (CSng(lvwOrder.Items(intCounter).SubItems(1).Text) * _
            CSng(lvwOrder.Items(intCounter).SubItems(2).Text))
        .DrawText(FormatCurrency(curItemTotal.ToString), 7, 3.5 + _
            (intCounter * 0.25))

' Add the amount of this line item to the running total.
        curTotalAmount = curTotalAmount + curItemTotal
    Next intCounter
```

One of the cool features offered through the PrinterCE.NetCF component is the ability to produce your output in any order. In the next code snippet, you add the total amount of the invoice to the upper-left corner of the invoice. This is easily accomplished even though you print the box in which this value is placed far earlier in this routine.

```
' Add the total amount.
    .JustifyHoriz = PrinterCE_Base.JUSTIFY_HORIZ.CENTER
    .FontSize = 16
    .FontBold = True
    .DrawText(FormatCurrency(curTotalAmount), 6.6, 0.4)

    .JustifyHoriz = PrinterCE_Base.JUSTIFY_HORIZ.LEFT
    .FontSize = 16
    .FontBold = False
    .DrawText(cmbCustomers.Items(cmbCustomers.SelectedIndex), _
        0.5, 1.2)
    .DrawText("1217 5th Avenue")
```

```
   .DrawText("New York, NY 10010")

' Add line between header and order content.
   .DrawWidth = 0.01
   .DrawLine(0, 3, 7.5, 3)

' Complete the print document.
   .EndDoc()
 End With
End Sub
```

At the end of the module you see where the EndDoc method is called to send the invoice to your printer, just as was done in the simple example shown earlier in this chapter.

TIP   *Since PrinterCE.NetCF doesn't include a graphical design component, designing and implementing complex printed output is frequently a tedious task. To simplify this process, I would suggest sending output to a network printer rather than your target mobile printer. Network printers, with their Ethernet connections and high-speed print capabilities, make the process far more tolerable than the slow printing speed and IR or Bluetooth interfaces found in most mobile printers.*

Summary of Printing with PrinterCE.NetCF

PrinterCE.NetCF offers mobile application developers a vibrant toolkit of printing functionality. Simply stated, with PrinterCE.NetCF you can produce any report that you have the imagination to conceive and the time to code. This component offers the powerful combination of support for industry-standard printers, communication methods, and printing functionality. I recommend that you visit the vendor's Web site for further details on the capabilities and uses for PrinterCE.NetCF.

Now that you've seen the longhand approach at printing reports, let's look at a less-complicated approach to application-controlled printing, HP's Mobile Printing Toolkit for .NET.

Printing Reports with the Mobile Printing Toolkit

The second alternative for direct printing control is the Mobile Printing Toolkit for .NET from Hewlett-Packard. This option is somewhere in the middle between

PrinterCE.NetCF and Report CE. On one hand, it enables developers to control the printing process, much like PrinterCE.NetCF. On the other end of things, the toolkit prints complete files, much like Report CE prints reports from templates.

The Mobile Printing Toolkit is best suited for situations in which your application needs to print preexisting documents or you can send your report output to one of the file formats supported by the toolkit.

The toolkit is designed to simplify the process of printing files. It enables developers to quickly and easily integrate printing into their mobile applications. With the HP Mobile Printing Toolkit, developers can create applications that print using IR, Bluetooth, and network connections. You can print a wide variety of file types including Pocket Word, rich-text format (RTF), simple text, Microsoft PowerPoint, Microsoft Word, and even Adobe Acrobat.

The Mobile Printing Toolkit for .NET is available at Hewlett-Packard's Web site, http://www.hp.com.

To give you an idea of how easy it is to work with the Mobile Printing Toolkit, I've created a sample application called HP Print Demo.

NOTE *You'll find this project under the **Chapter 22** folder in the **Samples** folder for this book. See Appendix D for more information on accessing and loading the sample applications.*

NOTE *To use this sample, you'll need to obtain both Hewlett-Packard's Mobile Printing Toolkit for .NET from the HP Web site and IntelliProg's RichInk control from their Web site at* http://www.intelliprog.com.

Examining the HP Print Demo

Unlike the HTML and Northwind demos, this demo application doesn't actually generate a report. To simplify the key function, printing using the Mobile Printing Toolkit, I use a preformatted report. In the case of this example, the report is an invoice, which is already stored in a file in Rich Text Format (RTF). As I mentioned earlier, RTF is just one of the many file formats supported by HP's Mobile Printing Toolkit.

Figure 22-5 shows the interface to the HP Print Demo application as it first appears to the user. The interface is comprised of three controls: one of IntelliProg's RichInk controls and two Buttons. Among other features, the RichInk control can be used to create and display RTF content.

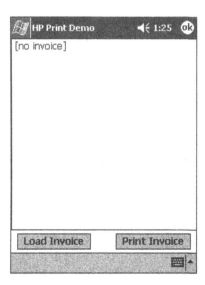

Figure 22-5. The interface of the HP Print Demo application

Tapping the **Load Invoice** button causes the preconfigured invoice to be loaded from file into the RichInk control. Figure 22-6 shows an example of this.

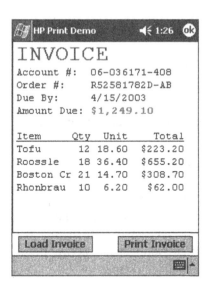

Figure 22-6. The invoice displayed within the HP Print Demo application

While the Mobile Printing Toolkit offers several methods for implementing printing within a mobile application, I've chosen what I feel is the easiest approach, which involves the following steps:

1. Add a reference to the HPMobilePrintSDKInstaller. Note, this is only required if you want the SDK to be automatically deployed to the device while you are testing.

2. Add the HPMobilePrintSDKWrapper DLL and the **HPMobilePrintSDKWrapper** code module to your project. This simple wrapper provides access to two functions provided by the DLL, PrintJob and GetLastError. PrintJob initiates the printing process. GetLastError provides the status of the last printing process.

3. To print your report, add code to call the PrintJob function.

Step 1: Adding a Reference to HPMobilePrintSDKInstaller

The Mobile Print Toolkit is a fairly involved component. It has its own installation utility that you can either manually install, or as I've chosen here, include in your project during testing. To add the reference to this component, perform the following steps:

1. In the Solution Explorer window, right-click the **References** folder. A pop-up menu displays.

2. From the menu, select **Add Reference**.

3. The **Add Reference** dialog box displays. Select the **HPMobilePrintSDKInstaller** component.

4. Click the **OK** button to add the selected component to your project.

Step 2: Adding the HPMobilePrintSDK DLL and Module

All of the printing functionality you'll need is accessed through the HPMobilePrintSDK DLL. There are two functions in this library that I'll be demonstrating: PrintJob and GetLastError. I've created a small code module that defines both of these functions for you in the file HPMobilePrintSDKWrapper.vb.
To add the DLL to your project, perform the following steps:

1. Under the Project menu, select **Add Existing Item**.

2. From the Add Existing Item dialog box, select **HPMobilePrintSDK.DLL**.

3. Click the **Open** button. The DLL will be added to your project.

4. In the Properties window, configure the Build Action of the DLL to be **Content**.

To add the code module to your project, perform the following steps:

1. Under the Project menu, select **Add Existing Item**.

2. From the Add Existing Item dialog box, select **HPMobilePrintSDK.vb**.

3. Click the **Open** button. The module will be added to your project.

Step 3: Printing Your Report

As I stated at the beginning of this section, I chose to present what I consider is the easiest method of printing using the Mobile Print Toolkit. That method involves making a single function call as shown in Listing 22-10.

Listing 22-10. Calling the PrintJob Function

```
Private Sub btnPrintInvoice_Click(ByVal sender As System.Object, _
  ByVal e As System.EventArgs) Handles btnPrintInvoice.Click
  Dim PrintError As HPMobilePrintSDK.HPP_RESULT
  Dim PrintWorked As Boolean
  Dim ErrorMessages() As String = _
    {"There was no error in submission", _
    "Memory error - probably out of available memory", _
    "The user canceled the submission", _
    "There is no content transformation available for the document type", _
    "There was a NULL pointer error in the HP Mobile Printing SDK module", _
    "There was a problem reading the document", _
    "The printer is currently busy and cannot be used", _
    "There was an internal error in the HP Mobile Printing SDK module", _
    "The background printing process is currently busy and can't be used"}

' Print the document.
  PrintWorked = HPMobilePrintSDK.HPMobilePrintSDKWrapper.PrintJob( _
    "/Windows/Start Menu/Programs/Apress/invoice.rtf")

' Check the status of the print request.
  If PrintWorked Then
    MessageBox.Show("The document was printed successfully.", "Print Status")
  Else
    PrintError = HPMobilePrintSDK.HPMobilePrintSDKWrapper.GetLastPrintError()
    MessageBox.Show(ErrorMessages(PrintError), "Print Status")
  End If

End Sub
```

At the top of the procedure shown in Listing 22-10 are descriptions of the various errors that can occur during the print process. Next is the call to the PrintJob function. You pass a single argument to this call—the name of the file to print.

The PrintJob function returns a result of the print request. By checking this response, your application can determine the outcome of the operation and, if necessary, call the GetLastPrintError function to obtain details on the error that occurred.

There are two other pieces of code that I want to discuss, the **HPMobilePrintSDKWrapper** module and the procedure used to load and display the invoice.

The HPMobilePrintSDKWrapper Module

The two print functions that are used by this application are defined within the **HPMobilePrintSDKWrapper** module as shown in Listing 22-11. Both of these functions are found in the HPMobilePrintSDKWrapper DLL.

Listing 22-11. The HPMobilePrintSDKWrapper Module

```
Imports System
Imports System.Runtime.InteropServices

Namespace HPMobilePrintSDK
  Public Enum HPP_RESULT As Byte
    HPP_NOERROR = 0            '!< There was no error in submission
    HPP_MEMORY_ERROR          '!< Memory error - probably out of available memory
    HPP_USER_CANCELLED        '!< The user canceled the submission
    HPP_CT_NOT_AVAILABLE      '!< There is no content transformation
    HPP_NULL_POINTER          '!< There was a NULL pointer error
    HPP_DOCUMENT_ERROR        '!< There was a problem reading the document
    HPP_PRINTER_BUSY          '!< The printer is currently busy
    HPP_INTERNAL_ERROR        '!< There was in internal error
    HPP_PRINT_SUBSYSTEM_BUSY '!< The background printing process is busy
  End Enum

  Public Class HPMobilePrintSDKWrapper
    Public Declare Function PrintJob Lib "HPMobilePrintSDKWrapper.dll" _
      (ByVal szContentName As String) _
      As Boolean
    Public Declare Function GetLastPrintError Lib _
      "HPMobilePrintSDKWrapper.dll" () _
      As HPP_RESULT
  End Class
End Namespace
```

NOTE   *For more on calling functions in DLLs, see Chapter 17.*

Displaying an Invoice

While this isn't an integral part of this application or of the printing process, I wanted to be able to demonstrate some of the functionality provided through IntelliProg's RichInk control. Listing 22-12 shows how easy this control makes displaying Rich Text Format. The RichInk control provides two methods, **LoadFile** and **SaveFile**, which make working with RTF format content simple.

Listing 22-12. Displaying the Contents of an RTF File

```
Private Sub btnLoadInvoice_Click(ByVal sender As System.Object, _
  ByVal e As System.EventArgs) Handles btnLoadInvoice.Click

  Load the demo invoice.
  RichInk1.LoadFile("/Windows/Start Menu/Programs/Apress/invoice.rtf", _
    Intelliprog.Windows.Forms.RichInkStreamType.RichText)
End Sub
```

The Mobile Print Toolkit User Interface

Up to this point, everything that I've showed you has to do with the developer side of this application. To fully understand what the Mobile Print Toolkit offers, we need to look at the user aspect of the Mobile Print Toolkit, or what the user sees after tapping the **Print Invoice** button on this demo application.

Figure 22-7 shows the interface presented to users when they tap the **Print Invoice** button. They have the option to either configure a new printer, select an existing printer definition, or to cancel the print operation.

Figure 22-7. Selecting a print device

Tapping the **Configure** button will cause the configuration interface to display as shown in Figure 22-8. From this interface, the user can either modify the configuration of an existing printer or define a new printer.

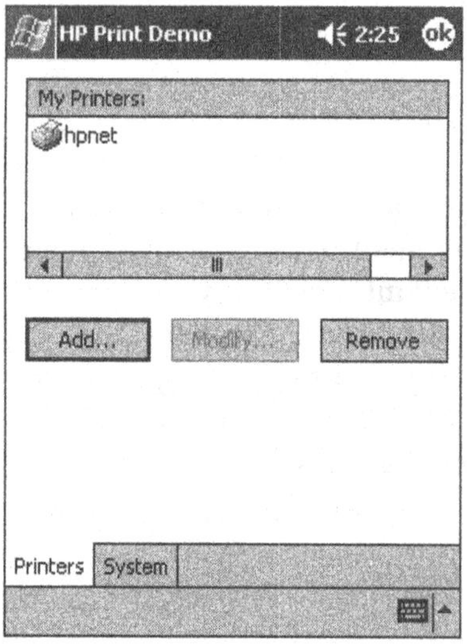

Figure 22-8. Configuring a printer

The user can tap the **Add** button to define a new printer. Doing so will display a selection of supported printer communication methods, as shown in Figure 22-9.

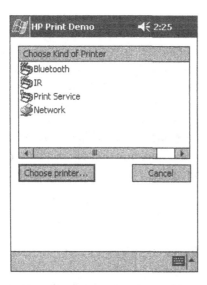

Figure 22-9. Specifying the communication method to use with a printer

Each type of printer (Bluetooth, IR, Print Service, and Network) has its own configuration screen that enables users to specify details on their print device. An example of the Network print configuration is shown in Figure 22-10.

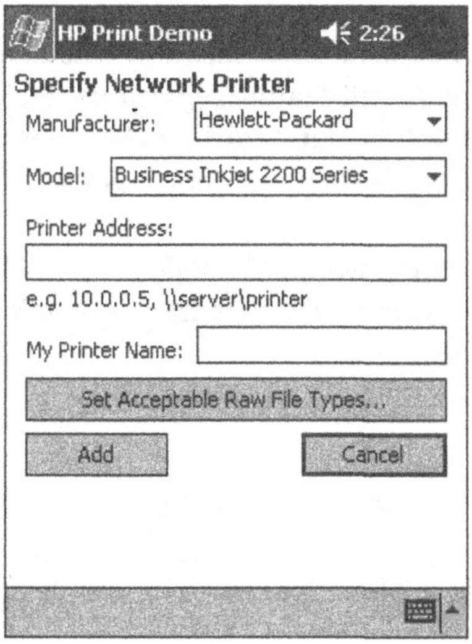

Figure 22-10. Specifying configurations for a network printer

Summary of Printing with the Mobile Printing Toolkit

If your application needs to print existing files, particularly industry-standard files such as Microsoft Word or Adobe Acrobat formats, then Hewlett-Packard's Mobile Printing Toolkit for .NET is one option you'll want to check out. As I demonstrated in the preceding sections, it's powerful and easy to use. One obvious drawback is that, unlike PrinterCE.NetCF, it supports only HP printers.

We've got one last printing option to examine, one that offers a far more development-friendly method for producing reports. That product is Report CE from Syware.

Pocket PC Report Generation with Report CE

Report CE from Syware offers mobile application developers the closest thing available to a report generation tool. It provides a scaled-down version of what you have come to expect to find in products such as Crystal Reports.

Report CE allows you to create report templates, which you can subsequently call to produce reports from your mobile applications. You can print your reports via the device's IR port or Bluetooth, or to a network printer. Optionally, you can send your report through e-mail, which is seriously cool, or save it as text to a file. Report CE supports producing color reports.

The data that you use within a report can come from either enterprise or local data sources. Reports can include a header, footer, data, and calculated data sections, just as you would expect from a full-feature reporting tool. Report CE's filtering capabilities allow you to control the data shown within a report. For more information on Report CE, visit Syware's Web site at http://www.syware.com/ prodlib/win_ce/rpt_ce/rpt_ce.htm.

While Syware doesn't offer a trial version of Report CE, it does offer a 30-day money-back guarantee. You can purchase Report CE online from Syware's Web site at http://www.syware.com/olstore/olstore.htm.

The Report CE Demo

To give you a flavor of what Report CE has to offer, I've created a sample application called Report CE Demo.

NOTE *You'll find this project under the **Chapter 22** folder in the **Samples** folder for this book. See Appendix D for more information on accessing and loading the sample applications.*

NOTE   *To use this sample, you'll need to obtain Report CE from Syware. This demo calls the Report CE engine on the device to generate the report.*

Examining the Report CE Demo

The process of leveraging Report CE for your mobile application's printing needs involves very little in the way of code. Most of the real development work is done within the Report CE design interface. Figure 22-11 shows an example of this interface.

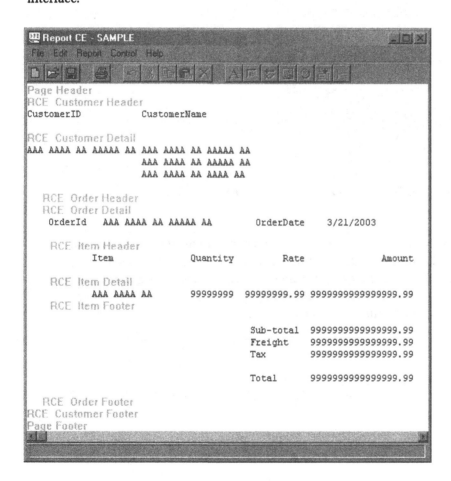

Figure 22-11. The Report CE design interface

The report is divided into sections: header, detail, and footer, just as you would expect to find in the larger desktop report-generation tools. Each section can in turn be divided into subsections as required by your reporting needs. Sections can be configured to automatically calculate and insert totals. Values can be retrieved from databases. Fields where data values are displayed are defined within the body of the report. For each field, you can define the type of data it will display along with the font to use.

Your reports can include filters as shown in Figure 22-12. This enables you to selectively restrict the data included in your reports.

Figure 22-12. The Filter dialog box shown when a report runs

Figure 22-13 shows the output produced from the template shown in Figure 22-11. You should note that this is a simple example, using a single font type and size. You can easily enhance your reports by varying your fonts. Report CE doesn't give you as much formatting functionality as PrinterCE.NetCF, but it more than makes up for that shortcoming with its graphical design element.

```
CustomerID          CustomerName

C04                 ABC Books
                    57 Ocean Drive
                    Lincoln RI

    OrderId   R41                    OrderDate    5/15/1999

          Item           Quantity        Rate          Amount

          Paper               10         2.85           28.50
          Pencil              50         0.05            2.50

                                     Sub-total          31.00
                                     Freight            10.00
                                     Tax                 0.00

                                     Total              41.00

    OrderId   R42                    OrderDate    9/1/1999

          Item           Quantity        Rate          Amount

          Pen                100         0.25           25.00
          Paper                5         2.85           14.25

                                     Sub-total          39.25
                                     Freight             5.00
                                     Tax                 0.00

                                     Total              44.25
```

Figure 22-13. Sample output produced by Report CE

NOTE   *While I haven't even touched on the report template design process here, rest assured that Report CE does come with a detailed tutorial that walks you through the process of creating and configuring report templates.*

Adding a Report to Your Mobile Application

As I've already stated, the coding part of working with Report CE is minimal. All that you need to do is launch the Report CE application, passing the name of the report as a command-line argument.

You use the same approach to accomplish this as was demonstrated with the HTML reporting example. Adding the **CreateProcess** module to your demonstration project makes starting the Report CE executable easy, as shown in Listing 22-13.

Listing 22-13. Printing a Report Through Report CE

```
Private Sub btnRunReport_Click(ByVal sender As System.Object, _
  ByVal e As System.EventArgs) Handles btnRunReport.Click
  Dim pi As ProcessInfo
  Dim si() As Byte
  Dim intResult As Int32

' Launch the Report CE engine, passing to it the sample report.
  intResult = LaunchApplication("\Program Files\Report CE\ReportCE.exe", _
    "\Windows\Start Menu\Programs\Sample.rce", Nothing, Nothing, 0, _
    0, Nothing, Nothing, si, pi)

End Sub
```

NOTE *You could also specify the criteria for the filter as part of the command line, enabling you to programmatically control the data included in the report.*

Figure 22-14 shows how the report appears to the user before it's printed. Report CE offers the user the option to print, save, or e-mail the report.

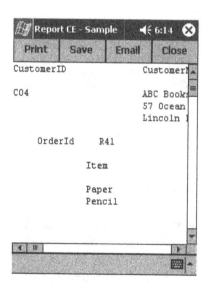

Figure 22-14. A sample report within Report CE

Selecting to print the report presents the user with the dialog box shown in Figure 22-15. From this dialog box, the user can select the target printer and the method to communicate, and even control the configuration and appearance of the print job.

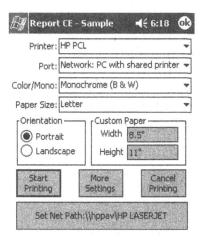

Figure 22-15. The print dialog box interface of Report CE

If users desire, they can send the report via e-mail simply by tapping the **Email** button from within the Report CE interface. Doing so will cause the e-mail dialog box to display as shown in Figure 22-16. From this dialog box, the user can select the recipient of the e-mail from a list of names drawn from the Pocket PC's contact list. The report is placed into the Outbox on the device, and will be sent the next time the user synchronizes the device.

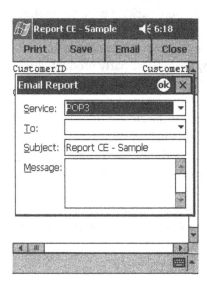

Figure 22-16. The e-mail dialog box interface of Report CE

Summary of Printing with Report CE

While Report CE doesn't offer the flexibility of the PrinterCE.NetCF component, it does offer both ease of design and use. With Report CE, you can create reports that group and summarize data without requiring any code. As you saw in the demo included with this section, incorporating a Report CE report into your mobile application involves nothing more than the few lines of code required to launch an application.

The combination of its price, royalty-free use, ease of design, and ability to produce output to printers, files, and e-mail make Report CE a viable reporting tool for every mobile developer.

Summary

While neither printing nor report generation are natively supported by either the Pocket PC or NETCF, that doesn't mean you have do without. Several good reporting options are available to mobile application developers.

HTML-based reports provide a flexible option in situations where your reports don't need to be printed. This approach is similar to both ASP and ASP.NET in that it's based on formatting data using HTML tags.

The PrinterCE.NetCF component from Field Software offers developers a printing option with support for a wide variety of mobile and network printers. On the plus side, this component is flexible and provides developers with nearly limitless possibilities for formatting reports. As a negative, working with PrinterCE usually requires a fair bit of coding to accomplish the desired effects.

The Mobile Printing Toolkit for .NET from Hewlett-Packard provides mobile developers with an easy-to-use printing tool for printing files in a variety of industry-standard formats. While it does require you to produce reports first to file, this part of the process can be simplified by other third-party products such as the RichInk control from IntelliProg. The primary limitation of this tool is its support for HP printers only.

Report CE from Syware offers mobile developers the closest thing to a report generation utility. Its graphical design environment enables you to easily construct reports. It's reasonably priced and easy to incorporate into applications written with NETCF. While it doesn't offer the range of flexibility found in PrinterCE.NetCF, it does offer a quick way to design and deploy reports.

Regardless of the method you choose, this chapter demonstrates that the Pocket PC can be a powerful extension of your enterprise reporting functionality.

Setting Up Your Development Environment: A Quick Step-Through

THIS MAY VERY WELL BE the shortest appendix in the history of publishing. Well, that may be an exaggeration, but this appendix will be short and to the point. The purpose here is to give you a feel for what you need to have installed to do a particular job in the world of .NET Compact Framework programming. The way to do that is to give you step-by-step instructions for what you need to do to get your environment up and running.

Install a Decent Operating System

By "decent," you might be thinking that I mean you shouldn't use Windows if you want a decent OS. Sorry, but no snide comments here! What I mean is you shouldn't use Windows 95 or Windows 98. Visual Studio 2003 requires you to use one of the following operating systems:

- Windows XP Professional

- Windows Server 2003

- Windows 2000 Professional (SP3 or later)

- Windows 2000 Server (SP3 or later)

It's possible to use Windows XP Home Edition, but if you do, you won't be able to write or host ASP.NET pages or Web services.

Install Visual Studio .NET 2003

This should be obvious, but I want to be complete. It's also important to note that the .NET Compact Framework is part of the 2003 release of VS .NET. The previous version, called the Smart Device Extensions, was provided as a separate add-on and installation to Visual Studio 1.0.

For some "official" information on Visual Studio .NET 2003, you can check out either of these two Microsoft Web sites:

- **Visual Studio .NET Home Page**—http://msdn.microsoft.com/vstudio/

- **Support Center for Visual Studio**—http://support.microsoft.com/ default.aspx?scid=fh;EN-US;vsnet

Install ActiveSync

ActiveSync is the software that synchronizes the data from your desktop computer to your PocketPC. Download the latest version of ActiveSync from http://www.microsoft.com/downloads/details.aspx?FamilyID=67e9e87c-ca96-48b4-b5d4-f3e047ca5108&displaylang=en and install it on your computer.

And really, that's all that is *required* to get started. The remaining tools you need are included in Visual Studio 2003. Of course, you may want to install some optional packages, and we'll discuss those next. You might also find a significant number of "toys" and other downloads interesting. The last portion of this appendix will contain links to some of those items.

Install SQL Server and SQL Server CE

If you don't plan on using SQL Server or SQL Server CE, then you don't have to worry about this section. But if you have a desire to use SQL CE by itself or to synchronize data with SQL Server, then this might be worth reading.

With the problems that exist from a variety of hacking attempts and successes, everyone should have the latest service pack for SQL Server installed. At the time of writing, that is SP3. As was discussed in Chapter 11, installing SQL CE over SP3 can get a bit dicey. You can find a description of SP3 and a link to download it from this Web site: http://www.microsoft.com/sql/downloads/2000/sp3.asp.

Now, when you install SQL CE 2.0, you have to install client and server tools. If you installed SP3, then you can use the SQL CE installation for client tools, but you *must* install a service update on the server that is hosting IIS. The following links point you to the important pages on the Microsoft Web sites that provide detailed information:

- **General SQL CE site**—http://www.microsoft.com/sql/ce/

- **SQL CE 2.0 download site**—http://www.microsoft.com/sql/ce/downloads/ce20.asp

- **SQLEC service update**—http://www.microsoft.com/sql/downloads/ce/sp3.asp

When you install these upgrades, they will bring your Microsoft Data Access Components (MDAC) up to version 2.7.

Install the eMbedded Tools

No, I don't know why Microsoft capitalizes the *M* and not the *e*. But I do know that you should install eMbedded Visual Tools 3.0 on your development machine. If you've previously used the embedded tools, you know that they include a variety of tools that let you look at processes, files, and other details of the emulator or device. These tools aren't included in Visual Studio 2003, and in time you'll need them for debugging or curiosity, whichever comes first. You can set up the Tools menu in Visual Studio to launch the utilities from right inside the IDE.

The SDKs that get installed with the tools also provide you the header files that can be used to build your own Declare or DllImport statements to call unmanaged code. Two versions of the eMbedded tools are currently available. Version 3.0 is the old standby that has been used for years to write applications for devices. The new kid on the block is eMbedded Visual C++ 4.0. This version, with Service Pack 2 installed, lets you target Windows CE 4.0, 4.1, and 4.2. At this time, Visual C++ 4.0 doesn't have an SDK to allow you to target the Pocket PC or Smartphone.

Following are the URLs you'll need to access and learn more about the eMbedded Visual Tools:

- **eMbedded Visual Tools Web site**—
  http://msdn.microsoft.com/vstudio/device/embedded/default.aspx

- **eMbedded Visual Tools 3.0**—
  http://www.microsoft.com/downloads/details.aspx?FamilyId=F663BF48-31EE-4CBE-AAC5-0AFFD5FB27DD&displaylang=en

- **eMbedded Visual C++ 4.0**—
  http://msdn.microsoft.com/vstudio/device/embedded/datasheet.aspx

- **eMbedded Visual C++ 4.0 SP2**—http://microsoft.com/downloads/details.aspx?FamilyId=CE7F1AAA-54EB-4989-812B-7F955605DCB8&display-lang=en

Once you digest all of the preceding Web sites and pages, you can get a general overview of application development for devices from the following site:

- **Device development overview**—http://msdn.microsoft.com/vstudio/device/overview.aspx

Summary

This short appendix covers everything you need to get started. There are many sites that you can visit for downloads, help, and tools. Rather than add a large list of URLs here that you would have to type in by hand, you can get a list of links at either http://www.larryroof.com or http://www.forestsoftwaregroup.com. Appendix D tells you the exact location of these sites, from which you can also download versions of the source code.

Working with the Emulator

THE FOCUS OF THIS APPENDIX is to show you how to get the most out of the emulator. Before we get started, let me say that I'm not a big fan of emulators. Obviously, if you don't have a device, they're your only option. While I may grant this consideration for students, I can't see any possible scenario in which corporate or commercial developers would be without a device.

The obvious and most important reason for testing on a device is that no matter how good a job the emulator does, it isn't a device. You don't interact with an emulator using a stylus; you use a keyboard and mouse. You don't hold it in your hand; it sits on your virtual desktop. It has different processor capabilities.

With that said, I have to tell you that I have from time to time used the emulator. In situations where you don't want to hook up a device, such as on an airplane, the emulator is a nice alternative. Additionally, the emulator provided with the Smart Device Extensions is a vast improvement over previous Pocket PC emulators.

Launching the Emulator

You can launch the emulator in two ways: from within the Visual Studio .NET IDE and from the command prompt.

Launching the Emulator from Within VS .NET

There are two ways to launch the emulator from within the Visual Studio .NET IDE. The first way is as follows:

1. Start a Smart Device Extension project.

2. Select **Pocket PC 2002 Emulator** from the Deployment Device combo box, which is located on the toolbar.

3. Run your application.

The emulator will be automatically loaded in preparation to running your application.

The second way to launch the emulator is to attempt to establish a connection to the emulator from within the Visual Studio .NET IDE. This can be accomplished by clicking the **Connect to Device** button, which is located on the toolbar, or through the **Connect to Device** menu item on the Tools menu.

TIP *To speed the development process, it's best to leave the emulator open and running between builds and tests of your application. I've found that the slow start time of the emulator interferes with the build, test, refine, and repeat development process.*

Launching the Emulator from the Command Prompt

To launch the Windows CE emulator from the command prompt, perform the following steps:

1. Open the command prompt.

2. Either define the path to, or navigate to, the directory where the emulator executable resides. By default, the emulator resides in the following directory: C:\Program Files\Microsoft Visual Studio .NET 2003\ CompactFrameworkSDK\ConnectionManager\Bin.

3. Enter the command **emulator**, along with any command-line arguments, and press Enter. The emulator will start.

Table B-1 shows command line arguments for the emulator application.

Table B-1. Emulator Command Line Arguments

ARGUMENT	DESCRIPTION
/CEImage	Represents the path to the operating system image to load into the emulator. The image must match the target device. This argument is required.
/Ethernet	Enables or disables an Ethernet adapter for use with the emulator. Acceptable values are none, shared, virtualswitch, or the MAC address of an adapter to use.
/Skin	Specifies the XML file defining the skin to use with the emulator.
/Video	Defines the resolution and bit depth for the emulator; for example, 240×320×16.

Default images, along with their skins, are included under the default folder hierarchy of C:\Program Files\Microsoft Visual Studio .NET 2003\ CompactFrameworkSDK\ConnectionManager\Bin\Images.

Running the Emulator Without a Network Connection

The emulators provided with Smart Device Extensions will not operate unless the development PC on which it's running has a network connection. If your PC doesn't have a network connection, you can still use the emulator by installing the Microsoft Loopback Network Adapter. This adapter simulates a network connection and effectively fools the emulator into running.

Installing a Loopback Adapter Under Windows 2000

Under Windows 2000, the process for installing the Microsoft Loopback Network Adapter is as follows:

1. From the Control Panel, click **Add/Remove Hardware**.

2. On the Welcome page of the Add/Remove Hardware Wizard, click **Next**.

3. Select **Add/Troubleshoot a device** and click **Next**. The process will pause while your system is scanned for plug-and-play devices.

4. From the Choose a Hardware Device page, select **Add a new device** and click **Next**.

5. On the Find New Hardware page, select **No, I want to select the hardware from a list** and click **Next**.

6. From the Hardware Type page, select **Network adapters** and click **Next**. There will be a brief delay while a list of network adapters is generated.

7. On the Select Network Adapter page, first select **Microsoft** from the Manufacturers list box, then select **Microsoft Loopback Adapter** from the Network Adapter list box. Click the **Next** button.

8. From the Start Hardware Installation page click **Next**. The loopback adapter installs.

Configuring a Loopback Adapter Under Windows 2000

Like any network adapter, installing a loopback adapter is only half of the process. You also need to configure your new adapter. Perform the following steps to configure the loopback adapter:

1. From the Start menu, select **Settings**, then **Network and Dial-up Connections**, and finally **Local Area Connection**. The Local Area Connection Status dialog box displays.

2. Click the **Properties** button. The Local Area Connection Properties dialog box displays.

 CAUTION *At this point, check to make sure that you're working with the right connection. The **Connection Using** field of this dialog box should read **Microsoft Loopback Adapter**.*

---

3. Select **Internet Protocol (TCP/IP)** and click the **Properties** button. The Internet Protocol dialog box displays.

4. Configure the IP address properties.

5. Click the **OK** button to close the Internet Protocol dialog box.

6. Click the **OK** button to close the Local Area Connection Properties dialog box.

7. Click the **Close** button to close the Local Area Connection Status dialog box.

Configuring the Emulator

You can divide the topic of configuring the emulator into two categories: configuring the "hardware" environment and configuring the instance of the Pocket PC operating system that's running in the emulator. I'm not going to discuss the process of configuring the operating system, as it's identical to how you would configure an actual device. Instead, in this section I'm going to focus on configuring the hardware environment—that's to say, the virtual device on which the emulator runs.

Defining the Emulator's Hardware

The hardware configuration of the emulator is defined through the Visual Studio .NET IDE. This configuration defines the virtual device in which the emulator runs.

In most cases, you can simply use the default settings, which define a device with 32 megabytes of RAM, a 240×320 screen with 16 bits of color depth (as shown in Figure B-1), and no COM or parallel ports.

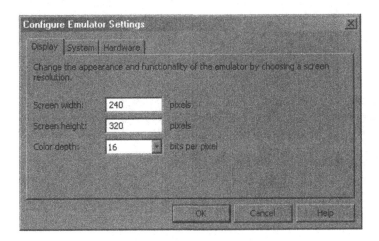

Figure B-1. Default emulator settings

To alter the hardware configuration of the emulator, perform the following steps:

1. From within the Visual Studio .NET IDE, select **Options** from under the Tools menu.

2. Under the **Devices** folder of the Options dialog box, select **Devices**.

3. In the Devices list box, select **Pocket PC 2002 Emulator**, as shown in Figure B-1.

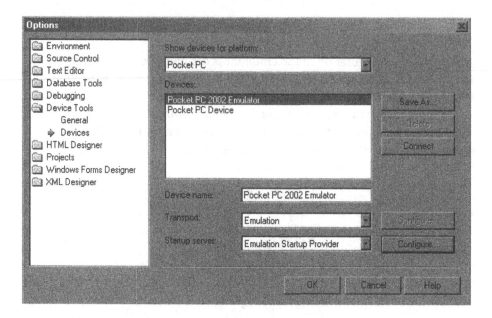

Figure B-2. Specifying the device in the Devices list box

4. Click the **Configure** button.

5. The Configure Emulator Settings dialog box displays. Define your new emulator settings and click the **OK** button.

The Configure Emulator Settings dialog box has three tabs: **Display**, **System**, and **Hardware**. On the **Display** tab, you can specify the size and color depth of the emulator screen. From the **System** tab, you can define the emulator's memory size and the host key, which provides a shortcut to emulator control features (see Figure B-3). The **Hardware** tab allows you to associate serial and parallel ports on your development PC to the emulator (see Figure B-4).

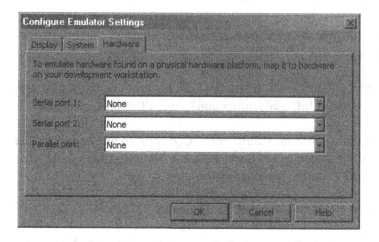

Figure B-3. System tab settings

Figure B-4. Hardware tab settings

NOTE *As with actual devices, the Pocket PC emulator is limited to 64 megabytes of RAM. Even though the dialog box will allow you to set the amount of memory to 256 megabytes, the emulator will in fact only have 64 megabytes. This is a limitation of the Pocket PC 2002 operating system, which applies as well to the emulator.*

TIP *A common reason to increase the memory size configuration of the emulator is to handle testing applications that make use of large SQL Server CE databases.*

Setting Up an ActiveSync Partnership

You may need to establish an ActiveSync connection to the emulator to test specific features or functionality of your application. To create a connection to the emulator, your development PC needs at least two COM ports. The emulator and the development PC will each need a port for use with the ActiveSync connection.

To establish the physical connection between your development PC and the emulator, perform the following steps:

1. Connect a null modem serial cable between the two serial ports.

2. Configure the emulator's hardware to include a serial port. This will be the emulator's ActiveSync connection.

3. On your PC, launch the ActiveSync application.

4. Under the File menu of the ActiveSync application, select **Connection Settings**.

5. On the Connection Settings dialog box, confirm that the setting **Allow serial cable or infrared connection to this COM port** is selected.

6. Using the combo box, configure the COM port to one of the COM ports on which you connected the serial cable. Note that this should NOT be the port you added to the emulator.

7. Click the **OK** button to close the dialog box.

To establish a partnership between your development PC and the emulator, perform the following steps:

1. Start the emulator if necessary.

2. Press and hold the control key (CTRL) on your development PC.

3. In the emulator, click and hold on the clock in the upper-right corner of the title bar. After a brief pause, a shortcut menu displays.

4. From this menu, select **Run**.

5. In the Run dialog box, type **repllog**. The repllog executable is the device-side component of ActiveSync. It initiates the connection to a PC.

6. The ActiveSync module on your desktop PC will detect the emulator's attempt to connect. The New Partnership Wizard will start.

7. Complete the wizard, specifying the types of data to synchronize between the emulator and your development PC.

At this point, you have a functioning ActiveSync connection between the emulator and your development PC.

NOTE *You should use ActiveSync version 3.6 or later when working with Smart Device Extensions and the .NET Compact Framework.*

Changing the Emulator's Skin

This is another one of those things that falls into one of two categories: Either you have too much time on your hands or you're being paid by the hour.

The emulator allows you to modify and customize the skins used by the emulator. If you're not already familiar with the term, *skins* define the appearance of an application. In this case, that application is the emulator.

You define the skin for the emulator with an XML file. Listing B-1 shows an example of the default skin shipped with Visual Studio .NET. Through this file, you can configure the size and position of the emulator, the graphical images that define the interface, and tooltips.

TIP *You may choose to define custom tooltips in situations where your application is taking control over the hardware buttons.*

Listing B-1. The Default Skin

```xml
<skin>
<view titleBar="Pocket PC 2002" displayPosX="56" displayPosY="61"
 displayWidth="240" displayHeight="320" displayDepth="16"
 mappingImage="pda_3.bmp" normalImage="pda_1.bmp" downImage="pda_2.bmp">
  <button toolTip="rocker-up" onClick="0x48" mappingColor="0x00FFFF" />
  <button toolTip="rocker-down" onClick="0x50" mappingColor="0x00FFD7" />
  <button toolTip="softkey 1" onClick="0x3B" mappingColor="0xFF00FF" />
  <button toolTip="softkey 2" onClick="0x3C" mappingColor="0xFF00D7" />
  <button toolTip="softkey 3" onClick="0x3D" mappingColor="0xFF0000" />
  <button toolTip="softkey 4" onClick="0x3E" mappingColor="0xD70000" />
  <button toolTip="dpad-up" onClick="0x48" mappingColor="0xFFFF00" />
  <button toolTip="dpad-down" onClick="0x50" mappingColor="0xFFAF00" />
  <button toolTip="dpad-left" onClick="0x4B" mappingColor="0xFFD700" />
```

```
    <button toolTip="dpad-right" onClick="0x4D" mappingColor="0xFF8700" />
    <button toolTip="dpad-action" onClick="0x1C" mappingColor="0xFF5F00" />
</view>
</skin>
```

 NOTE *For more information on creating skins, see the emulator help file, which is accessible through the Help menu from the emulator.*

Resetting the Emulator

Like regular Pocket PC devices, you can reset the emulator. This can be either a soft or a hard reset. The soft reset restarts the emulator while maintaining any existing configurations. The hard reset restarts the emulator while restoring it to its original state. That's to say, you'll have to go through the Startup Wizard and will lose any existing configurations.

You use both of these resets just as you would on a device, to restore a testing environment.

Saving the Emulator State

When you exit the emulator, you'll be prompted to save the current configuration, or state, of the emulator. The saved state automatically restores the next time the emulator starts. This feature enables you to create and reuse a specific emulator configuration that is best suited for your testing needs.

A single file stores the state of an emulator. This file is placed in the following location:

```
C:\Documents and Settings\<account name>\Application Data
```

where "account name" is the name of the user account under which you logged in; the filename for the state file is {GIUD}.vsv. You'll notice this file by its relatively large size.

Moving Files to the Emulator

The last topic that I want to discuss is how you go about moving files to the emulator. These files, used for testing purposes, might include anything from simple text files all the way to databases.

Earlier versions of Windows CE/Pocket PC emulators offered two distinct approaches to creating the emulator environment. The first generation of emulators used a closed environment, which was inaccessible from standard Windows-based file management tools found on the development PC. Any files that you needed on the emulator had to either be created within the emulator or copied to the emulator using specialized utilities that were included with the eMbedded Visual Tools.

Second generation emulators provided a more open environment, one that was accessible using common tools, such as File Explorer. The emulator directory structure existed in a subdirectory on the development PC. Copying files to and from the emulator was a simple drag-and-drop operation.

The emulator included with Smart Device Extensions returns you to the closed emulator environment. To complicate matters, unlike earlier versions of the eMbedded Visual Tools, Smart Device Extensions doesn't include a file management tool. This absence requires some creative workaround on your part.

There are three common ways to provide files within the emulator environment. One way is to create the files through applications that run on the emulator. I don't believe that this approach requires any additional discussion here. You can use any of the other approaches detailed throughout this book to create text, XML, or database files.

What I'm going to focus on in the remaining part of this appendix is the other two ways of providing files within the emulator: adding files to your project and copying files from a share.

Adding Files to Your Project

The easiest method to move files to the emulator is to include them as part of your project. The other advantage to using this approach is that in the event that you perform a hard reset on the emulator, you simply need to rebuild your project to resume testing.

The process for using this approach is as follows:

1. Open your project within Visual Studio .NET.

2. Under the Project menu, select **Add Existing Item**.

3. From the Add Existing Item dialog box, select the file that you want to copy to the emulator.

4. Click the **Open** button. The file will be added to your project.

5. In the Solution Explorer window, select the file you added.

6. In the Properties window, verify that the **Build** property is set to **Content**. Items configured as "Content" are copied to the target device as separate files. Items configured as "Embedded Resource" are part of the application's executable.

7. Build the project. The file copies to the device along with your application.

Copying Files from a Share

The second approach offers more flexibility with a minimal amount of additional work. It makes use of the network file sharing functionality built into the Pocket PC operating system, which subsequently is made available through the emulator included with Smart Device Extensions.

There are two parts to this approach: setting up a share on your development PC and then accessing that share through the emulator's File Explorer.

Setting up a share requires two configurations. First, you must configure your PC to enable sharing. Second, you must configure individual folders to share.

To enable sharing on a development PC running Windows 2000, perform the following steps:

1. Under the Start menu, select **Settings**, select **Network and Dial-up Connections**, and then specify your local area network connection.

2. From the Local Area Connection dialog box, click the **Properties** button.

3. From the Local Area Connection Properties dialog box, enable **File and Print Sharing for Microsoft Networks**.

4. Click the **OK** button to close the Local Area Connection Properties dialog box.

5. Click the **Close** button to close the Local Area Connection dialog box.

At this point, you've configured your development PC to allow file sharing. Next you need to share the folder in which you'll place the files you wish to copy to the emulator. To share a folder under Windows 2000, perform the following steps:

1. Launch File Explorer.

2. In File Explorer, right-click the folder you wish to share.

3. A pop-up menu will display. From this menu, select **Properties**.

4. From the Properties dialog box, click the **Sharing** tab.

5. On the **Sharing** tab, select to share the folder and provide a name for the share.

6. Click the **OK** button to close the Properties dialog box.

With your development PC configured, you're ready to copy files. First, you'll need to place all of the files destined for the emulator in the shared folder. Then, to move the files to the emulator, perform the following steps:

1. Launch the emulator. Refer to the instructions on launching the emulator at the start of this appendix, if necessary.

2. From within the emulator start File Explorer.

3. From the File Explorer menu, select **Open**.

4. The Open dialog box will display. Specify the name of your development computer followed by the name of the share you created using this format: **mycomputer\myshare**.

5. Tap the **OK** button.

6. Depending upon the security settings on your development PC, you may be prompted for a user name and password before being allowed to access the share.

At this point, you're ready to copy files to and from the share on your development PC and the emulator.

 NOTE *These same approaches for copying files work equally well with a device with one known issue. Pocket PC devices by default have a device name "Pocket PC". Unless you change this name, you won't be able to access a share.*

APPENDIX C

Resources

THIS APPENDIX PROVIDES YOU with a variety of sources for information and products that relate to either the .NET Compact Framework or mobile development.

 CAUTION *As with any printed materials that include references to Web sites, there is always the possibility that a URL will have changed between the time a book goes to print and the time you purchase and read that book. For an up-to-date list of mobile development–related resources, check out* http://www.larryroof.com.

Newsgroups

The most active newsgroups of interest to the NETCF-based mobile developers are all sponsored by Microsoft. They include the following:

- `microsoft.public.dotnet.framework.compactframework`—Discussions on developing with the .NET Compact Framework.

- `microsoft.public.mobility.miserver`—Topics on Microsoft's Mobile Information Server, the server-based ActiveSync manager.

- `microsoft.public.pocketpc`—General information about the Pocket PC, focusing on the hardware and operating system.

- `microsoft.public.pocketpc.developer`—A somewhat useful forum for Pocket PC developers. Although, unlike the .NET Compact Framework newsgroup, this newsgroup isn't product specific, it's useful in that it covers a variety of topics, including working with hardware, Pocket Internet Explorer, and the eMbedded development tools (eVC++ and eVB).

- `microsoft.public.smartphone.developer`—Provides discussions on Smartphone-related topics.

- `microsoft.public.sqlserver.ce`—Focuses on the SQL Server CE product. The best source for mobile database–related questions.

- microsoft.public.webservices—While technically not a NETCF or a mobile group, in situations where your mobile solution needs to leverage a Web service, information found in this newsgroup may be helpful.

- microsoft.public.windowsce.app.development—You'll find discussions on general Windows CE–related topics within this newsgroup.

- microsoft.public.windowsce.embedded.vb—The newsgroup for developers working with eMbedded Visual Basic (eVB).

- microsoft.public.windowsce.embedded.vc—The newsgroup for developers working with eMbedded Visual C++ (eVC++).

Web Sites

Numerous Web sites provide useful information for mobile developers. In this section, I've divided these sites into several categories for easier reference.

Web Sites: Developer Programs

If you're developing commercial applications that target the Pocket PC, you may be interested in participating in one or both of the following two programs:

Microsoft's Mobile Solution Partner Program is a worldwide initiative designed to aid you in the development and marketing of mobile solutions. You can obtain additional information on this program at http://www.microsoft.com/mobile/partners/default.asp.

Microsoft's Mobile2Market Program is a comprehensive program for the certification and delivery of mobile applications designed for Pocket PC and Smartphone. It connects independent software vendors to mobile operators and retailers, strengthening the marketplace for mobile applications by creating new revenue opportunities for mobile applications, reducing your time to market, and improving your customer's user experience. For more information on this program, see http://www.microsoft.com/mobile/developer/developerprograms/mobile2market/default.asp.

Web Sites: Developer Information and Tools

Following is a list of sites that cater to mobile developers, offering articles, sample applications, and forums:

- `http://smartdevices.microsoftdev.com`—Microsoft's Web site for smart device development, where you will find articles, downloads, and other items for developers who are targeting the Pocket PC, Pocket PC 2002, Pocket PC 2003, Pocket PC Phone Edition, Smartphone, Handheld PC, and other devices running Windows CE version 4.1 or later.

- `http://samples.gotdotnet.com/quickstart/CompactFramework`—Microsoft's site that targets developers who are just starting to work with the .NET Compact Framework. The QuickStart site provides guidance in a variety of areas. It offers mobile development techniques and workarounds for differences between the full .NET Framework and the .NET Compact Framework.

- `http://msdn.microsoft.com`—Microsoft's MSDN site contains a number of articles and white papers on working with the .NET Compact Framework and SQL Server CE. On this site, you'll find the MSDN Voices column "Two for the Road," which presents monthly articles on mobile development.

- `http://www.devbuzz.com`—A comprehensive repository of articles, samples, and forums on the .NET Compact Framework and SQL Server CE.

- `http://www.innovativedss.com`—The forums offered at this site include a variety of topics related to the .NET Compact Framework.

- `http://www.larryroof.com`—Here you'll find links to Larry Roof's articles on developing with the .NET Compact Framework and SQL Server CE.

- `http://www.forestsoftwaregroup.com`—Dan Fergus's site offers a variety of code examples and articles on working with NETCF.

- `http://www.opennetcf.org`—A site that provides a repository for information and open-source projects specifically targeting the .NET Compact Framework.

- `http://www.pocketpcdn.com`—This site offers a large number of articles that focus on mobile development. While NETCF content is minimal, this site still is a good source for Pocket PC–related topics.

- `http://pocketprojects.pocketgear.com`—Here you'll find a large variety of forums on mobile development, including the .NET Compact Framework.

- http://www.microsoft.com/mobile/assets/PocketPC_SoftApp_Handbook.doc—
  This link brings you to "Designed for Windows for Pocket PC, Handbook
  for Software Applications," Microsoft's guidelines for developing applications that target the Pocket PC.

- http://www.ragingsmurf.com/vbcsharpconverter.aspx—This site will convert
  code written in C# .NET to its VB .NET equivalent. This feature can be of
  great aid in situations where the only sample of a particular technique
  that you have is in C# and you want to work in VB.

Web Sites: Pocket PC Software

Although you'll find a number of Pocket PC software sites on the Web, three of
these sites merit mentioning for their usefulness to mobile developers:

- http://www.pocketpc.com—The "home" site of the Pocket PC. This site
  includes everything from "getting started" tips for the end user, to brief
  development articles, software updates, and development kits and tools.

- http://www.handango.com—The premier commercial portal for software
  that targets the Pocket PC. Whether you are looking for end-user software,
  developer tools, or a market for your applications, Handango is the place
  to start.

- http://www.microsoft.com/mobile/catalog/—Microsoft's catalog of applications certified for the Pocket PC and Smartphone. This catalog is a showcase
  of products that carry the Microsoft Designed for Windows logo certification and is part of the Mobile2Market Program discussed earlier in this
  appendix.

Web Sites: Pocket PC Hardware and Accessories

In this section you'll find links to information about commercial and industrial
versions of Pocket PC, as well as miscellaneous equipment for your mobile device.

Commercial Devices

A large number of companies now make some variation of Pocket PC devices.
I'm not going to list them all here, as the list of vendors and the models they provide change on a regular basis. Instead, I would recommend you reference the

following page on Microsoft's Pocket PC site that provides a fairly up-to-date listing of current products offered by Pocket PC vendors. The link is http://www.microsoft.com/windowsmobile/buyersguide/compare/default.mspx. From this page you can select from various global regions to obtain information on devices that are marketed in your area.

Industrial Devices

There are several manufacturers that make industrialized versions of Pocket PC devices.

- **Symbol**—Provides a wide variety of ruggedized devices that incorporate barcode scanning, wireless networking, printing, magnetic strip card reading, and GSM/GPRS connectivity. Symbol offers an SDK for developers working with the .NET Compact Framework that makes it easy to incorporate their devices' hardware features into your mobile solutions. For more details, see http://www.symbol.com/products/mobile_computers/mobile_computers.html.

- **Intermec**—Provides a complete product line of ruggedized devices, like Symbol, that offer scanning, wireless networking, printing, magnetic strip card reading, and GSM/GPRS/CDMA connectivity. Intermec offers developers components to use with the .NET Compact Framework for leveraging the features of their devices. For more product information, see the Intermec site at http://www.intermec.com.

- **TimbaTec**—Offers an industrialized, all-weather device that incorporates wireless networking functionality. The TimbaTec device is completely sealed so that it can be used in extreme climate conditions. You can select from a variety of plug-in modules, including barcode and serial port functionality, that extend the capabilities of this device. For more information, see TimbaTec's site at http://www.timbatec.com.

- **Amaga**—Offers a rugged, expandable device for both military and industrial use. Available add-ons include wireless networking, GPS, GSM/GPRS/CDMA, and Bluetooth. For more information, visit the Amaga site at http://www.myagama.com.

- **Casio**—Provides a number of industrial devices based upon the Pocket PC form factor. Most units are expandable so that you can add barcode scanning, wireless networking, or a magnetic strip reader. See Casio's site at http://www.casio.com.

Miscellaneous Equipment

This category includes CF cards, PC Cards, cases, keyboards, modems, and other equipment that extends or enhances the effectiveness of a Pocket PC. Listing all of the vendors that provide such equipment is beyond the limits of this appendix, and such a list would be out of date the day that this book went to print. Instead, I would suggest visiting the Mobile Planet Web site at http://www.mobile-planet.com. Mobile Planet offers a comprehensive assortment of equipment for the Pocket PC.

Developer Tools

While the number of third-party companies that cater to mobile developers is but a mere fraction of the volume of companies providing aid to the desktop market, you should be aware of certain key products and companies, as we'll discuss in this section.

Hardware Tools

The most important hardware tool that I would suggest you consider as a mobile developer is to add an Ethernet connection to the device you're using for testing. Whether that connection is tethered or wireless depends upon your project needs, but whichever you choose, you will find that developing over Ethernet dramatically improves your productivity.

While a number of manufacturers offer both tethered and wireless CF Ethernet cards for use with the Pocket PC, I'm particularly fond of the offerings from Socket. They are battery friendly, meaning they are designed to use as little power as possible. You can find out more about Socket's offerings at http://www.socketcom.com.

Programming, Testing, and Deployment

While not a large number of tools are available for mobile developers, you may want to consider adding a few key products, discussed in this section, to your creative arsenal.

Pocket Controller

This utility is comprised of two components, desktop and device. This pair of components works together, providing both a visual and input interface between a desktop PC and a device.

Two main benefits are offered through Pocket Controller. First, it enhances your productivity, as it allows you to enter data from your PC rather than from the device. What this means is that you can use your computer keyboard and mouse instead of the stylus, enabling you to speed up your testing processes.

Second, Pocket Controller is ideal for presentations, as it allows you to project the screen of a device through a connecting PC. All that you need to do is attach a projector to your computer to demonstrate applications running on a Pocket PC.

Additional features include

- Ability to remotely capture and print screens

- Support for both portrait and landscape view

- Four levels of zoom off the device interface

- Ability to transfer data between desktop and mobile device clipboards

- File transfer support

- Ability to remotely activate or stop applications and processes

- Ability to create video recordings of screen activities as they occur on a device

Pocket Controller is a product of Soti and is available online at http://www.soti.net.

P/Invoke Wizard

If you need to incorporate Windows CE API function calls into your mobile solutions, then you should consider purchasing the P/Invoke Wizard offered by Paul Yao, at http://www.paulyao.com. The wizard works by reading values found in the include (.H) files of Visual C projects. It takes the various C/C++ declarations and produces a compatible .NET version in your choice of C# or VB .NET.

One of the hardest parts of being able to use Windows CE API functions from within a .NET Compact Framework application is the process of translating the calls from their native format to the format required by NETCF. This wizard makes quick work of that process and is a tool that will pay for itself many times over.

PocketConsole

Microsoft provides a console, or what is frequently thought of as a DOS prompt, with Windows CE. Unfortunately, the Pocket PC OS doesn't. While not in great demand for mobile developers, in certain situations you'll need such a console as part of your mobile solutions.

PocketConsole, from SymbolicTools, provides a console device for Pocket PCs. This console manages input and output for character-mode applications.

For more information on PocketConsole, see the vendor's Web site at http://www.symbolictools.de.

EzSetup

This free setup utility allows you to create installations for your Pocket PC applications. The installations generated by EzSetup are easy for your end user to follow. This utility allows you to include readme files and licensing information and generates compressed, self-contained, self-extracting installations.

Installations can be created for a variety of languages and integrated with the installation component of ActiveSync. Best of all, this setup utility is free.

For more information, see http://www.softspb.com.

Controls and Components

The selection of third-party controls and components for use with the .NET Compact Framework is steadily growing. Following are some of the more useful controls available.

CFCOM

This component provides a solution to one of the largest limitations of NETCF—being able to use COM objects and ActiveX controls. With CFCOM, you will be able to

- Use ActiveX controls in NETCF applications.

- Use COM components in NETCF applications.

- Build your own managed controls and components based upon ActiveX controls and COM components.

- Support both ActiveX and COM events.

- Include full designer support for Visual Studio .NET.

Included with this utility are complete examples with source for wrappers for ADOCE, Pocket Outlook, and Media Player. You can obtain CFCOM from Odyssey Software at http://www.odysseysoftware.com.

ADOCE .NET Wrapper

This component provides both read and write access to Pocket Access databases from your NETCF applications. With this component, you can also access underlying system tables that are stored in the Object Store.

The ADOCE .NET Wrapper uses an object model that is similar to ADOCE itself, making development easier for eVB programmers switching over to the .NET Compact Framework. The wrapper provides support for NETCF features such as data binding, providing you with the best of both worlds from ADOCE and NETCF.

The ADOCE .NET Wrapper is available from InTheHand Software at http://www.inthehand.com.

Pocket Outlook .NET

Pocket Outlook .NET is a set of .NET classes that enable you to incorporate the appointments, contacts, and tasks that are stored in Pocket Outlook into your NETCF applications. Delivered as a DLL wrapper to the underlying POOM COM component, Pocket Outlook .NET provides a set of classes, methods, and properties that make it easy to query, add, and update information stored within Pocket Outlook.

Pocket Outlook .NET is available from InTheHand Software at http://www.inthehand.com.

Document List

Products such as Pocket Word and Pocket Excel make use of a standard list interface for displaying available documents. InTheHand Software offers a lightweight component, Document List, that allows NETCF developers to easily incorporate this interface into their applications. Using this component rather than OpenFileDialog will dramatically improve the appearance of your user interfaces.

Document List is available from InTheHand Software at http://www.inthehand.com.

Identity

Stored away in the registry of every Pocket PC is the device owner's information. Using InTheHand Software's Identity component, you can access this information easily from your NETCF application. You can use this information to customize your application and to perform key-based registration, such as that used by Handango.

The Identity component is available on InTheHand Software's Web site at http://www.inthehand.com.

DateTimePicker Control

One of the many controls that didn't make it into the .NET Compact Framework, the DateTimePicker control is a mainstay of user interface development for mobile applications. IntelliProg, realizing this shortcoming, was quick to provide an alternative for use under NETCF.

For more information, see IntelliProg's Web site at http://www.intelliprog.com.

HTMLViewer Control

While certainly not as robust in functionality as the Web controls offered with the .NET Framework, IntelliProg's HTMLViewer control enables you to render and display HTML content within the interface of your mobile applications.

For more information, see IntelliProg's Web site at http://www.intelliprog.com.

RichInk Control

NETCF is incredibly limited in the ways it provides developers for displaying text content. IntelliProg addresses this shortcoming with its RichInk control. This control supports entry, editing, and display of text in a variety of formats including Rich Text Format (RTF). An additional feature of this control is its support for ink, enabling your users to enter content in written form.

For more information on the RichInk control, see IntelliProg's Web site at `http://www.intelliprog.com`.

IP*Works

This suite of controls from nSoftware greatly simplifies the development of Web-enabled applications. Included as part of this package are controls that implement the HTTP, FTP, SMTP, POP3, and NNTP protocols, as well as many more. You can obtain more information on IP*Works at the company's Web site: `http://www.nsoftware.com`.

Training

If you are looking for either face-to-face or video-based training to jump-start your development projects, then look no further than `http://www.larryroof.com`, where you will find the finest in NETCF application development training.

Larry Roof's 5-day training class will enable you to quickly begin developing robust mobile solutions using the .NET Compact Framework. You'll be led through the complete process of developing effective Pocket PC applications, from design, through development, and finally to distribution. You'll learn firsthand from one of the industry's best.

Are you unable to get away from work to attend a 5-day training class? Then let Larry bring his training to you in the form of his industry-leading video training. This isn't simple computer-based training as you seen offered by other vendors; instead, it's high-quality, DVD-based content that is unmatched by anyone today. You can purchase the full set of training modules or only the topics you're interested in. If you just need to learn how to work with SQL Server CE, or to create Web services, then you can buy just those modules.

For more information on either Larry's face-to-face or video-based training, visit Larry's Web site at `http://www.larryroof.com`.

Sample Applications

THE SAMPLES THAT ACCOMPANY this book are available as a download from three sources: the Apress Web site, Larry Roof's Web site, and Dan Fergus's Web site.

The Apress Web site is at http://www.apress.com. Once there, you'll need to navigate to the page for this title. On that page, you'll find a Source Code link. Clicking that link will take you to a page from which you can download the source code.

You can also get the samples from either Larry's or Dan's Web site. If you go to http://www.larryroof.com, on the left side of the main page, you'll find a menu. From this menu, select **published works**, then **books**, and finally **The Definitive Guide to the .NET Compact Framework**. The page that details this book will load. From that page, select **Download the Source**. At Dan's site, http://www.forestsoftwaregroup.com, navigate to the samples by using the Publication link on the main page's left-hand menu. That will take you to a page giving details on the book and directions on how to access the sample applications.

Unpacking the Sample Applications

You receive the source for this book as a zipped archive. You'll need a utility, such as WinZip (http://www.winzip.com), to uncompress the archive.

The archive will unzip to a series of individual folders, with each folder containing the samples for a chapter.

Obtaining Sample Updates

To correct errors and omissions, updates to the samples may be made available periodically. These corrections will be bundled into a samples archive and will be available from the two sources detailed earlier in this section.

Loading a Sample Application

All of the samples are in the form of a completed VB .NET project. You can load an individual project by performing the following steps:

1. Start Visual Studio .NET.

2. From the File menu select **Open**, and then **Project**.

3. Through the Open Project dialog box, navigate to and select the sample project you wish to load.

4. Click the **Open** button to load the desired project.

Running a Sample Application

Almost all of the sample applications provided for *The Definitive Guide to the .NET Compact Framework* run without any additional configuration. In some instances, particularly with the database-related samples, you may need to configure either the sample and/or the target server before running the sample. In those instances, details provided within this book specify the steps you need to perform.

To run a sample application, perform the following steps:

1. Select either **Pocket PC Device** or **Pocket PC Emulator** from the Deployment Device combo box.

2. Select **Release** from the Solution Configurations combo box.

3. Click the **Start** button.

The individual projects are configured to load to the **\Windows\Start Menu\Programs\Apress** folder on either your device or in the emulator. This allows you to manually launch applications through the Start menu later. Simply tap the Start menu, then **Programs**, tap the **Apress** folder, and finally tap the desired application.

Removing an Application

Applications built and deployed from within the Visual Studio .NET IDE are not "installed" on the device. They are simply copied to the device. To remove an application from your device, you only need to delete its executable. You can use the Pocket PC File for this.

To remove an application, perform the following steps:

1. Start File Explorer.

2. Navigate to Windows\Start Menu\Programs\Apress.

3. Tap and hold on the application you wish to delete.

4. From the pop-up context menu, select **Delete**.

5. From the Confirm File Delete dialog box, tap **Yes** to complete the deletion.

Problems with a Sample Application

If you run into any problems with a sample application, first verify that you have performed any additional configurations. If you are still having trouble, you should check to see if there is an update to the book's samples available. If you have the latest updates and still can't resolve your problem, you can register your problem at http://www.larryroof.com. On the left side of the main page, you'll find a menu. From this menu, select **published works**, then **books**, and finally **The Definitive Guide to the .NET Compact Framework**. The page that details this book will load. From that page, select **Request Help with a Sample**.

APPENDIX E

Error Handling

NO DISCUSSION ON DEVELOPMENT would be complete without including a conversation on error handling. By definition, the mobile development environment is prone to runtime errors. Think about it; you're mixing wireless networking, cell phone communication, database synchronization, Web services, custom communication modules, battery-powered devices, and mobile users all together in one environment. As far as development goes, if this isn't asking for trouble, I don't know what is.

The bad news is that you're going to have to lace your mobile applications with error handling. The good news is that the .NET Compact Framework offers a robust set of tools for addressing this need. It combines the best of the Visual Basic world (On Error GoTo) along with the new .NET-based exception handling (Try, Catch, Finally). If you're an eMbedded Visual Basic developer switching over to NETCF, let me just say that you're in for a treat.

Now, I should take a moment to point out a key terminology difference between Visual Basic and VB .NET. *Error handling*, as you have come to know it in your developer journeys, is *exception handling* in the world of the .NET Compact Framework. Whether you refer to it as error or exception handling, it all boils down to the same thing: handling problems that occur during the running of your application.

Handling Errors Visual Basic Style

The .NET Compact Framework provides support for what I like to refer to as "old school VB error handling." The foundation of this style of error handling is the On Error Goto Label statement. Obviously, the key benefit to using this approach is that Visual Basic developers are already familiar with how it works, what it offers, and how to use it within an application.

VB-style error handling will certainly appeal to eMbedded Visual Basic developers migrating over to the .NET Compact Framework. After all, they've survived for years on the minimalist version of this, the On Error Resume Next statement, what I affectionately refer to as the "crash-and-burn school of error handling."

NOTE *The .NET Compact Framework does provide support for the On Error Resume Next statement, although for the life of me I couldn't think of a good reason to use it.*

Is this VB style of error handling the best approach to error handling offered by the .NET Compact Framework? Certainly, it's not. Is it a suitable approach to error handling? Usually it is. I guess what I'm saying is that if you're a VB or eVB developer switching over to the NETCF world, struggling with the idiosyncrasies of .NET, and are searching for development techniques that you're already familiar with, this might be just what you're looking for. Certainly, though, at some point, you should learn the new approaches to error handling offered through the .NET Compact Framework.

Implementing VB-Style Error Handling

The easiest way to understand the VB style of error handling is through the examination of a sample. Listing E-1 shows the basic structure of VB-style error handling.

Listing E-1. Implementing VB-Style Error Handling

```
Private Sub Button1_Click(ByVal sender As System.Object, _
  ByVal e As System.EventArgs) Handles Button1.Click

  Dim sw As System.IO.StreamWriter

' Enable error handling.
  On Error GoTo ErrorHandler

' Open the file.
  sw = New System.IO.StreamWriter("\Storage Card\text.tmp")

' Add some text to the file.
  sw.Write("This content was written at: ")
  sw.WriteLine(DateTime.Now)

' Close the file.
  sw.Close()

' Jump over the error handler code.
  Exit Sub
```

```
ErrorHandler:
  Select Case Err.Number
    Case 76      ' Cannot access the CF card.
      MsgBox("Please insert the CF card into the device and tap OK.", _
        MsgBoxStyle.Exclamation + MsgBoxStyle.OKOnly)
      Resume

    Case 101     ' Another common error.
      Resume Next

    Case Else    ' Handle general purpose errors here.
      MsgBox("Number: " & Err.Number.ToString _
        & " Description: " & Err.Description)
  End Select

End Sub
```

It all starts by enabling error handling, which is to say letting NETCF know that if any errors occur, you'll handle them. You accomplish this with the following statement:

```
On Error GoTo ErrorHandler
```

What this statement does is redirect the execution of code to the label ErrorHandler when a runtime error occurs. Usually, you'll find this statement near the top of a procedure, placed such that it will enable you to handle any and all errors that occur within the procedure.

The label serves as a declaration point for your error handling code. It's located near the bottom of Listing E-1, in a common place for this type of code. You implement labels by including the name of the label followed by a colon.

Now, I'd like to point out a key component to this style of error handling. It's what I refer to as the "error handler speed bump." This single line of code prevents your application from erroneously executing your error handling code. You place the speed bump directly above the start of your error handler as shown in Listing E-1. Its comprised of a simple statement, either Exit Sub or Exit Function. It's sole purpose is to exit the routine in which it's placed, skipping past your error handling code.

Trapping errors is only half of the problem. Handling errors is the other half. At the bottom of Listing E-1 is the code that handles errors. Typically, this will be a Select Case statement, with a set of individual Case statements handling all of the errors you anticipate encountering.

The Select Case statement evaluates the **Number** property of the Err object. This property holds the number of the last error that occurred. Note the inclusion of the Case Else branch with this statement. To handle errors that you might not have anticipated, it's always good practice to include a fail-safe branch in the form of a Case Else statement.

The Err Object

At the heart of this legacy form of error handling is the Err object. This object provides access to details on the last runtime error that occurred within your application. Table E-1 lists the key properties of this object.

Table E-1. Key Properties of the Err Object

PROPERTY	DESCRIPTION
Description	The description of the error
Number	The error number of the error
Source	The source of the last error

TIP *The easiest way to determine runtime error numbers encountered by your application is to add a simple error handler with ONLY a Case Else branch. Within this branch, display the **Number** and **Description** properties of the Err object.*

There are two key methods of the Err object: **Raise** and **Clear**. The **Raise** method is useful in generating a runtime error within your application, such as from within a custom control, with the purpose of passing the error back to the hosting application. The **Clear** method resets the Err object and is most useful in situations where you are using the On Error Resume Next form of error handling.

NOTE *Use the **Raise** method within controls, components, and DLLs to force a runtime error to occur, which in turn passes back to the host program. For an example of using the **Raise** method in this fashion, see Chapter 5.*

Recovering from a Runtime Error

Within your error handling code, you'll need to define how to respond to various runtime errors encountered. Listing E-2 provides a simple example of the most commonly used options.

Listing E-2. Recovering from a Runtime Error

```
ErrorHandler:
  Select Case Err.Number
    Case 76      ' Cannot access the CF card.
      MsgBox("Please insert the CF card into the device and tap OK.", _
        MsgBoxStyle.Exclamation + MsgBoxStyle.OKOnly)
      Resume

    Case 101     ' Another common error.
      Resume Next

    Case Else    ' Handle general-purpose errors here.
      MsgBox("Number: " & Err.Number.ToString _
        & " Description: " & Err.Description)
  End Select
```

In this example, two errors, numbers 76 and 101, have specific handlers. All other errors will fall into the Case Else branch of the Select statement. The error handling code for the 76 error includes the Resume statement. Error 101 has the Resume Next statement. These two statements differ in a subtle way.

Executing a Resume statement causes your program to go back to the offending line, which is the line of code that originally caused the runtime error. Commonly you would use the Resume statement in situations where your error handling code resolves the root cause that generated the error in the first place.

Take for example an application that stores its data on a CompactFlash (CF) card. If the CF card isn't in the device when the application attempts to open a file on that card, a runtime error will occur. All that you need to do to correct this runtime error is 1) instruct the user to insert the card back into the device, and 2) reexecute the offending line of code.

In comparison, the Resume Next statement causes the execution within your program to resume at the line of code immediately following the line that generated the original runtime error.

CAUTION *In general, you should do nothing within your error handling code that could potentially result in the generation of a runtime error. Handling such a situation is at best problematic. At its worst, it will result in the termination of your application.*

The Try, Catch, Finally Statements

Now that we've looked at the legacy approach to error handling, let's look at the far more powerful, elegant, and flexible functionality provided through the .NET Compact Framework.

The foundation of error, or exception handling, as it's referred to within the world of .NET, is implemented through the trio of Try, Catch, Finally statements. This combination of statements allows you to handle exceptions encountered while executing a body of code.

Listing E-3 shows a simple example using these statements. At the top of the example is the Try component. Within the Try section, you would place your application's code. For example, you might be opening a database connection or establishing a connection to a Web service.

Listing E-3. The Try, Catch, Finally Statement

```
Try
' Implement some functionality.
Catch ex as Exception
' Handle general exceptions.
Finally
' Executed regardless of whether an exception occurred.
End Try
```

The second part of this example is the Catch component. The code within this section executes when, and only when, an exception occurs. Your exception handling construct can include a single Catch statement or multiple Catch statements. When you define a Catch statement, you specify the type or category of exception that it handles. The example shown in Listing E-3 defines a single, general-purpose exception, ex. This argument contains information on the exception that occurred.

The third part of the example is the Finally component. The code within this section executes all of the time, regardless of whether an exception occurs. You use this section to perform cleanup operations.

Catching Exceptions

As I noted in the previous section, you use the Catch statement to handle exceptions that occur. There can be one or more Catch statements as part of a Try, Catch, Finally structure. Having multiple Catch statements allows you to handle specific varieties of exceptions, where each type of exception may have details specific to that exception.

Listing E-4 provides an example of using multiple Catch statements. In this case, there are three Catch statements. The first Catch statement handles exceptions related to the **SqlClient** namespace. The second Catch statement addresses exceptions from the **SqlServerCe** namespace. The third Catch statement handles all other exceptions. This approach of using a single general-purpose Catch statement followed by a series of specific Catch statements is common to Try, Catch, Finally constructs.

Listing E-4. Multiple Catch Statements

```
Try
' Implement some functionality.
Catch ex As SqlClient.SqlException
' Handle exceptions related to the SqlClient namespace.
Catch ex As SqlServerCe.SqlCeException
' Handle exceptions related to the SQLCE Client.
Catch ex As Exception
' Handle exceptions.
Finally
' Executed regardless of whether an exception occurred.
End Try
```

NOTE *Matching and performing the code within a particular Catch statement terminates checking all remaining Catch statements. Because of this, you should place Catch statements in the order of 1) selectiveness, and 2) preferable execution.*

TIP *You should always include a general-purpose Catch statement as part of your error handling. While namespace-specific Catch statements are useful in isolating and handling exceptions, you need some way to handle those errors that you just don't think of.*

Handling Exceptions

Catching an exception is only half of the solution. The other half involves identifying and possibly handling the root problem. This brings up a key point: Not all exceptions are terminal, nor for that matter unexpected.

Take for example the following scenario: You've created an application for use in a warehouse. This application talks to an enterprise server via a wireless Ethernet connection to store data. The application is simple. It scans bar codes and sends the scan on to the server. As is often the case, the wireless coverage within the warehouse is less than complete. There are dead spots where the device can't connect to the network.

When the device can't connect to the network, it obviously can't access the enterprise server, and can't store data. Is this a fatal error? Yes. Is it an application ender? No. You know that there are dead spots in your network. You also know that the user has to scan in these areas, so you had better handle these situations.

That's where Catch statements come in. They allow you to 1) identify when an exception occurs, 2) determine what the exception is, and 3) respond in an appropriate manner.

To identify the occurrence of an exception, you specify an exception condition with a Catch statement.

There are two ways to determine the exception. The first way is to have a Catch statement that checks for a specific type of exception. Listing E-5 shows an example of this. In this example, a Catch handles the **FileNotFoundException**, which occurs, as you might expect, when a file that your application attempted to reference isn't found.

Listing E-5. Checking for a Specific Exception

```
Try
' Implement some functionality.
Catch fileNotFound As System.IO.FileNotFoundException
' Handle exceptions related to a missing file.
Catch ex As Exception
' Handle exceptions.
Finally
' Executed regardless of whether an exception occurred.
End Try
```

This is a perfect example of handling a specific type of exception through the Catch statement.

The second way to determine what exception occurred is through the argument provided by the Catch statement. The **Message** property of the exception is a good place to start because it defines the exception. Listing E-6 shows an example of displaying the **Message** property.

Listing E-6. Displaying the Message Property of an Exception

```
Try
' Implement some functionality.
Catch ex As Exception
' Handle exceptions.
  Dim mb As MessageBox
  mb.Show(ex.Message)
Finally
' Executed regardless of whether an exception occurred.
End Try
```

TIP *Whenever possible, find ways to not code Finally statements. You'll find that by doing so you get into the habit of cleaning up your objects.*

How you respond to an error depends on your application's needs. On the simple end of the scale, you may just display an error message. You know, one of those "something real bad has happened, so call someone who cares" deals.

On the more robust end of the scale, you may perform any number of activities to guarantee that you deliver the data gathered through your application. In our wireless scenario, that could involve queuing data up in a local SQL Server CE database, placing it in an XML file, or dropping it into Microsoft's message queue (MSMQ).

Remember, as with the error handling techniques used with Visual Basic and eMbedded Visual Basic, it's possible within the Catch statement to gracefully handle and correct the root cause of exceptions.

The more complete you can make the exception handling and recovery, the more likely your application will be successful. This isn't an area of development where you should scrimp.

Creating an Exception "Safety Net"

Whether you're using the old style of Visual Basic error handling, or the new exception handling functionality provided through the .NET Compact Framework, any unhandled runtime errors have the same effect—they terminate your application.

If I may state the obvious, having your application come to an abrupt halt is never a good thing. Having it crash with some obscure message is even worse. You can rectify this problem with a few lines of simple code, creating what I like to refer to as a "safety net" for your application.

To be able to handle runtime errors appropriately, it's important that you have a solid understanding of what happens within your application when an error occurs.

Applications built upon the .NET Compact Framework handle errors in the following manner. First, they look for an error handler within the procedure where the error occurs. If either that procedure has the legacy-style On Error GoTo statement or the new Try, Catch, Finally statements, control passes to that code. If error handling code doesn't exist, then control is passed to the calling routine, which is the routine that called the procedure in which the runtime error occurred. This process continues until either error handling code is found or the top of the calling chain is reached. In the event that there's no error handling code found, an unhandled exception message is generated, and your application terminates.

Providing a "safety net" for your application is simple. All that you need to do is add a few lines of code into the **Main** subprocedure, which is responsible for controlling the launch of your application. Many of you may not be familiar with this procedure. It's added automatically to Pocket PC projects, existing with the Windows Form Designer–generated code region of a form.

By default, the **Main** subprocedure appears as shown in the following code snippet:

```
Public Shared Sub Main()
  Application.Run(New Form1())
End Sub
```

Adding a "safety net" to this procedure requires only a few lines of code as shown in Listing E-7. A Try, Catch construct handles any errors that may bubble up to this level, keeping your application from ending in an uncontrolled fashion. Note, in this example, I'm still halting the application. I'm just providing a more descriptive error message, something that hopefully will help in the process of determining what went wrong within the application.

Listing E-7. An Application-Wide Exception Handler

```
Public Shared Sub Main()
  Try
    Application.Run(New Form1())
  Catch ex As Exception
    MessageBox.Show("An fatal error occurred. Please contact tech support " & _
      "and provide them with this information: " & ControlChars.CrLf & _
        ex.Message.ToString & ControlChars.CrLf & "Application is terminating."
    Application.Exit()
  End Try
End Sub
```

Obtaining Detailed Error Information

In order to keep the .NET Compact Framework as compact as possible, Microsoft moved error strings to a separate DLL. This DLL, System.SR, is by default *not* configured as part of new NETCF projects. You'll need to add a reference to your project.

If this DLL isn't present on the target device, all exceptions will contain the message "Cannot load resource assembly." Obviously, this is less than helpful as part of a debugging process. Microsoft's idea here is to allow you to add the System.SR DLL during your testing process and exclude it when you distribute your application, saving the space required by the DLL.

Tracking Exceptions

Developing mobile applications presents developers with a completely new set of problems to overcome, including how to handle errors that occur when the user is in the field. By "in the field," I mean anywhere away from the office. They might literally be in a field avoiding muck, or they could be on a delivery route in a truck. Maybe they're at a customer's site or in their hotel room at night, in the user's car or showing off tech toys at the bar. What happens when they encounter a problem? It isn't likely they can walk down the hallway and talk to you, or for that matter can you get up from your desk and walk to them.

You might not know when an error occurred, for what reason it occurred, or how your application responded. At best, users might tell you at a later date and time that "something went wrong." On questioning users, they will probably give the typical responses of "I don't know what I was doing" (or the ever more popular "I wasn't doing anything"), followed up by "I don't remember what happened next." Ah, just the detailed information you need to successfully debug an application. And you wonder why they don't let tech support personnel carry sidearms.

How you handle the problem is one thing. How you find out that exceptions did, in fact, occur is something completely different.

When designing an application, I like to build in some type of exception log. This log records exceptions when they occur. It doesn't need to be anything fancy. A simple log with date-stamped records will suffice. It can be nothing more than a comma-separated text file. I like to include the exception, the source, and any other pertinent information. Periodically you'll need to upload this log to a server for processing. This can be incorporated into your data synchronization process.

It doesn't take much work to create a general-purpose routine that implements this type of functionality. You can use this routine with all of your applications. Listing E-8 demonstrates a simple audit trail function, LogError.

This function accepts as arguments the path to the audit trail file, the exception/
error message, the source of the error (which I commonly use to store the
offending procedure's name), and any additional comments that you might have.

Listing E-8. The AuditTrail Class

```
Public Class AuditTrail

  Function LogError(ByVal LogFile As String, ByVal Message As String, _
    ByVal Source As String, ByVal Comments As String) As Boolean
    Dim strLogRecord As String
    Dim sw As System.IO.StreamWriter

    Try

  ' Open the log.
      sw = New System.IO.StreamWriter(LogFile, True)

  ' Add the item to the log.
      strLogRecord = Now.ToString & "|" & Message & "|" & Source & _
        "|" & Comments & "|"
      sw.WriteLine(strLogRecord)

  ' Close the log.
      sw.Close()

  ' Return a positive result.
      LogError = True

  ' A runtime error was generated. Return a negative result.
    Catch
      LogError = False

    End Try

  End Function
End Class
```

New entries append at the bottom of any existing entries, just as you would
expect from an audit trail. To accomplish this, you must open the log file in
append mode.

NOTE *For more on working with simple text files, refer to Chapter 8.*

Arguments that comprise an entry are separated with pipe (|) characters, instead of the more commonly used comma-separated approach. This allows you to use commas within log file output. Figure E-1 shows the contents of the log file after running this sample application.

Figure E-1. The contents of the audit trail

 NOTE *Make sure that you periodically purge or delete your audit trail. If not, it may cause memory use problems down the road.*

Listing E-9 shows the **Click** event routine used to test the audit trail routine. A Throw statement triggers the exception, which in turn results in the Catch statement executing.

Listing E-9. Testing the AuditTrail Class

```
Private Sub btnLogError_Click(ByVal sender As System.Object, _
  ByVal e As System.EventArgs) Handles btnLogError.Click
  Dim at As New AuditTrail

' Generate an exception for testing purposes.
  Try
    Throw New System.Exception("A test error.")

' Handle the exception by writing an entry to the log.
  Catch ex As Exception
    If Not (at.LogError("\My Documents\audit trail.log", _
      ex.Message.ToString, _
      "btnLogError_Click", _
      "testing log file...")) Then
      MsgBox ("Could not write to the audit log.", MsgBoxStyle.Exclamation)
    End If

  End Try

End Sub
```

NOTE *The examples in this section are from the Audit Trail project, which is included under **Appendix E** in the **Samples** folder.*

Causing Exceptions to Occur

At initial glance, this topic may seem to be counterproductive to the rest of this chapter. After all, we've been focusing our efforts on controlling and limiting errors. Suddenly, I'm talking about purposefully causing exceptions.

Bear with me. There are good, practical programming reasons for triggering exceptions. Commonly, you'll find this technique used within components designed for use within other applications. I'm using the word *components* here in a fairly broad fashion. By components, I mean controls, class modules, DLLs, or any other self-contained programming nugget.

The key point here is that you use these components within another application, which might be your own application or someone else's. Since these components are just a part of another application, you most likely will want to pass runtime errors and exceptions onto the host application for processing. There are two common ways of accomplishing this: using either the **Raise** method of the Err object or the Throw statement.

Triggering a Runtime Error Using the Err Object

The Visual Basic approach to triggering a runtime error is through the **Raise** method of the Err object. The syntax for this method is

```
Err.Raise(number, source, description, helpfile, helpcontent)
```

Table E-2 describes each of these parameters in further detail.

Table E-2. Raise Method Parameters

PARAMETER	DESCRIPTION
Number	An integer value between 0 and 65535. The range between 0 and 512 is reserved; this will be accessible to the developer through Err.Number.
Source	Defines the source of the error; I like to set this to a combination of the control and property names; this will be accessible to the developer through Err.Source.
Description	The description of the error; this will be accessible to the developer through Err.Description.
HelpFile	Path to a help file that provides additional information on this error; this parameter is of no use with mobile applications.
HelpContent	Context ID that defines a topic within the help file; this parameter is of no use with mobile applications.

Following is an example of calling the **Raise** method:

```
Err.Raise(vbObjectError + 1234, "scheduler.rating", _
  "An invalid property value was provided")
```

Triggering an Exception with the Throw Statement

The .NET Compact Framework equivalent of the Err object's **Raise** method is the Throw statement. The syntax for this statement is

```
Throw expression
```

The single part required by the Throw statement, **expression**, provides information on the expression to throw.

Following is an example of the Throw statement. In this example, I'm causing a custom error to occur. I could just as easily trigger a specific error.

```
Throw New System.Exception("A test error.")
```

Summary

Whether you call it error or exception handling, whether you use legacy Visual Basic or new .NET Compact Framework approaches, it's paramount that you include robust error management within your mobile applications. I happen to think that it's even more important than with desktop applications, due to the combination of the complexity of the mobile environment and the fact that the mobile user frequently is without ready access to the help desk.

Regardless of whether you're using the VB or the NETCF approach to error handling, it's important that you make error handling a part of your design and development process right from the start. It's only then that you'll have effective error handling that integrates itself seamlessly into your applications.

Custom Controls in C#

CHAPTER 7 PRESENTED A TUTORIAL that built a custom button using Visual Basic code. The only problem with VB, as we discussed then, is that you can't create a design-time control that can be dropped on your form. The problem? Both the VB and C# compilers generate warnings when you compile the code for design mode. The difference is that C# ignores the warnings and Visual basic treats them as errors. This problem means that if you stick with Visual Basic, you can't build a design-time component for your custom controls.

This appendix will show you how to create a C# button control, identical to the one in Chapter 7, and also how to build a design-time component. To make the comparison with Chapter 7 as obvious as possible, I'll walk you through the same steps that you did in Chapter 7. But instead of adding VB code, you'll add C# code in the project. In addition to the original 12 steps, you'll perform a few more steps that will add extra code to make the design-time component. Once completed, I'll walk you through the command line compile that you need to do to create the control.

Step-by-Step Tutorial: Creating a New Button

In this tutorial, you'll create a new Command Button control that has rounded edges and a colored button surface. This control will have multiple properties related to its visual appearance, (e.g., colors, enabled state, etc.), and will also handle various events. This tutorial will not go into detail about portions of control development that were covered in Chapter 5. Any new features of control development will be covered, but this tutorial is meant to be strictly a graphics tutorial.

Step 1: Starting a New Project

In practice, you would want to create a separate project for your control and a project to test the control. So, to keep this tutorial as realistic as possible, you'll develop two separate projects. Begin this step-by-step exercise by creating a new project using the following steps:

1. Start Visual Studio .NET if necessary.

2. From the Start Page, select **New Project**.

3. From the New Project dialog box, select **Smart Device Application**.

4. Specify the project name **RoundButton Demo**.

5. Select a location to create the project

6. Select the project type **Class Library** and click the **OK** button

Step 2: Adding References

To configure the target output folder for your project, perform the following steps:

1. In the Solution Explorer, right-click **References** and click **Add Reference**.

2. Select **System.Drawing** from the Component Name column and then click the **Select** button.

3. Select **System.Windows.Forms** from the Component Name column and then click the **Select** button.

4. Click the **OK** button.

Step 3: Configuring the Project

Because you created your project as a class library, only a small subset of references were added by the wizard. To add the references to your project, perform the following steps:

1. Under the Project menu, select **RoundButton Properties**.

2. Under the Device page of the Text File Property Pages dialog box, set the output file folder to **\Windows\Start Menu\Programs\Apress**.

Step 4: Naming Your Control Class

To change the control's name from Class1.cs to RoundButton.cs, perform the following steps:

1. Click the filename **Class1.cs** in the Solution Explorer.

2. Change the filename in the Properties window to **RoundButton.cs**.

3. Open the **RoundButton Class** module.

Step 5: Inheriting the Control Class

The RoundButton control is based upon the **Control** class. You accomplish this by adding a single line of code to your **Class** module.

Perform the following steps to add the line of code to inherit the **Control** class:

1. Open the **RoundButton Class** module.

2. Insert **: System.Windows.Forms.Control** in the **Class** module as shown:

```
public class RoundButton : System.Windows.Forms.Control
{
}
```

Step 6: Creating Class-Level Variables

You need variables to hold the enabled and disabled color of the button. You also need to track the button state as either up or pressed. (You'll see why later.) Add the declarations to the editor so that your code appears as shown:

```
public class RoundButton : System.Windows.Forms.Control, IDisposable
{
    bool _buttonDrawnDown = false;
    Color _btnColor = Color.LightGreen;
    Color _btnDisabledColor = Color.DarkGreen;
}
```

 NOTE *There is no step telling you to add the using statements (analogous to the Imprts statement in VB) at the beginning of the file, so I'll remind you here. Be sure to add imports for System, System.Drawing, and System.Windows.Forms.*

Step 7: Adding the OnPaint Event

You need to draw the control in several other locations rather than just in the
OnPaint event. Keeping that in mind, you have a very small and simple event to
code. Perform the following steps to add this procedure:

1. Open the **RoundButton Class** module.

2. Add the following code to the **Class** module:

```
protected override void OnPaint(PaintEventArgs e)
{
    DrawButton(e.Graphics, this.ForeColor, _btnColor);
    base.OnPaint (e);
}
```

This procedure calls out to your DrawButton routine, which we'll get to
shortly. In the meantime, notice that you are passing three arguments to the
method. The first is a Graphics object that you pull from the **PaintEventArgs**
parameter. The second argument is the control's own foreground color. Since
you are deriving it from **Control**, you can use the control's existing colors, among
other properties, by referencing your base class through the **Me** keyword.

Step 8: Creating Your DrawButton Method

You need to draw the control in several other locations rather than just in the
OnPaint event. Keeping that in mind, you have another very small and simple
event to code. Perform the following steps to add this procedure:

1. Open the **RoundButton Class** module.

2. Add the code in Listing F-1 to the **Class** module.

Listing F-1. Custom Drawing Your Own Button

```
public void DrawButton(Graphics g, Color foreColor, Color backColor)
{
    //    Use the button height as the diameter of the round end.
    int bRadius = this.ClientRectangle.Height / 2;
    int aTop = this.ClientRectangle.Top;
    int aLeft = this.ClientRectangle.Left;
    int aWidth = this.ClientRectangle.Width;
    int aHeight = this.ClientRectangle.Height;
```

```
Brush sb = null;
Font fnt = null;
Try
{
    if( this.Enabled )
        sb = new SolidBrush(_btnColor);
    else
        sb = new SolidBrush(_btnDisabledColor);

    g.FillEllipse(sb, aLeft, aTop, 2 * bRadius, 2 * bRadius);
    g.FillRectangle(sb, aLeft + bRadius, aTop, aWidth - (2 * bRadius),
aHeight);
    g.FillEllipse(sb, aWidth - (2*bRadius), aTop, 2*bRadius, 2*bRadius);

        //      Now write the text to the button face.
    fnt = new Font(this.Font.Name, this.Font.Size, this.Font.Style);

    SizeF siz = g.MeasureString(this.Text, fnt);
    g.DrawString(this.Text, fnt, new SolidBrush(foreColor), _
        (aWidth - siz.Width)/2,
        (aHeight-siz.Height)/2);
}
catch
{
}
finally
{
    fnt.Dispose();
    sb.Dispose();
}
}
```

Step 9: Adding the OnEnabledChanged Event

The basic button is now done and will work. However, you want it do more than just sit there. If the user changes the state of the button, you need to force the button to change its color appropriately. Perform the following steps to add this procedure:

1. Open the **RoundButton Class** module.

2. Add the following code to the **Class** module:

```
                    protected override void OnEnabledChanged(EventArgs e)
                    {
                        Graphics g = this.CreateGraphics();
                        Try
                        {
                            DrawButton(g, this.ForeColor, _btnColor);
                        }
                        catch
                        {
                        }
                        finally
                        {
                            g.Dispose();
                            base.OnEnabledChanged(e);
                        }
                    }
```

The **OnEnabledChanged** event is raised when the **Enabled** property of the
control is changed. This can occur from code or at design time.

You don't have a Graphics object passed to you in this method, so you need
to create your own. Your form has a **CreateGraphics** method that you use to get
a current Graphics object. Remember, you need to dispose of the object when
you are done. Just like your mother always told you, "Clean up after yourself!"

Step 10: Handling More Events

Since this is a graphics tutorial, we'll skip the explanation of some of the work in
adding multiple events. What is important here is that you see how you need to
force a redraw of the button face again after the mouse has touched or released.
Again, let me emphasize the fact that you need to create a Graphics object, pass
it to the draw routine, and then dispose of it. It's also important to call the base
class's **OnMouseUp** and **OnMouseDown** events to let the base control do its processing. Add the following code to the **RoundButton Class** module:

```
protected override void OnMouseDown(MouseEventArgs e)
{
    Graphics g;
    try
    {
        g = this.CreateGraphics();
        DrawButton(g, Color.White, Color.Black);
        buttonDrawnDown = true;
    }
    catch
```

```
        {
        }
        finally
        {
            g.Dispose();
            base.OnMouseDown(e);
        }
    }


    protected override void OnMouseUp(MouseEventArgs e)
    {
        Graphics g;
        try
        {
            g = this.CreateGraphics();
            DrawButton(g, this.ForeColor, _btnColor);
            buttonDrawnDown = false;
        }
        catch
        {
        }
        finally
        {
            g.Dispose();
            base.OnMouseUp(e);
        }
    }
```

Step 11: Adding Two Simple Properties

You need two properties to set the button face color when it's enabled and disabled. Add the following code to the **RoundButton Class** module:

```
public Color ButtonColor
{
    get
    {
        return _btnColor;
    }
    set
    {
    _btnColor = value;
    }
}
```

```
public Color DisabledButtonColor
{
    get
    {
        return _btnDisabledColor;
    }
    set
    {
        _btnDisabledColor = value;
    }
}
```

 NOTE *Having this property return a Color object has a very nice side effect. When this control is selected on the form, the **ButtonColor** property in the Properties window will display the color palette, the same as any standard .NET control does when selected. All without writing any code—cool huh?*

Step 12: Moving the Stylus Off of the Button

When the stylus touches the button and is then "rolled" off the button face, the button needs to revert to its normal color state. It then needs to be painted back to its depressed state when the stylus again moves over the button. That takes some fancy code, which you can add now to the **RoundButton Class** module:

```
protected override void OnMouseMove(MouseEventArgs e)
{
    try
    {
        if( e.Button == MouseButtons.Left )
        {
            if( (e.X < this.ClientRectangle.Top ||
                e.X > this.ClientRectangle.Width) ||
                (e.Y <      this.ClientRectangle.Top ||
                e.Y > this.ClientRectangle.Height) )
            {
                if( buttonDrawnDown )
                {
                    Graphics g = this.CreateGraphics();
                    DrawButton(g, this.ForeColor, _btnColor);
```

```
                    g.Dispose();
                    buttonDrawnDown = false;
                }
            }
            else
            {
                //    Moving inside the button
                if( !buttonDrawnDown )
                {
                    Graphics g = this.CreateGraphics();
                    DrawButton(g, this.ForeColor, Color.Black);
                    g.Dispose();
                    buttonDrawnDown = true;
                }
            }
        }
        base.OnMouseMove(e);
    }
    catch
    {
    }
}
```

Updating the Code for Design Time

You need to perform two extra steps to take this control and make a design-time component. First, the code needs to include an attribute that, when compiled, will mark your class as a control that can be added to the toolbar in the IDE. The first attribute you'll add is the one that gives your control a name. The following code snippet should be added to the source code just before the class definition:

```
#if NETCFDESIGNTIME
[assembly: System.CF.Design.RuntimeAssemblyAttribute("RoundButton,
    Version=0.90, Culture=neutral, PublicKeyToken=null")]
#endif

public class RoundButton : System.Windows.Forms.Control
{
}
```

That takes care of signing your control and letting the runtime know that this is an assembly that is to be used at design time. The RuntimeAssemblyAttribute also lets you specify the version of the assembly along with setting the assembly's culture and a public key. This attribute is exclusive to NETCF, taking the fully qualified name of the runtime assembly. This example will not be using the Culture or PublicKeyToken fields of the attribute. The import fields are the name and the version.

Now, what would a design-time control be without some properties that you can set during design? To mark the properties that you're going to expose through the Properties window, make the following additions to your code.

Before the **ButtonColor** property, add the following attribute:

```
#if NETCFDESIGNTIME
[
System.ComponentModel.Category("Appearance"),
System.ComponentModel.Description("The color for the Button face when Enabled")
]
#endif
```

Before the **Disabled** property, add the following attribute:

```
#if NETCFDESIGNTIME
[
System.ComponentModel.Category("Appearance"),
System.ComponentModel.Description("The color for the Button face when Disabled ")
]
#endif
```

Building Your New Control

Along with the attributes that you added, you also added a preprocessor variable with each attribute. The **NETCFDESIGNTIME** variable is set to true when you are building the design-time control so that the attributes aren't included in your runtime version of the control. This allows you to use the same code to generate two distinctly different controls.

The build step must accomplish three major objectives. First, your script should build the runtime version of your control. You'll see a little later why this is important. Second, the script must build the design-time component, and third, it must copy the newly built design control to the designer reference path so that .NET can find it. If you've never written a batch file or done any command line compiling, this build script may be a little daunting, but never fear. It's designed so that all you need to do to make this script work for any new control you write in the future is to change four of the first six lines to use the name of the new control being built. As the old saying goes, "How do you eat an elephant? One bite at a time." So let's take the first bite of this build script.

Before anything else is done, the script sets five variables. The first is a name for the control. In the following portion of the script, the control is named Apress.RoundButton.dll.

```
@ECHO OFF
CLS
SET BLDCTRL_DLL=Apress.RoundButton.dll
SET BLDCTRL_SRC=RoundButton.cs
SET BLDCTRL_ASM=AssemblyInfo.cs
SET BLDCTRL_SLN=RoundButton.sln
SET BLDCTRL_PFX=Designer

ECHO Batch Build for .NETCF Designer Controls
ECHO.
ECHO ————————————————
ECHO Round Button Example
ECHO The Definitive Guide to the .NET Compact Framework
ECHO Apress, 2003
ECHO Dan Fergus and Larry Roof
ECHO ————————————————
ECHO.
```

The next three variables are set to tell the script what files are to be compiled. BLDCTRL_PRX is a designation that is prefixed to the name of the control to signify that it's a design-time control. The next series of script lines are output lines that dump information to the console window during the build.

NOTE *While I'm the one showing this batch file now, the original version was included as a sample that ships with Visual Studio .NET. This version has been modified a little from the original. You can also find all of the C# code, titled RoundButton, along with the batch file, in the **Appendix F** folder of the **Samples** folder for this book. See Appendix D for more information on accessing and loading the sample applications.*

This build script must be run from a particular command prompt that has all of the paths set correctly for the compiler to run and find the required files. You can find this command prompt from the Start Menu by selecting **Microsoft Visual Studio .NET 2003** and **Visual Studio .NET Tools**. The script file verifies this before doing the compiling.

```
IF "%VSINSTALLDIR%"=="" GOTO NoVSEnv
SET NETCFDIR=%VSINSTALLDIR%\..\..\CompactFrameWorkSDK\v1.0.5000\Windows CE\
```

The **NETCFDIR** variable is the location to which the controls will be copied. Now it's time to build the controls. Your script will build the design-time version of the control.

```
ECHO.
ECHO [BUILDING %BLDCTRL_PFX%.%BLDCTRL_DLL% from %BLDCTRL_SRC%]
csc /noconfig /define:NETCFDESIGNTIME /target:library
    /out:%BLDCTRL_PFX%.%BLDCTRL_DLL% %BLDCTRL_SRC% %BLDCTRL_ASM%
    /r:"%NETCFDIR%Designer\System.CF.Design.dll"
    /r:"%NETCFDIR%Designer\System.CF.Windows.Forms.dll"
    /r:"%NETCFDIR%Designer\System.CF.Drawing.dll"
    /r:System.Windows.Forms.dll
    /r:System.dll
    /r:System.data.dll
    /nowarn:1595

ECHO.
ECHO [COPYING %BLDCTRL_PFX%.%BLDCTRL_DLL%]
COPY "%BLDCTRL_PFX%.%BLDCTRL_DLL%" "%NETCFDIR%Designer\"
IF EXIST ".\%BLDCTRL_PFX%.%BLDCTRL_DLL%"
    DEL ".\%BLDCTRL_PFX%.%BLDCTRL_DLL%"
```

Command line compiling can look rather complex, especially with the variable names being used in this code. The C# compiler, csc, defines the **NETCFDESIGNTIME** variable so that the code, when compiled, includes the attributes, thus making it a design-time control. The output name is built by joining the various variables that were defined in the first part of the script. After this, the required references are specified. Note that the references aren't the standard references that you would specify in a project. They are all system assemblies targeted exclusively at building design-time controls.

When you build a project in the IDE, the references are added to the compiler command line without your being aware of it. But when you build using the command line compiler, you must be sure to specify all required references.

The most inconspicuous portion of the compiler command line, and the most important, is /nowarn:1595. This is why Visual Basic can't build design-time controls. The C# compiler can simply ignore this warning, but the Visual Basic compiler can't. The VB compiler sees this as an error and therefore can't build the control.

Once built, the design-time control is copied to the designer folder in the CF directory, and the local file is deleted.

The next step is to build the runtime version of the control. The command line for this is very similar to that of the design-time control. The name of the control doesn't have the prefix added to it, and the **NETCFDESIGNTIME** variable isn't defined. The big difference is the references. Note that there are a larger number of references and that they are the ones you should be used to seeing from adding them in the Visual Studio IDE.

```
ECHO.
ECHO [BUILDING %BLDCTRL_DLL% from %BLDCTRL_SRC%]
csc /noconfig /target:library
    /out:%BLDCTRL_DLL% %BLDCTRL_SRC% %BLDCTRL_ASM%
    /r:"%NETCFDIR%mscorlib.dll"
    /r:"%NETCFDIR%System.dll"
    /r:"%NETCFDIR%System.XML.dll"
    /r:"%NETCFDIR%System.Data.dll"
    /r:"%NETCFDIR%System.Drawing.dll"
    /r:"%NETCFDIR%System.Windows.Forms.dll"
    /r:"%NETCFDIR%Designer\System.CF.Design.dll"
    /r:"%NETCFDIR%Designer\System.CF.Windows.Forms.dll"
    /r:"%NETCFDIR%Designer\System.CF.Drawing.dll"
    /nowarn:1595

ECHO.
ECHO [COPYING %BLDCTRL_DLL%]
COPY "%BLDCTRL_DLL%" "%NETCFDIR%"
IF EXIST ".\%BLDCTRL_DLL%" DEL ".\%BLDCTRL_DLL%"
ECHO.
```

Once the control has been built, it's copied to the control's directory under the NETCF folder tree and the local copy deleted. You now have two new assemblies, one for design-time use and one for runtime use. It's time to test these controls.

Using the Batch File

There is a trick (isn't there always) to making the development and debugging of the control work smoothly. Instead of opening Visual Studio and pointing to a project or solution, this trick takes a slightly different approach. Open a Visual Studio command prompt and navigate to the folder containing the control's code. From this command window, run the batch file. To work with the code, start Visual Studio by either typing **start roundbutton.sln** or by typing **roundbutton.sln**. When changes have been made and you want to rebuild the design-time control, close the IDE and run the batch file. To debug and test, start the IDE backup and run the code.

The reason behind this approach is simple: When your design-time control is loaded in the Toolbox, Visual Studio has a reference to it so you can't copy the DLL over to the design control's folder. Closing the IDE and then running the build file makes everything work fine.

It's time for the last step, testing the design-time control.

Step 13: Testing the Paint Job

Create a new Smart Device Extensions Windows Application. Move your mouse over the Toolbox and click the right mouse button. You should see the context menu shown in Figure F-1.

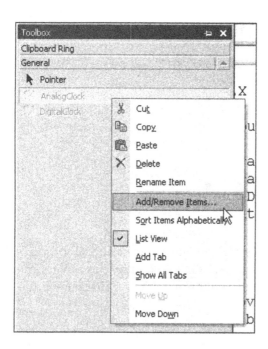

Figure F-1. Adding an item to the Toolbox

Choose the **Add/Remove Items** menu item. In the Customize Toolbox dialog box, click the **Browse** button to locate and add the control. You can refresh your memory about where the file is located by looking back at the batch file description. Once you select your control, notice in the dialog box that your control has a checked box next to it, as you can see in Figure F-2.

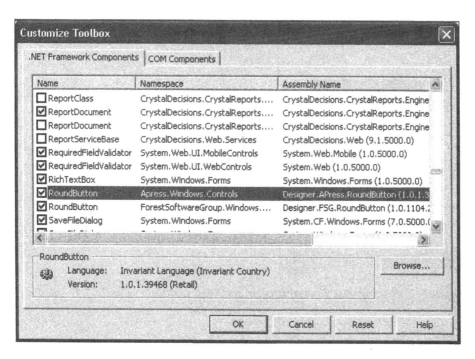

Figure F-2. Finding your control to add

Click the **OK** button, and you'll be able to see your control listed in the Toolbox.

NOTE *Don't be disturbed if the Toolbox has your control disabled. It will not show as enabled until you have a form open in the designer.*

When you open the default form in the project, double-click your control in the Toolbox, just as you would with a *real* control, to add it to your form. Your design-time control will magically appear on the form's designer surface. You can double-click the button to add an event handler for the button click. Add the following code to the form:

```
private void roundButton2_Click_1(object sender, System.EventArgs e)
{
    MessageBox.Show("Button Pressed");
}
```

Run the test project, and you should see the message box shown in Figure F-3.

Figure F-3. Viewing your new control on the form surface

Summary

While the procedure described in this appendix by no means results in a complete, production-ready control, it does show you the basics of creating both a runtime and a design-time control using C# and the .NET Compact Framework. Writing a C# application isn't that much different from writing Visual Basic .NET application. *If* you don't want to learn, you can probably find someone to help you with writing the C# code. As you work with VB controls on a form, without having the design component, you'll find how difficult it can be to lay out a form and make it work at runtime.

Maybe the VB compiler will get an upgrade in a future version of .NET, but until then, you might want to consider creating a design-time component—how you decide to do it is up to you.

Index

forums.apress.com

JOIN THE APRESS FORUMS AND BE PART OF OUR COMMUNITY. You'll find discussions that cover topics of interest to IT professionals, programmers, and enthusiasts just like you. If you post a query to one of our forums, you can expect that some of the best minds in the business—especially Apress authors, who all write with *The Expert's Voice*™—will chime in to help you. Why not aim to become one of our most valuable participants (MVPs) and win cool stuff? Here's a sampling of what you'll find:

DATABASES
Data drives everything.

Share information, exchange ideas, and discuss any database programming or administration issues.

INTERNET TECHNOLOGIES AND NETWORKING
Try living without plumbing (and eventually IPv6).

Talk about networking topics including protocols, design, administration, wireless, wired, storage, backup, certifications, trends, and new technologies.

JAVA
We've come a long way from the old Oak tree.

Hang out and discuss Java in whatever flavor you choose: J2SE, J2EE, J2ME, Jakarta, and so on.

MAC OS X
All about the Zen of OS X.

OS X is both the present and the future for Mac apps. Make suggestions, offer up ideas, or boast about your new hardware.

OPEN SOURCE
Source code is good; understanding (open) source is better.

Discuss open source technologies and related topics such as PHP, MySQL, Linux, Perl, Apache, Python, and more.

PROGRAMMING/BUSINESS
Unfortunately, it is.

Talk about the Apress line of books that cover software methodology, best practices, and how programmers interact with the "suits."

WEB DEVELOPMENT/DESIGN
Ugly doesn't cut it anymore, and CGI is absurd.

Help is in sight for your site. Find design solutions for your projects and get ideas for building an interactive Web site.

SECURITY
Lots of bad guys out there—the good guys need help.

Discuss computer and network security issues here. Just don't let anyone else know the answers!

TECHNOLOGY IN ACTION
Cool things. Fun things.

It's after hours. It's time to play. Whether you're into LEGO® MINDSTORMS™ or turning an old PC into a DVR, this is where technology turns into fun.

WINDOWS
No defenestration here.

Ask questions about all aspects of Windows programming, get help on Microsoft technologies covered in Apress books, or provide feedback on any Apress Windows book.

HOW TO PARTICIPATE:
Go to the Apress Forums site at **http://forums.apress.com/**.
Click the New User link.